Lyndall Gordon is the prize-winning author of six biographies, including *T. S. Eliot: An Imperfect Life*; *Virginia Woolf: A Writer's Life*; and *Vindication: A Life of Mary Wollstonecraft*. She has also  women's friendship in her native fellow at St Hilda's College, Ox Literature and a member of PEN.

'As Gordon tells it, this story of the terrible fascination Dickinson exerted on her heirs is as rich as a novel by Henry James . . . Perhaps for the first time since Dickinson's death, she invites us to meet the poet head-on'

Robert Douglas-Fairhurst, *Daily Telegraph*

'Gordon brings the advantage of distance and a fresh and tough-minded perspective to her fascinating study . . . She offers clear and boldly original answers to the "unanswered questions" of Dickinson's life . . . by clearing away much that is speculative, projected or contentious about the life, will open the way for new approaches to the woman she calls "the poet next door"'

Elaine Showalter, *Guardian*

'This is a work of literary detection . . . illuminating . . . The Dickinson genius, courtesy of Gordon's dexterity, survives the hazards of "biographical contexts". Here is the definitive biography'

Ronald Frame, *Scotsman*

'*Lives Like Loaded Guns* will shake up an already formidable body of work on Dickinson and her family . . . Gordon brilliantly shows how the subsequent feud determined Dickinson's legacy as a poet. If she was invisible before, Gordon in this book gives Emily Dickinson the startling clarity of one her own poems'

Frances Wilson, *Sunday Times*

'Gordon's biography proposes a theory to account for the enigma of Emily Dickinson's life as a notorious recluse which is so brilliant that, if this were a novel, a reviewer would be duty-bound not to reveal a thrilling twist . . . This book is unforcedly and powerfully original'

Caroline Moore, *Sunday Telegraph*

Lives Like Loaded Guns

EMILY DICKINSON
AND HER FAMILY'S FEUDS

LYNDALL GORDON

virago

VIRAGO

First published in Great Britain in 2010 by Virago Press
This paperback edition published in 2011 by Virago Press

Copyright © Lyndall Gordon 2010

The moral right of the author has been asserted.

A CIP catalogue record for this book
is available from the British Library.

ISBN 978-1-84408-454-8

Typeset in Spectrum by M Rules
Printed and bound in Great Britain by
Clays Ltd, St Ives plc

Virago Press
An imprint of
Little, Brown Book Group
100 Victoria Embankment
London EC4Y 0DY

An Hachette UK Company
www.hachette.co.uk

www.virago.co.uk

'My Life had stood — a Loaded Gun'

EMILY DICKINSON

'It was a devilish situation for everyone concerned'

MILLICENT TODD BINGHAM

In memory of
Diane Middlebrook,
biographer and friend

CONTENTS

LIST OF ILLUSTRATIONS

PLATE SECTION ONE

Austin Dickinson: Todd-Bingham Picture Collection (MS 496E). Manuscripts and Archives. Yale University Library

Susan Gilbert: © 2001 Barton Levi St Armand

The Dickinson Homestead: lithograph by John Bachelder, 1858. Jones Library Inc., Amherst

The Evergreens: Jones Library Inc., Amherst

James Jackson: Massachusetts General Hospital, Boston

Zebina Montague: Amherst College Archives and Special Collections. Identified by Margaret Dakin.

Emily Dickinson's conservatory: Jones Library Inc., Amherst

Replica of the poet's writing table: photograph by Jerome Liebling, from Liebling et al, *The Dickinsons of Amherst*

Lavinia Dickinson: Amherst College Archives and Special Collections

PLATE SECTION TWO

Mabel Loomis Todd: Todd-Bingham Picture Collection (MS 496E). Manuscripts and Archives. Yale University Library

David Peck Todd: Todd-Bingham Picture Collection (MS 496E). Manuscripts and Archives. Yale University Library

Austin Dickinson: Brown University Library

Mabel Todd with Ned and Mattie Dickinson: Todd-Bingham Picture Collection (MS 496E). Manuscripts and Archives. Yale University Library

Gib Dickinson: Todd-Bingham Picture Collection (MS 496E). Manuscripts and Archives. Yale University Library

Kate Scott Turner: from Richard B. Sewall, *The Life of Emily Dickinson*

Samuel Bowles: MS Am 1118.99b (6), by permission of the Houghton Library, Harvard University

Otis P. Lord: MS Am 1118.99b (55), by permission of the Houghton Library, Harvard University

Mary Bowles: MS Am 1118.99b (5), by permission of the Houghton Library, Harvard University

Maria Whitney: Historic Northampton

Elizabeth Holland: Amherst College Archives and Special Collections

Dr Josiah Holland: Amherst College Archives and Special Collections

Thomas Wentworth Higginson: MS Am 1118.99b (45), by permission of the Houghton Library, Harvard University

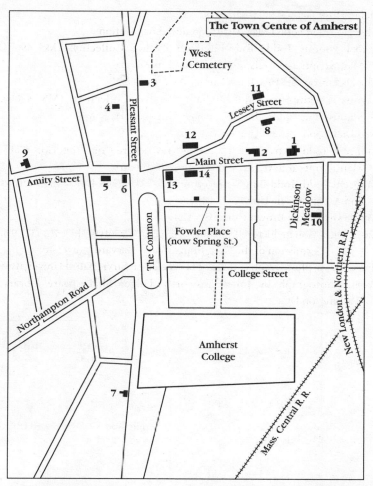

The Town Centre of Amherst

West Cemetery

Pleasant Street

Lessey Street

Main Street

Amity Street

The Common

Fowler Place
(now Spring St.)

Dickinson Meadow

College Street

Northampton Road

Amherst College

New London & Northern R.R.

Mass. Central R.R.

1. Dickinson Homestead
2. The Evergreens
3. Emily Dickinson's home, 1840–55
4. Primary school
5. Amherst Academy
6. Amherst House, where the Todds lodged
7. Birthplace of Helen Hunt Jackson, née Fiske
8. Sweetser house
9. Cutler house, where Susan and Martha Gilbert lived
10. The Dell, built after Emily Dickinson's death in 1886
11. The Lessey house, rented by the Todds in 1884–5
12. The Lincoln house, rented by the Todds in 1885–6, called by Austin '3dh' (third house, i.e. next to the two family houses)
13. Austin Dickinson's one-time legal chambers
14. Montague house, where Zebina and Harriet lived

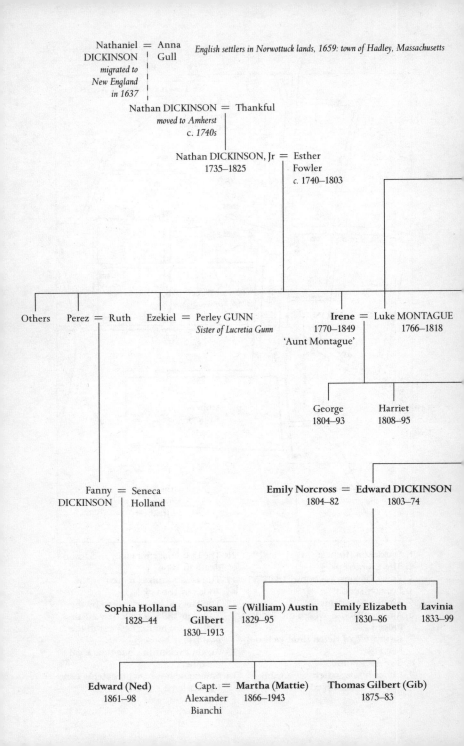

Nathaniel = Anna
DICKINSON ┊ Gull   *English settlers in Norwottuck lands, 1659: town of Hadley, Massachusetts*
migrated to
New England
in 1637

Nathan DICKINSON = Thankful
moved to Amherst
c. 1740s

Nathan DICKINSON, Jr = Esther
1735–1825   Fowler
                         c. 1740–1803

Others   Perez = Ruth   Ezekiel = Perley GUNN   **Irene** = Luke MONTAGUE
                                  Sister of Lucretia Gunn   1770–1849   1766–1818
                                                     'Aunt Montague'

                                                     George   Harriet
                                                     1804–93   1808–95

Fanny = Seneca   **Emily Norcross** = **Edward DICKINSON**
DICKINSON   Holland   1804–82   1803–74

Sophia Holland   **Susan** = (William) Austin   **Emily Elizabeth**   **Lavinia**
1828–44   **Gilbert**   1829–95   1830–86   1833–99
                     1830–1913

Edward (Ned)   Capt. = **Martha (Mattie)**   **Thomas Gilbert (Gib)**
1861–98   Alexander   1866–1943   1875–83
                   Bianchi

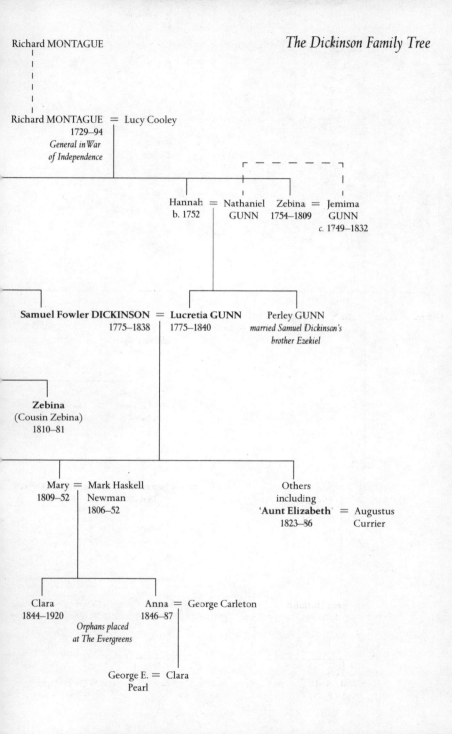

The Dickinson Family Tree

Richard MONTAGUE

Richard MONTAGUE = Lucy Cooley
1729–94
*General in War
of Independence*

Hannah = Nathaniel   Zebina = Jemima
b. 1752   GUNN   1754–1809   GUNN
c. 1749–1832

Samuel Fowler DICKINSON = **Lucretia GUNN**   Perley GUNN
1775–1838   1775–1840   *married Samuel Dickinson's
brother Ezekiel*

Zebina
(Cousin Zebina)
1810–81

Mary = Mark Haskell   Others
1809–52   Newman   including
1806–52   **'Aunt Elizabeth'** = Augustus
1823–86   Currier

Clara   Anna = George Carleton
1844–1920   1846–87
*Orphans placed
at The Evergreens*

George E. = Clara
Pearl

IN ORDER OF APPEARANCE*

WILLIAM AUSTIN DICKINSON: Only brother to the poet, Emily Dickinson. Lived next door at The Evergreens in Amherst, Massachusetts.

SUSAN (SUE) HUNTINGTON DICKINSON (NÉE GILBERT): Girlhood friend, sister-in-law and keen reader of Emily Dickinson's poems. Shared books with the poet.

LAVINIA (VINNIE) DICKINSON: Emily's devoted younger sister.

MABEL LOOMIS TODD: Co-editor and then editor of the first volumes of Emily Dickinson's poems and letters. Austin Dickinson's mistress.

DAVID PECK TODD: Professor of astronomy at Amherst College and philandering husband of Mabel Todd.

EDWARD DICKINSON: Formidable father of Austin, Emily and Vinnie.

MRS DICKINSON: Emily Norcross Dickinson, wife of the above.

COUSIN ZEBINA MONTAGUE: An invalid of sorts living with his sister Harriet, almost opposite the Dickinsons.

---

* It is difficult to know what to call writers who share surnames with men known in their own right. It is therefore often convenient to use first names but all reference to them as authors will use the names on their books.

MARY LYON: Founder of South Hadley Female Seminary, now Mount Holyoke College, in 1836 and still presiding in 1847 when Emily Dickinson arrived.

JANE HUMPHREY: Schoolmistress. Emily Dickinson's beloved friend.

BENJAMIN FRANKLIN NEWTON: Young lawyer in Edward Dickinson's office and first mentor to the poet after college.

MARTHA (MAT) GILBERT: Elder sister of Susan Gilbert. Confidential girl-hood friend of Emily Dickinson.

KATE SCOTT TURNER: A young widow, one-time school-friend of Susan Dickinson.

SAMUEL (SAM) BOWLES: Editor of the *Springfield Republican*, who published some of the poet's most daring works in the early 1860s.

MARY BOWLES: Unhappy, invalidish wife of the above, alternately teased and comforted by Emily Dickinson.

LOUISA (LOO) AND FRANCES (FANNY) NORCROSS: Cousins and intimates of Emily Dickinson.

JAMES JACKSON: Distinguished Boston physician, consulted in difficult cases. Emily Dickinson saw him when she was twenty years old.

THOMAS WENTWORTH HIGGINSON: Boston man of letters, sympathetic to aspiring women. Co-edited the first volumes of Dickinson's poems.

HELEN HUNT JACKSON: Amherst schoolfellow and supporter of Emily Dickinson. Well-known writer on the wrongs of Native Americans.

JUDGE OTIS PHILLIPS LORD: Friend of the poet's father, who became a suitor of Emily Dickinson.

EDWARD (NED) DICKINSON: elder son of Austin and Susan Dickinson, nephew to Emily Dickinson.

MARTHA (MATTIE) DICKINSON (MADAME BIANCHI): only daughter of Austin and Susan Dickinson. Loyal to mother and 'Aunt Emily'.

MAGGIE MAHER: Servant to the Dickinson sisters.

MILLICENT TODD BINGHAM: Studious only child of David and Mabel Todd. Inherited her mother's chest of Dickinson Papers.

ALFRED LEETE HAMPSON: Companion to the poet's niece Mattie Dickinson Bianchi. Heir of the Dickinson Papers. Married Mary Landis.

WILLIAM (BILL) MCCARTHY: Agent for the Dickinson Papers.

GILBERT MONTAGUE: Donor of the Dickinson Papers to Harvard.

WILLIAM JACKSON: Curator of the Houghton Library, who acquired the bulk of the Dickinson Papers.

NOTE ON TYPOGRAPHY AND PUNCTUATION

Since Dickinson's poems were almost all unpublished in her lifetime, and since she did not authorise the forms in which the ten printed poems appeared, there can be no secure typography and punctuation. Only a facsimile edition or scanning could include the variety of Dickinson's dashes. Since no typographical equivalent exists, I resort to a long dash for poetry, so as to register a signal more significant than an ordinary dash between the words.

Dickinson's subjective capitalisation is preserved in all quotations but not her lineation where it is impossible to be certain whether a line ends or runs on at the edge of her manuscript page.

Dates of Dickinson's writings are approximate, the cumulative but uncertain fruit of scholarship since the late 1880s.

I: A POET NEXT DOOR

In 1882 Austin Dickinson, in his fifties, fell in love with a young faculty wife. Twenty-six years before, Austin had married Susan Gilbert, the friend of his sister. The Evergreens was built to accommodate the married pair next door to the family home on Main Street in the country town of Amherst in western Massachusetts. By the 1880s Austin was the leading figure in the community; townsfolk called him 'the Squire', a standing he inherited from his father. No one was more respected than the tall Squire when he appeared in his black hat at a straight angle over his eyes. There was a spring to his stride, led by a cane, along Main Street. His mouth turned down and the expression on his lined face was austere. A devout member of the church, he reproved laughter on Sundays; of late he had turned his considerable taste to improving the graveyard. In every particular, Austin Dickinson appeared an unlikely candidate for the folly of passion.

Watchful eyes in a New England town of only four thousand meant that assignations had to happen in strictest secret. The only safe place was the irreproachable Homestead, next door to The Evergreens, where the Dickinson sisters continued to live. Even there, nothing was said to acknowledge the romantic and then adulterous nature of Austin's attachment to Mrs Todd. A fiction was maintained that Mrs Todd was no more than a special friend to all the Dickinsons. But one member of the family refused to collude: Austin's distraught wife. When protest, then humouring, proved useless, rows exploded in the privacy of The Evergreens.

The rows came to a head in the winter of 1885. On the night of 25 January, Susan Dickinson's nails gashed the wallpaper in the hallway, the rents gaping for any caller or servant to see. Her husband, being the pink of propriety, had to capitulate. Ostensibly it was an issue of refurbishment, but really about silence: a husband's refusal to speak to a protesting wife. Three days later, the last of the marital decor had been stripped from the walls. Dark-red wallpaper with a fashionable William Morris design was brought in from Galloway & Fitch to cover the damage.

Susan's breakout hardened her husband. Their son, prone to seizures, sided with her but was helpless against his father and nothing could stop the course of havoc Austin Dickinson was cutting through his family. Following the wallpaper incident, Susan and her son sank into poor health in the course of that winter.

There was no paving on the Dickinsons' side of Main Street. Townsfolk had to walk farther off on the other side of the road. A hemlock hedge, planted in the sixties, linked the two houses and protected their privacy. Behind the hedge, and invisible to curious eyes, was a home-trod path between The Evergreens and Austin's sisters next door in 'the paternal mansion'. Cross this path and enter the Homestead, an older house built of brown brick in the handsome Federal style. Climb its well-swept stairs and along the top landing turn right into a bright room with four windows. The front two look out across hedge and street at the snowy sweep of the Dickinson meadow and the Pelham hills in the distance. The side windows look at The Evergreens. Here is another, and sicker, invalid who has lain in her bed since October. Her hair flames against the pillow, for though she is fifty-four there's no sign of grey. This is Emily Dickinson, reclusive, unknown to the reading public in 1885 but soon to burst into fame as a poet. She expects fame and more: nothing less than immortality, and sometimes she can't sleep at night for thinking of immortality. 'Exterior — to Time —', she shuns intruders. Shutting her door on distractions, for thirty years she has honed her genius in the privacy of this room:

> The Soul selects her own Society —
> Then — shuts the Door —
> To her divine Majority —
> Present no more —
> Unmoved — she notes the Chariots — pausing —

> At her low Gate —
> Unmoved — an Emperor be kneeling
> Opon* her Mat —
>
> I've known her — from an ample nation —
> Choose One —
> Then — close the Valves of her attention —
> Like Stone —

Who is the One with her? Another poem, addressed to 'Sue' (Susan next door) and signed 'Emily', confides the answer in no uncertain terms. A divine 'Guest' keeps her company. She wants no other:

> The Soul that hath a Guest
> Doth seldom go abroad —
> Diviner Crowd at Home —
> Obliterate the need —

Against the wall stands a locked cherrywood chest, two of its drawers packed with forty handmade booklets into which she has copied many of her earlier poems, together with a huge assortment of loose manuscripts, a lifetime's unpublished oeuvre. Here is her secret 'Fortune'. Nearby is a small cherrywood table where she writes poems and letters. This year, though increasingly weak, she will write often to Susan Dickinson, her long-time neighbour and friend of her youth, the woman who had married her brother. Their attachment lies behind their lives, deep and not quite fathomed.

To another correspondent, the poet conceals her condition. 'I do not know the Names of Sicknesses', she waves the question away, but the present ill was said to be different from a recurring illness since her youth.

*

Emily Dickinson is now recognised as one of the greatest poets who ever

---

* ED's consistent spelling for 'upon'.

lived, yet her life remains a mystery. She continues to be encased in claims put out by opposed camps fighting for possession of her greatness. These camps originated in the clash between Austin Dickinson and his wife, who had been the poet's intimate and her keenest reader. Out of this clash a lasting feud developed, and it was the opponents in this feud, their allies and warring descendants, who devised the image of the poet as her fame grew and endured. What began as a split over adultery turned into a feud over who was to own the poet: in the first instance, who was to have the right to publish her works; in the second, whose legend would imprint itself on the public mind.

A fixed image has separated Emily Dickinson from family dissension, setting her apart to make art alone like the Lady of Shalott.* Yet given her compassion for those in distress and the closeness of her attachment to members of family caught up in the feud – her brother, her sister Lavinia (who sided with Austin), and the fraught children of Austin's marriage (who sided with Sue) – it simply cannot be so. Austin and Emily both had an eruptive vein, which Emily channelled into poetry. Her letters show that she cultivated adulterous emotions, if only in fantasy, for a married 'Master'. Did this affect her response to her brother's active adultery? And how did the ensuing feud strike the poet, who died at the height of its impact on her family? She did live long enough to know that what had happened could not heal.

To approach Emily Dickinson through the feud, to search out why it happened and to follow its consequences to the present day, is one of many possible stories. A feud, at least, is verifiable. People who knew the poet, then their daughters, heirs, and followers, did fire at one another, and went on firing when positioned to do so. But what is the link, if any, with a poet who said, twenty years before the feud began, 'My Life had stood — a Loaded Gun —'?

There are other explosions, if we turn our eyes from her tame visible life,

---

* Tennyson's famous poem, 'The Lady of Shalott' (1842), romanticised the solitary lot of a creative artist who may not – at her peril – engage in life and love. (ED read Tennyson in 1848, at the age of seventeen.)

flitting about the Homestead, or kneeling on a blanket outside while she tended her plants, or sending timely notes, flowers and goodies to friends and neighbours. What she termed 'Existence' was something else. Of that there are only hints and guesses. An unseen but decisive event, a 'bolt' or 'Bomb' that she had to 'Hold' and 'calm', vetoed a life she might have led outside her home, while it opened up the secret life she devised as a poet. There is the velocity of letters aimed at correspondents she marked out for her own, a gunman's 'yellow eye' narrowing at the target. There is the explosive image-cluster in her poetry: the earthquakes, the rumbling volcanoes, Vesuvius, Etna and the poet's voice like lava, coming in spurts through the 'buckled lips' of a crater.

'Abyss has no biographer —', Emily Dickinson said. Truth is bottomless, and she herself almost invisible. After her death, letters from correspondents were burnt according to her instructions and soon legend replaced living fact. The public learnt to revere a harmless homebody who shut off from life to suffer and contemplate a disappointment in love. Who, then, is there if we pare away the sentimental story that sees the poet through one or other man in her life, or the counter-story that cuts out men in favour of sister-love? Only the poet herself can tell.

'Tell' is one of her words, playing around her flaunting of secrets. The 'I' of her poems leaps out at us with startling disclosures: 'I'm Nobody! Who are you?', she asks. 'Nobody' she may be, but no innocuous nonentity, and the roles in her repertoire are many: the confrontational Nobody with a capital N; the tease speaking in riddles to those who would know her; the flirt who exults in the role of a 'Wife — without the Sign!'; and above all, the not-so-veiled boasts of volcanic power controlled by poetic form. Yet for all the poems' confessional aplomb, a secret slips into silence even as the poet points to it in one of her most telling poems. 'I tie my Hat' is about an explosive Existence coexisting with the speaker's visible life as a nineteenth-century woman. Modest domesticity is her cover for the soul's immensity, breaking through her clockwork routines:

I tie my Hat — I crease my Shawl —
Life's little duties do — precisely —
As the very least
Were infinite — to me —

I put new Blossoms in the Glass —
And throw the Old — away —
I push a petal from my Gown
That anchored there — I weigh
The time 'twill be till six o'clock —
So much I have to do —
And yet — Existence — some way back —
Stopped — struck — my ticking — through — . . .

A double life is not surprising: it's almost inevitable with intelligent women of Dickinson's homebound generation. She was drawn to Jane Eyre, and Maggie Tulliver, George Eliot's provincial girl whose 'eyes were full of unsatisfied intelligence and unsatisfied, beseeching affection'. All these aspiring nineteenth-century women struggle for self-control and contrive to do their duty. What's stranger in Dickinson's character are the silences surrounding almost every word in the climactic couplet about the nameless thing that 'struck' a tick-tock life.

Unanswered questions resonate in the wake of lives, and no one more elusive than Emily Dickinson. To approach a biographical absence, the first responsible step was to map her social landscape. This enterprise was initiated in *Emily Dickinson's Home* (1955) by Millicent Todd Bingham, and carried forward by her executor, Richard B. Sewall, who filled in a detailed background in his two-volume *Life of Emily Dickinson* (1974), where the poet is not born until the second volume. Then Alfred Habegger reconfigured the factual portrait with enormous detective flair in 2001. To track down verifiable facts has been an impressive achievement of the last half-century.

A complementary venture lies ahead: to risk 'the Abyss', the biographic sources of a creativity we can never fully explain. In that sense, the poet is right to warn us off, yet the enigma she presents beckons: its teasing insistence suggests something to be solved. Early biographers got lost in the byways of fancy but there are two securer openings to the larger truth of her buried life: one will explore what the poet confides in letters and poems about her 'sickness', how it strikes her and the strange lift it offers her work. A linked approach will be through archival records of a different sort of disruption: a family feud in which she was interfused.

This material has been tapped by one interest or another, but this is the first attempt to tell the whole story. The actors happen to have been incessant recorders in letters, diaries, journals, unfinished autobiographies, reminiscences, interviews and taped memoirs. The abundance of archival record makes it possible to know the actors close up, to see the scenes they played and hear them speak. Exchanges may be set out in dialogue, as in drama or fiction, but all words, scenes and claims of participants in the feud are documented in source notes.

Though the feud began with adultery, Emily Dickinson became its focus after her death, each side battling for her unpublished papers. The issue was not so much money as the right to own the poet – the right to say who she was. Each side claimed to know, and fought to promote its legend. These legends still guard the entrance to the Abyss, for the feud persists even now. It started with a newcomer to Amherst who was drawn to the Dickinson family, and even more to its invisible poet.

In the late summer of 1881 Mabel Loomis Todd, aged twenty-four, arrived from Washington. It had been a two-week journey, by boat from Baltimore and across the Long Island Sound; then by train to Hartford, Connecticut; on to Springfield, Massachusetts; and from there deep into rural New England. The last part of the journey had to be by stagecoach from Northampton. Reluctantly, on the evening of 31 August, Mabel stepped down from the coach in the college town of Amherst, surer than ever that her husband should not have accepted a low-paid post in astronomy.

'What have I done?' she asked herself in her journal.

Her sturdy, fair-haired husband was more hopeful. David Peck Todd had been lured by a hint that a donor stood ready with $300,000 or more to build a new observatory. It was a wily hint, for President Julius Seelye of Amherst College had judged correctly that Todd was an ambitious man without means. Then, too, to be approached by what had been his own college had appeared to Todd in a flattering light. So, when the new astronomer presented himself at the start of the academic year, he was disconcerted to find himself cast not as a rising star, more a workhorse carrying three extra courses in mathematics and making do with an outdated observatory.

His young wife was free of burden. Amherst House, where the couple lived, was a boarding house, so Mabel had no domestic duties. She had long had a presentiment of a special fate: some stardom of her own, yet to emerge from her array of talents. These included a command of Washington card-dropping etiquette. Where Washington was blithe and elegant, Amherst appeared plain and critical, apart from Mrs Stearns, a welcoming widowed schoolmistress who had lived in Bombay and furnished her house with carved teak and Eastern embroideries.

The newcomer had light brown hair and warm, reddish-brown eyes. Though not tall, she had a distinctive presence, thin nosed, extending an immaculate white glove with a sidelong smile and the dressiness of an urban beauty maintaining standards in what appeared to her a negligible village full of retired clergymen and elderly academics.

Mabel Todd, in flounces over tight lacing, her fine, floppy hair elaborately coiled and puffed out to balance her hat, was invited everywhere, and ready to choose whom to favour. She was taken with 'regal', 'magnificent' Austin Dickinson and his wife's dark poise, set off by a scarlet India shawl, when they called on the Todds at Amherst House on 29 September, later than the town's lesser inhabitants. Behind Austin's back, children mocked his auburn wig and sniffy stride, tapping his cane as he went, but such was his dignity that no child would have dared to look him in the face. As a trustee and the treasurer of Amherst College, Austin Dickinson was influential, not to be overlooked in view of the fact that the appointment of David Todd was on a trial basis.

Mabel wore her thinnest white dress for her first call at The Evergreens on 3 October 1881, an event she recorded in her journal. She was entranced with the house: its Italianate design, its intellectual refinement, the abundance of books and pictures, the grace of Susan Dickinson's small hands, her literate talk and her husband's polished sarcasms. And whenever Mabel called at The Evergreens she saw next door, planted on a rise, the Homestead where Austin's sister, a poet-recluse, lived with a more accessible younger sister called Lavinia. It was said that the recluse had not left the house for the last fifteen years. The town spoke of her as 'the myth', but The Evergreens had the privilege of intimacy.

Susan ('Mrs Dickinson', as Mabel addressed her) liked to read aloud:

> Exultation is the going
> Of an inland soul to sea,
> Past the houses — past the headlands,
> Into deep Eternity —

Extraordinary utterances of this kind had been sent across from the recluse. Mabel's new acquaintance had a large collection of unpublished poems.

'Her talk and her writings are like no one's else,' Susan Dickinson said. The poet was 'quick as the lightning in her intuitions and analyses'.

Susan Dickinson described 'Emily' as a genius no one had recognised. 'She seizes the kernel instantly, almost impatient of the fewest words by which she must make her revelation.' Mabel caught fire. She thought of Schubert, who went unrecognised in his lifetime. Musical publishers were deaf to 'this great soul'. And here, it appeared, was another great soul next door. How intently Mabel listened when Susan Dickinson spoke of an old bond going back to girlhood, before her marriage to the poet's brother.

Susan Dickinson liked to mix with people of intelligence, and no sooner did she meet Mrs Todd than she took her up and drove her along back roads in the Dickinson carriage. When they'd had their fill of fall colours Mabel obliged her new friend by singing to her for three hours.

Everyone at The Evergreens was entranced, in turn, by the newcomer's talents: she sang solos in the church choir, played the piano with brilliance, painted flowers with professional skill and published stories and travel pieces in magazines. Her readiness to foster the arts in local society delighted Susan. 'She admires me extravagantly', Mabel wrote in her journal, 'and I love and admire her equally. She is a rare woman, & her home is my haven of pleasure in Amherst.'

After the many courses of Washington dinners, Mabel took to 'teas' at The Evergreens. They began at 8 p.m. and, later, light refreshments with oysters would be brought in and placed on little tables beside each guest, a style of entertaining reminiscent of early nineteenth-century England: Emma offering scalloped oysters to her father's guests in Highbury.

At these teas Mabel and Austin Dickinson were often together, Mabel attentive to what was said, her lower lip (as photos show) a little open and her brown eyes melting. She was eager to share Austin's love of nature: the misty hills in autumn, the red leaves and the sound of crickets. He hoped, he said, to have crickets chirping about his grave. He spoke clearly but with a note of shyness in his bluff manner. His diffidence was part of a refinement beyond anything she had encountered. 'He is delicate beyond expression', she thought. He seemed to live 'on the heights', reigning over a New England world of Puritan descendants who respected elevation.

The responsive Mrs Todd seems to act out a familiar plot, the seduction of a man in power, but what differed in this instance was the presence of another and grander form of power, that of a poet who selects her society then shuts the door. To an enthusiast such as Mabel, that shut door, and the elect intelligence behind it, offered another irresistible challenge. So one sunny day, 10 September 1882, a year after the Todds' arrival in Amherst, Mabel crossed the path, fortified by Austin's escort. Curious, filled with anticipation, she stepped through the Homestead door and was admitted to the parlour.

In this long room looking towards The Evergreens she seated herself at the poet's square piano and let loose the trills of her trained voice. It rang out through the big, silent house, and as it did so Mabel became aware 'that Miss Emily in her weird white dress was outside in the shadow', while her mother, bedridden for years, was listening upstairs. Mabel records the scene in her journal: 'When I stopped Emily sent me in a glass of rich sherry & a poem written as I sang.' Its first stanza acknowledges the lure of a blissful voice – 'Elysium is as far as to / The very nearest Room' – but in the second and concluding stanza the poet spells out a presentiment of her own: a step is heard; a door is opening to an oncoming intrusion she must 'endure':

> What fortitude the Soul contains,
> That it can so endure
> The accent of a coming Foot —
> The opening of a Door —

Sure enough, the very next day Mabel offered Austin her warm, waiting hand outside The Evergreens. She had been invited for the evening, and Austin had called for her at her boarding house. The pair slowed down as they reached The Evergreens and walked past the gate. In his diary for 11 September Austin left a space at the end and then set down a fateful word: 'Rubicon'. These few steps sufficed to carry them across the barrier of marital fidelity, before they went inside to play a game of whist with the unsuspecting Sue.

It was raining so hard, Mabel reflected afterwards, 'I could not see even a step ahead. But I did not want to see.' It quickened her pulse not to know 'what was coming – either on the glistening sidewalk, or on that other mental path which was to lead me – even now can I say where? Yes. I entered it boldly and happily', because the emotion of this austere personage offered an 'opening so strange, so unexpected' that she saw herself on course for an 'exceptional' experience. Once inside The Evergreens, playing cards and chatting with the family, she sensed 'a whole new future'. It felt 'tenacious and vigorous', the sort of future that 'came to stay – not a day only or even a year, but always'. No hesitation interrupts this train of thought.

With Mabel at The Evergreens nearly every day, Susan continued to talk of Emily Dickinson's poetry as the rarest of treasures. Report of the newcomer's enthusiasm reached the poet herself, who was accustomed to circulate her poems to a number of chosen readers. She sent Mrs Todd a few poems, possibly with a view to drawing her in. Lavinia said that her sister was 'always watching for the rewarding person to come'. This was Mabel's impression, and when she calls it 'friendship' it's not necessarily as fanciful as it would seem. For Emily Dickinson did conduct her ties through handwritten copies of poems sent to those she admitted to friendship.

'She writes the strangest poems & very remarkable ones', Mabel wrote in her journal on 15 September 1882, four days after her initial visit to the Homestead. 'She is in many respects a genius. She always wears white, & has her hair arranged as was the fashion fifteen years ago when she went into retirement. She wanted me to come & sing to her, but she would not see me. She has frequently sent me flowers & poems, & we have a very pleasant friendship in that way.'

It was only a matter of time, Mabel was sure, before she saw the poet face to face.

Mabel Todd's entry into the Homestead looks politely obliging beside her attachment to Austin, but it was to present a parallel and more lasting threat to family cohesion. In the course of the following year Mabel would prise open the seclusion of the Homestead and establish herself as an habituée of the house, in a position to claim one of its rooms for three or four hours at a time. Until then the poet had controlled all contact with others. Her reclusive existence had served to release her gift and hold it at its explosive edge. But in the course of 1883 and 1884 she came up against the unstoppable momentum of this takeover. This advance of sexual energy on more sensitive forms of life – the Darwinian tragedy – presents a real-life drama nearly twenty years ahead of Chekhov's *Three Sisters* where a robust female, a brother's choice, takes over a family of three sensitive women. To what extent did Emily Dickinson resist the intrusion? Later, Mabel Todd would take possession of Dickinson's papers and market them on her own terms, so that the strange nature of the poet became obscured.

*

To see the poet through a family upheaval that was to determine her image, we need to go back and back in time. Thirty years before Mabel Todd won Austin Dickinson, he had been in love in much the same way. Clever and ardent, with a moody arch to his lower lip, and determined to see his love through, whatever the obstacles, he had married a girl whose father had died a bankrupt alcoholic. If this had been almost any other place beside New England the bridegroom's family might have opposed such a match. But in this region of rural Massachusetts during the 1850s, what mattered was faith.

Six years before the marriage of Austin and Susan a religious revival had gripped Amherst. In August 1850 Austin's upright father, Edward Dickinson, had been moved to fall on his knees and declare himself a miserable sinner. Despite this gesture, his minister was not entirely pleased with the dry manner of Edward Dickinson's salvation, as though this lawyer were arguing a case. But there could be no doubt about the feeling of Susan Gilbert, a girl of twenty dressed in black for a sister who had died from childbirth the previous month. For an orphan who missed her mother and, still more, the dearest and most protective of her sisters who had replaced her mother, a promise of reunion in the afterlife was an answer to loss. Edward Dickinson, kneeling in the same group and unaccustomed to public shows of emotion – he was reserved even within his family – was struck by the girl's seriousness and the grace of her words. So it was that when Austin cast his lofty eye on Susan Gilbert his father not only approved, he positively wished for the match. So did all the family, including self-effacing Mrs Dickinson, her vehement elder daughter Emily and her second daughter, Lavinia, to the extent of closing in on Susan with insistent persuasions.

'Susie – we all love you – Mother – Vinnie – me. <u>Dearly</u>!' Emily urged, her insistence quite as heated as Austin's.

Emily Dickinson had a reason of her own for drawing Susan into her family: she was a discerning reader. 'With the exception of Shakespeare, you have told me of more knowledge than any one living', she told Susan later. 'To say that sincerely is strange praise.' A poet in the making, she befriended Susan as her fellow reader and other self.

'I want to think of you each hour in the day,' Emily pressed her. 'You say you walk and sew alone. I walk and sew alone.'

If she could have painted her feelings, 'the scene should be – <u>solitude</u>, and the figures – solitude – and the lights and shades, each a solitude. I could fill a chamber with landscapes so lone, men should pause and weep there . . .'. In her fantasy, she and this most necessary friend would walk invisible, 'seeing yet unseen'.

In contact with Susan – a 'Sister' married, eventually, to her brother and settled next door – Emily Dickinson fired a poetic voice '<u>at the White Heat</u>'. Susan met this rarity with her own 'torrid spirit', hot enough for the poet to dub her 'Domingo', as stimulating as rum for a poet intoxicated with words. Excitement was mutual. Next door, at The Evergreens, Susan read Sister's poems aloud to the public men of Boston or Springfield – the philosopher Ralph Waldo Emerson, it might be, or Samuel Bowles, editor of the *Springfield Republican*, a newspaper admired for its independent editorials – when they chanced to stop over in the staid college town.

So it went on for twenty-five years, with two families in adjoining houses: the quiet, old-fashioned Homestead of the elder Mr Dickinson, his wife and two daughters; and the vibrant, much-visited home of Austin, Susan, and their children. From the late 1850s The Evergreens functioned as the prime outlet for Emily Dickinson, home to her poetic eruptions. Letters and poems (some with Sue as subject) took the path trodden by the two women's feet between the houses, and Sue was the sole member of family to take the temperature of Emily's venture. Brainy, curtailed Maggie Tulliver reads avidly, and Sue's wants were Maggie's wants: books with '*more*' in them. As a reading partner, Sue was on intimate terms with George Eliot, Elizabeth Barrett Browning and the Brontës. As such, 'Sister' could speak to a secret self bent on immortality.

It's known that she shut herself in her father's house and that she eventually produced 1789 poems, most of them secreted in that locked chest of drawers. On the face of it, her life seems uneventful and largely invisible, but a forceful, even overwhelming character stirred below her still surface. She called it a 'still — Volcano — Life', and that volcano heaves, close to the surface, throughout her poetry and a thousand letters. Stillness, for

her, was not a retreat from life but a form of control. Far from the helplessness she played up at times, she controlled her dramas, taking on the
head of her college, other strong women and men who were leaders in the
publishing and legal worlds. But there came a time when this control was
threatened by a young woman who admired her poems and offered to sing
for her delectation.

Once The Evergreens and then the Homestead opened their doors to
Mabel Todd, emotions — a lethal mix of passion, jealousy and rage —
erupted during the last years of the poet's life, perpetuated by descendants and the authorities they co-opted or persuaded. To crack through
accreting claims, to find what Dickinson called the red 'Fire rocks' below,
we must go back to acts of adultery that changed, changed utterly, the
lives of her family and those who were to be the first keepers of her
papers.

Within a year of Mrs Todd's advent in Amherst she was on course to an
unassailable position as Austin's mistress. His sisters could not help knowing that Austin turned against his wife, and then against his children when
they sided with their mother. Emily tried to soothe Susan with messages.
'Will my great Sister accept the minutae of Devotion, with timidity that it
is no more?' she offered. And again, as the first reverberations of what was
to come shook the ground, 'Your little mental gallantries are sweet as
Chivalry . . .'. This could not mend matters.

How was it possible to blow apart a family who lived in its set ways as
upright citizens in a New England town?

Mabel was no fictional femme fatale. Not the veiled and sometimes
dangerous lady in decorative distress who glides into the sanctum of
Sherlock Holmes. Not even the subtle Madame Merle whom James
brought into his *Portrait of a Lady*, playing the piano with such startling
bravura in 1881. Madame Merle wins the friendship of the innocent
American girl; without this move, Madame Merle would not have been
close enough to set her plot ticking. But Mabel enchanted a living family,
and real life can be in its way more extraordinary than fiction. For the
temperament to devise high drama did not reside with Mabel alone.

There's so much of performance in what followed, such roles to be played before a wondering public – the eccentric poet, the dressy adventuress, the top man in town, his vulnerable son, his outraged wife – we must not start by taking sides. These actors and the companies they gathered around them will tug us to do so, for they are – all – adepts at stories. Although Mabel's adventuress aspect does stand out, the success of her narrative depends upon the nature of the family on whom she intrudes.

As Mabel inserts herself between husband and wife, and then between poet and 'Sister', and as a fissure in the family cracks and then breaks open early in 1885, it's puzzling how this could have happened from the Dickinson side. Instinct is only the commonest part of it, an autumnal flush in a middle-aged man, and yet Austin, like all the Dickinsons, prided himself on rising above the common. They were close-knit, introspective people who exercised immense control in all they did; Austin himself, a cautious lawyer like his father before him, was the opposite of rash. He was a sticker, one of those who, by nature, mate for life: such creatures are closed to alternatives, so loyal are they to their attachments. Austin would have considered before he acted on a passing impulse, so what scenarios took over his mind? The deeper cause of the fissure in the family lies in their past.

II: 'A STILL — VOLCANO — LIFE'

1

THE FIRST FAMILY

In the mid-nineteenth century Amherst held out against the metropolitan tolerance of Boston. As Amherst's first family, the Dickinsons were true to the Puritan rigour of provincial New England. Her father's heart was 'pure and terrible', his daughter Emily said. 'I do not expect or wish for a life of pleasure', Edward Dickinson told his wife-to-be before their marriage. He was never seen to smile. When she was old, Lavinia mimicked for Mabel how her father sat for a photograph: head held in an invisible brace, eye unflinching. 'Could you – smile a little?' the photographer asked. 'I *yam* smiling,' Mr Dickinson replied through set jaw. Later, when a man of letters came all the way from Boston to visit the poet, Mr Dickinson gave him a grim, almost wordless welcome. He ruled the household – after he died, when Emily was forty-four, she still spoke of living in 'my father's house' – but did he dominate her? Or did she take on something of his power?

Her spaced eyes and large, full mouth were too keen for the passivity admired in women of her time. The well-known daguerreotype taken when she was sixteen bares the face of a person who, as her brother put it, 'saw things directly and just as they were'. Her sister called it a 'startling' face. There was a widening divide between people she wished to know and those she didn't. She abhorred sham: social talk instead of truth; piety instead of 'the Soul's Superior instants'. Her directness would have been disconcerting if she did not 'simulate' conventionality. This she could do:

as a girl longing for valentines, or tinkling out 'a sweet little song' ('Maiden Weep No More'), or playing to the solemnity of pious girls, she appeared indistinguishable from her contemporaries, yet she grew less inclined to make the effort. Though she disparaged herself as the 'only Kangaroo' amid Beauty, she had the creature's long, sloping neck holding up a sensitive face with the full eyes of a watcher. Another self-image is consciously charming, with eyes like sherry at the bottom of a glass, she said, and hair the colour of a chestnut burr. She sees herself in colour, but adjusts this to contemporary taste, for her hair was red like her brother's. She had the pale skin and summer freckles that go with red hair.

A schoolmate recalled her voice as high and clear. It had 'a strangely indefinable quality of surprise – almost an accent of consternation'. Austin's voice had a similar interrogative lift. What the schoolmate thought strange was a teasing irony.

One of her poems pictures herself as a wren: small, neat, with eyes and head on the alert. The daguerreotype shows the delicate frame of a girl who, from time to time, was removed from school for reasons of health. As she moved through her twenties, when she was fanning her poetic fire, she would have made no concession to the ringlets and doll-like crinolines of the 1850s. Her full, slightly jutting lower lip would have firmed as she grew older. The assurance and humour of her mature writing suggests an air of composure, unlike the vulnerable girl.

The vulnerable image encouraged the pathos woven into her popularity. How the public loves wounded genius! How it loves her all the more if she be unmated, seething with love denied, an all-time poet unrecognised in her lifetime. But the Emily Dickinson who speaks through her letters makes no concession to helplessness. This is not a person so frail, so wrapped up in writing that, in time, she would sidestep the rupture in her family. Nor is she unmindful of her family's standing: a status too secure for ostentation or the ephemeral absurdities of fashion: the one surviving dress confirms her continued simplicity. Her curly hair, cut short in her early twenties, was long again in her late twenties, parted in the centre and drawn back over her ears in smooth bands. The uprightness of her posture suggests New England correctness. This young woman has gentility – more distinguished in its way than aristocratic gentility because there is nothing above it, nothing between it and the superiority of superior instants. Who amongst us can face her steady, watchful eye? For there's something at the back of that eye that warns us to be very, very careful. How does the propriety fit what's wild in her poetry? The two could only be conjoined in a force-field where control (the tight net of the quatrain) and the uncontained ('Wild nights — Wild nights!') are both in play, not in conflict, for control deploys as well as holds down secrets surging to the surface. One flares for a second, a fuse packed in riddling turns of phrase, when she calls Aunt Elizabeth (her father's bossy youngest sister, registered at birth as male) 'the only male relative on the female side'.

As a young man Mr Dickinson had chosen a wife after a different mould. Mrs Dickinson followed the cult of true womanhood as laid down by the Revd John Bennett in his *Letters to a Young Lady* (1789), reprinted in 1824, four years before Emily Norcross came as a bride to Amherst. This small white advice book, which she brought with her (together with her grandmother's Bible and Watt's *Psalms carefully suited to Christian Worship*), helped to shape the generation of self-effacing Mrs Dickinson and, through her, the model of womanhood that her daughter Emily inherited – and countered. The Revd Mr Bennett warns women not to write anything loftier than letters. Turning prohibition to advantage, Dickinson would define poetry as her 'letter to the World' and transmit her poems through letters. A minister like Bennett could not fault her, yet it's not exactly the modesty he'd had in mind. In so far as a letter speaks from the present instant to eyes at a distance, it carries life or death, the poet warned, 'for what is each instant but a gun, harmless because "unloaded," but that touched "goes off"?'

Her mother had conformed more closely to the mild virtues of the advice book: she had been commended at school for punctuality, application and discreet behaviour (though amongst her obedient notes on sermons there is a scribbled appeal to a young teacher: 'Oh! Caroline, remember me for forever'). At the age of twenty-two she met Mr Dickinson, aged twenty-three, who was seated next to her at a chemistry lecture during a visit he made to her home town of Monson, Massachusetts. That year, 1826, he was setting up as a lawyer in Amherst, and ready to take a wife. She too was ready to marry a trustworthy man who may not have shown his feelings but knew his mind.

His overture was 'unexpected', she told him; there had been no 'intimations' of interest. 'When I reflect that I am writing to one with whom my acquaintance has been so short, I can hardly exercise the freedom I would desire. Still I will say to you that I realised much happiness in your society while at Monson.' She asked if she might defer a more definite response until she was permitted to see him again, 'yet I am sensible that you have conferred your friendship upon one who is undeserving'.

Becomingly modest as she is, her voice is not entirely passive when she intimates a need for 'freedom' of expression between herself and the near stranger who might become her husband. Though both were of marriageable age, it was not a quick courtship. This was not necessarily because they were too restrained for undue urgency, but most likely for the practical reason that a man had to prove his ability to support a family. Emily's father Joel Norcross was prosperous, while young Mr Dickinson, though able, had to deal with what used to be called embarrassments: debts. It was a matter of honour to clear his father's debts. So, for two years, Edward Dickinson rode the twenty miles from Amherst to visit Emily Norcross every four or six weeks. She had a private reason for delay. At long intervals, and with undemanding quietness, she voiced an unsatisfied need: 'I am sensible that I have never exercised that freedom which I presume you have desired me to.'

Presume? It's a troubled question, with a light finger on the pulse of a relationship. It's doubtful if Mr Dickinson entertained this desire for when, eventually, he made his formal proposal of marriage she hesitated for two months. She even withheld an answer during one of his visits, before she picked up her pen.

'I think you must be convinced ere this that your intercourse with me is mutual although I have not explained to you my views as I have wished . . .'. She did not think it immodest to tell her future husband that she looked forward to his parting kiss, but though he may have felt the same or more he could not bring out so intimate a word: he looks forward to a '-s'.

Mr Dickinson, insulated by reserve, was not one to enquire into feelings, though he had them. His manner was stern; with hard, keen sense and practical energy he rapped out his intentions. The Revd Mr Bennett counselled 'discipline of the imagination'. Unless a woman reined in her imagination she would be exposed to disappointments that, he warned, 'create disgust' – a disgust that can erode a wife's taste for 'the solid duties of your condition'. Nothing in Mr Dickinson's replies suggests that his bride's barely stated wish for freedom of expression had been heard, much less answered, when they married on 6 May 1828.

For his part, Mr Dickinson would have expected domestic competence as well as wifely compliance; his wife, as attentive to home and table as he could wish, deferred to him as 'my dear'. Her first child was their only son, William Austin Dickinson, always called Austin after one of Mrs Dickinson's dead brothers. He was born in 1829, a year after the marriage, closely followed on 10 December 1830 by a girl, Emily Elizabeth. Her second name was after Aunt Elizabeth. This connection did not endear her wilful aunt to a niece only seven years her junior and with a will of her own. A third Dickinson child, another daughter, was named after Mrs Dickinson's lively younger sister Lavinia. This was to be a close tie. Lavinia Norcross opened her home to her nieces, and Emily's affection for this loving aunt would extend to her children who would become part of the poet's inner circle of correspondents, the chosen audience for her poems.

After Lavinia's birth in 1833, Mrs Dickinson languished. Two years later there were still questions about her condition, as if she had undergone an illness serious enough to have been a blight on the household. Since there is no sign of physical harm, it sounds like postpartum depression. Her suppressed wish for expressiveness suggests that Mrs Dickinson was not the cipher she has seemed. Her daughter the poet would define a wife as one who rose to her husband's 'Requirement', dropping 'The Playthings of Her Life', and if she missed anything in her day-to-day life it fell outside the accepted vocabulary. Only a poet determined to re-invent language, riding metaphors that carry her to the frontier of a buried life, could articulate an 'unmentioned' thing: a submerged self, 'Fathoms beneath the sea'.

This generation of mothers and daughters would be the first to respond to a new kind of man capable of saying to a repressed young woman: 'I think you will learn to be natural with me, as I find it impossible to be conventional with you.' *Jane Eyre* flashed on Emily Dickinson like a mirror in which she saw, bared, a soul to be preserved.

'If you were God' on the receiving end of prayers that the author might be saved 'would you answer', she asked the junior lawyer in her father's office who had lent her his copy of the novel in 1849. Five years after the author's death in 1855, a still-fervent Dickinson imagines the benefit for heaven when Charlotte Brontë arrived:

> Oh what an afternoon for Heaven,
> When 'Bronte' entered there!

When Jane Eyre calls Rochester 'my master' the word conveys no sense of tyranny; rather, a master of character. For Mr Rochester, riding out of darkness, can detect the invisible woman behind the schooled façade of Victorian conformity. Charlotte Brontë and her sisters – born halfway between the dates of Mrs Dickinson and her daughters – were spokeswomen for submerged words, a voice Emily Dickinson would take up with a 'Master' of her own.

At a guess (it has to be a guess since there is little record of Mrs Dickinson) she was not naturally effaced, and in the aftermath of childbirth, when emotions swim to the surface, needs she had learnt to control overtook her. Her husband thought the answer was retreat from life: women were safest, he thought, if they stayed at home, and to stress this he gave his wife another advice book, *The Mother At Home: Principles of Maternal Duty*. The aim is to firm up mothers with wilful children, and to achieve this a mother must bring her own feelings 'under a system of rigid discipline'. If she keeps her mind 'unimpassioned' she will bring up better children.

*

The seriousness of Mrs Dickinson's condition is suggested by the fact that, unusually for a time when their kin on both sides had eight to ten children, the Dickinsons stopped at three. Mr Dickinson would have been considerate of his wife's health. He was minutely concerned with the health of his family and realistically so, given high mortality in chilly, tubercular New England, with risks increased for women weakened by constant childbearing. But what looks like a responsible decision to have no more births may have constricted their relationship. They were then no more than twenty-nine and thirty years old. Some years later, their daughter Emily was amused at the sight of them on Sundays sitting in state in the parlour, 'perusing such papers only, as they are well assured have nothing carnal in them'. As the years passed, Mr Dickinson's pure and abstinent life stilled his face: white and hollow of cheek, silent at times. It was a controlled household (apart from Mrs Dickinson's tendency to tears) and this, conceivably, was to have consequences for their children, who gave vent, later, to extravagant passions: Austin and Lavinia overtly, Emily in a more private manner of her own. One of her poems pictures a child craving emotional nourishment:

> It would have starved a Gnat —
> To live so small as I —
> And yet I was a living Child —
> With — Food's necessity . . .

The craving is upon the child 'like a Claw' it cannot remove. If there is any interior truth in this surreal impasse, the mother, the usual provider of emotional nourishment, is strangely absent. In the spaces of the poem there is something unexplained. Did this child take up her mother's craving? Another imaginary childhood wrong is to be 'shut up' in 'Prose' – in this context the prosaic, a smallness of mind the poet often associated with Mrs Dickinson ('My Mother does not care for thought', she alleged at the age of thirty-one when she approached a man of letters with her poems). The poem pictures a girl with a free spirit, like a bird's, who finds herself 'caged' in a domestic destiny. In the privacy of her soul the girl's brain (with a capital B) remains active; she defies her stilled positioning:

> . . . Still! Could themself have peeped —
> And seen my Brain — go round —
> They might as wise have lodged a Bird
> For Treason — in the Pound — . . .

These poems are dramatised, not to be read literally. Emotional repression in their parents did not inhibit the children from saying what they thought. All three were clever and ready to air their wits. Austin and Lavinia inclined to the cutting; Emily to the merry and irreverent. At two and a half she had been fearless at the sight of lightning which she called delightedly 'fire'. As a child she was attracted by the 'cordiality' of the Sacrament, and when a clergyman invited 'all who loved the Lord Jesus Christ to remain' she recalled, 'I could scarcely refrain from rising and thanking him for the to me unexpected courtesy, though I now think had it been to all who loved Santa Claus, my transports would have been even more untimely.'

Only Mrs Dickinson, it appears, being a wife and not of the blood royal, had no part in the Dickinson aplomb. While unmarried, Emily Norcross had enough curiosity to attend a chemistry lecture; as Mrs Dickinson, she gave herself to home and children. There's nothing to explain what happened to that curiosity, beyond the historical fact of Tocqueville's astonishment when he visited America in 1831 and observed how free-spoken American girls curtailed themselves on marriage. Why, Tocqueville wondered, should this girl, freer than her European counterpart, constrict herself in so willed a way? Her daughter's poems take a dim view of what it was to become a wife: 'Born — Bridalled — Shrouded — in a day'. The pun on 'bridalled' seals her fate.

Abruptly, overnight, the bride – the one-time Emily Norcross – was moved twenty miles away, to find herself dependent on a husband with troubles of his own. He was too busy to drive her to see her family, even when her mother, Betsey Norcross, was dying. Despite her sister's urgings that Betsey was asking for her, she was able to come only the day before her mother's death. The younger sister, still at home, saw a 'burning tear' of guilt mixed with grief slide down her married sister's cheek.

Soon after Emily Norcross married Mr Dickinson, prospects began to open up for women with higher education, an opportunity her elder daughter would approach with dreaming eagerness. The 1820s was the last decade in which no college for women existed. The first, now Mount Holyoke, was founded not far from Amherst, in 1836. This is not to suggest that Mrs Dickinson might have welcomed the higher education of women – there is no way to know. Yet the very existence of the college (following a new array of academies providing a high-school education for girls, and opening up posts for women teachers) must have shifted ideas for women's future. Emily, her daughter, spoke of herself as 'old-fashioned', and this image has charmed many of her admirers. In a Broadway play, *The Belle of Amherst*, an archly feminine poet hardly knows what she says, so keeps busy with baking. No slight to baking. Emily, like Emily Brontë before her, preferred it to housework, for baking and, even more, gardening, complement the life of the mind with more practical kinds of creativity.* Yet what remains odd is the poet's care to fit the effaced model of womanhood that shaped her mother's generation of the 1820s, in so far as 1830 (the year of Emily Dickinson's birth) is said to mark the end of an era of domestic retirement for New England women.

To go through the Revd Mr Bennett's rulebook is to see how ironically the poet fitted herself, point for point, with all the extravagance and precision of her character. The minister directs girls' attention to volcanoes to awaken a sense of awe. With apparent obedience the poet internalises the volcano. But the latent explosiveness of 'A still — Volcano — Life' is not what he had in mind. The same with plants. 'Pore on plants,' advises the minister, 'and I will engage you to become, in your turn, one of the most beautiful flowers in the creation.' As a child, Emily works away at her herbarium and delights in her flourishing plants; later she will take on the character of 'Daisy': an eroticised Daisy, turning her petals towards 'the man of noon'. Not the minister's idea, for sure.

* Similar to the practical diversion Virginia Woolf was to find in setting type for the Hogarth Press.

The most fertile loophole in the minister's advice leaves his dear young lady free to engage in one kind of writing: 'To write letters is a very desirable excellence in a woman . . . A man attends to the niceties of grammar . . . a woman gives us the effusions of her soul.' Emily Dickinson arrogates this liberty, but deploys the ungrammatical deliberately to invent a language of her own. So, Dickinson both obeyed the rules and pushed them to the edge with a kind of flagrant glee. One rule, though, she disobeyed outright.

'Poetry I do not wish you to cultivate', Bennett advised. 'A passion for poetry is dangerous to a woman.' It heightens her natural sensibility to an extravagant and sickly degree, he explained, and then repeated in his most forbidding manner, 'I do not wish you to become a poet.' Yet he could not shut off the beat of the Isaac Watts hymns that had been adopted by the First Church of Amherst. Each Sunday that combination of scripture and hymn metre fell on the ears of a child who would one day deploy that metre as the poet she was to be.

At home, the prime arbiter was, of course, Mr Dickinson. Emily was not cowed by her father's adversarial style. It was his way to intimidate opposition with a battering of sarcastic questions, speaking with the brevity of a curt, not expansive mind – not the inspired brevity of his daughter. Point one, he'd say, point two, when he addressed legal clients or when he rose to speak in the Massachusetts legislature or in Congress, where he served a term from 1853 to 1855. Logically, and with impeccable rectitude, he built a case against the extension of slavery to Western states entering the Union. His tone was habitually severe: one day, avarice is the worst of sins; another day, laziness. Whichever the sin, we turn to Jesus, and we do so not with love but in fear of damnation. Emily was unafraid of his fierceness: 'Father steps like Cromwell when he gets the kindlings', she joked, and she read his reticence with understanding. When Austin left for boarding school she detected a father's feeling in the grave way he walked towards the barn, and returned 'looking very stately – then strode away down [the] street as if the foe was coming'. Emily's own brand of fearlessness stirred unlooked-for pleasure in her father.

Mr Dickinson came from a line of venturesome men who led their communities. Their sense of status, more indwelling than show, overlaid a legend of primacy. Dickinson ancestry, they fancied, might be traced to the first voyage from Europe to the Americas, and to the first Normans in England. The European progenitor the Dickinsons chose was none other than Rollo the Dane who in 901 sailed to the shores of New England, and went on to conquer Normandy, entrenching himself as its first duke. Dickinson fantasy then fixed on his descendant in the next century, Walter de Caen, who accompanied William the Conqueror to England where the family — by the name of Dykenson (literally, de Caen's son) — became hereditary owners of a Saxon manor called Kenson, in Yorkshire. This grand family history does not explain how a nobody called Nathaniel Dickinson emerges from the soggy fenlands of Lincolnshire and sails for New England in 1637.

He and his wife and children joined a party of fifty-eight families who pressed deep into the territory of the Norwottucks in what is now western Massachusetts. They called their settlement Hadley; Nathaniel became its first recorder, its town magistrate and a trustee of the school. He lived to mourn two sons — the elder born in England, the younger in America — killed in the Norwottuck raids of 1675.

In 1742 his great-grandson, Nathan, moved north-east to what became Amherst. He was accompanied by his wife Thankful and son, Nathan Jr. The latter lived to ninety and fathered many children, three of whom married into the same family, the well-connected* Montagues whose ancestors had been fellow settlers in seventeenth-century Hadley† and who reappear in Emily Dickinson's story and the feud that follows. Nathan Dickinson's daughter, Irene Dickinson Montague, known to Emily as 'Aunt Montague', had three children — one, an invalid in Amherst. His name was Zebina, and when he was thirty-two he makes a dramatic appearance in Emily's first surviving letter, written at the age of eleven in 1842.

* In the network of cousinage in New England, reaching down from the colonial period, the Montagues were linked with the leading families, including the Norton and Quincy families; Abigail Adams, wife of the second president; and Abigail Adams Cranch, grandmother of T. S. Eliot.
† A plan of the new settlement in 1663 shows Richard Montague's eight-acre plot on the North Highway to the Woods and Nathaniel Dickinson's eight-acre plot on the Middle Highway to the Woods (*The Genealogy of the Montague Family*).

'Cousin Zebina had a fit the other day', she reports, 'and bit his tongue into.' Clearly she'd overheard an exaggeration: 'bit his tongue in two'. Mr Dickinson feared fits as he feared croup – as though fits were contagious – and warned his wife to keep Vinnie out of their way.

The achiever amongst Nathan's brood was Irene's brother, Samuel Fowler Dickinson, who became Emily's grandfather. In 1802 he reinforced the blood ties with the classy Montagues when he married Lucretia Gunn, whose mother was a Montague and whose home town was Montague, Massachusetts. Grandmother Gunn was tart and ill-tempered, and later generations of Dickinsons tended to excuse their outbursts by saying it was Grandmother Gunn 'coming out'. It would not have been beyond the poet to joke about this explosive inheritance in her line, 'My Life had stood — a Loaded Gun'.

Her grandfather was tall and spare, plainly dressed, plain to look at, but a man of ideas and principles and a ferocious worker. He graduated summa cum laude from Dartmouth College, which he pictured as a seat of the sciences amongst 'the savages' of the New Hampshire wilderness. 'It is still ours to inquire into the nature of man and springs of human action', he declared in an oration to his class of 1795. Such was his respect for education that he bankrupted himself to found Amherst College. In 1816 he and Noah Webster (the compiler of dictionaries) backed the idea, and it was Samuel Dickinson who had the vision and will to promote it, but in order to do so he was not only reckless with money but also involved members of his family in his debts. In 1833, when Emily was two years old, her grandfather was forced to sell half of his mansion on Main Street and go out west. He ended his days as steward to the Western Reserve College in Ohio. A daughter guessed that 'his depression of spirits' had brought on his early death.

Before he became entangled in business, Samuel had excelled as a lawyer. His eldest son, Edward, followed his father in this profession. By the age of thirty-two he was trusted for his probity and responsibility, and these qualities, enhanced by the afterglow of his father's sacrifice for Amherst College, led to Edward's appointment as college treasurer, not a task for which he was especially suited. Though more cautious than his father, he was also too scrupulous – some might say too honourable – to

handle finance. He did, however, manage well enough with his legal practice and owned some of the finest horses in the area. He would drive
through Amherst, spare, erect, the reins taut behind the high heads. In
time, he paid off his father's debts and settled his family in the right half of
the Dickinson Homestead (sometimes called the Mansion) built by his
father in 1813. It was the first brick house in town and stood apart on a rise
in Main Street, three blocks east of the village centre and looking out in
front over a large field, called the 'Dickinson meadow'. The Mack family,
who had bought the left half of the house, then went on to buy the
Dickinsons' side in 1840. Edward Dickinson moved his family to more spa-
cious quarters, a white clapboard house in West Street (now North Pleasant
Street) where his daughter Emily spent the formative years between nine
and twenty-five.

Her room overlooked the graveyard. Funerals took place nearly every day.
After each funeral she saw a 'Swelling of the Ground' to house the dead for
all Eternity. When, she wondered, would Death take her? There was the
untimely death of the gardener's baby, and with a keener shock Emily
entered the sickroom of a dying cousin, Sophia Holland. Visitors were forbidden when Sophia could no longer communicate intelligibly:

> Then it seemed to me that I should die too if I could not be
> permitted to watch over her or even to look at her face. At length
> the doctor said she must die & allowed me to look at her a moment
> through the open door. I took off my shoes and stole softly into the
> sick room.
>
> There she lay mild & beautiful as in health & her pale features lit
> up with an unearthly – smile. I looked as long as friends would
> permit & when they told me I must look no longer I let them lead
> me away. I shed no tear, for my heart was too full to weep . . .

When Sophia lay in her coffin it hit Emily that she could not call back a
schoolmate whose thoughts and feelings were her own, or so she fancied.
Unable to speak her feelings, she 'gave way to a fixed melancholy'. Her

condition was bad enough for her to be removed from her school, Amherst Academy, and sent away to recuperate with Aunt Lavinia, who was now married and living in Boston. There Emily remained 'down-spirited' and unable, she said, 'to busy myself about anything'. At such times she seems to have felt cut off from expressive warmth. Though warmth was her aunt's strength, the melancholy Emily had brought with her was, by now, hard to budge. She turned to a new arrival at Amherst Academy, Abiah Root from Springfield, asking that letters be 'long' and thanking Abiah repeatedly for her affection.

Mrs Fiske, the mother of another schoolmate, Helen, was consumptive. As her strength failed she kept Helen with her, out of school. She hoped to cheer her younger child Ann with a birthday party on Christmas day, but by then was too weak. By way of compensation she wrote to ask the Dickinsons if Ann could visit Emily and Vinnie. This didn't come off, and Mrs Fiske died a few weeks later. Emily's letters to Abiah remark the loneliness of yet another schoolfellow who had lost her mother, and the girl's longing for one more glimpse of her.

Mortality was rife in Amherst, its proximity inescapable, and this in part contributed to the pervasive speculation about immortality. Thinking back to 'the early spiritual influences about a child', Emily later said: 'The angel begins in the morning in every human life.' Her visionary gleam glanced off small things and heaven was close: 'How small the furniture of bliss! How scant the heavenly fabric!' An autobiographical poem recreates the extraordinary firmness of the child's hold on her private life, curbing her smile at talk of worldly riches since she knows the value of interior Gold:

> It was given to me by the Gods —
> When I was a little Girl —
> They give us Presents most — you know —
> When we are new — and small.
> I kept it in my Hand —
> I never put it down —
> I did not dare to eat — or sleep —
> For fear it would be gone —

I heard such words as 'Rich' —
When hurrying to school —
From lips at Corners of the Streets —
And wrestled with a smile.
Rich! 'Twas Myself — was rich —
To take the name of Gold —
And Gold to own — in solid Bars —
The Difference — made me bold —

We sense her breathing presence, especially in the spaced line 'I did not dare to eat — or sleep —', as though, with each dash, something nameless is breaking through the crust of words; as though language were a crater, unsafe and stirring. Emily Dickinson is telling us that she lived on the lip of this crater from childhood on, long before she began to preserve her poems.

The boldness of her early character solidifying around 'it' – childhood's visionary gift – had little in common with the preacher, aloft in his pulpit, blighting children's spirits with an avenging God and possible death that very night. Emily recalled that 'no verse in the Bible has frightened me so much from a Child as "from him that hath not, shall be taken even that he hath." Was it because its dark menace deepened our own Door?' Her awareness of her home's barricades against that encroaching and ever-visible 'menace' brought mortality home yet again, reinforced by the death of Aunt Lavinia's eldest child, aged four, from the dread scarlet fever.

There were evening prayer meetings and in midwinter, when the snow was two to three feet deep, four weeks of protracted prayers imploring sinners to undergo a change of heart they called conversion. Sinners clumped through the snow at a time when there was no street lighting. For the farmers who stayed for afternoon service on Sundays there were circular seats about a red-hot stove and talk 'in low sad tones. A meagre lunch would be drawn from large, yellow muffs, while small soap-stones, drawn also from muffs, were re-heated for the sleigh-drive home in the winter dusk.'

Emily was often excused from church on account of the cold. Once, when her father did command her attendance, she begged off until both were weary. Suddenly she disappeared and the family had to go without her. On their return they searched for her with increasing alarm. At last she was found rocking in a chair in the cellar.

When Emily was twelve Jane Humphrey, a younger sister of one of the teachers at Amherst Academy, arrived for a spell at the school. Jane stayed with the Dickinsons, and after she left Emily wrote to her: 'what good times we used to have jumping into bed when you slept with me. I do wish you would come to Amherst and make me a great long visit'. And again: 'I miss you more and more every day, in my study in play at home indeed every where I miss my beloved Jane – I wish you would write to me – I should think more of it than a mine of gold.' It took courage to persist without winning a reply.

Emily found it even harder to give up on a group of five fourteen-year-olds, including Sabra Palmer, Harriet Merrill, Sarah Tracy, and Abby Wood, who had adored their teacher, 'our dear Miss Adams', for two happy terms in 1844. Miss Adams, aged thirty-three, was an experienced teacher who could meld girls into a group. As it happened, the 'five' dispersed (three left Amherst) and ties faded but, once more, Emily reached out through letters, reminding the others of bonds that continued to vibrate in her imagination.

At this point she initiated a practice that was to dominate her adult life as a writer: sending her work out to friends with a view to binding them to her as a circle of readers. An encouraging teacher like Miss Adams would have given the signal for a consensus of praise. But left to themselves girls of fourteen are unlikely to have welcomed essays from a fellow pupil arriving, unsolicited, through the mail. As yet Emily did not take in the strangeness of unconcealed originality: ordinary girls of that age tend to be indifferent if not cruel to oddity, and especially so at a time when female ambition was odd in itself.

So when Emily pressed her 'papers' on schoolmates there were few or no replies. Sabra did visit, 'but as usual she went off in a hurry'. Abiah, who had returned home to Springfield, was invited to stay, with a promise to 'entertain you to the best of my abilities, which you know are neither few nor small', but Abiah saw only Sabra, to whom she was related. These are the first indications that, however uncommon Emily might be – 'you know how I hate to be common', she remarked to Abiah – the world out there would not be inclined to respond. 'This is my letter to the World / That never wrote to Me —', she would later write.

In June 1846, when Emily was fifteen and a half, she began to dream night and day of higher education. In some haste she began to revise arithmetic and move on with algebra, geometry and ecclesiastical history.

'I am fitting to go to South Hadley Seminary [as Mount Holyoke was known], and expect if my health is good to enter that institution a year from next fall', she confided to Abiah.

Her health in fact was 'very poor' all summer, accompanied by the usual 'bad feelings', and she was removed from school for the summer and autumn terms, altogether about six months. She expressed her dismay to Abiah: 'It cost me many a severe struggle to leave my studies & be considered an invalid, but my health demanded a release from all care & I made the sacrifice.'

Though 'sacrifice' may seem over the top, girls of this generation did not take education for granted. They spoke of loving school and their teachers who were friendly, intelligent young women, most of them not much older than their pupils. These were not career-teachers; after a while they would depart to make their 'wedding gear', and this relatively short space of pink-cheeked independence in their lives offered a captivating model. One such 'preceptress' was Miss Rebecca Woodbridge, the twenty-year-old daughter of a clergyman. Emily described her as tall and slender with 'rose bud' cheeks and dimples 'which come & go like the ripples in yonder merry brook – & then she is so affectionate . . .'. Emily dwelt on 'affection' with the intensity of a girl for whom attachments are tenacious.

'I am always in love with my teachers', she was not shy to declare. When Miss Adams left to be married it seemed to Emily 'lonely and strange'. Not even the dimples of Miss Woodbridge could quite make up for this loss. One compensation was to write long letters to 'Biah, more because Abiah was loyal than because the two girls were alike. She had initially appealed to Emily by arriving at school bedecked with dandelions arranged as curls when she was due to perform at one of their Wednesday sessions of

Speaking and Composition. Abiah had further endeared herself to the future poet with a secret: she was writing a romance. Then, all too soon, she succumbed to the pressures of conformity. Once Abiah found herself saved the two had less to say to each other.

Emily felt obliged to talk of 'the shining company above' who tune their 'golden harps' to a redeemed sinner. A physical fondness for pretty, fresh-faced Abiah remained: 'I could not wait to press you to my arms.' All the same, Emily was so put off by her effort to lend herself to Abiah's terms, mouthing clichés of regret for remaining unsaved, together with hopes that her better self will conquer the temptations of worldliness, that there came a day when, throwing phoney phrases aside, Emily tossed a mad letter to Abiah. It was mad in that she unleashed a visionary superiority meant to disconcert the tamed girl Abiah had become.

'God is sitting here', Emily strikes up, 'and I dont dare to look directly at him for fear I shall die.' Abiah, she thinks, may be tempted to laugh. 'I cant say I advise you to laugh, but if you are punished, and I warned you, that can be no business of mine.' There are vexations that can 'choke up the love for friends'. An unknown Emily is rising: 'Wouldn't you love to see God's bird, when it first tries its wings?' Then a witch-voice (from *Macbeth*) casts doubt on the bird's integrity: 'I put my treasures away "till we <u>two</u> meet again".'

An undisguised intensity cuts through the courtesies of communication. The letter is shot through with clichés in inverted commas — 'You will excuse . . . all <u>want of friendly affection</u> in the sight of the verse "the deepest stream stillest runs"', throwing dead words back in Abiah's face. It's surly, she acknowledged. 'I love to be surly — and muggy — and cross', Emily could say defiantly. It's also a gift, sharing her sparks, 'treasures' the poet would bestow in future on more favoured correspondents.

2

A SCIENTIFIC EDUCATION

To what extent did greatness depend on the special advantages this girl enjoyed? Emily attended a private school and had the same classical and scientific education as her brother. On the classics side, the sexes were not separated at Amherst Academy. Emily took classics for three to four years, while Vinnie remained on the English side.

'We have a very fine school,' she told a friend. 'There are 63 scholars. I have four studies. They are Mental Philosophy, Geology, Latin, and Botany.' Many images in Dickinson's poems would be drawn from geology – volcanoes, earthquakes, coral reefs, anthracite, quartz – and she had a lifelong passion for plants. She studied Edward Hitchcock's *Catalogue of Plants Growing without Cultivation in the Vicinity of Amherst College* (1829) and collected specimens for her herbarium: Indian Pipes, wild strawberry and the yellow ox-eye daisy mounted with crossed stems.

When Emily was a schoolgirl geology was the hot subject, and here again Edward Hitchcock was the author of her textbook, *Elementary Geology* (1840). Hitchcock himself, with his beak nose and jutting chin above his dark stock, was a well-known figure in the Amherst of Emily's schooldays. He was professor of chemistry and natural history at the college, which he made a leader in the natural sciences, on a par with Harvard and Yale. The prominence he gave to science influenced the curriculum at Amherst Academy. At the same time Hitchcock encouraged women's education and invited local schoolgirls to sit in on college lectures (along the sides, to avoid the impropriety of sitting amongst the men).

He spoke of a timescale reaching 'far back into past eternity'. His evolutionary chart looked at plants and animals side by side. At the base of both is 'Quartz Rock'. Reptiles and 'tracks of birds' — creatures the poet would observe minutely — appear halfway up the chart, and corals in the historical period at the top. Professor Hitchcock taught a precision narrative, starting with 'distinct Propositions', then 'Definitions and Proofs', followed by successive 'Inferences'. Logic along these lines taught pupils 'to condense the matter', and this mental training is evident in the bold propositions, swift logic and startling inference in Dickinson's poems.

In the late 1830s geologists such as Charles Lyell had come upon incontrovertible evidence of the timescale of pre-history and, nearly twenty years before *The Origin of Species* (1859), Hitchcock spoke a pre-Darwinian language. 'Species', he said, were gradually 'fitted to adapt' to peculiar conditions. Hitchcock foresaw the conflict with the creation story in the Bible, and warned religious teachers to keep up with the enquiring young. To him, as an ordained minister, the 'eternity of matter' did not preclude a deity. Even if continents arose from natural causes, the creation of life 'must be regarded as the highest act of omnipotence'. As a 'transcendent naturalist', the professor urged pupils to seek 'the Divine character' through examining formations of rocks.

Our earth is a mass of lava, Emily learnt. We are protected from its incandescent heat only by a layer of cooled crust, with the lava exploding in 'paroxysmal' outbursts, making 'the future destruction of the earth by fire a not improbable event'. Volcanic power must be deeply seated beneath the earth's crust, since volcanoes throw out more matter at a single eruption than the whole mountain melted down could supply. A figure in the Hitchcock textbook illustrates earthquakes, their holes in the landscape. She read of the 'red hot lava which flows over the rim of the crater'. Here are future landscapes for recurrent eruptions in Emily Dickinson's poems: 'Etna's scarlets' and the lava of Vesuvius as a measure of her own 'Lava step'.

Hitchcock lingered over the famous eruption of Vesuvius in AD 79, which buried Herculaneum and Pompeii. Mount Etna was doubly terrible. Eruptions in the 1660s killed 77,000 people across an area of eighty-four square miles.

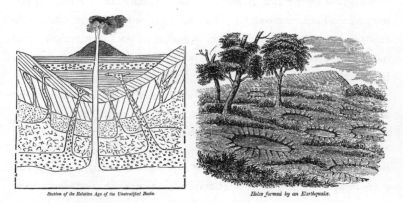

Section of the Relative Age of the Unstratified Rocks.   *Holes formed by an Earthquake.*

Volcanoes and earthquakes in Emily's schoolbook of the 1840s. A source for her poetic images at a time when geology was disproving the Biblical story of Creation.

A figure (*above*) demonstrates the underground tunnelling of volcanoes from one stratum to another. Most of their mouths are sealed, representing old and extinct eruptions, but one at the centre, shooting straight up from deep in the earth's core, erupts with extreme violence. Emily Dickinson would repeatedly draw on volcanic eruptions as metaphors for poetic expression .

Already, as a girl, her brilliance was recognised. Her compositions, said to be unlike anything ever heard, were applauded at fortnightly performances that were central to the Academy's curriculum: pupils took turns to read either their own essays or extracts from books of their choice. Emily participated keenly – and critically. At twelve, she sassed a boy who read a piece on thinking twice before you speak. The boy pictured a gullible youth who thinks nature has formed a certain young lady to perfection, but who should have remembered that roses conceal thorns. To Emily he appeared 'the sillyest creature that ever lived I think. I told him that I thought he had better think twice before he spoke.'

At fifteen she lengthened her skirts and teased other girls with a flawless front: 'I have grown tall a good deal, and wear my golden tresses done up in a net cap. Modesty, you know, forbids me to mention whether my personal appearance has altered.'

That year Mr Dickinson gave her a square piano, and always supplied most of the books she wanted, even if he remained somewhat uneasy. He was 'too busy with his Briefs – to notice what we do –', his daughter said later. 'He buys me many Books – but begs me not to read them – because he fears they joggle the Mind.'

Mr Dickinson believed a woman's place was at home, but when Emily approached him with her dream to study at South Hadley Female Seminary he did consent. At sixteen and a half, at the end of September 1847, Emily entered the country's first women's college. Mary Lyon, the founder, had the conviction of those capable of realising a dream. Her dream was women's greatness at a time when to many a great woman was a contradiction in terms. In her fifties, her dark hair was secured at the back by a neat, white cap with a lace frill just wide enough to have the effect of a halo around her bared face. Its widely spaced, awake eyes were balanced by a wide mouth, unsmiling but by no means severe. Professor Hitchcock had been her mentor as she came into her own as a scientist and educator, and it was with his backing that she had opened her college for women in South Hadley, Massachusetts, only nine miles from Amherst. It was this college that became Mount Holyoke.

There, Emily found 235 girls up against rising academic standards: if they failed the frequent examinations they were sent away. The college held assessments of new students soon after their arrival; Emily was nervous but coped easily. Apart from ancient history and rhetoric, she took all science courses: algebra, Euclid [geometry], physiology, chemistry and astronomy. The aim of all this, according to Miss Lyon, was to prepare girls to be good mothers, a diplomatic line that proved its effectiveness in her growing number of applicants: as many as five hundred in 1847. In practice, the prospect of motherhood did not interfere with an exacting routine that began at six each morning. In nearly every way, the college was an enlightened institution: Emily remarked on the interest of the work, daily exercise and 'wholesome & abundant' food. Yet there was an insuperable drawback.

Massachusetts at this time was the scene of a religious revival opposed to the inroads of science. Dickinson later makes her allegiance clear:

> 'Faith' is a fine invention
> When Gentlemen can <u>see</u> —
> But <u>Microscopes</u> are prudent
> In an Emergency.

Unfortunately for Emily, Miss Lyon was bent on pressing students to be 'saved'. The overwhelming majority succumbed; Emily did not. On one occasion, Miss Lyon called on all who wished to be Christians to rise. Emily Dickinson remained seated – the only one, so the story goes.

'They thought it queer I didn't rise,' she reportedly recounted the scene to her family. 'I thought a lie would be queerer.'

'Have you said your prayers?' Miss Lyon demanded during this or a similar confrontation.

'Yes,' she answered, 'though it can't make much difference to The Creator.'

Extra meetings took place in Miss Lyon's room and targeted girls were required to indicate in advance, with a note, if they wished to attend. On 17 January 1848, at the end of her first term, Emily attended a session for those who 'felt an uncommon anxiety to decide'. Either it was politic to undergo this session or Miss Lyon really did manage to induce some concern.

'Many are flocking to the ark of safety,' Emily said in a letter that same day. 'I have not yet given up to the claims of Christ.' Again, on 16 May, she felt compelled once more to own her failure: 'I have neglected the <u>one thing needful</u> when all were obtaining it.' It seemed that other girls desired only to be good. 'How I wish I could say that with sincerity, but I fear I never can.' Her tone is rueful. It was not amusing to be a moral outcast when Miss Lyon consigned her to the lowest of three categories of students: the saved, the hopeful, and a remnant of about thirty no-hopers.

*

Miss Lyon had founded the college with the help of an evangelical network of donors who saw it as a recruitment centre for missionary work of every kind. Emily, holding out against recruitment, continued to be the object of pressure, and yet she speaks of kind teachers and scientific gains. Her troubles in college had nothing to do with learning: her progress proved so rapid that by the close of the academic year she was ready for Senior work.

Curiously, she formed no lasting ties with her fellow students. There were 'many sweet girls', but something in the atmosphere of the college led her to guard against intimacy. Her childhood bedmate Jane Humphrey was there, but since she was a Senior they saw little of each other. In any case, Miss Lyon discouraged exclusive friendships. Emily was ready to 'love' a teacher called Miss Fiske from Amherst, who visited her in her room and went out of her way to cultivate their common ties, as Emily put it humorously to Austin: 'Miss Fiske told me if I was writing to Amherst to send her love. Not specifying to whom, you may deal it out, as your good sense & discretion prompt.'

For all her amusing self-possession, she says nothing of another persistent trouble: some form of ill-health. In mid-April 1848, an Amherst visitor to the college informed the Dickinsons that Emily had been ill all winter. At once Austin appeared 'in full sail' to fetch her. Protesting and in tears, she was hauled away from college and kept at home, an invalid, for a whole month. Every day a physician came to examine her and every day her father dosed her in his forceful way.

What made Emily ill? Why did the physician come back so frequently? Was her illness difficult to diagnose? A pattern of withdrawals from formal education precedes the pressures of college. If the illness is the same it's never named, apart from Emily's mention of her 'fixed melancholy' (in reaction to Sophia's death) when she was fourteen. In the spring of 1848, when she was seventeen, she joked about a fading cough intimidated by the force of Mr Dickinson's dosings, yet a cough sounds too slight to warrant her father's alarm. Critical opinion that she had 'pulmonary episodes' stretches thin facts; most inhabitants of Amherst would have had the odd cough without it interrupting their lives. The poet, as an adult, was not tubercular, on any evidence we have: in a place rife with small-town gossip, no whisper of consumption follows her. To go on what her letters give out, as though an answer were to hand, is to block off the mystery.

Tantalisingly – irresistibly – her voice draws us towards a secret that 'struck' the regulated course of her life. Was it a genuine secret, an unnamed ill concealed by her misleading report of a cough?

When Emily is removed from college at the age of seventeen, there's a gap in the record surrounded by questionable facts. Her tears and pleas when Austin comes for her show her resisting her family's fear, though under other circumstances she's glad to go home. Worth noting too: her sickness does not incapacitate her from studying at home, as proved by her performance in the examinations of the following term.

On Emily's return to college after the spring vacation, her invalid cousin Zebina sends her a 'long' letter in June. She replies, though this letter does not survive. Why does Zebina write at length – why does he write at all? As far as we know, they were not correspondents.

Another unexplained oddity: Emily's ill-health over the winter had not been apparent to college authorities. There were daily checks on health, and in addition a college rule – an unpopular rule, insistently enforced – that girls had to report on one another. If a student objected she was welcome to leave, Miss Lyon would warn in her address to newcomers. A vigilant eye on pupils penetrated even the privacy of their rooms: girls had to sleep with doors ajar and teachers would now and then patrol the corridors. Spying, to put it plainly, was threaded through the fabric of the college. A bad and persistent cough is unlikely to have escaped detection. The trouble, it seems, did not lie in her lungs.

What Emily confessed more readily was homesickness compounded by loneliness. 'A desolate feeling comes home to my heart, to think I am alone,' she told Austin.

Surrounded as she was by intelligent girls of the same age, why was this student quite so alone? The reason is obvious. As a non-convert who remained impenitent, she would have been made to feel uncomfortable in the sweetly enquiring style of fellow students. Their questionings and proddings would have been part of the pressure to succumb during Emily's second term, when the revival reached its peak.

Emily was wary of these girls. 'Their tones fall strangely on my ear & their countenances meet mine not like home faces . . .'.

She roomed with an apparently considerate Norcross cousin, another Emily, who, unknown to her, was reporting on their conversations, using the trust of a family tie and their intimacy as roommates to prise open Emily's reluctance to declare herself a Christian. Her cousin proved a conscientious informer on Emily Dickinson in a letter to members of the prayer meeting in Monson, Mrs Dickinson's home town. Emily's sister Vinnie later said there had been 'real ogres' at the college, and if this be true one of the ogres is likely to have been Hannah Porter, in a beribboned bonnet and richly trimmed black stole. With a concave chest and down-turned mouth, Mrs Porter lacked the impressive purity of Miss Lyon's bearing but she was a tireless leader of revivals. Emily's Monson relations were members of her First Female Praying Circle. According to her roommate's reports to this group, Emily's unbudging answer was that she felt 'no interest', the code phrase for having no intimation of grace. To fellow students who rejoiced in their own intimations, Emily Dickinson seemed unregenerate, even wicked, as she at times felt obliged to own.

'It startles me when I really think of the advantages I have had, and I fear I have not improved them as I ought.' This is how she spoke, adopting a politely sorrowful tone. 'Many an hour has fled with its report [of the saved] to heaven, and what has been the tale of me?'

What Emily rejects is not religion, but coercion. Signalling from behind her public failure is an intelligence collected enough to combat bullies who want to take over her mind and hardwire into it a formulaic 'tale' — the 'tale' of all fundamentalist faiths that close down the right to freedom of judgement. This negates the intellectual development for which she had come to college and, at the same time, negates notions of self-reliance she had come upon in the essays of Emerson. She talked appreciatively of visits from her fellow students, but sensed that these attentions were not friendship as she understood it. Though she did have the moral support of her father and brother, they were not on the scene and undoubtedly the strength to face this out alone came from herself: 'I generally carry my resolutions into effect', she had reminded her brother in a lighter mood. It's an accurate self-estimate of a young woman of extraordinary integrity and firmness.

Emily's refusal to conform coincides with the official start of the women's movement in America (marked by the Seneca Falls declaration of June of that year); the ferment of women's rights fuelled by the 1848 revolts in Europe; and the appearance of *Jane Eyre*, with its self-contained, rebellious heroine. Emily read it eagerly at the time of her own revolt against the housekeeping that awaited her at home: '. . . so <u>many</u> wants – and me so <u>very</u> handy – and my time of so <u>little</u> account – and my writing so <u>very</u> needless'. She was writing, then, at the ages of eighteen and nineteen.

Commencement on 3 August 1848 was the cut-off point: it brought to an end the scientific study she had pursued every day till the second night bell. Convalescing in the spring, she had read 'The Princess' (published in December 1847), where Tennyson seems briefly to concede women's blocked aspirations through the outcry of Lilia, who wishes she could be a mighty poet. Women's inferiority, Lilia believes, is all a matter of education:

> It is but bringing up; no more than that . . .
> Ah, were I something great! I wish I were
> Some mighty poetess, I would shame you then,
> That love to keep us children! O I wish
> That I were some great princess, I would build
> Far off from men a college like a man's
> And I would teach them all that men are taught;
> We are twice as quick!

Tennyson goes on to spoof the possibility of a women's college. His fantasy of unfit women is a far cry from the academic success of South Hadley. For Emily, though, it was over. That August, housework replaced classwork. Astronomy, the last of her courses, was irrelevant to the tasks her mother assigned. As sole daughter at home (Vinnie was still away at boarding school), Emily was expected to make herself useful; duty was to rule her days, not learning. To encourage her, Mr Dickinson bought his daughter a volume of *Letters on Practical Subjects*, inscribed to her on April 18, 1852. At this stage he cooled her taste for poetry, as she reported to her brother: 'we do not have much poetry, father having made up his mind that its pretty much all <u>real life</u>. Father's real life and <u>mine</u> sometimes come into collision, but as yet, escape unhurt.'

It did not escape Emily that her father did not take kindly to a woman who made herself conspicuous in public. At the age of twenty she accompanied him to hear the Swedish nightingale Jenny Lind perform one thundery night in Northampton. Mr Dickinson found that he was discomforted to see a female on stage. A gift was no excuse for a woman to exhibit herself. So what was his daughter to do with the gift that seethed inside her?

There was tenser friction with her mother, who was trying to introduce her to the finer points of housekeeping and whose care for the creature comforts of visitors often interrupted more interesting conversation. Were a visitor's feet cold? Wouldn't he like to warm them in the kitchen?

Emily turned to him. 'Wouldn't you like to have the Declaration of Independence to read? Or the Lord's Prayer repeated?'

Mrs Dickinson would have taken pride in the spotlessness of her house, its welcoming fires and the home produce on the table. It was customary for middle-class women to work alongside their servants, in keeping with the New England work ethic. Reproving elders urged Emily to *sweep* if her spirits were low, and visit the halt and lame, the old and infirm, the ugly and disagreeable '– the perfectly hateful to me – all <u>these</u> to see – and be seen by – an opportunity rare for cultivating meekness – and patience – and submission'.

There was an alternative: after Commencement, Jane Humphrey, like her sister before her, took up a teaching post at Amherst Academy. Over the following school year, 1848–9, she and Emily drew close. They would sit of an afternoon on the doorstep of the Dickinson house, their voices too low to disturb the birds singing in the tall cherry trees. The birds took fright only at their brushing dresses. Emily was blissfully unaware that Jane had a job to do. Her friend was to be a 'rock, support' for Emily who pours out her anger against the demands of housekeeping. This lava, carried by molten bursts of ardour, burns out friendship's need for reciprocity.

It could not escape Emily that she lost one friend after another. Sarah Tracy and Sarah Pynchen had moved away, leaving a mysterious silence. She wondered with 'inexpressible regret' what it was that prevented their answering her letters. Nor was there acknowledgement of a paper she sent to Hatty Merrill. It's the unique character of the personal letter to reflect the correspondent, and though Emily's letters are wonderfully imaginative and amusing, they do not often call up her correspondent. Jane, for one, remains a faceless 'darling'. Not for long. Without warning, Jane 'ran away', and her departure to take up other posts provoked Emily to a comic explosion of outrage, as much about retrieving control over Jane as about loss.

She caricatures her own incredulity and mounting fury to find Jane 'gone – gone! Gone <u>how</u> – or <u>where</u> – or <u>why</u> – who saw her go – help – hold – bind – and keep her – put her into States-prison – into the House of Correction – bring out the long lashed whip – and put her feet in the stocks –and give her a number of stripes and make her repent her going!'

Emily then cools off with a humorously defiant self-characterisation as a tempter to be avoided. '. . . I didn't mean to make you wicked – but I was – and am – and shall be – and I was with you so much that I could'nt help contaminate. Are you ever lonely in Warren [Massachusetts] – are you lonely without me . . . I want to know.'

The shift to tenderness is compelling, especially Emily's whisper about a secret script: 'silent', unwritten letters, full of affection and confidence. She will try, she says, a pen-and-paper letter, 'though not half so precious as the other kind. I have written <u>those</u> at night.' Silent letters are more vehement, since there's no need to whisper or shut the door. She wonders if Jane is awake and writing to her at the same moment 'with that spirit pen – and on sheets from out the sky. <u>Did</u> you ever – and were we together in any of those nights?'

Expressiveness, intelligence, intimacy, all these Emily offers Jane, as she had offered the same to the Amherst girls who had roused her feelings.

She saw herself storing 'treasures' for them. Yet, sooner or later, they contrived to escape an emotional power venting itself and catching them up in its whirlwind.

Since Emily Dickinson rejected distortion with huge courage, her delight in the genuine was correspondingly intense. She would have been on the look-out for it. 'Experiment to me / Is every one I meet / If it contain a Kernel?' She regarded others in the light of nourishment, as a squirrel regards a nut: '. . . Meat within, is requisite'. No kernels to be had at college, only the grid of uniform piety. There, Emily Dickinson had felt 'alone' in preserving intact the fruit of her soul. Released, she'd rediscovered Jane with a love concentrated, projected, on target, like a volley of buckshot or a beam of light picking out a doe in the dark. The object of such attention would be transfixed by the light (as Abiah Root was stilled too long for her own good) or else, like Jane, the marked-down creature would 'run away'.

When Jane took up a new teaching post in Willoughby, Ohio, in 1852, Emily accused her of caring too little. She consoled herself with an image of Jane as sad stranger in the Midwest. Jane's readiness to take up a post far away was a venture Emily found incomprehensible. Her own 'desolation' away from home and recurrent sickness had closed off any such course. Her father comforted her further with a possibility that he might send her to complete her studies elsewhere. Nothing came of this, and at the age of twenty, she rebelled against the narrow-mindedness she encountered in Amherst.

In a Shakespeare reading group a righteous young man tried to censor the bawdier lines. One of those present, Emily Fowler, recalled 'the lofty air with which the future poet ended the debate, saying, "There's nothing wicked in Shakespeare, and if there is I don't want to know it."' For the others it carried the punch of an exit line.

At home, an unending tide of cleaning closed over and seemed to obliterate her. She tried to practise 'kind obedience', doubtful if her act was convincing, and mocking herself as 'the Queen of the court, if regalia be dust, and dirt'. She could see herself through the eyes of the saved as she slunk away, 'one of the lingering <u>bad</u> ones' who pause and think, and think and pause, drawn neither to heaven nor the world. Her real prayer was 'God keep me from what they call <u>households</u>.'

There were 'cross' days when she didn't hide her frown, and her nearest and dearest were made to hear 'how loud the door bangs whenever I go through'. When she neglected to attend the winter season of the Sewing Society, who kept themselves pleasantly occupied with offerings for the poor, hints of hard-heartedness followed her, as well she knew: 'I am already set down as one of those brands almost consumed.' Nothing, she began to see, would rescue her from 'this wilderness life of mine' but a waking dream when she lived 'in the books the Shadows write in'.

At the time Emily was banging doors she talked to a young lawyer who was gaining experience in her father's office. Benjamin Franklin Newton, aged twenty-eight, was ten years older than Emily. As a reader he was in contact with 'the Shadows' – enough for Emily to confide something of her own book-life and to accept Newton's guidance in her reading. During 1848–9, he became her mentor, with Emerson one of their common topics.

Emily had put Emerson's belief in 'the integrity of the private mind' to the test at college. Whether consciously or not, she had proved herself a model of Emersonian self-reliance. Throughout her ordeal she had resisted the entrenched Puritanism (revived by Jonathan Edwards as a counterblast to the optimism of Unitarians when this form of faith took over in eighteenth-century Boston). As a Unitarian and an Emerson enthusiast, Newton would have understood Emily's private revolt against dogmatism; as her mentor, he would have reinforced her private declarations of spiritual independence – 'wicked' in the puritanical terms of their locale.

Emily Dickinson's private confrontation with the puritanical community was not peculiar; it's in a long tradition of American dissent, going back to an early English settler, Anne Hutchinson. Soon after her arrival in the Massachusetts Bay Colony in 1634, Hutchinson set up a weekly meeting to discuss the previous Sunday's sermon. Preachers seemed to her ministers of the letter, not the spirit. She stood for grace freely given. For a self-taught woman, however well-versed in the scriptures, to bypass and comment on the words of properly educated men struck the Puritans as

enthusiasm, opening minds to delusion. They called it antinomian, meaning beyond the law. Anne Hutchinson's claims for the private spirit and her
trial in 1637 came to be known as the Antinomian Controversy. Dissent was
to prove a tenacious and ultimately triumphant strain in America and
Emily Dickinson's freedom of mind at college is part of it, but to resist the
collective will of a community takes enormous courage. Hutchinson stood
her ground with disconcerting brilliance. It didn't help: her community
expelled her for sedition.

Nathaniel Hawthorne stirred the controversy over female free-thinking
through the outcast figure of Hester Prynne in *The Scarlet Letter* (1851). Emily
Dickinson's spiritual freedom seems quirky but exists in this contemporary
context. Women educated at the level of educated men were a new phenomenon in her generation, which may explain the concern of their
elders, including Monson's Female Praying Circle (filled with the Norcross
faithful), to police the college and stamp out any tendency on the part of
young women to think for themselves. It so happened that Monson's
Female Praying Circle wanted a report on Emily Dickinson in particular. If
she already nursed the dissenting spirit of Anne Hutchinson she would
have taken care to speak the communal language with no sign of sedition
as it could have led to expulsion from college. The most useful lesson she
had learnt there was how to protect a private self at odds with the pieties
of her society.

The pressure against forwardness still held sway. In 1830 Hawthorne
had published a diatribe against a 'monstrous regiment' of female scribblers
who had entered the literary marketplace. More insidious than his ridicule
of shallow sentimentality was Hawthorne's attack on the indelicacy of
public utterance. A woman writer stripped herself 'naked'. Charlotte
Brontë, Madame Dupin and later Mary Ann Evans and Olive Schreiner –
in fact almost all women writers – had to publish under male or neutral
pseudonyms if they were to avoid censure as women exposing themselves
in the public arena.

Dickinson had this dual challenge: as a woman, she was compelled to
avoid public utterance; at the same time, to find a voice of her own she had
to trust herself, as Emerson urged. During her college ordeal and after, she

aligned herself with a creed of her own, opposed to the sermons and missions closing in about her. Dinning in her ears was the old, grim conviction of innate depravity. All the while, away in Boston, Emerson and other lapsed Unitarian ministers were proclaiming the reverse: our perfectibility, what Emerson termed 'the infinitude of the private man'. Where earlier in the century the Unitarian minister William Ellery Channing had spoken of man's 'likeness unto God', Emerson asserted that man *is* god, and a god most of the time in chains. In his thrilling 'Divinity School Address' of 1838, Emerson had proclaimed that every person has the divine spark within. A person who recovered it would possess the creator's power.

Benjamin Newton gave the young Dickinson a volume of Emerson's poems (the first, published in 1847). A challenge about substance is pasted on the flyleaf:

All can write autographs, but few paragraphs; for we are mostly no more than *names*.

B. F. Newton

August 1849

It was Emerson, Emily said, who 'touched the secret Spring'. Emerson sanctioned 'stinging rhetoric', 'laconic and brisk' words as opposed to the pale language of literary magazines. He called for words that, if cut, would bleed; not tripping speech but 'a shower of bullets'. At college the young poet-to-be had looked into Emerson as into a secret self. 'In silence we must wrap much of our life,' he acknowledged, 'because we cannot explain it to others, and because somewhat we cannot yet understand.' In his central statement, 'Self-Reliance', he declares that his life 'is for itself and not for a spectacle'; therefore, he advises, keep 'the independence of solitude'.

The headiest element in Emerson is an offer of power if an individual remains unfixed, unaligned, in a state of becoming:

> I tire of shams, I rush to be.
> I pass with yonder comet free,
> Pass with the comet into space.

Power resides in the act of transition from one inward state to another. It refuses to settle or be defined – consistent with Emily's refusal to define herself in the expected way. In his poem 'Merlin', Emerson conjures up an American poet more forceful and innovative than he himself. He prophesies a poet who will strike the chords 'rudely and hard', one of the roughs taking his passage through the American scene. Whitman answered this call, saying famously, 'I was bubbling, bubbling, and Emerson brought me to the boil.' Towards the end of 'Merlin' Emerson calls up a 'sister' poet, a spinner of words who uses rhymes 'with ruin rife'. Did this encourage Emily Dickinson to devise the off-rhymes unknown – and unacceptable – to her time?

Newton, acting in effect as Emerson's emissary to the untried Emily Dickinson, urged her to become a poet. He spoke to her secret self, not in an alluring Rochester manner but more as an elder, or so she later gave out, together with protestations of deference to his wisdom. After Newton left Amherst to set up a legal practice in Worcester, Massachusetts, he wrote to her. At first her parents put a brake on her side of the correspondence: she was not to write for at least three weeks. When that time was up, she confided to Jane in January 1850, 'I shall.'

She was just nineteen, raring to write to Newton and seething with unused dramas during this particular month. It was the same month as she wrote her 'wicked' letter to Abiah as well as an even weirder letter to a Monson uncle, Joel Norcross, who had recently visited Amherst. He was a young uncle, about the same age as Newton, but unlike the high-minded Newton he was an importer of fancy goods. Emily relays a 'vision' of young men who 'kept gay stores, and deceived the foolish ones who came to buy' and, amongst these, 'one man [who] told a lie to his niece'.

What the lie was she doesn't say, but her letter mounts two dark dramas. First comes the Puritan drama of depravity. Here, she plays up the power of its warning voice and in a frenzy denounces her mother's brother for crimes that will hurl him into hell. In her dream he's already there: 'up from the pit you spoke'. There's a punitive relish in unmasking this merchant: 'You villain without a rival – unparraleled [sic] doer of crimes – scoundrel . . . promise-breaker . . . I call upon all nature to lay hold of you – let fire burn –. . . and hungry wolves eat up – and lightning strike – and thunder stun – let friends desert . . .' and so on until murder is justi-fied: 'I shall kill you'.

Having sentenced her uncle, the voice calms a little and contemplates the consequences. Her dear Aunt Lavinia will miss her brother, to be sure, 'but trials <u>will</u> come in the best of families – and I think they are usually for the best – they give us new ideas – and <u>those</u> are not to be laughed at.' Laughed at? Further calm is in order, for she's on the verge of rampant hilarity. Instead, a deliberate exercise in forethought firms up for the kill, the dramatic sequel. Where Macbeth displaced responsibility on to the supernatural – the witches who incite him to murder – Emily displaced responsibility on to the *weapon*. She does it airily, almost comically, amused by this mental trick. If she were to stab her uncle while he slept 'the dagger's to blame – it's no business of mine'. It would be different if she wrenched out his heart with her own hands. She concocts a corroborating story in which a man pointed 'a loaded gun' at another and 'it' killed him. People hanged the gun's owner 'for <u>murder</u>'. This is misplaced justice for, Dickinson argues, a gun has an independent existence, if only the 'stupid' world could understand. 'My Life had stood — a Loaded Gun —', com-posed thirteen years later, originates in this fantasy.

What sounds mad in prose works as poetry, where the gun acts for its 'Master' – acts as a divine agent who tracks the Master's targets. The speaker's life, loaded with shot and chosen for that reason, stands at the ready: 'I speak for Him —'. The pleasure of speaking is like a volcanic eruption; at such times the speaker shows 'a Vesuvian face'. Although Dickinson seems to speak as a lone voice, lava and fire were political cur-rency for activists of her generation. One of the first French cartoons of feminists in 1848 shows armed women erupting from a volcano, while a group of young women workers unfurl a banner naming themselves the *Vésuviennes* (women of Vesuvius). Dickinson's usage is at the contemporary cutting edge, in the American context of Emerson's individualism which sanctions lawlessness in so far as others are less real than the self: 'No law can be sacred to me but that of my nature.' Thus Emerson. Thus Dickinson in her frenzy. Her force is formidable, unswerving.

The poem makes sense if the shot or lava stands for the poet's emotional and verbal utterance. 'She felt a dangerous power inside her,' the critic Christopher Benfey saw, 'a great unleashing of the imagination that filled her with mingled power and dread.' Operating at the edge of existence, it's to be a life of extremes, given entire to a 'Master' who deals out our inescapable mortality. Her gun may be less enigmatic in the light of this letter she wrote at nineteen, soon after the bullying she had endured at college. Her ordeal had been sanctioned by her praying relatives in Monson whose spy had been planted in the privacy of her bedroom. Had she reason to hate her uncle in particular, beyond a broken promise to keep in touch following his visit? Or was she projecting onto his departure her loss of Ben Newton – could Newton have been more important to her than we can know?

None of the correspondence with Ben Newton survives. What does survive is an extraordinary confidence in a letter to Jane Humphrey in April 1850, intimating a heaven-sent 'joy':

> I have dared to do strange things – bold things, and have asked no advice from any – I have heeded beautiful tempters, and do not think I am wrong . . . Oh Jennie, it would relieve me to tell you all . . . and confess what you only shall know, an experience bitter, and sweet, but the sweet did so beguile me – and life has had an aim, and the world has been too precious for your poor – and striving sister! . . . Nobody thinks of the joy, nobody guesses it, to all appearance old things are engrossing, and new ones are not revealed, but there now is nothing old, things are budding, and springing, and singing . . .

Throughout Emily Dickinson's poetry there are hints of a secret, a transforming experience connected to heaven – whatever heaven meant to her which she won't or can't articulate. Here is evidence of something 'new' and so momentous during the winter–spring of 1850 that it gave a purpose to her life. This semi-confession is a test for Jane, whose warm heart she has felt 'beating near me' with 'music in its quiet ticking'. Emily's

alternating outbursts and sealed lips jolt Jane, as she would jolt later correspondents, alerting them to the limitations of language as verbal
consensus. Would Jane respond to this alert?

Emily knew that Jane's father was dying when she teased her with this
confidence and, as it happened, he died that very day. Emily opens with
cursory attention to Jane's grief together with a tight-lipped excuse for not
coming to Jane's side – not 'permitted now' – but Emily's chief focus is her
own rarer drama, to which Jane is to be admitted in a helpmeet role as 'my
friend . . . my rock, and strong assister!'

A warning closes the letter: Jane should not be tempted to think she can
get away. She won't be permitted to bury her past with the Dickinson sisters as she might more ordinary folk: 'Dont put us in narrow graves – we
shall <u>certainly rise</u> if you do, and scare you most prodigiously, and carry
you off perhaps!'

A month passed and Jane did not answer. From now on she kept clear
of Emily Dickinson. Nor did she take up the challenge of interpretation.

So, what do we make of Emily's secret? There's an afterthought to Jane –
another hint, harking back to a young man called James Kimball. She and
Jane had called him their 'Theologian'. He had made up to Emily, then disappeared. Emily assures Jane she feels nothing but indifference. 'Something
else has helped me forget <u>that</u>, a something surer, and higher, and I sometimes laugh in my sleeve. Dont betray me Jennie.'

My guess is that in January 1850, when Emily received her 'beautiful'
copy of Emerson's poems from Newton, together with a letter, she under-
went an Emersonian conversion. She found heaven in her own soul,
reversing the sense of depravity that chastened the faithful around her
and claimed her sister and father later that year. Privately she questioned
her society's abasement before its image of a paternalistic Omnipotence
who shames disobedience and prompts the polarising of the saved and the
sinners: 'bright halos' on one side; cast-down eyes on the other. Whatever
Ben Newton meant to her as a man, he certainly backed her individualis-
tic hotline to the colossal substance of Immortality. In Emersonian terms,
that godlike character was latent in all beings, be it man or woman or
child, with the courage and imagination to elicit a transcendent being.

Then, a bolt. Newton contracted tuberculosis in 1851 and then, on 4 June, he made a move that took Emily aback.

'B.F.N. is <u>married</u>', she broke the news to Austin. His choice was Sarah Warner Rugg, a woman twelve years older than himself. As an ill man he needed steady care more than the excitements of twenty-year-old Emily Dickinson, who was periodically ill herself. This is no more than a guess. In truth, we know nothing beyond the fact that the bond with Emily Dickinson existed, that he 'often wrote' and that what he said was formative for the future poet. Ben Newton was a master of phrases, with the power to imprint themselves on her memory. Nine years after his death she recalled proudly, 'My dying Tutor told me that he would like to live till I had been a poet . . .'. She must, then, have shown Newton her poems, none of which survive from this period (though conceivably she recopied some when she started to store her work in the late 1850s).

Newton sent her a message from Worcester in the last week of his life. She could quote his words twenty-three years later: 'If I live, I will go to Amherst – if I die, I certainly will.'

For a married man to figure Amherst – that is, Emily – as his heaven confirms her secret status. '*Title divine — is mine! | The Wife — without the Sign! . . . | Betrothed — without the swoon | God sends us Women — . . .*'. We can't be sure what biographical experience lies behind this later poem, only that the poet cultivated this kind of possessiveness and that Newton's message seems to license the first instance. There was no communication between Mrs Newton and Emily, who seems not to have expected Newton's death on 23 March 1853.

'Oh Austin, Newton is dead', she wrote when the news reached Amherst four days later.

Nine months later she still longed to find out his final state of mind. Possibly she hoped for a deathbed message. Not wanting to contact his wife, Emily approached Newton's distinguished minister, Edward Everett Hale. It was a determinedly disarming letter that she mailed to the minister in January 1854, presenting herself as a passive recipient of manly instruction. It's an overdone performance. She had been 'but a child' at the time of her tie with Newton, she insists, though in fact she had been an eligible young woman and he an eligible young man whose tastes were congenial beyond anything she had so far known. She pictures a humble little innocent, at the knee, as it were, of a 'gentle, yet grave Preceptor', teaching her what to read, which authors to admire, 'and that sublimer lesson, a faith in things unseen'. These truths mingle with her child-fiction.*

If, at fourteen, Emily had gazed at the dying Sophia, a death that brought home to her the fact of mortality, so at twenty-two she had to take in the silencing of Newton's voice, another who had seen and sanctioned the creature she felt herself to be. 'My life closed twice before its close', she wrote. 'Parting is all we know of heaven, / And all we need of hell.'

Emily Dickinson looked on marriage in the same coercive light as organised religion: to be 'bridalled' was to be 'shrouded'. Men, she waved away as '<u>boots</u> and <u>whiskers</u>'. No living man would ever again fertilise her poetry with Newton's conviction, none short of 'Papa above', with whom she continued to wrestle. As a poet she rejected the set conversion narrative in favour of a biblical drama of her own choosing, that of Jacob who, in a dream, wrestles all night with a man and at daybreak finds his thigh out of joint. He limps away saying, 'I have seen God face to face.' There's a spirit strong enough to take on the divine, resulting in an onrush of superhuman strength. Dickinson has the nerve to claim more. As day breaks, her astonished Wrestler finds that he has 'worsted God'.

If the traditional authority of 'Papa above' provoked the contender in Emily Dickinson, women were another matter. Ever since her childhood bed-play with Jane, Emily warmed to women with whom she could strip her mask. This included her young teachers at Amherst Academy, whose own lives were yet in the making. While still at college, she romanticised her one-time teacher Helen Humphrey Palmer, Jane's elder sister, widowed soon after her marriage. How beautiful Helen would look in mourning, Emily mused, preferring the husbandless to the 'bridalled'. Her

---

* If Hale replied, his letter would have been destroyed after ED's death, along with all other letters to her.

imagination circled around chosen intimates whom she wooed with let-
ters. '*The Soul selects her own Society* — | *Then* — *shuts the Door* —'. In this decisive
manner she swung from reserve with fellow students towards the 'kernel'
people who nourished her expressiveness. What exactly she required, and
how to make it her own, remained in question.

This poet had extraordinary strokes of fortune, not least the advantage of
an education closed to women in other countries. Her volcanic temperament was cooled and tautened by scientific training. Her wit won her
father's support and she had the luck to come upon a timely mentor.
Newton's impact was brief, yet enough to get her poetry going.
Perfectionist as she was, she needed only the spur of a reader's assent to the
sublime spark she already had when she was 'new — and small'.

Circumstances can't explain genius, but they helped her preserve it in a
society with a habit of fundamentalist bullying. Her 'Difference' from
others, far from blocking her, made her 'bold'. How boldly confident she
was as she refused to succumb to successive revivals, waiting on the fruit of
her soul. But this 'Present' from 'the Gods' was, as she knew, precarious. It
remained for her to devise the shell – the outward life – to shield so rare a
kernel.

3

SISTER

As a girl Emily Dickinson did not disguise her character from Jane Humphrey: her boldness, her revelling in the dreams of 'blessed' night and her 'wickedness'. During another religious revival, in April 1850, she stood alone 'in rebellion', gazing enviously but still unyielding at those of her circle, including her sister Vinnie and friend Abby Wood, who went about with softened, tear-filled eyes and gentled voices, manifesting holiness.

Her brother, to whom she sent a philosophic letter, slapped her down with the carelessness of a young man who might have occasion to mention 'the author in me'. He could not comprehend her, he complained, so would she speak in a simpler style?

Did he expect her to be a 'little ninny', she replied in mock indignation, 'while I pant and struggle and climb the nearest cloud, you walk out very leisurely in your slippers from Empyrean, and . . . request me to get down! As simple as you please, the simplest sort of simple – I'll be . . . a little pussy catty, a little Red Riding Hood, I'll wear a Bee in my Bonnet, and a Rose bud in my hair, and what remains to do you shall be told hereafter.'

Her determination to 'do' was already a counter to caricatures of femininity – pet, victim, dimwit and rosebud – who don't venture to 'climb'. Emily's education gave her the confidence to tease the superiority Austin began to assume after his graduation from Amherst College that summer.

Suppose 'Topknot' should condescend to speak to his sisters? Suppose this 'most ungrateful of brothers' should 'doff his crown, and lay down his lofty sceptre'? So she wonders, and then puts on a display of deference if such is what he wants. 'Permit me to tie your shoe, to run like a dog behind you. I can bark, see here! Bow wow!' A young woman who casts herself as domestic pet 'dare not' climb on high to where Austin sits like Jove on Olympus. From behind this teasing camouflage an irrepressible sister shoots down Austin's importance.

'Fear the King!' came his command.

'Exit <u>Sue</u>!!!' Emily flashed back, aware he had an eye for a girl who was not one to put up with kingship.

Susan Huntington Gilbert, born in the same month as Emily, was the orphaned daughter of Harriet Arms and Thomas Gilbert, a veteran of the War of 1812 who had taken on various public offices and kept an inn at Old Deerfield, ten miles from Amherst. The Gilberts were an established family in the area and there were some educated and prosperous relations but, like the Dickinsons' grandfather, Thomas Gilbert fell into bankruptcy in his last years – hastened, in his case, by drink. He and his wife both died young, leaving six children. 'Susie', their youngest, was eleven. The two sons went out west and prospered. The four daughters were brought up by their mother's sister, Sophia Arms Van Vranken, in Geneva in upstate New York. Sue was schooled to a high standard: in recognition of her abilities she was sent for one year, 1846–7, to Amherst Academy, where she studied with the boys on the classical side. She then completed her formal education at the Utica Female Seminary, known as Miss Kelly's, which emphasised teacher training. There, from 1848 to 1850, Sue excelled in mathematics, so much so that one instructor, a Yale man, told her that she ought to go to Yale College. Sue also had a way with words: what letters survive combine humour with alertness to what others feel. If any girl should have gone to college Susan was suited, avid as she was for books – eventually she would amass about three thousand volumes. Though Emily Dickinson recognised the limitations of approved novels she still read them – novels, she joked, about irreproachable girls who did not indulge in low-voiced questions. Sue's taste was surer: she read works of literature as they appeared, especially the poetry of Elizabeth Barrett Browning and everything by the Brontës. She had little money and spent nothing on clothes, but she did lay hands on books of lasting quality. This was a girl who could tell the difference between the page that perishes and the page that endures.

For all her intelligence, Susan Gilbert could not expect the advantage of higher education, and neither she or anyone in her family considered it. Where Emily Dickinson approached a discerning father, Susan was blocked as an orphan. She did look to her eldest brother as to a father, but he was too far away and she too proud to beg more than small favours. Her manner to him did not presume on the affection she offered; it was gravely respectful and uncomplaining, a serious voice with none of Emily's sass. She could never permit herself to forget the weak position of a poor relation.

In 1848 Susan's eldest sister Harriet had married an Amherst merchant called William Cutler. This brought Sue back to Amherst when the time came to leave Miss Kelly's. She was to live with Harriet, together with her two older sisters, Mary and Martha. Mary, the elder of the two, was clever like Sue and mothered her as the baby of the family. In September 1849 Mary married a schoolmaster called (appropriately) Mr Learned. They settled in Sunbury, North Carolina, and the following July Mary gave birth. A few days later she died of puerperal fever, with Martha present. While Martha joined their brothers in Grand Rapids, Michigan, Sue, in shock, remained with Harriet in Amherst and looked for consolation in the latest revival. In August 1850, kneeling in her plain, black dress, speaking her loss in well-turned words, she caught the attention of Mr Dickinson. From the first, the Dickinsons, who thought themselves unlike other people, recognised – or thought they recognised – a likeness in this bookish young woman who had come to live amongst them.

Over the following four months, while Martha was away, Sue was drawn into friendship with Emily: two girls of nineteen who were inwardly unlike their society. Each recognised in the other the molten emotions of transformation: Sue, newly converted and reaching out to a heaven that held her sister; Emily freshly in touch with what Emily Brontë calls 'the

God within my breast'. Again, Emily was 'in love' as she sat beside a friend on the doorstep of the Dickinson house.

When Martha came back to Amherst in December 1850 she and Sue bonded so inseparably that Emily teased them as 'twin-Martha' and 'twin-Susie'. On the day of Martha's return, Emily feared to intrude an 'unwelcome face' on their reunion, even as she pleaded with the Gilberts not to forget the Dickinsons' invitation to join their own 'little world of sisters' – not excluding the angel face of 'dear Mary – <u>sainted</u> Mary'. How could they resist? It was not only grief that opened the hearts of the Gilbert sisters; they were unhappily placed with their brother-in-law, a business-man with a company called Sweetser & Cutler. Vinnie's diary, recording a visit to the Cutlers on 27 February 1851, finds that one word can sum up Mr Cutler: 'dreadful'.

Mr Cutler looked on his wife's sisters as unwanted dependants. He was tight-fisted, and their sense of oppression was almost physical: the Cutler house was stuffy, over-heated to a degree that Sue longed to escape. She resolved to support herself and found a post teaching mathematics at a private school, Mr and Mrs Archer's Boarding and Day School for Young Ladies at 40 Lexington Street, Baltimore.

Like Emily, here was a young woman filled with possibility, but where Emily was expressive and exhilarating – merry to the point of hilarity – Susan was sober, a reserved Jane Eyre aware of an orphan's position as visitor in others' homes and therefore very careful, very proper. There were two plots open to her: she might marry or she must earn her living as a teacher, the course her superior brain seemed to dictate. Her distaste for Mr Cutler, followed by Mary's wreckage ten months after her wedding, were hardly inducements to marry. Sue, buttoned up to her tight, white collar, her shining hair pulled back from the straight line of its centre parting, ignored family protests and signed up for the 1851–2 school year.

Where Emily was 'bold' in spirit, Sue was bold in action. In the summer of 1851 there was as yet no railroad to Amherst, and it was an arduous journey – a girl of twenty travelling alone, protected only by her barrier of mourning and propriety – as, stage by stage, she made her way south to Maryland. She faced an unbroken year away from twin-Martha, since they could not afford to meet during school vacations. The pay for women teachers was less than for men. She could save next to nothing, Sue found, once the costs of board, lodging and laundry were deducted from her earnings.

Emily offered a lifeline in her frequent letters: an unbreakable bond between two women on the biblical model of Ruth and Naomi. 'You won't cry any more, will you, Susie, for my father will be your father, and my home will be your home, and where you go, I will go, and we will lie side by side in the kirkyard.'

Emily's appeal was this breath of intimacy – friendship to the death and beyond, renewed by acts of memory: the doorstep, the evergreens over-head and their cultivation of reverie in line with Emily's favourite book, Ik Marvel's *Reveries of a Bachelor* (at twenty Emily thought it hardly worth living if 'Ik' – as Donald Grant Mitchell styled himself – should stop turn-ing out novels). Her letters to Sue keep up a bombardment of longings, refusing to conceal their absurd violence. In October 1851, when Sue had been away about three months, Emily let loose a humorously jealous attack on Sue's preoccupation with 'stupid' pupils.

'I fancy you very often descending to the schoolroom with a plump Binomial Theorem struggling in your hand which you must dissect and exhibit to your uncomprehending ones – I hope you whip them Susie – for <u>my</u> sake – whip them <u>hard</u>.' In May 1852, when Sue had been away for nine months, she heard that Emily would not permit anything to <u>blossom</u> till her friend's return, and meant 'to go out in the garden now, and whip a Crown Imperial for presuming to hold its head up, until you have come home'.

Austin's letters vented parallel longings. Both treat letters as appeals, hotting one plea then another; they draft and re-draft compulsively, with Emily carrying fragments of half-composed letters about the house in her pocket as she mulls over them whilst she dusts and bakes. Their aim was the same: to possess Susan Gilbert.

'Nothing could take me from you,' Austin told Sue, 'how I value only <u>your</u> love & how all others offered me or that I could have for the taking I care not a dross . . .'. Sue, he assured her, had never failed to answer and

<u>more</u> than answer all his dearest dreams of joy. He dreamt of 'those days when we will be together – how gentle & tender I'll be with you!' He liked to think of 'all the little ways I'll try to please you'.

One way was to read her favourite passage in Charlotte Brontë's *Shirley*, with its independent and outspoken heroine. Often, though, Sue appears unreal in his letters, an interchangeable object of desire. What Austin desires is a superior woman moved by his performance as a lover. In so far as it's his drama, not hers, Austin is like Duke Orsino (in Shakespeare's *Twelfth Night*), mooning over his chosen object, Olivia, in a way that exasperates her. For Olivia can pick up the difference between wooing as rhetorical power-play and genuine eloquence – words welling from buried desire. The Duke's agent, Viola, releasing her own unspoken desire, can move Olivia, where the Duke, for all his melancholy and all his worldly props, fails.

So there was Austin with a stray lock over his brow and a down-turned, contemptuous mouth. Tempestuously handsome in this moody style, the most eligible bachelor in town, he could not command Sue. To Emily he confided, first, that 'the world is hollow', and second, that Sue would not play the love-game.

'Dollie [Sue's pet name] is stuffed with sawdust,' he grumbled.

In their confidences, Austin and Emily were aligned in their poor view of society in general and their sister in particular. Austin dismissed Vinnie for triteness and Emily agreed. In fact, in the early months of 1851 (the sole year Vinnie kept a diary), her reading included *Pilgrim's Progress* and *David Copperfield*, a good step up from Ik Marvel. At eighteen she was back home from boarding school, blooming and more sociable than her sister and brother. She had abundant, wavy hair (dark brown, not red like theirs) with a tilted little nose and round, creamy cheeks. Emily, warning Austin against the <u>danger</u> of ice cream, joked about Vinnie's plumpness compared with her own '<u>skin and bones</u>': '. . . For our sakes Austin wont you try to be careful? I know <u>my</u> sake a'nt much, but Vinnie's is considerable – it weighs a good many pounds . . .'.

Vinnie was 'perter and more pert every day'. She had a tart tongue of her own, but it didn't deter Amherst students in their velvet collars and beaver hats. The President of the College forbade dancing on the Sabbath but it went on in private. To preserve secrecy, dances were called 'P.O.M. Meetings': Poetry of Motion. Vinnie favoured the attentions of a Yale graduate, handsome curly-headed Joseph Lyman who often returned to the Homestead. He was a distant connection of Mrs Dickinson and Austin's schoolmate at Williston Seminary. As a schoolboy of sixteen he had been part of the Dickinson household ('that charming second home of mine') for two months, gratified by the understanding of the Dickinson sisters and appreciative of Mrs Dickinson's food, which he praised as 'delicate' – a flair she passed on to her daughters.

From 1846, when Vinnie was emerging from childhood, until Lyman took off for the South in the spring of 1851 he courted, won and dropped her, though for years to come, until he married a restrained Southern girl in 1858, he remembered Vinnie with occasional regret – whenever his Romeo inclinations replaced the stern ambitions of a Caesar, his preferred posture. To cultivate power he forced himself along what he called a flinty path and chose a sturdy wife to support a rising lawyer – a cerebral choice, he was unkind enough to tell her. At thirteen, Vinnie had responded to him with the passionate commitment of a Juliet. The passion held, but when she was eighteen – of marriageable age – it occurred to him that so much excitement might prove distracting. He was insecure financially and unsure what exactly was due to him from a wife, but as the years passed he came to think that what must matter most was a woman who would push him. Vinnie had been so young and so in love, and his intelligence so channelled to public success, that he had failed to detect the strength in her. Having characterised her as a creature of love, he did not notice the telling excellence of the books she was reading in 1851. What is known of Lyman's lingering tie to Vinnie (as late as 1854, after a three-year absence, he still thought to marry her) comes from later, instructional letters to his bride-to-be warning her about bereft girls like Vinnie who had insufficient regard for his ambitions – who failed, as he puts it, to 'come up to snuff'. A weak man rules by caprice. Lyman found it easy to fault an admirer in New Orleans who had shown herself too sexy, while Vinnie, though unmistakably a lady, had been too keen in her attentions. Another time, he blamed Vinnie for neglecting to write as often as she might. If he defected it would be her fault. Then, plumping for a cooler bride, he was perverse enough to prod her reserve with nostalgia for Vinnie's warmth.

Vinnie had been openly in love with Lyman, at his side, hanging on his arm or placing a red ottoman close by his chair so that she might lay her book — Virgil, at one time — against his chest, her arm across him, while she read aloud, looking up into his face. Her arms were plump and soft, Lyman noticed, and her soft mouth and kisses were 'very very sweet'. She liked to sit on his lap, pull out the pins from her long silken tresses and bind the loosened strands around his neck. To shake out long hair was the voluptuous gesture of the day, like Hester Prynne pulling off her Puritan cap when she meets the minister, her former lover, in the woods. For Vinnie to unpin her hair made her wildly different from the way girls of good family were expected to behave.

The reserved Dickinson parents had somehow produced these rampant offspring. Emily was not an oddity amongst them; all three were intense in the ties they cultivated. Austin spoke of 'long fainting for tenderness': 'I have never before received any – from any *body*.' At home, Austin's moodiness was tempered with wit. He set his family laughing over his antics as a temporary master at the Endicott School in the poor North End of Boston. Austin caricatured his power over cowering Irish boys whose families had fled the potato famine of 1847. Emily played this up, urging him to whip the boys just short of death and assuring him the temptation to kill was reasonable.

'. . . I should like to have you kill some [Irish boys] – there are so many now, there is no room for the Americans, and I cant think of a death that would be more after my mind than <u>scientific destruction</u> . . . Wont you please to state the <u>name</u> of the boy that turned the faintest, as I like to get such <u>facts</u> to set down in my <u>journal</u> . . . I dont think deaths or murders can ever come amiss in a young woman's journal.' She is sorry to have little news at the Amherst end, but since it's mid June 'it is almost time for the cholera, and <u>then</u> things will take a start!' This was the grim humour the Dickinsons relished. 'We laughed some when each of your letters came – your respected parents were overwhelmed with glee.'

Virulence was a family joke, drawing in 'the folks', as Austin and Emily called their parents. As a lover, Austin put aside this vein. A man, he thought, had to adopt an overwrought manner towards a candidate for romance: he spoke like a languishing knight and wished 'Lady Susan' to play fairy-enchantress. What Emily called Austin's 'very high style of rapture' was so fixed that even in the presence of tart sisters and a practical mother he clung to his notion of a creature who must be fed nonsense till she's netted. The less his overtures appeared to engage Sue, the louder and more persistently Austin roared out romantic platitudes.

If it was Emily's parallel fancy to possess Susan, it never occurred to brother or sister that they competed; on the contrary, they saw in their responses to Sue complementary affirmations of their choice. Austin was content to assume 'spiritual converse' between his sister and Sue. True, of course, but Austin might have been surprised by the ardour of Emily's letters. Nor would he have realised how her intimacy would have compensated for his own effusions.

While Sue was away for the school year, Emily and Austin took on Martha Gilbert as a sort of understudy. Although she and Sue continued to wear identical black dresses, with tight white collars pinned with the same oval brooch at the throat, their looks belied their twinning. Martha had slanting, rather attractively narrow blue eyes and a delicate mouth. Her centre parting was less straight, her hair softer than her sister's severity. Susan had heavy, dark eyes and plush lips. Her features were almost thick, the sort of dramatic handsomeness that was to become fashionable in the twentieth century when women put on trousers: womanhood veiled by the masculine guise. Sue seemed to inhabit a space between the sexes, a shade away from masculinity. Her coolness would have been all the more provocative clothed in the demure, doll-like corset and full skirt of the 1850s. Provocative, too, the sheath of black, in which she moved, an unpierced seal of grief.

All the while Austin was writing to a remote Susan he encouraged her sister's shy responsiveness with letters, drives and a bracelet of scented beads from Boston – Martha's blue eyes were alight, Emily reported to her brother. That month, September 1851, Austin writes to thank 'Mat' for a bouquet she sent him and reminds her of a ride 'too pleasant to seem real'. For the next forty years he kept the drafts of these letters. Though Austin always preferred Susan, it was comforting to induce a response in her 'twin' and to ready Mat as first reserve at a time when Sue appeared to prefer a career. Emily too took comfort in Mat's proximity and encouraged her attraction to Austin, suggesting it would do him good — away in Boston — if they kept him alive in their hearts with constant talk. At the same time she stoked her brother's interest.

'She thinks a great deal of you,' Emily confided. 'Martha loves you, and we both love Susie, and the hours fly so fast when we are talking of you.'

A month later she told Austin, 'I give all your messages to Mat — she seems to enjoy every one more than the one before . . .'. And so it came about that what had been a three-cornered tie became four-cornered in the course of 1851–2: Emily and Austin entranced with Susan; Martha entranced with Austin; Susan *not* entranced with Austin and drawn more by Emily's irresistible intimacy.

With Mat so plainly in love, Emily could broach a subject Sue had avoided — physical desire — as she and Mat sat close together on the front door stone one light evening in early June.

Afterwards they shared 'a bit of Heaven' as they walked 'side by side' westward along Main Street 'beneath the silent moon' a short distance towards Martha's home in Amity Street, a continuation of Main Street on the other side of town. Talking led each to dream of 'that great blessedness' of a permanent union 'by which two lives are one'. The possibility came close; it seemed almost upon them: 'how it can fill the heart, and make it gang wildly beating,' Emily said, 'how it will take *us* one day, and make us all its own, and we shall not run away from it, but lie still and be happy!'

Curious, emboldened by Mat's responsiveness, the next day Emily took this up with Sue. 'You and I have been strangely silent upon this subject, Susie, we have often touched upon it, and as quickly fled away, as children shut their eyes when the sun is too bright for them.'

Having ventured thus far, Emily now probed further. 'I have always hoped to know if you had no dear fancy, illuminating all your life, no one of whom you murmured in the faithful ear of night — and at whose side in fancy, you walked the livelong day; and when you come home, Susie, we must speak of these things.' Did Sue secretly respond to Austin, as Mat did? Or did Sue draw back in fear? 'Oh, Susie, it is dangerous,' Emily acknowledged. 'It does so rend me, Susie, the thought of it when it comes, that I tremble lest at sometime I, too, am yielded up.' Her willingness to share the fear tempts Sue to reveal a more troubled state than Mat's romantic love.

'You have seen flowers at morning <u>satisfied</u> with the dew, and those same sweet flowers at noon with their heads bowed in anguish before the mighty sun; think you these thirsty blossoms will <u>now</u> need nought but – <u>dew</u>? No, they will cry for sunlight, and pine for the burning noon, tho' it scorches them, scathes them; they have got through with peace – they know that the man of noon, is <u>mightier</u> than the morning and their life is henceforth to him.'

Susan did not enter into this fantasy. What Emily's letters recall of their confidences as they'd sat on the door stone was, in fact, stone: two young women of twenty-one left cold by gallantries.

'I guess I'm made with nothing but a hard heart of stone,' Emily had said, 'for it don't break any, and dear Susie, if mine is stony, yours is stone, upon stone, for you never yield . . . Are we going to <u>ossify</u> always, say, Susie – how will it be?'

In a lowered voice Emily had proposed a different dream, 'a big <u>future</u> waiting for me and you'.

This is what the grasses growing at the corner of the door stone had heard, trusty grasses who would not *tell*. In April 1852 Emily sent Sue 'a sad and pensive grassie', not quite so glad and green as when they used to sit there. She imagined how some spruce plantain leaf won its young heart away and then proved false. In her herbarium she had crossed a tall plantain leaf with a frail stalk of a flower, arranging the two to resemble a courting couple: the leaf upright and dominant; the flower bent. The flower's small triangular head is so pliant it's about to drop. It's like a nineteenth-century lady's head with flowerets on either side and furry filaments, exquisitely delicate. The leaf is broader, especially in the torso, and narrow-hipped.

Men meant marriage, and marriage meant childbirth, and childbirth could mean death. One strain in Sue's and Emily's tie was their absorption with death: Emily stamped with the graveyard under her window; Sue stamped with Mary's fate. For Sue it was a brand of nature's betrayal: the agony and mortality in wait for dream-filled girls at the end of the romance road.

Not surprising, then, if Sue shrank from contact with the 'man of noon'; not surprising if Emily confessed 'I so love to be a child' when childhood friends, now in their twenties, succumbed to what womanhood would do to them. Contact with their own sex was safe. Sitting close and sharing beds was normal in the nineteenth century. Women often spoke like lovers to each other, endearments tripping off their lips, with no sense of deviance. It was easy for Emily to hold Sue, as she says, 'to my heart'; or to crack time away with her little whip till she brings Sue back. Freely she cries out against the weeks she must get through: 'I need her – I must have her, Oh give her to me!'

Desire, anger, the whip and ambition too: these were emotions good young women were not supposed to feel. Her beckonings to Sue and Martha, as to Jane Humphrey before them, drew them into her arena of improper extravagance.

When school closed Sue returned to Mr Cutler's house with nothing to show for the last ten months, beyond taking herself off his unwilling hands. Another alternative occurred to her the following winter while she visited the Bartlett family. Mrs Bartlett had been Mary Learned, sister-in-law to Sue's beloved Mary. As early as 1851 Mrs Bartlett, often ill, had conceived an idea of inviting Sue Gilbert to stay in the capacity of guest-helper. At that time Sue had preferred to pursue a career of her own, but after school-teaching failed to support her the Bartletts renewed their invitation. In the winter of 1853 they, with a new baby, were living in Manchester, New Hampshire. Sue now agreed to join them, a little apprehensive at the prospect of a stay with strangers but willing to try her hand at babycare. She took the unusual step of exposing her vulnerability in the hope of securing a sensitive welcome.

'Has it occurred to you that perhaps we shall not like each other,' Sue wrote to Mary Bartlett a month before going. 'I really begin almost to fear meeting people I have never seen, but think I shall have courage for the encounter when it comes.' Her voice took courage from the new candour in women's writing, coloured perhaps by the voice of Elizabeth Barrett Browning whose recent volume of *Poems* (1852) she carried with her on the journey northwards.

Fear proved unnecessary. Sue found herself in a gentle place, so much so that she fell in love with the whole family. The intellectual taste of the Revd Mr Bartlett was particularly congenial to a bookish young woman deprived of higher education. He was a Dartmouth graduate who later became president of the college. The family had been alerted by Julius Learned that Sue was 'some punkins' (outstanding), and Mr Bartlett's talks with her must have confirmed this for he gave her a copy of Charlotte Brontë's newly published *Villette*, the story of an outwardly cold orphan called Lucy Snowe who discovers her buried ability when she goes abroad in search of a new way to support herself. Miss Snowe, who ventures alone, geographically and mentally, defines herself as 'a rising character'. Sue responded with unaccustomed extravagance: after she left she let the Bartletts know how much they suited her buried life – a hint of her wish to belong to them, in accents of barely veiled desperation:

> . . . I am really lonely to go back to you and it will be the work of
> weeks, to get possession of a contented spirit, and my old resigned
> temper of mind. I loved you and Mr. Bartlett, as I have no others
> save my own brothers and sisters, and if I live the years of
> Methuselah I never shall forget the sympathy and affection I found
> with you . . . There was something in the atmosphere of your home
> just suited to my life – something so kindly and gentle (laugh at me
> if you will) I can't think of you all without crying like a child.

Susan's declaration that 'no others' had evoked this depth of attachment is surprising in the context of the passionate letters Austin and Emily Dickinson had penned and, more particularly, Emily's captivating invitation to share her poetic destiny. It came to her as a voyage out, a promise of sailing together 'On this wondrous sea', the poet as pilot, towards a timeless shore. Intrepid, resolute, they would find their own *terra incognita*:

> Thither I pilot <u>thee</u> —
> Land Ho! Eternity!
> Ashore at last!

She sent this poem, the first of many, to Sue in New Hampshire in March 1853. Yet Sue turned like a needy child to the Bartletts. Her declaration to them can't have been mere gratitude or flattery; she obviously cared for them too much for her own good. It seems that she really did prefer this 'gentle' family to the Dickinsons, whose emotions were molten and rumbling underground, audible to those in their emotional vicinity. If Sue wished to seek safer ground she was less at liberty to draw away than a succession of earlier intimates who had left town. Sue, in fact, appreciated Mr Dickinson, who turned away from emotion.

The Bartletts were pleased with their visitor and in time invited her back for another stay, but it never occurred to them to go so far as to offer her a permanent home. Sickly Mrs Bartlett, who welcomed Sue's help with the baby, was not about to adopt a young woman of twenty-two in need of a life. Wrenching herself away in March 1853, still in her buttoned-up mourning, Sue was once more travelling alone. Her route back to Mr Cutler took her via Boston, and she stopped overnight at a hotel called Revere House, a questionable situation for a young woman on her own. Here, in Boston, was Austin Dickinson, newly admitted to Harvard Law School. When they met that night, 23 March, Susan consented to be engaged.

'Those hours, Sue, let us never forget – & I can never be unhappy,' Austin wrote after she left, 'those sweet kisses you, leaning over me imprinted on my forehead – our parting that night – how warmly you let me press you to my heart – & how passionately you clung around my neck – and held my lips to yours let me never forget – Let me never forget it all – and I never shall doubt that the deepest, strongest love . . . has been given to me –'. It seemed to him a miracle that their sharp-edged characters should come together.

The time had come to set himself straight with Mat, as his sisters had advised. On 27 March, four days after the tryst with Susan, Austin drafted an eight-page letter to the sister who loved him more:

> Forgive me now Mattie will you for not writing to you before. It is not because I have not thought of you – nor because I do not love you – I do love you Mattie – just as well as Emily and Vinnie . . . you all enter into all Sue's & my plans for the future – . . . You shall be with us then Mat if you have chosen no other, fuller home – and live as much like a spoiled child as love & indulgence can induce you . . . The world is very wide & Fortune very kind and fears & doubts are for the weak and wicked . . . [Sue and I] love each other Mattie with a love that knows no cessation – no abate – that is larger with every new morning, & sweeter with every coming evening – that makes all things possible . . . We have loved each other a long time.

Martha did not reply for two months, and then was forced to comply by another disingenuous nudge from Austin, offloading his guilt on to his future sister-in-law, to whom he had always felt so brotherly that he can't understand her silence at news of the forthcoming marriage. Martha joined her brothers in Grand Haven, Michigan, and did not return to Amherst for the rest of 1853. She lived another four years in Amherst but spent more time with her aunt in Geneva, and then married a Geneva merchant called Smith. The bond with her 'twin' was unbroken, and whether Martha showed Sue the letters Austin sent her, or whether Sue regretted the impulse to yield to a man her sister had desired, we can't know – only that his choice had been driven by a capacity for hero worship inherited from a Puritan father. This much Susan discerned as the years passed. Every autumn twin-Sue who became Mrs Dickinson would visit Geneva, but twin-Martha who became Mrs Smith did not often return these visits. Martha's was not a visible tragedy. She did not go into a decline; nor did she retire from the world to nurse disappointed love.

What Emily thought of this is unrecorded, but it's clear that she closed the door on Martha, beyond the odd pleasantry: she might, for instance, remark to Sue that she hadn't heard from Martha for a long time. A cooling, then, after their intimacy. Her first loyalty was to the brother in whom she had long recognised an ascetic tendency, susceptible to stern pledges of renunciation. Attraction to women was the obvious antidote, and so long as he remained uncommitted Emily had advised Austin not to let ties block any spontaneous liking. It wasn't the old double standard; more, her determination to stop her brother from stiffening into a replica of what was pure and terrible in their father. When he had been flirting with both Gilbert sisters Emily had teased him with a prospect of twin-Martha flinging herself off a cliff in the Green Mountains (of Vermont), while the apparently calmer twin-Susan was mired 'in <u>most deep</u> affliction'. Emily assured Austin that whatever should happen, 'I will never desert Micawber'.*

In the summer of 1854 Austin was about to take his final examinations at Harvard Law School. His professional qualification would have raised the prospect of firming up his plans. These are likely to have included a prospective date for a wedding, since by now he and Sue had been engaged for over a year. It was during this summer, while Austin was still in Cambridge, that Sue fell ill with what her doctor diagnosed as a nervous fever. She lay prostrate, too feeble to dress and unwilling to eat.

To Emily, it was an inflated drama. She mimicked Mrs Cutler's anxious voice asking her to relay an important message to Austin: 'Sue has eaten broth *twice* today and a chicken leg – She designs eating a wing tomorrow.'

Harriet Cutler and other fussing females had assigned Austin the role of 'missing Saint', Emily told him, 'and as none of them speak of you . . . without plentiful tears, I have considerable work to arrange my emotions'.

Emily's comedy rides over Sue's frame of mind, at the centre of the clamour around her. No symptoms are mentioned, and the illness appears

---

* The comical vehemence of Mrs Micawber, loyal to her endearingly helpless husband in *David Copperfield* (1848).

to be some sort of breakdown. There's a strain and restlessness in Sue, not to be satisfied by Emily's calling and calling to her to be her 'darling'. Sue could not be healed by the prospect of future sistering – Emily's share of Austin's trophy.

A suggested cure was for Sue to join her brothers in the area of Grand Rapids and Grand Haven on the shore of Lake Michigan. Sue hesitated between her need to get away and guilt on Emily's account.

'Sue – you can go or stay,' Emily told her, dreading her loss in line with former friends who had backed away from Dickinson intensity. 'There is but one alternative – We differ often lately, and this must be the last. You need not fear to leave me lest I should be alone, for I often part with things I fancy I have loved, – sometimes to the grave, and sometimes to an oblivion rather bitterer than death – thus my heart bleeds so frequently that I shan't mind the hemorrhage . . . Perhaps this is the point at which our paths diverge.'

Once Sue left, Emily had to disguise the rift. When the good folk of Amherst enquired after Sue, she was obliged to invent vaguely plausible answers. Yes, Susan had reached Michigan safely. Yes, Susan was better every day. Six months passed and still Sue kept her distance. Emily wrote twice, in her usual vein. To write felt futile, like bringing a thimbleful of dew to quench 'the endless fire'. Not once does she enter into Sue's collapse. Was this tact? Or was Emily too loyal to her brother to want to know? Sue kept these letters but remained silent, like Jane Humphrey before her. Emily wondered if Sue's departure could be permanent.

Elements of the Dickinson legend appear in these letters of 1854: a bereft and disappointed persona developed, it appears, before she became a poet. Added to this persona is the 'old-fashioned' air enacted in a final letter to Abiah Root, in which Emily declines an invitation to visit. 'I'm so old fashioned, Darling, that all your friends would stare.' In place of the tart young woman she was, Emily constructed this caricature complete with spectacles, work basket, and pussycat. Already, at twenty-three, she was rehearsing the part of retiring quaintness, beloved by posterity.

Austin went west in December 1854 to seek out Sue and explore the possibility of starting a legal practice in Chicago. On Austin's return, Emily pressed him with questions, as she relates in a humorous letter to Austin's adored in late January 1855.

'How did Sue look?'

'As she always did,' Austin answered shortly.

'What was she wearing?' Two months after her engagement to Austin, Sue had taken off the black dress she had worn for nearly three years, and acquired a white dress, a white straw hat with a ruched ribbon, and a mantilla of fawn silk. Emily had noticed how 'very lovely' she looked.

'I never did notice what people wear,' said Austin flatly.

'Did Sue wear a basque?' Vinnie prompted.

'She *did* have on a black thing.'

'What did she say of *me*?' Emily badly wanted to know, not having heard a word for half a year.

Austin remained vague. 'She said I must tell you *everything*.'

'A message?'

'No.'

Emily sighed over 'a good-for-nothing fellow' who, a moment later, would be firing off raptures to Sue. A new wedding date had been set for the following autumn. Conceivably, Sue had joined her brothers, hoping to take refuge from pressure. But since her brothers offered handsome handouts on her marriage to a promising young lawyer of good family they are likely to have encouraged it. Her brothers' wishes would have weighed with Sue in the way such wishes weighed with any unmarried girl who did not want to become a permanent financial burden on her family. Everyone but the prospective bride wanted this marriage, and Sue returned to her Amherst fate in February 1855.

That month, Mr Dickinson wished his daughters to join him in Washington. From 1853 to 1855 he served in Congress, representing his district of Massachusetts as a conservative Whig. In new clothes, Emily felt like a reluctant peacock in borrowed plumes. As a stranger at Mr Cratchett's boarding house, amid the turmoil of the capital, she was 'unwell'. Again, silence as to symptoms. Whatever they were they excused Emily certain gaieties, though she and Lavinia did meet Christopher Dawes Eliot, who shared rooms with her father. From these rooms at Willard's Hotel the pair were in the process of founding the anti-slavery Republican party.*

After three weeks in Washington, in March the Dickinson sisters went on to Philadelphia to stay with cousins called the Colemans. Since Emily rarely left home there has been huge interest in this episode, though almost nothing is known beyond the fact that, while there, she encountered the Revd Charles Wadsworth, then pastor of the Arch Street Presbyterian Church. It was his habit to withdraw from his congregation by way of a trapdoor after a theatrical sermon, an insistent solitude that Christopher Benfey likens to Hawthorne's gloomy minister who isolates himself behind a black veil.

Emily was attracted to these trappings of solitude. 'You are troubled,' she ventured to say to this man sixteen years her senior.

'My life is full of dark secrets.' He shivered as he spoke.

She was impressed with the vehemence of sorrow, and even more with secrets. Later, by letter, she confided to him a 'sorrow' of her own. He had no idea what the 'affliction' of 'Miss Dickenson' could be, conveyed with so much emotional urgency, but offered his sympathy and prayers.

In October 1855 Emily was ecstatic to receive a visit from Jane Humphrey. Jane had returned to Amherst before taking up a post at an elite Massachusetts school at Groton. To see her again revived all the acuteness of Emily's attachment: 'Jennie – my Jennie Humphrey – I love you well tonight, and for a beam from your brown eyes, I would give a pearl.' It made her weep to think of the friends she had lost, 'the longing for them' – all those 'who stray from me'. At nearly twenty-five, it was coming home to her that all her efforts to develop an alternative life based on women's friendship were doomed in the face of an economic system based on marriage. Should she contrive to kiss a joy as it flies, or exert a firmer hold?

* Mr Eliot's brother was William Greenleaf Eliot, who had left their native Boston in order to found the Unitarian Church in St Louis. His grandson was to be the poet T. S. Eliot. The link of the two poets may seem tenuous, but both were part of the network of New England families rooted in the Puritan period and imbued with its high-minded habits of spiritual search.

'I try to prize it, Jennie, when the loved are here, try to love <u>more</u>, and <u>faster</u>, and <u>dearer</u>, but when all are gone, [it] seems as had I tried <u>harder</u>, they would have stayed with me.'

Holding still to the intimacy of their past, Emily urged her once more to renew their tie. 'No day goes by, little One, but has its thought of you, and its wish to see you. When shall you come again?' Tenderly, calling her 'my Child', Emily made a final plea for words: 'will you write me instantly?'

Jane never replied. She went on teaching until 1858 – ten years in all – and then resigned when, at twenty-nine, she married.

Deacon Mack, who had bought half the Dickinson Homestead in 1833 and then the other half in 1840, died in November 1854. This had far-reaching consequences for the Dickinsons and, ultimately, for Austin's fiancée. In April 1855 the Homestead came on the market and Mr Dickinson bought it back for $6000 (helped, it's thought, by Mrs Dickinson's recent inheritance from her wealthy father). In the grounds adjacent to the Homestead stood a cottage built in 1847, worth $900, which Mr Dickinson rented out. Mr Dickinson now made two proposals to his son: he offered to build Austin and his bride a next-door house that would incorporate the cottage kitchen and dining room. At the same time Mr Dickinson, who had recently lost an election and would not be returning to Congress, offered Austin a partnership in his local law firm. So ended the plan to settle near Sue's brothers. She was to live next door, as part of an extended Dickinson family. To allow for renovations and building, the wedding was postponed once more.

In November 1855 the Dickinsons moved into the Homestead. It was only a walk around the corner to where Emily had lived before she was ten, but she felt like an immigrant trundling out west in a wagon: a '<u>gone-to-Kansas</u>' sensation. Humorously she pictures herself with a lantern, looking for 'deathless me'. Mrs Dickinson, however, was depressed. One possible cause was grief for her father; another, the loss of a home she'd made her own; and then, too, there was the probable use of her inheritance for what her husband wanted. There's a hint of the sick passivity of a wife overruled. She lay on the sofa while Emily and Vinnie took control. In fact they found the house in fine condition, thanks to Mr Dickinson's up-to-date improvements. In the front parlour he had put in French windows opening onto a veranda to catch the afternoon sun. Directly above, Emily had a corner room filled with light from four windows and heated by the latest Franklin stove, a novelty that put fireplaces out of fashion. From one set of windows, at the front of the house, she had an uninterrupted view of the Dickinson meadow or, looking down, of passers-by along Main Street. From the side set of windows she looked out on the groundwork and rising front tower of the house for Sue and her brother. Here, in a room of her own, Emily read her letters in private and wrote at her cherry table, only seventeen and a half inches square – sometimes on Sundays while the rest of the family went to church. She was excused (for unspecified reasons of health) any time she chose, and she exercised this liberty at will. Many of her letters comment on her lifting spirits in the stillness of the emptied house with no company but 'Pussy'. Her best companion, she remarked, was her lexicon.

At some point it became her habit to start writing at three in the morning. The invisibility of the night set her free. 'My Wheel is in the dark', she begins one poem. She can't see the spokes of the wheel, but knows its 'dripping feet' (the feet of the rhythmic line) go round and round, with the poet's foot 'on the tide' – the tide of words and metaphors: the dark, the wheel, and the 'unfrequented road' to an imagined 'Clearing'. Is 'Clearing' the clarification at the end of her poems? In this instance it's also an end point in her poetic journey. En route she sees ahead some who give up ('Some have resigned the Loom'); some whose spirit dies; and the enviable few who proceed to immortality. Their 'stately feet' (no longer 'dripping') pass 'royal' through the gate of the immortals, and in doing so they act on the strugglers they leave behind, 'flinging the problem back, at you and I'. You and I may well be Sue and Emily, for Emily sent this poem to Sue, yet it speaks more widely to the challenge of imaginative endeavour: how to lift work in the direction of the 'royals'.

So, equipped with lamp, book and little else, Dickinson picks up her pen and, as she puts it to paper, a fund of phrases falls to her. The confidentiality of this windfall is part of its appeal. Her 'Banker' is a divine being with whom she's engaged in private converse,

> So stationed I could catch the mint
> That never ceased to fall — . . .

The face is hidden; only the voice is heard. Other all-time poets have counselled invisibility as the condition of truth. 'Flee from the prees [crowd],'
Chaucer advised, 'and dwelle with sothfastnesse.' 'I am a crowd, I am a
lonely man, I am nothing,' Yeats declared. None pursued invisibility as
strictly as Dickinson. *The soul selects its own society, then shuts the door.* 'Noteless'
behind that door, she's immured against celebrity: 'I could not bear to
live — aloud — / The Racket shamed me so —'. In this way she would pass
nine undisturbed hours, broken only by her sunrise task of waking the
household with 'that shrill morning call' sleepers were 'sure to hear'.

To free herself of morning duties, she had to have the backing of her
father; his assent was decisive for her future as a poet. A poem of about 1858
has the following dedication:

To my Father —
to whose untiring efforts in my behalf, I am indebted for my
<u>morning hours</u> – viz – 3.AM – to 12.PM – these grateful lines
are inscribed by his aff[ectionate]
    Daughter

To marry would be to lose this freedom to follow her natural rhythm;
no husband would have tolerated her timetable as her father did, and soon
there would have been babies to fill the hours. The poet Julia Ward Howe
found herself silenced by her husband Samuel Gridley Howe after she published *Passion-Flowers* in 1854. 'The Heart's Astronomy' reveals a wife's affinity
for a 'comet dire and strange' as she paces round and round the house,
while children smile from its windows. The book made a sensation but Mr
Howe was so displeased to hear of 'wild, erratic natures' tethered to domesticity ('Between extremes distraught and rent') that he delivered an
ultimatum: if his wife continued to publish in this vein he would end the
marriage and take the children. His threat about her children brought
Mrs Howe to heel. From then on she brought out only public verse like

'The Battle Hymn of the Republic'. When Mrs Howe asked her husband how he could have been so sympathetic to Florence Nightingale, his reply was that had Miss Nightingale been his wife he would not have allowed her to nurse the sick and wounded.

The time came for Susan to face once more the prospect of her wedding to Austin Dickinson. Sue's postponements of this event over the three years of their engagement did alert Austin to the problem of sexual fear. There's some evidence that he tried to cross the barrier of silence.

Was she, he put it delicately in a draft letter, 'troubled by the thought of giving yourself away to me. Does it now, Sue? Does it ever seem to you you could live happier – better – unmarried . . . Is there anything in the . . . relation of wife that gives you sometimes gloomy thoughts – and if there is can I say something that will relieve them'?

His unrealistic offer was that she remain a virgin, 'if so you are happier – then I will ask nothing of you, take nothing from you – you are not the happier in giving me'. This 'sacrifice' he was prepared to make if she would go through with the wedding. 'Don't ever be discouraged, Sue, to thinking of "a man's requirements" – I ask nothing but your love – just the love you are giving me now – and I offer in return all I am – & all I can accomplish – without reserve – without qualifications.' Sue was sufficiently alert as a reader to have picked up his hope of a wife who is 'happier' in giving herself.

The Gilbert brothers sent $6000 towards furnishing the new house with an oak sideboard, Gothic chairs, Victorian paintings and a green marble fireplace adorned with Canova's *Cupid and Psyche*.

In the end, after prolonged hesitation but encouraged by Emily and the rest of the Dickinson family, Susan Gilbert married Austin Dickinson on 1 July 1856. Her grave eyes looked out from a bonnet like an inverted basket with festoons of flowers tucked under the brim. Austin stood tall, his brooding stare set off by his flaming locks. It was a quiet wedding, attended by the bride's brothers and sisters at Mrs Van Vranken's home. After a few days in the Cataract House at the honeymoon resort of Niagara Falls, followed by a night at the Donegana Hotel in Montreal, the couple settled at The Evergreens.

They named the house for the spruce and pine around it. It was the most stylish house in town, one of the earliest examples of Italianate domestic architecture and the first to install built-in closets on either side of the front door and a bell-pull in the library. The steps of the front path lead up to a square tower and the height of the hall is dramatic, looking up through two storeys. Here Sue welcomed visitors. Her hospitality flowered, making The Evergreens a centre of social life in Amherst. Across the hall was the library, looking out towards the Homestead.

It did not take long for the back path to be trodden into the grass between the two houses as private communications between Emily and Sue raced back and forth. Books were part of their exchange. Sue was quick to acquire *Aurora Leigh*, the novel-poem in the first person by Elizabeth Barrett Browning, published in 1857. Its heroine is a poet who defies the triviality of women's lives and takes her domestic way into the larger issues of existence. Aurora Leigh playfully makes herself a poet's crown, a signal of possibility to Emily Dickinson who plays queen in later poems.*

Sue and Emily read this keenly, and one of them has marked 'the burning lava of a song'. A double line picks out the need for candour above all: 'if we say a true word, instantly / We feel 'tis God's, not ours, and pass it on . . .'. When Robert Browning met Elizabeth Barrett, he had admired an emotional candour he could not, he said, bring himself to risk. A Dickinson poem of this time, 'I think I was enchanted / When first a sombre Girl —', celebrates a 'Foreign Lady' who opens up possibilities for a woman poet. Dickinson marks a 'change' tantamount to 'Conversion of the Mind'. From then 'The Days — to Mighty Metres stept —'.

Elizabeth Barrett Browning was a poet whose voice had reached a wide public from her sickbed. Her success, turning seclusion to advantage, may have served as a model for the way of life Dickinson would devise for herself as poet. Her hair, cut in 1851 and again in 1853, was long again and she began to wear it parted behind and looped over her ears in the style of

---

* Another secret queen of the 1850s, Lucy Snowe in *Villette*, sits on her throne in an attic, declaiming to the garret vermin.

Elizabeth Barrett Browning. Vinnie followed suit, folding the two ends of her abundant tresses into a bow-knot at the back.

During the unmarked year of 1857, a year that has left no trace apart from books, certain reclusive voices of authentic womanhood and spiritual trial converged on Emily. Sue gave her an 1857 reprint of *The Imitation of Christ* by the fifteenth-century mystic Thomas à Kempis, and in the same year Sue bought Charlotte Brontë's first novel, *The Professor*, published posthumously. The following year Anne Brontë's *Tenant of Wildfell Hall* joined the Dickinson collection, together with Emily's dark-brown copy of *Wuthering Heights*. That year, too, Emily gave Mrs Gaskell's new *Life of Charlotte Brontë* to Sue, inscribed 'Sister, from Sister', while Sue gave Emily a copy of *Villette*, where the buried fire of Lucy Snowe encounters the blazing fire of the actress Vashti, modelled on the actress Rachel whose explosive performance had thrilled and shocked Charlotte Brontë in London, as Mrs Gaskell relates. It was fitting that another of Sue's gifts to the burgeoning poet was Rachel's *Memoirs*, published in New York in 1858. In this period after Charlotte Brontë's death Emily Dickinson thought of the moss creeping over her grave,

> The little cage of 'Currer Bell'
> In quiet 'Haworth' laid.

She imagines her 'returning' – the continued existence of this rare bird in the unseen space:

> . . . not in all the nests I meet —
> Can Nightingale been seen —

At some stage Dickinson acquired a rare copy of the first edition of the Brontë sisters' poems published privately (at Charlotte's instigation) in 1846, when Emily Dickinson had been a schoolgirl of fifteen. Here she would have come upon Emily Brontë's visionary poems of 'the world within', the closest to Dickinson's rising poetic gift and most inspiring of all preceding poets. Mrs Gaskell reports Charlotte's wonder at poems not 'at all like the poetry women generally write'. Charlotte had been stunned by a voice starker and more dauntless than her own. It was like a blast on a trumpet. Unlike the weak diffusiveness and wordiness of popular poetesses, these poems were 'condensed and terse, vigorous and genuine' – an obvious model for Emily Dickinson.

She was young and still in the making when she encountered the Brontës' assent to the hidden alien in women, and discovered in Emily Brontë a poet fixed on 'infinity'. Left to herself, this was a poet who would have secreted her poems through her lifetime. Fiercely private, she saw the impossibility of spiritual wholeness in a shallow world she shunned; for her, wholeness had an absolute existence beyond life. When a biography eventually appeared in 1883, Dickinson snapped it up at once, finding this life 'more electric far than anything since "Jane Eyre"'.

At the time when Susan and Emily Dickinson were reading in unison and setting up the next-door habits of their sisterhood, they had a private meeting place at the Homestead: the back serving hall, a dark room with alternative exits through which they could slip at the sound of footsteps. Emily spent many an evening in Sue's library, with its books and paintings. There was a convenient glass door facing the Homestead through which Emily, lantern in hand, would arrive for evening games of battledore and shuttlecock with Sue and a favourite visitor, Samuel Bowles, the owner of the daily *Springfield Republican*. He was four years older than Emily and Sue, a hard worker who sometimes went to bed at three in the morning. He had taken over his father's newspaper at the age of twenty-five, in 1851. Having missed out on college, he liked to report on the annual Amherst commencement – the 'Gravities', Emily joked. She was unimpressed with professors who lost themselves in 'wherefores'. She and Sue preferred a man like Bowles with his hands on the ropes. Bearded, bright of eye, he liked the company of intelligent women and often printed women's poems.

One evening in January 1859 a young widow in mourning sat beside the fire – 'the Maid in black', said Emily. The visitor was Kate Scott Turner from Cooperstown in upstate New York. She and Sue had met at the Utica Female Seminary. Kate warmed to the rarity of Emily's character as she improvised at the piano.

'My heart votes for you,' Emily told her. She was 'Condor Kate', an habituée of distant crags. Here was another candidate for a secret society of outsiders and pilgrim souls. Kate was to be amongst 'my girls' who antici- pate the March sisters in *Little Women* in playing Pilgrims – only these girls, as Emily conceives them, take their way outside society: 'All *we* are *strangers* – dear – The world is not acquainted with us, because we are not acquainted with her.' In such company, Emily's secret self could emerge. 'I am pleas- antly located in the deep sea,' she said, 'but love will row you out if her hands are strong, and don't wait till I land, for I'm going ashore on the other side –'. Kate, like Sue, was invited to follow the poet's voyage out to eternity, leaving the safer shores of society behind.

'Those were unnatural evenings,' Emily thought after Kate had gone, 'Bliss is unnatural.' She knitted Kate a pair of garters and sent them with a humorous verse: '. . . When Katie kneels, their loving hands still clasp her pious knee — / Ah! Katie! Smile at Fortune, with two so knit to thee!'

Sue used her new home to set up a salon. One member refused to read *Adam Bede* (1859) on hearing of its author's ungodliness. Defiantly, Sue bought the novel for Emily in 1860 and then both bought copies of the newly published *Mill on the Floss*. Sam Bowles stoked this enthusiasm by giving Sue these two novels as well as the earlier *Scenes of Clerical Life*. Emily put a picture of George Eliot on the wall of her room (along with Elizabeth Barrett Browning). Otherwise, George Eliot was little known in Amherst for some time. Sue, craving intellectual company beyond the limitations of the town, had the idea of inviting writers and editors to lecture, and in time leading men and women of the day came to the drawing room at The Evergreens: Harriet Beecher Stowe, author of *Uncle Tom's Cabin* and *The Minister's Wooing*; the Revd Henry Ward Beecher; Mrs Frances Hodgson Burnett, author of the children's books *Little Lord Fauntleroy* and *The Secret Garden*; Thomas Wentworth Higginson who frequently published in the leading cultural magazine, the *Atlantic Monthly*; Sam Bowles; Dr Josiah Gilbert Holland, assistant to Bowles and quarter-owner of the *Springfield Republican*; and Helen Hunt, another successful American novelist whom the Dickinsons would have remembered as Helen Fiske from the Amherst of their childhood.

On 16 December 1857 Emerson himself came to lecture on 'The Beautiful in Rural Life', and stayed at The Evergreens. It seemed to Emily 'as if he had come from where dreams are born'.

The later 1850s was a difficult period for Sue. She marked these lines in her copy of *Aurora Leigh*:

> . . . There are fatal days indeed
> In which the fibrous years have taken root
> So deeply, that they quiver to their tops
> When'er you stir the dust of such a day.

While Sue tuned into the voices of unconventional women, including her sister-in-law, Austin gave her *The Angel in the House*, upholding the selflessness of the ideal wife. 'Someone has been watching us, Sue,' was Austin's inscription for Christmas 1857 – wishful, certainly, but not necessarily deluded, since Sue did pour her talents into domesticity. She created a garden and filled it with choice flowers. Oysters brought from the New England shore awaited Austin's return from his office in Palmer's Block. Sue's food was stylish, while next door at the Homestead the emphasis was on home-grown produce, preserves, puddings and baking – in 1857 Emily won a prize for her Indian bread at a local food fair.

Sue bore her first child in the summer of 1861, so abstinence was certainly at an end by the latter half of 1860. Austin later alleged an attempted abortion, and this is likely: Sue's horror of childbirth made it a potentially fatal trap she had long tried to avoid. At the time she fell pregnant, she apologised to Emily for seeming to turn away from a kiss.

'If you have suffered this past Summer – I am sorry – *I* Emily bear a sorrow that I never uncover – If a nightingale sings with her breast against a thorn,* why not we?'

This much they told each other of hidden pain, perhaps little more. There's a hint of reproach for a certain degree of oblivion on Emily's part.

---

* This image comes from Hans Christian Andersen's story, 'The Nightingale and the Rose'.

Sue's part was to encourage the poet's verbal power, but that power, and the self-absorbed intensity that went with it, was something Sue had to contend with if she was to hold her own. Others before her had felt over-powered, sapped, upstaged, a common experience for those drawn into the force-field of genius. The poet was a brilliant deviser of psychic situations. As prime reader, Sue backed these; still, it seemed to her right that Emily should not neglect to see what Sister did not say about her marriage. Sue might have said – if such things could be said – it was a marriage to Emily's benefit. Sue might have said that it was a union Emily had urged despite their mutual understanding that marriage was 'dangerous'. Emily's word. In 1858 one of her early poems had imagined marriage as an obligatory martyrdom from which the poet is happily exempt:

> By such and such an offering
> To Mr So and So —
> The web of life is woven —
> So martyrs albums show!

Once married, Susan was subject – sooner or later – to what used to be called a husband's rights, and subject also to her father-in-law's plans. He was legal guardian to four orphaned nieces, daughters of his favourite sister and her husband, a wealthy Brooklyn bookseller called Newman. Initially Mr Dickinson had placed the girls (with a chaperone) in an Amherst house he owned, but at this time he split up the household. The two eldest were placed with another member of the Dickinson family, while the two younger girls, Clarissa (Clara) and Anna, aged sixteen and about twelve, he placed with Sue and Austin. As guardian, Mr Dickinson had borrowed about $6000 from his late brother-in-law's estate, which was the amount it cost to build The Evergreens. He could have justified this as providing a home for his wards. They did not settle well. It's possible that they vented on Sue some resentment at Mr Dickinson's borrowing from their inheritance to build his son's home.

So it happened that two dressy girls from Brooklyn were living with

Susan within a year of her marriage. At only twenty-seven, Sue had to put up with their mulish faces and the prospect of their company day and night for the foreseeable future. At the Homestead the girls would have been an intrusion, to judge from Emily's impatience with Cousin Pliny Dickinson of Syracuse and his two daughters, who stayed only a few days: 'Fortunate for us indeed that his business feels the need for him, or I think he would never go.' She thought Clara and Anna pleasant enough but 'not *like us*'. It appears that Mr Dickinson protected the privacy of his household at Sue's expense. There was friction with the girls, who later complained of Sue while retaining respect for Mr Dickinson. Susan signed her maiden name in a copy of Goethe published three years after her marriage. To herself she was still 'S. H. Gilbert'.

This is the secret sharer who urged Emily Dickinson on as she swims away from land towards the deep sea of her solitude. In 1858, the year the poet began to save selected poems in home-made booklets, she celebrates Sue in a sister-poem and sent it to her, most likely on Sue's twenty-eighth birthday. It was amongst the first of the 276 poems that would follow across the grass between the two houses:

> One Sister have I in our house —
> And one, a hedge away.
> There's only one recorded,
> But both belong to me.
>
> One came the road I came —
> And wore my last year's gown —
> The other, as a bird her nest,
> Builded our hearts among.
>
> She did not sing as we did —
> It was a different tune —
> Herself to her a music
> As Bumble bee of June.

Today is far from Childhood —
But up and down the hills
I held her hand the tighter —
Which shortened all the miles — . . .

Their tie is not unmarred. The poet owns, 'I spilt the dew — / But took the morn'. 'Spilt' and 'took': the monosyllabic verbs are hard, wilful. The speaker has no compunction about appropriating her Sister's freshness. Yet this acquired Sister is no weakling: she keeps up her 'hum' and brings back the 'Violets' – the old fragrance of mutual feeling that, to tell the truth, has 'mouldered' for some years. For a poet in the making it's more than enough, a family circle in adjoining houses and a guiding star for what she is to 'do':

. . . I chose this single star
From out the wide night's numbers —
Sue — forevermore!

Sue's two reminiscences of family and Amherst life show a flair for memoir. She had a humorous eye for detail. Where Emily Dickinson soars into luminosity, Sue sees other people. Over the course of the 1850s she had the intelligence to see Emily Dickinson. It was Sue's extraordinary fortune to encounter a mind of this calibre; it was her misfortune to have it possess and shape her fate, for Sue's marriage was in part the work of Austin's sister. Nothing in Emily's poems and letters to Sue suggests that she might be other than the one who offers the rum – the choice 'Domingo' – to intoxicate 'the little tippler' of a poet. Dickinson's poems to Sue are shot through with rum and heat brought home from a West Indian island of the imagination.

There's a strange exception to the poems sent across the grass: a more possessive poem to 'Dollie' (Sue), which Dickinson kept to herself. Dollie is called to join the poet in her grave. It's a call from beyond the poet's life-time, reaching out for Dollie in a way that's all the creepier for Dollie's assent to the poet's power to 'take':

. . . Trust the loving promise
Underneath the mould,
Cry 'it's I,' 'take Dollie,'
And I will enfold!

Deathless love, like the 'rocks beneath' in *Wuthering Heights*, is invisible to a society based on marriage and procreation, in which the affinities of twin souls have no institutional habitation.

Whether this attachment was physically erotic as well as ardent and infinite remains in question. What is unquestionable is the primacy of this relationship for the genius that began to show itself in the late 1850s. 'No Words ripple like Sister's,' Emily told Sue in later years. To a poet nothing had mattered so much as words, and their genealogy was 'very sweet to trace'. Far back, at the start, Sue's words had been 'Silver' to 'the lone student of the Mines'.

Their bond was a day-to-day affair, reinforced as a family and neighbours' tie that was to last thirty-six years. But what was formative for a poet starting out in her twenties was to find (or induce) in 'Sister' a response to light her fire.

4

'WIFE WITHOUT THE SIGN'

In her early thirties, between 1860 and 1863, Emily Dickinson wrote 663 poems. Amongst them were many of her greatest, rising to 'My Life had stood — a Loaded Gun —' late in 1863. The fiery output of four years produced more than a third of her complete works. What prompted this? In 1863, when the poet was thirty-two, she shows off that well-conducted woman tying her hat as she goes about the duties of her clock-bound day, with an air of having so much to do; yet mild domesticity guards the 'Bomb' in her breast for which no words exist but which she demonstrates with an explosion of dashes as she recounts how, some time back, 'Existence — stopped — struck — my ticking through —'. This is thought to have been the transforming experience in three letters of 1858–61, addressed to an unidentified 'Master', which enter into a forbidden love, impossible in this world but directed at the next.

The three letters – drafted, maybe unsent – reveal that she cultivated a desire, if only in fantasy, for a married 'Master'. He is bearded; he has a public face to maintain; and sickness disables him from time to time. Sickness is a bond for Dickinson, many of whose poems in the early 1860s have to do with the unexplained onset of dysfunction.

Both the love drama and the unnamed dysfunction play into a pervasive drama of secrecy. To 'tell' or not to tell: that is Dickinson's repeated question. What she does tell, almost obsessively, is that a secret has shaped her

Existence, an eventful hidden life of 'Fire, and smoke, and gun' at odds with her event-less visible life. It's a secret often on her lips. Now, the poet's lips are sealed; now, they crack open in 'a quiet — Earthquake style —'. If open, the 'lips' are 'buckled' – distorted – by the remade landscape of her inner life. The curiosity of neighbours, the 'praters' and 'babblers', must go unsatisfied. 'Tell the truth but tell it slant' is her way. To 'tell' is a tease, for she's often unintelligible, even if intensely confessional. Her more intimate communication is relayed in riddling, fragmentary terms which call into question our customary stories.

'I am alive I guess', she starts abruptly, lifting her head. 'I felt my life with both my hands . . .'. She leans into the glass to judge her features, releasing the curl of her hair from its tight folds and pushing her cheeks with both hands to smooth away her mother's dimples – gazing into a different face – before the dimples 'twinkled back'.

Confessional gestures in the many poems starting with 'I' or 'My' beckon us towards an unseen life. *He touched me* . . . The intimacy is palpable. *I groped upon his breast* . . . Only, the confession comes missing what a biographer would see as the crucial fact: the identity of 'Master'; or the diagnosis of a 'sickness' that makes the body 'dangle' or drop; or what exactly it was that 'I' *knew* when, after 'dropping down', she 'finished knowing then —'. This tantalising (and characteristic) cutting off of confession with a dash invites us into a situation we have to imagine. Her earthquake style throws up fragments of buried life about, say, 'Wild Nights — Wild Nights!'

> Rowing in Eden —
> Ah — the Sea!
> Might I but moor — tonight —
> In thee!

Does she mean a lover or the divine Guest? The one often means the other. To put such fragments together in order to compose a coherent story about a secret love affair with 'Master' is a dubious exercise. For these fragments are not biographic facts; they are states of being consequent on events closed to us. It's uncomfortable not to know what the poet '<u>knows</u>';

and so uncomfortable to biographers and scholars, who pride themselves on knowing, that successive commentators have contrived to weave a romantic fiction around Charles Wadsworth, the Philadephia minister. Dickinson liked him enough to confide some distress, and he paid her one visit in 1860 (a good while before he moved to California in 1862) and another in 1880, but none of these facts adds up to much. Pasty-faced and beardless, with a beautiful, supportive wife, Wadsworth obliged her with a routine pastoral letter, signing it 'in great haste' – hardly the language of romantic love. He sounds kindly attentive, no more, too busy to share sorrows in the way Dickinson may have hoped. Those who plumped for Wadsworth had to believe in instant love (the poet spent only two weeks in Philadelphia), followed by chaste renunciation. Here, ready to hand, was a story fit for a proper New England spinster.

It's a mistake to read the Master letters literally. The voice is too absurdly abject not to be a performance. It amuses her to prod the power relations between the sexes. Master's skin is so swollen with self-absorption that it must be soothed with the balm of feminine humility and sacrifice, delivered to him in the modest manner of nineteenth-century ladies. Master does not notice that her words are over-the-top, just short of hilarity.

Prior to the first surviving letter to 'Dear Master', thought to be in 1858, the writer has tried to communicate in the language of flowers. If he cannot understand, she blames the flowers for failing to communicate. 'They were disobedient. I gave them messages.'

In the second letter, written early in 1861, the writer names herself 'Daisy', the girl-in-waiting in the fantasy Emily had confided to Sue in their early twenties (three years before she encountered Wadsworth, and six years before she came to know the newspaperman Sam Bowles, another leading candidate for 'Master'). Daisy's freshness, like early-morning dew, will be drained by the rising sun of desire. As she lifts up her petals to the burning ray, her 'dew' gives way to thirst and she yields to 'the man of noon'. That's as far as the fantasy went in 1851. In this second letter, ten years on, 'Master' appears responsible for a 'gash' and drops of blood from Daisy's body. Daisy refrains from explicit blame – though she's on the verge of it – as 'Master' knows, and resents.

'Oh did I offend it – [Did'nt it want me to tell it the truth]'.

Daisy puts on an apologetic act, calculated to placate Master even as she shames him by the overdone abasement he seems to require. Daisy, who once sat on Master's knee, now kneels to him. 'Low at the knee that bore her once . . . Daisy kneels a culprit . . . but punish don't banish her'. A coloratura voice soars to a top note as she asks Master to kill her if he thinks she deserves this.

It's a non-stop act. Daisy is not really cowed. She points to the wound by boasting that, on parting, she contrived to hide it. Daisy 'never flinched'. The noble pathos is operatic; her letter, in effect, an aria. She has at her command an abundance of affecting words, and after she's abased herself for long enough, and told Master that he fills her brown eyes with tears, the moment arrives for a dramatic gesture: she uncovers a weapon.

'I've got a Tomahawk in my side'.

It now comes out that so long as she's been brave enough to conceal the tomahawk, Master has been taking advantage: 'her master stabs her more'. The tomahawk and blood suggest a virgin's defloration. (There is similar violence in Dickinson's botanical dramas: 'My Fuschzia's Coral Seams / Rip . . .', Dickinson observes as she tends her garden, 'My Cactus — splits her Beard / To show her throat —'.) Master's stabs continue though he's aware how small she is. He did see that she 'had no pounds to spare'.

It's by no means certain that this protest comes from the writer herself, even though Emily Dickinson herself was small and thin, weighing about 107 pounds. She is as capable of entering into the elation of 'Wild Nights!' as of lending herself to sexual fear. The Dickinson parents would never have mentioned sex. Her most likely source would have been 'Sister'. When Sue confides to 'Sister' of the thorn in her flesh, it's not the voice of a contented wife.

The scene switches from the tomahawk assault of frontier narrative to *Wuthering Heights* and strains of deathless love. 'Let me in!' pleads Catherine Linton from the other side of death. In Dickinson's second letter, a ghost voice pleads with the wrongly married Master to take her in for ever. Heaven is not for her 'because it's not so dear'. In the background the twenty-third psalm wafts into the airwaves: 'I shall not want'. This love is heaven-sent, the only heaven worth having.

The third letter, supposedly a month or two later, in the summer of 1861, imagines togetherness at night. Instead of the marital 'frost' Master must endure, Daisy would breathe beside him. Her mood is now playful, rather cosy. She would then be nearer than his new coat, but this is 'forbidden me'. If this love is heaven-sent, adultery is not at issue. The true reason it's forbidden she can't say.

'Vesuvius don't talk – Etna – don't – one of them – said a syllable – a thousand years ago, and Pompeii heard it, and hid forever – She could'nt look the world in the face, afterward . . .'.

This voice erupts in a blaze of destructive scenarios, flashing too fast for coherence: a woman in white – a bride it may be – could be shut in a chest; alternatively, there's the dungeon of Chillon, Byron's scene of long-term imprisonment; a 'bullet' hits a Bird; a 'gash' stains Daisy's bosom. Master seems impervious to the damage in his vicinity, so Daisy offers to exhibit a tell-tale drop of blood. To tell or not to tell? Dickinson herself concealed what she called, in confidence to her cousin Loo Norcross, 'that old nail in my breast' (like Susan in her role as the nightingale who sings with a thorn in its breast). What's genuine in the hidden pain of 'bullet', 'nail' or 'tomahawk' should not obscure the bravura of the poet's professionalism: the way these letters draw on a dazzling array of historical and literary models. What appeared to be love letters may in fact be closer to exercises in composition.

Though the Master letters play variations on the romance plot, they also confirm Dickinson's aversion to weddings and marriage. 'Master' is neither tender nor considerate. Nor can he hear what his correspondent is saying.

All the same, there was huge benefit from 'Master': what Dickinson gained was fuel for a new phase of her oeuvre. As Yeats would say of his unrequited love for Maud Gonne, there was an advantage to so much effort to verbalise his feelings: 'I have come into my strength, / And words obey my call.' Since, in this sense, the poet's life is there, what links may be found between the facts of Dickinson's life and her leap between setting up her private poetry base in 1858 and the poetic immortality she knew she had achieved by the end of 1863?

The starting point must be the fact that Emily Dickinson wasn't required to earn her living in the drudging ways then open to women; she was also relieved of the pressure to marry. In her domestic seclusion, white dress, and Daisy manner, hers seems a womanish life, but it hides another, as proved by the lifetime's work discovered after her death. 'I cannot dance upon my toes', she writes in 1861, 'No man instructed me', and then continues with a long list of all the things she can't do. Untaught by men, she can perform none of the acts of female contortion: no platform for her; no applause. Not for her the 'claw upon the air', the wilted arabesques of the ghosts in the white act of *Giselle*, who have lost their lives to lovers' betrayals. They glide across the stage like snow on wheels, automatons with frozen hearts. Dickinson will not line up as one of them. Yet though no one knows her 'art', it's 'full as Opera —'. Affirmation comes from herself alone, shooting down negations from the public arena. Her complete works – not a mere opus, but 'Opera' in the plural – are filling an inward space, stretching to the full, in the pregnant silence of the final dash.

I think she spoke the truth when she said 'no man'. For a long time biographers and critics empowered a 'Master' with responsibility for her output. They speculated about his identity, choosing one or other from seven candidates, none of whom seems right. My sense is that Master was largely, though not completely, a stirring fantasy, all the more intriguing for what it reveals about a passionate woman who played games of femininity but kept herself free from sexual artifice. I don't think any existing man in her circle of recognisable husbands – a kindly minister and three literary authorities hooked on trite rhymes – could have lent himself to the royal extravagance of her desire.

This does not necessarily mean that Emily Dickinson did not see potentialities in a man (or men) she knew. It is clear from her draft letters to 'Master' that she had a real man in mind, and the critic Judith Farr has made a convincing case for newspaperman Sam Bowles. If we put the Master letters side by side with the twenty-five letters, many with poems, sent to Sam Bowles between 1858 and 1864, it's plain that Bowles provided a model for at least some aspects of 'Master'. Bearded, opinionated, with a close stare, he looked the part ('You have the most triumphant Face out of Paradise,' Dickinson told him), and he had a way with intelligent women, drawing them out, rereading *Shirley* and backing women's rights.

In the summer of 1858, Austin and Sue welcomed him to The Evergreens as a friend of Austin's father, an habitué of Washington and the political world beyond the confines of Amherst, informed on state secrets and in touch with other editors, college presidents and notable writers such as Bret Harte. Sue was stimulated by Bowles's 'free and shaggy manner', iconoclastic, robust, struggling. His talk excited Austin to combats lasting long after midnight.

It's likely to have been Sue who sent Bowles one of Sister's poems, 'Nobody knows this little rose', without divulging her name, and he printed it in the *Springfield Daily Republican* in August 1858. The explanatory heading plays up the intrigue: 'To Mrs.– , with a Rose [Surreptitiously communicated to The Republican.]'

'Has girl read Republican' – Sue, triumphant, sent a note to Emily across the grass, settling an appointment to meet next day. They had to talk 'without witnesses'.

Though Sue was party to Sister's greater poems, she had wisely chosen a modest verse. Bowles also published Emily Dickinson's earliest surviving poem, a humorous valentine of 1852. These came closest to the anodyne verse Bowles put out for mass consumption, while nourishing himself on lasting words. Sue introduced him to the Brownings, while he read aloud his favourite passage from *The Mill on the Floss*: 'The great problem of the shifting relation between passion and duty is clear to no man who is capable of apprehending it . . .'.

His first duty was to his wife. In 1850 he had married Mary Schermerhorn, whose family had a home in Geneva, the town where Sue and her sisters grew up. There's no sign that their paths had crossed, and Sue would hardly have found it appealing to read of Mary's most recent childbirth in one of Bowles's earliest letters. It had come on 15 May 1859 after a ghastly day ending in the delivery of a dead boy (Mrs Bowles's sixth birth and third stillbirth in the nine years since her marriage). What's odd about this letter is that instead of comforting his wife with every bit of love he can offer, Bowles is tucked away in his study asking pity from the Dickinsons with whom he and his wife are not yet on first-name terms. All his letters to the Dickinsons lean to confession.

No letters to Emily have survived. Those to The Evergreens are scrawled fast, almost illegibly, in a large, cramped hand, as though he were coiled in upon himself as he raced in his many directions. Why so forthcoming a man should have picked an unforthcoming wife like Mary is hard to understand. Bowles was unusually adept at drawing women out. Mary may have presented the hardest challenge and he may have been won by his own success with unpromising material. Sadly for Mary, such efforts did not survive marriage. She became a poor creature, asthmatic and so constantly giving birth that she took to the role of chronic invalid, vying with her husband for attention.

Mary Bowles had a washed-out face and a thin plait tightly coiled, like a platter glued to the back of her head. The side hair was flattened to her forehead like colourless drapes. A photograph exudes unhappiness, not a passing mood but a gutted self. Because she felt unloved and therefore unlovable, Mrs Bowles was prickly in company. Late in 1858, Emily had been at the gate to greet her when Bowles had brought his pregnant wife to visit Sue and Austin. It had been meant to cheer her. It hadn't. Bowles's correspondence with The Evergreens reveals the surge of emotional excitement he exercised in contact with others, and the trouble this caused in his marriage. Mrs Bowles was forced to hear Sue's answering claims for 'the higher life of humanity', as befitted an admirer of Maggie Tulliver.

'I cherish you for keeping up my faith and hope in the higher, future woman!' That's the encouraging way Bowles spoke in letters to Sue Dickinson.

Mrs Bowles felt her deficiency. With an animated woman her husband would be all attention, resting his head on one hand and stretching out the other to touch hers. His wife's misery left him a little guilty from time to time, but not so guilty as to change his ways.

'I have made [women] shed many tears,' he owned, 'hated myself for it, – and that was not the least of the wrong they did me. A man does not enjoy hating himself.'

Mary Bowles was conspicuously ungrateful towards her pale cousin, Miss Whitney, who came to nurse her for long stretches. Maria Whitney was the same age as Emily Dickinson, born in November 1830, the daughter of a Northampton banker, Josiah Dwight Whitney, and related to Mrs Bowles through the Dwights. She had the intelligent eyes of a reader, large, grey eyes with a steady, rather sombre expression and level brows. Her hair was drawn back over the tips of her ears in a clean line, setting off a decided chin above a narrow, round collar. Sam Bowles rewarded Miss Whitney with his usual attentions, and it was whispered that she was in love with him. Mrs Bowles had reason to be jealous, for her cousin carried herself with sophisticated elegance. She was Europeanised in a serious way, having made a study of Old High German and steeped her mind in the German higher criticism of the scriptures. Her two bachelor brothers were professors at Harvard and Yale, and eventually, when Smith College was founded, she became its first teacher of French and German in the spring semester of 1876. Soon after, she and Emily Dickinson would begin to exchange heartfelt memories of Bowles.

Maria Whitney was attached to the house she shared with her brothers, adjoining the old house of Jonathan Edwards in Northampton. But duty compelled her, as a single woman, to be on call whenever married people had need of help. When she left Mrs Bowles to nurse another needy member of her family, Sam Bowles said: 'Her going has been a trial to me.' She had left him bereft, he complained to the Dickinsons, 'a day of torture and blueness'.

At The Evergreens his gaze had followed Sue's schoolfriend Kate Scott Turner ('the late flirtatious widow') who came on another visit. He hoped to meet her again and, to Austin, mulled over the moral question of pursuit.

'Mrs Bowles is very liberal at her government. Would it be fair to take advantage of it to go forty miles to see beauty & grace . . . in that most enticing of mortal packages, which the elder Weller has so immortally warned all susceptible Samuels against?* I put it to you, as a loyal husband – would it do?'

---

* He alludes to Sam Weller in *The Pickwick Papers*.

While Kate took no notice of his signals, the Dickinsons urged Bowles to forget her.

'I would not, if I could, – & could not if I would,' was his quick comeback.

Later, when his life seemed to limp along, he asked wistfully to be commended to 'the two Utica schoolgirls' (Kate and Sue). His were emotional infidelities, arguably as bad if not worse than physical adultery. As his flirtations stacked up, he began to fear the Dickinsons might come to think him 'wanton & fickle'.

The Dickinson sisters he referred to collectively as 'the girls from the paternal mansion' or simply 'the girls'. The few times he singled out Emily, his messages were distanced, rather jocular, as though wary. It's the tone of a man who wants to signal appreciation – or more – yet does not want to be drawn too far into the dramas her poems devised. She was sending him many of her poems at this time.

He teased her in lieu of encouragement: 'to the Queen Recluse my especial sympathy – that she has "overcome the world." – Is it really true that they sing "Old Hundred" & "Aleluia" perpetually, in heaven . . . and are dandelions, asphodels, & maiden's [vows] the standard flowers of the ethereal?'

A printing office allowed little opportunity for the 'spiritual manifestations' the Dickinsons discussed. Bowles wanted them to know these did 'live ever & for an age in me'. He must have made this known also to Emily, for he sent remembrances (via Austin) 'for the sister of the other house who never forgets my spiritual longings'. He was not without an affinity for her, as he once confessed to Austin: 'I have been in a savage, turbulent state for some time – indulging in a sort of divine disgust at everything & everybody – I guess a good deal as Emily feels.'

At the time she drafted the second Master letter, in the spring of 1861, her poems began to heighten the romantic stakes. Once, when Bowles was next door, she assumed her Daisy character in a poem dispatched along the path between the houses. 'If it [you] had no pencil', came wrapped around the stub of a pencil, inviting Bowles to try hers, worn out though it was with 'Writing much to thee'. Daisy's voice is as arch as in the Master letters, and plays the same Little Me role.

If he can return no word, she asks, would he draw her a daisy as diminutive as she'd been when he'd 'plucked' her?

Her ways of reaching out for dramatic material, though more secluded and intense, are essentially no different from the habits of any number of writers who work up the dramas in their lives. As Henry James said, 'art makes life'. We have no way of knowing what, if anything, lay behind a poem about a fight to the death, apart from the curious fact that Dickinson gave the poem to one person only, saying, 'I cant explain it, Mr Bowles —'.

> Two swimmers wrestled on the spar
> Until the morning sun —
> When One turned, smiling, to the land —
> Oh God! the other One!
> The stray ships — passing, spied a face
> Opon the waters borne,
> With eyes, in death, still begging — raised,
> And hands — beseeching — thrown!

Part of a poem's meaning lies with its recipient, in this instance Bowles, yet to pursue biography is not what this poem asks us to do. The conflict is perfectly distilled from the context of its composition and designed to terminate in us, her readers, dredging up our own, sometimes silenced confrontations – anything we might have experienced of damage and abandonment.

Dickinson's counter-drama against abandonment is a series of poems where 'I' is knit to a Master figure. It's an imaginary drama about an intruder on a marriage, told from the intruder's point of view. 'I'm "wife" . . . I'm Czar — I'm "Woman" now —'. She posits an alternative marriage as a permanent translation from earth to heaven. While Dickinson draws on a long poetic convention in which human and divine love explain each other, the voice is cool. She exults to be rid of girlhood with its attendant pain. Now and for ever, she has her 'comfort': 'I'm Wife! Stop there!'

The wedding night of this alternative bridal is rehearsed in a 'Master'

poem of 1861, 'A wife — at Daybreak I shall be—', which Dickinson recopied with variations in 1862 and 1863. Midnight's transforming hour is at
hand with Master mounting the stair to where his destined mate awaits
him in her room. This is the last moment she's still a child; the next, she
will be transformed for ever: 'How short it takes to make it Bride!' Is he a
human bridegroom who's approaching, or is it a ghost of a love that might
have been, or is this a visionary encounter? The bride looks to her 'Victory'
at sunrise, an elevating turn to the east. Here (in first draft) is what she's
thinking as the footsteps approach:

> The Vision flutters in the door —
> Master — I've seen the face before —

In the end this is not about a wedding night. It's not about the love of
man and woman. Dickinson was inspired by some more general conception where 'I', as a mortal being, meets an eternal force: in later drafts
'Master' is interchangeable with 'Saviour'. Yet, as the dashes suggest, any
sentence on this subject must remain unfinished. Her model could be
Emily Brontë, who was not writing about ordinary human love when
Catherine dies and her servant feels 'an assurance of the endless . . . hereafter – the Eternity they [the dead] have entered – where life is boundless
in its duration, and love in its sympathy . . .'. Dickinson too yearned for
infinities and dreamt up a Master to yearn with her.

The real biographical question is not the identity of 'Master', who van-
ishes into an array of dramas, particularly as bridegroom of the spirit (a
drama utterly beyond Bowles or any other of the candidates). No, what
matters is when something happens that should *not* have happened, and
that is when the control Emily Dickinson exercised over every detail of her
life slipped. This was rare, but did happen. It happened when the imaginative life of poetry, feeding to some extent off ordinary life, spilt into an
actual relationship on the ground. She was more scrupulous than other
poets – Shelley and Byron, say, wreaking havoc around them – in holding
herself apart from what we'd ordinarily call life. But now and then imagination crossed the boundary, as in her 'gun' letter to what must have been

a bewildered Norcross uncle – a threat that belongs in our lawless fantasy life and nowhere else. Dickinson's 'wife' poems celebrate an emotional bond that transcends social and legal ties. The bond prompts a breakthrough of the speaker's buried fire, her private character as 'Vesuvius at Home'. Fuelling the poetic eruptions from well below the surface there's an adulterous fantasy, dangerous if let loose in real life, as it proved when Emily intruded on Mrs Bowles.

At the height of Dickinson's 'wife' drama, between the second and third Master letters, Bowles again brought his wife to visit the Dickinsons. This, in early May 1861, turned out as much a disaster as her first visit in 1858.

'You must make some allowances for her peculiarities,' Bowles defended his wife to Austin. 'Her very timidity & want of self-reliance gives her a sharper utterance. The porcupine I take it is really a very weak & . . . distrustful animal, & so puts out his fretful quills to hide his soft heart. – I think she was somewhat disappointed in her Amherst visit – it did not turn out so pleasantly, as she meant to have it.'

He did accept some of the blame: his wife, he owned, wished him to 'manage' her 'as she wanted to be managed', but this concession, coated in the mild language of the pleasant, leaves out the torment he inflicted on a wife whose face was drear, as though drained of life.

In the autumn of 1861, when Bowles was out of reach in a Northampton sanatorium, Emily turned her attention to his again pregnant wife, who found her 'alarming'. Emily, amused, played up to Mrs Bowles's alarm. She pretends to be advancing on this wife, alone and unprotected at home; scary Emily is on the road; she's at the gate; she has her hand on the door.

Early in March 1862, when Sam Bowles once more went away, to Washington, a little earlier than expected, Emily wrote another strange letter to Mrs Bowles. It was an excuse for having sent 'a little note' to Mrs Bowles's husband, which the wife would have intercepted. Her husband – Emily was now aware – would have left before the note in question arrived. It was his habit to keep Emily's notes and letters, but this one has disappeared. Presumably Mrs Bowles did not see fit to pass it on when her husband returned.

The purpose of the note, Emily attempts to explain, had been merely to ask a favour. What she wants from Mr Bowles's wife is reassurance that she has not been troubled. It's the poet's attempt to cover up her intrusion into Mrs Bowles's legitimate space. To glance at another of Emily's notes to Bowles at this time (many of them including poems or slipping into poetry) is to see why Emily felt uneasy. It's filled with emotion, tensely intimate underlinings about the limitations of words, for the deepest feelings don't 'move' into overt expression:

Dear Mr Bowles.

I cant thank you any more – You are thoughtful so many times, you grieve me <u>always – now.</u> The old words are <u>numb</u> – and there <u>a'nt</u> any <u>new</u> ones . . .

When you come to Amherst, please God it were <u>Today</u> – I will tell you . . . – if I <u>can,</u> I will –

'<u>Speech</u>' — is a prank of <u>Parliament</u> —

'<u>Tears</u>' — a trick of the <u>nerve</u> —

But the Heart with the heaviest freight on —

Doesn't — <u>always</u> — move —

   Emily.

Her manner to Mrs Bowles, by contrast, is commanding and at no loss for words. The poet does not wish this wife to have cause for complaint, so insists that Mary Bowles favour her with an exculpatory statement, a token of cordiality, which, she knows, Mrs Bowles won't want to write. The tone then changes from insistence to menace as she reminds this wife, grieved by stillbirths, how vulnerable her new baby could be. Playfully, the poet moves into fairy-tale mode, sending a rose for the baby boy's hand. His mother is to place it there when little Charlie goes to sleep, 'and then he will dream of Emily – and . . . we shall be "old friends"'. She's aware that Mrs Bowles might not wish her to take over Charlie's mind, any more than she can bear Emily's bombardment of her husband with letters and poems. Emily makes it clear to Mary Bowles that these aren't about to stop.

Dear Mary –

Could you leave 'Charlie' – long enough? Have you time for
me? . . . Don't love [Charlie] so well – you know – as to forget us
[Dickinsons] – We shall wish he was'nt <u>there</u> – if you do – I'm
afraid – <u>shant</u> we?

I'll remember you – if you like me to – while Mr. Bowles is
gone – and that will stop the lonely – <u>some</u> – but I cannot agree to
<u>stop</u> – when he gets home from Washington.

Goodnight – Mary –

You wont forget my little note – <u>tomorrow</u> – in the mail – It
will be the <u>first one</u> – you ever wrote me in your life – and yet –
was I the little friend – a <u>long time</u>? <u>Was</u> I – Mary?

Emily.

Her punctuation should never be underestimated. The inverted
commas around 'Charlie' were a reminder to the baby's mother that Emily
wished the little boy to have a different name. Emily's choice was Robert,
after Browning, the rescuer of the poet Elizabeth Barrett from her invalid
seclusion in her father's house. Emily was reminded of this drama at just
this time when Elizabeth Barrett Browning died in Florence, leaving
behind a little boy, the son of the two poets, whose name was Robert.
Emily's insistence on her right to name the Bowleses' child is further evidence of a poet's fancy intruding on poor Mrs Bowles, alone and
unprotected from this onslaught of words. In this period Dickinson sent
Bowles 'Title divine is mine! / The Wife — without the Sign!'

'Here's what I had to "tell you"—,' she added beneath her transcript.
'You will tell no other?'

It's one answer to Master's complaint, 'You do not tell me all.' Since 'all'
was a tall order for a 'reticent volcano', telling remains a tease. She would
always hold a deeper secret in reserve.

Bowles told Austin he must withdraw from the Dickinsons. His health,
he said, required him to abstain. 'You ought to know without my explain-
ing,' he added, unwilling to specify his reasons. 'You are certainly not
ignorant of them. I must respect them; so must you.' He was probably

recalling a confidential outburst to Austin, when they had been riding on their own on the outskirts of Amherst.

'My nature revolts at a divided, contradictory loyalty,' he had said. 'But my life, to be happy & harmonious at home, must have friends abroad, – & yet it must be happy at home.'

The future of the tie, as Bowles spelt it out, is similar to Emily Dickinson's prospect in her Master poems: to see a special person less and yet to 'have as much as ever, or rather more, in eternity'.

Many of her letters to Bowles contained poems pertinent to what she had to 'tell' – not just anyone, but what she had to tell this heartfelt man, this susceptible husband, this editor with a national reach. During these brilliant years she composed poems with an eye to him: the exultation of the 'Wife without the Sign'; the divine furore of the 'soul's superior instants'; the sickness, collapse and longing. Message after poetic message had flown his way. Could he understand her? Could he – while continuing to publish verse with a sugar-coating of sentiment – wake up to these blasts of candour?

One poem she sent him appears to be resigned to her failure to quicken his interest: 'I've nothing Else, to bring, you know — / So I keep bringing these — / Just as Night keeps fetching <u>stars</u> — / To our <u>familiar</u> eyes.' Was she too familiar for him to see the star quality? Perhaps Bowles would only <u>mind</u> [notice] these poems if they didn't *come*.

Privately, Bowles disliked 'Lady-writers' and counted himself lucky they wrote at home and out of sight: 'it is treading upon eggs all the time to deal with them,' he grumbled, 'they receive the unvarnished truth as if it were a red-hot bullet'. Could this be the sort of bullet that hit the Bird in a Master letter?

Dickinson went on trying for quite some time because Sam Bowles exuded promise, attracted as he was to intelligence in women. In conversation, in person, his attentiveness, his 'Arabian' looks and a feminine quality appealing in a man who is unafraid of it, made Bowles unlike the local pedants, whom she called 'manikins'. A welcome gesture from Bowles was a message to the poet to send him one of her 'little gems'. If he did pause to read, truly read, the poems Dickinson sent, she thought he'd be as 'puzzled' as she – wouldn't he just – to find their stars pointing 'Our way Home!' Home to her? Or to an eternal home? Home is one of her words that carry a residue of private connotation.

She sent some of her wildest poems to Bowles at this time and he published five, including the emotional intoxication of her 'little tippler / Leaning against the — Sun' (4 May 1861) and her mockery of a deadly heaven in 'Safe in their alabaster chambers' (1 March 1862). The newspaper preserved the poet's anonymity, but imposed banal or misleading titles like 'The May Wine', as well as chiming rhymes. Editorial fiddling 'robbed' her, she said, of her Snake sliding across his boggy acre. Her indignation is legendary.

One problem with Bowles is that he employed a literary editor called Fidelia Cooke, who was clueless about poetry. It was typical of Bowles's public support for women that he appointed a woman (the second ever, after the Boston writer on women's rights, Margaret Fuller) to be on the staff of an influential daily newspaper; unfortunately, Cooke published the kind of sentimental tosh that far from advancing women's intelligence kept it and readers in their place. It could be that Bowles, impressed with public excitement over Elizabeth Barrett Browning and Charlotte Brontë, was lending himself to a new fashion for women's writing, albeit without much discernment. Bowles himself was content with 'tit-bits' of poetry, the staple of *The Household Book of Poetry*, his gift to Sue and Austin. He thought every household should have such a collection of tit-bits. Then, too, Bowles exercised his empathy with a number of women besides Emily: Susan Dickinson and Maria Whitney were his favourites. He really had too many soulmates to qualify for the kind of commitment the poet had in mind.

There is yet another fact which rules out Bowles as the sole source for Dickinson's 'Master': his home in Springfield, Massachusetts. 'Master' lives at a greater distance, for Daisy suggests he come 'to New England' to see her.

Dickinson's poems, like Shakespeare's sonnets, occupy a mid-space between experience and imagination. The same with Shelley who, as Ann Wroe has shown, fills his poems with scenes and figures that 'begged to be decoded', but which are likelier to be figments or symbols 'than actual fragments of his past'. In Dickinson's letters to 'Master', the emotional force of 'I' seems to authenticate her confessions, but though, as readers, we lend ourselves to the intimacy of this voice, we can't forget that Dickinson's letters are as close as letters come to the inventiveness of the poems that are her 'letter to the World'. An erupting voice burns away the life/art distinction. The fact that Dickinson placed the Master letters with her poetry rather than with her correspondence suggests he was largely invention.

Instead of plumping for an actual Master, we might feel our way into a woman's desire for character. The poet is enlivened by the imagined harshness of Master's character in a way that stimulates fertile imaginings of a potential situation that might have grown out of an initial situation we aren't meant to recover. Biography is not exactly irrelevant, but bound to be misleading with poems that throw the onus of introspection back into the lap of the reader: they compel us to recognise how our cherished emotion of love – even (or especially) deathless love – is largely imagined, a fictitious vessel for our tastes and dreams. If this is so, then friendship, and the kind of love that grows through friendship, are bound to prevail over a master-love in a woman's daily heartland. That back-door track between Emily and Susan, the path worn, step after step, day after day, by the poet's feet, could have been in reality more compelling than the perhaps tenuous contact behind her Master letters.

In the third Master letter she imagines herself as queen, sleeping beside 'Plantagenet', their bodies breathing together. Why Plantagenet, rather than another royal name? A Plantagenet is a member of a royal line opposed to the line of Lancaster in the civil wars of fifteenth-century England. The name implies strife ahead, the Wars of the Roses. Dickinson was enthralled with Shakespeare's *Henry VI*, which re-creates these wars. Crookbacked but active and pitiless in *Henry VI* is the future Richard III who murders his kin, other Plantagenets who stand between him and the crown. He will fight to the death, the last of an embattled line of killers and victims.

Daisy, meanwhile, is enthroned on Master's knee. There are no scruples about his legitimate wife and no inhibitions. All the same, she continues to conceal something she cannot communicate to Master. Her secret outlasts the Master letters.

Vinnie said, 'Emily never had any love disaster.' So long as the lovelorn image holds sway, Vinnie's statement sounds like a cover-up, but could she be right? With strong-willed imaginations it's vital to stress the gains that accompany the pains of denial and longing. During these extraordinary years the poet is distilling theorems of experience from her life: desire, parting, death-in-life, spiritual quickening, the creative charge and creative detachment just short of freezing. I want to propose that her poems work when a theorem is applied to a *reader's* life. It's a mistake to spot Dickinson in all her poems; the real challenge is to find our selves. She demands a reciprocal response, a complementary act of introspection. For the poem to work fully we have to complete it with our own thoughts and feelings. Her dash is not casual; it's a prompt, bringing the reader to the brink of words; there is the need to speak, if only to ourselves. This can be especially effective when we are in touch with feelings as intense as the poet's own: it might be abandonment or grief or fear of losing control. A Dickinson poem can open out into any number of dramas to fill its compelling spaces. As a woman unmodified by mating, a stranger to her time, speaking for those who are not members of the dominant group, Dickinson's dashes push the language apart to open up the space where we live without language.

This act of daring takes off from a logical argument along the tightrope of the quatrain. She flaunts her footsteps. Her poetic line is a high-wire act: a walker pretends to hesitate, stop, and sway; then, fleet of foot, skips to the end.

In April 1862 she claimed that her poetry had been impelled by 'a terror – since September – I could tell to none'. She sings, she said, because 'I am afraid'. The date is specific: September 1861. What happened to leave her with a sense of deadness – 'palsy', she called it?

It may or may not be relevant that in September 1861 Bowles found himself 'a wreck'. It was the result of stress affecting his heart, as well as sciatica. A temporary measure was to retreat to Dr Denniston's sanatorium in Northampton; a longer-term plan was for Bowles to visit Europe the following spring. The poet may have felt abandoned. If so, it was a repeat of her sense of abandonment by friends whom she'd bound to her with maximum intensity: when Jane Humphrey had left for Ohio and Susan had gone off to Michigan, their letters had stopped; distance had dissolved ties vital to her Existence; immured as she was at home, it seemed to her a kind of death. Now Bowles, on the receiving end of insistent dramas and unable to cope with the attachments he'd roused, was to go. Her 'palsy' does follow the final Master letter, undated but thought to have been written in the summer of 1861. What brought the series of Master letters to an end? Did long-suffering Mrs Bowles nerve herself to make a stand? Mary Bowles kept that wicked-witch letter and could have used it as a weapon against a rival 'Wife'. Her husband came to see Emily as 'half angel, half demon'.

Awaiting his farewell call before Bowles sailed, Emily, Vinnie and Sue sat together downstairs at the Homestead, listening for his knock. When a knock came Vinnie tipped Pussy off her lap in her haste to open the door, while Emily held tight to her chair, putting out a petal (in her Daisy character). Alas, the knock turned out to be a delivery. Bowles failed to come and Emily let him know that 'Hearts in Amherst — ache . . . If we could only care — the less — it would be so much easier'. Tears, she said, were still dropping from black, blue and her own brown eyes.

Yet no sooner did Bowles sail, on 9 April 1862, than she found a new correspondent in a Boston man of letters, Thomas Wentworth Higginson. He was to be her lifeline to the publishing world Bowles had formerly represented. Her need — to her a matter of life or death — was the stimulant of sustained private contact with that public space. It was to this stranger, Higginson, that she blurted out the 'terror' since September that had nearly finished her. The date of this her first letter to him, 15 April 1862, is commonly explained as a response to Higginson's tips for young writers in a recent issue of the *Atlantic*. True enough, but Bowles's departure six days earlier could have been a keener incentive. Exit one leader of opinion. Enter another.

After seven months Bowles returned. On 17 November he came to the Homestead, expecting the heartfelt reception he had missed.

'I cannot see you', was the message Emily sent downstairs, though tuned to his voice below. But why, when one of her letters had cried out to him to return at once? Such agitated feeling could have led her protective father to ban further contact. She did not see Bowles face to face for the next twelve years – so long as her father lived. It was part of her image to be an obedient daughter, but she exercised her own control. For the best part of a year Bowles had put himself beyond her reach. We can picture the fade-out of the attention her writing deserved and had to have. Here lies the real disappointment: not love, not visits. What she craved were letters in answer to hers, above all an editor's signal of faith in her powers as a poet.

Once she'd sent Bowles a rare first edition of the Brontë sisters' *Poems*, their first book, self-published in 1846, which sold only two copies. 'Keep the Yorkshire Girls, if you please, with the faith of their friend and yours.' The message is plain: as a friend to the Brontës, he should take note of a parallel situation, the unrecognised poet who was at this moment writing to him.

Bowles missed the point when he returned the volume.

'Please to need me . . . you denied my Bronte', she'd reproached him. 'Teach us to miss you <u>less</u>.'

Her letters to eminent men auditioned them for roles as master and mentor to the future star of the 'Opera', and further, these letters devised the blueprint for her legend. In the early 1860s people began to notice her shut door. The burning life of the 'Ethiop within' was belied by the façade of the woman in white: 'Ourself behind ourself, concealed—'.

What does she conceal, and so fixedly that her lips are 'soldered'? Intimate as she is with 'Master' (at least in fantasy), he does reproach her for holding back something she will not 'tell'. Nor would she tell Sam Bowles why she would not see him on his return. What word cannot pass her lips or shape itself on paper, even in drafts for her eyes alone? If 'Master' was largely fantasy, what was it that 'struck' her ticking 'through'? Legend had it that Dickinson closed off from life to languish over disappointed love. But there was a simpler reason for seclusion.

5

'SNARL IN THE BRAIN'

The ticking of the hours as she folds her shawl about her shoulders and tends her flowers, at thirty, thirty-one, thirty-two, has little to do with 'the bolt' of her 'Existence', to be found in the hinterland of the past or in what we might today call the DNA of the Dickinson family. Dickinson myth posits a wraith who is singular, but what if we tracked 'the bolt' into the plurality of family: the inescapable network of inheritance, the time-bomb of innate traits? DNA can be a form of tragedy. Yet during these blazing years of the early 1860s, Emily Dickinson transformed sickness into a story of promise:

> My loss, by sickness — Was it Loss?
> Or that Etherial Gain —
> One earns by measuring the Grave —
> Then — measuring the Sun —

Convalescing after another bout of sickness early in 1865, she mulls it over ('As One does Sickness over'), still open to Gain: the 'Chances' of an emergent 'Identity' (as poet and visionary) which health ('blessed health') would have obscured.

Sickness is always there, unnamed, shielded by cover stories. In youth, a cough is mentioned; in her mid-thirties, trouble with eyes. Neither came to much. A love drama seems to explain her poems of collapse, but what if these dramas change places? What if the poems of collapse were the primary drama – what if sickness *is* the story? If so, her life shifts. A different reason for seclusion stares us in the face.

Collectively, in her poems, there's a history of a mechanism breaking down, a body dropping, in one of her clock poems, when the ticking stops. It 'will not stir for Doctors'. In 'A Clock stopped' it's a clock with miniature figures who appear on the hour. The figures dangle, hunched in pain, like puppets bowing. Not the clock on the mantel, Dickinson says, pressing her point: it's the body that seizes up.

'Agony' is her truth in a poem about telling the truth: 'Men do not sham Convulsion, / Nor simulate, a Throe —'. Could her volcanoes and earthquakes, the unexploded Bomb in her Bosom and her life as Loaded Gun, repeat this truth? The capitals, like the distinctive nature of her 'Existence', are deliberate: 'Convulsion', she says, 'Throe'. 'Transport' is taught 'by throe'. Even without her explicitness we hear the jolting rhythms of poems with protracted breaths between spasms of words. Their spacing is unprecedented as a verbal performance. To the poet's professional contemporaries, the performance was bizarre. 'Spasmodic', was the verdict of the Boston critic, Higginson, on the first batch of poems she sent to him, 'uncontrolled'. These are the words she shoots back in her deadpan reply on 7 June 1862:

> 'You think my gait "spasmodic" – I am in danger – Sir – You
> think me "uncontrolled" – I have no Tribunal.'

When biographer Mark Bostridge identified Florence Nightingale's chronic illness, he warns that 'posthumous diagnoses are rarely successful in establishing with any degree of certainty the nature of an illness experienced by a person long dead'. The same caution is necessary in naming 'sickness' in Dickinson's letters and poems. What she calls 'Dying! Dying in the night!' invites a diagnosis, yet in this case there is also 'Gain'. In the gifted, long-term illness, and the apartness it brings, is subversive, and as such transforming. It turns the sufferer into a solitary forerunner of 'some strange Race'. To faint, she says, is to look deep into the darkness where things shape themselves. A jolt projects her from an abyss into an uncharted region of the mind, a purified alertness.

If the twenty-first century is to explore unknown pathways of the brain, Dickinson's poetry is replete with information about dysfunction and recovery. Here is what she has to tell: 'I felt a Funeral, in my Brain'. A plank in reason broke, she says, and 'I dropped down, and down —'. She feels a 'Cleaving' in her brain, as though the lid of the brain gets 'off my head' and can't re-attach. Logic and its sequential language are disrupted.

> I felt a Cleaving in my Mind —
> As if my Brain had split —
> I tried to match it — Seam by Seam —
> But could not make them fit —
>
> The thought behind, I strove to join
> Unto the thought before —
> But Sequence ravelled out of Sound —
> Like Balls — opon a Floor —

One poem records what seems like a Throe: its slow but relentless onset, its drumming in the head, its deceptive pause before, again, a full-on bolt 'scalps' its victim. It's not the victim's fault, another poem argues; it's Nature who imposes the blight on the young: 'Nature — sometimes sears a Sapling — / Sometimes — scalps a Tree —'. There's talk of constant 'Dread'. She must control the Bomb in her body, as well as hide it: 'to simulate is stinging work'.

Allowing for the poet's resolve to 'tell it slant', through metaphor, are we not looking at epilepsy? The word, from the Greek, means seizure, and the onset, which the poems describe, is what doctors call the aura. Dickinson's word is a 'Presentiment': a Shadow indicates 'that Suns go down —':

> . . . The notice to the startled Grass
> That Darkness — is about to pass —

In Greek, aura means 'breeze'. In Dickinson this intensifies, as 'Winds take Forests in their Paws —'. A 'Thunderbolt' blacks out consciousness ('The Universe — is still —'), and then an 'electric gale' wafts the body beyond 'its dull — control'.

If this, at least in part, is what was secret, the conditions of Dickinson's life make sense: sickness is a more sensible reason for seclusion than disappointed love. A seizure can happen with little warning: about a minute. Too short a time to take cover. This is why those who keep the condition secret would fear to go out, even to join callers in the parlour. During the annual summer Commencement, when Mr Dickinson, as College Treasurer, entertained visitors at home, Emily would emerge, walk swiftly through the crowd and disappear. What seemed eccentric was simply dread. Marriage for epileptics was discouraged and some American states prohibited it by law.* She saw herself 'by birth a Bachelor'.

In its full-blown form, known as *grand mal*, a slight swerve in a pathway of the brain prompts a seizure. As Dickinson puts it, 'The Brain within its Groove / Runs evenly', but then a 'Splinter swerve' makes it hard to put the current back. Such force has this altered current, it would be easier, she thinks, to divert the course of a flood, when 'Floods have slit the Hills / And scooped a Turnpike for Themselves'.

As the Throe comes on, consciousness is not wholly extinguished. The speaker in these poems is alive to 'Murder by degrees', like a mouse in the teeth of a cat who will tease it before she 'mashes it to death'. Part of this torture is the space for breath to 'straighten' and the brain to 'bubble Cool' before the kill re-starts. In another poem it's as though the body is a house haunted by an 'Assassin' of the Brain, who prowls its corridors until the tormented Body 'borrows a Revolver' and prepares for a secret shoot-out behind a bolted door.

In the poems that recount the various stages of 'Dying in the night', the horror lies in the onset and aftermath. The Throe itself is brief – 'The

---

* A leading London authority, Edward Sieveking, stated the reasons in *On Epilepsy* (1858): the excitement of the 'marital act' might cause fits in those susceptible. Marriage was discouraged also for the sake of the partner and potential offspring.

Maddest — quickest — by —', and in its course the body sheds the flesh and becomes an immortal soul. A sign of divine favour, she would not wish to exchange this for what we call normality.

Afterwards, the brain sinks into a 'Fog'. A dimness envelopes consciousness, she says, as mists obliterate a crag. In this state, the soul seems to abandon the body to a death-in-life she calls 'Languor' or 'the Hour of Lead'. Languor and visions, Throe and art co-exist in ways understanding of the brain can't, as yet, follow.

The Boston doctor and poet Oliver Wendell Holmes said in 1891: 'If I wished to show a student the difficulties of getting at truth from medical experience, I would give him the history of epilepsy to read.' The ancients called it 'the sacred disease' because of the visions, and the artist Raphael depicts the proximity of sick and sacred, the association of extreme otherness, in *The Transfiguration* (1517): a boy with a swivelling eye undergoes a seizure while Jesus, in radiant light, hovers on high.

The oldest recorded idea (on a Babylonian tablet in *c.* 650 BC) is 'possession' – a demon to be driven out, indicated by an eye moving to the left and the jerking of the body. Hippocrates (*c.* 460–370 BC) resisted the supernatural when he deduced a physiological basis in the brain. In *Julius Caesar* it's called 'the falling sickness', as Dickinson, a constant reader of Shakespeare, would have known:

CASCA: He fell down in the market-place, and foam'd at the mouth, and was speechless.

BRUTUS: 'Tis very like, he hath the falling sickness.

CASCA: . . . And so he fell. When he came to himself, again, he said, if he had done or said any thing amiss, he desir'd their worships to think it was his infirmity.

Shakespeare refers to the infirmity again when Iago goads Othello into the frenzy of jealousy. 'My lord is fall'n into an epilepsy,' Iago tells Cassius. Emily Dickinson pitied 'the throe of Othello'.

Traditionally, epilepsy has carried a stigma. In the Middle Ages it was seen as a form of demonic possession and seizures played a part in convicting witches. In the nineteenth century, epileptics were sometimes incarcerated in asylums, and the more advanced asylums segregated them: too disturbing for the mentally ill. Females especially provoked genteel aversion as they broke the rules of ladylike control. Families therefore colluded to keep the condition a lifelong secret. Dickinson's poetry speaks of a 'reticent' volcano: though its explosiveness would be relevant to her condition, the volcano's still, temperate façade compels her imagination even more: the tremendous power of suppression 'when upon a pain Titanic / Features keep their place —'. The Loaded Gun of her art has the deceptive stillness of a 'Vesuvian face'.

In Emily's youth the sickness was described in violent terms. The victim falls 'as if hit by gunshot', followed by 'spasmodic throes'. These appear as if a creature, recently dead, were subjected to 'the shocks of a galvanic battery'. A spark as to a 'barrel of gunpowder' will 'induce the explosion'. Fingers are clenched and eyes, 'suffused' with moisture, swivel.

From her schooldays, when Emily was not well, she stayed for long periods in Boston with her Aunt Lavinia and little cousins Loo and Fanny Norcross. Between 4 and 22 September 1851, when Emily was twenty and staying with her aunt, she consulted Dr James Jackson, a man of seventy-four, dressed in a long-tailed coat and old-fashioned white neckcloth. He had been Professor of Physic at Harvard Medical School, President of the Massachusetts Medical Society and co-founder of the Massachusetts General Hospital. This, then, was an eminent physician, not to be consulted for anything trivial. He was thought of as the last resort in chronic cases from all over New England. His best-known book, *Letters to a Young Physician* (1855), has a chapter on epilepsy.

Jackson was a doctor who practised medicine with delicate attention to the patient, eliciting facts without intrusive questions. Everything about him suggests how suitable he was for Emily Dickinson. His looks were grim, reassuringly like her father – not one to overdo a bedside manner. At this time she had lost confidence in the local Amherst man, Dr Brewster, and in Dr Wesselhöft, a Boston homeopath urged on her by Aunt Lavinia.

It was Dr Jackson's practice to converse with the patient for a whole hour without taking notes, so as not to deflect attention from every nuance of the patient's history. He welcomed subjective details; it was his way never to fault the patient even in tone of voice. Alert to character and to the effect of the mind on the body, he treated each case as individual. Following no formula, his habit was to listen and then to communicate 'principles rather than rules'. After discussing at length the patient's mode of life, he could satisfy an incurable patient without any prescription for a drug. In the case of epilepsy, he told his patient at once not to use any drug to *remove* it.

His strict adherence to the good of the patient was exceptional, for though Jackson had the curiosity of a scientist he would not try this or that in ignorance of side-effects. Because he was intelligent enough to admit the limitations of medical knowledge, he refused 'idiot medications', over-dosing and disregard of relief through the natural processes of the body. From his youth he had been impressed by Robert Boyle's ideas on the healing power of nature and the advantage of a simple regimen of hygiene, outdoor exercise and rest.

He said, 'I am convinced that all active interference, during the fit, is use-less and may be injurious.' When he faced a patient who had 'at all times a liability to the epileptic paroxysm', he put the question to himself: 'can this liability be removed?' Sympathetic though he was to the distress of the patient and the family's need to overcome this 'dreadful' liability, the answer had to be no. He warned against experiment. Once the disease had begun, there was no stopping its course. The best practice was to avoid whatever might aggravate or prolong attacks: agitation, fright, fatigue and excitement.

After assessing a case, he would state the truth plainly. He claimed that in no instance had a patient made him regret candour when there was no cure. Where other doctors who treated epilepsy at the time spoke glibly of 'cures', Dr Jackson had more sense. He preferred to speak posi-tively about devising a mode of existence that would mitigate and comfort suffering. In such a situation, he believed, the taste and inclination of the patient should be indulged. Patients left his rooms ready to meet trials bravely. It could have been Dr Jackson who persuaded Emily Dickinson to accept the prospect of seclusion and singleness in the hope of doing something with the intellectual and creative gifts that this doctor had the capacity to discern. Here was just the person to help this young woman devise the way of life to which she adapted with such extraordinary results.

Dr Jackson's authority would have weighed with Mr Dickinson, who agreed to relieve his daughter of the household tasks and empty social gatherings she loathed. Instead, he indulged the priority she wished to give to poetry and promoted mild exertion in the fresh air: daily walks with her dog Carlo (named after St John Rivers's dog in *Jane Eyre*) and her taste for gardening. For her sake Mr Dickinson added a conservatory in a corner between the dining room and the library, with indoor access through the library, so that she might continue to garden during the winter.

Dr Jackson gave Emily a prescription which was filled at a drugstore in Tremont Row (now Center Plaza, across from Boston's City Hall), near to where Dr Jackson lived on Hamilton Place. She delivered the prescription to her father and took the mixture with confidence. 'I have tried Dr Jackson's prescription and find myself better for it,' she wrote to Austin (then teaching in Boston) on 7 October, in the month following the consultation. 'I have used it all up now, and wish you would get me some more . . . I should like to have you get <u>three or four</u> times the quantity contained in the Recipe, as . . . I think it benefits me much.'

This bit of paper, which survives, is a crucial clue to Dr Jackson's diagnosis. What he prescribed was half an ounce of glycerine diluted with two and a half ounces of water. Glycerine has many uses, but one of the medical uses in those days was for epilepsy. In a nineteenth-century listing of 'Medicinal Uses of Glycerine' in Amherst's Jones Library, there is a recommendation for epilepsy: dissolve half an ounce of chloral (a sedative) and twenty-five drops of peppermint essence (for flavour) in four ounces of glycerine. This use of glycerine in the treatment of epilepsy (as distinct from its use for TB) has gone unnoticed. In treating both diseases the substance would have been futile, though it had a placebo effect on Emily

Dickinson, a consequence of her trust in Jackson together with an urgency to be cured. She used the prescription until 1853 with diminishing confidence. The editors of her letters thought that her prescription was a hand lotion, but she would hardly have troubled an eminent physician for something so trivial. Then, too, her dosage, as discussed by Dr Norbert Hirschhorn in the *New England Quarterly*, was too small for external use. It had to be a dose taken internally: a teaspoon a day.

Dr Hirschhorn asks an extremely pertinent question: why did Dickinson persist in asking Austin to send her this medication from Boston even though there was an adequate drugstore at home in Amherst? This practice was sanctioned by her father, who carried the prescription to Boston on at least one occasion. Dr Hirschhorn admits that if TB were the case (an idea he generally favours) her action is puzzling, since no stigma attached to TB. It was all too rife in distinguished families: Emerson's brothers and first wife, the Adams family in Quincy and indeed Emily's well-off Norcross relations. The question of secrecy about her medication is therefore still open. The undeniable stigma of epilepsy could be the answer, given its shaming associations at that time with 'hysteria', masturbation, syphilis and impairment of the intellect leading to 'epileptic insanity'.* This would explain why she wished this prescription to be filled in Boston, away from the small-town tattle of Amherst.

The main regimen recommended by authorities was what they called hygiene, and central to this was cleanliness. In *On Epilepsy*, the London authority Sir Edward Sieveking is almost obsessive in his warnings against what's unclean, including 'unsanitary' theatres, concerts, balls and parties. Other people are unclean; places where other people congregate are unclean – in contrast to the spotless Homestead. A simple and entirely

---

* This sinister diagnosis permitted the incarceration of epileptics in asylums. Women were more susceptible than men, in the view of the French psychiatrist Jean-Étienne Esquirol in 1838, and women were more numerous in his National Asylum at Charenton. Of 385 epileptic female patients placed in this asylum, forty-six were diagnosed as 'furious' and thirty-four as 'hysterical'. Anger and hysteria would have appeared contrary to the prevailing model of passive, compliant womanliness.

unromantic reason for Emily Dickinson to wear white could be sanitary, the same reason why white would be worn by doctors and nurses: to show the presence of dirt in situations where it presents a threat to health.

In a case of incurable sickness, Jackson advised, 'it affords much consolation to have one to watch over them'. This is a consolation Emily Dickinson experienced from 'Sister' in the late 1850s. Susan Dickinson, as a member of family, must have been in the know, to judge from her central role in the earliest poem 'Sister' wrote on the subject. 'Dying! Dying in the night!' (c. 1860) is a humanist take on God's absence ('And "Jesus"! Where has <u>Jesus</u> gone? / They said that Jesus — always came') in contrast with the comfort of hearing Sue's step. At this moment, she's 'Dollie' again, the pet name of those who'd loved Sue as a girl:

> . . . Somebody run to the great gate
> And see if Dollie's coming! Wait!
> I hear her feet upon the stair!
> Death won't hurt – now Dollie's here!

Epileptics are often attached to a member of family, who makes it their lifelong task to care for them. In the Dickinson Homestead, Lavinia took this on. Because the diagnosis was rarely uttered, still less put on paper, there's little chance of explicit evidence. In any case, epilepsy was often misdiagnosed, and still so. Well into the twentieth century, there's a common misapprehension that seizures could be deflected by self-control, extending the sufferer's torment with a moral obligation to stop what physiologically can't be stopped without medication. Since poetry was all-important to Dickinson, it was in a sense fortunate that she lived before barbiturates came into use in 1912 for, in sedating the brain, drugs dulled it.

Whatever Dickinson may have endured in loss of control before, during and after a Throe, some part of her brain remained, as she said, alert. Sufferers like Dostoyevsky can be visionary, as well as plumbing hellish depths. The range of experience opened to the gifted can't be tabulated.* Dickinson's oxymorons defy definition: calm bomb; quiet earthquake; reticent volcano. Still, if she did suffer from epilepsy it would explain her claim that Existence struck through the daily ticking of her life. 'Struck, was I, nor yet by Lightning — / . . . Maimed — was I — . . .'.

On the surface of that life nothing to see but a closed door; and behind the door, writing at a small cherrywood table, a woman in white; and 'it', the unmentionable, waiting there in her room like a loaded gun. She was proud of 'it'. 'I like a look of Agony,' she said, because Agony opened up what lies beyond the limits of language: visionary states of mind she would not otherwise have comprehended and which became prime material for poems. We might guess that during the four years when she produced so much of her greatest work, her sickness was at its height. In later years it was less active, as was her poetic output. By her fifties, the 'Torrid Noons' of her early thirties had 'lain their Missiles by —', though the Thunder that once brought 'the bolt' did rumble still.

To see epilepsy as part of Dickinson's secret Existence cannot explain genius, only certain conditions that facilitate it: freedom from the demands on a nineteenth-century wife; freedom to keep odd hours; and the seclusion she had to have if she was to take poetic risks that were certain to jar

---

* Dickinson's words correlate with Dostoyevsky's extraordinary record of epilepsy in *The Idiot* (1868), part two, chapter 5 (Penguin Classics, 263–4). Both stress a breakthrough into what Dickinson called 'Existence' and what Dostoyevsky called 'a higher existence': at once, a supreme rationality and vision. Dostoyevsky reports a stage immediately before the seizure when the brain 'seemed to burst into flame' and with a jolt all vital forces tensed together. The sensation of life and of self-awareness increased almost tenfold. But these moments 'were merely the presentiment of that final second (never more than a second), with which the fit itself began'. Afterwards, Prince Myshkin would ask himself if he had experienced a violation of the normal condition. 'What does it matter if it's an illness then,' he decides, if the result yields an unheard-of completeness, proportion, reconciliation and ecstasy? In the very last conscious moment he could to say to himself: 'Yes, for this moment one could give up one's whole life!' Myshkin does not insist on this conclusion because of the aftermath when the fit subsides into 'stupefaction' (what Dickinson calls languor). He's left with the question of what to do with this 'reality'. In both writers, the 'moment' opens up a sense of the timeless. Myshkin quotes from *Revelation*, x: 1–7 – 'there shall be time no longer' – and conjectures a similar revelation for 'the epileptic Mahomet': 'in that very second he was able to survey all the habitations of Allah'.

public taste. She was fortunate in her father. Traditional and formidable though he was, he supported her, we might guess from the respect and security she enjoyed in a home she always called 'my father's house'.

The shock of discovering a lifelong condition of this kind is the subject of one poem. Evidently Dr Jackson did not name it, because she invents a name, drawing, she says, on a residue of Latin from her schooldays. She does not tell us the invented name, only that to put the unmentionable into Latin helps to distance the blow. She turns over this word – 'it' – in her mind, trying to adapt to the diagnosis:

> It dont sound so terrible — quite — as it did —
> I run it over — 'Dead', Brain — 'Dead' . . .
> How like 'a fit' — . . .

A *fit*. So close did her lips come to utterance. The victim promises herself that what looms so horribly at present, in a year's time will be a verbal habit.

The daring of genuine confession fuels such poems from well below the surface. She got away with explicitness by telling it 'slant'. For she plays on the ambiguity of 'fit' in the context of wearing an outfit. 'Murder – wear!' She will 'fit' herself to 'Murder', another code word for 'dying in the night'. In a later poem, 'I fit for them', she again draws on the double entendre of fitting herself to certain conditions, as though she had chosen them. At thirty-five, helplessness becomes agency: 'I fit for them — I seek the Dark / Till I am thorough fit.'

Does 'thorough' imply a full-scale fit, as distinct from averted ones? It's impossible to be certain because her words and grammar are undergoing transformation. Even that's too weak for her purpose which is nothing less than transfiguration, as though the poet were inventing a sacred text. For the ideal outcome of 'fit' (a familiar noun transformed as a verb, infused with a verbal power to 'do') is to produce 'a purer food' (poetry) for read-ers' souls. At the same time, there's a calm acceptance that should she not succeed, she has still had the 'transport of the Aim —'. Again, the final dash registers her leap beyond language into the lacunae of unknown modes of being.

And yet she never got over her fear of 'it' and in time her constant apprehension of 'a Fitting' turns out to be 'terribler' than when it's on — when she's 'wearing it'. She was forty-three when she set this down in the first person; the fair copy shields 'I' with 'we':

> While we were fearing it, it came —
> But came with less of fear
> Because that fearing it so long
> Had almost made it fair —
>
> There is a Fitting — a Dismay —
> A Fitting — a Despair —
> 'Tis harder knowing it is Due
> Than knowing it is Here.
>
> The Trying on the Utmost
> The Morning it is New
> Is terribler than wearing it
> A whole existence through —

On 4 February 1864 Emily and Vinnie returned to Amherst from Boston, following a consultation with New England's foremost ophthalmologist, Henry Willard Williams, then in his mid-forties. He was a big man and a forcible speaker, the first to introduce a clinical course in ophthalmology in America and one of the first to use ether as surgeon to the City Hospital. In 1864 he founded the American Ophthalmic Society — another distinguished doctor. From April to November 1864 and for a similar period in 1865 Emily, aged thirty-three to thirty-four, spent the better part of two years in Boston for treatment of her eyes. Eyes? She never wore spectacles, and though she may have used Dr Williams's (commonly prescribed) eyewash, there is no other confirmatory sign of a disability grave enough to justify this level of disruption for a person who didn't take kindly to leaving home. 'Bereaved of all, I went abroad —': death-in-life awaits her in the form of lodgings in a strange street. There's no repose there, because 'it'

goes with her, even when she takes sleeping draughts ('Cups of artificial
Drowse / To steep its shape away'):

> I waked, to find it first awake —
> I rose — It followed me —
> I tried to drop it in the Crowd —
> To lose it in the Sea — . . .

She stayed in a Cambridgeport boarding house with her orphaned
cousins Loo and Fanny Norcross, and went for treatment to the doctor's
rooms at 15 Arlington Street near Boston's public garden. But can eye
treatment alone necessitate such prolonged stays in Boston, when the distance from Amherst was not so great as to prevent her father's coming and
going? Common sense suggests a major disability, and a concerted attempt
at a cure.

Epileptics' eyes are vulnerable to stimuli. During the aura they might
see spider webs, thin clouds, spots, fiery circles or other premonitory signs.
Charcot, the celebrated professor of the nervous system at the Salpêtrière
in Paris, said that the visual abnormalities accompanying epilepsy are 'like
so many sphinxes' defying anatomical investigation. Alternatively, a fit
can start with a spot of blindness known as scotoma. A physician would
shine his ophthalmoscope (developed during the 1850s, and newly in use
for searching out diseases of the brain) into a dilated pupil in order to
examine small blood vessels at the back of the eyeball, the only vessels visible without surgery. In 1865 Dr Williams won a prize for his treatise *Recent
Advances in Ophthalmic Science*, announcing a new dawn of discoveries and
cures, which Mr Dickinson bought for his library. Here, Williams investi-
gates what he terms 'hyperaesthesia of the retina' (amongst a range of
ills). He describes how contraction of the blood vessels at the back of the
eyeball activates nerves going to a troubled part of the brain. For a person
who was predisposed, repeated flashes of light would set off convulsions,
and if this were so in Emily's case it would have been logical to approach
her problem through an initiating symptom. If the patient could be cured
of her photosensitivity, the attacks might be stopped.

At first Dr Williams was enthusiastic about a cure, and ordered Emily Dickinson to avoid sunlight as well as snow light – the glitter coming off the snow affected her eyes. A poem of 1864 talks of those who must 'forget the color of the Day'. This would have suited her preference for the dark hours of the night. In the same poem the speaker labours by night to fatigue the 'glittering Retinue of nerves' and 'put a Head away'. ('Retinue', aurally close to 'retina', would be typical of Dickinson's aural word-play: a half-note off like a sharp or a flat.) For this speaker, there's 'No Drug for Consciousness', only death, and the voice in this poem despairs of other relief. Her words suggest more than eye trouble: 'Affliction', she calls it, 'Being's Malady'. If the poet's eye problem was a symptom, not the prime ill, it would explain why there's no sign of serious eye trouble before and after this period.

What does seem evident before she went to Boston is an almost desperate hunger to feast her poetic eye on all that exists under the sun,

> As much of Noon as I could take
> Between my finite eyes —

There's a before-and-after narrative in this poem, 'Before I got my eye put out': before, the poet 'liked as well to see — / As other Creatures, that have Eyes'. In the context of her submission to Dr Williams it's tempting to read this poem literally. The poem is posited on a conditional clause: if she 'might', if she were told she might, if she were allowed 'to look at when I liked', her Heart would split as it took in the crowded sights of her release. 'I tell you', she says. As it is, she has adapted to certain constraints on seeing and developed the traditional 'other way' of the blind seer. The poem ends with a contrast of soul versus eyes, deprecating the 'safer' enclosures of the soul:

> So safer Guess —
> With just my soul opon the Window pane —
> Where other Creatures put their eyes —
> Incautious — of the Sun —

Though she endured the treatment, she found it hard to share the surgeon's hopefulness. Throughout this ordeal, she maintained that she was neither better nor worse. The treatment, whatever it was, made her eyes water, so that the doctor had to wipe her cheeks – to protect her hat, he said.

Dr Jackson, by now almost ninety, had always warned that experiments could be injurious in the case of incurable sickness, and so it proved. Not only did Emily force herself to undergo a nightmare protracted over two years, but Williams disrupted a creative life at its peak. It seems not to have occurred to him that the instrument of diagnosis, powered by gaslight or sunlight (first tried in 1860), would itself have been likely to set off the contraction of the retinal nerves it intended to examine. Since his patient was sensitive to light, examination would have been stressful, even painful, which, in turn, would have affected the tissues the doctor observed. In 1865, Dickinson sent Sue this rebuttal of scientific observation:

> Perception of an Object costs
> Precise the Object's loss —

An act of observation is an act of transformation. Her proposition anticipates the Uncertainty Principle of Heisenberg, that an act of measurement will, in the process, alter the object measured. There's consolation in the next couplet: a recompense for a loss of objectivity is an enlargement of the fund of the imagination. 'Perception in itself a Gain / Replying to its Price —'. The third proposition strengthens the second, 'The Object absolute — is nought — / Perception sets it fair'. This was articulated most famously by Coleridge: the imagination, he declares, 'is essentially *vital* even as all objects (*as* objects) are essentially fixed and dead'. Romantic theory views the object as nothing until it receives its character from the subjective mind. Dickinson's conclusion overthrows this. An object has, after all, a wilful life of its own. Subjectivity, confounded,

> . . . then upbraids a Perfectness
> That situates so far —

'Situates' is a passive construction refusing passivity. In the end the poem questions the efficacy of observation. It rejects the allure of Romantic subjectivity and reverts to the opening premise, fusing it with a Puritan belief in the unknowable: 'Perfectness' – unobservable and immeasurable – defamiliarises the more ordinary 'perfection'. This may be the most brilliant theorem Dickinson distilled from experience, applicable to any observation a reader might make. At source, the poem came out of the poet's eye problem at the time it was written.

In the end Dr Williams's cure was so ineffectual that he fell back on a standard defence: blame the victim. Her problem lay in her attitude, the doctor decided; it required a change of mentality on her part. At first, Emily had tried to be positive in the face of long discouragement.

'Emily wants to be well,' she had told Vinnie in July 1864, during the first phase of the cure. 'If any one alive wants to get well more, I would let Him first.'

By March 1865 a disappointed Vinnie had taken the doctor's side: 'I cannot see why you don't get well,' she reproached her sister.

Emily reported these words to her sympathetic cousin Loo, adding ruefully, 'This makes me think I am long sick, and this takes the ache to my eyes.'

Dr Williams further subscribed to the current medical view that too much thinking could damage a woman. 'Down thoughts', he told her.

It was as though he had told her, 'heart be still'. To be parted from thoughts and books (for he also forbade reading)* was an exile to 'Siberia'. His prohibitions put an end to the booklets. She never resumed this alternative to publication, and though she did continue to write poems, the great surge of the early 1860s came to an end. Dr Williams, in the vanity of the latest know-how, simply didn't *see* her. The invalid Alice James confided to her diary: 'I suppose one has a greater sense of intellectual degradation after an interview with a doctor than from any human experience.'

---

* Since reading can lead to changes in the brain, there was a belief that reading excited the brain in a way that prompted attacks in those who were susceptible. (Scott, *The History of Epileptic Therapy*, 134).

One of the degrading diagnoses concocted for women was 'hysteria', from the Greek for womb. Respectable doctors, even Dr Jackson, believed that epilepsy could be hysterical in origin. They spoke of 'hystero-epilepsy'* or 'hysteric convulsions' and since, as they fancied, a distension of the vessels of the brain occasioned attacks, they fancied by analogy that turgid blood in the uterus and genitalia might bring about spasmodic motions.†
There's an implication that women who are highly sexed are more liable to aberration. This would appear to place the onus on a woman who, the theory assumes, is indulging in the kind of thoughts that lead to turgidity. A misogynist diagnosis will lean to punitive treatment. The best treatment, doctors advised, was to remove the patient from the sympathies of her home so as to encourage a wanting self-control.

If the guess about epilepsy is right, then the reason Emily's treatment failed is because epilepsy was not curable. Drugs, developed later, merely suppress seizures which often happen with the depression of consciousness at night. Dickinson's poem, 'It struck me', explains how 'it', the electrical discharge, slit through sleep and spread like fire, leaving miasma in its wake:

> It burned Me — in the Night
> It Blistered to My Dream
> It sickened fresh upon my sight
> With every Morn that came —

---

* A supposed disease, 'hystero-epilepsy' was part of the proliferation of hysteria as a diagnosis reserved for women in the nineteenth century. Charcot, in Paris, emphasised the passions – wrath, fright, lust, disgust – as a cause of epilepsy. He implied that epilepsy was psychological, self-induced and, as such, controllable. This message was coercive: a woman should exercise decent control. (In a letter to her friend Abiah Root, Emily Dickinson mentions feeling unwell from time to time, her understanding that she should control the 'feelings' and then, ruefully, confesses her inability to do so when the 'feelings' come upon her.) If she was enduring a physically uncontrollable sickness such as epilepsy, she was fortunate not to have been exposed to a reproving diagnosis. The price of protection, to take cover at home, would have been the natural choice.

† In the prostitute setting of 'Sweeney Erect' (1919), Eliot's poem revives the link between female sexuality and an epileptic attack.

Epilepsy has a genetic component, and two others in Emily's family were subject to seizures. Cousin Zebina Montague, immured at home – he, too – across the road into town from the Homestead was a son of Irene Dickinson ('Aunt Montague'), sister to Emily's grandfather Samuel Fowler Dickinson. There were three unions between Montagues and Dickinsons in that generation. Emily's grandmother, it will be recalled, was the irritable Lucretia Gunn. Lucretia's mother Hannah, Emily's great-grandmother, was a Montague and elder sister to Luke Montague, who married Aunt Irene Dickinson. Intermarriage alone cannot cause a recessive disorder, but if a gene for epilepsy happens to be latent in a family's DNA, inter-marriage can lead to homozygosity – the doubling of a gene – activating it in following generations.

After his graduation from Amherst College in 1832, Zebina became a rector of an academy in Tennessee; then almost at once he left off teaching, rid himself of his goods and joined his brother, a merchant in Georgia. There the well-read Zebina, keen on Latin and English literature, worked in a store and then as assistant cashier in a Georgia bank. Soon this restless man volunteered to fight some escaped Creek Indians in Florida, but was assigned only camp duties. Returning to the bank in Georgia, he became engaged at the age of twenty-nine. His blue-eyed fiancée, aged nineteen, came from a family of wealth and social standing. He will draw a veil over what happened next, he says, for it was then, in 1839, that 'dreadful disease' struck: he was disabled and the marriage was off. The veil consists of one inadequate word of explanation: he was 'paralysed'. Whatever actually happened, it left him '*blank*', and when he could not recover, a devoted slave (whom he'd taught to read and write) undertook to convey the sick man a distance of some fifteen hundred miles – an interminable journey in bumping coaches – to a sick and ageing mother in the Montague homestead in Amherst. Until he began to apply the alternative stimulus of cold water, his nights were troubled 'with spasms and *starts* most horrible'. He was a 'mystery', it was said at his graveside, for this supposedly sick man went on living for a very long time – another forty years. His paralysis was said to be 'partial', without indicating, as people usually do, what (if any) part of his body was visibly affected. Tall and helpless, his case is far from clear.

When Emily, aged eleven, heard that Zebina, aged thirty-two, had bitten his tongue in the course of a fit, secrecy was not preserved – not in the family. The word 'fit' was in the air in 1842, and an alert child picked it up. It's impossible to know if the fit was epileptic or caused by some other chronic condition. What is certain is that it was not a fatal condition.

From his late twenties until his seventies Zebina rarely left home, and therefore needed that sort of support in which one member of family puts her life at the service of another. Zebina's sister Harriet did this. He didn't marry and neither did his sister.

Zebina wrote Cousin Emily a long letter, we recall, after ill health had forced her to leave college for a month when she was seventeen. If she were showing symptoms of permanent illness he would have wished to enlighten her so far as he could. His situation was hardly cheering. In Amherst he and his sister were regarded as oddities. 'Poor Harriet and Zebina', Emily said in 1863. They were a 'genteel' pair, given to sighing reminiscences, punctuated by 'God help us.'

Then another member of the family turned out to be afflicted: young Edward (Ned) Dickinson, born to Austin and Sue in 1861. At the age of fifteen, in mid-February 1877, Ned had a fit, to his family's dismay. 'It seems he went to bed as well as usual Sunday night,' a caller was told, '– in the night was taken with a fit, followed by another on Monday morning' while the doctor was present. Dr Fiske feared the fit was linked to Ned's weak heart, the result of rheumatic fever in 1874. By the following day, the caller reports, the family, though anxious, began to think 'the trouble might not be so serious'.

Emily wrote to her nephew after a few weeks, hoping he'd recovered, but the fits returned. It can't have helped that his parents' marriage was strained. The preceding autumn, while Susan and the children had paid their annual visit to Geneva, New York, Austin had lived at the Homestead for four weeks. This is when Emily noticed a change in her brother: he'd withdrawn and she could no longer reach him. It felt 'antediluvian' to have Austin back in his childhood home, and yet his sisters missed him while he stayed, and then missed him after he left. 'Curious' was all Emily was prepared to say.

Instinctively she sided with Austin, who looked burdened, waiting for a 'crumb' of sympathy from his sisters, while Susan was said to be over-charged with 'scintillation'. Watching Austin's mood in the autumn, Emily took in his picture of a wife entering on a buzz of activities while the put-upon husband retreats into relative seclusion. This image of a shallow socialite is not entirely convincing in light of what is known of Susan as a serious reader and sensitive mother. Were her excursions and parties an effort to cheer up the children in the face of a father who looked on darkly? When their daughter Martha (Mattie), aged ten, accompanied her father on a visit to Northampton he rebuked the child's spirits: he was 'much ashamed' of her. On their return, Mattie confided to Aunt Emily and Aunt Vinnie that *she* had been much ashamed of *him*. Her father's manner was increasingly austere as he tried on the crown descending from his grand-father through his father, both of whom had faltered in their financial management towards the end of their reigns. Austin, like his father before him, intended to make good what came to him in disarray: the college accounts. Jollities disrupted his right to quiet. They were an affront to domestic propriety.

Susan's 'scintillation'– alien to family reserve – reinforced a graver accu-sation stirring in Austin's conscience. Refusing to consider if Ned's epilepsy was inherited through his side of the family, he cultivated a suspicion that Sue had caused it by an attempted abortion. It's not known at what point this medically untenable notion came to Austin, but it served to forestall guilt – especially if the Dickinsons had kept the blight from Susan before she married into the family. It was nineteenth-century practice to conceal shaming diseases: madness (in *Jane Eyre*) and syphilis (in Ibsen's *Ghosts*) as well as epilepsy. Here is a buried seed for an efflorescence of blame yet to come. For the abortion story became the position Austin was to articulate in the 1880s, when Mabel Loomis Todd arrived on the scene, as one justifi-cation for turning against his wife. Susan, drawn into the family with pressing eagerness in the 1850s, was now re-categorised as alien, in a sense re-orphaned, and for Austin to exclude her emotionally meant that motherhood – her undeniable claim as mother of Dickinson children – had to be eroded. Forgetting Sue's old terror of childbirth and his one-time idea of a *mariage blanc*, Austin's tone was righteous: his wife had perpetrated an immoral act with terrible consequences.

Austin kept a record of Ned's seizures in a diary of 1880 when his son was nineteen and a student at Amherst College. The eight seizures that year happened at night, about one hour into sleep. At the sound of Ned's awakening cry, Austin would leap over the rails at the bottom of the bed he shared with Sue and rush upstairs. It was always Austin who went and he never got used to the groans from Ned's room, the foaming mouth, the spasms of mouth, neck and chest, and the strained breathing that followed convulsions 'distressing to see'. Later, Mabel observed Austin's own nervous system as 'exquisitely delicate & high-strung' with a tendency to 'night-horrors'.

Ned's seizures were unpredictable, though Austin records after one attack: 'I noticed his eyes an hour before bedtime last night as very black and bright.' Black indicates a dilated pupil. Ned was not told he had epilepsy. He'd wake in the morning with no sign beside a sore tongue and sometimes a headache, which Sue would treat with a 'fomentation'. It could happen that a headache preceded an attack and heavy breathing might follow. Some seizures were mild enough for Ned to go to classes next day. Some were so violent they shook the house.

We can't know if Emily Dickinson suffered as her nephew did. There are many forms of epilepsy, and the mild *petit mal* does not involve convulsions. Much depends on what region of the brain is affected, and where it spreads. If it's the motor region at the top of the brain sufferers, like Ned, undergo the visible jolts we associate with the condition. The mildest manifestations are absences. A friend of Dickinson's youth, Emily Fowler (later Mrs Ford), recalled that she dropped crockery. Plates and cups seemed to slide out of her hands and lay in pieces on the floor. The story was designed to bring out her eccentricity for, it was said, she hid the fragments in the fireplace behind a fireboard, forgetting they were bound to be discovered in winter. This memory is more important than Mrs Ford realised because it suggests absences, either accompanying the condition or the condition itself.

What's clear, on the evidence of Dickinson's writing and the sheer volume of her output, is that she coped inventively with gunshots from the brain into her body. In 'My Life had stood — a Loaded Gun —', the 'power to kill' makes the gun a 'deadly foe', but since this gun outlives its Master it's no ordinary gun. Can it be the poet's art? By late 1863, when this poem was probably written, the poetic force is sure of itself, exultant when it dares to expose its 'Vesuvian face'. To write this kind of poetry is a form of action, an act of pleasure 'every time I speak for Him' – 'Him' (the owner or Master) being the mortal self.

So it was that art and life converge at this point, when poetic immortality is certain. Poetry is not only celebrated for its explosiveness; it's also the protective gun that guards the 'head' by night (art's ability to protect against outbreaks of sickness), and this guardianship is preferable to the shared pillow of matrimony. By day this force roams the 'Sovereign' woods. It's not reclusive, it's adventurous; it 'roams', and its arena claims the same regal status Dickinson confers on her 'Queen' role in other poems. A poem like this outlives the body, though for obvious reasons the body, art's vessel, must continue as long as it can. The poem itself has 'no power to die' – it's an immortal power, wielded by a killer eye and thumb, that is the control art imposes on the ephemeral, the mortal, passing across its field of vision.

In this way, 'My Life had stood — a Loaded Gun —' turns an explosive sickness, its recurrent dramas of 'Revolver' and 'Gun', into well-aimed art. *I fit for them* . . . The secret is on her lips or it's kept like a bomb in her breast – a timebomb ticking softly in some of her poems, yet 'calm'. Art is made at the interface of abandon and decorum: the abandon of mind and feeling under the control of form, a tight form like Dickinson's four-line stanza, the beat of hymns thrumming in the veins of her forebears. Contained further in her own domestic order, propped up by her protective father and sister, Emily Dickinson saved herself from the anarchy of her condition and put it to use.

6

TELLING

The Dickinsons were not her readers. In his youth Austin had fancied himself a writer; Emily had seen he was not and changed the subject. He knew of her poems and sometimes when his wife read them aloud to visitors Austin must have been present, but he did not think her great. Austin was to be surprised by his sister's fame.

Vinnie was not told of the manuscript booklets and sheets of poetry her sister was piling up in her chest of drawers. Though it was known in the household, and eventually in Amherst, that 'Miss Emily' wrote poems, the family, led by Mr Dickinson, would have regarded precarious health as the main fact in her life. That her poems did not interest her kin so long as she lived might have happened for ordinary reasons – familiarity, conventionality, or respect for reserve – but their incuriosity might also have been associated with their attitude to her condition: abnormal poetry born of an abnormality to be kept out of sight. What would the family have made of a poem about a sex change, an operation that must 'rearrange' a 'Wife's' make-up?

> Amputate my freckled Bosom!
> Make me bearded like a Man!

Modest blushes are swept aside by the speaker's pride in a 'constant' love that 'never leapt its socket' and by acceptance of a gender shift 'when they dislocate my Brain!' Here is another secret: 'Big my Secret but it's <u>bandaged</u>' for the rest of her life. Dramatically, a 'Wife' – a socially unac-knowledged wife – blurts what she stifles. Conjoining issues of sickness and gender, this poem was not published until 1945.

The more daring her imagined confessions, the more the poet had to guard the facts of her life. She cannot name 'Master'. Nor can she name her sickness. The sacred or falling sickness was always unnameable when it struck a female. With males, secrecy was less strict, and fame in a few – Caesar, Mahomet, Dostoyevsky – over-rode the stigma, but a woman had to bury herself in a lifelong silence. It's therefore remarkable that Dickinson developed a voice from within that silence, one with a volcanic power to bide its time.

Publication, under the circumstances, had to be postponed indefinitely. When Higginson suggested that she delay to publish, she assured him that publication was as foreign to her intentions 'as Firmament to Fin'. She owed it to her father's name not to expose her oddities: 'A modesty befits the soul / That bears another's — name —'. A deeper reticence held up this shield of modest womanhood, and it was not an act; she could defer to others while protecting her gift. In this she was not all that unusual amongst women writers. But she stood alone in her avoidance of print. Conceivably, this was not so much a matter of modesty, nor even a matter of poetic irregularities, but the intractable block of a taboo.

Amid the thousands of details amassed about the poet's family and local environment, one link has been overlooked. It's the curious fact that living within yards of one another were three semi-invalids who belonged to the same family, each with a member of family attached as carer. If we look at a well-known British case of the period, the poet Edward Lear, there's the same closed-off family solution: Lear's sister became his lifelong carer. Since these were middle-class families who could afford outside help, the issue was not economy but secrecy. A diagnosis, if made, would not have passed a family's lips. And yet, if this guess is correct, the poet talks about 'it' all the time in her poetry, the pronoun pointing to its namelessness. ''Tis so appalling — it exhilarates —'. All the same, 'it' is no more than vir-tual death, unlike men dying 'externally' in the Civil War. The actuality of their deaths is a fact 'of Blood', whilst 'it' is playing 'kill' and the dreamer is playing 'shriek'. A dreamer has the option of opening her eyes – safe after all, and mocking her safety: this is 'Dying in drama — / And Drama — is never dead —'.

Dickinson tells it 'slant', but to tell it at all is an act of disclosure, justified only by refraining from publication and certainly not under her own name. As disclosure 'it' becomes exemplary of any extreme ordeal of those who live in sight of death, but more significantly for a poet, 'it' is formative for the jolts or leaps across space to open new pathways.

Emily Dickinson was an avid reader of Shakespeare and took similar liberties with English grammar, as when she coins 'perfectness' to convey a uniqueness too intractable for standard 'perfection'. In that poem on the impossibility of objective perception ('Perception of an Object costs') she transforms the passive voice of the verb 'is situated' into an ungrammatical active form, 'situates'. Each transformation has its rationale. 'Situates', like 'perfectness', conveys a wilful distance from definition – a disruptive energy crucial to her art. It turns the noun into a verb. Research on Shakespeare's grammar, in particular his use of a noun as a verb (say, 'foots it' for dance), has demonstrated a measurable surge in the brain of his reader or audience. This research is still at an early stage, but one idea is that nouns and verbs may be processed in different regions of our brains, which means that when the usual connection is challenged a new pathway opens up. A 'surge' in the brain registers on an electro-encephalogram one six-hundredth of a second after we hear a novelty of transformed grammar.

This surge is said to be a kind of syncopation. In jazz, the jolt of syncopation interrupts the glide of musical pathways. This rhythm, as vital to jazz as to Dickinson's start-stop lines, has made her appealing to composers, from John Adams's *Harmonium* with its marvellously objective choral treatment of 'Because I could not stop for Death', to pop stars who adapt her lines. The British pop star Pete Doherty, interviewed on his release from prison in 2006, owned to stealing a copy of Dickinson from his Bedford school (as well as a copy of *Crime and Punishment* from Her Majesty's Prison library).

'Actually, I nicked one or two of [Dickinson's] lines,' he whispered, sipping a Guinness in London's Boogaloo bar. 'Aargh, she's outrageous man! She's fuckin' hardcore! Can't ignore her.'

What did he pinch?

'I took one Draught of Life, paid only the market price,' he quoted. 'I added, "now I'm estranged".' He delivered each word with a point in the air, like an invisible karaoke ball. 'Bom bom bom bom bom bom.' He saw his present-day life – estranged, imprisoned, finding solace in words – in what Dickinson had to tell of her life in 1862:

> I took one Draught of Life —
> I'll tell you what I paid —
> Precisely an existence —
> The market price, they said . . .

Curiously, Doherty expresses a Dickinsonian aversion to public eyes. To perform in public is a nightmare, like war, 'but to sit down and write in solitude is like a dream'.

The lyrics of pop stars and the handwritten poems of Dickinson function outside the standardising rules of print. Polished as her poems are, they remain at odds with publication. Their explicit claim on immortality turns on the question of transmission. Dickinson famously resented editorial interference in the matter of a comma in one of the poems Bowles published. With so few poems printed in her lifetime and none of them reliably, there is the extraordinary phenomenon of an entire oeuvre without the finalisations of print. This leaves her poems provisional, as in fact they were.

The manuscripts exist in variant versions sent to different recipients. Many words keep in play a choice of variants listed at the bottom of her page. Even after Dickinson copied poems in her booklets she continued to alter them, dividing long stanzas into quatrains, shifting punctuation, substituting words. Her lineation too must remain in question as her hand reaches the right-hand edge of the page: is it a run-on line or the start of a new line? No one can be sure. Most debatable of all: what is the meaning of her idiosyncratic punctuation, the variegated dashes standardised in print?

The only solution would be to shun print culture. The Dickinson editor and critic Martha Nell Smith makes a persuasive case for reading Dickinson's manuscripts as scans posted on the internet. From this point of view the standard three-volume edition with its laborious apparatus (and even more a 'reading' edition) becomes the unsatisfactory alternative: a construct of print conventions and editorial decisions which may or may not accord with the poet's intention.

Dickinson's distance from print retains the manner of improvisation. A confessional ferment invites reciprocity from readers who, ideally, will apply the ferment to our own lives. Dashes, pushing the language apart, create spaces for readers to fill. To join with her can give an ordinary mind an amazing surge. Print culture, by contrast, renders the reader more passive, an inert receptacle for the book trade. Virginia Woolf, a hands-on publisher who often set the type herself, suggests that Caxton's press (established in 1478, the first in England) ended the improvisations of the anonymous. As she put it, 'Caxton killed Anon'. The spontaneity of Anon is revived by Dickinson's hand as it moves across her page. The brevity of her provisional statements, sustained by the long pause – the interrogative wait of her dash, like the 'interrogative' note in her live voice – tugs us to participate, while her transformations of grammar stir up our brains.

The participatory 'surge' in the brain, drawing on Dickinson, is marked in the innovative theatre of British director Katie Mitchell. Her staging of *The Idiot* as '. . . *some trace of her*' uses Dickinson to extend Dostoyevskian intensity on the verge of seizure. A screen-filled photograph behind the actors distils a poetic image from the time-tied action on stage. Mostly, the scenes fixed on screen derive from the slow routines of nineteenth-century domestic life, much the same as Dickinson's home-body in 'I tie my Hat — I crease my Shawl — ' who puts new flowers in the glass, not expecting a strike to the soul. On Mitchell's stage, basins are brought in for washing, tables are laid and disassembled, yet these scenes are shot through with extremes of experience like Dickinson's whose voice 'tells': the shadow on the grass announcing what is to 'pass'. On stage, a full-blown seizure embodied in a swiftly fluttering hand co-exists with mental suffering on a par with Dickinson's 'Hour of Lead'; in the darkness of the auditorium we're compelled to participate in an act of creation. The point of each poem or scene is not so much the passing impact of horror and sublimity; more the continuous improvisation of a lit-up brain.

For Dickinson, the vital open-endedness of improvisation outweighed the permanence of print. Here was a positive reason to develop an alternative to publication: the well-established practice of circulating manuscripts. This was customary, of course, before Gutenberg invented printing, with one of the first books as we know them, Malory's Arthurian legends, coming off Caxton's press in 1485 and reaching a readership beyond the purview of the author. Private circulation of manuscripts would seem to be superseded; still, the practice did not end. During the Renaissance, aristocrats circulated sonnet sequences amongst themselves. In the early nineteenth century, Byron, as an aristocrat, scorned publication and affected to toss off poems with careless ease, though he did stoop to publish – upon persuasion – and in 1812 famously woke up famous. Dickinson outdid Byron in shunning the marketplace: 'Publication', she said, 'is the Auction / Of the Mind of Man —'. In the first half of the twentieth century innovative Modernist works like *Ulysses* circulated in avant-garde milieus – Pound's 'Men of 1914' and the Bloomsbury Group – before they were published, at first, in coterie magazines. It was part of the Modernist ethos to speak only to discerning readers, while in the Soviet bloc dissident literature was disseminated privately because publication was dangerous.

So, for aristocratic, political, or experimental reasons, texts continued to exist in private hands, often associated with contempt for the compliant herd. This elitism puts the unpublished text above the masses; it reverses the educative mission of print, to be found in mid-nineteenth-century novelists like Dickens, whom the Dickinsons read and quoted. All the same, despite his pleading for the poor, Dickens did not jar the well-to-do; he upheld social divisions.

It was not only sickness that kept Dickinson apart. She could not lend herself to the 'surrounding Bog' of banalities and she thought less well of her mother for wanting to hear the stale words of visitors. She threw 'donkeys' over her shoulder as she fled them. 'The Soul selects its own Society / Then shuts the door'. That door of her intelligence opens to Susan, to whom she writes as 'Rare to the Rare'; they are 'sovreign People'. A poem jokes at the 'altitude of me —' when her speaker hangs a Christmas stocking too high for Santa Claus to reach.

Imagine this elevation conjoined with the status of royals, and we approach the private importance the Dickinsons felt. It capped that sense of importance to advance in the religious life. Emily Dickinson did reject the bombardments of evangelism; she did shake off the creepy hand of Miss Lyon fingering her soul; yet that soul does, after all, late in 1862, signal its election:

> Mine — by the Right of the White Election!
> Mine — by the Royal Seal!
> Mine — by the sign in the Scarlet prison —
> Bars — cannot conceal!
>
> Mine — here — in Vision — and in Veto!
> Mine — by the Grave's Repeal —
> Titled — Confirmed —
> Delirious Charter!
> Mine — long as Ages steal!

In her late teens Dickinson had declared herself wicked in the terms of her society; in her late twenties she had conceived her adulterous drama with 'Master' and morally deserved to wear the Scarlet Letter; nevertheless she had some unmistakable sign: a vision or visitation. 'The Wife — without the Sign' was to be saved at about the time she shut her door on Sam Bowles when he came to see her on his return from Europe. In 1873 Mr Dickinson was still preparing for election in his plain style: 'I give myself to God.'

The New England Puritans, taking their moral pulse, made distinctions between church members, cutting off sinners from the chosen. This distinction is definitive for the Dickinson family (as for others of their kind, like Eliot). Exclusive habits of mind encouraged Dickinson's freedom to choose her readers.

With poems copied in her own hand, Dickinson reached out to others. 'I grope fast, with my fingers, for all out of my sight I own – to get it nearer – ', she explained to Sam Bowles. *I own*. Her verbs assert her estate: 'my friends are my Estate', she declares, extending the boundaries of friendship as friends become her readers. Sue made her think of Peruvian mines; Bowles, the Roman mines in North Africa; each had gems for this poet. Sue had taught her, as the poet saw it, to 'esteem' her 'poverty' for the sake of 'Life's Estate – with you!' Her reach is an act of possession. Lassoes of letters went whirling out from the Homestead to more than forty correspondents. A lifelong correspondent, Elizabeth Holland (whose Amherst family had been old friends of the Dickinsons), was tugged back when she slipped out of reach, retrieved with this lasso:

c. September 1873

. . . I have lost a Sister. Her name was not Austin and it was not
Vinnie. She was scant of stature though expansive spirited and last
seen in November – Not the November heretofore, but
Heretofore's Father . . .
    Possibly she perished?
    Extinction is eligible . . .
              Emily

Mrs Holland, who had moved to New York a year earlier, and Jane Humphrey, teaching in the Midwest, took advantage of physical distance. Sue had tried to do so when she took refuge with her brothers in Michigan in 1854 and would not reply to Emily's letters, but Austin managed to reel her back. From then on, the family possessed this restive orphan, an acquired Sister only 'a hedge away'. The in-house sister and the reader-sister: both, the poet insists, 'belong to me'. In 1877, she still exults to 'own a Susan of my own'.

Poems were part of the owner's letters, and the person to whom she sent a poem is part of its meaning: Bowles or Sue are imagined participants, not passive readers. The poems cast Sue as one who appears stranger the closer you get, flashing gifts of mind and shadowed by an un-acted part in another life she might have lived.

Sue believed that poems addressed and sent to her were written for her exclusively. Many were, but on occasion the poet would adjust the pronouns and send the same poem to Bowles or someone else. The intimacy was not always as exclusive as a recipient might have thought.

Her letters to Bowles cast him as consort to a 'Title divine'. It was part of his appeal that he responded so readily, looked so 'Arabian' as he exercised his responsiveness, and appeared so romantically wretched in the misery he was making at home. Bowles, teased too far by the poet's beckonings and refusals to see him, roared up the Homestead stairs in 1877, 'I've travelled all the way from Springfield to see you. Come down at once, you damned rascal.' She did come down, so the story goes, conversed with even more than her usual wit and signed her next letter 'Your "Rascal"' – leaving out the 'damned'. A note at the foot of the letter draws attention to this: 'I washed the Adjective.'

Her claim on her readers does not evoke a fragile creature shut off from the world. She invited, even demanded, attention, passing on her 'bolts' to correspondents. Her most active year was 1863, when she sent out no fewer than 295 poems. Receiving a letter was an event to be relished to the full behind a closed door. Only through letters – many revised with the professionalism she gave to poems – was she able to control distribution to her audience, mainly 'sisters', an obscure form of life addressing other obscure forms of life. 'Are you — Nobody — too?' 'Nobody' was superior to a 'Somebody'. Her Nobodies included Loo and Fanny Norcross in Boston. It was common at the time for private letters to be circulated to far-off confidantes (in the way Charlotte Brontë passed on letters to her friend Ellen Nussey for comment or Emily Dickinson was allowed to read Cousin Loc's letters from Maria Whitney: 'We will preserve them carefully,' she promised Loo. *Preserve*. She expected no less from others.)

Her circle of Nobodies included, also, Sue's schoolfriend Kate Scott Turner, whom Dickinson had approached as a 'Candidate' for her society of '<u>strangers</u>'. This is how she envisaged an alternative audience. 'My heart votes for you,' she'd told Kate, drawing her towards the deep-sea passage to her habitations. Love would row her out. Her letter 'touches' Kate's face, puts a cheek to hers, strokes Kate's hair. This tender love comes easily into being at the same time as the poet dreams up a wounded love for a stern 'Master' bound to her by drops of blood. To Bowles she offers a drama of Martyrs who, fixed in their destined course, resist 'Temptation' and 'Convulsion'. What was he to make of this poem-letter that begins: 'Because I could not say it – I fixed it in the Verse – for you to read'? The verse tells, yet does not tell, what 'it' is. The riddle did for a time exert its hold, but there's a risk in refusing to solve a riddle. A busy journalist like Bowles, at first intrigued, was bound to turn away.

She understood her own 'mad' manner well enough to be suitably cautious with her new mentor, Thomas Wentworth Higginson. Her first letter included four poems, including her spoof of a deadly heaven in 'Safe in their Alabaster Chambers' (published in Bowles's paper six weeks earlier). 'Are you too deeply occupied', she asked, 'to say if my Verse is alive? The Mind is so near itself – it cannot see, distinctly – and I have none to ask.'

Higginson's response to her originality was heady enough to bind her to him. She had 'few pleasures so deep as your opinion', she replied, close to tears. At the same time he warned against 'spasmodic' rhythms and idiosyncratic grammar. Though she thanked him for his 'surgery', she made none of the changes Higginson advised. When he invited her to join Boston's literary society she declined. She could not tell him why she could not leave her house, not even to hear Emerson.

One of the first things she did tell Higginson was untrue. It was the same untruth she'd told Newton's minister, Mr Hale, when she'd presented herself as a child-friend: the same cover of a harmless, humble Little Me. To Higginson she presented herself as an unambitious amateur in need of advice. She listened with apparent submission when he thought her poems uncontrolled, disorderly, 'wayward'.

She needed, she nodded, to be ruled. 'I had no Monarch in my life, and cannot rule myself, and when I try to organize – my little Force explodes – and leaves me bare and charred –'.

He chided her for owning to small mistakes, unaware of her larger ignorance.

She had only just then begun to write, she lied, warming to her role. 'I went to school,' she told Higginson, 'but . . . had no education.' She asked this new 'Master' to 'punish' her poems. It's like the master–pupil drama in *Villette*: an accomplished teacher in one of the world's great cities and a provincial young woman, unassuming, untrained in the way of formal discipline, who reveals an irresistible gift for expression. It stuns her teacher. The erotic undercurrent of this exposure – the excitement of being seen for what she feels herself to be – would explain the edgy propriety of Dickinson's tone: the snowy heroine who is rising, burning, speaking to a teacher commensurate with her buried fire.

This was the fantasy scenario. In reality, Higginson – Colonel Higginson, as he became in the Civil War – was a man of principle and, if not her match, an attentive friend to Dickinson, as biographer Brenda Wineapple has shown in a reassessment of the relationship that rightly refuses to see Higginson off as the blunderer he has appeared. He was a high-minded man who fought for the rights of the disenfranchised: freed slaves and women. He backed women's suffrage and education (and was later a founder of Radcliffe College). As a militant abolitionist he was to lead a regiment of nine hundred freed slaves in an assault on Jacksonville in Florida: the First South Carolina Volunteers, the first federally authorised regiment of former slaves. He bore out Mr Dickinson's anti-slavery politics – more, in fact, than Mr Dickinson's son who, like many who were drafted, paid another man to take his place in the Union army. It was during Higginson's service in the army that he contributed to the preservation of Negro Spirituals by copying dialect verses and music he heard sung around the campfires. This, then, was a man unusually alert to unrecognised forms of poetry.

Emily Dickinson kept up this tie. 'Sweetest of Renowns to remain Your Scholar –', she ends a letter when she was forty-five and for the last eighteen years had been writing what well she knew were great poems. At least twice she had to tug Higginson back. After she had sent him five insistently remarkable letters over the first six months, to four of which he had duly replied, he paused. There would have been other matters on his mind: he was about to take off for the battlefields of the Civil War in November 1862. Just then, his 'plaintive' correspondent – unconcerned, it appears, with Higginson's imminent participation in a war that was piling up ghastly death tolls and would kill more than half a million men – roped him with the politest of queries:

6 October 1862

Did I displease you, Mr Higginson?
But wont you tell me how?

Your friend,

E. Dickinson –

About ten years on, when Higginson again paused, she was as terse and more direct: 'Will you instruct me then no more?' was all she wrote on a card.

For his part, he was impressed enough to stick with the somewhat ineffectual role she imposed on him as decipherer of letters tending to the impenetrable. He represents the public world at its kindest as she opens up her flashes of originality. One of the poems she enclosed was 'Dare you see a soul <u>at the White Heat</u>'. Higginson both dared and feared, and was honest enough to admit his mystification.

May 11, 1869

Sometimes I take out your letters & verses, dear friend, and when I feel their strange power, it is not strange that I find it hard to write . . . I have the greatest desire to see you, always feeling that perhaps if I could once take you by the hand I might be something to you; but till then you only enshroud yourself in this fiery mist & I cannot reach you . . . Every year I think that I will contrive somehow to go to Amherst & see you . . . I feel . . . always timid lest

what I <u>write</u> should be badly aimed & miss that fine edge of
thought which you bear. It would be so easy, I fear, to miss you.
Still, you see, I try. I think if I could once see you & know that you
are real, I might fare better.

It is hard to understand how you can live s[o alo]ne . . . Yet it
isolates one anywhere to think beyond a certain point or have such
luminous flashes as come to you . . .

Write & tell me something in prose or verse, & I will be less
fastidious in future & willing to write clumsy things, rather than
none.

Ever your friend

TW Higginson

He could not quite stifle a contrary impulse. Amongst his Boston-
Brahmin set he called Dickinson 'my partially cracked poetess at Amherst',
and he did not stop his wife when she asked why he encouraged lunatics.
He mocked too a message Dickinson had sent with a gift of Emerson's
Representative Men for sick Mrs Higginson. Emily had called the book 'gran-
ite for you to lean on'. Apt, we might think.

No one could be more loyal to those she knit to her. At the same time,
she felt words so keenly that she could not relay them in a tepid conver-
sational temperature. This led her to write an occasional rejection letter.
One went to Joseph Chickering, the professor of English at Amherst, who
proposed to call on her.

'I had hoped to see you,' she said, 'but have no grace to talk, and my own
Words so chill and burn me, that the temperature of other Minds is too
new an Awe —'.

As a young woman she had refused an invitation from Abiah, by saying
that she never left home. As it happened, she had recently stayed with the
Hollands — he, an editor. Dickinson may have hoped he would read her
poems. In fact, he judged her poems 'unsuitable' for publication: 'too ethereal'. He was fixed in the common view that 'the genuine classics of every
language [are] the work of men and not of women'. *Jane Eyre* and *Aurora Leigh*
may have 'set the world in a flutter' for a time, but their appeal was bound

to be ephemeral, for women could not create 'the permanent treasures of literature'. Dr Holland's belittlement of women shows up in his political judgements: after the Civil War he opposed legislative reform that gave wives control over their earnings and property; he was also against women's suffrage. So, the most powerful editor in touch with Emily Dickinson was closed off, ideologically, to her greatness.

Did her chosen readers have anything in common beyond their attachment to the poet? Readers who knew of her sickness would have had biographic access to certain poems and metaphors. At the age of twenty-five, her first mention of her machinery getting 'slightly out of gear' was a half-joking plea to Elizabeth Holland: 'please . . . some one stop the wheel'. She spoke to her Boston cousin Loo as one who had seen her through a lot, and later, in about 1873, she wrote to Loo's sister Fanny: 'I was sick, little sister, and write you the first that I am able.' The sickness was so secret that those who cherished her felt all the closer. They need not have been adept as readers of poetry; it was closeness that mattered, that and the loyalty of secret-sharers, like Sue close at hand. 'Sue makes sick Days so sweet, we almost hate our health,' Emily told her. On such an occasion, early in 1873, she apologised for her untidy appearance.

'I felt so sick,' she excused herself. 'How it would please me if you came once more, when I was palatable.'

An artist as original as Dickinson must create her audience. She would have chosen readers attuned to the inward life. While Julia Ward Howe was writing her 'Battle Hymn of the Republic' and Whitman his *Drum Taps*, Dickinson demolished feats of heroism: no golden fleece, and Jason a sham. Her friends shared or tolerated her repudiation of dead words, especially the sayings of unthinking faith: dull heaven, mindless obedience, meekness and blind belief in the resurrection were all targets. She told Higginson she shunned people 'because they talk of Hallowed things, aloud – and embarrass my Dog'.

Higginson, who thought he had been corresponding with an apologetic, self-effacing pupil, was puzzled to find himself 'drained' of 'nerve-power' after his first visit to her in 1870. He was unable to describe the creature he found beyond a few surface facts: her light steps had pattered as she approached; she had two smooth bands of auburn hair and no good features; she had been deferential and exquisitely clean in her white piqué dress and short light-blue cape (crocheted with a draw-string neck); and after an initial hesitation she had proved surprisingly articulate.

'Could you tell me what home is?' she had asked. 'Is it oblivion or absorption when things pass from our minds?' She'd read Shakespeare and thought, 'why is any other book needed'?

It should have been exciting, but Higginson was trying to reach her through everyday talk. Not easy, especially as he sensed that questions might make her withdraw. She, for her part, had no qualms. Without his touching her she drew from him, noting with concern how he *tired*.

'Gratitude is the only secret that cannot reveal itself,' was her parting flourish. Why complicate thanks with this insistence on her secret? It seems of a piece with her wish and refusal to 'tell'. Poor Higginson was baffled. She had said a lot of strange things, from which he deduced an 'abnormal' life. He left relieved not to live near her.

It's obvious from this meeting why Dickinson found it preferable to communicate through letters and letter-poems. The question of contacts has intrigued later generations of readers. Who was being trained in her unique mode of communication? Who provoked her to further communication? Susan Dickinson above all: more than a friend of her youth, more than the sister she became, she remained a prime reader throughout the thirty years of the poet's output. Sue, she said, looking back from their fifties, had shared the sense of 'Infinity'; had *been* infinity. An initiation in infinitude was the gift Dickinson offered to the few she admitted to intimacy. Contrary to the usual view that people changed her, it was she who operated on others for the brief periods they could bear it. She created certain people in the same way as she created her poems, many of which function as letters and, in fact, were enclosed in letters as extensions of them. She half-found, half-invented a receptive reader in Susan Dickinson, 'Only Woman in the World', to whom she sent more than twice the number of poems sent to anyone else. In a similar way she half-found, half-invented the man she called 'Master'.

The existence of an alternative audience prompts questions. One is whether certain members of her chosen audience fell short: did Bowles, for example, fail her when he preferred sentimental tosh and when his paper conventionalised the few poems that he published? Did Susan fail her when she advised Dickinson to cut the second stanza of 'Safe in their Alabaster Chambers'? This is a poem about the lifelessly obedient who will lie unrisen, for ever, in their graves. Susan's instinctive move closer to the fire was a humorous response to the chilling subject. Though she failed to see that the wheeling, oblivious universe in the second stanza is integral to this definition of death, Susan responded with eloquence and warmth:

> I am not suited dear Emily with the second verse – It is remarkable as the chain lightening that blinds us hot nights in the Southern sky but . . . it just occurs to me that the first verse is complete in itself . . . You never made a peer for that verse . . . The flowers [Emily sent] . . . look as if they would kiss one – ah, they expect a humming-bird – Thanks for them of course – and not thanks only[,] recognition sister . . .
>
> Susan is tired making <u>bibs</u> for her bird [her son] – her ring-dove – he will paint my cheeks when I am old to pay me –
>
> Sue –

Susan isn't Emily's hummingbird now. She's a mother. It must have disappointed the poet to find Sister's attention straying to her baby ring-dove. And what made Dickinson say that Katie 'betrayed' their love? Was it simply that Kate remarried in 1866, when their friendship seems to have ended? Ten years on she lamented that loss in a poem which admits 'Treason' on her own side: she closes her door to this friend, as to others, unable to speak of her sickness. This is an unsent letter-poem, signed 'Emily', written when Katie was visiting Amherst in 1877:

> I shall not murmur if at last
> The ones I loved below
> Permission have to understand

For what I shunned them so —
Divulging it would rest my Heart
But it would ravage theirs —
Why, Katie, Treason has a Voice —
But mine — dispels — in Tears.

With Susan there were renewals and entrancing affirmations. 'Rare to the Rare —', Emily addressed her in 1869. At forty, custom could not stale this neighbour. 'To see you unfits for staler meetings. I dare not risk an intemperate moment before a Banquet of Bran.' At forty-three or four, her ardour for Sue seems undimmed in a note of three words, quoting Shakespeare's Antony to Cleopatra: 'Egypt — thou knew'st'. She could rely on Sue's reading to call up the fullness of that love:

> Egypt, thou knew'st too well,
> My heart was to thy rudder tied by the strings,
> And thou shouldst tow me after. O'er my spirit
> Thy full supremacy thou knew'st, and that
> Thy beck might from the bidding of the gods
> Command me.

In later years, Emily entered into a different kind of friendship, the result of her circulating manuscripts. From about 1866 Higginson was copying and passing on Dickinson poems to Helen Hunt, who was, at the time, regarded as the foremost woman poet in America. She was the same age as Dickinson and had grown up in Amherst, the Helen Fiske whose mother had died while her daughters were at school. Helen remembered Emily at Amherst Academy, but recalled Vinnie more clearly as a playmate of her younger sister Ann. As a young married woman living in Washington DC, Helen Hunt had avoided calling on the Dickinson sisters when they'd visited their father in 1855. Vinnie had appeared to her merely a 'fat little country lassie'. Then, on a visit to Amherst in 1860, Helen, together with her husband Major Hunt, had attended a reception at the Homestead. Emily told Higginson that she thought Mrs Hunt's verses better than any by a woman bar Elizabeth Barrett Browning and Mrs Lewes (as George Eliot was known).

Mrs Hunt, in turn, admired Dickinson's poems and all the more for what she took to be the propriety of modest retirement. She herself published behind the 'shelter' of her initials in 'the crowded obscurity of print' and she refused to speak in public. Yet even as she abjured publicity, she was not unaware of 'H.H.' as a brand. As with other successful women writers – Mrs Gaskell, Charlotte Brontë, George Eliot and Constance Fenimore Woolson (great-niece of James Fenimore Cooper) – ambition and retirement co-existed. All held off from public women demanding rights and suffrage: Brontë thought Harriet Taylor Mill manifested a heart of leather in her 1851 essay 'The Emancipation of Women'; Helen Hunt satirised American feminist leaders Susan B. Anthony and Elizabeth Cady Stanton in 'Good-by, Leather Stockings!'; while Dickinson 'avoided' the feminist writer Harriet Prescott Spofford. Domestic values drew Helen Hunt and Emily Dickinson to each other. Like an earlier vindicator of women's rights, Mary Wollstonecraft, Helen Hunt stood for the values of home – the domestic affections, nurture, listening, justness – as the right levers to 'move the whole world'.

Some twelve years after Helen was widowed, she married a Mr Jackson of Colorado. Emily tossed off a monosyllable of joy, followed by a three-line verse muttering obscurely about 'doom'. The bride made bold to return the verse for explanation. None was forthcoming, but after a while Dickinson threw out a lasso to Mrs Jackson who, she said, had 'averted' her head. Not a bit, came Helen Jackson's reply; she had merely neglected to write while setting up home in Colorado Springs. Emily was touchy about friends who married, expecting neglect. Helen Jackson made it plain that she expected their friendship to go on as before and pressed her friend to publish – the only creative writer at the time to recognise Dickinson's genius.

When Higginson came face to face with Dickinson for the second and last time, in 1873, he asked her how she coped with lack of occupation, day by day within the same walls. She was astonished and gave him to understand that such a question had never occurred to her. Though by then Higginson had corresponded with her for twelve years and read a good many of her poems, he was unaware that her inward life was so active, and her attention to events of nature so constant, that she felt no lack of occupation. She gardened, kept a flourishing conservatory, made the household bread since her father preferred hers and, then too, she added rather dreamily, 'people must have puddings . . .'.

Her main occupation, of course, was her work, starting before dawn. One poem 'The Birds begun at Four o'clock' celebrates the 'multiplicity' of their music when there's no one to hear: 'The Listener — was not —'. Patently untrue, because the poet, singing at the same hour, is awake and present. Nor was it true that her voice had no audience, her poems ephemeral as birdsong. She ensured that five to six hundred fair copies were entrusted to her friends and, as a further precaution, half of her poems (presumably those she most wished to preserve) were in hand-sewn manuscript booklets tucked away at home, which would sing, she knew, in time to come.

By six o'clock the dawn chorus is over; the 'Band' has gone; the sun rises; day takes over. The poet, the unmentioned witness, is left to balance loss and achievement. This she does with perfect equanimity, closing with a neat full stop:

> The Miracle that introduced
> Forgotten, as fulfilled.

She tells us, generations on, exactly what we want to know: the Miracle of composition overrode public obliteration during her lifetime. Composition was not only an end in itself; it was an 'Extasy':

> Nor was it for applause —
> That I could ascertain —
> But independent Extasy
> Of Universe, and Men —

7

ROMANCING JUDGE LORD

With no warning, Mr Dickinson, aged seventy-two, died on 16 June 1874. He was stressed at the time. As the years passed he had not managed to repay what he had borrowed from the inheritance of his wards who had lived at The Evergreens. This pressed upon him in 1874 when Anna Newman, the youngest, married. Then too his accounts as Treasurer of Amherst College had been in disarray when he resigned in 1872, a repeat of the unhappy situation of his own father, who had then left town. Samuel Dickinson had died far from family and all he held dear. Edward Dickinson too was away from home, serving in the Massachusetts legislature, when his heart stopped.

His last letter from Boston had been written in his dry lawyer's voice:

June 8.74

Dear Family,

    The day is extremely hot – I came down from the House, about 5 o'clock, & found Louisa & Fanny . . . at the 'Tremont House' [hotel] . . . Nothing more to-night.

Yours affy,
E. Dickinson

Crowds came through the gate of the Homestead for the funeral: all the worthies of Amherst, fellow members of the legislature and the senators for Hampshire County and Sunderland. An overflow from the house sat on chairs and sofas on the lawn. The coffin was open and a reporter (probably Bowles, who saw Emily for the first time in twelve years) observed that Mr Dickinson looked 'as self-reliant and unsubdued as in life'. A wreath of white daisies from the Dickinson meadow were the only flowers allowed.

The Revd Mr Jenkins read from the first book of Samuel: 'Samuel died, and all the Israelites were gathered together and lamented him, and buried him in his house at Ramah.' Like the high priest, Mr Dickinson had administered justice and maintained integrity in his position as 'Father to Amherst'. His alarming manner, the minister went on, had concealed a 'hidden gentleness'. It was 'not a gentleness that expended itself in pleasant speeches and manners assumed for effect, but a gentleness that felt others' pains and losses, and exerted efforts for relief'. The Puritan in him, simple, stern, had abjured sentiment, while delicacy concealed choice feelings. Unconventional in his faith, not caring for ceremony and doctrine, Mr Dickinson had been (in his own words) 'melted to tears' at the remembrance of his conversion: 'what we saw and felt of the working of God's spirit among us in 1850'.

The sermon ended with a warning to survivors: 'A great burden which strong shoulders have borne hitherto is rolled upon us . . .'.

Shaken, unprepared, Emily remembered that the day before her father left for Boston she had wanted to spend time with him, and as the afternoon stretched out he had said, 'I would like it to not end.' She still heard his voice at prayers. 'I say unto you,' he would read in such militant accents he would startle her — she who startled others with words of her own. Without him, home seemed 'a House of Snow'. She recalled a scene in April: unseasonal snowstorms had brought birds to the kitchen door one frozen morning. She had spied her father in slippers, on his way to the barn to fetch them grain. Now she saw this protector removed to the 'Palace' of his coffin, to a narrow prison in the 'Marl House'.

Then, on the first anniversary, with grief as cutting as ever, Mrs Dickinson had a stroke that left her paralysed. She would need to be nursed for the rest of her life. A line from the Psalms echoed in Emily's head: 'He giveth to the beast his food and to the young ravens which cry.'

Their mother had only to sigh and Emily heard it, which meant that she no longer shut her door unless Vinnie were there, feeding, washing, combing. Responsible Vinnie, knowing 'no shadow – brave – faithful – punctual' was 'spectacular as Disraeli and sincere as Gladstone'. Emily's hyperboles set domestic affections above politics, even George Washington. If his name came up, she flashed back, 'George Who –?'

Vinnie, she said, was more hurried than Presidential candidates and 'in more distinguished ways, for *they* have only the care of the Union, but Vinnie the Universe –'.

Tenderness was the only God whom Emily was prepared to know, a faith for a household of women. While Vinnie undertook the hands-on care, Emily read to her mother, fanned and encouraged, so that it seemed to her she had hardly said, 'Good morning, Mother' when she heard herself saying, 'Mother, good-night.' As the years passed it was a relief each morning to find that timid face awake on the pillow.

The sisters had sufficed for each other before their father's death. Emily had explained to Mrs Holland what Vinnie meant to her: 'She has no Father and Mother but me and I have no Parents but her.' Now the sisters stood closer than ever. They had long relieved their mother of household care, with the help of an Irishwoman, Margaret (Maggie) Maher. She too called Mrs Dickinson 'Mother'. Warm and wild and noisier than the Dickinsons, 'the North Wind of the family', Maggie alone was in the poet's confidence about the booklets in the bedroom chest of drawers. She agreed to secrete them in her trunk.

By the 1870s, the existence of poems in the Homestead had got about and Miss Emily had begun her long career as 'the myth'. Curiosity grew about the recluse, the kind of talk that would captivate Mabel Todd when she arrived in Amherst. House guests continued to stay: for one their father's sister, Aunt Elizabeth, tall, imposing in royal purple, leaving behind her an atmosphere of court martial. In her forties she had married a tame widower. 'Eagles have the right idea,' she said to her miserable stepdaughter. 'They push the eaglets out of the nest.' Aunt Elizabeth was now Mrs Currier, but called privately 'Aunt Glegg' (after Maggie Tulliver's carping aunt in *The Mill on the Floss*), her bossiness so invasive that visits had to be borne as a joke. Aunt's heels clunked up and down the stairs. There was no stopping her. But no one would detect poems in the servant's room.

In business matters the sisters now leant on their brother, who took over his father's partnership in the law office. He had already taken over his father's post as treasurer, a position commanding all college decisions. Austin Dickinson's appointment in 1872 was not uncontested, but when it came to finance he proved able. He sorted out his father's accounts and landscaped the college grounds. Like Emily, he had botanical taste and expertise.

Another man to rely on was Mr Dickinson's old friend Otis Phillips Lord, a judge in the Massachusetts Supreme Court. Lord had studied law at Amherst just before Emily was born and during the first eighteen months of her life. He had graduated in 1832, a classmate and friend of Cousin Zebina, and Amherst had conferred on him an honorary Doctor of Laws in 1869. He was married to Elizabeth Farley, a high-minded descendant of John Leverett, president of Harvard. They were childless and lived near the witch-house in Salem, the town famous for the witchcraft trials of the 1690s. The Lords from Salem used to stay at the Homestead, and after Mr Dickinson died 'the dear Lords' continued to come. The Judge appears to have come on his own for a week in October 1875 when Emily, far from reclusive, spoke of his visit as being 'with me'.

Since Lord had known Emily all her life he did not hesitate to enquire after her health in a fatherly way. She was dreaming of her father every night (always a different dream) and prone to forget what she was doing during the day, 'wondering where he is'. This absence of mind may have troubled her sister, since it was with Vinnie that Lord raised his concern: '. . . Knowing . . . how unwilling [she is] to disclose any ailment, I fear that she has been more ill, than she has told me. I hope you will tell me particularly about her.' Unsure what her sickness was, he wished Vinnie to report *fully*, though he respected Emily's reticence on the subject.

'Emily never thinks of herself,' he remarked to Vinnie in March 1877. He thought her an angel, like his wife, who had rheumatism and other ills. Mrs Lord died in December 1877, on Emily's forty-seventh birthday.

Over the next few months she turned to the handsome widower – not as a father but as a suitor of sorts. Later, a granddaughter of Dickinson's confidante Mrs Holland suggested that Lord's tenderness had 'long been latent in his feeling for her'. Dickinson expert Christopher Benfey has asserted this possibility more strongly, suggesting the attraction went back to the summer of 1862 when Otis Lord came to Amherst as Commencement speaker.

Eighteen years her senior, his grey hair was shading into white; his expression calm and contained – not a man to exact attention, though his grave and upright bearing subdued others, not only the guilty, as he passed judgement. To Susan he looked forbidding, casting gloom over guests at The Evergreens; stern 'as the Profile of a Tree against a winter sky', Emily ventured to say. He appeared as rigid as Mr Dickinson, but she had a way with elders of this sort, breezing through their barest branches. Her amusing darts disarmed men of law who were accustomed to wither lesser beings; the drafts of her letters to Lord are witty, confident, open (not coded like letters to 'Master') and playfully physical – hardly the way modest women were meant to behave. Gossip had it that Susan had been taken aback to break in on the supposed recluse, the image of white-frocked chastity, in the Judge's arms.

Three people claimed to have heard Sue deplore that embrace: one was Mabel at the start of their friendship in 1881; another was Mrs Halls, an Amherst neighbour; and the last, the Judge's niece Abbie Farley. Emily, the niece is reported to have said, had not 'any idea of morality'. She was bound to take this view for Miss Farley, aged thirty-five, was the Judge's heir. She and her mother, Mrs Lord's sister, were due to inherit jointly $23,000. Together with another niece on the Farley side (due to inherit $10,000), they kept house for the Judge. If he remarried he would have new claims.

'Little hussy', Abbie fumed over a copy of Emily's *Poems* decades later when her own chief heir, Mrs Stockton, questioned her about the celebrated poet Abbie had once known. By then Abbie Farley had become Mrs West, elaborately dressed and married into a leading Salem family. 'Loose morals,' Abbie remembered. 'She was crazy about men. Even tried to get Judge Lord. Insane too.'

'I went there one day, and in the drawing room I found Emily reclining in the arms of a man', Susan reportedly warned the Todds when Vinnie asked them to call. Mabel Todd had had no reason to distort this report. There's a gap here, something unsaid that remains in question. Did Emily's demonstrative ease lead Susan to suspect an improper spark while Mrs Lord had been alive? Was Susan jealous? In succumbing to marriage, one consolation for Sue had been Emily, who had knit herself to her friend and 'Sister'. Yet now, improbably, Emily had someone else: not the figment 'Master' had largely been, but a man in love with her.

To Emily herself Lord's love was 'Improbable'. It would have been unthinkable in Mr Dickinson's lifetime: his carefully protected daughter permitting such licence, and with his old friend. The voice of judgement, 'I SAY UNTO YOU' thundering through the startled air at morning prayers, had cleansed impurities from the minds of Mr Dickinson's listeners. As Emily put it humorously, 'Fumigation ceased when Father died'. Now, four years on, that voice no longer ruled. In her late forties and early fifties she found herself free to partake of the forbidden tree.

Lord, too, appeared to have relinquished his public character. Emily perceived, as she put it, Calvary and May struggling for supremacy. In his courtroom he was 'merciless' against fraud and dishonesty, and did not hide his contempt for legal technicalities that obstructed justice. 'His dynamite was all in his eye', according to colleagues on the bench. He could detect a fallacy at a glance and strip a case of irrelevant matter. A witness rarely left the stand with any fact concealed. To search out 'the secret springs of action' was more demanding, more subtle, he considered, than the mysteries of science: 'he that becomes master of the human mind and human passions has achieved a greater triumph than he who has discovered a planet'. Susan thought him 'a perfect figure-head for the Supreme Court, from his stiff stock to his toes'. His individuality, she said, was 'so bristling, his conviction that he alone was the embodiment of the law, as given on Sinai, so entire, his suspicion of all but himself, so deeply founded on the rock bed of old conservative Whig tenacities, not to say obstinacies' that he could not 'coalesce' with others at The Evergreens. Here was a man disposed to entertain the Dickinsons at table by reciting a hymn beginning 'My thoughts on awful subjects roll / Damnation, and the dead', accompanied by nervous laughter from his listeners.

With Lord, Emily was unafraid to speak up, inviting a glint of humour she called 'the Judge Lord brand'. A smile broke when she teased him with the solemnities of courtroom language. 'Crime', 'confess', 'punish', 'penalty', 'incarcerate' were the words she applied to his supposed trial of her as a wanting lover. 'I confess that I love him,' she has to admit, but cannot pay the 'debt' she owes him. Can her 'involuntary Bankruptcy' be a crime? Will he 'punish' her? 'Incarcerate me in yourself — that will punish me,' she makes bold to suggest. The prospect of this 'rosy penalty' elates her: 'the exultation floods me', she confides, 'I can not find my channel — The Creek turned Sea at thoughts of thee . . .'.

Flashing repartee of this sort exploded into intimacy within months of Mrs Lord's death. That year, 1878, there's immediate talk of consummation. She's expressive about 'hunger'. Restraint, she's aware, fans desire.

Dont you know that you are happiest while I withhold and not confer — dont you know that 'No' is the wildest word we consign to Language?

You do, for you know all things — [top of sheet cut off] . . .

The 'Stile' is God's — My Sweet One — for your great sake — not mine — I will not let you cross — but it is all your's, and when it is right I will lift the Bars, and lay you in the Moss — You showed me the word.

I hope it has no different guise when my fingers make it. It is Anguish I long conceal from you to let you leave me, hungry, but you ask the divine Crust and that would doom the Bread.

Her letter reports to him her nephew's curiosity, reflecting something of the family's astonishment: such a figure of rectitude, such a paragon of the law, to be consorting so unconventionally with his aunt.

'Aunt Emily,' Ned asked, 'does Judge Lord belong to the Church?'

'I think not, Ned, technically.'

'Why I thought he was one of those Boston fellers who thought it the respectable thing to do.'

'I think he does nothing ostensible, Ned.'

'Well, my father says if there were another Judge in the Commonwealth like him, the practice of law would amount to something.'

'I think it probable,' she murmured, recalling (as she put it in her next letter to the Judge), 'I had never tried any case in your presence but my own, and that, with your sweet assistance . . . Dont you know you have taken my will away . . .? Should I have curbed you sooner? "Spare the 'Nay' and spoil the child"? Oh, my too beloved, save me from the idolatry which would crush us both –'.

During 1879 she was following *Scribner's* serialisation of *The Europeans*, a comedy of New England manners by Henry James. What amused her most was the chill rectitude of Mr Wentworth, a replica of Mr Dickinson. 'I fear I must ask with Mr Wentworth, "Where are our moral foundations?"' she joked to Mrs Holland, whose husband edited the magazine. The Hollands now lived in New York, out of touch with what had happened to her.

'Should you ask what had happened here, I should say . . . sweet latent events – too shy to confide –'.

She wasn't shy when she drafted her letters to Lord: 'lift me back, wont you, for only there [in your arms] I ask to be . . .'. He was her 'lovely Salem'; she, his 'Amherst'. Weekly letters, directed to arrive on Mondays by the Judge's habits of punctuality, bonded Salem and Amherst. Emily's 'little devices to live till Monday' – attempts to concentrate on work – gave way to 'the thought of you'. So she said to herself, if not to Salem, in a pencilled scrap which breaks into verse celebrating the nature of love (fleet, indiscreet, wrong and joyful), drawing out a 'glee' lurking in Salem's corners and capable of eluding the scourge of a puritanical religion – shades of her father warning her mother not to look for pleasure in marriage:

> How fleet — how indiscreet an one —
> How always wrong is Love —
> The joyful little Deity
> We are not scourged to serve —

Embraces sealed the nearness of words when, now, at more frequent intervals, Salem – 'sweet Salem' – came to Amherst. As a single man it was no longer proper for Judge Lord to stay at the Homestead; he and Emily met in the parlour. There, they held each other while the air about them fanned the question of marriage.

It was different from her feelings for 'Master'. Lord was emotionally more guarded and this blocked the kind of desire she hoped to promote (like her mother before her): 'How could I long to give who never saw your natures Face —', she tried to say in a draft of a letter she may not have sent. At the same time his physical presence intensified in August and September of 1880, when he practically lived in Amherst.

During this time they may have entered into some kind of private engagement. Softly, her thin hand is offered to him in response to what she calls 'your distant hope'. He leaves saying it had been a 'heavenly hour'. How sweet was his candour, she wrote. It was a new fashion 'in delight' to hear a man call her beautiful. 'I never heard you call anything beautiful before', she scribbled a day or so after. 'It remained with me curiously'. By 'curiously', she meant a dream where she was asked to 'unvail' his posthumous statue. She couldn't bring herself to unveil him, she confessed: 'I said what I had not done in Life I would not in death when your loved eyes could not forgive.' It was important for her to convey that she would not take advantage of this intimacy; he was not to be used as material for poems. This was strictly a private pleasure and part of her pleasure was to release a clarity of statement that reflects a judge's demand for directness. He would have had a lifetime's experience in courtroom questioning – pressing for truth – but he had the sensitivity to refrain from power. He might have been a Master, but wasn't.

Emily Dickinson had led 'Master' and Mr Higginson a merry dance, beckoning then giving them the slip – her superior instants furled in riddles they could not read. Her abjection as the humble little Daisy or the worshipful posture of 'your Scholar' teased these leaders of the literary marketplace. The Judge, with dynamite in his eye when it came to character, would have seen through such dramas. With him, she was honest.

'I have done with guises', she declared at the time the relationship moved forward in 1878. 'I never seemed toward you', she confirmed in the course of 1880.

Was she too frank for her own good? The fear did cross her mind, and it's possible that she edited the surviving drafts or didn't send them. Whether she did or not, her father's friend gave her emotions a 'fair home', replacing the vacancy in what she still called 'my father's house'. And yet he was not like her father. His racy talk, familiar to colleagues on the bench, called out an unfamiliar side to Emily Dickinson.

'I will not wash my arm', she said, ''twill take your touch away –', and again: 'It is strange that I miss you at night so much when I was never with you – but the punctual love invokes you soon as my eyes are shut – and I wake warm with the want sleep had almost filled . . .'.

She speaks like a guilt-free child – childlike in the Romantic sense, untrammelled by what Wordsworth called the prison-house: capitulations to social norms that blight the innocent who comes into the world trailing clouds of glory 'from God who is our home'. To lie in Lord's arms, to evoke his touch in bed at night was as spontaneous, as free of definition, as the way Dorothy Wordsworth lay beside her beloved brother or held his head against her breast.

Wafting through the poems is a woman playing a counter-role: this purified creature has to freeze the life of the 'Ethiop within'. Abandoned to solitude, she retires from existence; puts on purity in her white dress; assumes 'Cobweb attitudes'; and hangs her head in ostensible submission. In this poetic role she enacts the appealing helplessness and self-effacement of nineteenth-century womanhood, but a cutting voice finds the role absurd: 'such was not the posture / Of our immortal mind —'. All the same, the white legend was to linger: as late as 1976, in the Broadway play *The Belle of Amherst*, a 'shy', 'chaste', 'frightened' poet charms the audience with her feminine winsomeness. The playwright called it an 'enterprise of simple beauty'.

The sentiment of this cult invites satire. A giant (sixty-foot) puppet of the Belle of Amherst, in the signature white dress, pops out in the 1999 movie *Being John Malkovich*. Demurely, book in hand, this famous 'Nobody' decries 'Somebodies' who croak about themselves the livelong day. Then, in 2008, 'EDickinsonRepliLuxe', a futuristic tale by Joyce Carol Oates, imagines the mass-marketing of a Dickinson robot half the poet's size. This diminutive Belle in her dimity apron is designed to be a harmless pet, a consolation for wives buried in suburban deadness – so unlike the ardent woman who flung out her lassoes.

After a springtime visit to Amherst in 1882 the Judge conducted a trial in Springfield, as reported daily in the *Republican*. On 29 April he sentenced the accused, Dwight Kidder, to twenty years for the manslaughter of his half-brother Charles. Emily Dickinson wrote to Lord the following day, a Sunday, unsure whether he was still occupied with the case or whether he had returned to Salem. Her letter is again extraordinarily frank in its strange allusiveness and innuendo: she appoints him 'the judge' of their varied moments, and herself the advocate for contentment with the status quo.

30 April 1882

. . . To write to you, not knowing where you are, is an
unfinished pleasure – Sweeter of course than not writing, because
it has a wandering Aim, of which you are the goal – but far from
joyful like yourself, and moments we have known – I have a strong
surmise that moments we have <u>not</u> known are tenderest to you. Of
their afflicting Sweetness, you only are the judge, but the moments
we had, were very good – they were quite contenting . . .

    I am told it is only a pair of Sundays since you went from me. I
feel it many years . . . I have been in your Bosom . . .

    <u>Heaven,</u> a Sunday or two ago . . .

'Impregnable' was a word of the moment. She placed it between them, teasing a legal mind for whom words have precise connotations. 'Could we yield each other to the impregnable chances till we had met once more?' Anticipation might open up fantasy. This was admissible: the space, between meetings, to stage what they will. As Emily concedes that Sweetness she and Mr Lord had *not* known – aware of his more 'afflicting' frustration – his letter arrived from Salem. The following day she continues:

Papa [another private name] has many Closets that Love has never
ransacked. I do – do want you tenderly. The Air is soft as Italy, but
when it touches me, I spurn it with a Sigh, because it is not you . . .
Our life together was long forgiveness on your part toward me. The
trespass of my rustic Love upon your Realms of Ermine, only a
Sovereign could forgive . . . Oh, had I found it sooner! Yet
Tenderness has not a Date – it comes – and overwhelms.

The question of marriage came up more seriously in November–
December 1882, after Mrs Dickinson died. Eyeing Emily's thinness, he
teased her as 'Emily Jumbo' (the famous elephant, Jumbo, in Barnum's
circus had recently appeared near Amherst). She tossed the joke back.

'Sweetest name, but I know a sweeter – Emily Jumbo Lord. Have I your
approval?'

He assumed that she was now freed to live with him. He replied, 'I will
try not to make it unpleasant.'

She was touched that he could invite her into his 'dear Home' with
'loved timidity'. Her answer, as often when she was moved, almost falls
into verse.

'So delicate a diffidence, how beautiful to see! I do not think a Girl
extant has so divine a modesty. You even call me to your Breast with apol-
ogy! Of what must my poor Heart be made?'

His delicacy made her reproach herself. He was the 'tender Priest of
Hope', and his offer needed no further glow. Meanwhile, in the bitter cold
of mid-winter, the love she felt must keep him 'sweetly warm', though she
hoped he'd wear his furs as well. His love for her was 'a treasure I still
keep . . .'. Writing to each other, as was their custom, on a Sunday, she willingly transferred her worship. 'While others go to Church, I go to mine, for
are not you my Church, and have we not a Hymn that no one knows but
us?'

Her 'No' to marriage was never final. She 'lies near' his 'longing'; she
'touches' it, but then wills herself to move away. It would have been natural to hope that her condition would lessen as she grew older but she'd
had a blackout, perhaps a seizure, in April 1881, brought on by the blaze of

a fire in Phoenix Row, with a wind blowing the burning shingles. Afterwards she had lain on her pillow for more than a week, while Vinnie had closed her lips even to Loo and Fanny, who were familiar with 'the cause'. When Emily was able to lift her head she apologised to them for Vinnie's secrecy.

In the end she did not tell Lord why she could not 'bless' their union, only that not to do so 'would be right'. To keep epilepsy the secret it had to be, she must remain at home as long as she lived. But she may have had other considerations as well: the incursions of the spirit are often associated with a particular place and Dickinson's room may have been for her thus hallowed. All that's certain is that she had to control the tie with Lord. The forgiveness she asks for refusing to consummate their union addresses a divine Spirit rather than a leader of men.

Was Lord vital to Dickinson or was he an aftermath to her soaring? Was this a comfort after her father's death, the slow fading of her mother and the premature death of Samuel Bowles, at fifty-two, on 16 January 1878, a month after Mrs Lord died? It's telling that Lord does not enter her poetry. From that point of view he was a latecomer, competent, humorous, honourable and devoted, who offers the woman – not the poet – a new drama. For the first time she experiences a man's touch and re-experiences it at night in her imagination. Lying in the dark, she thinks of Lord's need and goes to meet it with a readiness both like and unlike that of Daisy, an innocent, eager for a momentous experience, yet uneasy at the looming Man of Noon. At forty-seven, forty-eight, forty-nine and into her fifties, she tried out a prospective husband; his desire held up a mirror to a 'want' of her own but she could not forget the red 'Fire rocks' of her 'volcano' that bound her still to 'solitude'. By now, solitude was her habit. In the haunted house of her imagination, a bridegroom would mount her stair at midnight. He's her poetic 'Future'; the consummation she anticipates is posthumous. No ordinary bridegroom could compete with the footfall of the afterlife. All her days she heard it coming.

8

SPLIT IN THE FAMILY

Susan and Emily had remained keen readers of George Eliot. For Emily only one word could do justice to *Middlemarch*: 'glory'. She cast George Eliot as 'the Lane to the Indes. Columbus was looking for'. The great novelist died in December 1880 and Emily watched for her biography with such intentness – 'like a vulture' – that she wrote to a Boston editor, Thomas Niles of Roberts Brothers, to ask when it was due. It was during this watching time that Mabel Todd, an unashamedly ambitious young woman publishing scenes and stories, burst upon Amherst. Her trained voice broke upon the stiff parlours of the New England country town. Her solos soared above the church choir. Mabel's full-bodied sails made straight for the Indies.

To come from Washington, to bear a cultivated air of the capital, may have caused a stir in a quiet provincial town, but this brightness faded out a tough reality: Mabel had no money and, for all her ambition to rise in the world, she had married an unmoneyed man. Her parents had always lived on the verge of indigence. Throughout her childhood, Eben and Mary Loomis could not afford to buy a home of their own, nor could they afford to rent an apartment. Mabel grew up in the cramped space of a boarding-house room – one boarding house after another.

Eben Jenks Loomis had been a farm boy held back by lack of opportunity. He'd craved education and why it had not been available to him at a suitable level remains unknown. The gaps in what Mabel writes about his background suggest some misfortune that she kept under wraps. Eben's father, Nathan Loomis, had been no ordinary farmer; he wrote about agriculture and may have felt obliged to experiment. He was also a mathematician and one of the original (human) computers* of the American Ephemeris and Nautical Almanac† after Congress authorised this in 1849. Eben's sister Collette had been amongst the first women to go to college. So the Loomises valued education, and in the past it seems there had been the means to pursue it.

Eben did manage one or two mathematics classes at Harvard's Lawrence School, but these were external classes designed for practical use, not the theoretical learning reserved for Harvard undergraduates. Then, too, external students had to pay, and Eben couldn't. During that time in Cambridge he heard lectures by Henry Wadsworth Longfellow and Louis Agassiz, celebrities of poetry and science who spoke so closely to him that afterwards he recalled them as his companions. After that, he was employed as a clerk in the Nautical Almanac Office in Washington and there he remained for fifty years, calculating planetary movements and minding the records. He didn't have the education to rise beyond a senior clerkship, though his family called him 'Professor Loomis' and he didn't object. He did feel professorial in his attachment to astronomy; he had a nature that yearned to lift up his eyes to see more than might meet the ordinary eye; he quoted and wrote verses; and had a Whitman-like air of the unworldly seer. He was that kind of American, a seeker and dreamer, and though he once took a walk with Whitman (during Whitman's stay in Washington in the 1860s), Eben was not footloose and not one of the roughs, which is to say that he had a tidy wife.

Mary Alden Wilder Loomis came from a prouder family. Her mother, Grandma Wilder, a widow who lived with her daughter, was wheeled out as a descendant of John Alden, one of the Mayflower pilgrims. Grandma's

* Together with Benjamin Pierce of Harvard. Their work began in Cambridge, Massachusetts.
† A table showing the places of a heavenly body for every day of a given period.

husband had been the Revd John Wilder, the minister in Concord, Massachusetts – home to Emerson, Thoreau, the Alcotts and the less blithe Hawthorne – during the town's Transcendentalist heyday. Grandma Wilder had been friendliest with the Thoreau family and remained on visiting terms with Thoreau's aunts, placid Aunt Jane with a close cap over her white hair and sharp Aunt Maria, whose wide cap was festooned with purple ribbons over a 'front' of dangling curls. The sisters liked to recall how Thoreau had made the most of robust home meals during his experiment in stripping existence to its essence at Walden Pond. Thoreau himself had invited Eben Loomis to join his expedition to the Maine Woods, and he'd held baby Mabel in his arms before handing her over with a relieved groan. Mabel could recall the velvety biscuit the Thoreau sisters put in her hand when the Loomis family visited them in Boston's Bowdoin Square.

The Concord connections fed reminiscent stories on the part of Mary Loomis, who was not always truthful. She was apt to embroider the past: Grandma Wilder, it should be known, had been the belle of society before she married a clergyman, and the line of Mr Loomis could be traced 'straight back . . . to Richard Coeur de Lion'. No mention of the unmarked progenitor, one Joseph Loomis, who arrived in Boston in 1638. It was Mrs Loomis rather than her husband who contrived an appearance of gentility. Their only child, Mabel, was beautifully dressed, for Mrs Loomis was skilled with her needle, and so winning was this child that her parents could deny her nothing. They struggled to save and occupied meagre rooms so that Mabel might have three winters at Miss Lipscomb's school in Georgetown, where girls were modelled as sprightly, mannered Southern ladies while they took in a curriculum of astronomy, chemistry and geometry.

The Loomises then scrimped to send their daughter to the Boston Conservatory of Music. Grandma Wilder, who accompanied Mabel as chaperone, introduced her to another Concord figure, Louisa May Alcott. Mabel was astonished by Alcott's humorous admission that she had never had a lover. Pathetic, Mabel thought; from the age of fifteen she'd found it easy enough to attract admirers, with her soft, slightly projecting lower lip and arched upper lip so that her mouth lay appealingly open. Seven years after the publication of *Little Women*, Mabel would have been alert to Alcott's fame but the novel was not for her. She had only contempt for domestic women and no intention of being 'little' or unnoticed; not for her the hidden life of goodness, appealing to women of the preceding generation who shared George Eliot's faith that half the good in the world is done by those who lie in unvisited tombs. Henry James's cousin Minny Temple, writing her selfless letters to James in 1869–70, was another devotee of George Eliot. Neither Minny Temple (in her twenties) nor Emily Dickinson (in her forties) was 'little' of course – James recognised in Minny a '*grande nature*', great enough to be his model for an American girl who will 'affront her destiny', while Dickinson saw herself as 'Queen' – yet neither expected to advance onto the platform of public action in the manner of New Women of the next generation.

In 1874 Mabel, at eighteen, was taking shape on the cusp of a new era when women began to emerge from domestic seclusion into politics or the workplace or, in her case, performance. Propriety dictated that it had to be a ladylike performance. The theatre, her natural arena, would not have entered her mind. To play or sing in drawing rooms, excelling beyond the range of an ordinary Miss, was her first ambition.

At the Conservatory, Mabel lamented when her parents could not pay for courses in harmony and theory required for a diploma. Later she wrote a story about a singing girl whose parents can't afford the 'extras' girls of less talent enjoy but whose private diligence wins out. Her voice grows 'stronger and clearer, filling every corner . . . with bird-like music'. Conscious of 'repressed power', Mabel's heroine longs for 'an opportunity to exercise it'. When the opportunity comes, 'the audience almost held its breath, until with a last cadenza of thrilling purity, she ceased in a tumult of applause which speedily became an ovation'.

Though Mabel left the Conservatory after two winters, she emerged with a trained voice and sufficient brilliance in playing the piano (she could play by ear) to stand out in social gatherings. Back in Washington, she was co-opted by a society hostess to 'receive', a role she performed with verve.

Predictable as Mabel's narratives were (the incidents in her journal build towards conquest or applause) she did have the sensibility to look up to her

Portrait of the Dickinson children by Otis A. Bullard (1840). *Left to right:* Emily (aged nine), Austin, Lavinia.

Top left: Edward Dickinson. Her father's heart was 'pure and terrible', Emily Dickinson said.

Top right: Mrs Dickinson, née Emily Norcross, had to suppress her youthful need for expressiveness. 'I have never exercised that freedom which I presume you have desired me to,' she put it to Edward Dickinson before their marriage.

Dickinson family home (1840–55) in North Pleasant Street, Amherst.

Daguerreotype of Emily Dickinson at the age of sixteen. Her sister thought hers a 'startling' face. Her brother said that she 'saw things directly and just as they were'. The 'only kangaroo' amongst beauties, Dickinson declared herself.

Mary Lyon, founder of South Hadley Female Seminary, the first college for women. Emily Dickinson was there 1847–8. The date coincides with the declaration of women's rights at Seneca Falls, but she found herself beset with coercive fundamentalism.

Professor Edward Hitchcock was an early supporter of Miss Lyon and women's education. He was also the author of Emily Dickinson's geology textbook, a source for her volcanic images.

Broodingly handsome Austin Dickinson, the most eligible bachelor in town.

Thoughts of men turned Susan Gilbert to 'stone', so her friend Emily
perceived, yet she wanted Sue to be her 'Sister'. Sue looks gravely uneasy in
this wedding photograph (1856). '. . . Bridalled — Shrouded — in a Day',
Emily came to see marriage from a woman's point of view.

The Dickinson Homestead on Main Street, Amherst. *Below*: The Evergreens, next door.

Eminent Boston physician James Jackson, whom Emily Dickinson consulted at the age of twenty in 1851.

Cousin Zebina Montague (front row, second from right) along with his friend Otis Lord (front row, far right), at an 1852 reunion of the Amherst College class of 1832.

Her conservatory.

A replica of the poet's writing table (18 inches square) in her bedroom.

Beautiful Lavinia Dickinson in the 1860s, abandoned by the unstable man she'd loved with demonstrative ardour.

father: his reading, his preference for poetry. All the same, she fell in with her mother's wish that she better herself. The obvious route was to marry well, and here Mabel met an obstacle to her sense of destiny. Pretty, well-dressed and accomplished, she appeared everything potential suitors could desire when they encountered her in Boston or at seaside resorts where she, her mother and Grandma Wilder shared one room. At Casco Bay in Maine men were happy to dance and flirt with her, but no sooner did they detect poverty than the most princely amongst them melted into the distance.

One rainy June day in 1877 when she met her father at the Almanac Office he introduced her to a young colleague by the name of David Todd. He saw a devoted daughter in an old blue raincoat, clasping her father's arm. When she smiled her mouth curled to one side. Mabel was away over the summer and when she returned in November she and Mr Todd met again at the home of the astronomer Simon Newcomb, on the north-east corner of N and 11th street, where Todd lodged. She noticed that he had nice teeth, even though the set of his mouth was too straight a line.

It was a relief to have a genuine suitor, even if he had no money. Her parents were less taken with Todd – her father was disturbingly silent – but Mabel persuaded them this was her man. During her absence, in August 1877, Mars came close to Earth and it had been Todd who recognised that a point of light near the red planet was an unknown satellite. When Mabel met Todd again he was in the afterglow of this discovery, and appointed over her father to a position as professional astronomer. He had a bent for mechanical gadgetry – Newcomb called it 'celestial mechanics' – and planned to develop recent advances in photography to record the movements of the stars, especially the eclipse of the sun. He had recently rejected another opportunity that might have suited him better: his contemporary, Thomas Alva Edison, an employee at Western Union in Newark, New Jersey, was trying out his early electrical experiments and Todd might have joined his team of young assistants, but he could not resist the world's most advanced telescope at the Naval Observatory in Washington.

Then, too, he was not a team man. At college he had not joined a fraternity. His lack of social life may be explained by the fact that he was up at night, observing the stars, and slept during the day, but as an excuse it rings less true than a private disturbance: the break-up of his home as a result of his mother's mental illness. He related to other men only as mentors and preferred the company of women.

David Todd was a short man who appealed to women. They sensed how much he liked them in every way, most of all physically. When he scented readiness, he could bring it on. It was his way to take on well-off, married women, those who were bored with their husbands yet had no intention of leaving them. Such women could be relied on to make no claims. With Todd it was not a matter of discrimination – he had a taste for what Mabel would later call 'low' women – but he took care to preserve his respectability. For this reason marriage was the best cover.

Some hint of Todd's promiscuity may have been what worried the Loomis parents, and made them resist him in unspoken ways that Mabel meant to withstand. Although she had flirted a lot, she believed in the ideal of girlish purity. Her fiancé's expertise awakened her senses and she surrendered to him before their wedding. Given the mores of her society and background, this had to be an act of trust on Mabel's part. In their engagement photograph she looks like a trusting, furry little dog with doggy brown eyes. What reassured her was the ambitious core to David Todd, and his assent to her sense of destiny.

She expressed 'a strong intuition' that her life would be 'full of romance and uncommon adventure . . . There are capacities in me, I know, which I've not yet begun to feel . . . I shall yet *do* something which will be heard of – that I know.' It meant she would never give herself to domestic trivia – a bold declaration at the time and for almost a century to come. Here David Todd excelled: he encouraged plans for her own significant future.

What he revealed of his sexual history came as a shock, so much so that David scissored out a good many entries in his diary for 1878. Uncomfortable rumours led him to hasten the date of the wedding. As a bachelor he may have been less careful than he became. There were three daughters in the house where he lodged and as a single man he'd been well placed to make up to one or other before Mabel caught his fancy; it would explain why their father, the influential Newcomb, did not offer David a permanent post – why, we might ask, did David move to a low-grade post in Amherst when he had a patron in the capital?

Mabel didn't enlighten her parents but confided to her journal, in unusually muted tones, her hope that David would turn faithful. She intended to 'purify' him with her love. Voicing her disgust with loveless sex, she gave him a biography of Madame de Pompadour. So, when David renewed his philandering after their marriage, she might have left him had she not found herself pregnant. She had been determined to prevent this and her account of her failure to do so (in her journal and a 'Life of Millicent') shows her flair for writing about sex with ease and finesse.

When they conceived Millicent (named after the British suffragist, Millicent Fawcett), 'it was not at all from uncontrollable passion', but to prove a theory of contraception. Mabel expected to be fertile only 'at the climax moment of my sensation – that once passed, I believed the womb would close, & no fluid could reach the fruitful point'. A parallel theory was that the womb closed after menstruation, so that on the eighth day of her cycle a woman would be safe. Accordingly, on 15 May 1879 the Todds took themselves upstairs after breakfast to test these theories, with Mabel, as she records, receiving 'the precious fluid at least six or eight moments after my highest point of enjoyment had passed, and when I was perfectly cool and satisfied, getting up immediately, thereafter, and having it all apparently escape'.

So firmly did she hold to these misguided ideas of contraception that she refused to recognise her pregnancy until the fifth month, when she could no longer ignore her thickened waist. During these first months she tried various forms of abortion: vaginal suppositories of belladonna and morphine, jumps and prolonged immersions in boiling baths, all the while telling herself and her doctors that menstruation had stopped for other reasons. The doctors accepted her version, against all medical indications. (One physician of fifty years' experience, her uncle Dyer Loomis, responded to her complaints of nausea by prescribing quinine for a supposed residue of malaria in her system.) Her persuasiveness with these doctors is characteristic of the power she could exercise over others: it's the power of conviction conveyed with an irresistible combination of eloquence, tact and the lift of her head and breast as she sailed confidently into consulting rooms.

As well as their child, there were three other reasons to remain with her husband. First and foremost is the traditional reason of dependence. Mabel had nothing to live on: she did love her parents and, like women before her, would not have wished to become a burden. She was proud enough to keep David's affairs from them. Then, too, David convinced her that he was committed to their compact to promote her professional future along with his. At the same time, he pressed home his skill as a lover who was also her husband, sealed by letters signed 'l/h' ['lover/husband']. Was there a trial of wills in a scene where David drew Mabel towards his own practice, a reverse of the scene in *The Golden Bowl* in which the wife of an adulterous husband resists his embrace? This wife sees that if she does not resist 'she should somehow give up everything for ever'. Every throb of her being prompts her to give way but, unlike Mabel, she does hold out and achieves 'the feat of not losing sight of what she wanted' – that is, fidelity.

A contrasting scene took place when the Todds were alone in their two rented rooms at Amherst House. At night he undressed her on the Turkey rug before the fire, then wrapped her up to keep warm while he put hot bricks in the bed. In the morning there was baby talk and play as David spread her clothes around the fire and then brought her grapes, figs and apples to eat in bed. Their child never interrupted these pleasures: it was convenient to leave her behind in Washington with her doting grandparents.

So it was that Mabel succumbed in the face of infidelity, a signal of acquiescence that was to have consequences both for Mabel and for those whose lives she was to change, because acquiescence cut her off from her upbringing and innocence. Where the Jamesian wife eats of the tree of knowledge and is not corrupted, Mabel Todd ate of the tree of knowledge and contrived not to find the fruit bitter.

'At first I used to suffer', she would recall eleven years on, having accustomed herself to her husband's habit 'of falling immensely in love with someone else, & having a very piquant time out of it'. She had to accommodate a husband who remained 'absolutely blind to matters of morality'.

David Todd's infidelity was a blow she concealed, even in her journal, for a long time.

The faithful of Amherst would have welcomed David Todd's direct descent from Jonathan Edwards who, as a minister in Northampton, had led a Puritan revival in the 1740s. New England had reeled from his sermon on 'Sinners in the Hands of an Angry God'.

Cutting a slight figure and unassuming in manner, Todd grew a beard to frame his face and, soon after his arrival in Amherst, began to cultivate the jutting ends of his moustache and curl them down towards his lips. He encouraged his wife to flirt; it diverted him, and provided tacit support for his conquests. But while Todd assumed they were two of a kind, Mabel continued to crave fidelity. This was the initial appeal of Austin Dickinson. When they met, she looked into his blue eyes and saw a man 'who could be forever trusted'.

As a portionless girl, it had pained Mabel to see admirers back off at fashionable resorts; now that she was safely married, men vied to waltz her around Washington ballrooms when she paid her parents a two-month visit in the spring of 1882. Her slanted smiles and light curves warmed their pulses, while her manners assured them she was a lady. The artistic novelty of her clothes invited admiration: a white camel-hair dress with satin shoulder panels and cuffs on which she had painted a design of sweet-peas. 'I have simply felt as if I could attract any man to any amount', she exults in her journal. Disempowered by her husband's susceptibilities to other women, she felt 'bottled up' and restless until she retrieved her power in what seemed to her an 'innocent' way. She was too ambitious not to see the limitations of ballroom conquests: 'feverish like a caged eagle', she sighed 'for more worlds to conquer'.

Her two-year-old daughter Millicent accompanied her return to Amherst in June. To Mabel's disappointment, the child was not pretty. Millicent's mouth was a straight line, unlike her mother's charmingly curled lips. When Millicent smiled her lips remained closed over her teeth. All the way to Amherst, Mabel prepared Millicent to meet the youngest child at The Evergreens, Gilbert (Gib) Dickinson, aged seven. Excited at the prospect of a friend so much older than herself, Millicent could not stop talking about 'Gildud'. But when the two were introduced Millicent was struck dumb. Mabel would have liked to see female wiles: was Millicent coy? But the child's huge black eyes were hesitant. She was silent in company, waiting to judge whom to trust. Mabel found reserve strange; it was not her way to hang back. Millicent would have to be taught a more pleasing vivacity. After another speechless encounter with 'Gildud', Millicent began to cry. How could she disappoint this beautiful Mamma? Missing 'Muggler', her grandmother, Millicent clung and fell ill. Mabel, impatient to take up an invitation to stay with the Dickinsons during the Commencement festivities, hired a nurse.

'I have not the quality of motherhood sufficiently developed,' she excused herself. 'I do not in general care for children.'

Released, she shot off to The Evergreens. Whenever there, she saw a house and way of life that was everything she might have wished for herself, had she made a better marriage. As an orphan without funds, Susan Gilbert had once been in a weak position but had married a gentleman who could bestow on a wife all the advantages of his family. Sue had flourished. She grew prize flowers, turned out elegant feasts, invited out-of-town thinkers to The Evergreens and was rearing three children: Ned (Edward), nearing twenty-one; Mattie (Martha), aged fifteen; and little Gib. Sue continually praised Mabel as a model to Ned and Mattie, who were soon running over to see Mabel every day. Mattie was attached enough to spend the night once or twice a week and Ned undertook to improve Mabel's waltz in the latest style. Whenever she came to The Evergreens there was a whirl with Ned in the hall while Mattie played the piano. Though still a boy, he was graceful in his attentions to his sister and mother, and extended these graces to Mabel who was charmed to find a 'knight errant' in the Dickinson family. Triumphantly, her journal records his declarations and her replies.

Ned told Mabel she had his 'every thought'. It made him restless, inattentive in class. After his family went to bed he would go downstairs to the library and commune with Mabel's photograph, as he confessed to her in the direct manner of the Dickinsons.

'Oh! Mrs Todd, I'm afraid I love you, and what shall I do?'

'I'm very fond of you,' Mabel assured him.

'Ah, what you are kind enough to call your affection for me is nothing for you to give; but I love you as you love your husband.'

'I don't know but I ought to be stern and disagreeable,' Mabel offered. 'To cure you.'

'You could not cure me.'

Accustomed to flirtation, Mabel was a little taken aback by Ned's emotion, all the more so because he was so innocent. Since he meant no harm, he thought love could not be wrong.

Once, dressed in velvet pantaloons and riding boots, Ned was visiting Mabel when Mattie's red hat appeared at the window. Mabel dashed outside to head off Mattie , so that Ned might slip away.

Susan, meanwhile, went on thinking it a fine thing for her son to have (as Mabel put it to herself) 'a brilliant & accomplished married lady for his friend'. She did feel some unease over Susan's blindness. It would take years for Ned to get over this, Mabel realised, and she was honest enough to admit to herself, 'I am vain & selfish enough to be glad.'

Tiring a little of Ned's needs, Mabel cast her eye on the Squire, a more challenging figure. When Mabel glanced at Austin Dickinson she saw his superiority. Tall, sour, contemptuous, he felt no need to prove himself. Mabel's history had sharpened her sensitivity to social codes and hierarchies. As much as the Dickinsons were drawn to Mabel, she was entranced by them: the uprightness of their ties and intensities; their family pride; their challenging, interrogative tones; the rhetorical questions they put to themselves as they trod the paths of introspection; their strength of will — flaunted, not kept like her own under wraps; their witty sarcasms; their fine horses and carriages; and the narrative paintings Austin had selected for his walls.

Susan had come into all of this. Since Susan had no money of her own and her father had been bankrupt, Mabel fancied a simplified scenario: Susan, she assumed, had lifted herself from low origins to the top of Amherst society. Every time Susan's rise crossed her mind her origins sank lower in Mabel's fancy until she came to believe that Mr Gilbert had been a despicable stable-keeper. Mabel both admired and envied Susan's rise. Her welcome into the Dickinson family had been secured by her friendship with Austin's extraordinary sister, and this was still alive. Mabel could sense it in the way Sue spoke, the exhilaration of her bond with the unknown poet. When Susan exhibited some of the gems amongst her collection of poems Mabel was quick to value what Susan had been privileged to see in all its rarity, and this privilege put Susan on a different plane from the society women Mabel had imitated and courted. Her wish for social acceptance found in the Dickinson family a surprisingly unobstructed and fertile place.

Here Mabel's 'presentiment' put down its roots. A fancy became a possibility, then intention, to seed herself in Susan's place. It was not long before an alien plant reared against the pale New England sky. One of the tendrils it put out curled around the heart of Sue's grown-up son. Physically, it was a weak heart, having to withstand the stress of seizures. One took place on 24 May 1882 just before Ned turned twenty-one. His mother cheered him with a party, much to his father's annoyance. Austin frowned on the disruption. He loathed jollities. Ned, turning away from his father's down-turned mouth, took Mabel riding.

Sue then invited the Todds to join the Dickinsons in the country during their summer vacation in Shutesbury. On 26 July, at five in the morning, Austin drove Mabel and Millicent in his carriage, leaning over to converse above the child who sat speechless between them. At Shutesbury Susan organised a picnic for young 'philosophers'. The scene recomposed in a studio photograph shows Mabel as a figurine shepherdess in white with bunched panniers, a tucked bodice buttoned to a round collar and sleeves to her elbows. An enormous white hat shadows her face. Susan sits at the centre of her party, her dark hair drawn back, rounded, maternal. Her arms are folded around Gib with his angel face and fair locks. Her face, in profile, is turned towards her children. On her left is Mattie, fresh-faced in a round hat with a fan on her lap, while Ned lies on the ground at her feet. Both have racquets. David Todd is natty in a straw boater pulled over his eyes.

At another of Sue's picnics, Mabel and Austin, watching the sun set, drew close until, for a second, she brushed against him. In late August, the obliging Mabel sang in The Evergreens' drawing room. The family sat rapt, even 'the Cynic Austin' (as Emily called him). On the evening of 8 September he sat with Mabel on the loggia until late. It was a small but significant step to acknowledge their feelings on 11 September as they lingered in the rain, on the glistening sidewalk outside the gate.

In November, while David Todd was away at the Lick Observatory in California – he was recording the Transit of Venus and sporting with the wife of a colleague – Mabel was in and out of The Evergreens, almost one of the family. Susan kept a bed made up for her and Mattie, turning sixteen, had piano lessons with Mabel, who exulted in a letter to David that the Dickinsons had 'thrown open to me their home, their horses, & their hearts with a truly touching and magnificent generosity'.

As quietly as she had lived, Mrs Dickinson died next door and Mabel attended the funeral at the invitation of Austin and Lavinia (Emily did not appear). Her participation in their loss brought her closer to Austin. Touching hands and looking deep into the other's eyes, they would mark that November as their private anniversary.

Intensity was sharpened by a degree of danger. So far, her husband's partiality for Mabel had pleased Susan. After the funeral, when the Revd Mr Jenkins teased Austin for his alacrity in seeing Mabel home, Sue said that she was only thankful there was someone Austin actually liked. Romance did not occur to her, still less the rivalry building up between father and son. When Ned took Mabel for a row on Freshman River, Austin brought out his carriage to escort her home. And when Ned took Mabel to hear a preacher in Northampton on a Sunday night, 19 November, Austin went after them.

'Why should I!' Austin put it to himself. 'And why shouldn't I!' He often posed questions in this exclamatory way. 'Where is the wrong in preferring sunshine to shadow!'

He had no plan to bed Mabel. Austin's desires were contained by moral refinement. Mabel found herself treated with 'the most delicate courtesy'. The Dickinsons were respectful to women and the family habit was lifelong commitment. When Austin had crossed his 'Rubicon' the previous September he switched to an unknown narrative, one he would have to invent as it went along (in somewhat the way his sister invented a secret narrative). Austin's new drama would depend on the character of his leading lady, especially her sexual character.

Mabel responded to men with alacrity. It was apparent in the way she moved and had her being, and it was part of her charm that her alacrity was graceful, never gross. Millicent's conception had proved to Mabel that her fertility peaked on about the eighth day of her menstrual cycle – that is, uncommonly early – so that she had no fear of pregnancy if love-making took place during the final ten days of the cycle. David Todd called this her 'auspicious' period and planned his travels around it. For all the sexual confidence she exuded, Mabel had not slept with any man besides her husband. This together with Austin's purely romantic intentions towards Mabel would have permitted him to assure himself that nothing improper was on the agenda. He believed that God alone could have brought on this passion stirring behind the disapproving curve of his mouth.

As his father's son he continued to quell laughter. One evening, when Judge Lord was a dinner guest and Austin in bed with a cold, Vinnie convulsed the party with her imitation of the church choir at its grimmest, singing 'Broad is the road which leads to death'. Austin rang his bell and sent along a message to remember, please, this was Sunday!

Neither the austere Austin nor his reclusive sister in her neat, white dress with practical pockets would have appeared likely to invite passion in the late 1870s and early 1880s. Emily, aged fifty-two, in the arms of her father's friend in the Homestead parlour; Austin, aged fifty-three, reaching out to Mabel's warm, waiting hand as they trod past their proper destination, the gate of The Evergreens: neither scene could have been conceivable during their father's rule.

Austin's secret bond with Mabel was similar to Emily's earlier idea of a 'Wife without the Sign'. A wife without the sign is precisely how Mabel came to see her relation to Austin Dickinson, but in its first phase, from September 1882 until early December 1883, any label would be misleading. Legally, Austin's response to Mabel and hers to him could not be construed as active adultery, however intense their emotions. The correspondence of

Austin and Mabel, like Emily's letters to 'Master', avoids names. Not for nothing are these members of a legal family. Where their father was wholly cautious, Emily and Austin cultivated a blend of caution and abandon. Emily, in her epistolary character, sleeps with 'Plantagenet' who is (or is soon to be) king. Austin becomes 'my King' to Mabel. These outbreaks of sister and brother seem linked in some way with the Dickinson dream of royal descent. To follow Austin's shift from romance to adultery, it's necessary to go back to the year their father died.

In November 1874, five months after Mr Dickinson died, Austin and Susan conceived Gib. Susan was almost forty-four. The long gaps between their three children suggest her continued reluctance to give birth – eight years had gone by since the second child, Mattie, was born. At some point in that year Emily sent Sue a number of consoling notes, without saying why Sue needed solace, but pregnancy would have upset her. That autumn and winter of 1874–5, Austin's sisters first saw he had become a vacant shell. Sue herself could not cure her husband's hollowness, yet his heart did fill towards the child born to grieving middle age. Everyone adored Gib. 'Our' child, Emily said, for he consoled them all. She rejoiced in what she called his 'soar'. He was the child she might have had, 'panting with secrets', wordplay, repartee. She loved his retorts when Aunt Vinnie questioned him about her cat.

'Weren't you chasing Pussy?'

'No – she was chasing herself.'

'But wasn't she running pretty fast?'

'Well, some slow and some fast,' said Gib beguilingly.

'Pussy's Nemesis quailed,' Emily reported to Susan. 'Your Urchin is more antique in wiles than the Egyptian Sphinx.'

Aunt Emily had red flowers in bloom. Gib raised his hat and asked if he might smell them.

'Yes, and pick them too,' she said.

When he declined to pick, it seemed a sign of the blood royal: 'Tudor was not a Beggar'. Her fancy ignores the realities of Tudor greed: the stinginess of Henry VII and the acquisitiveness of Henry VIII. So long as the child was royal.

When Gib was eight, rows between his parents rent The Evergreens. They began in December 1882, when Ned told his mother what was going on between his father and Mabel Todd. She was a flirt, Ned said. Sue's coldness surprised Mabel when she visited on the evening of 5 December, yet the following day Sue accompanied Mabel to observe the Transit of Venus through the telescope at the college observatory. No one in the party could see: Venus was obscured by clouds. Meanwhile, Mabel turned up the volume to Austin.

'Oh I love you *thrillingly*,' she wrote in secret, 'I give you a kiss such as we know at this moment.' It would be 'easy' to prove her love if he were with her.

'It was no fault of yours or of mine that I could not take this in at first,' Austin excused his caution. 'My experience of life was too firm & encrusted to permit it. It contradicts everything, revolutionizes everything.' At this moment Mabel's declaration arrived: 'Great Heavens, my darling, I am transported by it, almost overpowered. We love.'

Face to face once more during a stolen meeting on 11 December, Mabel said it was 'wicked' to have to postpone their bliss. 'What do you suppose I am dreaming! I want you . . .'.

This Monday message followed a weekend of renewed friendship with the Dickinson women: on the Saturday Mattie had stayed overnight with Mabel at her boarding house, after which Mabel had spent all of Sunday with Sue at The Evergreens and then slept the night there.

She was in Washington again for Christmas and came back to Amherst on 6 January 1883. David Todd, returning from California, intercepted her train. The following day, the Todds called at The Evergreens, expecting their usual welcome. Austin was away and Susan Dickinson alone rose to greet them, her politeness so frozen it withered Mabel even as civilities flowed.

'The evening was too horribly chilling', Mabel complained to Austin the following day. His wife had been 'cruel' and 'pitiless'. She'd wept 'the bitterest tears' into her pillow. 'What new thing has occurred to make everything so dreadful?'

The chill was so pointed that Mabel was obliged to ask the reason. There followed a 'frank' talk on 13 January. Mabel would have reassured Susan, not without truth, that she loved her own husband. She commended Sue's manners. Both managed to speak civilly to each other.

For a short while Mabel's protestations of innocence soothed the situation. On Saturday 20 January Sue and Mattie called on Mabel and they all went for a sleigh ride in the afternoon. That evening Mabel sang once more at The Evergreens. Mabel was convincing because she believed in her script from the moment it took shape in her mind. So she disarmed Susan, though not completely, since Susan, aided by her daughter, kept her eyes open. Their vigilance daunted the lovers who could no longer meet with any safety.

In a secret letter to Austin, delivered by Vinnie, Mabel confessed 'an immeasurable feeling of wrath' when she thought of Ned, 'the one person to whom it was all due in the first place'. As frustration grew, blame spread from Ned to his mother and sister, whom Austin and Mabel called privately 'the Powers'. Their enemy was plural, with Susan cast as the 'leading Power', fortified by Ned and Mattie.

Ned and Mattie were drawn into the struggle between their parents. They stood by their mother as their father withdrew his love. Austin made it a test of allegiance; as he saw it, Ned and Mattie failed to choose him. Gib, who was not expected to understand the issues, was exempt from this test. Turning from his elder two, Austin loved his youngest the more; he told himself that Gib alone cared for him.

While Ned's revelation was still new, Austin justified his love in heaven-sent terms. Their love, he told Mabel, was a holy thing, a holy of holies they agreed. Mabel played back this script. Austin's language is banal compared with his sister's, but Mabel's ready fervour built up this drama.

'I trust you as I trust God,' she told Austin in March 1883. This was a time of trial for all concerned. Whenever Mabel ventured out she found Sue and Mattie in her path, so watchful there was no evading their surveillance. Austin smuggled a message to Mabel: 'I am famished for you.' Anxious and impatient, Mabel felt a dual deprivation because she was losing the bond with Sue, whom Mabel admitted to Austin she still loved.

'I do – she stimulates me intellectually more than any other woman I ever knew. She is fascinating to me. I would do *any thing* to make her like me again. She has such pretty feminine hands and wrists, and she had some very pretty little quaint bracelets last night. I could have kissed them at any moment.'

What fascinated Mabel above all was Susan's friendship with the recluse. Mabel's repeated insistence that the poet was her 'friend' has the sound of a rival claim. She was accustomed to have her way, and as her annoyance swelled rivalry displaced regard. This adversarial role of 'the Powers', with three members of the family campaigning against the godly pair, allowed Mabel to cast herself as victim. In fact, Susan was now in a weaker position as an unwanted wife than as a dependent girl thirty years before.

Back in the 1850s, Vinnie had joined forces with Emily in persuading Susan Gilbert to marry Austin. Now, Austin expected their assistance in deceiving Susan. What Emily thought of this remains to be seen. Vinnie, meanwhile, provided the necessary cover. She permitted Mabel's love letters to be addressed to her and delivered through the sisters' post office box (number 207), to which no one but themselves and their brother had access. Usually Austin collected the mail and delivered it to his sisters, but if Austin was away or unavailable Vinnie was responsible for finding the letters from Mabel and passing them on. Vinnie also undertook to pass on letters in the reverse direction, from Austin to Mabel. He uttered the same fervid love-calls as to Susan in the 1850s and Mabel played them back with unflagging eloquence.

Mabel befriended the go-between. To Vinnie, in need of company, the warmth of these overtures was irresistible. From Mabel's point of view, friendship with Vinnie was vital. If Mrs Todd, as Vinnie's particular friend, was often at the Homestead, and Austin continued to pay his brotherly calls, no one could object if these legitimate visits happened to coincide. So it was that on Valentine's Day 1883 the lovers converged before the fire in the dining room (warmer than the parlour and used as a sitting room in winter). Possibly Mabel's presence was observed because three days later, when Mabel appeared at The Evergreens, Susan's 'utter coldness (combined with unimpeachable courtesy)' reasserted itself. The atmosphere was so icy that Mabel thought several times she would have to leave.

Austin now had to face Susan's protest. She interrupted another tryst at the other house (as the Homestead was often called) on 27 February, when she sent for Austin to escort her to a college event. 'After which, a night of it', Austin noted in his diary. Upholding Susan was the sanctity of the marriage vows and Austin, who shared her faith, would have found it hard, in principle, to disagree. Trained to introspection, they were accustomed to question secret sin. Susan was versed in the classics of moral debate and Austin was temperamentally a moral being like his father. This was the challenge Mabel had to confront in her smuggled letters.

After the first chill, on 15 December 1882 her voice took on a strange timbre, as though she were reporting an impersonal fact: 'It is months ago now that you heard some one say she had come to stay.'

'I have come to stay', Mabel repeated after the freeze, on 17 January 1883, and a third time on 28 January: 'As I told you long ago – I have come to stay.'

It was as simple as that: she was immovable, like a rock in restless waters.

'I came to stay,' she reminded him yet again in April.

There was no going back to his wife. If Austin did soften to Susan's protests or acts of kindness, he could find himself in Mabel's power. He would go all his days in the shadow of their secret: their deep looks into the other's eyes, the shady drives along back roads, the kisses and pressures of the hand they had exchanged. There was no overt threat. Mabel's commitment shone with promise. All the same, there was a claim. Austin Dickinson was too astute a lawyer not to recognise his danger.

Bad as this was for Susan, she had one effective weapon: she cut Mabel socially. In a small community this could not go unnoticed, and Mabel was quick to feel the hurt. Not only personally, for Mabel was wary of damage to a lady's reputation: once disfigured it would be hard, if not impossible, to retrieve. To prevent public notice of Susan's snub Mabel was forced to leave town. In mid-March 1883 she retreated to Washington.

From there she sent Susan a box of arbutus in mid-April. No thanks came. Instead, Susan rebuffed her by sending money to pay for Mattie's past piano lessons.

Mabel did not allow her chagrin to show. 'I am sorry that you have given money for what was only a pleasure to me,' she replied. 'You have done for me that which no number of lessons could repay, & I hoped you would allow me the satisfaction of this slight return.'

To Austin alone Mabel showed her mettle: 'This week will not last forever, not this month, nor this year. I came to stay; and sometimes you will look back upon all these days of pain with exultant, triumphant happiness in their entire banishment from your life.' In the meantime, he must compel his family to keep up a façade of outward courtesies. 'I should like to have [the members of your family] call, at least with an appearance of cordiality. I *think* they will do this. But I am very anxious to have nothing occur to cause an open ceasing of all civility. That I could not bear.'

Susan must have refused, since Mabel stayed away from Amherst for six months. Not for a second did Mabel waver; her letters urged Austin to defy his family for the sake of happiness to come. What he had to endure in the way of 'nervous tension' as he tore his family apart was, she promised, a 'portal' to bliss. In June she passed through Boston en route for Hampton Beach in New Hampshire and there – after a separation of three months, with another three months to go – Austin met her.

The lovers' pretence of nothing between them came to an end with this assignation in the summer of 1883. Abruptly Austin exchanged the tactics of secrecy for confrontation. On the morning of 29 June he walked with Mabel for several hours on Boston Common. Afterwards he was ready to have it out with his wife, as he confided in a letter to Mabel. On his return to Amherst that evening the presence of a visitor silenced the couple, but at breakfast next morning Susan faced him squarely.

'Did you see Mrs Todd?'

'Certainly,' said Austin who had expected the question. 'That is what I went to Boston for.'

Susan was confounded by such unhesitating frankness. It took her a while to rally.

'She told me she was to spend a few days in Boston before going to Hampton and I concluded you would see her.'

'Yes, I *said* I did.'

When Susan continued to hold out against courtesies to Mabel, Austin felt called upon to deliver blows on love's behalf. On 12 July, in an outburst of chivalry mixed with self-pity, Austin fired off a series of blasts against his family. He demanded that they welcome Mabel in an agreeable manner. 'I cannot but believe they will,' he reassured her.

'I suffer for every wound you have received from my family, but for the time have seemed powerless to prevent them,' he excused himself, and then a torrent of resolve burst out. 'What strength I have however will be pitted against any more of them. I will straighten the matter out before the summer is over, or smash the machine – I had rather be under the wreck than under what I am. There would be several other broken heads, certainly, and I would take the chance of coming out on top.'

Vinnie pitied her brother, who wasn't strong. Missing the 'shine & affection' Mabel had brought into her life, she was up in arms on Mabel's behalf: 'I think if the real reason for your absence was known, there would be great indignation,' she had written to Mabel on 30 April. By July she succumbed to the lovers' slander of Sue: 'The same terrible influences prevail about me,' she wrote to Mabel. A plan was forming for Susan and the children to return to Shutesbury for their summer vacation and Vinnie declared that she could not wait for Sue to go: 'I shall sing amen all the day of freedom,' leaving Austin as 'our guest' at the Homestead.

At Shutesbury there was an accident. Gib fell backwards out of a wagon and was dazed with a headache the next day. Then, early in October, Gib went down with typhoid. His fever rose. The child seemed to have no resistance to the disease, and as he sank rapidly on the night of the 4th Emily, with a lantern, crossed the grass for the first time in years. The smell of the sickroom activated her sickness and she collapsed at three in the morning. Gib died a few hours later.

Over the next six weeks Austin had no wish to live. Susan, in blackest mourning, no longer cared to save the marriage, no longer cared about anything. To escape the gloom of The Evergreens Austin went to sit with his sisters, so bleak himself that Vinnie sent for Mabel.

She was at this moment the star of Amherst following an amateur production of *A Fair Barbarian*, based on the recent novel by Frances Hodgson

Burnett. On Thanksgiving Day, 29 November, she reminded Austin of what she had to offer in contrast to his sad wife.

'I thank God that my part in your life has been a joyous and helpful one,' she said. 'I rejoice more every day in the immensity of the love which you have given so magnificently. You have made me grander and nobler every day . . .'.

'Yes, darling,' he agreed, 'I *have* something to be thankful for . . . this sad day, with my boy gone, and except for you, alone. I have *you*. Would to God I had you close – in my house, at my hearth, in my arms! Would not this be too much? *Would* it! . . . We have indeed come to the holy of holies . . . We were made to give joy to each other.'

Further contact brought them 'before the veil of closest intimacy'. For a few more days Austin held off as he turned his face from death to life: 'All my business must be to keep the white heat which engulfs my being from flaming in the surface.' *White Heat*. It's his sister's phrase. Her volcano seethed underground, erupting in poems. Her brother's volcano, activated by the burdens he inherited from his father, erupted when Mabel offered to restore him. She was saving his life, he said, and central to this rescue was sexual consolation.

Mabel's actions were considered, not impulsive. She had to feel justified, and this habit of firming up her position in advance (as when she conceived Millicent) banished other considerations. Accordingly, Mabel planned adultery with her husband's consent.

On 10 December they discussed this prospect until the early hours of the morning. Neither saw it as infidelity. There were two considerations for David Todd. He had been disappointed with the donkey work assigned to him by Amherst College. Restless with ambition, he meant to use his technological inventiveness, particularly in the developing field of photography, to lead research on the sun. The first act Austin had performed for Mabel had been to exercise his power to David Todd's advantage. A letter to Todd in Washington bombards him with patronage, including support for Todd's wish to absent himself from teaching in term-time for the purpose of research. At the same time the patron allows himself a sly dig.

Amherst Oct 13 [18]82

My dear Todd,

Why don't you speak, and say something! Where are you! What are you about!

Are you going to California! And when! If not, why not! And what then!

Trustee meeting yesterday – and you go on to the new catalogue Ass[is]t[ant] Professor of Astronomy and Director of the Observatory.

Is that better!

My October greetings to Mrs Todd, and with them assure her from me that the Comet is only a vain show got up by imps . . . The Astronomy is all very well as gymnastics for the imagination but we come home to Moses and the prophets.

Pleasant remembrance to Mrs Wilder [Mabel's grandmother] also and a straight look for Millicent.

Cordially

Wm A Dickinson

Austin had not only secured Todd's promotion but also a raise to $1000 a year, no great sum – less than the $1500 some part-time teachers received at nearby Smith College – but a distinct improvement on what Todd was earning. So Todd was not displeased to find a benefactor in love with his wife. He believed that his own benefit was his wife's prime motive in taking the romance further. It did not escape him that Austin had more power at Amherst College 'than all the Trustees put together'. There was no end to possibilities and promotions in the treasurer's gift.

As Todd always came back to Mabel, so Mabel, he trusted, would always come back to him. He saw in her plans a mirror of his own exploits. What Todd did not see was the intensity of attachment in Austin Dickinson. David Todd never saw the passionate letters, only those written for his benefit in Austin's hearty voice. In reality, Austin and Mabel were about to consummate an alternative marriage. With Austin, Mabel could repudiate ephemeral love, returning in her own way to her parents' ethos. The depth of emotion she evoked in Austin compensated for her husband's light-weight attachments, an inexpressible humiliation visited on the early years of her marriage. Since she couldn't trust a 'sweetly unmoral' spouse, she felt justified in taking a lover who was a moral being. Part of Austin Dickinson's appeal was his high-toned fidelity. To switch his marital attachment from Susan to herself was an unprecedented act on his part.

Austin might not have contemplated adultery had it not been for Gib's death. Shattered, his spirit close to death, he came to see physical love as a comfort when home was comfortless. His wife had withdrawn into grief. This blanked-out figure in black did not appear to him a woman he had once loved; she had become something bound up with death, against whom he had to pit himself if he were to live.

So, on the evening of 13 December 1883 Austin, aged fifty-four (the same age as Mabel's father), and Mabel, aged twenty-seven, met in the dining room at the other house; they shut the door; and in front of the fire they fell on a black horsehair sofa. Emily, Vinnie and the servant Maggie kept out of the way until the lovers opened the door and left. On his way home Austin noticed the grass between the houses appeared as green as in spring. In the deepest winter of his being life sprang up in all its promise, while back at The Evergreens his wife appeared a 'great Black Moghul'.* The label served to obliterate Sue's local identity, and denied her bereft state, for though 'Black' was the mourning she continued to wear for a long time, 'Moghul' distances Sue as a foreign potentate. She was pitied by her remaining children and by a broken Emily, who sent note after note.

'Perhaps the dear, grieved Heart would open to a flower, which blesses unrequested, and serves without a Sound.'

Hopelessness, she told herself as much as Sue, 'has not leave to last'

---

* Moghul or Mogul is derived from the Mongol empire in India, and 'Great Mogul' was a sixteenth-century phrase used by Europeans for the emperor of Delhi who ruled over most of Hindustan. In the seventeenth century the phrase came to mean an autocratic ruler. Dickens used the word in this pejorative sense: 'your sister comes the Mogul over us'. A picture of the Great Mogul was on the wrapping of the best playing cards, and since Susan gave card parties Mabel could have seen the image there.

because it would close down the Spirit. As yet they were moving in the dark, like boats at night loaded with grief – two boats on no discernible course.

Austin, meanwhile, took the course Mabel offered. Three times, when he left his office towards evening on 13, 17 and 19 December, the lovers took over at the other house before Mabel boarded a train on the 20th to spend Christmas in Washington.

'My life has a sort of consecration now, & all outward things seem changed,' she reflected in her journal. Austin had 'recovered from the blow enough to live *for me* . . . His love for me is something sacred; it dignifies me & elevates me.' A starring 'me' takes the stage, radiating the character and emotions her lines give her. It's a script for a threesome including a contented husband in a 'peaceful & satisfying' marriage.

Offstage, silenced for the time being, was her one-time friend, the wife she'd ousted.

III: MABEL'S REIGN

9

EMILY'S STAND

Where does Emily Dickinson stand when the feud breaks out? With her sister a go-between for their brother and his mistress, is it possible for the poet to maintain a neutral or unknowing position?

From the consummation of her brother's romance at the end of 1883, and through 1884 and 1885, most assignations take place in the poet's house: about twelve a month, usually between two and four-thirty in the afternoon, often followed by a call in the evening— Austin calling on the Todds. It's not explicit, but these calls would be attentions to David as well as to Mabel, reassuring David that Austin has no intention of detaching his wife. On the contrary, he reaches out to David with friendliness and favour. There's a singular atmosphere of propriety and graciousness in the conduct of this three-way attachment, but, more than that, the calls are affirmations of an unfailing after-sex glow noted in both Austin's and Mabel's diaries. 'Never eaqualled [sic]', Austin comments, and another time, 'the most perfect ===='.

The lovers are both keeping records: Austin's parallel lines in his diary, Mabel's single line in hers. On Sunday 3 January 1886 Austin reports, 'at the other house 3 to 5 and + =====XXX'.* Mabel's diary adds the fact that they'd made love before the fire in the dining room . 'A most exquisitely happy and satisfactory two hours'.

* Not all the code signs can be interpreted.

All the while Mabel continues to sleep regularly with her husband, and until late in 1884 she sustains a practice of numbering these occasions, starting with number 1 in the new year and leaving off at 75 at the end of August. David's diary excludes his own love life. It's a record of work, reading (Tennyson's *In Memoriam*, Thoreau's *Walden* and George Eliot's *Letters*) and church (he loved the organ, especially Bach). As an experienced womaniser he's discreet, but it's also likely that sex, much as he enjoys it, is peripheral to ambition – common in those who use the chase and conquest as fuel for political or intellectual power. David was not lying to Mabel when he said that sex on the side didn't matter.

Lovemaking with both men quickens over a few days each month, which must be the safe days of Mabel's cycle. The precision of Austin's records allows him to remind Mabel of the time as well as date of one scene, the early afternoon of 7 August 1884: 'we met at the other house just after two, and had two sweet hours there = = = = = . . . How simple the great things of life are! and with the right conditions, how easy to be had.' Recalling this a year later, he's moved to call her 'my sweet wife'. She wore his ring on her wedding finger, having moved her wedding ring to her right hand. Mabel's diary adds another visit to the Homestead in the evening: 'Went to see Lavinia after dinner —. Took some jelly & some Indian pipes for Emily.' And that's not all, for her diary on that 7 August records number 69 with her husband.

How did Mabel Todd bring off the feat of keeping two husbands happy at the same time, as well as the even more difficult feat of fending off public opinion? As the affair went on, Mrs Todd did incur suspicion and snubs, but conspicuous hymn-singing and wifely devotion gave these the lie. Then, too, Austin's unassailable public standing protected her along with him. So, although her reputation felt precarious, she managed to avoid exposure, unlike New England's most famous adulteress. In the seventeenth-century setting of *The Scarlet Letter* an A marks the bodice of Hester Prynne, exposed on the public scaffold. What Mabel shared with Hester Prynne was secret defiance: 'What we did had a consecration of its own,' Hester assures her lover, as Mabel assured Austin. No stab of guilt comes off the page in Mabel's letters and journal. She had no sympathy for Sue once her hold tightened on Sue's husband; on the contrary, she considered that a woman of Sue's 'low' background had no business with so fine a husband. It remained a continued annoyance that Mrs Austin Dickinson had the right to ride out in the Dickinson carriages, while she, Mabel, the wife without the sign, had no carriage of her own nor was like to have. When Austin took her for drives it had to be along back roads.

Once, when Austin had told Sue that there was no time to drive her, she and Ned, in the Dickinson sleigh, came upon the lovers strolling along a back road. (It was 20 December 1883, the day after they'd made love for the third time.) Austin had brushed off the awkwardness as amusing – too amused to notice the consternation of his son when he could not protect his mother. His mother did observe Ned's distress, and packed him off on holiday, saying 'all will be well' and Papa would write to him.

So long as nothing was said to disturb Austin at home – and nothing *was* said – he felt content. His comforts were seen to and he observed with satisfaction a little air of discouragement that this would make the slightest difference to his detachment. He was teaching his family a lesson. They had not got him 'under' and this assertiveness, which Mabel had urged, he brought her as an offering. She called him her 'God', her King, the granter of her 'nobility', the transformer of her soul – so she claimed, adapting the local script of spiritual drama. Austin had promoted her to a higher platform not open to the masses who were suitably policed by law and religion. 'Conventionalism is for those not strong enough to be laws for themselves, or to conform themselves to the great higher law where all harmonies meet,' this lawyer decreed in private, determined to justify adultery as heaven-sent in his own case.

This was no ordinary affair, the pair assured each other; they were amongst the world's great lovers: Antony and Cleopatra, Abelard and Héloise, Chateaubriand and Madame de Récamier. Mabel's 'dream of a perfect manhood / That I realize in you' never failed to enchant Austin; while Austin declared himself already 'through the shining gates'. As the pair polished their self-styled roles as king and queen of 'pure' love, it never occurred to them that they were leaning on a servant. For the assignations at the other house relied on the service, the fires and discretion of Maggie Maher, whose Catholic confessor would have condemned the adultery. Maggie's witness to what was taking place, and for how many hours, would not be forgotten.

Meanwhile, Mr and Mrs Dickinson lived on in the festering silence of The Evergreens. Separation was not an option for a wife with no income of her own and Austin would not have agreed to a visible split. Ned longed to assuage what she bore. 'Such superhuman efforts to keep up & cheerful, for those around her, mortal eye never witnessed,' he reported to Mattie, away at boarding school. 'I would willingly lay down my life for her.' He too was ill and suffering in the winter of 1885, at the limit of endurance.

What remains unknown is whether there was any link between the stress at The Evergreens and the poet's insufficiently explained collapses into long periods in bed. Was the tie between Emily and Susan strained by the newcomer in their lives, knocking and knocking at the door of the Homestead in order to make love to Susan's husband in the safety of his sisters' home? The Dickinson sisters were dependent on Austin. How dependent they were, and in what ways, remains in question – it's a question pertinent to Emily Dickinson's position. Austin paid their considerable bills (almost as much as those of The Evergreens) and took care of their finances as their father had done. It was customary for Austin to have tea at the other house after his day at the office. At this time, he took to visiting 'Em' and 'Vin' two or three times a day, and told a gratified Mabel that he and his sisters would 'talk you over – always . . . you are the constant theme'. He did speak of sisters in the plural. If so, Emily could hardly have been blind to the affair. To what extent did she cooperate or, like Lavinia, condone? She and Lavinia certainly took in Austin's emotional shift from The Evergreens back to the Homestead: as though their brother had never left home, they agreed.

The facts of Vinnie's complicity and the acts of adultery in the Homestead have been available since the correspondence of Austin and Mabel was finally published in 1984, a century after the affair began. Yet the question of the poet's stance has remained unasked. This happened because Dickinson legend has kept the poet untouched, oblivious to her brother's affair. The time has come to recognise her inevitable part in the family feud. What did it mean to an experienced fender-off of intrusion to find Mabel Todd occupying the dining room in the Homestead? To add to the intrusion, this happened to be the room where the poet had a second writing table, at a corner window shaded by honeysuckle.

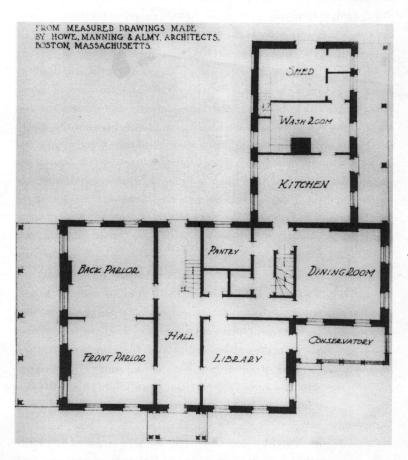

Downstairs at the Homestead, and Emily's conservatory: the layout at the time when adultery made itself at home.

The lovers' alternative venue was the library. This was the room Emily had to pass through en route to her conservatory. Next to her room upstairs, this was her space, central to her daily life. But for two to three hours of a morning or afternoon the lovers might be there. The door would be closed. This means that during these hours the three women who lived in the house could not walk freely downstairs, particularly Emily, who was determined never to meet Mabel. It's one thing to flee the 'donkeys' of the town; quite another to evade a person who frequents the main rooms of the house, coming through the front door into the hallway, opening and closing doors at any moment. In one or other of those rooms to the right of the hallway a fire would be lit.

The lovers did not make use of the parlour, running the length of the house, to the left of the hallway. That was Emily's domain when the Judge came. Occasionally Mabel entered the parlour to play the square piano that Mr Dickinson had bought for Emily. She played Bach, Scarlatti and Beethoven, and sometimes she lifted her voice and sang. The trained voice, resonant with the vigour of a fulfilled life, reached into every cranny of the house. She sang, she said, for Emily, whom she pictured seated, all attention, on a step of the staircase. Afterwards the poet sent in a glass of wine, and with it either a piece of cake or a rose, and sometimes also a few lines of verse. Mabel liked to think the verse impromptu, called out by her own voice.

There were, then, these non-encounters. Emily's successful avoidance of Mabel means that she could not have been uninformed of her visits. For her policy to work as it did, there had to be some sort of understanding. To Mabel, the fact that Austin discussed her in the Homestead implied that his sisters accepted the affair. Or did it? Vinnie certainly, at this stage, was charmed by Mabel and bent on obliging her brother. If Vinnie felt compunction about Sue, her conduct as go-between gives no hint. Her letters to Mabel are partisan, recruited to the power base Mabel was building up against the wife she meant to replace more completely.

What Emily thought is less certain. If Mabel was telling the truth (always questionable), Emily too was charmed. Mabel watched people fall under her 'spell', women as spellbound as men. Up to a point it's fair to assume the poet's response to Mabel's songs and eagerness to read her poems. But Emily's letters – to Susan, to Ned, to Mabel herself and, surprisingly, also to Mabel's parents – suggest a different story.

Can it be that Emily Dickinson was the first target of Mabel Todd's takeover? With writing ambitions of her own, she was gripped by the poems Sue shared soon after Mabel's arrival in Amherst. She began to put herself in the way of the recluse. That first autumn of 1881, when Mabel was about to depart on a visit to Washington, she ventured to send the poet a message of farewell. The reply was a rebuff to any delusion of intimacy Mabel might cultivate. 'The parting of those that never met, shall it be delusion, or rather an unfolding of a snare whose fruitage is later?'

This is well before the men in her family fall for Mabel. Such prescience seems uncanny, but there's no mystery here: supremely alert, the poet is a decoder of signs – a lurking intention. Ignoring the snub, Mabel persists in believing that Emily Dickinson pined for her when she went away. What Dickinson called 'delusion' was actually something Mabel had in common with the poet: invention. The situations Mabel invents carry artistic conviction – enough, almost always, to see them through – though there's all the difference in the use of words. The poet's words stab us awake; Mabel's words are imitations of others' scripts, just as her manners imitate society ladies'. Refinement and courtesy are manifest, but not always that care for others that marks real manners. Mabel could be impervious to what did not impinge on her self-making, while the poet, secluded though she was, took in everything.

This was apparent on 10 September 1882, when Mabel entered the Homestead for the first time. The poet hears fateful footsteps coming through the door and foresees the necessity for 'fortitude'. It's as though Dickinson scents Mabel's appropriation of herself and conveys what she can, within the bounds of politeness, to ward her off.

Later that month, Mabel sent her a painting of Indian Pipes. She would have gleaned from Austin or Vinnie that this was the poet's favourite flower, a white woodland plant native to New England. As a child Emily had pressed and labelled it *monotropa, uniflora*. Hers are ghostly white in the shadow of their bold, dark stalk, unlike Mabel's painted, full-bodied Pipes (*below*). The gift obliged Emily to thank her: 'I know not how to thank you. We do not thank the Rainbow, although its Trophy is a snare.' Again, a snare. Dickinson warns the many-hued Mabel that she spots it.

When the adultery was underway Mabel tried a second gift, a yellow jug painted with red trumpet-vine blossoms. Dickinson's acknowledgement is once more a coded rebuff: it characterises Mabel as 'Egypt', as Cleopatra, mistress of 'the entangled Antony'. Antony's sister could hardly be more explicit in pointing the blame. Cleopatra is, of course, no mean power: to a poet who characterises herself repeatedly as 'Queen', ruler of her private realm, here is a rival queen positioning herself on her territory, first as a family friend, then the chosen of her brother, then stepping some twelve times a month through the Homestead door.

Once Austin entered into his affair it was impossible to be direct. Austin was head of the family. His wife and children, who opposed Mabel openly, had found themselves in the poor position of rejected dependants. The poet encased her rebukes in riddles. It's Hamlet's ploy, bound as he is by ties of nature to the family a usurper has destroyed. Like Hamlet, she puts on an antic disposition, her words so opaque and apparently incoherent the speaker appears to be deranged. This absolves her of responsibility for what she says. It's in this Hamlet sense that the poet appears to be outside the action. Not unknowing, as legend had it; on the contrary, words are a form of action. Her verbal antics, like Hamlet's, oppose the usurper.

> Dear friend —
>> Nature forgot — The Circus reminded her —
>> Thanks for the Ethiopian Face.
>> The Orient is in the West.
>> 'You knew, Oh Egypt' said the entangled Antony —

There's no certain solution to this riddle but what is unmistakable is the curtness, unlike Dickinson's warmth to other correspondents. A possible decoding could be that the poet had forgotten this 'friend' (with her 'circus' of show-piece accomplishments) until nudged by a gift. Her reply calls up the ('Ethiopian') Queen of Sheba bearing gifts to a king renowned for wisdom. This alien seductress with the Oriental wiles of a Cleopatra ('Egypt') has come 'in' – intruded into – the poet's home in her native West. The verbal combat returns Mabel's blackening of Sue as 'great Black Moghul'. Here, Sue's defender exposes Mabel's 'Ethiopian Face': the real foreign potentate who, through sexual conquest, has an unnatural sway in the Dickinson family. The poet's 'thanks', though obligatory, is shot through with sarcasm.

When other overtures from Mabel compelled replies, Dickinson wrote acidly, 'Will Brother and Sister's dear friend accept my tardy devotion?' and again, in 1885, she addressed Mabel as 'Brother and Sister's Friend!' Not her own friend (after Mabel had been haunting the Homestead for three years). Dickinson's signature on this letter is unprecedented: she signs herself 'America', ostensibly because Mabel was abroad at the time, but 'America' implies independence. In this sense the signature seals the warning: Mabel, as 'Egypt', may have disarmed 'Antony', representative of Rome, but she can't take over 'America'.

This is the only drama in Dickinson's life that's not of her making, ever

since Miss Lyon's attempt to command her soul in 1848. As a girl, Emily had
been free to turn her back on Miss Lyon, but this conflict of mature people
with a lot to lose – 'Sister', wife, children, reputation, peace of mind, privacy – has worked its way inside her home.

Some of Dickinson's readers, like Sue, were admitted to intimacy; to
others, like Mabel and Thomas Wentworth Higginson, Dickinson wrote in
her most riddling manner. Where Higginson was willing to own his bewil-
derment, Mabel did not. It was part of her script to act the favourite.
Impossible to know to what extent Mabel could decode Dickinson's stabs
and sarcasms in every instance, but one diary entry records the receipt of
'some adder's tongue sent over by Lavinia'. Adder's tongue is a plant, but I
think Mabel is referring to a pencilled poem. If so, Lavinia would have
been an innocent pawn in this war of words, with no idea what the poem
was saying, but Mabel did, it seems, detect the venom of the following
riddle:

> Their dappled importunity
> Disparage or dismiss —
> The Obloquies of Etiquette
> Are obsolete to Bliss —

Again there's no certain reading, but we may surmise that when it
comes to 'them' [Mabel and her lover] there are only two possible
responses for the poet: she can 'disparage' or 'dismiss' their devious ['dappled'] and persistent intrusion ['importunity']. The slanders ['Obloquies'] –
presumably Mabel's detraction of Austin's family – that are part of Mabel's
manners [a sardonic take on her taste for 'Etiquette'], have nothing to do
with the soul's superior instants ['Bliss'] the poet enjoys, however insistently the lovers claim theirs to be a higher love. The poet, therefore,
scorns the lovers' project.

Even so, Mabel was not to be put off. She meant to gain access to the
poet in one way or another. It was simply a matter of waiting.

Meanwhile, there was another determined woman with an eye to

Emily. Helen Hunt Jackson, as we know, recognised Dickinson's stature. 'You are a great poet', she wrote on 28 March 1876, '– and it is wrong to the day you live in, that you will not sing aloud. When you are what men call dead, you will be sorry you were so stingy.'

Dickinson sent her some poems, and Helen was one of the few she would see. On 10 October of the same year Helen sat face to face with Dickinson, who looked so pale that her fellow poet felt 'like a great ox talking to a white moth, and begging it to come and eat grass with me to see if it could not turn itself into beef!' Stupid, she admitted, and also 'very impertinent' to have accused the moth of living away from the sunlight. Yet Helen couldn't resist another try: 'You say you find great pleasure in reading my verses. Let somebody somewhere whom you do not know have the same pleasure in reading yours.'

When Helen returned to Amherst in October 1878 she called on Dickinson once more, this time with her husband. It was not Dickinson's habit to see a stranger, yet she enjoyed 'a lovely hour' when the winter strands in Helen's hair seemed banished by the warmth of her undiminished summer. Helen came as a professional writer – she brought Dickinson her latest book, *Bits of Travel at Home* (1878), and there was a professional purpose to this visit.

By 1878, Dickinson had written over fourteen hundred poems. Helen had been urging her to publish a poem or two anonymously in a collection called *A Masque of Poets*. 'I will copy them – sending them in my own handwriting – and promise never to tell any one, not even the publishers, whose the poems are. Could you not bear this much publicity? Only you and I would recognize the poems.' A candidate for publication was 'Success is counted sweetest / By those who ne'er succeed'. It looks as though this poem came up during a visit from Helen on the morning of 24 October, because the following day she redoubled her plea.

'Now – will you send me the poem? No – will you let me send the "Success" – which I know by heart – to Roberts Bros . . . I ask it as a personal favor to myself – Can you refuse the only thing I perhaps shall ever ask at your hands?'

Dickinson finally agreed – with reluctant waves in Higginson's direction – and she did, after all, make her identity known to the editor Thomas Niles, a partner in the Boston publishing firm of Roberts Brothers. The collection, selling at one dollar, came out at the end of 1878. It was part of a 'No Name Series', advertised as anonymous poems by the great of Britain and America. Its epigraph came from the recently published *Daniel Deronda*: 'Is the Gentleman anonymous? Is he a great Unknown?' Sadly the poems collected fell foul of greatness. One preceding Dickinson's, 'Avallon', is fake medieval, hopelessly sub-Tennyson; other poems are absurdly trite, along these lines:

> Oh! To-day is too delicious,
> Fill'd with little winds and birds
> And the far-off hum of herds,
> [. . .]
> Oh! Today is too delicious,
> [. . .]
> Let to-morrow be malicious.

As a sample of the editor's taste, it's only fair to add that he wasn't alone. Nor was Niles alone in seeing fit to change Dickinson's phrasing. When she wrote to thank him for a copy of this volume he was polite enough to speak of her 'valuable' contribution. Reviewers thought it by Emerson, and Helen Hunt Jackson singled out 'Success' for praise in an anonymous Colorado review that reprinted the poem. Privately she owned to Dickinson that she was unable to recognise greatness in most of the others.

She went on praising her friend to Niles, who wrote to Miss Dickinson on 24 April 1882: 'she wished you could be induced to publish a volume of poems . . . I wish also that you could.' Surprisingly, Dickinson followed this up.

'The kind but incredible opinion of "H.H." and yourself I would like to deserve – Would you accept a Pebble [her poem, "How happy is the little Stone"] I think I gave to her, though I am not sure.'

The editor apparently expressed no interest and a year later, in mid-March 1883, Dickinson initiated another approach when she wrote to ask once more for news of the forthcoming life of George Eliot by her husband John Cross. In reply, Niles sent a different biography of the novelist which Roberts Brothers was about to publish. Her thanks enclosed two more poems 'Further in Summer than the Birds' and one of her great works, which she entitled 'Snow' ['It sifts from Leaden Sieves']. Niles preferred the minor bird poem. Hoping to elicit a keener response, she asked him to 'efface' the others and then, trying her hardest to please, she sent Niles the same treasure she had offered to her first editor, Samuel Bowles: the first edition of the Brontë sisters' *Poems* (1846), whose greatness at the time had gone unrecognised. The covert message would have been the same: an editor should not fail to recognise another poet of the Brontë calibre.

'I thank you heartily,' Niles replied on 31 March, 'but in doing so I must add that I would not for the world rob you of this very rare book . . . If I may presume to say so, I will take instead a M.S. collection of your poems, that is, if you want to give them to the world through the medium of a publisher.' Again she offered only more samples, including another bird poem – a great one – 'A Route of Evanescence'. The editor replied with formal courtesy:

23 April 1883

My dear Miss Dickinson
 . . . I am very much obliged to you for the three poems which I have read and re-read with great pleasure, but which I have not consumed. I shall keep them unless you order me to do otherwise, in that case I shall as in duty bound obey.
Yrs very truly
T. Niles

Thomas Niles had a mulish face with a slightly protruding lower lip, concealed at the corners with a walrus moustache, its hair rather prickly in contrast to the straight hair combed neatly across his crown. In 1868, when Louisa May Alcott had sent him the first dozen chapters of what

became *Little Women*, he had thought them dull. Fortunately he showed
the chapters to his niece, Lillie Almy, who laughed and cried. Niles
revised his opinion and Alcott went on with the book. In 1881, Helen
Hunt Jackson submitted a book exposing ill-treatment of Native
Americans. She showed how they had been displaced from their lands;
how this contravened the international law of prior occupancy; and a
chapter on 'Massacres of Indians by Whites' revealed how often Native-
American violence had been provoked. Roberts Brothers rejected *A
Century of Dishonor* as too controversial. Published by Harper & Brothers,
the book established Helen Hunt Jackson as an authority on Native
Americans. She was then appointed as the first female commissioner for
Native Americans in Southern California, where she extended her
domestic values of compassion and listening in a political arena. Here she
found material for her bestselling novel *Ramona* (1884), which Dickinson
read.

Up to the age of fifty-two, Dickinson had managed not to expose herself to outright rejection. She was silent on the subject, but the
encounter with Niles had to be destructive, in the same way as public dis-
paragement of *Wuthering Heights* had to have been destructive of Emily
Brontë – publication (resisted at first) hastening her course towards
death in 1848. Dickinson's long-held affinity for this predecessor
mounted in her own last years, when she liked to quote the final stanza
from 'No coward soul is mine'. The self-satisfied bore with dead eyes
who looks out of Niles's photograph had no idea of damage to so fine an
instrument. For genius is no protection against its denial, especially for
those writing in their bedrooms and diminished by nineteenth-century
notions of 'little' women. It's not that Dickinson would have doubted
her gift, but she had put herself in a false position: a supplicant with an
unwanted offering.

She made no further attempt at publication. What is clear, though,
from the abortive encounter with Niles is the poet's willingness to speak to
a wider public and to us far off in the future. Emily Dickinson was *not* shut
away from publishing; she was in touch through her initiative with Niles,
through sustained ties with leading editors and men of letters, Higginson,

Bowles and Dr Holland, and in her last decade through a professional friendship with Helen Hunt Jackson.

To Helen's credit, she never stopped trying. In September 1884, after falling down the stairs and breaking a leg, she could still put her mind to her friend. 'What portfolios of verses you must have,' she guessed correctly. 'It is a cruel wrong to your "day & generation" that you will not give them light.' She offered to be Emily Dickinson's executor. 'Surely, after you are what is called "dead," you will be willing that the poor ghosts you have left behind, should be cheered and pleased by your verses, will you not? – You ought to be.' The poet did not take this up, nor in the same month did she consent to see Bleecker Van Wagenen, from the publishing firm of Dodd, Mead and Company, who turned up at the Homestead with his wife, Mrs Holland's daughter. Emily teased Vinnie for being over-impressed by the gentleman of the vast name.

There was one other editor who could have published Dickinson during her lifetime. Maria Whitney, the cousin of Mrs Bowles who had nursed her dutifully and adored Sam Bowles, was often in touch with Dickinson from the time of Bowles's death in 1878.

'I hope you may remember me, as I shall always mingle you with our Mr Bowles,' Dickinson said. 'Affection gropes through drifts of Awe, for his tropic Door –'.

Maria suggested that those who had loved Mr Bowles be more closely each other's.

'Your touching suggestion is a tender permission,' Dickinson agreed. 'You will be with us while he is with us and that will be while we are ourselves – for Consciousness is the only Home of which we now know.' To be at home with Bowles was to recall how one glance of his could 'light a world'.

Tacitly she acknowledged Maria's superior right to grieve. In truth, Dickinson had more than adequate consolation in Judge Lord, while Maria was bereft for the rest of her life. Hers was a self-contained scholar's life directed towards Old High German, studiousness alleviated by a flash of red petticoat brought back from fashionable Europe to the disapproval of old-fashioned Northampton. When Bowles had been failing, Maria Whitney had gone to see him in Springfield three times a week. It had been a tragic time whilst she'd kept going at Smith College.

After she resigned this post in 1880 she edited the literary pages of the *Springfield Republican* where, two decades before, Bowles had published a few of Dickinson's most daring poems from the early 1860s, a time when she deluged him with offerings. Whitney had been close enough to Bowles, as well as to the Norcross cousins, to have known of Dickinson's poetry; the fact that Dickinson wrote was not secret. Although Whitney and the poet were intimate correspondents in the early 1880s, Whitney never included her poems in the newspaper. Her taste was probably too correct, in the light of Dickinson's comment on an unnamed female scholar (and Whitney was the only one she knew): this scholar 'had the <u>facts</u> but not the <u>phosphorescence</u>' of books. That phosphorescence illumines every letter Dickinson sent to Whitney. So here was another editor whose door failed to open to a great poet. Only three readers fully recognised her greatness during her lifetime: Sue Dickinson, Mabel Loomis Todd and Helen Hunt Jackson.

After the Springfield murder trial hit the news in April 1882, Judge Lord collapsed unconscious on 1 May following his return to Salem. On 3 May the *Republican* had reported little hope for his recovery. Vinnie heard this from Austin en route to catch a train (as Emily Dickinson reported this scene in a letter). Vinnie came indoors and stood in front of her sister who was smiling as she read a letter from the Judge, delivered with that morning's post.

'Emily, did you see anything in the paper that concerned us?'

'Why no, Vinnie, what?'

'Mr Lord is very sick.'

She grasped at a chair that seemed to be passing, for her sight seemed to slip. Her smile froze and then slowly faded. Tom Kelley, Maggie's brother-in-law, came in at that moment, and she ran to his blue jacket, as she put it, 'and let my Heart break there . . .'.

'Don't cry, Miss Emily.' He had never seen her like this. 'I could not see you cry.'

At that moment the doorbell rang and she heard a stranger's voice saying, 'I thought first of you.' It was Professor Chickering from the English Department at Amherst College, who had made several unsuccessful attempts to see the poet. This time he came with an offer to telegraph Abbie Farley in Salem. Mechanically, she 'asked the Wires' how the Judge did, and attached her name.

Abbie's reply gave cautious grounds for hope. Emily searched the paper for news each day, hoping silence boded well. Then, on 8 May, Austin read aloud to his sisters a report on the Judge: he had survived the crisis. At once, Emily dashed off a letter:

Monday

Dear Abby —

   . . .Were our sweet Salem safe, it would be 'May' indeed — I shall never forget 'May Day.'

   All our flowers were draped [in mourning] —

   Is he able to speak or to hear voices or to say 'Come in,' when his Amherst knocks?

   Fill his Hand with Love as sweet as Orchard Blossoms, which he will share with each of you — I know his boundless ways —

   As it was too much sorrow, so it is almost too much joy —

Lovingly,
Emily

By the 14th, Lord had recovered enough to hear from her directly: her 'rapture' at his 'return'. 'The fear that your life had ceased, came, fresh, yet dim, like the horrid Monsters fled from a Dream.' At the age of seventy it seemed sensible to retire. His health deteriorated during 1883 and, aware that he was slipping away, Emily Dickinson — cut off in Amherst — longed for a last opportunity to break through his reserve. In a rare poem addressing him, she fights like a biographer against the 'reportless Grave': it's a matter of urgency to find the right question that will 'still' — 'still' she repeats — 'wrest' from him what she needs to know:

Still own thee — still thou art
What Surgeons call alive —
Though slipping – slipping — I perceive
To thy reportless Grave —

Which question shall I clutch —
What answer wrest from thee
Before thou dost exude away
In the recallless sea?

Lord died in Salem on 13 March 1884. His last words to Emily were 'A caller comes'. She inferred it to be 'Eternity, as he never returned'. At the first 'dart' of grief she 'hardly dared to know' her loss, 'but anguish finds it out'. She was in a 'place of shafts'.

If the sun came out after rain, it barbed her loss afresh. There was no escaping the heartless renewals of nature. Outside the robins sang, but the poet, writing to Mrs Holland, can summon only 'a drooping syllable'. In the past ecstasy had come as though it pervaded all existence, but now she realised 'he [Judge Lord] was the cup from which we drank it'. To be an ecstatic with no access to ecstasy was to feel deprived of life. 'Abyss has no Biographer —', she called across the years to Sue's sister, Martha Gilbert Smith, who had suffered in silence when they were young. No words were adequate, only Mark Antony's cry, 'My heart is in the coffin there with Caesar.' She comments, 'I never knew a broken heart break itself so sweet – '.

There was no consolation in formal religion. The 'waylaying Light' of her visions had removed her from doctrine and official versions of the supernatural. 'When Jesus tells us about his Father, we distrust him,' she said. 'When he shows us his Home, we turn away, but when he confides to us that he is "acquainted with Grief," we listen, for that also is an Acquaintance of our own.'

Mourning provided an excuse for the Homestead to close the door to Mabel. The lovers had to go elsewhere – but where? The Todds' room in their boarding house was out of the question. Austin's law office was out of bounds to Mabel (though at the start of the affair she'd found reasons to drop by, compelled by the drama of risk). In the spring of 1884 Mabel cast her eye on the Lessey estate, graced by columns, trees and two acres on the far side of Lessey Street, curving behind the Homestead. Mrs Lessey was ill, and in late May Mabel's expectations were met: Mrs Lessey was no more. Acting swiftly, the Todds took possession of the Lessey house in June. The lease was for a year. Mabel borrowed from the bank in order to revamp the property, requested her furniture from her parents and when they could not bear to part with certain items sold them to her parents for six hundred dollars – deaf to their pleas, for they could not afford this.

Mabel's interiors had curtains from woven wall-hangings and rather tired ostrich feathers in vases. An upright piano stood in a corner of the parlour with a cover laid loosely over the stool. Rush mats, gathering dust, covered the floor; bits of crocheted lace adorned the mantel. Though Mabel was dainty about her own clothes she despised housekeeping, and so pleased was she to have a servant – and so inexperienced as an employer – that she did not inspect too closely. She informed her mother proudly that the servant had all cleaning finished by the time the Todds sat down to breakfast. The effect was a mite tatty in contrast to the spotlessness of The Evergreens (where, David Todd used to complain, he'd felt obliged to wipe his feet all the way up the garden path) or the crisp whites of the Homestead. In the Todds' bedroom tacky curtains drooped from conspicuous rails. More ostrich plumes, ragged with age, were tucked behind a nondescript painting of the seashore.

One Saturday in mid-June, while Emily was baking a loaf cake with Maggie, she saw 'a great darkness coming'. She blacked out for many hours until, late at night, she woke to find Vinnie and Austin bending over her, together with an unfamiliar physician, Dr Fish. Emily gave out that this was the first time in her life that she 'had fainted and lain unconscious'. She had certainly never lost consciousness for that alarming length of time. The doctor called it a revenge of the nerves. Her sister was sick *differently*, Lavinia told their cousin Clara Newman Turner, the elder of the two orphans who had lived at The Evergreens and who was therefore familiar with family ills. There were headaches, vomiting and convulsions – signs of more than one disease. Some have suggested hypertension; kidney failure, known as Bright's disease, was the diagnosis at the time but new evidence – drugstore prescriptions from 1883 until 1885 – suggests that the invalid was treated also for epilepsy. A chronic sickness would have complicated whatever 'different' disease she had contracted.*

From childhood, Dickinson had contemplated mortality. During the

---

* Dickinson prescriptions (amongst others from the period 1882–5) are pasted into a record book belonging to the Adams drugstore in Amherst. This was not the only drugstore in town but it served the Dickinson family, and it's possible to list, with dates, certain drugs prescribed for Emily Dickinson. These tally with contemporary treatments for epilepsy. The drugstore records during the last years of her life show that Amherst's Dr Bigelow, who often treated the Dickinsons, prescribed glycerine (the same medicine Dr Jackson had given her in 1851) on 28 June 1884 – that is, during her prolonged fainting sickness that summer.

On 15 October 1884, when she began a second long-term spell of sickness, lasting until January 1885, Dr Fish prescribed two drugs then in use for epilepsy: hyoscyamus (an anti-spasmodic recommended since 1858 by London authority Sir Edward Sieveking in his treatise *On Epilepsy*) and 'extract ustilago', a compound of ergotine and bromide (used also for headaches). A *Dictionary of Medicine* published in 1883 (Dr Bigelow owned a copy) recommends three to six grains of 'ergotine' for epilepsy in an article by a respected French neurologist, C. E. Brown-Séquard. One of the Amherst doctors prescribed glycerine once more on 23 January 1885.

Other prescriptions given in this period also correspond to drugs then used for epilepsy, though these were common medicines used for a variety of ills. The extracts were crude; treatments look dangerously hit and miss, especially the use of poisons, and we might well wonder what effect these poisons had on Dickinson's premature death.

Arsenic (used also in tonics) is recommended for epilepsy in the *Dictionary of Medicine*: 'arsenic alone can do much against any form of epilepsy'. Dickinson was prescribed 'Fowler's arsenical solution' on 9 October 1883 when she collapsed after Gib's death.

The same applied to strychnine (recommended in *On Epilepsy*, though used also in tonics). Strychnine is an ingredient in Nux vomica (from an ulcerated nut). Dickinson was given 'Nux vomica' on 12 October 1883, three days after the arsenic. This prescription was for 'L Dickinson', obviously Lavinia, who would have obtained medicine on her sister's behalf. Strychnine was prescribed on two other occasions in this period: 9 January 1883, when the first scenes of the family feud broke out, confirming Dickinson's apprehensions; and 17 August 1885, when she was shocked by news of Helen Hunt Jackson's unexpected death.

Digitalis was prescribed on 30 January 1885. Digitalis is usually prescribed for the heart and also for kidney failure, which Dr Bigelow isolated as the cause of death.

next weeks of faintness and weakness – sometimes in bed, sometimes in a
chair – mortality now became her companion, as attached as Gib: 'The
little boy we laid away never fluctuates, and his dim society is companion
still.' As for the future, it remained the mystery on the other side of death.
She kept an open mind:

> The going from a world we know
> To one a wonder still
> Is like the child's adversity
> Whose vista is a hill,
> Behind the hill is sorcery,
> And everything unknown,
> But will the secret compensate
> For climbing it alone?

After eight weeks she could reassure her Norcross cousins that she was
'now staying'. At this time she told Susan all she'd meant to her:

> Show me Eternity, and I will show you Memory —
> Both in one package lain
> And lifted back again —
>
> Be Sue — while I am Emily —
> Be next — what you have ever been, Infinity —

From a formative age they had shared a language untrammelled by falsehood: 'No Words ripple like Sister's —', she'd written to Sue. 'Their Silver
genealogy is very sweet to trace—/ Amalgams are abundant, but the lone
student of the Mines [the poet] adores Alloyless things—'.

When Sue sent a cardinal flower to the recuperating invalid, Emily
flashed back: 'Except for usurping your Copyright – I should regive the
Message, but each Voice is its own –'.

Would Emily join her, Sue asked, in supplying material for a forthcoming biography of Sam Bowles?

Emily agreed. 'Go to Mine as to your own, only more unsparingly –'.
She foresaw the result would be 'like a Memoir of the Sun, when the Noon
is gone' (exactly what the biographer, George Merriam, produced: a faded
composite of fact). In private Emily shared the living memory with Sue:
'You remember his swift way of wringing and flinging away a Theme, and
others picking it up and gazing bewildered after him, and the prance that
crossed his Eye . . .

> . . . No vacillating God
> Ignited this Abode
> To put it out —

This feeling letter to Sue ends,

> Remember, Dear, an unfaltering Yes is my only reply to your
> utmost question –
>   With constancy –
>   Emily –

Given the clash of interest between Sue Dickinson and Mabel Todd, it's
telling to compare Emily's assents to Sue with the emphatic negations of
her latest riddle for Mabel.

While in danger, and almost too weak to write, Emily had roused herself on 19 July to confront Mabel. This was the only letter she managed to
write during her dark passage when death stood by. Defiance was on her
mind. It consists of two sentences and four lines of verse about the last
stand of the Greeks at Thermopylae. A lone group of Spartans [the
Dickinsons] who are about to die at the hands of the Persian invader [Mabel
Todd], and whose stand will make them 'the Deathless', declare their
purity of purpose: nothing now can stain their spirit, not the 'Dart' of an
enemy spear, nor the uncertainty of the afterlife. The stain comes from 'an
adjourning Heart' [Austin's withdrawal from his family]. Again, there's no
sure answer to this riddle, but the fact that Dickinson sent this message to
Mabel alone suggests the speaker's distress over a brother whose heart is

removed from his family. It's there the damage will be found: not her own sickness, not the advance of mortality, but estrangement. Her accompanying verse points to emotional betrayal:

> Not Sickness stains the Brave,
> Nor any Dart,
> Nor Doubt of Scene to come,
> But an adjourning Heart —

During Dickinson's bout of sickness she was healed by the opposite: the fellow-feeling of her Norcross cousins and a neighbour, Nellie Sweetser, who offered 'precisely the tenderness most craved'.

In October 1884 the Todds threw open their new residence to seventy-five inhabitants of Amherst, who were offered a lunch of chicken salad. Mrs Loomis came for this event and was as amazed as Mabel could have hoped, yet worried. To a mother who had scrimped all her life, the grandeur of the Lessey house and grounds was disturbing. How could Mabel afford this on her husband's salary? Who had funded it?

It didn't take Mrs Loomis long to deduce that Mabel had acquired a protector. At once she summoned Mabel's father from Washington. Appalled questions drew in Austin Dickinson, who gave Mr Loomis his lofty assurance that nothing was amiss. It's inconceivable, he protested, that a gentleman of his standing and probity could corrupt their daughter. The problem lay with the Loomises, who had fixed on adultery where there was nothing but friendship.

Meanwhile, Emily Dickinson signalled in her own way with warm notes to the Loomises. Careful not to mention Mabel, she expressed her 'trust' in their sense of 'Right'. These are not riddling letters. Her warmth to these strangers signals how firmly she sides with them in their battle for their daughter's virtue.

At least twice Eben Loomis confronted Austin, who was taken aback to be considered 'a sneak, and an improper person, given to mischief, and treachery'. To Mabel, Austin confided his distaste for 'vulgar minded people' who think too much of the body. Outwardly he practised the accommodating politeness of one whose patience is tried:

> My dear Mrs Loomis
>   If it may afford you the least satisfaction to supplement our Sunday afternoon talk by any word unspoken, any question unasked, or unanswered then, any new thought – you may command me for such time as you will, after 5 o'clock this or tomorrow ev[en]ing.
> Very sincerely,
Wm A Dickinson

In truth, Austin was somewhat put out to hear of an informant (probably Grandma Wilder, who had been staying with the Todds before the Loomises arrived). He used a lawyer's tactics, requiring the kind of evidence that could prove an allegation in court, unpicking evidence and continuing to manoeuvre Mr Loomis into a defensive position. If Austin is spied late at night with Mrs Todd on the porch, if he comes back day after day through an inconspicuous door, it is because they like each other – what harm in that? David Todd, after all, condones it, and sometimes joins them. It offends Mr Dickinson that a friendship so pure and elevating should be maligned by little minds.

He formulated Mabel's denial: 'There is nothing to the whole of it, beyond the fact that we are earnestly interested in each other . . . if he [her father] has heard differently, he has heard wrongly.'

Eben Loomis, not taken in, sent Mabel a 'terrible letter', which she probably destroyed. It left her gloomy for weeks. For all that, Mabel kept up her hymn to Austin as her God; his love a sign God loved her. Defiantly, the lovers assured each other of their purity.

Mr and Mrs Loomis left Amherst on 5 November. Dickinson wrote to them: 'Parting with Thee reluctantly, / That we have never met . . .'. How different had been her parting words to an un-met Mabel as an intruder laying a 'snare'.

Grandma Wilder remained behind at the Lessey house and reported on Mabel to her parents. Restricted by surveillance, the lovers were forced to return to the Homestead. Again this shift took place while Emily Dickinson had another bad spell, from October 1884 to January 1885.

'The Dyings have been too deep for me,' she explained, 'and before I could raise my Heart from one, another has come.'

Death had always been a mystery the poet longed to solve, the undiscovered country she'd seen Sam Bowles and her father enter. She had wondered where they were, and had coursed to the verge of 'boundlessness' when Gib died. Wanting to take Sue with her, she was unable to do so at a time when Gib's father, isolated by grief, slid finally and irretrievably into Mabel's waiting arms. The quarrels of the last year deepened into a permanent rift: on one side, Susan, Ned and Mattie; on the other, Austin, served by Vinnie. The rift manifested as rows between Sue and Vinnie, and in late January Sue's confrontation with her husband, when she had ripped the wallpaper of the hall in The Evergreens.

'NO NEWS', Ned reported the following morning to his sister Mattie at boarding school. The ironic heading is in decorated capitals. Ned conveyed his news with joking discretion: he had been called in to assist at 'the fall of the old reigeime [regime] – A reluctant consent was obtained by Father'. Ned's spelling is erratic, his hand unformed with a childish roundness belied by his sardonic ironies. He had what would now be recognised as a kind of dyslexia that becomes more pronounced under stress. Word formation and spelling were wildly disrupted by the rows Ned was too discreet to specify. It was an 'unpleasant' day, damp and moist. Joking platitudes issued from Ned's nib: 'What can't be cured must be endured. No use crying over spilt milk. Ha Ha never say die.'

Close to midnight he wrote to his sister once more, unable to conceal his wretchedness any longer. Their parents had turned 'wild' at a troubled letter from Mattie delivered to The Evergreens during the day. Ned begs her to stop wailing (in her letters from school) because their mother can bear no more. 'When you see the Dearest thing in all the Earth slowly being destroyed by cruelty & no way in God['s] world to prevent it, & have to wear a smooth front all the time, then you know what it is to endure.'

Would that he could take what Mother had to bear upon his shoulders, he would be 'more than thankful'.

Three days later, Ned saw the hall 'in that most forlorn of all conditions'. On 28 January he had spent the day stripping the last of the marital decor. The new wallpaper did not signal a genuine revolution, more an obligation to paper over the split in the household. 'As for news the same applies as has applied heretofore. We're out. Very out.'

As Ned sickened that winter there was little comfort in a note from next door where Aunt Emily 'gasps out' that she has managed to get up. They are 'the Cripples'. His father ignored the deteriorating health around him. His was god-given love, on a par with Dante and Beatrice. He was proud to side with them.

David Todd's tolerance puzzled Susan. Knowing nothing of his sexual marksmanship, she dismissed him as ineffectual. 'Little dud David' was her taunt. He never forgot it.

Mabel took care to keep her husband in play. Her next move was to bring in a Boston cousin: plump, well-kept Caroline (Caro) Andrews, her rump encased in a striped black taffeta skirt. It rustled as she walked. Glossy black braids crowned her head and a wide collar of lace, edged with a frill, covered her shoulders. Caro was the daughter of a Congregational minister of Cambridgeport, and before her marriage had been on the editorial staff of a magazine. Bored with marriage to a wealthy merchant, she was typical David Todd prey. He immediately took up with Caro, whose apt middle name was Lovejoy. She came to stay on 16 April 1885 and that very evening David invited her to his observatory, while Mabel 'fixed the furnace' and entertained Austin. Caro and David, she notes, 'came back very late'. The following day, her diary goes on, 'David & Mrs. Andrews, Mr. Dickinson & I had a lovely drive all morning. Windy & fresh.' In the evening Mabel had a 'tremendous' little conversation with her husband and then the following day, while David took Caro away until five in the afternoon, Mabel had another conversation with Austin in the Todds' parlour. This involved 'Revelations' she does not reveal, but it appears that a 'strange relation' with Caro ensued, which Mabel dared not write out except to say (in her more reflective journal) it was 'more remarkable & almost unbelievable than any novel I ever read or dreamed of'. Mabel's excitement was such that she hardly ate. The editor of the lovers' letters has suggested a four-way relationship, and it looks as though attraction developed between the two women. Caro's visit, Mabel goes on, activated 'the whole beautiful rounding-out of some halves of things'. Caro then invited Mabel to accompany her and her husband when they sailed for Europe in June 1885.

Before leaving Mabel handed over Millicent and Grandma Wilder to Mrs Loomis, who passed through Boston en route to New Hampshire for the summer. The quayside saw a bitter exchange between Mabel and her mother, followed by a 'dreadful' fifteen-page letter in which Mrs Loomis reproached her daughter for selfishness, stubbornness, vanity and meanness to her child in cheap boots while Mabel sailed out in customary style. Mrs Loomis deplored not only Austin but also Lavinia as 'cynical, carping, irreligious people'. Mabel told Austin that since the letter every breath was an agony. She decided to pretend it never came. All Austin could offer was ardour: 'I kiss you all over.' Then, a longer letter than usual from Emily Dickinson reinforced the Loomis accusations with warnings to 'Egypt' from 'America'. It was written on 31 July and boldly enclosed in a letter from Austin. He'd hoped, he told Mabel, to prove the worth of her character by showing Emily her farewell letter: 'I shall let Emily read it sometime, when it comes right.' It never did come right.

That summer, while Mabel toured Europe, the Lessey lease came to an end and Austin supervised the transfer and storage of Mabel's sofa, chairs, dresses and pictures in his sisters' home. Austin assured Mabel that Emily liked to see her oil paintings of flowers and grasses.

When Mabel steamed towards Boston harbour on her return from Europe she had to choose which man was to meet her first. She gave priority to her husband, and it wasn't only a gesture of wifely correctness: 'How I will kiss you & caress you when I once more get you within reach!' Mabel stirred his anticipation. 'How you shall <u>feel</u> all that I think now about you from afar.'

To Austin, nine days later, she was a little apologetic: 'policy considered', she must put her husband first. She sent Austin, too, his boost. She will write twice more '– and then – oh! then!'

Accordingly, when the ship docked in Boston on Sunday 13 September she spent the night with David Todd, who left at dawn to be on time for a Monday morning class at Amherst, while Austin's dawn train from Amherst to Boston sped in the opposite direction. Austin's train got in at 9.40 a.m., in time for a few hours with Mabel before she left later that day to join her mother and Millicent in New Hampshire. So, a blissful reunion at night for one man; and bliss next morning for the other.

Austin was considerate towards David Todd, as David to him – no sign of friction where it might be expected. The Todds moved into the Lincoln house near the bottom of Lessey Street, the neighbouring house to the west of The Evergreens that Austin calls in his diary the third house or '3dh' (as distinct from the 'other house' to the east of The Evergreens). Convenient, of course, for Austin's assignations, yet the proximity to his family would have provided further scenes for observation.

While Mabel was abroad she'd turned over the idea of building a house of her own.

'Dear heart, sweet-heart,' she appealed to Austin. 'Oh! I do so hope things will be arranged for me . . . I am really thinking a good deal about a house – one or two requirements being so necessary.' It's a hint about their need for a permanent place to meet.

Austin agreed to deed a plot of Dickinson land to the Todds, but to do so he required signatures from his sisters. Since his father had died intestate in a country where there is no law of primogeniture, these were co-heirs. Austin wished his sisters to oblige his mistress and could count on compliance from Vinnie. Emily alone held out, as she'd promised her nephew in a staunch letter of August 1885 while he was away at Lake Placid, in the Adirondack Mountains in upstate New York.

'Dear Boy,' she started, 'I dared not trust my own Voice among your speechless Mountains, and so I took your Mother's, which mars no Majesty – So you find no treason in Earth or Heaven.' Emily is at one with Ned's mother in wanting to protect his future inheritance. 'No treason' must be allowed to mar his fragile peace of mind, for Ned had suffered another seizure on 9 June. Emily repeats the assurance that he will not encounter treason from her: 'You never will, My Ned'. And then, a third time, she promises to hold the fort, positioned as she is to defend his interests:

And ever be sure of me, Lad –

> Fondly,
> Aunt Emily.

Emily's refusal to sign the deed was not known outside the family and this act remained unnoticed by biographers. But it's vital to see her great moral courage, like her acts of moral courage at college, as she took a stand against her brother. The necessity for this stand means that her brother had urged her to give the land to his mistress. We can't know the degree of pressure she felt, but she did not yield even when her health declined. Her sympathy with Sue, known to her nephew at least, is evident in a request he made before he went away.

'You will look after Mother?' he asked.

Emily shared this with Sue. Nothing so sweet, she said, 'as the last words of your Boy'.

At the same time she maintained her loyalty to Austin in her Shakespearean riddles. They cast him as a man of power whose passionate nature makes him susceptible to manipulation. Antony came to mind, then her favourite, Othello, 'who loved not wisely but too well'. The next month, September 1885, Emily pencilled one line to Mabel: 'Why should we censure Othello [for strangling his wife], when the . . . Lover says, "Thou shalt have no other Gods before Me"?'

It's hard to believe that Emily sent this solely for her own satisfaction. Her riddles go beyond verbal ingenuity. Their emotional energy goes beyond a game. She meant Mabel to feel the hit, assuming an adversary with the intelligence to do so. To enter into a duel implies a compliment of sorts to an opponent who is in on the code, and up to it. Mabel, alert to attention from the recluse, kept every letter.

As Emily sank over the next ten months, Austin's visits were rather infrequent. According to his diary, he sat with Emily every ten days or two weeks during the last months of her life. This is oddly sparse for a brother living next door, and we may wonder if Austin was displeased by Emily's refusal to sign the deed or see his mistress face to face as she wished. Contrast the two or three visits a day back in 1883 (before the poet's home became the venue for adultery), when Austin spoke of Mabel to his sisters.

Meanwhile, the lovers again took advantage of Emily's increasing sickness to settle in once more downstairs. In January 1886 Austin arranged an assignation in a note to Mabel, careful as ever not to mention her name: he asks if his 'client' would accept an appointment for 2.15 p.m. in his sisters' library? Vin, he says, consents, though the wording leans to the negative: 'there is nothing in her case to interfere with my seeing my client in the Library after Lunch if our business seems to require it'. He has satisfied himself that Emily is not too sick for this to happen.

Mabel replied with an unsigned note, dated 14 January. 'I will come at 2 & risk it. I think I can arrange it well. At any rate I'll come.'

A follow-up note from Austin to Mabel conveys a measure of coolness on Vinnie's part. 'Vin is sort [of?] nervous – Things are edgy [?] over there.'

A daytime assignation would not have been invisible from The Evergreens, and could have contributed to Ned's outrage. On 17 January 1886 he had another seizure.

The next month, as Emily worsened, Mabel offered Austin a return to youth. She spoke of spring, buds, blossoms. Renewal would come, she promised, if they could be permanently together, if there were no one to 'say us nay'.

Even now, Mabel tried to soften Emily with yet another gift. On 11 February she painted a bronze plaque with thistles and dispatched it to the Homestead four days later. Emily's first answer, from her sickbed, was a hyacinth, but ten days later she rallied to her most brilliant rebuff. It was only half a line: 'Or Figs of Thistles?' The clue to this riddle is the complete line from the New Testament: 'Do men gather grapes of thorns, or figs of thistles?' No nourishment, then, from thorns or thistles forced down her throat. This is Emily Dickinson's last and most cutting thrust at Mabel Loomis Todd. *She dealt her pretty words like blades.* Did Mabel get it? She certainly noted the adder's tongue sent over from the Homestead, though she was politic enough to claim an unblemished friendship with the poet. Dickinson herself foresaw a doomed stand, yet to make the stand in the face of death was a Thermopylae of her own.

If Emily cultivated adulterous emotions for a forbidden 'Master', did this affect her response to her brother's outbreak into active adultery? An answer lies in her Shakespearean retorts to Mabel. Here, there is sympathy for the 'entangled' Antony, the susceptible Roman whose command is tarnished by his affair with the enemy queen, Cleopatra. There is sympathy too for the worked-up Othello.

Another question: how did the ensuing clash strike the poet, whose collapse during 1884 coincided with the height of its impact on her family? She did live long enough to know that what had happened could not heal. All the same, loyalty to her brother did not stop her reaching out to Sue: 'The tie between us is very fine, but a Hair never dissolves.'

There were short breaths of empathy in her messages to Sue: 'Emerging from an Abyss, and re[-]entering it – that is Life, is it not, Dear?', and then the last pencilled notes to Sue made their way across the grass: 'How lovely every solace! . . . Thank you, dear Sue – for every solace –'. Her health gave out with the break-up of the family, compounded by a succession of deaths that cut too deep. 'Because I would not stop for Death — / He kindly stopped for me —', so she'd set the scene when she was young, undercutting irony with triumph: 'The Carriage held but just ourselves — / And Immortality.' In her last illness she spoke differently of 'the great intrusion of Death'. Some gardens, she observed, were willing to die in autumn: 'I do not think that mine was – it perished with beautiful reluctance, like an evening star –'. She died on 15 May 1886, when she was fifty-five.*

---

* The final prescription, from Dr Bigelow, was 'chloroform olive oil' [Leyda, ii, 470] two days before Dickinson's death, when she was breathing in a way that horrified her family. Chloroform, according to Bigelow's *Dictionary of Medicine*, might serve to rectify the jagged, partially asphyxiated breathing that warns of an oncoming fit.

The next day was a Sunday; Mabel appeared all in black in the church choir, and so grieved that she found it hard to sing. On Tuesday, the day before the funeral, she cried herself 'sick', and that evening, when Austin came to call, she 'let go utterly' and 'cried frantically'. The grief may seem excessive for one who had never laid eyes on the poet, yet Mabel was perceptive and prescient too, when she writes in her journal: 'Rare Emily Dickinson died – went back into a little deeper mystery than that she has always lived in.'

Susan prepared the grave with fragrant boughs but did not attend the funeral, aware that Mabel would be there. Higginson, who came, sensed something 'pure and strange' in the atmosphere of the Homestead as a more elevated House of Usher. (In Poe's ominous tale, the House holds a dead sister and living brother who are conjoined in overwrought family affinities in a home poised on the edge of ruin.)

Emily Dickinson, long unseen by some, was visible in the open coffin at the funeral. There were violets at her throat and Vinnie put two heliotropes by her hand 'to take to Judge Lord'. The poet looked young for her years, her red hair untouched by grey and no wrinkle on her beautiful brow. Mabel, costumed again in black, looked haggard in her role as prime griever for so dear a friend.

In fact, this death opened the way for Mabel to acquire her plot of land. The handover went ahead after the funeral on 19 May. The deed is dated 8 June 1886. It's made out as though the Todds were buying the plot for $1200, but it was a gift. By 14 June contractors were standing by, and the following month Austin sent Mabel $100 'as per request', assuring her (on college treasurer stationery) that she could request more as needed. This followed a wail from Mabel that building was held up because the cost had climbed to $300 more than the original estimate. At some point Austin gave her a further $1500 from the Dickinson coffers, waving gratitude away: 'Don't say a word.' He'd already cut a private road through his father's meadow, an eastern extension of Fowler Place (named in honour of his grandfather; now Spring Street), bisecting what had been an open stretch in front of the Homestead. There, in the second half of 1886, the Todds' house sprang up. Painted red, it stood out on the meadow. Austin had pictured a modest cottage but Mabel had other ideas. She called it 'a little house of thirteen rooms' and gave it a cottagey name, The Dell, as though it were tucked away in the small ravine (known as 'the dell') at the bottom of its garden. In fact, the house was three storeys, with a striking geometric design: a wide half-moon window beneath the roof echoed in the curve of its wide entrance. Mabel's desk, a gift from Austin, stood at a big south window looking towards the Holyoke hills.

A back stair had been planned to provide outside access to the second storey. Polly Longsworth, who edited the lovers' letters, saw that 'some kind of *ménage à trois* arrangement was contemplated' when Austin, Mabel and David spent Sunday evenings together at the Lincoln house. There are ten occasions during 1886 when Austin adds 'with the witness' to the parallel lines in his diary, and the witness – it can only have been David – reappears in Austin's diary of 1888 (the diary for 1887 has not survived). Like 'client' as cover for mistress, 'witness' uses a familiar legal word as cover for their experiments with voyeurism. Mabel's diary corroborates these Sunday evenings in her own code. She leaves the church choir between eight and eight-thirty, goes home and 'up to bed at once'.

David often said that he loved Austin 'more than any other man', and Austin said more or less the same when he described 'a sort of unspoken sympathy' that seemed to grow up between them: 'He has seemed to lean upon me – and confide in me beyond anything I have known among men, and I make a point of looking after him.' Reciprocal benefits – Austin improving David's position without being asked; David yielding up his wife to what he persisted in seeing as light diversion – underpinned a deepening tie between the men. There's no knowing whether their bond was a by-product of the allure Mabel exuded, or her contrivance, or whether it grew of itself as the men came into closer contact. David would 'clear the track' when Austin asked. Sometimes Austin stayed the night while David was at work. At daybreak David would hum an aria before entering the house, a signal to the couple upstairs.

An outside stair could have allowed a lover to avoid the inconvenient child at The Dell, but Austin was all too evident. Afternoon assignations meant the silent presence of Millicent Todd, home from school. 'Hello,

Child,' Austin would say, and then he would lead Mamma upstairs while she murmured 'my King!' Then they would close the door. Millicent felt his 'awful omni-presence' as much upstairs as when he was visible. Her later fragments of autobiography recall Austin's spare, erect figure, tall and awesome with his red side-whiskers and wig of coppery hair standing out like a halo around his austere face. He wore a long gold chain about his neck and soft kid shoes cut to fit his narrow feet. On his head was a brown velvet cap that he left at The Dell; Mamma kept it in her music case in the back parlour. His lofty manner meant less to Millicent than her sense of him as 'the somewhat terrible center of the universe'. This was not to be questioned, Millicent said, 'but I felt the weight of him and carried it throughout my childhood'. All that time, he hardly acknowledged her existence. This is what she told herself, discounting Austin's attempt at a tease when he would return her 'straight look'. A smile from him was unthinkable. Yet the active contempt came from the opposing camp when Millicent encountered the other inhabitants of The Evergreens.

Mrs Dickinson and her daughter would pass the child with heads high. Millicent sensed the snub had something to do with Mamma. She tried to avoid them, and if her way lay along their part of Main Street, she walked— stiff-faced, with solemn eyes— on the opposite side to The Evergreens (the paved side for public use). Nothing was explained to the child who longed to protect Mamma and rescue her from the hate seething about them.

Only the recluse had reached out to Millicent. Though adamant about Mabel, she did see the child and once, in a letter to Mabel, pointed to her familiarity with 'the quaint little girl with the deep Eyes, every day more fathomless'. Millicent was welcome to enter a side gate and trot through the back door to the apple-green kitchen. There, a cookie or flower was put in her hand. She was only six when the poet died, and later, when Millicent became her mother's champion in the ongoing feud, all she could recall was the fiery hair in a brown chenille snood, with tassels swinging behind each ear, as Emily Dickinson bent towards her.

10

LADY MACBETH OF AMHERST

'Mabel Loomis Dickinson' – Mabel set out the name on an envelope with a photograph of herself, taken ten to fifteen years earlier when she had been about fourteen.

Obviously the way to become Mabel Loomis Dickinson was to marry Austin, but there was what Mabel termed 'an obstacle' in the shape of the present Mrs Dickinson. Her elimination was not an idle fantasy. Mabel had long had a 'presentiment' of future distinction, and in November 1885 – two years after she became Austin's mistress – it revived. She trusted that the day was to come when she would take a public role as consort to Austin.

Mabel's campaigns intensified and speeded up in the wake of Emily Dickinson's death, as though Emily's stand did have some effect in holding her back. From Emily she'd had warning after warning that an invisible Dickinson saw through her moves. Once Emily was buried, Mabel got the land and house, but she wanted a stronger powerbase. The fact that she called Austin her 'King' casts something of a Lady Macbeth light on what Mabel willed to happen.

She devised her campaigns away from Amherst: the farther away, the more ambitious her dreams. It had been in Europe in the summer of 1885 that she'd planned a house of her own on a plot carved out of Mr Dickinson's meadow. Two years later, she urged Austin to deal with the 'obstacle' to her future reign with 'my King' – the King of Amherst. The time had come for Susan's exit.

When she left on a journey to Japan in 1887, Mabel infused Austin with a promise of deathless love. Her farewell letter on 5 June promises to be together for 'eternities' because 'it is in the great foundations of things that you and I shall be mated'. His nerve must not fail. 'Impediments' (his wife and children) would kill what was 'not of God, partaking of His ever-lastingness'. Austin should now grasp the 'glories' ahead, and have no doubts.

'No, sweetheart, we are one for <u>always</u> – I know it, and I trust in Him – and you.'

She looked to an act of God, in line with Austin's belief that their tie was God-given, 'pure'. With God on the lovers' side they must now secure 'positive' not 'negative' happiness. Mabel was adept at transforming definitions of this sort. Austin must be convinced that their thriving affair was a lesser joy; that it was a 'negative' way-station en route to a 'positive' union, and to achieve that 'positive', a public tie, Austin was pressed to let his wife fade, as surely she would if she were made to feel the lethal force of rejection. Mabel's pressure is slant, subliminal; she wanted it to become a purpose Austin would make his own.

It's unclear how David Todd would have accommodated to 'Mabel Loomis Dickinson', but it would be in character for Mabel to convince him, once again, that her plans were to his professional advantage.

In a tensely expectant state, Mabel felt herself advancing towards her destined part, planted permanently in The Evergreens and acknowledged by everyone in town.

From the start, Mabel had transformed the 'Sister' and 'Mother' who was Sue into the 'great black Moghul'. The image distanced Sue, as though she were alien to her own home and town. It also blocks pity for Sue in black, the figure in mourning. Mabel, dressed in white, had struck Austin as a beacon of purity on the piazza of the Lessey house, as he had come towards her by night. An angel, Austin had said, enraptured to think she was waiting for him. Mabel was 'pure white' and 'thinking no evil', he assured her, when her mother and grandmother criticised the vanity and selfishness they associated with her shame. While her mother spoke, Mabel gazed out of the window at the rain weeping 'in sympathy'.

For a long time after Gib's death Sue hardly went out, but when she did Mabel reported her to Austin as 'parading' in the town, as though it were pushy to show herself at all. Her black dress loomed, an emblem of moral darkness. So Mabel put it to Austin, who inclined his ear to a lover who looked like an innocent flower – like the flowers she painted on her person: a daisy on her bodice, rosebuds on her sash.

Sue's visibility troubled Mabel. Protected only by the dignified reserve of the Dickinson family, Mabel feared for her reputation. To forestall or damp down gossip over Sue's ending their friendship, Mabel put it about that Sue was faithless: a person who wooed friends, only to drop them. Such rejections were arbitrary. Nothing to do with Mabel, who had been too trusting, one of Sue's social victims. This slander was to stick: to this day Sue is made out to be untrustworthy, a manipulator inflicting damage.

Another tenacious slander played up the family tensions present before Mabel arrived on the scene. Austin and Sue were still sharing a bed at least a year before Mabel's arrival, but there were certainly tensions signalled by the change in Austin's behaviour following his father's death. He became withdrawn, sombre, forbidding pleasure and resentful of Sue's sociability, her 'scintillation'. In her youth Emily had foreseen an ascetic strain in her brother, a recapitulation of their father, and to balance her brother Emily had encouraged his attraction to Martha Gilbert and the over-riding passion for Sue. But as Mabel had it, she'd come upon this dysfunctional family and found it in her to comfort Austin who'd had the misfortune to marry a low-born creature, 'the Spoiler' of his life.

Mabel didn't make this up; it was what Austin had told her. 'He has begun to feel that it does not do for persons of entirely different social grades to marry,' Mabel reports in her journal of 1885. She was given an impression that Austin's sole motive for his marriage had been to inject 'bodily vigor' into his family. Sue had 'made him marry her, in spite of his terrible repugnance to doing it'. According to Mabel's journal, Austin likened his wedding to an execution. Austin, it appears, has told her nothing of the way he pursued Sue in the 1850s. But then, nothing in Austin's hand was ever on paper to confirm this melodrama of the doomed bride-groom.

Mabel set down things he'd said: Austin's 'entire disappointment' in the marriage, and his entrapment, as a fly caught in a spider's web. The truth, of course, is that it was Sue who'd been reluctant and in the end unable to escape the marriage. But Austin was not one to tell a deliberate lie. Thirty years on, this must be what he'd come to believe. It was easier than attempting to explore why Sue didn't adore and make love with him. Mabel includes abortions in the list of accusations, with no apparent re-collection of her own attempts to abort Millicent. Mabel relays Sue's fear of childbirth as Austin's grievance. Her 'morbid dread of having children has hurt & distressed his life to the quick. She caused three or four to be artificially removed before Ned. And she did everything in her power to rid herself of him – to which efforts all his ill-health is attributed.'

Mabel fires up over her lover's alleged report that Sue's 'fits of horrible & entirely unrestrained temper have put Austin several times in danger of his life, & he says if anything should happen to him suddenly we may be tolerably sure she has killed him'. A specific accusation is that Sue once threw a knife at her husband.

Sue's temper has come down to us as a trait that estranged Emily. It's true that Sue's Christmas gift in 1880, Disraeli's *Endymion*, was inscribed to Emily 'who not seeing I still love'. That this amounted to estrangement is disproved by two letters in 1881, the year Mabel entered the scene. Emily had asked Dr Holland how he'd managed to snare William Dean Howells whose novel, *A Fearful Responsibility*, was serialised in *Scribner's Magazine*. The editor had replied:

Emily –
    Case of Bribery – Money did it –
                         Holland –

Emily shared this note with Sue who, she recounts to Dr Holland, 'took Ned's Arm and came across – and we all talked of Mr Samuel [Bowles] and you, and vital times when you two bore the Republican, and came as near

sighing – all of us – as would be often wise – I should say next door – Sue
said she was homesick for those "better days," hallowed be their name'.

There's a hint here of treading on eggshells with Austin next door, but
no coldness between Sue and Emily. If anything, Emily's tone is commis-
eration constrained by loyalty to her reserved and frowning brother.

'And you alone have found me out,' Austin told Mabel. 'I never revealed
myself to another – you know it – there was but one key. That you had.
You have turned it, and entered in. You have conquered me, by such sweet
winning ways.'

He was a person who oscillated between extremes of reserve and emotional abandon, a temperament similar to his sister's. Their volatility made
the stable routines of home all the more necessary. As homemaker Susan
had excelled, all the more keenly after her orphaned youth and discomfort
in her brother-in-law's house. To counter Sue's domesticity (something
Mabel always despised), she projects on to Sue the illegitimate ploys of a
mistress.

'It seems unfair that she should be cold and dreadful to me, and over-
poweringly sweet to you,' she put it to Austin. 'You are petted & cajoled,
and I am hated.'

How was Mabel to evict a wife so entrenched in The Evergreens? Susan
had channelled her considerable gifts of mind and taste into her home. The
Evergreens was a centre of culture: its dinners delicious, running to many
courses on gala occasions; a house and garden worthy of the leading man
of Amherst. To erode Austin's comforts, Mabel asked him to enumerate his
reasons for turning against his marriage. Her first request was from
Washington early in 1884, immediately after they had consummated their
union, when the idea of a documented case against Sue came to her. At the
time, Mabel had been elated by a sense of power as she'd swanned through
a succession of 'brilliant' social events, including a reception at the White
House given by President Arthur's sister. There had been a tea for four
hundred where she'd 'received', wearing a silk dress and the sash she had
painted with rosebuds.

Mabel wanted this case in writing, 'to use as a shield' against any
future 'attack' on their love. As always, she presents herself as the

innocent victim of his family's campaigns. Her allegations are persuasive
enough for her words to have reached beyond Austin to biographers
and critics of the future. This reach across the footlights of her own time
testifies to Mabel's skills as an actress who is the first to believe her words
as they issue from her mouth. How rare it is 'to be a lady to the core!' Her
class act upstaged Susan's 'wrath'. In her politely temperate tones, Mabel
regretted Sue's tantrums as too vulgar for a gentleman of Austin's refinement. They justified his defection. Mabel capitalised on every outburst,
commiserating with Austin on what he had to bear from the virago at
home. Mabel's drama of manners seeks to obliterate the darker drama of
betrayal.

Inconveniently for Mabel, Susan's protests did not continue. Successive
blows of death and betrayal had shaken her, but she found something to
live for in the love of her two remaining children. These ties strengthened.
Then there was the balm of Emily's support, with more notes crossing
the grass in 1885 than in any previous year. That year, following the wallpaper incident, Ned's nerves were 'perfectly worn out' by unavoidable
proximity to a 'storm-centre' (his father) moving their way. Ned's rheumatic condition worsened and his frame 'stiffened up', he noticed, in new
places. Alarmed, Susan found the strength to prop up the outer ramparts
of relations with Austin.

For all these reasons, as well as family rectitude, Austin replied to
Mabel's request with caution: '. . . Is it not better and nobler that I say
nothing which . . . reflects upon any other!' He did not want to 'offend or
wound'. They had 'so much to be grateful for', even if obliged 'to defer
some of our hopes – everything will come in good time'.

Mabel didn't let go. She pressed him once more for a 'wee' case against
his wife. 'Dear, forgive me, but have you put that little wee note in my
box yet?' she pleaded from London on 18 July 1885. 'You will, will you
not?'

Austin hesitated. In August, he offered Mabel emotional security when
he called her 'my sweet wife'. It was a private gesture when what Mabel
wanted was to move from the secret space occupied by a mistress into a
public space where her tie with the Dickinsons could be manifest.

Austin's reply was delayed until 13 September 1885, the day Mabel returned from Europe. Again he backed away. His past had been a 'wicked' failure, he said, and he wanted to put it behind him rather than 'involve any other unpleasantly' or risk 'the slightest injustice. Believe me,' he appealed. 'Believe me.'

Mabel was not to be deterred. Austin's family were 'encumbrances' and 'annoyances', while she, Mabel, who 'Oh!' loves him 'so tenderly', may die if 'deprivations grow insupportable'. In this campaign to cut family ties, Mabel called in a powerful supporter, none other than the Almighty.

Just 'one turn of God's hand' could secure what she wants. 'I wonder if He does hear prayers!'

Like fighters and armies from time immemorial, Mabel co-opts the deity as she prays for the enemy's death. It was indeed to be a fight to the death, led by the campaign of slander. This was in the air when Ned asked Aunt Emily to look after Mother while he was away. Emily fortified Sue with scripture: 'The World hath not known her, but I have known her, was the sweet boast of Jesus'.

Mabel's dark intent shows its face for an instant in November 1885 when she asks Austin, 'what can we do?' It appears a rhetorical question in the context of Mabel's threat to die if she has to wait too long to fulfil her 'pre-sentiment'. The tone is delicately balanced between resignation and covert challenge: would he 'do' something to prevent her dying?

A month later, Austin still had made no move. This is how Mabel came to advise on the minutiae of goodbyes and greetings at The Evergreens: hints on how to wither the life of his family.

During the last months of Emily's life Austin hesitated to leave Amherst, but he did make it twice to Boston. After he left The Evergreens on 15 December 1885 it occurred to Mabel that she had neglected to orchestrate his farewells to his family. He should be chilling their hearts, not indulging in family rituals: a touch, it may be, a pat on the arm, a wish for his safety, a promise of kindness on his return. In Boston again the following March, six weeks before Emily's death, Austin received Mabel's renewed strike at family customs. One such custom was to correspond when Austin and Susan were apart.

'You will not think it necessary to write [from Boston] to anyone but me in this town? Will you? I meant to have spoken of my hope that you would not . . .'. A day later, Mabel reminds Austin that her directive about farewells 'holds just as intensely strong about the kind of greeting you get on your return. <u>Please don't</u> have it . . .'.

As these tentacles reach into The Evergreens, Mabel pictures herself as passive in God's hands: it's God who creates their love, she tells Austin. The soar of Mabel's voice lifts them off the ground. This is the master-chord of her campaign, tuned to her lover's surrender to the Lord's will in accord with the prime drama of his milieu. As Mabel returns rave for rave, translating Austin's passion into her own eloquence, abundant inward fuel steams from 'that little star of a presentiment which never wholly leaves me'. She splurged her savings on a sealskin cape like Sue's, which Mabel had long coveted. The slur of blackness forgotten, Mabel's emergence in the black cape was a token of the identity in which Mabel's imagination dressed herself.

The black cape means more than fashion. It's a sign of Mabel's continued eye to Sue. Closer to hunger than to love, there's a possessiveness like that of a stalker or obsessive fan, potentially dangerous to its object. Mabel was fixed on the Dickinsons: on the kingly authority of Austin Dickinson, on the genius of the poet and more instinctively on Susan whose brain, enhanced by reading, had fitted her to join this family. The danger to Susan Dickinson was Mabel's need to *be* her. It's more than a simple wish on the part of a mistress to change her status; there's a compulsion to take on the very being of the person she wants to eliminate. If Mabel's imitation is more sinister than the shallow narrative of the femme fatale, what narrative does she devise? Her urgings are softer than Lady Macbeth's, not so forthright, not so commanding: a Lady Macbeth with the passive manner of nineteenth-century womanhood. Her wish at this point is still covert: when, oh when, will Austin remove the obstacle?

This didn't happen. Nine months later Austin can be found participating contentedly in summer activities with his family. In July 1886, unknown to Mabel, he accompanied Susan, Mattie and Ned on an overnight jaunt to arrange a vacation in Ashfield, Massachusetts, a lovely drive through the Berkshire hills; there was a picnic at Mount Sugarloaf in Sunderland; and Austin invited the same party and Lavinia (recently bereft of Emily) on a long evening drive to Leveritt (where he and Mabel had made love a month earlier). At his wife's invitation, Austin joined his family twice at Ashfield in August, and over Mabel's objection he went back a third time to help them home.

He told her bluntly, 'You've made a mistake.'

She grovelled at once. Fearing to lose him, her abjection was over-wrought. Only the alarm rings true; her outcry for forgiveness is too clamorous to be convincing.

From the late summer of 1886 and through the spring of 1887 Mabel was occupied with building and furnishing her nest on the Dickinson meadow. She continued to satisfy the giver of this bounty. But her renewed whis-perings to Austin suggest that to satisfy him does not satisfy her, and is secondary to an ambition she can't define, inflated with a delusion it can join with God.

'. . . I feel that there are, within me, divine possibilities which can only blossom through you', were her parting words to Austin when she and David left for Japan in June 1887. She followed this up three days later on a train to Montreal: 'I have a sort of of-<u>course</u> feeling, that pretty soon we shall be inseparably together . . . – a presentiment for this world, I mean, as well as Heaven, dear.'

A more forceful scenario grew on Mabel on the long journey across Canada and the Pacific to Tokyo. They took a new route from Vancouver, more direct than the route from San Francisco, but this far north it proved stormy even in summer: giant waves rose above the ship and broke over the deck. Mabel alone stayed on deck, in a hatchway, to witness the wild-ness. Unlike the other passengers, prone in their bunks below, she had the stomach for upheavals of the seas. The captain commended her appearance at meals. Even his seasoned wife couldn't make it.

As part of David's expedition, Mabel gamely climbed Mount Fuji (the first woman permitted to go beyond the sixth level) and then slept on the floor under mosquito netting in a Japanese inn in Shirakawa, where David was preparing to photograph a total eclipse of the sun. Here, far from Amherst, Mabel's mind was fixed on The Evergreens, awaiting the bolt from on high, the 'divine visitation' about to hit her 'enemies'. It's not escaped notice that if Austin was her 'God' he was particularly well placed to act on her behalf. A charitable view is that this was 'unconscious' on Mabel's part, but that's unlikely given her conviction that the obstacle had to go.

From Shirakawa, on 31 July 1887, Mabel sent a renewed death threat to Austin: he must intervene to secure her public position and subdue the 'bigoted spite' she experienced as his mistress.

'You have, as far as the outward circumstances go, the great advantage of me. You can rule & compel some things which I cannot . . . they make your outward life much more bearable than mine. I do not want my life to end so soon. I have capabilities which will grow in time into larger accomplishment, sometime. I mean to do something worth while.'

Up to now, Mabel's ambition had not shown full face to Austin. Where David supported ambition, Austin may not have known that New Women existed. He did do Mabel the favour of sending a manuscript to a contact at *Harper's* magazine when she went so far as to ask, but there's no sign Austin himself read it or saw her future in professional terms. It was well enough for Mabel to sing in church or drawing rooms, but he'd not have liked her on the stage. What he wanted was Mabel's resounding echo of his love-calls. For Mabel to reveal her separate ambition at this point shows how near the edge she was.

Ambition, she confessed, was eroded by 'morbid' fears over 'the terrible hatred of my three enemies. I can feel it pursuing me here on the other side of the world – the positive hatred & persecution, as well as the negative disgust. I feel it every moment, & it is killing me. Perhaps I am nervous, but I certainly do feel as if it would ultimately be my death. I do not know but that something is being done by them now, for my destruction – at all events, I have been most horribly conscious of their malignity for more than a week, so that some days I have hardly been able to speak for the crushing power of it.'

Before she left Shirakawa, on the afternoon of Sunday 21 August, she asked Austin to meet her ship when it docked if what she expected were accomplished. '. . . If any divine visitation occurs to the big black Moghul, you will come to Vancouver & meet us, won't you. In spite of my half-feeling that God has deserted me, I seem to be waiting for an answer to my prayers on that subject all the time.' Mabel continued to expect news of Susan Dickinson's death at every stage of the long return journey.

In Mabel's fantasy the threesome would then make a triumphal arm-in-arm progress towards their Amherst kingdom. When the obstacle remained in place, she was almost incredulous. Three times Austin held out against Mabel's call to action. First, in the summer of 1885, he had refused to attack his marriage with written evidence. Then, in the summer of 1886, he had refused Mabel's plea not to help his family at Ashford. Lastly, in the summer of 1887, Austin did nothing to undermine his wife's existence when Mabel, far away in Shirakawa, awaited developments. She had made it as clear as she could that if she is to flourish Austin must freeze or wither Sue's spirit to the point where health and hold on life give way.

Did Austin get the message? Was he stirred by Mabel's threat of her own death? Or was he reluctant to seize the dagger before him, the handle towards his hand? These are crucial questions, even if they leave us guessing. Austin's eruptive nature made him suggestible if deflected from his groove – he accepted, for instance, the novelty of group sex – but, unlike Macbeth, he was not susceptible to evil or injustice. To call Mabel 'my angel wife' placed a block of sorts on active malice. Yet during the two years of rehearsal for Susan's demise, Mabel did succeed up to a point: if she could not screw Austin's courage to the sticking place, she did narrow the scope of his emotional attachments until he could see only her. That summer, he tells her how far he has 'grown away from everything else; I have grown so entirely to you'. While Mabel is in Tokyo he repeats it. This is the message he's absorbed: 'There is nothing else. You transform, transmute, translate everything . . . you have made me yours . . .'

All other ties felt hollow. This may explain his curtailed visits to Emily when she was dying. The summer following her death, when Austin sits in her room, he doesn't think of her, as someone who has lost a sister might.

It's just a room, not too familiar, an emptied place where he can write to Mabel. All the time she was away he felt 'the power' of her love, 'its over-whelming, overmastering strength in and over me'.

David Todd's expedition to Japan failed in its main purpose, to photograph the sun's corona during a total eclipse on 19 August 1887. He had invented a forerunner of the motion picture machine to capture the event but unfortunately Mount Fuji erupted at just that time, filling the atmos-phere with obscuring fumes. Nor could any amount of planning or money avert clouds, and this happened time after time. He travelled to California, Japan and, later, Angola in the vain expectation of a fine day. It always eluded him. He remained hopeful of future expeditions but President Seelye of Amherst College was not impressed with his habit of chasing eclipses. Inconvenienced by his absence, the college was not inclined to cover his salary. David Todd therefore needed Austin Dickinson's backing on the Board of Trustees. Thwarted ambition lies behind David's agreement to Mabel's plans for new campaigns. Though he didn't fathom his wife's need for the fidelity Austin offered, he had reason to believe that she was backing him. Their marriage was true after its own fashion, true to the ambitious partnership on which it was founded. Their manner towards each other was rather chummy. With David, Mabel calls herself 'May-bill', a billing coo unlike the high-toned speeches she reserved for Austin. Mabel, meanwhile, was increasingly disconcerted to have no news of an act of God. 'I am pitifully helpless in His hands, & dare not even reproach Him.' There's a desperate note in her voice when she asks Austin – in his Almighty character – for a sign. No luck. Sue walked about Amherst with her usual vigour.

Failing this campaign, Mabel interested herself in Austin Dickinson's will. It was signed on 3 November 1887, when he told Mabel of its contents. The will left his wife almost everything apart from Austin's share in his father's estate: the Homestead and the meadow. These he left to Lavinia on an understanding that she would 'turn it over' to Mabel.

'She has promised to do this,' he reassured Mabel.

Accustomed to his sister's compliance, Austin trusted that this would happen after his death. The understanding allowed him to leave an impeccable will with no questionable obligations to a mistress. He merely left two paintings to Mabel Loomis Todd, as to a friend with whom he shared a taste for art.

Disappointed of a public claim, Mabel's thoughts now turned to the West.

The frontier was the American answer to trouble. Huck Finn lights out for the Territory, and back in the seventeenth century Hester Prynne, condemned for adultery, tempts her one-time lover, the Puritan minister, to find liberty together in the wilderness, away from a punitive society. 'I want to rush away into liberty with you,' Mabel had suggested to Austin towards the end of 1885, at a time when Emily was too ill for him to take off. Earlier that year, he'd had a similar fantasy when Mabel had been in Europe. If he'd gone with her, he said, 'I doubt if we should have returned'. If he'd thought about it in time he might have laid his situation 'clearly' before his sisters.

Could the lovers take off in the opposite direction? This idea became a possibility in November 1887 when Austin went west and south to look around. Behind him in the far past were pioneering forebears, old Nathaniel Dickinson in the seventeenth century and great-grandfather Nathan and great-great-grandmother Thankful Dickinson in the eighteenth century, but migration was not for Austin, any more than it would have been conceivable for his father. It had finished off his grandfather to leave his native place for Cleveland, Ohio. As Austin travelled from Cleveland and Columbus to St Louis, Des Moines, Indianapolis, Tennessee and Birmingham, Alabama, he was sending home almost daily letters informing Sue, in sharp barks, of his movements. To Mabel he continues in the vein of love letters, deferring comment on his impressions, but to Sue he opens up, as to a wife solicitous for her husband's well-being: he hasn't slept a wink due to a howling baby. He favours Sue with Western menus: a haunch of black-tail deer, hunter's style. Here he is from Wichita, Kansas: 'a great nasty, horrid human hoggery . . . My whole nature recoils from it.'

How appalling to find an all-wise Creator had made human beings so degraded and ignorant. 'The wild hogs . . . that haunt the woods and stand in the shallow streams here seem not out of place – but the wretched mass of humanity – '. Leaving Wichita on 15 November phrases erupt into dashes along his almost illegible lines. 'Dante's inferno is nothing –'. There's chagrin to find how unsuited he is to a life beyond the perimeter of Massachusetts.

'I wouldn't give a volume of Emerson for all the hogs west of the Mississippi,' he told Sue. Emersonian individualism was often co-opted to back commercial greed. Here Austin rescues individualism with the fearlessness of his sister.

Mabel had no idea of this correspondence, nor how decisively Austin's home thoughts put an end to running away. They show him turning to Sue as part of his habitual life – the life to which he will return. It was not what Mabel would have wished to hear.

Failing to bring off Sue's demise, failing to establish a recognised claim in Austin's will and failing to convince Austin to abandon his home, Mabel remained dissatisfied as the wife without the sign. There had to be some visible sign, and this time it was to be a Dickinson baby. In February 1888 this unmaternal woman resolved to conceive another child. The code phrase was 'the experiment'. Mabel's concern for her reputation was such that pregnancy would have been out of the question had David not agreed to pass off the child as his own. He would have been convinced, once more, that the scheme was in his interest. The Todds still had no money, sometimes not even enough to buy a ticket for a train. Austin's baby, if not Mabel herself, would have a claim as a Dickinson heir. A moral claim, of course, not a legal one, but the Dickinsons were moral beings. At the same time a child would provide an indissoluble bond with the Dickinsons, joining Mabel to the bloodline.

When the plan for conception went into action Austin was nearly sixty and 'frightened'. His children were grown up. Mabel, on the other hand, was only thirty-one and a child would have been a tangible fruit of their love. They were inordinately cast down in March, when conception didn't happen in the first month. They talked to each other of 'failure', and 'dis-appointment' ate into Mabel's morale when, despite hot baths to relax her body before their attempts, for month after month nothing happened. They agreed to go on with 'the experiment', but without much hope. Mabel became depressed in the course of the year; God, it seemed, had turned away.

Susan Dickinson, meanwhile, sustained a wifely correspondence with Austin while she and their children vacationed that summer at Claremont House in South West Harbor, Maine. She stressed how 'safe' they all were, as though their safety mattered. She was in the company of the Amherst elite, Mrs Seelye (wife of the college president) and Professor Stearns (ex-college president), and would be even more content were Austin to join their party. Her only cause for concern was Austin alone at home – even if he wasn't lonely. 'I am forevermore lonely[,] that goes without saying.' This one flash of sadness does not press him too hard. As a solicitous wife she won't trouble her husband, though she owes it to their past not to deny her continued attachment. If the likelihood occurred to her that, in their absence, Mabel would sleep with Austin at The Evergreens (as she indeed did), Susan ignored it. This path between honesty and diplomacy is deli-cately judged – for their children's sake if not her own. There's a reassuring message about the children. Mattie had written to him, and 'Ned and Matty send their good-night with mine – Sue.'

So it happened that instead of this wife withering in a freeze emanating from her husband, it was the mistress who grew thin and dejected. To supplement David's salary she took on music pupils and taught art at the Convent, the school run by Mrs Stearns (the widowed daughter-in-law of Professor Stearns). A photograph of Mrs Todd with her pupils shows her a little wasted in a row of robust schoolgirls.

On the evening of 22 October 1888 David Todd came home with what Mabel called a 'thunderbolt'. It was almost certainly what she always dreaded: some slur on her reputation. 'I was crushed', she records in her diary. 'Cried all night.' Mabel was sure it emanated from her 'enemies' at The Evergreens. God, she thought, should really take away 'that heavy incubus' who weighed her down all the time. 'I should do it if I had unlimited power.'

For the first time she allowed herself to resent Austin's unwillingness to exert his power on her behalf: 'how very easily it could all be straightened and made perfect'.

She continued to brood over this and a month later sent Austin her most urgent plea to act against his family:

> Thanksgiving morning [29 November] 1888
>
> . . . It almost seems to me as if there is a faint little shadow between us today — for the first time in six years. . . . I do trust you — fully, firmly, even when your judgement seems to me over-cautious. I have hoped for changes to better us all these years. They have never come, but a steady pull, down in the other direction. Is it any wonder that I am eager for you to attack the fatal cause of it all?
>
> . . . I urge you to save me . . . I see it becoming daily more impossible for me to live in the little town which is yours. I see myself more and more alone, and I know that it is all merely the deliberately planned result of a hatred and a threat made and begun many years ago. I see power over all this lying idly in your hands, and you the only person able to cope with this terrible thing . . . I see with eyes supernaturally clear that the day has come for you to use just a little of the strength which lies in you against the stronghold of all my hurts . . . Even when I have seen the most clearly, and waited the most breathlessly for what you should do, I have never had an impatient thought of <u>you</u>. You sit enthroned, always. But you have never seen the bitter necessity as I have.

From the vantage of his own security, Austin thought Mabel should look upon the world as too large and fascinating to trouble herself with the gossip of gnats and carrion birds. He suggested she control herself.

Mabel replied that he had no idea of 'the almost iron hold' which she kept on herself all the time. Her impatience, she added, was only 'the superficial froth' of a struggle 'too deep for words'.

Her problem, in fact, was not that she lacked the words. It had to do with Mabel's struggle to subject her eloquence to a concubine code: never reproach the King. This time she risked it.

'I have continually put down the suggestion in my own mind that much of this pain was unnecessarily given me by your reluctance to step in and relieve it in the one place which caused it all. I have never admitted a thing into my consciousness which could seem like a disloyal thought toward you. But oh! how gladly shall I see you do what you can in this line!'

The letter warns that if he does not act now, she will have to go away. She meant it.

Driven from town by 'heart-breaking discourtesies', Mabel spent an unhappy winter in Boston in 1889–90. There she lodged in a boarding house at 124 Boylston Street. It was not in her to do nothing. Austin bought her a season ticket to the Boston Symphony, she took weekly voice lessons at the Conservatory and she sang with the Handel and Haydn Society.* Mabel was keen to take on Bach's *Christmas Oratorio* and Gounod's *Redemption*, and she sang in Handel's *Messiah* during the festive season. Inspired by the music and by her long immersion in Dickinson's mystical love poems, she was moved to hand over her soul and its after-life to Austin. 'What Austin stirred was unappropriated; it was there . . . and it recognized him and went with a rush to its master.' She imagined that in 'the great spaces of the universe where souls live, his will find me and stay forever more with me'. Although she did miss her husband (away in Angola on another expedition), David Todd was not a monoga-mous animal and as such could not engage her spirit. At a distance from her 'dear men', she reflected on her need for both: 'I know what one is – I know what the other is, and two entirely separate sides of my nature go to them.'

In February 1890 she gave a public talk on her experience of climbing Mount Fuji. Mrs Loomis, who was present, told her daughter that she had 'found her genius', and it did prove to be the start of a twenty-three-year career in public speaking all over the country. Austin's response to her speaking was distinctly cool. 'I like it, and I don't know that I do.'

* Founded in 1815 in order to stage oratorios and other works in America.

If she weren't so womanly, he went on, it would detract from her womanhood, for a woman should be inconspicuous, under the shade of a boulder or by her fireside with her husband-lover. He ruled out her mother's encouragement. Mrs Loomis didn't know her as he did. Mrs Loomis was too 'shallow' to tell a duck from a hen. 'Shallow' was short-hand for the Loomis inability to appreciate the loftiness of their daughter's affair. Clearly Austin had not forgotten the Loomis opposition, their refusal to believe in his denials of the affair in the tone of a social superior who condescends to explain himself to the dismayed parents of his mistress.

For all Mabel's activity in Boston, nothing could assuage her apprehension about the power of her enemies to ruin her. Susan visited Boston that winter and Mabel, seeing her as 'the one person who has driven me away from my house and home', feared Susan would spread the damage. They visited some of the same people and Mabel dreaded to come 'face to face with my particular horror'.

Paranoia reached a maddening level when she visited her prosperous cousin Lydia Coonley in Chicago in March 1890. Mrs Coonley was President of the Chicago Women's Club, one of the first to be established. Although the cousins shared an interest in women's rights and Mabel was fêted for lectures on Japan to her cousin's circle, she fancied a snub on the part of one Mrs Ray, who'd met Mattie Dickinson. Mabel sent off another frantic plea to Austin to intervene on her behalf – she wanted him to pressure Mattie's acquaintance to invite Mabel to her house. Austin told her this would not do and assured her that Mattie had not the slightest idea of Mabel's whereabouts. He did not believe his daughter was orchestrating snubs from afar. As it turned out, Austin was right and Mrs Ray proved hospitable after all. Yet depression remained. It seemed to Mabel, in her early thirties, that she had wasted her youth and got nowhere. Austin, in his sixties, was puzzled about her limitation of life to youth: it seemed to him a female thing that life should depend on looks. He tried to reassure her but Mabel 'abominated' the middle-aged woman.

Her campaigns appeared to come to nought and her future looked bleak. Forced out of town, it was an act of endurance to return to Amherst in May 1890. Strangely, though, it was during this dark passage in her life from 1888 to 1890 that Mabel undertook a new task that would link her legitimately to the Dickinsons, and for all time: she began to decipher, date and type Emily Dickinson's poems, at first one or two, then a few, then hundreds. The poems themselves drove and sustained her 'mentally and spiritually. They seemed to open the door to a wider universe' and had 'a wonderful effect' of release from her depression. In place of her failure to produce a baby with Austin Dickinson, she could bring forth the creative offspring of Emily Dickinson. This venture was different from the succession of campaigns conceived at a distance from Amherst. In her own Amherst house, in sight of the Homestead, in easy reach of the poet's sister and brother, she began in a small way with a borrowed typewriter, a new invention for the office and newer still for domestic use. It was the unlooked-for answer to her 'presentiment'. For it was not as Dickinson consort but as Dickinson editor that Mabel Todd was to thrive.

11

MABEL *IN EXCELSIS*

During Emily's last year Vinnie had heard her muttering worriedly, 'Oh, Vinnie, my work, my work!' When Helen Hunt Jackson offered herself as literary executor, Dickinson's reply avoids the subject. Unfortunately, Helen Jackson died in August 1885, nine months before Dickinson. Her efforts on her friend's behalf (with doubting Mr Higginson, the supposed celebrity volume and Thomas Niles, head of the Boston publishing firm of Roberts Brothers) had all failed through no fault of her own. Dickinson had every reason to have no confidence in that or any other route to publication.

This left Sue, Dickinson's prime reader, as the likely person to transmit the poems to posterity. Vinnie lent her the forty booklets threaded with string – 'the little volumes' – which came to light within a week of Dickinson's death. These contained about eight hundred poems. Other poems were copied on separate sheets and assorted fragments were scribbled on the backs of envelopes, bits of wrapping paper and suchlike scraps. Much of this went to The Evergreens. Together with Sue's own hoard of two hundred and fifty, she had in hand more than a thousand poems. A large part of a lifetime's oeuvre sat there, at The Evergreens, awaiting attention.

Sue had no doubt of the poet's genius. 'A Damascus blade gleaming and glancing in the sun was her wit', she said in her eloquent obituary for the *Republican*. 'Her swift poetic rapture was like the long glistening note of a bird one hears in the June woods at high noon, but can never see.' Sue had stood with her on the brink of 'Infinity' but, turning with Emily to face the public, Sue was daunted. In 1886 she sent a poem by Emily Dickinson to the finest New York editor of the day, Richard Watson Gilder. He had the taste to serialise *The Bostonians* by Henry James in *Century* magazine. Dickinson he rejected.

A professional writer like Mabel Todd would have been used to rejections; Susan was not. The impact of rejection for a novice can be incalculable. It's common for the rejected never to try again, particularly women on their own or housewives or provincials who venture without support. It's not that Susan would have thought a jot less of the poems themselves, but the great world out there in which men made their uncomprehending judgements would have appeared to close the door. Higginson feared the poems were 'un-presentable' to readers attuned to smooth rhythms and chiming rhymes. ('Alcohol' does not rhyme with 'pearl', a critic complained of Dickinson's ecstatic 'I taste a liquor never brewed'.) None had an ear for the silence of dashes that defy the march of standard meanings in order to open up a space for vision and veto – for all that lies beyond the frontiers of language. No critic had an ear for dissonance. It never occurs to them that dissonance could be deliberate, in accord with playful or disruptive thoughts. This was three decades before Eliot burst upon the public ear with the jolts and stops of *The Waste Land*, he, too, bent on transgressing aural frontiers in tandem with 'the frontiers of consciousness'. If the fellows of All Souls College, Oxford, declined to elect Eliot to a fellowship in 1926 because they thought his poetry peculiar, how could the guardians of convention in the 1880s lend themselves to originality in a woman who was 'wayward'? Dickinson had not seen fit to follow the advice Higginson, with patient kindliness, had laid out for her over the course of twenty-five years. The label 'wayward' stuck to her well into the years of her fame.

Dickinson herself had said nothing to anyone when Mr Niles could not 'consume' her poems. In 1883 she'd had the sense to submit only three (instead of the requested collection) to an editor who had participated in the celebrity scam of the No Name series. She had survived by keeping her poems apart from the marketplace, and Susan would have felt for the mode of transmission the poet had chosen.

Lavinia, alone in her father's house, was 'sometimes weary, always full of longings'. In her time she had been a demonstrative woman, ready to touch hands and lips, and, like Emily, keen to express and receive love. So Lavinia welcomed visits from Mabel and the expressiveness Mabel offered when she swept around Austin's vegetable garden between The Dell and the Homestead. Here, once more, is the young woman whose desire Lavinia has facilitated. One day Mabel remarks that she's teaching herself to typewrite (a new word in 1887) on a borrowed Hammond machine that turns out print. Would Vinnie like a preview of her heart's desire, to see her sister in print? Vinnie would. She reads a few of Emily's poems aloud to Mabel and then on a bright, cold Sunday, 13 February 1887, Mabel returns to hear a few more. On that day Vinnie must have entrusted Mabel with some poems because the following Thursday Mabel records typing Emily Dickinson's poems for the first time. This fact is tossed off amid the other activities of that day, but it marks the start of Mabel's role as authorised editor of Emily Dickinson:

17 February 1887: Finished attic curtains in the morning & made David put them up. In the afternoon a few of Emily's poems copied on the typewriter . . . Lovely sunny day. Lay on the bed & rested after. Call [from Austin] at 7.30. Choir rehearsal at 8.30.

18 February 1887: Heavy snow storm. At five went over to Vinnie's with some copied poems.

Closeness to Vinnie is part of this venture and Mabel does feel it. When Vinnie feels sick and blue, Mabel takes care to visit every day at two for the best part of a month. Her understanding of Vinnie's impatience with Sue, and of Vinnie's wish for publication, is irresistible. This is not to suggest a deliberate campaign. Early in 1887, other campaigns claim the forefront of Mabel's mind: to induce Austin to wither the remains of his marriage or, failing that, to escape out west, leaving Sue and the children behind.

On the very day of Austin's disgruntled return from his Western journey, Mabel picked up the poems and from then on her commitment grew, as her diary indicates.

30 November 1887: Copied two or three more of Emily's poems, & took them over to Vinnie's.

22 January 1888: Vinnie gave me more poems.

15 February 1888: Wrote a number of Emily's poems on the typewriter. At two went to Vinnie's, & had a lovely visit until 3.30.

11 March 1888: Typed a lot of Emily's poems.

'No publisher will attempt to read poems in Emily's own peculiar handwriting, much less judge them, Mabel advised Vinnie. 'I should have to copy them all.'

Her know-how, her commercial approach to publication, was more to Vinnie's mind than Susan's leaning towards private publication. The latter option would cost a lot, and Austin was unlikely to contribute.

Susan continued to read the poems to guests at The Evergreens. Since Vinnie had never participated in her sister-in-law's salon, Susan did not invite her now. Alone in the Homestead, Vinnie felt excluded. Why should Susan have the privilege of selecting what poems to read, without consulting the legal heir to the manuscripts?

This adversarial thought, dropping into Vinnie's mind, did its bit to change her plan.

In 1888 she retrieved the manuscripts she had placed in The Evergreens and turned them over to Mabel Todd, who proceeded to transcribe hundreds of poems. Mabel worked at first on the borrowed Hammond typewriter, then on a more primitive 'World' machine that cost her $15. She had to turn a pointer manually to each letter, and then stamp the letter (capitals only) on to paper through an inked rubber sheet. It was laborious, exhausting. In the spring of 1888 Vinnie sent trusty Maggie

Maher to stand in for the untrained and sometimes absent servant at The Dell. For Maggie it was thankless work. Where the Dickinson sisters had been accustomed to work alongside Maggie – Emily baking, Vinnie house-keeping – Mrs Todd did not value domestic work and offered Maggie nothing for her efforts. And again it did not occur to Mabel that signs of adultery – the closed door to the bedroom upstairs – would jar on a servant, in the same way as it never occurred to her how that door, with Austin Dickinson behind it, jarred on Millicent, aged eight, when she came home from school.

During October 1888 Grandma Wilder came to stay, making assignations at The Dell impossible. On the 16th Mabel's diary, careful as ever to avoid Austin's name in any intimate context, mentions two assignations on the same Tuesday at the Homestead: a 'call' at twelve, at Vinnie's, and 'and one at five, up stairs'.

What never ceased to worry Mabel was Susan's power to damage her reputation. During 1888 Mabel, it will be recalled, looked rather wasted, none too fertile for a woman trying to conceive. Yet however much snubs preyed on her spirits, however unfair it was that Austin's gender and social pre-eminence should exempt him from blame, and however frustrating that Austin did nothing further to squash his wife, Mabel was never tempted to end the affair. It meant more than sexual loyalty, much as she wanted that; its hold on her had to do with a dream derived from her father who cared for poetry and the life of the mind. The word 'presentiment', and the aspirational resonance it carried for her, had lacked a focus until she encountered the Dickinsons. At the heart of that family beat a destiny she had to grasp – she'd heard it instantly in the voice of Susan Dickinson reading the poetry aloud, as though she were its legitimate channel. Todd ventured to become the legitimate channel when she decided to copy hundreds of poems.

She had the staying power and energy to carry through a challenge of this magnitude. It required exceptional patience to pore over a difficult hand and unfamiliar usage where nouns, say, might appear as verbs. Mabel refused to be damped by Higginson's warnings to Vinnie and by Austin's resistance. For Austin's family pride shrank from exposure and the failure he anticipated.

Pause. Pause for what lies between the scenes, the unseen space where so much happens. No facts come down to us from 1888 and 1889 as Emily Dickinson is hauled to the surface – the great lines swimming into focus as Mabel Todd types 'My Life had stood — a Loaded Gun —' . . . 'Mine – in Vision and in Veto' . . . 'Vesuvius at Home' . . . 'My life closed twice before its close'. For Mabel to have kept going, day after day for two or more years was an extraordinary feat. It was fuelled by a sure response to the poems. Mabel Todd's venture was completely under wraps because, of course, Vinnie was deceiving Susan, compounding her betrayal in the matter of adultery. Throughout these years, Vinnie feared Susan, and her master plan was not to reveal Mabel's part. In the end, the poems would be published, and no one was to know how they had come to be presentable to editors.

Here, Lavinia erred: she took Mabel's enthusiasm, genuine as it was, for granted. The relationship was unequal in that Lavinia owned the manuscripts; Mabel did not. Lavinia did witness Mabel's effort, she saw how long it took, but as an old-fashioned gentlewoman Lavinia had no idea that Mabel Todd, as a New Woman contributing two to three years of her professional time, might expect recognition.

The mistake was not entirely Lavinia's fault. It was Mabel's habit to project a ladylike passivity. Others approach her, others ask her to do things, and when they don't it's destiny taking a hand, like the impulse that compelled Austin to take her warm, waiting hand that rainy evening at the gate of The Evergreens on 11 September 1882 – that Rubicon moment that changed the Dickinsons' lives. Far off in the future people would say that Lavinia Dickinson approached her brother's mistress and asked her to take over the editing – in secret – from her sister-in-law. Mabel Todd complied as a favour to Lavinia, a huge favour, people would say. This was the Todd story in retrospect. Afterwards she reassured Higginson that Sue 'gave it up definitely. Then Lavinia came to me . . . So you see Mrs. Dickinson can have no real cause for complaint.'

Mabel Todd is a plausible propagandist for her story because she sticks close to the truth, deviating, often, with one word. Apart from 'definitely' in this case, it's the apparently insignificant word 'then' that shifts the sequence in favour of innocent passivity. *Look like the innocent flower.* To us in the future, the manoeuvre can look like the merest slip of memory. Only it's there too often to be a slip. It's an almost automatic untruthfulness, the insignificant cog driving the wheel of a plot Mabel sets in motion.

At the time, Mabel told Vinnie that she was copying hundreds of poems for the love of what she was doing. This statement was largely true. And Lavinia believed it, and took pleasure in conferring on Mabel this privilege. But, well below the surface, there was a darker motive to these earliest transcriptions of Emily Dickinson: a pattern of campaigns on the part of Mabel Loomis Todd who wanted to be 'Mabel Loomis Dickinson' or linked in some indissoluble way to the Dickinson family, to the extent of trying to conceive a Dickinson child throughout these years when she was transcribing the poems. Later she'd claim that the poet herself asked her to do this. A lie like this stands close to some sort of truth, for the years she gave to Emily Dickinson convinced Mabel Todd that she was indeed – in literal deed – the true poetic heir.

This co-exists with Mabel Todd's confident response to the poems themselves. From the start she had envied Susan's intimacy with Dickinson's poetry. If it's correct that Mabel wished to *be* Susan, she was now on course. Mabel had what it took to pursue this through the dark, depressed, uncertain years from 1888 to 1890. It remained as secret as her other campaigns but, unlike them, this was creative, fertile, healing. She felt, she said, the poems' greatness; she was 'uplifted'.

By night, under cover of darkness, Vinnie crept over to The Dell to inspect progress and urge Mabel on. Though Vinnie had colluded in the love affair, this was closeness of a rarer kind: two women, one middle-aged, one young, joined in an enterprise that was to burst on an unknowing public. In their secret intentness both were in a way closer to the poet than in life, as readers are when they live from day to day with a writer who speaks to them: in this instance, a writer who speaks – blasts – directly to the soul.

*

In July 1888 Higginson visited Lavinia to discuss an edition. He was too busy to take this on himself, but agreed to reconsider the possibility if someone undertook the labour of copying the poems. Since no one knew what might be there until it was transcribed, Mabel realised that she would have to commit herself to Dickinson's whole oeuvre, or at least that large part of it in her hands.

Vinnie would bring baskets of poems to The Dell and dump them on the floor in front of the fireplace in the back parlour. David would then compare Mabel's transcription with the original; if there were errors Mabel would do it again. Certain poems Vinnie would not let out of her house, and Mabel transcribed them there under Vinnie's eye. If they spied Susan coming the poems were hustled out of sight.

During the first six months of 1889 Mabel hired a copyist, but Harriet Graves had no sympathy for 'Emily's mad words', and seemed to Mabel a shade worse than an insentient machine. So Mabel dismissed Miss Graves and pressed on. Millicent, aged nine, helped with the copying and there was help too from David Todd, consistent with their pact to promote each other's careers. He helped to sort hundreds of scraps of paper. This wasn't only helpfulness; this astronomer had fixed on what his wife called Dickinson's 'comets of thought'. At this time he was drawn to another boldly original woman, Olive Schreiner, a semi-invalid who lived in isolation on the South African veld. From that lone spot her feminist fables spoke to avant-garde thinkers. David Todd wished to write to her and asked Roberts Brothers for her address. They obliged, apologising that they did not know her street. In fact, Matjesfontein was only one street behind a railway stopping in the midst of thorn bush stretching to the horizon. Such solitude had proved no bar to addressing the world through her pen.

In October 1889 David left for Angola. It was yet another expedition to photograph the sun's corona in the course of an eclipse. David expected Mabel's help, as in Japan, but this time he sailed in a naval vessel that refused to have a woman aboard a man-of-war. (Her father, Eben Loomis, was allowed to join the expedition in the capacity of instrument maker.) This was when Mabel was oppressed by Amherst snubs and took herself off to Boston for the winter.

There, on 6 November, Higginson came for an hour to discuss the tran-scripts with Mabel at the opulent Beacon Hill house of her cousin, Caro Andrews. He warned once more, 'The public will not accept even fine ideas in such rough and mystical dress, so hard to elucidate.'

Mrs Todd rose with graceful aplomb. Moulded in a corset perfectly judged between womanly yield and ladylike tightness, she leant a little for-ward in performance mode, picked up the poems and began to read a dozen of her favourites aloud. Addressing the ear, not the eye, the rhyth-mic glide of a trained voice smoothed out the jolts of the Dickinson line and protected Higginson from the sight of the experimental punctuation Dickinson had neglected to alter. Mabel was in her element as performer. Her voice was persuasive, her accents soothing, unlike the startling ques-tions the poet had put to Higginson until he felt drained.

He was astonished. He had no idea, he said, 'there were so many poems in passably conventional form'. He asked her to classify them as A, B and C, and on that basis would look them over.

Held up by illness for much of the winter, he eventually did this in April 1890 while Mabel was Chicago. Higginson's initial selections were not all in agreement with hers. At this point, with David still abroad, it was six months since Mabel had left Amherst. Austin urged her return. On 24 April he brushed off her need to confer with Higginson in Boston: 'I don't know what you mean about "the poems" and their possibly delaying you. That is of no consequence.'

Austin was impatient to repeat the 'experiment' and thought publica-tion a whim of Vinnie's, to inflate herself. In fact Vinnie participated discerningly in the editors' selections. By May a volume of about two hun-dred poems was ready for submission and Higginson chose the prestigious publishing firm of Houghton Mifflin, where he acted as a reader. They said no. Next Todd tried Roberts Brothers, who had published Dickinson's 'Success' and then could not 'consume' her other poems.

Mr Niles reaffirmed his adverse opinion. He had always thought it 'unwise to perpetuate Miss Dickinson's poems. They are quite as remark-able for defects as for beauties & are generally devoid of the true poetical qualities.' The reader's report by Arlo Bates, a poet favoured by the firm, noted Dickinson's 'crudity of workmanship'. He foresaw no possibility of making a stir but did concede that this was the real thing, a power near to genius. Had she published – had she learnt the conventions of punctuation and rhyme – 'she would have stood at the head of American singers'. In a grudging tone, Mr Niles offered to bring out a small edition on condition that the sister paid for the typographical electroplates and agreed to forgo royalties on the first five hundred copies. Bates halved the number of poems to be included in a collection, rejecting some of the best including 'I died for Beauty'. Mabel, exasperated, restored a few with the help of Vinnie, bringing the final number to 116. Mabel handled the negotiation for Vinnie, who had 'about as much knowledge of business as a Maltese pussycat'.

That summer Mabel remained in Amherst, toiling over five proof stages which, she insisted, were necessary, since the typesetters kept correcting the poet's inventions. Even though the editors themselves had deviated from the manuscripts to bring Dickinson more into line with their own tastes and those of the day, Mabel Todd was rigorous when it came to printing.

Sue, still in the dark about the volume nearing publication, sent 'There came a Day at Summer's full' to *Scribner's*. It was published in August, and Sue was paid $15, which she kept, even though this sum should have gone to Vinnie as legal owner of the papers, and Vinnie's rights acknowledged. As this poem happened to be in the forthcoming volume, Mabel Todd had to seek permission from *Scribner's* for its inclusion.

When the final proofs came in September the editors were jubilant. Higginson now wrote a diplomatic preface asking readers to excuse the grammatical oddities for the sake of daring thoughts. Candour compels him to point out the 'rugged' frame of the poems and to regret that lyric flights are not smoother. Yet he assents generously to the poet's persistent refusal to hear his advice: here is a recluse who is true to herself.

The first volume of Dickinson poems, bound in white leather and published on 12 November 1890, was handled in just the way that had put the poet off publication during her lifetime: the editors had tampered with the inventive punctuation and off-rhymes of the volcano speaking through 'buckled lips'. Words were changed 'to make them smoother' (as Mabel Todd put it) and dashes eliminated. There were trivialising titles like 'With a Flower', 'Playmates' and 'Troubled about many things'.

For all this, Dickinson spoke to readers. Her sudden revelation, as one reader put it, was like 'a shaft of light sunk instantaneously into the dark abysm'. 'Much madness is divinest sense', people read, 'A wounded deer leaps highest' and one of the exultant poems sparked by the Master letters: 'I'm wife . . . I'm Czar, I'm woman now'. Other 'Exultation is the going / Of an inland soul to sea', or there's the fight to the death of 'Two Swimmers on a Spar'. 'Men do not sham convulsion / Nor simulate a throe' when the brain swerves from its 'groove'. And, always, oncoming mortality and certain immortality: 'Because I could not stop for Death / He kindly stopped for me'. Death does have the power to halt the speaker whose immortal powers are all the sharper for her vulnerability to human attachment:

> I never lost as much but twice —
> And that was in the sod.
> Twice have I stood a beggar
> Before the door of God!
>
> Angels — twice descending
> Reimbursed my store —
> Burglar! Banker — Father!
> I am poor once more!

The volume was a huge success, to the surprise of Houghton Mifflin who had rejected the poems, Niles who had grudgingly published them and the still rather offhand Austin. Five hundred copies of *Poems* were sold on the day of publication; the volume was reprinted eleven times in the first year; and the total sale, astonishing for a poet publishing a first collection, was almost eleven thousand copies. Public interest was fanned by Higginson's modest account of his correspondence and contact with a naively gifted recluse who had a 'quaint and nun-like look'. This was published in the *Atlantic Monthly* in October 1891, to promote a forthcoming second volume. Public interest was fanned further by Mabel Todd's talks and articles. A Boston reporter who attended one of her talks noted the sympathetic keenness and wit with which she explained Dickinson's elusive genius to her audience. 'As she stood there – an almost girlish figure in her black lace dress whose sole adornment was a small bunch of her favorite jonquils – every tone and gesture revealed not only the intelligent critic but the loving friend.'

The name of Mabel Loomis Todd will always be linked with that of Emily Dickinson. Vinnie, apprehensive of Sue's reaction to the secret undertaking (Sue, she thought, would want to 'kill' her), had tried to keep Mabel Todd's name off the title page. Higginson had insisted it must be there, putting Todd's name first. Her painting of Indian Pipes, tooled in silver, took pride of place on the cover. For the next few years Mabel promoted the poems together with the image of a shy creature, reclusive, eccentric, asexual, whose 'friend' she had been. Dickinson had indeed been reclusive with Mabel, though not with Helen Hunt Jackson and Lord.

Only when pressed did Mabel admit that they'd never met face to face. At most, she'd 'once' glimpsed her object 'flitting' away. 'Flitting' fits the legend of shyness, a shrinking creature, but the cutting edge of the Dickinson voice conveys the opposite: it's bared, at the ready.

William Dean Howells, the well-known American novelist, recognised a lasting voice. He was the first to see her improvising manner as intentional and masterly. 'If nothing else had come out of our life but this strange poetry we should feel that in the work of Emily Dickinson, America, or New England, rather, had made a distinctive addition to the literature of the world.'

This influential review had been prompted by Mabel. In the summer of 1890 she'd met Howells, who was staying at the same boarding house as Mrs Loomis and Millicent. Howells and his wife, who had lost a beloved daughter aged ten, befriended Millicent, also ten. Mabel had found Howells genial and willing to lend an ear to the forthcoming Dickinson phenomenon.

In a letter to Vinnie from Rome, the painter and illustrator of *The Rubaiyat of Omar Khayyam*, Elihu Vedder, declared 'love at first sight' of the poems. 'They are barbed things these poems and strike and remain – not like some snowballs of poems that . . . break and melt and are gone[,] leaving you cold.' Niles had the happy idea of sending a copy to the English poet Christina Rossetti who, single and rather solitary, dramatising a lone, confessional voice, had much in common with Dickinson. She praised 'a very remarkable work of genius, – though I cannot but deplore some of the religious, or rather irreligious pieces'.

Vinnie bristled at the reservation. 'I'm sorry Miss "Rossetti" fails to comprehend "Emily" faithfully.'

Early in 1892 the brilliant invalid Alice James delighted in 'I'm Nobody! Who are you'. No tome of philosophy, she said, could match Nobody's antithesis:

> How dreary — to be — Somebody!
> How public — like a Frog —
> To tell one's name — the livelong June —
> To an admiring Bog!

The sureness of this farce from the 'highest point of view of the aspiring soul' was beyond the grasp of Somebodies, as Alice James saw, and she feared only for Dickinson's not being the flawless miracle a James was qualified to appreciate. She saw too a poet who must be rescued from editorial intervention.

'Her being sicklied o'er* with T. W. Higginson makes one quake lest there be a latent flaw which escapes one's vision.'

Though Alice James was then close to death, no one could relish more the bafflement of Dickinson's critics. In England, reviews followed the London publication late in 1891. 'It is reassuring to hear the English pronouncement that Emily Dickinson is fifth-rate,' Alice James said. 'They have such a capacity for missing quality; the robust evades them equally

---

* Hamlet is 'Sicklied o'er with the pale cast of thought'.

with the subtle.' The *London Daily News*, groping condescendingly in the right direction, thought Dickinson 'a kind of unfinished. rudimentary Brontë'.

The American papers, on the other hand, and particularly the Boston ones, sided with the common reader in their praise. Higginson told Mabel Todd, 'You are the only person who can feel as I do about this extraordinary thing we have done in revealing this rare genius. I feel as if we had climbed to a cloud, pulled it away, and revealed a new star behind it.'

For Susan, *Poems* came as a shock. Here was Emily wrenched away and twisted into shape for publication. She and Mattie stopped speaking to Lavinia, who held up her head but was not impervious to the pain.

With Higginson, Sue restrained her shock. As the poet's old friend, she took it upon herself to thank him 'for her' – for leading her in front of the curtain. Her criticism of the volume was measured and her claim undeniable.

'I think this much is due myself – my life long intimacy with Emily – my equally long deep appreciation of her genius. I am told that Lavinia is saying that I refused to arrange [the poems]. Emily knows that is not true. You are generous enough to be patient with my exegesis even if tedious to you. "The Poems" will ever be to me marvellous whether in manuscript or type.'

The editors were unaware of letters containing letter-poems as great as any. Susan had intended to set poems in the biographical context of the prose, a plan informed by insider knowledge. Higginson proposed that Mrs Dickinson be at least consulted on future volumes. Todd had no such intention. Her rival had lost her chance to 'unconquerable laziness'.

Susan fought back. Three months after *Poems* appeared, Susan selected a fair copy of a visionary poem, 'Just lost, when I was saved', from her private trove. On 8 February 1891 she sent it to William Hayes Ward of the New York *Independent*, with a further inducement: the manuscript might be kept by the editor's sister for her autograph collection. Written at the start of Dickinson's *anni mirabiles*, in the summer of 1860, it soars into a timeless region as later T. S. Eliot would speak of the wind from 'beyond the world'. Eliot and Dickinson were both soaked in the Bible, where wind and breath are the same. Dickinson recalls how the 'breath blew back'. She's 'as one *returned*' to report the vision. Unlike poets bereft of vision (as Eliot feels in

the aftermath of his 'moment'), Dickinson is heartened by her proximity
to Eternity, like a sailor on a voyage of discovery who comes back exulting
in her proximity to the 'secrets of "the Line"'. A metaphoric venture
beyond the equator floats her towards lines she is to write as 'Reporter' of
unknown modes of being. She speaks from the brink of immortality:

> . . . Therefore, as one <u>returned</u>, I feel,
> Odd secrets of 'the Line' to tell!
> Some sailor skirting novel shores!
> Some pale 'Reporter' from the awful doors
> Before the Seal!

Far from feeling, as Eliot, cast off by the timeless into a 'waste' of time-bound
routines, Dickinson looked to renewed proximity to the timeless realm:

> Next time to stay!
> Next time, the things to see
> By ear unheard —
> Unscrutinized by eye!
> Next time to tarry
> While Ages steal —
> Tramp the slow Centuries
> And the Cycles wheel!

It's to Susan and no one else that the poet 'reports' this crossing of the
'Line': the ultimate frontier. So when Susan offered this poem for publication early in 1891 it was not only for others to read, but also a validation of
her tie with the poet.

She identified herself to Ward in her twofold capacity as wife to
Dickinson's brother and a chosen reader who had been at one with
Dickinson's gift 'as I have known and felt it since our early girlhood inti-
macy', poems 'clear and crisp as soul's crystal to me'.

Susan protested more freely to Ward: 'All the more am I indignant at
the silly fear of the public or lack of ability to recognize the power of many

[poems] that were ruled out of the volume just printed.' Her hope was to establish a rival relationship with a powerful editor. 'I have many manuscript letter-poems from which I mean to make up into a unique volume as I can command the time.'

Todd, of course, could always command the time. Her advantage over Susan was not time or understanding, but the initiative to press on. Susan was not 'lazy'; her home, anyone could see, was a model of domestic industry. She did transcribe about eighty poems (eliminating the dashes and capitalisations) and selected another fifty-nine for typing, since her own difficult hand was unlikely to engage editors. Sadly this effort, coming from the source closest to the poet, could not surface. Susan Dickinson found herself silenced.

If Susan had expected Lavinia to be gratified by the timely publication from her private hoard on 12 March 1891, the spirit of strife proved stronger. It is hard to like a person you have knowingly injured, who then stops speaking to you. Lavinia assuaged her guilt by liking Sue less. Then, too, the triumphant outcome of co-opting Todd hardened her partisan position. At the time Mabel Todd undertook to edit a second volume of the poems and contemplated a volume of letters, Lavinia turned against Susan, the primacy of whose tie with Emily was ever more evident as letters came to light. Why had Emily confided in Sue and concealed this hoard from the sister who had protected her so faithfully?

So it was that Lavinia fired a shot against Sue's publication. Her protest to Ward laid out the law of ownership. A writer might give a manuscript to someone else, but the possessor is not the owner. Legally, the copyright on the writing remains with writer, and upon death transfers to the writer's heir. On the basis of Emily's will, which left Lavinia 'everything', Lavinia claimed (pushing the point) that Emily had granted her exclusive rights to her papers, and though Emily gave copies of poems to others they were given simply for private reading 'and not to pass the property in them, which is mine'.

Unsurprisingly Susan challenged this. She had lost her husband to Mabel. Her friendship with Lavinia was being destroyed and now the thing she held most dear, her private relationship with Emily, was being ripped from her. She sounds a little desperate as she writes to Ward: 'the sister is quite jealous of my treasure . . . All[?] [the poems and letters] I have are mine – given me by my dear Emily while living[,] so I can in honor do with them as I please.'

Ward, caught in the crossfire of these claims, politely declined further poems from the Dickinson papers. Sue apologised 'that I so innocently have drawn you into a hornets' nest. I beg that you will not be drawn into any correspondence with Miss Lavinia over the poems or allow yourself to be troubled by her foolish fits of temper . . . She feels a little baffled by my possession of so many mss. of Emily's and is very foolish in her talk of *law*. I am quite used to her vagaries, and while I pity her, I shall never yield a line in my possession to her . . . I have a little article in my mind, with illustrations of Emily's own, showing her witty humorous side which has all been left out of the book.'

Avoiding the 'hornets' nest', Mr Ward did not take up this offer. There were two consequences: Lavinia's principle of exclusive rights effectively blocked Susan's attempt to open up an independent route to publication. At the same time, the hornets began to sting outside the family.

Higginson's suggested title for the next volume, 'Indian Pipes and Witch Hazel', limits Dickinson as nature-poet. Fortunately the simple title *Poems: Second Series* prevailed. It was Todd's turn at a preface. As well as eloquent testimony to the poet's greatness, she offers facts about the five or six pages of notepaper Dickinson sewed together to make booklets for fair copies in the early 1860s. Todd called them 'fascicules'. It's not a word the Dickinsons used, but it has stuck.

Fired by success, Todd looked forward to ten volumes – there was an abundance of great poems. She also planned a selection of Dickinson letters. In a New England in which personal letters were looked on as 'a private trust never to be made public', this would have been impossible without the backing of Vinnie. In making the first attempts to date the letters Todd asked help from Dickinson's circle, almost all of whom were alive when she went to work in 1891. She took care to enter into relationship with certain correspondents such as Emily's schoolfriends Abiah Root (now Mrs Strong, and living in the Berkshires) and Emily Fowler (Mrs Ford), who could recall Emily as a girl in the 1840s.

A strange scene takes place in the middle of 1891, when the biographical project has barely begun. Mabel, with Austin's collusion, begins to tamper* with the overwhelming evidence of Emily's bond with Susan. A booklet containing 'One sister have I in the house / And one a hedge away' is taken apart so as to remove the poem. Emily's sewing holes are cut to disguise the poem's place in the booklet, but though the page is thus mutilated, and torn in two places, it's not destroyed for the sake of another poem on the verso. Using black ink the mutilator scores out all the lines and, most heavily, the climax 'Sue — forevermore!'

The text survives only because Susan retained the copy sent across the grass in the late 1850s. There are similar mutilations of many letters, especially Emily's early letters to Austin, written when he was in love with Sue, and letters to Sue filled with Emily's parallel, more entrancing ardour. All the mutilations are designed to obliterate the poet's attachment to 'Sister'.

In this adversarial atmosphere, the Lady Macbeth imperatives revived. Austin reported a 'trying talk' with his wife. 'I must entreat you not to let it accomplish nothing,' Mabel replied on 15 September 1891. 'It is certainly true that you have the power in your own hands if you will <u>only</u> use it – you <u>must</u> use it – you must bring out some of your weapons and <u>make</u> them of use . . . I expect you to – I know you will.'

More than five hundred letters passed through Mabel Todd's hands. She organised her selection on the basis of correspondents, arranged chronologically according to the date a correspondence began. Two formidable difficulties at once presented themselves: half the correspondence – the letters Dickinson received – had been destroyed and her own letters are undated after 1855. Todd had to determine dates, where possible, by way of postmarks or stamps, or on the basis of handwriting that

---

* 1891 is the date given by R. W. Franklin in his 1967 pamphlet on editing ED. He assumed that the mutilation was done by Austin because, he argued, Mabel Todd had too much respect for manuscripts to do so. This view (current in 1967, when Mabel's daughter was still alive and amassing scholarly support for her mother) underplays Mabel Todd's initiatives. Her persistent project was to replace Susan as the poet's intimate. It would be out of character for Austin to do this of his own accord; he was generally cautious about documents, as with his will.

changed three times, from the running hand of an older generation of gentlewomen to the curvy, hard-to-read hand of the 1860s and then, for the last twelve years of Dickinson's life, a spare hand with each letter detached as in print. Other clues to dating were events that are mentioned (the 1851 visit to Northampton to hear Jenny Lind, or the 1855 visit to Washington). But in some cases it took Todd as long as a month to date a letter.

Given the array of correspondents – Abiah Root, Mrs Holland, Sam Bowles, Maria Whitney, Mabel Todd herself and many minor figures – a distorting omission is the correspondence with Susan. Nowhere is she mentioned. It's a common temptation to editorial power to contrive a bias, sometimes in covert ways. Here the agenda is all too plain.

Another intense relationship was kept under wraps. No letters to Judge Lord were published for half a century, and by that time the renunciatory legend was so firmly established that Emily's delight in the Judge's visits and her candour about desire have been underplayed.

Austin required all reference to sickness be cut. Consistent with secrecy was the refusal of the Norcross sisters to let Todd see the letters in their possession. These remaining witnesses to Emily's ills in her teenage years, and to the treatment she endured in Boston in 1864 and 1865, shielded their cousin from biographical intrusion. Fanny Norcross was distant and scrupulous: she offered to read aloud from the extracts and letters she had copied so that Todd could check the proofs for the forthcoming volumes, but no eyes, she insists, will ever fall on the censored content. The following letter makes it plain that a huge batch of Dickinson's letters – the originals – are to disappear:

> Concord [Massachusetts]
> Aug.1, 1894

My dear Mrs. Todd,

. . . I cannot send the letters, not because I fear they will be lost, but because my sister and I are not willing that any one even Vinnie should have the free reading of them; many of them have whole sentences which were intended for no eyes but ours, and on our own account as well as Emily's no one else will ever read them. This we consider our right, and we must insist upon it.

I shall bring the letters which I copied almost as they are, and also those from which I made extracts, but I must retain the privilege of reading them to you. Of course the handwriting of the several periods of time will be open for your inspection . . .

> Yours very truly
> Fanny L. Norcross.

A week later, a tantalising scene ensued: Fanny Norcross holding Dickinson's letters in front of Todd, cutting out the confidences as she reads.

For all the omissions, Todd again performed a remarkable feat, not only of retrieval and ordering but also understanding. Her unpublished essay (or talk) on the letters points to the suggestiveness of a letter to Bowles where the women he attracts (Emily, Susan and Vinnie, all of them jumpy with expectation as they await his knock at the Homestead door in the spring of 1862, before he goes to Europe for his health) offer flower-cups for his relief and delectation. This offering shows once again how Dickinson's poetry is sparked by English women writers of her time. 'We offer you our cups' takes off from Christina Rossetti's most recent and celebrated poem, 'Goblin Market' (1862). But where Rossetti's beguiling sellers, all male, are sinister as drug dealers, Dickinson's sellers, all female, offer what a sick man craves – unconditional love:

> We offer you our cups, stintless as to the bee the lily, her
> new liquors.
>> Would you like summer?
>> Taste of ours.
>> Spices?
>> Buy here.
>> Ill? We have berries for the parching!
>> Weary? Furloughs of down.
>> Perplexed? Estates of violet trouble ne'er looked on!

Captive? We bring reprieve of roses!
Fainting? Flasks of air.
Even for death, a fairy medicine.
But which is it, Sir?

Todd's essay brings out the humorousness of Dickinson's home nature, and her way of playing with darker moods. 'With her, pathos lay very near to raillery and badinage, pain very near to delight.' Todd does not deny that Dickinson bared her soul but seldom, and offers this explanation: 'It was not so much that she was always on spiritual guard, as that she sported with her varying moods, testing them upon her friends.'

The essay was one of Todd's efforts to promote the *Letters*. She travelled in a snowstorm to Brooklyn to lecture to an enraptured audience; she sent out leaflets to women's clubs, with the help of fourteen-year-old Millicent who copied them out in a mature hand; and she made an imaginative proposal to Roberts Brothers: an 'Emily Dickinson Year Book', with 'comets of thought' appropriate to each day or season. 'Think of reading against some day in March "House is being cleaned: I prefer pestilence."' Todd stood ready to collect 'my 365 flashes'. Disappointingly, her publisher did not take up this idea.

Mabel Todd edited the *Letters* on her own. It was 'a peculiarly delicate piece of literary work' demanding 'an endless amount of thought and tact'. As she typed, she noticed how 'startling' the prose looked 'in the cold impartiality of print'. By the time she delivered the typescript to Roberts Brothers in August 1894, Todd had given the better part of seven years to the Dickinson papers. For all this work she had received, so far, $200 out of the $300 Lavinia had gained in royalties. Todd, as a professional writer who had to earn a living, quite reasonably felt that more was due to her, this time, in the way of copyright. The result of her claim was two versions of the contract with Roberts Brothers, arranged by E. D. Hardy who, that year, succeeded Mr Niles. One is the draft, sharing copyright and royalties with Todd. The other is the final version, in which Lavinia Dickinson retains exclusive copyright. The existence of two contracts was to provide ammunition for renewed battle in time to come. Mabel retained her copy of the draft contract which granted what she wanted. Lavinia retained her copy of the final contract which, in effect, deprived Mabel of what she wanted.

In the final contract it's agreed that the proceeds [the royalties] and not the copyright itself would be shared equally with Mabel Loomis Todd 'in consideration of the service rendered in preparing the manuscript and editing the said work'. Austin signed, as well as Lavinia.

For the first time in the succession of early contracts Austin took part in the negotiations, weighing in on Mabel's side. His presence is apparent in a query from Roberts Brothers on 21 August as to whether they should insert a clause to the effect that when Miss Dickinson dies 'the whole royalty is to go to Mrs. Todd'?

Lavinia refused. On 22 September she informed Mr Hardy of her final decision. The copyright for the letters was to be 'the same as the Poems': that is, in her name alone. 'I have talked with Mrs Todd,' Lavinia went on, 'she is satisfied with my wish.'

Mr Hardy did not believe Mrs Todd was satisfied. That very day he informed Austin that Miss Dickinson 'does not agree with your idea nor with Mrs Todd's'.

Austin, infuriated, apologised to Mr Hardy for Lavinia's change of mind. 'This may all seem very queer to you, and it is. We are a queer lot.'

His revenge was to cast Lavinia not as staunch promoter of their sister's greatness but as a rural dimwit thrilled to receive a publishing contract addressed to herself in a big envelope from Boston. Lavinia, he said, was 'disturbed by the feeling that somehow her glory and magnificence are dimmed by any other than her supreme self being recognized'.

In fact, Vinnie had been fending off what she saw as another encroachment on the treasure she'd inherited from Emily, and this by a couple with whom she had always sided, to the detriment of the family next door who now avoided her.

Austin, in backing Mabel, complained with some justice that Lavinia saw her as a flunky. The demeaning connotation of 'service' in the final contract does bear this out. Lavinia had no idea what editing entailed,

Austin raged to Mr Hardy. She thought it merely a matter of copying from manuscript and carrying the copies 'in a heap' to the publisher.

Lavinia was not quite so uninformed. The real problem was Todd's failure to acknowledge Lavinia's participation as prime mover in collecting letters. Her status as sister would naturally have been more persuasive to Emily's circle than any number of winning approaches on the part of a stranger. (Todd's own approaches were effective in part because they had Lavinia's support.) Lavinia insisted that Todd's preface should include a statement that Emily Dickinson's sister had collected the letters. Todd, unaccustomed to submit on demand, persuaded Roberts Brothers to reprint the letters with a different version of that sentence. It was to say that Emily Dickinson's sister had asked Mabel Loomis Todd to collect her letters, implying Todd alone had done the job.

To invite peace, Roberts Brothers was compelled to bring out more or less concurrent editions of the same book for the sake of this one sentence. The alteration appears negligible, but not so to the principals. Beneath these statements there rumbled adversarial claims of some importance: Lavinia resented the way Todd underplayed Lavinia's role in favour of her own. Money was not the main issue, nor even the prestige of association with strangely brilliant letters unlike any other. The crux was Mabel Todd's advance, a step further on to Dickinson territory: her first step had won Susan; her second step had won Ned; her third, Austin, with Lavinia's assent; a fourth step had failed to win over the poet herself, but Emily's death had opened the way for a takeover of her papers. From 1886 until 1894 Lavinia had seen herself in command of the papers, but in the summer of 1894 she detected danger signs: the challenge to exclusive copyright; the potential loss of family royalties at her death; the obliteration of the crusader role she had conceived and carried through since Emily died. Lavinia's stand in holding on to copyright in the late summer of 1894 was, in this context, shoulder to shoulder with Emily's last stand at 'Thermopylae'.

Roberts Brothers printed one thousand copies of the *Letters*: two small grey-green volumes, stamped once more with Todd's painting of Indian Pipes, this time tooled in gilt and even more prominent, centred on an otherwise empty front cover. (The name of the author appears only on the spine.) One volume carried a portrait of Emily; the other, a photograph of the well-kept Homestead on its rise above Main Street. Although copies sold quickly there was no continued demand, and this left Roberts Brothers a little in the red. Lavinia owed them $231.30. Years passed, and on 20 March 1899 the firm pressed Lavinia to settle the debt. At this point the firm was taken over by Little, Brown, and an alternative offered to Lavinia was 'transfer of copyright' to the publisher. Again Lavinia held on to copyright and the debt remained unpaid. When, later in 1899, she died intestate, copyright passed to her next of kin, the family at The Evergreens.

In her lifetime, Emily Dickinson had been called 'the myth'; when she died, Todd saw her disappear more deeply into her 'mystery'. Higginson introduced her to the public as a nunnish recluse who never thought of publication. He characterised her as 'whimsical', 'wayward', 'uneven' and 'exasperating'. Actually, the blueprint for this character goes back to the poet herself: the coy Daisy of the Master letters and the untaught-Little-Me who writes to Higginson.

Austin smiled at Emily's display of an 'innocent and confiding nature' in her letters to Higginson. He said, 'Emily definitely posed in those letters.'

The same posture directs 'This is my Letter to the World / That never wrote to me'. In 1863 the poet begs her 'sweet countrymen' to be kind to unassuming nonentity. Did she really think her countrymen sweet in 1863, at the height of the Civil War, biographer Alfred Habegger asks, adding, 'I wouldn't bet on it.' Though the poet had placed this poem in the middle of a booklet, Higginson and Todd gave it the status of an authorial preface to their first volume, as though it were Dickinson's authentic voice. Habegger rightly points out that it's a disarming but 'unreliable' construct of feminine modesty, devised at a time when she is supremely confident of poetic immortality.

Austin insisted on his sister's normality. Todd's preface to *Poems: Second Series*, her essay on Dickinson's letters, her review column ('Bright Bits from Bright Books') in the *Home Magazine* and her many public talks all publicised Austin's message that his sister was neither disappointed nor an invalid. He was right to deny disappointment as a reason for seclusion, but his assertions that seclusion was a 'normal' development do not ring true. Mabel Todd offers no explanation beyond this assertion of normality. She was probably in the dark. It's likely that little was disclosed, much less discussed, even in the family.

One small clue to seclusion was Austin's uneasiness about his sister's eyes. When Roberts Brothers wished to include a picture of Dickinson with the *Letters*, Austin ruled out the now famous daguerreotype taken when Emily was sixteen. Austin told Mabel it didn't resemble her and Lavinia concurred. In that image her eyes are large, wide, dramatically alert, rather like the spare facial structure of a kangaroo, the creature to which she likened herself at the time. There was an attempt to doctor the daguerreotype with a tint, and in 1894 an artist, Laura Hills, was asked to introduce curls on Emily's forehead in place of hair drawn straight back from a centre parting in a way that bares her face. Emily's brother and sister would have remembered her hair as curly – not evident in the daguerreotype – and they would have been aware that curly hair had come into fashion. Now, in the nineties, a curly fringe overlaid the bared brow of the 1840s, yet the family aim is less fashion than a wish to revamp Dickinson's image in the direction of tameness and femininity. The artist filled in the neck with a lace fichu. The girl's level gaze and sensuous, almost swollen lips are toned down to a faintly smiling sweetness.

In the end, the daguerreotype did not appear in Austin's lifetime. He insisted that a likeness to Emily was 'far better' in an oil portrait painted of her as a child, looking much like her red-haired brother and unlike their small dark sister. The child has a less distinctive look – she might be any 'normal', neatly turned out and reasonably placid little girl with short hair and a white frill about her neck – and this was the first image to be published, even though the unformed face of a child consorts oddly with the sophisticated verbal play of the letters. Curiously, even here, Austin expressed uneasiness. Todd, he said, must ask the artist at Roberts Brothers to 'soften the eye in some way'. It must be 'altogether softened'.

Lavinia remained dissatisfied with the 'revised' daguerreotype after she fell in love with a portrait that appeared in the pages of *Century* magazine in April 1897. It's a miniature of Mrs Lloyd Rogers, a beauty with propped-up rounded bosoms and curls tumbling over her forehead. Lavinia detected, she thought, a likeness to Emily, though the beauty's nose is narrower and her mouth small, set off by a stiff, upstanding ruff behind Mrs Rogers' head. Lavinia decided to have a miniature painted, prettying the daguerreotype further on the model of Mrs Rogers and her outfit. The bogus miniature of Emily Dickinson perpetrated in May 1897 was beyond Lavinia's 'highest expectations. It really seems as if Emily were here', she rejoiced. 'I think the artist can create some fluffy finish for the neck. Perhaps a ruffle half as high and not quite so full as Mrs. Rogers' would be the thing.' In time this became a ruff to cover up the exposed funnel of the poet's throat (and presumably the abnormalities coming out of it, what one reviewer called 'the neuralgic darts of feeling' voiced in 'curiously far-fetched' words spaced out by 'the hardly human dumbness').

From the first, Todd too concocted a 'picturesque' image – the white legend – speaking as one who had witnessed it. 'Dressed always in white, her graceful passing about the house seemed rather the coming and going of some gentle spirit than any mere earthly presence.' *Housekeeper's Magazine* picked this up and spread it further: Mabel Loomis Todd was one of the few privileged ones who were admitted to intimacy with the poet, 'a dear ghost, seen but scarcely tangible'. Hardly the Emily who welcomed Lord's touch.

At the same time, Todd did bring out the explosive character of the 'startling little poetic bombs', as though earthquakes, bolts, the revolver pointed at an unwanted self, and a life that stood a loaded gun had no con-nection with the ghostly writer. This blend of truth and evasion was to characterise future legend. Todd did encounter words like blades but, as mouthpiece for the family, never mentions this, any more than Jane Austen's family saw fit to mention her sarcasms. Nineteenth-century fam-ilies project an image of an authoress as retiring lady whose gift shades into an uneventful life. Nothing could be said of sickness, love, adultery or the rising fire of the feud.

*

What came to be called the War between the Houses took off with Lavinia's discovery of the poems in the Homestead. This made her the sole legatee of a treasure, the value of which she immediately perceived – value, that is, to literature. Only gradually did she realise it was potentially an asset of untold proportions. The clearer this became with the publication of successive volumes, the sourer Austin turned towards Lavinia. Despite all she had risked for him and Mabel, all it had cost her in the affections of her niece and nephew (for, like Emily, Vinnie was very fond of Ned) Austin disparaged her limitations. He declared that she knew nothing beyond what callers could tell her.

'My sister Vin,' he thought fit to inform Higginson, 'had no comprehension of her sister, yet believed her a shining genius.'

Happily, Emily's posthumous voice testifies against this: her sister's 'inciting voice' was part of her own courage, Emily had said. Without Vinnie, 'life was fear and paradise a cowardice'. Their bond was 'early, earnest and indissoluble'.

The more Austin failed to dent Lavinia's allegiance, the more he let loose against her. For Lavinia held her own when it came to the papers. She became what she felt herself to be, a warrior as fierce and fervent as 'Joan of Arc'.

Meanwhile, next door, Susan held on to her separate collection of poems and letters, amongst them some of the poet's most daring works. The lines were now re-drawn for the battles to come: Lavinia versus Mabel Loomis Todd who had the ear of Austin Dickinson. Although Austin had no interest in Emily's poetry he was Mabel's man and determined to control Lavinia.

In the 1880s the focus of the feud had been adultery; in the 1890s the focus shifted to the divided treasure the poet had left behind. Who had the right to possess her? Who had the right to say what she was?

IV: THE WAR BETWEEN THE HOUSES

12

LAVINIA'S STAND

So long as Austin Dickinson lived he continued to control Vinnie – up to a point. In 1894, when she refused to hand his mistress half the copyright in Emily Dickinson's letters, Austin let fly. Following that first stand Lavinia hesitated not at all in refusing Austin's next diktat, that she will her rights, away from the family, to Mabel Todd. From the start, Lavinia had found herself tugged into the lovers' camp, to the detriment of her bonds with Austin's wife and children. What could she have done? Lavinia's friend Miss Buffam, a schoolmistress accustomed to independence, noticed that not a cent in Lavinia's pocket was not meted out by her brother. As brother and co-heir of the Homestead, Austin could come and go as he pleased and his 'friend' (Mabel) came too, and the truth of their tie Austin did not offer to explain.

So it was that the affair was known – and *not* known. There was no evidence, not in legal terms. As a lawyer, Austin Dickinson was adept when it came to evidence. Love letters were locked in a safe-box in the vault of the bank, and the letters themselves took care to omit clues and names.

For a long time Lavinia had been more compliant than Emily. Where Emily had retained her closeness to Sue and Ned, Lavinia was positioned with her brother, and the more that position strained her ties with The Evergreens, the more dependent on Austin she became; and then, after Emily died, the purpose of her life was the joint venture with Mabel Todd.

Their faith in the greatness of Emily Dickinson ensured a bond with Mabel, reinforced by kisses and David Todd's particular affection. He came to fix her clock and once, in 1894, when she'd been ill, he gave her 'a lovely warm bath while her bed was changed'. It was a practical, hands-on act of kindness by a man at ease with women's bodies. Vinnie was not so conventional as to resist this attention. Mabel mentions it matter-of-factly. She was often at the Homestead to discuss the poems and Lavinia made return visits to The Dell, bringing bushels of Dickinson manuscripts in her basket. It was therefore no small matter for Lavinia, aged sixty-one, to take her stand in August and September 1894.

Lavinia was a fame-seeking fool, Austin exploded to Emily's publisher, Mr Hardy.

But Austin's heart condition and failing health changed the balance of power. For Mabel it meant an end to kingly protection. Lavinia, freed from her brother's rule, burst into action. This sister who had been in the background, tending others, advanced with unexpected aplomb towards the footlights of a public confrontation. From now on Lavinia Dickinson was centre stage.

As Austin lay dying in the summer of 1895 he sent a message of gratitude to David Todd. For twelve years Austin had believed in the primacy of his tie with Mabel, and Mabel's letters had endorsed this belief. Only once did Susan shake it. She pointed out that while Austin had rejected all physical and emotional attachment to his marriage, Mabel had not done so with hers. What Austin had taken to be no more than the dutifulness of wifely devotion continued to be, for David, an active tie. So Susan argued: Mabel claimed two men and 'had the best' of both their lives. In reporting this to Mabel, Austin owned to the awkwardness he was made to feel. He had no adequate answer. Nor did Mabel offer one.

During Austin's last weeks, confined to bed at The Evergreens where Mabel had no access, Lavinia still acted on the lovers' behalf, trying to carry letters from Mabel undetected by the rest of the family. Austin died on 16 August, when the Todds were away in New Salem, near Shutesbury, where David delivered a speech on the Dickinson dynasty.

In contrast to the relief at The Evergreens – an end to the daily pain inflicted by a father and husband who'd withdrawn his love – the Todds were shattered. 'My best friend died tonight, & I seem stranded,' David cried out in his diary, 'he touched and forwarded everything.' The funeral, on 19 August, struck him as the saddest day of his life. Millicent, aged fifteen, never forgot her mother's inconsolable weeping and pleas for her husband to fetch the love letters from the vault. Secrecy now compelled her less than what she needed: to make Austin's love known. Austin was never persuaded to make her 'Mabel Loomis Dickinson' – in effect, to go public. Once he'd gone, she was prepared to defy opinion in a new role as Austin's widow, an open rival of Susan Dickinson, back in her blacks.

So here is Mabel in a black dress, black cape and black hat. With a black mourning veil over her face and her lover's ring on a pointed finger when she draws off her gloves, Mabel goes about as Austin's rightful mate. Lavinia remonstrates in vain: 'It's degrading to Austin.'

'Austin wished it,' Mabel says. 'It was a promise between us.'

To flaunt her 'widowing' is, of course, provocative: insulting to Susan, embarrassing to her own husband and altogether indiscreet. Is this the woman who'd left Amherst in the winter of 1889–90 to avoid the whispers? Her public conduct in the late summer of 1895 reveals her as less than calculating: it's natural to her to extend a genuine loss and grief in turns and costumes. Mabel's all too manifest widowhood recalls her haggard appearance at Dickinson's graveside in May 1886. The theatricality to which she rose on occasion is not to say it was all an act.

Before Austin's funeral an acute and genuine anguish had thrust her into a dramatic scene. Defying the prohibition against her entering The Evergreens, she slipped inside while the family dined (in a room to the left) and dashed through the red hall, turning right, into what the family called 'the dying room', the dark old marital bedroom where the body lay. Here is her diary entry for Monday, 19 August 1895: 'My Austin is going to Wildwood [cemetery] – that is, his dear, dear body is. I kissed it a long, tender goodbye. <u>He</u> is here with me.' Intimacy with the dead deepens eleven days later when she says, 'I feel my eyes closing to Earth, and opening – to

Austin!' Then a cry of separation breaks from her on 4 September: 'I want Austin – I agonize for him – I call for him, I reach to him.'

Grief accompanied her on a second journey to Japan the following year. En route Austin seemed as near 'on a volcano in Hawaii as in our own meadow in Amherst'. No other soul would ever meet her 'real, innermost self' as this man had with his 'exquisite sympathy'.

'If only I could die this night!' she whispered to herself.

On the return crossing, more than a year after Austin died, she parted her hair and saw a few white threads under the brown, and peering closer into the small cabin mirror detected a line 'of pain' on her forehead. She would like to die, she thought again, 'but as long as I do live I must stay young. Youth is my role.'

Back in Amherst she plunged into thirty-five public talks over the following winter of 1896–7. Marking even now the stabs of pain, she saw them as 'signet royal of my closeness to my dear master'.

For all that Mabel suffered at the loss of a man who had loved her exclusively and with all his being for twelve years, it can't provide a reliable answer as to whether her prime attachment was to lover or husband. The abundance and fervour of her love letters to Austin declare to him (and to the readers she hoped one day to have*) that he was the love of her life. There are two reasons to question this.

One is that Mabel adapted her voice to her role. Austin's rampant emotion required arias of unconditional love tuned to the highest pitch of soulfulness. The operatic vehemence Mabel delivered day after day would not be realistic in domestic life. It's sustainable because the lovers could not cohabit, and sustained too by the vibrato of fantasy that separation invites. As recently as 1893, there had been Austin's renewed fantasy of escape out west when he welcomed an offer of a post in Omaha, Nebraska. At the age of sixty-four he'd been prepared to start a new life with Mabel. Then there was the lovers' fantasy of building a house on a hilltop near Amherst; and Mabel's failed fantasy of Susan's

---

* Mabel Loomis Todd's papers show that she planned to publish the love letters as though she were editing them at the request of the anonymous lovers.

death. 'A deaf God', Mabel cried at the close of a letter to Austin near the end of his life.

A more serious reason to question Austin's pre-eminence with Mabel is her continued devotion to her husband. Though this did serve as a cover for her affair, it was more than that. At the outset, Mabel chose David as a husband who would back her sense of destiny. Their commitment to promote each other's work was as much a pact as a marriage. David's adventures in romance and conquest were diverting, but stable attachment was reserved for his wife.

'And if my life is the success I hope it may yet be, I shall not rest until my ambition is gratified by seeing you in the highest degree honoured & appreciated for your full worth,' he assured Mabel.

Success. Honour. Worth. The language of aspiration is unremarkable; it's the reciprocity that's rare. In the late nineteenth century and well into the twentieth century many a woman had to choose between marriage and career. Not Mabel. On his return journey from Angola in 1890, David mailed a letter from Barbados reaffirming a marriage of mounting ambition on both sides. 'My advancements and the little successes of my life so far have all come of you. Eleven years more will, I venture, see us more thoroughly in love than now.'

David had reason to welcome his wife's liaison. To win the ear of the college treasurer was Mabel's effort for David's advance. As a young astronomer he had been lured back to Amherst by a mirage: a new observatory of his own. This had not materialised. Then, in the early nineties, President Seelye fell ill; there was an interregnum and Austin Dickinson took over. It's likely that he was behind an initial move to build an up-to-date observatory at the college. By 1894 Mabel was writing letters on stationery with an observatory letterhead, even though the building took another decade to complete. To encourage funding, she collaborated with David on a book, *Total Eclipses of the Sun* (1894), published under her name by Roberts Brothers in the same year as they published her selection of Dickinson's *Letters*.

To consider Mabel's allegiance to one man or the other may be the wrong question. She never compares husband and lover in the way of

Hester Prynne or Emma Bovary or Anna Karenina. Here is an unclassifiable phenomenon: not quite the femme fatale, not quite the gold-digger, and not so much the social climber as to leave her husband in order to cling exclusively to her 'King'. The constant in her history, far back, is that 'presentiment' combined with contempt for the domestic destiny of lesser women. Mabel's ambition, confirmed by an array of talents but starved of means, came nearest the bone. Money therefore meant a lot to her.

Alerted to this, Austin had wished Mabel to inherit the Dickinson meadow. In the 1890s it was open land where corn grew — apart from the Todds' plot which, as Vinnie stressed later, had been 'cut out' of what was now her property. Back in November 1887, when he'd made his will, Austin had assured Mabel she would benefit by his death since he'd arranged for Vinnie to hand over this stretch of seven to eight acres.

Austin covered his defection from his family with an impeccable will that left The Evergreens to his wife and the meadow to his sister. On the face of it, he was the responsible husband and brother. But Austin's plan was otherwise: to do his family down, and to use his sister to carry this out. The promise he extracted from Lavinia required her, in effect, to take over the moral burden for disinheriting his children of this ancestral land. Lavinia's niece and nephew, Mattie and Ned, were bound to be outraged, and Susan too on their behalf. Inevitably their anger would fall on Lavinia. Emily, it will be remembered, had stood by their nephew, assuring him there would be 'no treason'. '. . . *Ever be sure of me, Lad.*' If Lavinia acted on her brother's wish she would be at war with these, her closest relations and neighbours — hard on a lonely woman. It's unlikely Austin troubled himself to see beyond a scheme that shielded himself and Mabel from the scandal of an overt bequest of these proportions. He was, after all, accustomed to use Lavinia to further his affair.

When Austin's heart was giving out in the early summer of 1895 he had done the Todds a final favour. On his last legs he had staggered over to The Dell in order to verify David's survey of an adjoining strip of land including a great maple tree, the land Mabel wanted most. Austin had already landscaped and planted this strip as though it were part of the Todds' plot. His final intention is unknown: could this have been a fall-back if Lavinia would not yield the whole meadow? There was nothing on paper apart from the private promise Austin had given Mabel in November 1887. Lavinia had not signed it, so Mabel depended on Lavinia's assent to an instruction from her brother eight years earlier.

6 October 1895. Austin has been dead seven weeks. Mabel decides it is time to show Lavinia the letter from Austin: his private addendum to a will for an estate of nearly $34,000. It's not like Austin's other letters. He states their names: the letter is headed 'Mrs Todd' and signed 'Wm A. Dickinson' with an air of legal formality. Written in pencil, though, and unwitnessed, it has no legal validity. It's designed to weigh with Lavinia alone. After the funeral a moved Lavinia had seemed to agree to this bequest, yet the weeks pass and nothing more is said.

On this Sunday morning Mabel goes to see Lavinia with the letter and Lavinia refuses to hand over the meadow.

Vinnie is 'utterly slippery and treacherous', Mabel fumes in her diary. Austin always said so, always 'had entire contempt for her' but 'he did not think she would fail to do as he stipulated in this'.

Mabel had too much self-command to permit frustration to interfere with plans. If one plan failed she put a variation on the table. The handsome sideboard Lavinia's mother Emily Norcross, as a bride, had brought from Monson to Amherst had been moved to the dining room at The Evergreens.* Would Vinnie like her friend Mabel to find her a new sideboard?

Vinnie waved the offer away: 'I guess we won't have any trade of that kind.' She was not to be wheedled into accepting help in lieu of land.

All that autumn, Mabel came back to Lavinia with bonding ideas for their future folded in her endearing gaze. The only way to avoid Mabel would be to put up a pre-emptive barrier, as Susan and her children had done, not speaking, not seeing, and this Vinnie in her loneliness was not yet prepared to do. She needed Mabel Todd to edit a third volume of poems, a prospective delight after the recognition the first volumes had excited.

* Visitors to The Evergreens can see it there today.

How congenial it was to share once more in the selection. By now Higginson had bowed out, which meant that in the autumn of 1895 Vinnie depended on Todd alone.

With this volume nearing completion, Mabel Todd pressed her to do 'a lovely thing': to give the Todds the strip of the meadow, two hundred and ninety by fifty-four feet, that Austin and David had measured. It was to be a secret (in the same way as the editing of Dickinson had been a secret, to avoid opposition). One night, after dark so as to avoid detection, Vinnie took her turn at inspecting the site. Then, on about 29 December, Vinnie agreed to yield. Two days later Mabel Todd, hard-working and punctual as ever, delivered her typescript of *Poems: Third Series* to Dickinson's publishers.

The Todds were about to depart for Japan for six to seven months. In February 1896 Mabel was busy with the immense preparation needed for David's expeditions. As the March date for departure drew near, it was time for Lavinia to actually sign over the land. Mabel was taking no chance that, left to herself, Lavinia might back off once more.

There was another obstacle. Lavinia had a business adviser in place of Austin, another rather volatile gentleman, Dwight Hills, for twenty-four years President of the First National Bank of Amherst. Aware of the pressure on Lavinia to hand over land, he had warned her not to sign any paper without his knowledge. Hills spoke as a protector and Lavinia, rumour said, warmed to this attention from a mature bachelor who lived with his mother. In her youth Lavinia had been a demonstrative young woman with long black hair tinged with red. It was still long and luxurious, and sometimes she shook it out and aired it, combing it with her fingers to the tips. She would rather not annoy Mr Hills with the 'lovely thing' she would do for Mabel Todd.

Mabel could not afford to wait. She had to forestall the possibility that, at any moment, Lavinia might consult her protector who was certain to intervene. Another danger was Susan Dickinson, who would be angry, very angry, should she hear of a second transfer of land. Lavinia would be subject to family pressure. For these reasons Mabel Todd could not risk leaving for Japan with the deed unsigned.

Anger threatened Lavinia on three sides but at this point her first consideration still had to be the safety of the new volume of unpublished poems. In January and early February 1896, with Mabel's preface due, it was vital to satisfy her.

Mabel readied the deed of transfer. She had often handled these as Austin's unofficial assistant. (Trustees of the college would have been surprised to learn how much she knew of their business.) She had kept a spare blank and filled it in. Who might witness Lavinia's signature? Since the transaction was to remain secret this had to be done privately, not in a lawyer's office, and with a witness of unquestionable credentials, preferably from out of town. Mabel consulted a prominent lawyer, Everett C. Bumpus of Tremont Street, Boston.* Bumpus, in his early fifties, already had an eye to the animated and elegantly costumed Mrs Todd. They had met during the winter she spent in Boston in 1889–90, and when they'd met again for a meal in September 1895, a month after Austin's death, Mabel perceived that Bumpus longed to make love. Her journal crosses this out, but it's plain that Bumpus continued to be charmed. Now, for Mrs Todd's purpose, he suggested a colleague called Timothy Spaulding who practised law in Northampton and was a Justice of the Peace. Mr Spaulding was a polite gentleman whom Lavinia had not met but whose family was familiar. As a child she'd known his mother, who had lived in Amherst, and his father had been a friend of her father and brother.

Mabel arranged for Mr Spaulding to call on Lavinia on 7 February at 7 p.m., the usual time for social calls. No one who spied Mr Spaulding would suspect he'd come on business at such an hour.

'I don't think she'll sign it,' Mabel said to the lawyer as they walked over to the Homestead.

'Oh yes she will.'

When Lavinia opened the door Mabel introduced him.

He spoke to her about the old days, drawing her out by listening to what she had to say. In subsequent and conflicting reports of what transpired during this scene, there is no disagreement over one fact: Mr

* His name and Boston gentility prefigure the threatened sobrieties of 'The Love Song of J. Alfred Prufrock', Aunt Helen and Cousin Nancy in T. S. Eliot's early poems.

Spaulding appeared keen to discuss the poetry of Emily Dickinson with her sister. For Lavinia this was the absorbing subject of discussion for twenty to thirty minutes, the normal length of a social call.

Then Mabel asked Lavinia, 'Might I show Mr Spaulding your mother's blue china?'

The three went into the dining room. It will be recalled that this was the sitting room in winter and the scene of Mabel's embraces back in the eighties when Emily was alive. Here Lavinia keeps her writing materials. While the lawyer peers at dinner plates depicting the landing of Lafayette (in support of George Washington during the War of Independence), Mabel sets the deed on the table next to a pen and inkstand, and indicates where Lavinia is to sign.

Mr Spaulding, preoccupied in another part of the room, lifts his head to give Lavinia the routine caution. This is a deed to transfer a strip of land. It must be done of her free will. In Mabel's statement later, 'he said to her he should suppose she'd like to give Mrs Todd a little piece of land. He took it as an ordinary thing and didn't make much of it. She answered as an ordinary lady would as if it was alright and said she'd be glad to sign it.'

It did not occur to Lavinia to see the document in advance. Accustomed to her father's and brother's legal expertise and handicapped by poor sight (she didn't use spectacles), Lavinia was not in the habit of reading documents and she did not read this deed before she put her name to it in her sprawling hand – Mabel likened Lavinia's hand to a demented spider who has fallen into an inkwell.

Mr Spaulding talked a bit more about Emily Dickinson, and then walked off with Mabel to The Dell. Their exit together in a mood of friendship emboldened Mabel to make her last move: she asked the lawyer to delay registration of the deed. By that time Mabel was at a distance from the scene, on her way to Japan.

One morning in May, in the post office, Lavinia's loyal servant Maggie Maher heard talk of the deed. Hastening home, she broke it to Lavinia that talk in town gave out a Todd victory.

Lavinia was appalled. Instead of the 'lovely' little arrangement she'd been led to expect, and the congenial visit from Mr Spaulding in whose presence she had felt secure, the fierce terms of the deed were designed to wipe out any claim the Dickinson family might put forward to contravene Lavinia's gesture. Here are the terms to which she'd put her signature:

> Lavinia Dickinson of her free will gives Mabel Loomis Todd land, adjacent to land deeded to her by the Dickinsons on June 8th, 1886.
>
> The land is handed over 'in consideration of the sum of One dollar and other valuable considerations paid by Mabel Loomis Todd'. [What was 'paid' remains vague.]
>
> Miss Dickinson grants the land to Mrs Todd and her heirs 'to their own use and behoof forever', and Miss Dickinson's heirs [Ned and Mattie Dickinson] will defend Mrs Todd's heirs forever against 'the lawful claims and demands of all persons'.

Now it was public. Now Mr Hills would know the foolish thing she had done behind his back. Lavinia was distraught. She thought he would no longer protect her – an abrupt end to his protection. He would be furious, and more so her sister-in-law, dear nephew and determined niece. As Lavinia now saw, she had put her name to a document that betrayed her family, an act Emily, ten years before, had resisted to the death.

Mr Hills, as angry as Lavinia foresaw, told her there was but one way out: she could contest the deed if she had not understood what she was doing. This meant accusing Mabel Todd of misrepresentation or worse.

There was something Lavinia could not mention to Mr Hills: the fissure in the family, known to two or three editors who'd felt the sharp edge of conflicting interests but otherwise concealed. The Dickinsons had contrived to preserve an unblemished front. After the advent of Mabel they had lived outwardly as before. For thirteen years, ever since 1883, no one had attempted to cross the fissure between Austin and Lavinia on one side and, on the other, Susan, Ned and Mattie. To abandon Mabel and rejoin her family would be to cross that fissure. Looking across to the other side, Lavinia stood for a space alone.

*

Lavinia took this leap. That May she drew up a Bill of Complaint with the help of her lawyers, Hammond & Field. Here she invented a plausible story: she'd merely agreed to allow no building on the meadow adjacent to the Todds' house. She'd been willing to do so because she would never permit a building where there were 'sacred' shrubs (planted by her brother). Then Mrs Todd had come with an argument that Miss Dickinson might die, so it would help to have this agreement in writing. Under repeated pressure Miss Dickinson had agreed to sign a paper. She denied that she had ever agreed to deed the land; she did not recall hearing the word 'deed'. Mrs Todd had called it a 'paper'. She also alleged that Mrs Todd had prepared the deed secretly; it was in Mrs Todd's hand. The value of the land, for which nothing had been paid, was said to be $2000 (though actually worth, at the time, about $600). Miss Dickinson had not herself employed Timothy Spaulding to witness the signature. There had been a deceptively casual air to the business. She had no foreknowledge of the signing and had thought Mr Spaulding was coming, at his request, to discuss her sister's poems.

Far off in Japan, Mabel Todd worked away at the proofs of *Poems: Third Series*. She was scrupulous about checking against Dickinson's original manuscripts and it's likely that she took these with her to the other side of the world. By August the proofs were back in Boston, Todd ever prompt and professional. On 10 August 1896 Roberts Brothers drew up a contract with no reference to Mrs Todd. This, the fourth contract with the firm, was the simplest: all rights and royalties were lodged with Lavinia Dickinson alone.

That August, *Poems: Third Series* was announced for the autumn. This was the first volume of poems to be edited solely by Mabel Todd; it was, then, the first to go out minus the protection of Higginson's name, and now, at last, even before it was published, what Emily Dickinson had feared did happen. A lash from a newspaper was bound to chasten a woman immodest enough to enter the public arena. 'That singular anomaly, the Lady novelist,' sang

*Revived at the Savoy in London from July 1896.

the Lord High Executioner in *The Mikado*.* 'I don't think she'd be missed, I'm sure she'd not be missed.' The *New York Tribune* complained of Emily Dickinson in August 1896: why must the public be imposed upon yet again with 'mere trifles or experiments' from this 'minor' poet?

Ned, on holiday in Maine with his 'girls' (as he called his mother and sister), shuddered for Aunt Emily. As the man in the family, Ned was all too aware that he was not manly in the expected way. At thirty-five, a need to act for his family's protection reproached his long retreat from conflict. Throughout his twenties he'd been sunk, helpless, in a 'witchesmare'. Roused now to action by this slight to his aunt, Ned cut Lavinia to the heart with an accusation that she had brought shame on her beloved sister. This is what came of encouraging the Todds: 'these people', he calls them, as though the very name stuck in his throat. On a foggy morning in Maine, Ned typed the following:

> Hotel Claremont,
> Southwest Harbor.
> 27 August 1896

> My dear Aunt:
> . . . For the sake of my Grand-Father's good name, and for the peace of my Aunt, who shun[n]ed all vulgarity, it makes me shudder to think of having the family name dragged before an unwilling public, and by a woman, who has brought nothing but a sword into the family. You would be held responsible naturally for any such performance, and would do more to injure any just fame that may belong to Aunt Emily, simply from a literary point of view, than any thing that could be done. Excuse my warmth on the subject, but as I am the only man left to represent generations of strong, forceful men who have preceded me, I feel I have the right to make my protest . . .

> Very faithfully,
> Edward Dickinson

Mabel Todd returned to Amherst in October, bringing Vinnie a gift of Japanese pottery. Vinnie received her with the usual kiss. Not a word to Mabel revealed the bomb about to explode in her face. Soon after, in the same month, *Poems: Third Series* came out. Vinnie's waiting was now over. A few weeks later, when there was nothing more for the editor to do, Lavinia left town on a rare visit to Boston while Hammond & Field filed the Bill of Complaint on 16 November 1896. The Todds, it said, had obtained their new slice of Dickinson land by 'misrepresentation and fraud'.

Mr Bumpus of Boston helped Mabel to prepare a Defendants' Answer, registered a month later, on 14 December. She denied having made a request that no house be built on the land in question, and denied too that Lavinia was uninformed about the purpose of Mr Spaulding's visit. These denials ring true. Even more convincing was her story about the fate of Emily Dickinson's poetry. Mabel Todd knew how to put together a coherent story of daunting challenges and eventual triumph, a story to outdo the pathos of Lavinia's defrauding. It told of 'ten' years toil over poems and letters, for which Todd had received a paltry $200.*

The years she'd given to Dickinson had prevented her writing many 'lucrative' pieces, Todd declared. Miss Dickinson would urge her on, saying that Emily's friends were dying and soon there'd be none to care whether the poems were published. Her Defendant's Answer insisted that the editing had required discrimination, and it stressed David Todd's part in transcribing poems in type, to reinforce the claim that Austin Dickinson had wished to deed the Todds a second plot of land as compensation for their work. He 'had knowledge of the work, and complained because his sister failed to give Mrs Todd proper compensation. He agreed with Mrs

---

* This amount, it will be recalled, represented two-thirds of Lavinia's royalties on the first two volumes of ED's poems. By the time that the case came to court, Mabel Todd mistakenly believed that Lavinia had received as much as $2000 and that half of it was her due. In fact, royalty statements from December 1894 to June 1898 show falling sales after the first thousand copies of the two-volume selection of ED's letters. Lavinia was debited $604 for the electroplates. Mabel also mistakenly came to believe that the recent (fourth) contract had stipulated shared rights. (It's not known whether Todd made this up because she felt it her due, or whether Lavinia had spurred her on with expectations.)

Todd to give the latter the property in dispute, but before the deed could be executed Mr Dickinson died. In the autumn of that year [1895] the plaintiff [Lavinia] expressed to Mrs Todd acquiescence in her brother's purpose and agreed that the land should be conveyed to Mrs Todd.' The secrecy had been Miss Dickinson's wish.

The Todds had a strong case. Lavinia's allegations were, in the main, untrue. Mr Hills, who was so furious with Lavinia that he wished Mrs Todd to 'wallop' her, revealed that Lavinia had debated the land transfer in the autumn of 1895, before she signed the deed. (Testimonies conflict as to what Mr Hills had advised: so long as he favoured Mrs Todd, he claimed to have left the decision to Lavinia. She claimed to the contrary, that he'd warned her never to give land away to the Todds who, he said, were 'leeches, leeches, leeches'.) Miss Seelye, his housekeeper, and her sister supported Mr Hills by reporting an unguarded comment from Maggie Maher to the effect that Miss Lavinia 'knew perfectly well what she was doing when she signed the deed'.

Better still, Mr Spaulding stood ready to testify that he had conducted himself with legal propriety. This was never in question, and his evidence, given with a lawyer's acumen, would make him a formidable witness for the defence. He would undoubtedly claim to have spelt it out to Miss Dickinson that she was about to sign a deed to hand over land. There had been no scope for misunderstanding.

Witnesses gathering for the defence were not the only reason that Lavinia found herself in a weak position. Mabel Todd was holding on to a massive cache of about six hundred poems as well as a hoard of Dickinson letters. Mabel entertained certain notions about her rights, a residue perhaps of promises Austin had made, assuming the power to control Lavinia even as that power was fading. Mabel continued to believe in the validity of the draft contract of 1894 that had granted her half the copyright in Dickinson letters, and she continued to believe as well (or so she said later) in an improbable notion that Lavinia had made a will before Austin died, leaving Mrs Todd substantial rights in the whole Dickinson oeuvre.

Mabel was able to retain the manuscripts, since Lavinia had willingly handed them over. To Lavinia, of course, it was merely a loan. The papers were at The Dell so that Todd could go on with their long-term project of editing as many as ten volumes. What Lavinia did not consider, or not enough, was that the public humiliation of the editor might affect their future project. Lavinia took the view that to edit Emily Dickinson was an honour. She did not pick up on the shortness of cash in Todd's household, an oblivion soothed by Mabel's pride in drawing a genteel veil over the matter of money, much as her mother had done.

The stress of Lavinia's leap across the fissure, followed by preparations for legal battle, affected Lavinia's heart. Her physician declared her unfit for a trial. At different times, Bumpus tried to settle out of court: if Mabel would return the land and the Dickinson papers then Lavinia would drop her charge.

'All right,' Mabel agreed, 'but never until she admits on paper that she accused me falsely.' It would have to be 'an entire retraction'.

David said, 'We have too good a case. I intend to go through with it.' Yet for all the strength of the evidence in the Todds' favour, there was a flaw in the case for the defence.

Astonishingly, it seems not to have occurred either to Mabel or David that a person with a secret who cares about hiding it for the sake of her reputation should not stand trial. When Bumpus, acting as Mrs Todd's counsel, initially encouraged litigation he did not, it seems at that stage, know that Austin had wrested the prior plot of land from an unwilling family as a gift for Mrs Todd once Emily Dickinson was out of the way. No one outside the family knew that immediately following his sister's death, when Austin had signed over the plot to his mistress, Susan Dickinson had shut herself in her room. She did not emerge for a day or two, helpless to defend her children against a father who repudiated them: 'They never were my children,' he told Mabel. Bumpus had no idea of the bitterness festering at The Evergreens for ten years since this ill deed in June 1886. Nor did Bumpus know for some time that Austin's decision to give Mrs Todd a second gift of land went back to November 1887 — that is, *before* she began assigned work on the Dickinson papers.

The case due for February 1897 was postponed till the autumn, and then postponed again. Meanwhile, on 28 May of that year, a private cross-examination took place that was to have an immeasurable effect on the trial to come. Lavinia's counsel, Mr J. C. Hammond, and Mabel's counsel, Mr Bumpus, came to Northampton to take a deposition from Lavinia's chief witness, Maggie Maher, who was leaving Massachusetts for a while and might not return in time for the trial.

The defence was up against a forty-three-year-old Irishwoman who since the age of twenty-eight had stood by Lavinia Dickinson in all she had done for the comfort and care of her parents and sister. Having lived at the Homestead for these years, since 1869, Maggie had seen and heard at close quarters what there was to see and hear from the time Mabel began to use the house on a regular basis in 1883. Her testimony was devastating as she exposed Mabel and Austin's trysts. Since it was crucial to forestall speculation that the land was compensation for sexual favours, this undermined Mabel's insistence that the land was compensation for 'labor' on Emily Dickinson.

Maggie's testimony opposed this claim. She had heard Mrs Todd 'often' speak of her work on the poems as 'a labor of love'. When the royalties for the first volume arrived Miss Lavinia had handed the bills and money to Mrs Todd in the dining room.

'Is that right, Mrs Todd?' she'd asked, and Mrs Todd had expressed herself 'satisfied' with what Miss Lavinia had shared.

Maggie described working at The Dell over a three-month period, when she had been there helping the Todds every day from three in the afternoon until eight in the evening 'by Miss Dickinson's wish'. She was not paid for this work: 'I always told [Mrs Todd] I wanted no compensation; that I was doing it because she was editing Miss Emily's poems for Miss Dickinson.' Austin used to call between five and six, when Mr Todd would be in college. 'I would see [Mr Dickinson] coming; I never let him in. He generally came in at the side door . . . Mrs Todd let him in.'

'Did you observe any act of intimacy between Mr Dickinson and Mrs Todd?' Hammond asked.

'I remember at one time when Mr Dickinson brought some laurel to trim Mrs Todd's front hall stairs, and he placed the laurel there for her in a large vase, and she put her arms around him and kissed him and said, "You dear old man".'

Another scene had them embracing and kissing upstairs, 'on the second landing', as seen from the landing below. Maggie testified also that Mrs Todd had been alone with Mr Dickinson at The Evergreens when his family was away in 1893. He had asked Maggie to bring over lunch at one o'clock. She hadn't seen Mrs Todd but had heard her singing at the piano. Three hours later Mrs Todd had stopped by to see Miss Dickinson, coming from the direction of The Evergreens.

'Did you ever hear Mrs Todd say that she was not allowed by Mr Dickinson's family to come to that house?' Hammond interposed over sharp objection from Bumpus.

'I have heard her say she was not allowed to go there. She would say that she was very sorry she couldn't go there, and she didn't know why she couldn't. Miss Dickinson would answer to her, "You know the reason why."'

Maggie's most pointed testimony was that the pair had often been alone together at the Homestead. 'They met very frequently; probably three or four times a week, sometimes in the afternoon and sometimes in the fore-noon, either in the dining room or the library. Sometimes for three or four hours just as their consciences allowed them. They met alone; the door was shut.'

She also recalled scenes when Mrs Todd had run out of funds: 'I recol-lect another time she wanted to see him to get some money and she waited in the kitchen until she saw him come across from his house. They both went into the library, and an hour later she went home.'

Bumpus, with constant objections, did his best to obstruct what Maggie was saying, but she proved a careful, precise witness, not saying more than what she had observed. Bumpus could not block her acid remark as to what the consciences of the lovers 'allowed', since this moral opinion was embedded in a factual answer. No lawyer could have turned a defter phrase.

Hammond once more pressed Maggie 'whether or not at any time at Miss Dickinson's house you saw any act of intimacy between Mr Dickinson and Mrs Todd'.

Maggie recalled a scene that took place in 1891. The lovers hadn't seen her, though she'd been no more than a foot away. 'They came from the dining room to the kitchen. I was in the next room, which we call the wash-room, with the doors open. She put her arms around him and kissed him.' They did this in silence. 'They had been in the house about two hours.'

'Did Miss Lavinia Dickinson know that Mr Dickinson, her brother, and Mrs Todd were in her house in the way you have stated?' Bumpus demanded when it was his turn to cross-examine.

'She did know it, but did not like it.'

All this was disagreeable news to Bumpus, and he could neither stop it coming nor shake Maggie's integrity.

Did Maggie tell Miss Dickinson what she'd seen at The Dell?

'I never did.'

'You kept on working there afterwards?'

'Yes sir, I did.'

'I understand from your answers that you did not mention the kissing to Miss Dickinson and you remained in [Mrs Todd's] employ in spite of what you saw there?'

'I knew I was obliged to stay in her employ. I was doing it for Miss Dickinson, when Mrs Todd was working on the poems.'

Annoyed to have got nothing useful for the defence, Mr Bumpus tried confrontation. 'Isn't it a fact that you and Miss Dickinson have talked this matter over a great many times and you have told her in substance what you would testify to?'

Maggie stood her ground. 'No, sir. I have nothing to testify to but the truth.'

Austin and Mabel had enjoyed long drives in the country, sometimes in summer making love on the way. When Hammond enquired into these, Maggie said the pair often went out, mostly in the afternoon but sometimes for a whole day. 'Mr Dickinson would ask if she was ready, and she would answer, "Yes, always ready." I heard these things myself. Mr Dickinson asked Miss Lavinia and me to put up a lunch. We always put it up.' When they went in the afternoon they didn't come back until eight or nine at night.

Maggie's witness to these habits had the power to erode Mrs Todd's contention that Austin Dickinson had wished to give her land as compensation for her work on his sister's writings. Mabel Todd took every opportunity to stress her special relationship with Emily Dickinson. Maggie was emphatic in her denials that any such a relationship existed. This, ironically, was established by Mrs Todd's counsel, Bumpus, as he tried to firm up the basis of her defence: the intimacy with the poet behind Todd's work on the manuscripts.

'Was Mrs Todd intimate with Miss Emily Dickinson?'

'No. She was not.'

'Was she acquainted with her?'

'No. Only through notes.'

Bumpus questioned Maggie's own tie. 'Did *you* have anything to do with the poems or know where she kept them during her lifetime?'

'She kept them in my trunk.'

'How were they arranged or done up?'

'They were done up in small booklets . . . tied together with a string.'

The interview with Maggie Maher was long and probing. The result was remarkably consistent. It proved, first, the poet's trust in her servant in contrast to the distance she had put between herself and Mabel Todd. Secondly, it proved that the gift of land could not be dissociated from sexual favours. From the time this deposition was taken, it became as clear as Lavinia had intended that the forthcoming case about land was really about adultery.

13

THE TRIAL

Maggie's evidence handed the Dickinsons a loaded gun. They had the ammunition to shoot down the Todds, but it would have been unthinkable to shame Austin in public. It sufficed that this gun was to hand in the course of the trial to come. Even before the trial opened it had an impact on Mr Bumpus who understood, better than Mabel, how questionable was a gift of land that a lover meant to take from his rightful heirs in order to content a mistress. As the trial approached the good Bumpus backed away when he could, wary of his reputation.

How far Mabel grasped the effect of Maggie's disclosures remains doubtful. Later, when years had passed and facts had dimmed, Mabel would call Maggie a 'fool', an 'Irish Paddy', a nonentity who had told 'a pack of lies'. She denied Maggie's statement that she had played and sung to Austin at The Evergreens when his family was away. Mabel said she could recall only one occasion when she was there in the absence of the family, and Mattie Dickinson had locked the piano, so playing would have been impossible. A glance at the deposition filled her with such 'disgust' she did not care to read it.

Mabel resolved to sue Lavinia for slander and David Todd agreed. He was fond of Lavinia but, included as he was in the allegation of fraud, his blood was up. On 4 October 1897 Mrs Todd entered a suit against Miss Dickinson, asking compensation of $25,000. She alleged that it was Miss Dickinson's design to bring her into 'public disgrace and contempt', as well as exposing her to prosecution for a crime punishable as forgery. This injury to her reputation troubled her mind and body.

To sue is a form of therapy in the initial stage because the rhetoric of advocacy offers the balm of self-justification. This kind of rhetoric makes it impossible to imagine another or nuanced point of view, as opposed positions get set in stone. Seven witnesses were lined up on Mabel's side, two of them leading citizens of Amherst. They said that Lavinia had voiced her 'slander' to Mr Hills, in the hearing of his housekeeper Miss Seelye, and also to the respected headmistress Mary Stearns, who employed Mabel to teach art at her school. Mrs Stearns backed Mabel staunchly.

In the Amherst Slander Case, plaintiff and defendant were now reversed. Over the winter of 1897–8 the court decided to hear Mrs Todd's action against Miss Dickinson before it heard the Dickinson action against Mrs Todd. The slander case came up on 28 February 1898, in the Superior Court of Hampshire County in Northampton. Presiding was Justice John Hopkins of Millbury. Partisan heat, fuelled by gossip, ran high and the Connecticut Valley was divided into opposed camps: Toddites versus Dickinsonites. The court was packed: no case had ever excited such interest, given the standing of the adversaries and the seriousness of the charges. Lavinia was present; Mabel not – for reasons unknown. Her husband represented her so far as the court allowed.

Mabel's non-appearance calls up her vulnerability to reputation. The two related cases were going to be about her reputation. Austin's part in their affair was not to be discussed and nor was his reputation ever disparaged even though he was the guiltier party in so far as he had damaged and split his family. And though overtly David Todd supported Mabel, he too was safe, his reputation preserved with his wife's help. Mabel, then, had to stand alone to face judgement.

Mr Hills should have been a powerful witness in her favour but, pleading sick, he sent instead his housekeeper. Miss Seelye sported an opulent sealskin coat on the witness stand. Where did she get it? Her employer gave it to her, she said. There were hoots of laughter. A report of her employer's private opinion echoed through the crowd: *the Todds are 'leeches, leeches, leeches'*.

Mabel Loomis Todd, a talented young beauty from Washington, DC. She observed that every man she met wanted to make love to her.

David Peck Todd soon after his arrival at Amherst College.

Austere Austin Dickinson in his fifties. As the leading citizen of Amherst, he was called 'the Squire', as was his father before him.

Summer 1882: Austin and Sue Dickinson's children in the briefly harmonious glow of Mabel's entry into their home and family. *Back left*, Mabel; *front, left to right*, Ned (in love with Mabel) and Mattie (Mabel's music pupil). *Inset*: little Gib Dickinson, whom the poet called 'our' child.

'Condor Kate'. In the late
1850s the poet welcomed
Kate Scott Turner as a
secret sharer.

Newspaper owner Samuel
Bowles, who published a few
of the poet's best works and
was a leading candidate for
the correspondent she calls
'Master'. 'You have the most
triumphant face out of
paradise,' she told him.

Unhappy wife
Mary Bowles.

Judge Lord of the
Massachusetts Supreme
Court. He teased the thin
poet as 'Emily Jumbo' after
the famous elephant in
Barnum's circus. She teased
him back with a better name:
'Emily Jumbo Lord'.

Maria Whitney. First teacher
of modern languages at Smith
College and adorer of Samuel
Bowles. Dickinson wrote, 'I
have thought of you often
since the darkness [of Bowles's
death] — though we cannot
assist each other's night.'

Friends and Editors

Top left & right: The poet's friend Elizabeth Luna Chapin Holland and her husband, leading New York publisher Dr Josiah Holland, who thought ED's poems too ethereal.

Middle left: Thomas Wentworth Higginson, Boston man of letters and correspondent of the poet, lent his prestige as co-editor to the first two volumes of Dickinson's poems.

Middle right: Popular writer Helen Hunt Jackson was one of only three readers to recognise Dickinson's genius in her lifetime.

Bottom left: Boston publisher Thomas Niles could not 'consume' the poems Dickinson sent him in 1883. He considered them 'devoid of the true poetical qualities'.

First Generation: Battle in Court

Top left: Mabel Loomis Todd

Top right: Trusted servants to the Dickinson sisters. Maggie Maher (*left*) was chief witness in Vinnie's case against her brother's mistress. Beside Maggie is her brother-in-law Thomas Kelley, on whose shoulder the poet cried when Judge Lord fell ill.

Bottom left: Lavinia Dickinson in the 1880s, looking humorous and confident at the time she and Todd were preparing for the first publication of her sister's poems.

Bottom right: Ned Dickinson sickened after the trial.

Second Generation: Battle of the Daughters

Millicent Todd with Mabel. At forty, she married psychologist Walter Bingham in 1920. He warned her against taking on Mamma's feud, but it had for Millicent an 'irresistible compulsion'.

Intelligent, dignified Millicent Todd Bingham pursued the feud into her eighties. The photo on her desk is her husband, the portrait on the wall her grandfather Eben Loomis.

Mattie Dickinson ('Madame Bianchi'). Amherst College conferred on her an honorary degree (their first for a woman) as niece and editor of 'that rare and original spirit, Emily Dickinson'.

Legends

A sign of the poet's rising fame was an absurd post-centenary play, *Brittle Heaven* (1933). Emily supposedly vies with Amherst friend Helen Hunt for her husband, a trophy male in military uniform. Emily, covered in frills and bows, gives Lieutenant Hunt a dying duck look while Helen glares in the background.

From 1894 to 1924, as the poet's fame grew, the Dickinson family doctored the daguerreotype of Emily Dickinson with curls, fichu and ruff in an attempt to feminise her image and hide the long funnel of the poet's throat, through which words burst in spasms: 'And yet — Existence — some way back / Stopped — struck my ticking — through —'.

First edition of *Poems* (1890) with Todd's painting of Indian Pipes on the cover. This both asserted Todd's claim to intimacy with the poet and promoted an acceptable image of Dickinson as a nature poet.

Once Lavinia's adviser, and then Mabel's man, Mr Hills saw fit to retreat. 'He liked me', Mabel believed, but when the time came he hesitated to appear on her side. Maggie's deposition had done its work. A prominent banker could not be seen to side with an adulteress.

The same applied to a prominent lawyer. Though the records list Mr Bumpus of Boston as one of Mrs Todd's counsel, he saw fit to fade from her scene: urgent business called him to Washington, which prevented his appearing for Mrs Todd at the trial.

A local lawyer, Wolcott Hamlin, replaced Mr Bumpus. He argued the importance of the absent Hills and made a plea for a continuance at a later date. Lavinia's lawyers objected that Mr Hills was only one of seven witnesses and that he had not acted on their offer two days earlier to take a deposition in the presence of a doctor.

Judge Hopkins overruled the plaintiff's motion. Mrs Todd was called, but as she failed to appear her case was dropped.

The land trial opened on the next day, 1 March, in the same Northampton court with the same judge.

Lavinia, aged sixty-five, was seated between Maggie Maher and her friend Miss Buffam. Mrs Stearns was seated beside Mabel. Each opponent had co-opted a schoolmistress as her support. Called to the witness stand, Lavinia gave her age as 'about sixty'. She wore yellow shoes and an ancient dark blue flannel dress with a belt, which she kept for best. The dress was pleated in the plain style of Emily's white dress.

'How is your health?'

'My health is perfect.' Putting back a long mourning veil, she did appear remarkably fit, with an air of readiness, even enjoyment. She still did her hair as in the 1850s, parted and coiled over the ears with the ends coming together in a knot at the back in the style of Elizabeth Barrett Browning. She made a point of these associations and meant to play up what she was: old-fashioned, distinguished 'Miss Vinnie', the late Squire's remaining sister.

'Have you ever been accustomed to give attention to your own business and the care of your own property?' Mr Hammond, acting for her, asked.

'Not in the slightest.'

'Did you and your brother and sister sign a deed of that original [meadow] lot to Mrs Todd?'

'Yes, sir. My sister was not living.'

Mr Hamlin, acting for Mrs Todd, objected. 'I don't see what relation this has to this matter.' But it did, for Miss Vinnie had revealed two vital facts: one, that Mabel Todd had already received a plot of Dickinson land. Two, Miss Vinnie made it clear that Emily's death preceded the transaction. Her lawyers had prepared this trail towards a trap as yet out of sight.

One eyewitness at the trial was Mary Jordan, an early Vassar graduate who taught English at Smith College in Northampton. She thought Miss Vinnie 'ridiculous', exactly as Vinnie had intended in her role as helpless dupe.

'Miss Dickinson, is not this your signature [on the deed]?'

'Yes — that is to say, it's my *autograph*. I understood that someone in Boston wished my autograph, and thought that was what I was doing when I wrote it.'

'Can you confirm that this case is about a release?'

'Isn't that business?' Miss Vinnie asked in a wondering voice. 'I know *nothing* of business.'

'Did you not know that this was a contract?' Offered the more familiar term, Miss Vinnie batted it back.

'Isn't that business, too? Father always attended to business.'

'Miss Dickinson, did you never employ labor?'

'No.'

'Do you mean that you never hired servants?'

Miss Vinnie appealed to Judge Hopkins. 'Does he mean Maggie?'

Judge Hopkins was seen to contain his mirth. Yet professional men respected gentlewomen like Miss Vinnie. The quaint unworldliness of the New England spinster was as she should be. Endearing. Unpretending. Her crape mourning veil reminded the court of her loss: her brother's death had left her alone and unprotected.

Across the courtroom Mabel, in a stylish black hat surmounted with two white birds' wings, thought Lavinia looked absurd. In her later years, reminiscing to her daughter, Mabel recalled Vinnie's white, wrinkled face and wide mouth – too wide when she opened her mouth in wonder, showing too many teeth, some not her own. Mabel kept her lips even, as a lady should. She carried herself as tall as she could, like the New Woman of the day: a towering goddess whose upswept, puffed-out hair balanced a big hat, and whose arched bosom, like a straining bow, overhung a cinched waist. Taking her cues from Washington society, she didn't see that Miss Vinnie's indifference to fashion upstaged her. To a New England judge it declared a confidence in who she was, an authenticity and independence beyond the range of worldly cleverness.

Her junior counsel, Henry Field, remembered Miss Vinnie 'distinctly' in after years when he himself became a judge. He'd feared cross-examination might confuse her. 'But not at all. On the witness stand she appeared perfectly natural and composed, not in the least bit disconcerted by an array of opposing Counsel and a Court-room filled with curious spectators.' Thirty-four years later he reminisced to her niece:

> On the witness stand she appeared to be just what she was, a gentlewoman of breeding, refinement, culture and perfect manners determined to tell the truth as she saw it.
>
> As I recall it she was slight and delicate and on the witness stand made me think of one those little red porcelain miniatures in a gold frame.

Vinnie's masterstroke was to express herself as the innocent she was assumed to be – and, to some extent, was, though not entirely in this instance. Her innocence recalls Emily Dickinson's 'Daisy' role. Where Emily performed in her poetry and letters, her sister often did so for an audience of family and visitors. She was an accomplished mimic, and her satiric turns included the worthies of Amherst. She used to joke that she could deceive the elect with a look of her grey-blue eyes. 'Why,' she would say, 'I can make anybody believe anything.' In court Miss Vinnie was the put-upon gentlewoman, a part to play opposite a schemer, the role in which she cast Mabel. And Mabel did grimly recognise a fellow performer who 'came in . . . a crape veil with a forlorn look, playing the part of the "sur-viving sister".'

No, Miss Vinnie had never entertained any idea of transferring land, much less agreed to it. No, her brother had never asked her to do it.

David Todd testified to the contrary, that before Miss Vinnie had signed the deed she had inspected the site. From an east window in The Dell he'd spied her moving about by moonlight. She'd then come inside to say she'd agree to the transfer.

Miss Vinnie denied this in no uncertain terms. No, she did not inspect the site. Did the court believe that she would totter out in the bitter cold of December to take measurements by night? It was not her way to creep about in the dark. As townsfolk were aware, the Dickinson sisters did not venture out at night. She and her sister were known for their still, uneventful way of life. In this retiring role Miss Vinnie outplayed Mabel.

'State all that you knew about the purport of Mr Spaulding's call,' the court asked.

'I was told he came to see *me*,' Miss Vinnie answered promptly. 'I was asked if he could come and see me on account of his interest in my sister; he would like to talk with me about *her*.'

Speaking her lines, Lavinia warmed to the part. Those who witnessed her word-perfect performance said she was vivid, convincing. Every word told in her attack on Mabel Todd. Here in the courtroom is a woman who has been positioned as a willing dependant who's resolved to be put upon no longer. She has done things for Austin because he was her brother, and dedicated her life to Emily, the adored. But now Austin is no more, Lavinia feels used by Mabel Todd. In her self-centred way, Mabel has taken the land as her due. She seems to have forgotten the consideration due to Lavinia who 'did not like it' when Mabel used her home for adultery, and who still resents Mabel's failure to acknowledge her part in collecting Emily Dickinson's letters.

The court asked Mrs Todd, in turn, about the purpose of her visit with Mr Spaulding. 'The only object of your visit was to get the woman to sign the deed?'

'To get her to sign the deed was what we went for. That is what she knew we went for . . . I got Mr Spaulding there for that purpose.'

Was anything said about that purpose before the move to the dining room?

Mrs Todd admitted that neither Mr Spaulding nor Miss Lavinia said a word about the deed before she herself introduced the subject in the dining room.

'What was said?'

When Mrs Todd put the deed on the table and called Lavinia's attention to it, Lavinia said 'something like "Shall I sign it now?" I said, "Mr Spaulding is here. Perhaps now is as well as any time."'

'What did you say that for, if you knew that was what he was over there for – if you knew he came on purpose to sign the deed?'

'I knew I was going out of the country for six—'

The lawyer repeated the question.

'I suppose because then was the most convenient time.' Mrs Todd evidently found this hard to explain. 'She wasn't like the ordinary run of people . . . I knew Mr Spaulding was courteous enough not to hurry her, because he told me he had always heard she was very queer. If she hadn't wanted to be hurried I think he would have been willing to come again.'

Was Mrs Todd herself in any hurry?

'I don't think I was in a hurry. I wanted the deed before I left the country.'

Miss Vinnie's counsel drove it home that she had not employed Mr Spaulding to witness the deed. It remained, then, distinctly questionable how he had come to make a business visit to the Homestead at night. Miss Vinnie repeated the refrain of her script: the lawyer's visit had appeared to her in the light of a social call. While Mr Spaulding examined the china, 'Mrs Todd drew this little roll from under her arm and asked if now I would sign this little paper,' she told the court. 'It was not open. It was simply handed to me where to sign, and I never thought anything about it.'

When Mrs Todd alleged that Miss Dickinson had agreed that the deed was to be 'a secret from everybody a long time', Miss Vinnie denied it emphatically. 'No, sir, I never did anything of the kind.'

Where her opponent lied without hesitation, Mabel stuck as close as she could to the truth without disclosing her liaison. She was on the defensive, speaking more hesitantly than her wont, in contrast to Miss Vinnie's assured delivery. 'I think . . . it could have been . . .', she said as she picked her way through qualifications.

She was too astute not to realise when the case slid towards the cliff-edge of adultery, held back out of respect for Austin Dickinson and public propriety. Miss Dickinson dared to walk that edge in her reply to a question whether she had 'invited' Mrs Todd into her house.

'I can't tell. She always came,' she said. 'I can't tell whether I asked her because she was in the *habit* of coming.'

Ned Dickinson, who had been in love with Mabel before his father came into play, sat with his sister behind their aunt. From behind he was in a position to guide her with a whisper in her ear. Though he could not forgive Lavinia (he saw the trial as 'a good lesson to her'), Ned acted as Aunt Lavinia's man. This was his chance for retribution.

To win the day it was necessary to erode Mabel's claim on the land as compensation for her editing of Emily Dickinson. Taking her turn on the witness stand, Miss Vinnie denied flatly any such understanding. 'She never talked with me about its being pay for copying my sister's poems. There was never any talk of that kind between me and Mrs Todd.'

Her testimony scaled down Todd's editorial role. 'Mrs Todd asked the privilege of doing it,' she recalled. 'I wished [the poems] copied. Mrs Todd copied them. . . . We always used the words my sister tried first. She sometimes had others, and put crosses down for reference, but we always decided to use the first choice.' The collaborative 'we' took a stand against Todd's rightful 'I' claim to discriminating initiatives and professional expertise. Miss Vinnie conceded that she did not select the first volume of poems, but after that she had shared in the selection of poems for publication. 'The second and third volumes were the ones I chose,' she said. 'I furnished the letters.'

But then Mabel went so far as to claim that 'Emily' had actually asked her to edit her poems.

Mr S. S. Taft of Springfield, a well-informed member of the Dickinsons' legal team, cross-questioned Mrs Todd about her supposed closeness to the poet:

TAFT: You never saw Miss Emily Dickinson?

TODD: Except as I saw her flitting through a dark hall.

TAFT: You never saw her to *speak* to her?

TODD: She *has* spoken to me.

TAFT: You never *saw* her to speak to her?

TODD: I never spoke to her.

Vinnie and Ned had primed their legal team with Mabel's habits of acquisition. Emily Dickinson's death came up in court because the family was pointing to a pattern of behaviour: the fact that the Todds' land claims followed a Dickinson death, first Emily's, then Austin's.

'Was the original deed signed also by Miss Dickinson's sister?' Mabel was asked on the witness stand.

'Yes,' she lied.

Nothing was said explicitly about the family disagreement implied by Emily's refusal to deed the first plot of land to Mrs Todd, yet the force of this act of inaction was kept to the fore through the tenacity with which the Dickinsons' counsel fixed on a link between Emily's death and the Todds' acquisition. In the face of this pressure, Mabel's testimony tried to fudge her acquisition of Dickinson land for The Dell. The Dickinsons had 'sold' it, she'd stated in the Defendants' Answer. They had 'bought' it, she repeated in court.

Lavinia's counsel pounced on 'bought'. Clearly they were informed of Austin's insistence on a gift, and informed too of Emily's stand, forcing Mabel to wait until Emily died. Mr Hammond and his colleague Mr Taft cross-questioned the Todds persistently as to the value of the land, the question of payment and the precise date when they had obtained the first deed.

This is where Mabel faltered. Uneasy and on the defensive, she prevaricated. She claimed that she did not know whether the plot was 'bought' or not. It had been a transaction carried out between Austin Dickinson and her husband – nothing, then, to do with her. It was crucial to throw the court off the scent. Contrary to Mabel's display of widow's weeds two and a half years earlier, she now had to distance herself from Austin. Land must not be seen to be a gift of love. Quick to pick up the drift of the lawyer's questions, but wary of lying outright, Mabel could not, it appeared, recall exactly when the plot was obtained (even though she herself, in filling out the deed for the second plot, had set down the precise date of the first deed, 8 June 1886, a mere three weeks after Emily Dickinson's funeral).

Taft wanted to know if she had built her house 'after the death of Miss Emily?'

'I think the foundations were dug *before* she died. She died in May, 1886. I think it was dug in *April*.'

'That [plot] came to you from the Dickinson estate?'

'It did.'

'How much did you pay for that?' Taft pounced.

'The deed says twelve hundred dollars,' Mabel hedged.

Taft was not to be deflected. 'Whether anything was paid or not, you don't know?'

She stuck to her story. 'The first I knew was when Mr Todd told me he had bought the lot and we should have a house there.'

'The deed is in *your* name?' Taft pressed her.

'The deed is in my name. Mr Todd wished to have it so.'

David Todd, summoned to the witness stand, was compelled to come clean with the facts.

'How much did you pay for your house?'

'The deed . . .' David hedged.

'No,' Taft cut in. 'How much did you pay for it?'

'Nothing.'

'And you got it when?'

'In . . .' David hesitated. He could not bring himself to contradict his wife. He was willing to confirm her evidence that the land came their way in 1886. 'I can't give you the date within three months.'

'After Miss Emily died?' Mr Taft leant into this question as though he had the answer already. For David to deny this fact would be worse than futile.

'I should say yes.'

*

The courtroom was crowded on 3 March when the Todds' main witness, Mr Spaulding, took the stand. The scene in question turned on how the lawyer had cautioned Miss Vinnie. Mr Spaulding insisted that he had done so; she claimed to have heard nothing. The fact is that she was not sitting opposite him in a law office; there would have been little if any eye contact, with Mr Spaulding intent on the china; and his tone was likely to have been routine, rather automatic, believing as he did (from Mrs Todd) that the two women were agreed. His manner, Miss Vinnie said repeatedly, was social, not legal. Indeed, to the lawyer from Northampton these were not his clients; he was doing a favour to Bumpus of Boston, whose say-so, as conveyed by Mrs Todd, had reassured Timothy Spaulding that to witness the deed was a mere formality; and Bumpus at that date had known only what Mrs Todd had told him. Before he was enlightened by Maggie's deposition, his recommendation of a local colleague had been a favour to an attractive woman.

Miss Vinnie's counsel probed this web of favours when they asked Mrs Todd if Mr Spaulding, travelling from Northampton at her request, did this 'without compensation'?

'Mr Spaulding never sent any bill.'

One further fact revealed by Spaulding again took the court close to that cliff-edge of adultery. Asked what reason Mrs Todd gave him for not wanting the deed to be recorded at once, Spaulding mentioned 'her estrangement with the family of Austin Dickinson'.

Taft's summing-up savaged Mrs Todd for an hour: 'pounded' she felt 'in the face'. The *Republican*, convinced, commended Taft's 'lucid' solution to the problems the case presented. During the early afternoon of 3 March Taft put it to the court that since the testimonies were irreconcilable, the case should be judged on the conduct and character of the contenders: one, a picture of refined seclusion, unacquainted with business; the other, 'very much a woman of the world'.

On 3 April Judge Hopkins delivered his verdict. The deed Miss Dickinson had signed without understanding was held to be void. The court ordered

Professor and Mrs Todd to return the land to Miss Dickinson. The judge also ordered the defendants to pay the costs of the trial: $49.55.

Public opinion in Amherst on the whole favoured the judgment. Miss Vinnie may not have told the truth, townsfolk said, but she had a right to dispose of her property as she wished.

Mabel was astounded. 'Something was done in ways other than in court,' she suspected. The verdict 'kills me daily' she wrote in her diary later in the month. 'I cannot seem to get out from under it.' Lavinia had lied, while her own defence had been strong – so strong, she heard, that Harvard Law School used it to illustrate how a case weighted with truth and evidence on one side can go the other way. Mabel Todd felt with justice her right to recompense for the extraordinary effort of the last decade and the feat she had performed in bringing Emily Dickinson permanently before the world. In court, Miss Vinnie had deliberately minimised what Mrs Todd had achieved. Mrs Todd had 'asked' to do the work of copying. 'She asked the privilege of it' and Miss Vinnie thought Mrs Todd sufficiently rewarded. 'I knew that she thought it would be for her literary reputation to do it, and it made her reputation.' As far as Miss Vinnie was concerned, the largesse had been hers.

Mabel Todd had combated the copyist image with evidence of her evolving expertise on the Dickinson papers. She had explained to the court all she had done to order undated manuscripts, to transcribe a difficult and changing hand, to persuade and co-opt Mr Higginson, to struggle with printers who 'could not conceive as possible Emily Dickinson's use of certain characteristic words' and, finally, to promote the first volumes of Emily Dickinson with talks and readings, each and every time to excited applause. All this Miss Vinnie had dismissed when she told the court, 'the poems got there on their own legs'.

With Ned and Mattie literally behind her, Vinnie took the high ground, a Dickinson grandee waving away a presuming flunky. It was nothing less than a denial of the destiny Mabel Todd had fulfilled.

After the tongue-lashing from Taft on the last afternoon of the trial, Mabel left with head high and took herself off to tea with Mrs E. P. Harris, who was part of a circle who shared her outrage. Mrs Stearns and Mrs

Washington Cable (wife of the Southern writer of local-colour tales) had supported her throughout the trial. Others criticised her for showing her face. The Todds responded in fighting mode. Early in May, they instructed their lawyers, Hamlin & Reilly, to take the case to the state Supreme Court. Who would lose in the long run was yet in question.

A Supreme Court judge called Field was another to back away from an adulteress. His excuse for resigning from the case was that Caro Lovejoy Andrews (Mabel's cousin and David's sometime bedmate) had told him so much that he could not judge independently. As it happened, his place was taken by one of the great legal figures of the American scene. Justice Oliver Wendell Holmes, Jr, son of the poet-doctor Oliver Wendell Holmes, a Bostonian and Harvard graduate, was soon to be appointed to the Supreme Court of the United States. In September 1898 he presided over the Todds' appeal at the sitting of the state Supreme Court in Northampton.

Holmes made two astute observations. One was that Mrs Todd was too busy. Miss Dickinson appeared passive in the face of Mrs Todd's 'multiple' initiatives: getting the blank for the deed, filling it in, rounding up Mr Spaulding. The court noted the style of a social call arranged and managed in a manner too lulling to Miss Dickinson.

The other observation came from a lawyer's feeling that a sensible landowner does not give away valuable land for nothing. There was a weakness in a defence depending on a say-so from Austin Dickinson, who could have acted himself at any time before his death. What Austin Dickinson had wished and what the present owner wished were not identical.

'Seldom is there a case in which the reasons for a rule that weight should be given to the impressions produced by seeing and hearing the witnesses are so strong as in this case,' Holmes reflected. He was alert to the subtleties of 'temperament' and states of mind. It was indeed a case in which the routines of the law came up against a situation as intricate as any in novels of Henry James, where the greatest force lies in what is hidden. The outsiders who comprised the Supreme Court had to consider a clash of irreconcilable testimonies: did 'Miss Vinnie' lie on the witness stand?

Did Mrs Todd have the stronger case, as she had reason to believe? They had to elicit the truth from an unmentionable but pertinent history of adultery, a concealed family schism and shaded characters with their moral ambiguities.

Holmes had been close to Henry James during their youth in Boston in the mid-1860s. At that time, James had dropped out of his law studies at Harvard in favour of literature, with its more inclusive approach to truth than the binary right or wrong, guilty or not guilty of the courtroom. Holmes rose to what might be called the Jamesian challenge in this case, conceding, up to a point, his court's limitations.

'Habits of life', he directed, must determine judgement, and these a local court was better placed to discern. The outcome, on 21 November 1898, was to uphold the earlier judgement. The Todds, finally defeated, had to return the land and, once more, pay the costs: $86.73.

'Habits of life' picked up Miss Vinnie's coded words for adultery. Mrs Todd was '*in the habit of coming*' to the home of the Dickinson sisters as a safe place for assignations. What did *not* happen in court – the force of unexploded facts – turned the case into a judgement of character. So it was that the character of Mabel Loomis Todd in the familiar story of adultery triumphed over a rare story: her rescue of Emily Dickinson.

'I am perfectly crushed,' Mabel said the day the verdict came. For all her outward aplomb she had been all year as sensitive as a leaf. She had felt like a ballet dancer who has to be light and graceful with a chain around her ankle. 'I shall die standing,' she told herself. 'There will be no weak admission that persecution has killed me.'

14

DEFEATS OF THE FIRST GENERATION

After Mabel lost the case she was finished with the Dickinsons. She would have nothing more to do with them, she told herself, but this did not include returning the Dickinson manuscripts.

In 1897, with the case on the boil, confidence bubbling and the steam of her own slander action on the rise, Mabel Todd had still meant to edit a fourth volume of poems, or so she said in court in 1898. But then, when the judgement went against her, she stashed the manuscripts in a Chinese camphorwood chest and locked the lid on a huge cache of 665 poems as well as assorted letters, both those she'd selected for publication and those she'd left out. And there the treasure slept, untouched, unseen, as the seasons and firmaments wheeled round. Years, then decades passed. No one but Mabel Todd knew where the treasure lay. No one spoke of it. Memories dimmed and many who remembered died.

Mabel was not the only loser. The case hurt the winners as well, in the long run more painfully. The Dickinsons shrank from 'the disgrace of dragging the family name into court'. In the run-up to the trial, Susan, Mattie and Ned had escaped to Europe, but Ned had not been happy. He felt alien to the American men who idled in the Old World. On his return he had to take up the case against the temptress who had fanned his first romantic feelings and then destroyed his family. He sank into the 'witchesmare', the old nightmare: back in the winter of 1885 when he spies his father 'taking his usual drive. With his usual company.' His reports to his sister on the battles at home are sent in code: all quiet today on the Potomac. As a son of twenty-three, helpless before the storm-centre in his father, he's forced to witness what this does to his mother. At such times Ned gives up trying to get well.

He is stifled further by the 'smooth front' the family has to present, pretending that nothing is wrong. Part of the angst of the trial is to lay the adultery trail without a public disclosure that would dishonour an errant father. Austin's death had opened up a prospect of peace for a brief space before the woman who'd 'brought a sword into the family' started on her next round of initiatives: exposing Aunt Emily to public sneers and defrauding Aunt Lavinia.

Some of this Ned confided to a trusted friend, Theodore Frothingham, in coded words, taking care not to mention names. Ned warmed to Frothingham for hearing him out 'without making a row'. He writes in a mocking tone designed to make light of things, unlike the heavy ardour of his father. 'It rains too hard for scandals in high life, and the town alas has no low life.' So fond are these letters to Frothingham, they appear lover-like. But whatever he may have felt for Frothingham, at the age of thirty-six Ned was drawn to Alice (Alix) Hill, who had been Mabel Todd's assistant for *Poems: Third Series*. Mabel's diary shows them together almost daily, working, cycling and talking till two in the morning when Alice stayed the night.

Alice had a pale face and watchful expression like the young Emily Dickinson. She too had a strange, warning look about the eyes, though not so widely spaced – more hare than kangaroo. She wore a ruff about her neck, completely hiding it in the way Lavinia longed to hide that voice-funnel her sister had exposed in the scooped neck of the 1840s. Unlike Mabel's eye-catching headgear, Alice wore a flattish hat, dipped to the side with a modest plume towards the back. The effect was quiet and self-contained.

Ned hoped his mother and sister would welcome so dear a girl into the family. Just before the trial, in January 1898, they agreed to receive Alice, but their correctness fell short of enthusiasm. The visit left an uncomfortable silence at home. Ned declared to Frothingham he'd marry even if it hurt 'the world', while his troubled mother confided to Frothingham that 'the dear boy is rather too happy to be wise just now'.

Susan Dickinson was against the marriage for reasons we can only guess. Was it resistance to a girl who was friends with Mabel? Was there a fear that Ned might pass on epilepsy if he had children? Or fear for 'the Dickinson heart'? There may have been a consensus in the family that Ned was physically unfit for more than his quiet post as a college librarian. Mattie was less resistant to Ned's marriage than her mother and Ned liked to think: 'When the pinch comes, Sis can always be counted on to do the square thing.'

Susan took a tough line. At the end of January 1898 she exacted a promise from Ned not to see Miss Hill for three months. In this manner Ned was deprived of happiness at just the time he went through the ordeal of the trial. Obviously Susan hoped that separation would weaken the tie, but the stress of capitulating to his mother's demand, compounded by the humiliating publicity of the trial, impaired Ned's always precarious health.

Angina hit him in mid-April as the end to Susan's interdict approached. His agony was terrible. Two and a half weeks later, on 3 May 1898, poor Ned's heart stopped.

Strangely, the date on his tombstone is a year earlier: May 3, 1897. It can't have been a mistake because, in after years, Mattie kept up the fiction of the earlier date. This suggests that the altered date was deliberate. Ever since his early twenties his mother's care had consoled Ned for his father's rejection. Susan's coldness following her encounter with Miss Hill in January could have been too much for him. Either that or the case killed him.

'After Ned's death there were tragic battles between the two houses,' said a gossip, Mary Lee Hall, who lived in Amherst with her mother. 'I was called to Miss Vinnie's many times to quiet her nerves, and help her recover from Sue's *verbal* blows.'

Keen to be in on the kill and darting a beady eye about for blame, Miss Hall lighted on Sue Dickinson. This animus went back to an invitation to The Evergreens when Mary Lee Hall was not amused by the Dickinsons' mimicry of the worthies of the town, including President Seelye. How very disrespectful. With a mind too small to accommodate more than one point of view, and that the most proper, Miss Hall decided Sue and Mattie must be drunk. Escorted by her brother, she took her leave determined never to enter that house again.

In years to come Miss Hall frisked about Mabel Todd with offerings of partisan poison. Sue had been a 'blind alley' who gave Emily 'very little nourishment', and Lavinia nothing but a 'loyal drudge'. Miss Hall guessed at the deep, unhealed stab Mabel had sustained when Lavinia, her long-time ally, unaccountably crossed to the Dickinson camp. The balm Miss Hall offered was a witchlike concoction: it was Sue alone who was responsible for the trial, even though she had kept out of the case and never appeared in court. Mabel's defeat should be traced to Sue's wicked machinations. So Miss Hall said. Her vehemence made up for lack of evidence and fuelled Mabel's resentment, going back to 1883 when the young Mabel, with superior love to offer, could not see why she could not take over Susan's husband and remain still Susan's best pet and the happy, trilling songbird of The Evergreens.

Immediately after the trial, Lavinia had been elated. She had looked ten years younger, townsfolk noticed when they called to congratulate her. Then two pillars of her existence collapsed. First the disaster of Ned's death. Then, following the failure of the Todds' appeal, the foreseeable sequel: Mabel Todd's refusal to go on editing Emily Dickinson.

Ned's gentle and considerate nature had made him the most lovable of the Dickinsons; he'd been his mother's mainstay. He had stood by Aunt Lavinia throughout the trial. This had allowed her to feel she had done right in crossing the chasm between the houses. Had Ned lived, he would have continued, if not her champion, at least her kin. Ned's death did not open Susan's arms to her sister-in-law. Their grief could not be shared. Both had stressed Ned severely in different ways, and Sue in her wretchedness did not find it in her to forgive.

After Mabel Todd put an end to editing, Vinnie was left with a cache of poems remaining at the Homestead. This is how it happened that at the end of 1898 Vinnie approached Mary Lee Hall with the idea of replacing

Mabel Todd. Since Vinnie had looked on Mabel as little more than a copyist, she deluded herself that all she needed was another. Fixed in her
courtroom assertion that Emily's poems had made their way on their own
legs, Lavinia failed to appreciate Mabel Todd's editorial feat and the public
impact of her readings. Miss Hall had none of her predecessor's gifts. It's
not surprising that nothing came of this. After the adverse review of *Poems:
Third Series* in August 1896, and the subsequent protest from Ned, Lavinia
worried whether it might 'hurt Emily' to publish her again. There was no
one now to support the venture, and no healing the breach with Mabel
Todd. After the lawsuit Lavinia tore out the title page and introduction of
her copy of *Poems: Third Series*, bearing Todd's name.

'Did Miss Vinnie ever talk to you about the suit against my mother?' the
Todds' daughter Millicent asked Mary Lee Hall thirty-six years after the
court upheld Vinnie's complaint of fraud. '*Why* did she sue Mamma for that
piece of land – after all that Mamma had done for her?' Millicent still
could not fathom this action. 'Do you know why she did it? What was the
real motive? I have wondered and wondered about it. Though it has warped
my life, I have never fully understood it.'

Why . . . the question went on in Millicent's mind. 'Why did she turn
away from her best friends – my mother and even more my father who
was devoted to her?'

Miss Hall entertained no doubts. Sue was behind the trial, manipulating
Miss Vinnie, who regretted the break with Mabel. 'Millicent, you never will
know what an evil-minded person Sue was. You cannot imagine such a
fiend.' Sue drove Austin away by flirting with Samuel Bowles – so said
Miss Hall in the 1930s, still chewing on a morsel of Amherst gossip. Emily's
life was shortened by Sue's cruel treatment.

Such poisonous spume jetted from the lips of Mary Lee Hall when a
target offered itself to her notice. As a young woman at the time of the
trial, she had fed her fill on Lavinia's troubles, and what remained in later
years was voluble distortion. As Mary Lee Hall had been on the scene her
memories were canvassed. She was not a sensible woman. Hers was the
kind of stupidity that is busy and full of itself. If there's anything to be
retained, it's what spite does to elusive truth.

It suited Miss Hall to picture Lavinia as pathetic, since that enhanced her own role as comforter. This sorry view comes down to us as a banal contrast of brilliant poet and humdrum sister,* even though Emily herself thought Lavinia as 'spectacular as Disraeli'.

One way to think of the Dickinsons, one reason to approach them as a family, is because they had so much in common. Like her brother and sister, Lavinia was proud, passionate and caustic on occasion. A stillborn baby, she said, 'decided not to breathe when it entered this world'. It amused her to imagine a 'runaway corpse'. This was the grim humour of the Dickinsons, with an added drop of acid when it came to the minister's 'cancerous sermons'. Lavinia sniffed so much 'sewer' in these sermons it might be 'well to have a little chloral of lime sprinkled down the aisles'. Where Emily's acumen lit up abstractions, Lavinia's fixed on individuals: one acquaintance had 'shoulders high as gallows'; another was 'poulticed from head to foot'; and a certain female voice was so sharp 'it needed filing'.

Lavinia's sayings and mimicry were part of what Austin meant when he boasted how 'queer' the Dickinsons were. Emily had once directed a house-hunting old woman to the graveyard 'to spare expense of moving'. She'd relished Austin's cutting comments on his pupils and hoped he'd flog them to death – it had the brutal hilarity of a cartoon.†

Saddened though she was by Ned's death and shut off by Sue's continued distance, Lavinia retained enough spirit to attempt a new venture in 1898. Soaked in her sister's poems, she wrote seventeen poems of her own. 'As noiseless as the snow', the pines let drop their needles, which 'light the darkest paths'. Like Emily, she knows nature can be cruel: 'The ingenuity of pain / Groping for the tenderest nooks / Then plants its fangs . . .'. A tart, prosaic voice talks of wrong, disappointment and moral failure.

She often starts with a promising line – 'Indifference is as sure to kill / As

---

* In the novel *The Hours* there's a similar banal contrast where a distorted image of Virginia Woolf's demented genius is set off by a sister who shops – an image of a normal woman as obedient consumer.
† Eliot too plays on the brutal hilarity of cartoons when his potentially murderous Sweeney tests a razor on his leg in the brothel setting of 'Sweeney Erect'.

smokeless powder's mark,' – and then trails off into homily. There's the Dickinson secrecy, but without the excitement of her sister's play on the frontier of confession: Emily's on-the-brink urgency of intimate communication. Occasionally, there's a burst of confidence: 'Circumstances shatter vows'. Is she thinking of broken promises to Austin and Mabel Todd?

Mary Lee Hall kept Emily Dickinson's poems for about six months, until the end of May 1899. When she returned the manuscripts to the Homestead she advised Miss Vinnie to put them in a safe place. Some went into a box where Vinnie kept deeds and mortgages; others were hidden between the pages of a large book. So now a second treasure slept, untouched, unseen, as years, then decades passed.

This was Lavinia's last effort for her sister. That summer, aged sixty-six, she took to her bed. Attended to the last by Maggie, she died on 31 August 1899.

'Lavinia Dickinson died at six o'clock tonight', Mabel Todd noted. 'I have no feeling about it, one way or the other. Only I am glad it is she and not I, who had to go into eternity with perjury on her soul.'

This was not the end of it. In 1905, Mabel visited a medium who spelt Lavinia's name backwards and told Mabel that this woman from the spirit world, with beautiful dark hair falling about her, was clasping Mabel's knees and begging forgiveness for treachery.

'Let her entreat,' Mabel said. The scene left her 'furious'.

The case left no winners, and, trailing in its wake, two deaths. It could be said the case was a killer – no less than Jarndyce and Jarndyce, destroying the litigants in *Bleak House*. *'Whole families have inherited legendary hatred with the suit.'* Mabel chose to read this novel during her own legal drama. In life, as in Dickens, there is the obfuscation of truth, deferring justice. The quarrel goes on from generation to generation, the principals die, hearsay takes over, the fog thickens. Where the fog lies thickest the divided treasure, fading from memory, sleeps on.

Two of the first generation survived into the twentieth century: Mabel Todd, who was only forty-two at the time of the trial, and Susan Dickinson, by then sixty-eight. Susan, the youngest of the seven Gilbert orphans, was the last to remain alive. Soon after Austin's death in August 1895 her sister Martha sickened in their home town of Geneva in upstate New York. Susan was there to nurse her. Martha Gilbert, who had been in love with Austin in the early 1850s, and a girlhood confidante of Emily Dickinson, died that autumn. After Lavinia's death in 1899, a question arises about Susan. Lavinia, like her father, left no will, and this meant that all her property, including the rights in the Dickinson manuscripts, went to her next of kin at The Evergreens. If two parts of the treasure were buried and hidden, Susan had, we recall, her own hoard, and had long wished to publish these poems and letters. So why, now, didn't she?

There's no obvious reason why Susan should not have become an editor. As she grew old she did go on to publish stories and sketches, none of them superior to her vivid memoirs of Amherst, humorous letters and piercing obituary of Emily Dickinson. At the turn of the twentieth century the vogue for Dickinson seemed to be over. When David Todd said this to console Mabel, he voiced a current opinion. Dickinson's poems didn't go out of print – there were reissues – but when Little, Brown took over Roberts Brothers in 1899 they would have noted the poor sales of the two more recent publications. Todd's selection of the *Letters* had indeed sold quickly, on the strength of enthusiasm for the poems, but the publishers had not recovered their costs. Quirky and poetic, the *Letters* had needed more biographical context, while *Poems: Third Series* suffered, inevitably, when Todd's customary promotion was stopped by Lavinia's Bill of Complaint in November 1896 (yet another sign of Lavinia's oblivion to what Todd had contributed). All through 1897 Todd chose to lecture on Japan and kept off the subject of Emily Dickinson.

So, for want of confidence or some other reason, Susan's trove, the third part of the divided treasure, slept on at The Evergreens, while Susan travelled four times to Europe for prolonged stays. Her daughter Mattie accompanied her, in soft white frocks with a bared forehead and Austin's down-turned mouth. Her look was serious, verging on sombre. Austin's rejection of his daughter, along with his son, had left its mark on Mattie. After her schooling at the socially elite Miss Porter's, Mattie became an accomplished pianist and writer, and in her thirties published a collection of poems. They were competent, without her aunt's genius. Readers thought the poems sad. 'Life isn't merry', she admitted to Amy Angell Collier, a friend of her Geneva days, in 1900. After that she wrote romantic novels in which American girls try out the company of European grandees. This was the scenario for her own romance.

In March 1902, at the age of thirty-six, Mattie 'broke down', she confided a month later to Ned's friend Theodore Frothingham. Attempting an airy tone, she'd had, she adds, 'a bully time killing myself'. Her doctor ordered her to take a year's rest abroad, and in July this shaky woman sailed for Europe. She could afford it: as the last of the Dickinson line she had inherited everything her grandfather, father and aunts had owned. Before sailing, at a New York party she met Captain Alexander Emmanuel Bianchi (sometimes known as Count Bianchi). His name sounds Italian, but he was *echt* Russian, he said, and appointed by his country's government to a post in Boston – an odd place for a diplomat or emissary. Why not Washington or New York? What Mattie saw, however, was a cultivated European who played the cello. His military position, he claimed, had been earned in the Imperial Horse Guards of the Russian army. He owned an array of uniforms: in one, he appears in a double-stitched, double-breasted coat with many buttons, epaulettes on the shoulders and dark stripes on the collar. One hand carries a hard cap; the other is tucked in his pocket with just the thumb showing. His hair looks as though two brushes have stroked it, and his moustache is trained to steely points on either side of his mouth. It's the image of a pre-war grandee who confers distinction by his presence.

Bianchi pursued Mattie Dickinson to Europe and two months later they announced their engagement in Russian as well as in English. They were married on 19 July 1903 in Marienbad (though the announcement had promised a grander venue: the church of the Russian Embassy in Dresden). The bride's white satin wedding shoes came from Altman's in New York and her dress was exquisitely (and expensively) fashioned from lace and satin, enveloped in the long white cloud of her veil. All that showed of Mattie herself was a thin, rather tense profile and a puff of dressed brown hair over her forehead, held in place by the frill of her veil.

The couple returned to America. Later in 1903 Mattie was back in Amherst with a foreign husband who, she found, could not banish 'the heartbreaking associations' lingering in every corner of The Evergreens.

Nothing more is heard of the pair until early in 1907, when a Miss Charlotte Terry of New York sued Captain Bianchi for $3000. He had borrowed the money on the strength of a Dickinson connection with the Terry family. A cheque returning the sum was 'dishonoured', the newspapers reported. The Captain declared no cause for concern: he was importing a car for a millionaire, a company president in Philadelphia, who was to pay $8000 in cash for it. The car, already offloaded, was held by Customs in New York, awaiting $600 import duty. If Miss Terry could lend the Captain that further sum she would have the amount owing to her in ten days, the time it would take to deliver the car to its destination. So confident was the Captain, and so honourable the background of his wife, that Miss Terry actually obliged. The Captain gave her his promissory note, endorsed, as a blank, by Martha Dickinson Bianchi, and then, before ten days were up, he called on Miss Terry and in her presence drew an initial cheque for $675 on the First National Bank of Amherst. The additional $75 was a small gesture of thanks for Miss Terry's kindness. He offered this with Old World graciousness. This cheque too was 'dishonoured'.

In court it came out that the company president had no arrangement with Bianchi to take delivery of a car, and further that no such car had passed through US Customs. Somehow Mattie was persuaded to believe that the money 'owed us' was still coming from the reluctant millionaire, and that she and her husband had been 'victims of a really absurd persecution'. So she told her brother's old friend, Frothingham. As a respected New York lawyer, he provided her with a 'character' and the case went in her favour. In March she protested against what she termed 'unjust slanders' and 'gross misrepresentation', but by May she was again 'seriously ill'.

The following year, the Captain's financial embarrassments compelled him to return to Europe. He went alone, leaving behind his cello, a trunkful of uniforms and, naturally, his debts. New debts appeared and the Terry case came up again in 1912. The Captain (elevated, it appeared, to Colonel when the war broke out) sent Mattie an urgent plea for funds: in Belgium he had been arrested as a spy by his compatriots, or so he claimed. He finally dropped out of sight from about 1916.

At this time Mattie consulted a lawyer in New York. He was a distant cousin, Gilbert Holland Montague, who had married Mattie's old friend Amy Collier. It was decided that Mattie's fortune had been drained to the point where she was forced to sell the Homestead in order to pay for 'some' of her husband's 'fraudulent business transactions', as Montague put it. Though she divorced the fraudster in 1920, she remained 'Madame Bianchi'.

Of all who suffered in the course of the trial and its aftermath, it was the one who lost the case who was to thrive. A month before the trial, in February 1898, Mabel and David Todd moved from The Dell to Observatory House, far grander with a pillared entrance above a wide flight of steps. Charles Wilder, cousin to Mabel's mother, Mary Wilder Loomis, had willed $15,000 for this property adjacent to a prospective observatory. The house, reserved for the director of the observatory, put the Todds amongst the notables of Amherst. From 1903 to 1905 the observatory itself was rising at its side, the fulfilment of David's dream. By this time Mabel had launched a new career. Women's clubs were active everywhere, and she became their star turn, with fifty or so lectures each winter, including lectures for private schools and colleges across the country. On New Year's Eve 1900 she reflected on her success: she had found it in her power to cast a 'spell' on listeners as she opened up 'The Gateway to the Sahara' (Tripoli) or the floating houses of Siam, places she had visited in the course of husband's expeditions. When she stopped speaking she would hear a sigh, as though her audience woke up from a trance.

David told her, 'you positively seem to take our minds with you, and actually spread out the places before our own eyes. I believe it is half hypnotic.'

It was as though she transported her audience into the unvisited places of the earth, revealing the customs of the hairy Ainu in Esashi on the island of Yezo in northern Japan, twelve hundred miles north of

Yokohama, or the Negritos, dwarf aborigines in the Philippine archipel-
ago. At a time when anthropology was a new field, Mabel Todd was often
the first outside woman to penetrate the customs of these peoples.
David, with his expertise in photography, created slides to illustrate the
talks.

In the years after the trial her energies soared as a performer who wrote
her own scripts for these one-woman shows. Mabel, who knew the difference between talent and genius, recognised that in lecturing alone she
had the quality of genius. For sixteen years Mabel Todd gripped audiences,
at the same time as Mrs Pankhurst and her daughters, on platforms across
England, were demanding votes and openings for women's efforts. Mabel
Todd always supported the women's movement, and no woman was more
attuned to the rising agency of her sex. As she watched the days dawn and
sink behind the hills she felt, she said, unseen forces 'clasping me for a
higher flight. Is not mine the inheritance of the ages? Am I not the heir of
time, the participator in immortality?'

The talks made money. A newly affluent Mabel was able to fund her
husband's 1905 expedition to Tripoli. She continued also to promote her
husband's philandering. Mabel was expected to arrange visits of women
'friends' to their home. She balked, at last, when David took a fancy to a
typist in 1911.

This sign of 'low tastes' was too much for Mabel, as she confided to her
journal: David 'gave himself away to a fearfully common person far below
him'. It was 'one thing I had always pleaded with him to spare me'. Then,
with her usual caution, she tore out five pages and inked out some phrases.
The following remains:

For <u>thirty-three</u> years I have absolutely refrained from putting on
paper one single sentence which . . . could ever do [David] any
harm. I have even allowed misrepresentations and reproach to
attach to myself, to be thought the . . . flirtatious one of the two;
and never a word written or spoken, has come from me to show
that I had the faintest justification for anything I have been
supposed to do. If I could write out the facts it would be appalling!

This belated cry takes us back to Mabel as a bride, expecting to purify her husband. Her defeat, in the early years of marriage, had been her 'justification' for an attachment more elevating than David could conceive. To Mabel there could be no doubt: 'Austin was mine, mine and he is more mine now than ever before.' By this she meant his incursions from the afterlife 'where free winds blow that were never felt on earth'. To claim him so completely was to re-enact Dickinson's poetic drama of deathless love with its attendant pain. 'The scars,' Mabel said, 'cover my soul.'

This has been a story of secrets and explosions, culminating in the scandal of the trial. Where the loaded gun in the life of Emily Dickinson had been concealed, Austin showed no compunction in blowing up his family. There was no end to this, for Mabel shot off fresh slanders against Susan Dickinson: she was a drunkard like her father; she had an affair with Bowles; and then, too, she was a prude: 'Sue hated anybody that should fall in love. Thought it was disgusting.' Susan's resistance to Mabel's plans had long made it a fight to the death. 'Why God lets [Sue] live and go on, I cannot see,' Mabel exploded at the start of the new century: New Year's Eve, 1900.

Mabel did have reason to resent the 'killing' injustice of Susan's attempt in 1901 to have her name removed from the title pages of Emily Dickinson's poems. David threatened litigation and the press stood by Mabel. David assured her that her name was 'irrevocably' associated with the poems, but there remained 'a constant fight' against 'the wickedest woman who ever lived'.

The slander became crazed after Susan died, in 1913 when Mabel had a stroke while swimming: she claimed that an evil hand – none other than Sue's – had pushed her down. And, sure enough, it was the ghost of Sue who retarded her recovery. The stroke – mere 'sunstroke', Mabel gave out – left her too handicapped to play the piano or speak in public. Millicent was brought up to hate and revenge, she remembered in her notes for an autobiography she never completed. For Millicent, as for Martha Dickinson Bianchi, their mothers' wrongs called out to their daughters to take up arms.

15

TWO DAUGHTERS

Two daughters remained from the defeats of the first generation. Millicent Todd and Mattie Dickinson each bore wounds in their growing bones. Each tried to heal herself through a life of her own. Professional careers beckoned able women of their generation. Could they leave the feud behind or would loyalty to warring kin compel further action?

As a child, Millicent Todd was pained by what she knew. It was what she must not be seen to see and never, but never, mention. In any case, a girl in the 1880s had no words for it, as she sat in the Dickinson buggy between Mamma and the towering column of Mr Dickinson holding the reins. One stretch of road in the Pelham hills was imprinted on Millicent's memory and recorded in one of her many autobiographical typescripts: the fragrant pinewoods on one side of the road; a blueberry patch on the other. It was as though the positions of each plant and each cloud in the sky pierced her consciousness when Mr Dickinson and Mamma leant towards each other behind Millicent's stiffly arched back, stilled by tense elbows. Her eyes were fixed on the quivering ears of the horse ahead.

Mr Dickinson never bent down to see her solemn face and round brown eyes, watchful beneath a black fringe. He did not appear to know her name: at the Dickinson Homestead he called her 'the child' to his sister Miss Vinnie, whom Mamma visited so often that, one day, when Millicent herself is old, she will say 'my early childhood was spent largely in that house'. Miss Vinnie's coils of dark hair were streaked with grey. She was dressed as usual in black cashmere with knife pleats. Millicent saw Miss Emily 'every day' but not so far as to notice. The child's eyes were on her radiant Mamma, who was leaving her. For Mr Dickinson, as always, awaited Mamma in the dining room. There the shades were drawn so that Millicent could hardly make out the colour of the dark-blue china on the sideboard. Looming out of the dimness was the rigid, forbidding shape of Mr Dickinson. Then the door shut, leaving Millicent with Miss Vinnie and fat Maggie billowing about the apple-green kitchen. Holding up a candle, Miss Vinnie descended into the cellar. Her knotty fingers offered the child an apple. Miss Vinnie could not abide the sound of crunching so told the child to move off. This child was a ghost of a being, effaced yet gathering force to save Mamma from a miasma of disapproval infecting half the town.

Mr Dickinson's daughter – 'Mattie D', as townsfolk called her – was most to be feared: tall and spare like her father, her hatred stung the child with a venom that coursed through her veins. To encounter any of them was a shock. 'That they could be human beings, made of flesh and blood, never occurred to me,' Millicent recalled later. 'They were a race apart.'

Millicent spent long periods with Mrs Loomis, who was the daughter of a minister. Mary Loomis had failed to repress her daughter and was resolved to do better with her only grandchild. A photo of 1885 shows a grave, clean child on a footstool in Washington. On one side sits her bony, thin-lipped great-grandmother, the widow of Concord's minister; on the other side looms her blooming mother with a smile sliding up one cheek. Grandma, folding her hands in her lap, helpless over Mabel's shame, is determined to impress virtue on the soft, malleable substance of little Millicent, a more biddable character who seems entirely hers.

Grandpa, whom Millicent loved better than anyone, feared she cared too deeply. She preferred his 'dear quaking voice' to her mother's crystal trills. It lulled her to peace. *O hush thee my baby.* She'd clamber into bed between her grandparents and listen to Grandpa's stories. As a boy of ten he had a lamb. 'I raised it,' he said, 'and when I sold it, I had a dollar to spend. I walked seventeen miles to a bookstore, and found Shakespeare for a dollar and a half. "Sir," I said to the bookseller, "would you rather have the book or a dollar?"' Grandpa still read that book, puffing his pipe and learning speeches by heart. Often he walked up and down reciting.

At ten, Millicent came upon a small object in her mother's top drawer. It was a pot of rouge. It was not done to use rouge in Amherst, and confirmed the coquette in her mother. At the same time Millicent's loyalty to Mamma forbade anyone to say anything against her. She disliked Grandma for trying to explain Mamma's 'marriage within a marriage'.

Honour thy father and thy mother. Millicent prayed to love Mamma more dearly than she did. 'Make Mamma a more X woman', was how she put it. She had no word for X, only her 'inmost sense that something was utterly wrong'. The more watchful she was, the more determined she had to be not to know what in some way she did know. She was a neat, systematic child. Her thoughts, wishes, her very prayers were pigeonholed, each 'primly placed'.

At an extraordinarily early age, two or three, Millicent had the ear and voice to sing the upper part of a Bach fugue, yet she rarely sang above a whisper. She developed an aversion to her mother's music lessons: she wanted to kick and scream, though never did. When Mamma tossed off difficult runs on the piano or delivered her talks, Millicent silently shunned the applause.

Until Millicent could be of use to her mother she hung about in the wings, her eyes fixed on Mamma spinning her graceful scripts, gesturing and trilling in the spotlight. Millicent herself felt unlovely from the age of fourteen, when her father pointed out her square jaw at the same time as she began to menstruate. She was to blame for her jaw, he told her, because she had determined opinions. A girl at school asked her to raise her chin and made fun of its underside which, she crowed, 'looks like a frog's'. Millicent began to hold her mouth open so that her jaw would not fix in a permanent square. At dances she was not popular with college boys. The partners she might have had scented Mamma's allure, while her daughter sat unasked and conscious of her acne.

At the age of fifteen another girl told Millicent about sex. 'They say they enjoy it.'

'No, not that,' Millicent said. 'No.' She cherished romantic feelings for a future missionary called Alden. She prayed for him to notice her.

At fifteen she was required by Mamma to re-address a love letter from Austin, so that his hand would not be detected. Afterwards Millicent discovered *The Scarlet Letter* and read it by stealth, while her parents were out. Her cheeks were burning, for to read of sin seemed to her to partake in sin. She was transfixed by this tale of adultery that makes the adulteress the pariah of the Puritan community. It confirmed what Millicent knew: like Hester Prynne's daughter, she could not escape the sin bred in her through her mother.

There came a flash of hope when Austin died. 'Yes, I am all that Mamma has left now', she thought. Her lesser life might be of use.

At seventeen, Millicent knew nothing of the court case accusing her parents of fraud. In 1897 she was sent off to Miss Hersey's boarding school in Boston and she remained with friends during vacations. The trial was reported in newspapers, but no one mentioned it to Millicent, and later she wondered at her oblivion. Study was her refuge: she immersed herself in natural history. At the time her parents lost their appeal to the Supreme Court, in the fall of 1898, Millicent entered Vassar College in Poughkeepsie, New York.

Here, at a college for bright women, the fog of untruth at last appeared to lift: 'no cloaking under fine-sounding phrases, no uncertain expressions'. She thrived in an academic environment and chose to major in biology. Yet even here, around the clear pools of fact, a fog gathered. Parthenogenesis was the only mode of reproduction laid out in biology lectures. In 1900 it would be improper for young women to be informed of the facts of life, even in the lower species. Millicent went out into the world in 1902 wrapped in her unknowing.

When she asked herself what she wanted, it was to be unlike Mamma: no courting of status and flattery. 'Ugh! It is all obnoxious to the last degree,' she ordered her better self. 'Deliver me from push.'

Over the next decade she travelled extensively and taught modern languages at Vassar, Wellesley and Sarah Lawrence, but all the time and for the rest of her life her real wish was to write her own story: a daughter's authentic tale of a latter-day *Scarlet Letter*: the adulteress exposed to censure in her New England community; her lover, the impeccable leader of that community; the intensity of secret assignations; and the purity of their love, as they felt it to be. *What we did had a consecration of it's own*. But then, too, as Millicent had reason to know, there's what that love chooses to ignore. A truth-telling memoir surged continuously beneath the surface, but a daughter could not set it down because it would hurt Mamma.

Unlike Millicent, Mattie Dickinson was born to status and privilege. Aunt Emily called Mattie 'an imperial Girl' with a capital G. At fourteen, under a jaunty hat, she looked like the girl Aunt Emily would have liked to be. In the privacy of her room, Aunt raised a hand holding an imaginary key between thumb and forefinger, and turned her wrist as though she were locking her door.

'Just a turn – and freedom, Mattie.' A Dickinson daughter is privileged to be an exception: she is not to be 'bridalled'. Content and safe in her father's house, a writer holds to her vision.

There's a side to Aunt Emily that Mattie never mentioned: a moody strain, evident in one of her six letters to her niece. On Mattie's seventh birthday Aunt's prophetic voice had enjoined her 'to live in vain'. Aunt's tone had been distant and skittishly obscure, different from her fond letters to Ned and joy in 'our' Gib.

As the years passed, Aunt Emily saw less of Mattie than she saw of her brothers whom Aunt seemed to love unreservedly. At fifteen Mattie was keener to visit her responsive piano teacher Mrs Todd, whose cuffs racing up and down the piano were painted with flowers of her own design.

Mattie was shaping contentedly in this chrysalis when it was ripped away. Her pious, reproving father fell in love with Mrs Todd, crossed his 'Rubicon' and cut off his family. Mattie, still a schoolgirl in love with her teacher, found herself included in Mrs Todd's slurs on 'the Powers', thus punished for standing by her mother. To her father his two remaining children no longer felt to him as children. The dead Gib, he decided, was the only child he'd loved.

Aunt Emily called her teasingly 'our martial Mattie, / Flag and Drum in one'. When rows split the family Mattie was not weak like Ned, and she was not, like her mother, 'bridalled'. Mattie had therefore less to lose by cutting behaviour to Mabel Todd. Years later, when Mabel counted her scars, she declared that no one was as bad as Susan Dickinson except Mattie 'who is worse in all ways'.

It happened that Aunt Emily felt a warmer stir of kinship when Susan showed her Mattie's studio photograph at the age of eighteen. 'I knew she was beautiful; I knew she was royal; but I didn't know that she was hallowed.' Why didn't she know? Why should Mattie have ever appeared to her unhallowed? Following this affirmation was a note of caution: Aunt Emily still hoped that Mattie might be 'saved', but warned that salvation of the mind precedes that of the soul. Emily Dickinson never sent Mattie a poem nor shared her feeling as in notes to Ned. Mattie was not included in her audience.

For the next decade, until Mattie was twenty-nine, her father was sealed off, while she felt the hot breath of harm upon her life. Then came some kind of breakdown, followed by marriage to a confidence man and his drain on her inheritance. Yet she knew her mother cared for her, and she cared for her mother devotedly, anxiously, hardly daring to go out after Susan began to fail at the age of eighty.

When Susan died nothing was said of her intimacy with Emily Dickinson. It devolved on Mattie to revive this in *The Single Hound: Poems of a Life-time*, a selection of the dazzling poems Susan had received from the poet. Mattie published this volume to record the 'romantic friendship' of the 'dear dead women'. Dickinson's poem of *c.* 1858, 'One sister have I in the house, / And one a hedge away –', was entitled 'To Sue' and appears on its own like a dedication. It follows Mattie's biographical preface about a poet who had been visible only to those 'who dwelt with her behind the hedge'.

This remarkable preface lights up the poet: her bronze hair worn low in her neck, half-covered by the velvet snood; her cheek velvety-white with no vestige of colour; her long upper lip over regular little teeth 'like a squirrel's'. We see her lift up her hands when she jokes or scores a point. Her palms flash in triumph. We see, for a moment, her gesturing vivacity, and we see too her complicity with children. Her eyes 'smoulder' when a child feels wronged. When Mattie's too small to go to church she's left at the Homestead with her aunt, who stuffs her with sweets and cookies. At the age of four Mattie already knows it's naughty.

Her aunt's scrapes fascinate Mattie as a child. Tender to flowers but not to cats, Aunt Emily drowns four 'superfluous' kittens in a barrel of pickle brine in the Homestead cellar. Judge Lord happens to be visiting Mr Dickinson when the putrefying corpses make themselves known. Mattie's focus is the ease of Aunt's escapes: she would take to her room until quiet was restored. No repercussions. Old Mr Dickinson did not reproach Emily, as though this man of deliberation and policy had reason to calm her or permit her to calm herself.

A puzzling fact has been buried in an unpublished letter Mattie wrote to Frothingham in 1914. Mattie says that her mother had smiled on her in the days before her death, when Mattie had put a copy of *The Single Hound* into her hands. How could this be? Susan died in May 1913. The volume did not appear until 1914. What Mattie gave her mother must have been a manuscript completed by the spring of 1913 at the latest. During Susan's last year, from 1912 to 1913, she'd reread the poems and letters of Emily Dickinson 'with increasing indecision as to the final deposition of her treasury'. Should she burn those too intimate to share? Sue could not abandon them to strangers to edit.

An obvious solution would have been to bring in her daughter. Though Susan's part in this publication has to remain speculative, it's just possible that Susan smiled on a *collaborative* venture. If so, this neglected but choice selection with perceptive groupings of the poems, the first selection not to impose titles, could be the sole volume sanctioned by the poet's authorised reader. 'Dear Sue', the poet had said, 'Your praise is good – to me – because I <u>know</u> it <u>knows</u>'.

An opening group of poems on the life of the soul attended by its mortal incarnation tells us immediately who Emily Dickinson was. We glimpse here the sufficiency of the world within:

> Adventure most unto itself
> The soul condemned to be —
> Attended by a single Hound
> Its own identity.

The contents of this volume tell us too that Dickinson entrusted 'I fit for them — I seek the Dark / Till I am thorough fit' to Susan who 'knows'. The explosions of sickness open up the route through death's divide to what beckons the speaker beyond a mortal life. That other place will light up the panels of her grave.

Another group of poems has to do with darkness as the route to vision: the darkness before day or the dark of the mine. The mine puts the speaker through hellish but purposeful pain. This transformation underground, Dickinson could share with Susan, as well as an alertness to its opposite: the unchanging perfidy of the Devil who visits all who traffic in the world:

> The Devil — had he fidelity,
> Would be the finest friend —
> Because he has ability —
> But Devils cannot mend —

Mattie sent a copy to her mother's old schoolmate Kate Scott (now Mrs Anthon and living in the Lake District). She replied with heartfelt memories of early times at The Evergreens: Emily with a lantern coming through the glass door of the library and improvising strange music on the piano.

Two years after *The Single Hound*, Mattie had to sell the Homestead. In 1916 the Parke family moved in and the poet's things were carried across the grass to what Mattie designated the 'Emily Room' downstairs, behind the library. In this dark room with its black floorboards and blackish wallpaper, once the marital bedroom and then the 'dying room', the relics of the poet's genius commingled with the tragedies of The Evergreens. Here Mattie set out her aunt's writing table, her square piano from the parlour, the grey and white cameo brooch she pinned at her throat and the light blue crocheted cape she wore when she met Mr Higginson, the blue china that Emily Norcross brought from Monson at the time of her marriage to Mr Dickinson and the chest of drawers where Emily Dickinson had kept her poems. From 1916 until 1950 the Emily Room was the shrine for 'pilgrims'. A poet who had honed her narrative as 'Vesuvius at Home' foresaw her relics, buried like Pompeii, uncovered in time by 'some loving Antiquary' of the future. It was Mattie's fate to survive the volcano and live on in the interim as lone, aloof guardian of what remained.

She had to work hard if she was to remain in 'the beloved old spot', the home 'where the family were once with me'. She herself felt a relic of the past, fighting a death wish ('some of the days are harder alone than others'), yet there was a certain relief in solitude. 'Just the changing lights and shadows are complete companionship.' Sometimes she read Aunt Emily's letters to her mother, which Mattie thought of as letters 'to us'.

On the other side of town, on a hill near the college, Millicent Todd moved her mother's camphorwood chest to a purpose-built 'barn' beside Observatory House. Her father, increasingly unstable and given to aberrant behaviour, had lost his job and the Todds had to vacate their home. Millicent did the packing because the stroke had lamed Mamma's arm. Mamma never mentioned what was in the locked chest, nor did Millicent ask. The Todds then settled in Coconut Grove in Florida.

Millicent felt responsible for her damaged parents and resolved to pursue graduate studies so that she could support them in old age. Ever studious and intrigued by remote parts of the world where she had accompanied her father's expeditions, she began a doctorate in geography at Radcliffe, the sister college to Harvard. Her private life remained unsettled. In her twenties her ties were mainly with women, culminating in 'a passionate attachment' to a companion in Germany who proved 'brutal'. Millicent had needed to wrench herself away. In her thirties she hoped to find a man who could rouse her, but the tameness of academic admirers left her cold. She would not permit even a pressure of the hand.

After America entered the First World War, Millicent volunteered for service abroad. Fluent in French, she was sent to Base Hospital 27 at Angers.

At thirty-eight, in the uniform of the American Expeditionary Force, there was no sign of the uncertain shadow-being laid down in childhood. Miss Todd's mouth showed a straight line under the brim of an unbecoming black hat. She proved efficient, humorous and able to converse in German with prisoners of war. From eight in the morning until ten at night she was 'humbled' by the sights and sounds of young men who were returned from the front maimed, with backs blistered, their minds shell-shocked, their eyes blown from their sockets and, perhaps worst of all, their lungs burnt out by mustard gas.

One sergeant called Joseph Thomas, wounded at Château Thierry, was told that he would never walk again; helped by Miss Todd, he did. She felt for him 'a wild, reckless emotion, over which reason had no power'. He told her that he'd served in a regiment of engineers for two years and came from a military family, the son of Surgeon General Thomas in the Philippines, and grandson of General Thomas in the Civil War.

After the Armistice she stayed on as a lecturer in Grenoble with the United States Education Corps. In the summer of 1919 hundreds of American soldiers on furlough attended her course on the geography of France. She published a book on this subject, co-authored by the professor of geography at the University of Grenoble. The idea behind all this was an *entente intellectuelle* between two allies.

During these post-war months Millicent became engaged to Joseph Thomas. His kiss, sealing their future, was unlike anything she had ever experienced. 'That was, for me, the climax of my life.' Then, without a word, he disappeared. As she searched for him it became plain that all he'd told her was a lie. Eventually she tracked him down to Muskogee, Oklahoma. He didn't want her. It was 'utter annihilation'.

She turned to work, and then to an academic of her own age, Walter VanDyke Bingham, a founder of industrial psychology whom she had known seven years earlier. She had been with him to a winter carnival at Dartmouth (where he'd taught). He had been in love; she, not. Since then he had investigated aptitudes at the Carnegie Institute of Technology in Pittsburgh. He was long and lean, a good-tempered man with a benevolent smile breaking into long lines on either side of his mouth, the bottom half of which had a full jaw like a whale. He had the communicative skills of whales, and sang his whale song to Millicent about caring for his kind. It reverberated benignly through her solitary sea. In Maine during the summer of 1920 they rowed around Hog Island to the side facing the open ocean, and here he asked her to marry him. She was emotionally dead, she confessed. He didn't seem to mind.

For more than twenty years following the trial no one had mentioned the name Dickinson in her hearing. Walter Bingham was the first not to avoid it. It came as a jolt when he said, 'What is it that freezes you when I ask about Dickinson?'

In December 1920 she married him. Bingham, unlike her father, was a moral being. It felt a privilege to live with someone so good. Millicent was, all the same, her father's daughter in her scientific pursuits. In 1923 she was the first woman to gain a doctorate in geography from Harvard. She walked through the Yard, solemn and unsatisfied in her academic gown. A degree was not really what she wanted.

What did she want?

Could she yet give meaning to her existence, and could this be achieved only if she freed herself of her unruly parents whose needs pressed ever more insistently upon her? David Todd was deranged and too disruptive to be on the loose. He was put in Bloomingdale Asylum in 1922, then moved to various other institutions, none suitable. Hard on Millicent when her father with a white beard gazed at her, as it were, from behind bars: it was Millicent's fault, he said. She must release him at once. To look at him he seemed all there, with his stocky energy and the light of scientific curiosity alive in his eyes. He still had designs on the sun: how to capture its corona without the occluding clouds that had frustrated his many expeditions? In the mid-twenties he co-opted a pilot to take him and his photographic equipment above the weather. A photograph shows him smiley, hopeful as ever, preparing to board a fragile plane. He sent his daughter on scientific errands to friends here and there, but the friends turned out not to exist.

Meanwhile, Mabel Todd lived on in Florida, in fashionable Coconut Grove. She was now affluent after her years as star of the lecture circuit and she had the further support of wealthy Arthur Curtiss James, the yacht-owning sponsor of David's second expedition to Japan. Her beautiful house, Matsuba, had three great arches opening out on a palm-tree garden. Too handicapped to play the piano herself, she invited others to perform. A photo in 1922 shows her poised on a step in black lace with a pointed hem showing off her still-fine ankles. Her black hat is festooned with black lace at the edge, casting a shade of allure.

Millicent, in a plain summer dress and floppy hat, positioned on a step below, silently disparages her mother's get-up. It's a throwback, she thinks, to the dressiness of the nineties. As Mabel aged she remained beautiful, even more so, redolent of old-fashioned charm. The society photographer Bachrach captured this as she sits, facing the camera with all her old poise, a black velvet band about her throat and her unbobbed hair pinned up with combs and barrettes as though in an effort to tame its abundance. She had a new partner, a painter called Howard Hilder. Come summer, Hilder would drive her Buick all the way from Florida to Maine where Mabel had a second home on Hog Island.

Mabel made light of her lamed side. Millicent was astonished by the undimmed glow, this readiness, as though a leg that wouldn't move, a hand that could not hold, an ear that could not hear and teeth that clashed like china presented no problems. As though it did not matter that Mabel could no longer play the piano nor paint nor travel in her old intrepid way. As though Hilder were not inferior to the males who had buzzed around her blue-sky youth. Millicent frowned at Mamma's unwillingness to face facts. She was ashamed of her mother's hold on life, she owned to herself. 'It revolts and disgusts me.'

Nearly a quarter of a century had passed since Mabel Todd finished with the Dickinsons. She buried defeat in a recess of consciousness, unwilling to articulate the truth even to herself, let alone to her daughter. The truth she buried was this: the Dickinsons had their victory because, when it came to a public contest, lovely, gifted, industrious Mabel who had worked many years to bring recognition to Emily Dickinson was silently but effectively branded a scarlet woman. Her distinguished identity as Dickinson's first editor had failed to take precedence over what the servant to the Dickinson sisters had witnessed in the Homestead.

In 1922 Mabel Todd's editions of Emily Dickinson came out of copyright after twenty-eight years. This left the way open to Mattie Dickinson Bianchi to retrieve what she considered her right as sole heir to the Dickinson possessions. Part of these possessions were the poet's papers and Aunt Lavinia's copyrights to the four posthumous publications in the 1890s.

Mattie was now poised to right the wrongs she believed were done to her mother when (she thought) Mrs Todd, in secret, took over the editing from Susan Dickinson. Mattie's claim as the Dickinson heir, overtly a legal issue about rights, was backed by her sense of responsibility. As niece of the poet it was her responsibility to rescue 'my aunt, Emily Dickinson' from the clutches of Mabel Todd. Dickinson had left no instructions about her poems, yet three people – Vinnie, Susan and Mabel – each believed and declared herself the intended heir. This contest, quiescent from the time of Lavinia's death in 1899 until 1922, flared up when Mattie fired a double shot aimed to eliminate that interloper Mabel Todd.

In the course of 1922–3 word got round that Madame Bianchi was preparing a *Life and Letters of Emily Dickinson* for Houghton Mifflin, together with an edition of her *Complete Poems*. Unaccustomed to the demands of accuracy in non-fiction, Mattie rushed out the two books by 1924, and she managed to accomplish this by appropriating Mabel Todd's carefully researched editions.* The supposedly 'complete' poems were hopelessly incomplete. Content to do the job at second hand, Mattie bunged together Todd's three selections of the nineties with the addition of *The Single Hound*. Most of the *Life and Letters* turned out to be a reprint of the letters Mabel had gathered, dated and published in 1894. Out of 381 pages, 272 were taken from Mabel Todd's editions.

Both books were published under the name of Martha Dickinson

---

* Mattie's contribution was to remove all the invented titles to poems and restore an occasional word from manuscript. She told herself that these necessary measures amounted to 're-editing', for like Aunt Lavinia she underrated what editing entails.

Bianchi, as though she had done the editorial work. There was no acknowledgement to Mabel Loomis Todd. From Mattie's point of view, none was
due. Since Emily Dickinson had been invisible and unpublished in her lifetime, after her death whoever controlled the poet's papers felt empowered
to say who she was. The problem for Mattie is that the vivid portrait in *The
Single Hound* had more or less distilled all she knew at first hand. No one in
Nazareth thought much of Jesus, which is not peculiarly stupid of the
Nazarenes; it's human nature. In a similar way, Mattie, as a girl, hadn't paid
that much attention to an invalid aunt behind their hedge. What was
strange and intriguing to those on the other side of the hedge was, to
Mattie, ordinary in the sense of what had always been. When Aunt Emily
was sick in the summer of 1884 Mattie had carried over suppers devised by
Susan to tempt the invalid's appetite. Aunt's comment that she had
'scarcely seen' Mattie since her birth has to be an exaggeration, but it does
suggest that Mattie hardly visited her aunt of her own accord. When Emily
gave thanks for the suppers, what she didn't say is telling: if Mattie had
stayed to talk, if there had been more in the way of closeness, it would not
have gone unnoticed.

So when Mattie made her advance on Todd territory between 1922 and
1924 she was acting largely at a remove, as her mother's agent. What she
thought she knew, she knew to some extent from the gossip that had always
swirled around the recluse. This hearsay, suffused with Mattie's strongest
inheritance, the legacy of hate, could now be conjoined with legal claims
and it's this combination that re-ignited the feud in the second generation.

Mabel had never lacked initiatives and now, nearing seventy, she prepared to fight. The first big gun she moved into position was the poet Amy
Lowell, an outspoken fan of Emily Dickinson. Mabel's plan was to co-opt
Amy Lowell as her ally and stir her to undertake a rival biography. Miss
Lowell's celebrity and the social cachet of her Boston Brahmin family would
serve to outshine Mattie the minor novelist. Mabel moved as quickly as
ever. She needed no introduction because Amy Lowell was familiar with her
name as Dickinson's editor, and understood the impressiveness of that
achievement. Mabel, with her Harvard daughter in tow, was soon on visiting terms and both wrote to Amy Lowell with customary civility. By

January 1923 Lowell was turning over the idea of a literary biography, rereading Mabel Todd's volumes and admiring Dickinson more than ever. The poet's dramas, she remarked to Mrs Todd, are 'of course' contained in her heart and mind, which makes the life all the more interesting.

When Miss Lowell was disappointed to hear of the prospective *Life and Letters*, Mabel reassured her that Mrs Bianchi 'will perform a life which may satisfy some persons, while the real essence of [Dickinson's] elusive life must escape all except the elect. I *wanted* to have you do it!' She spoke familiarly of 'my dear mis-read Emily'. Mabel gave 'dear Miss Lowell' a manuscript poem, as though it were hers to dispose of.

Then, early in 1924, Mabel made a mistake. She was far from indiscreet, yet accustomed to talk over plans with her husband. At this time she mentioned to David Todd her wish for Amy Lowell to take up the Dickinson project and David, fired up, planned legal action against Houghton Mifflin to prevent their publishing Mattie's biography. Amy Lowell was aghast. Houghton Mifflin happened to be her publisher. She feared David would write directly to the press and begged a rather helpless Millicent to put a stop to this. In the end, though Amy Lowell remained tempted, she had to honour a contract for a biography of Keats.

No biography, then, was to challenge Mattie's highly coloured story of her aunt, which took up the opening quarter (about a hundred pages) of *Life and Letters*. Mattie burst into purple prose to promote her story of renunciation and single-minded love for the Revd Charles Wadsworth. He's not named but it's easy enough to identify the preacher whom Emily heard during her visit to Philadelphia in 1855. As a result, for the rest of the century Wadsworth remained a prime candidate for 'Master', a candidacy owing little to verifiable evidence and much to the legend Mattie published in 1924. The rumour of disappointed love had long been in circulation, but Mattie made it plausible by announcing that she alone, as the last of the Dickinsons, had entrée to a family secret. The identity of the lifelong lover was *the* secret, not discussed but taken for granted in the family. She entertained readers with a scene of Lavinia running next door to call Sue because 'that man is here' and Emily might run away with him. In the mid-1850s, the alleged date for this crisis, Sue was still unmarried and there was as yet no house next door. In fact, the Dickinsons had not as yet moved back into the Homestead. Such facts do not deter Mattie's fantasy; her pen races on, at ease with popular fiction.

'But the one word he [Wadsworth] implored, Emily would not say.' So he moves his family a continent away, and dies prematurely.

All that can be proved is that Emily respected the Revd Wadsworth, who did not die prematurely. After his death in 1883 she gave out that he had been 'my Shepherd from Little Girlhood' (a re-enactment of her little-girl role after her married mentor, Ben Newton, died) and famously called him 'my best earthly friend'. Since she was a master of extravagant declarations and made a good many over the course of her life, these are less telling than they might seem on their own. 'It's easy to invent a Life', Dickinson once said, 'God does it — every Day —'. But Mattie is too overcome by the dramatic intensity of the poet's confessional voice to consider inconvenient counter-statements. Here is Mattie in full flood:

> Certainly in that first witchery of an undreamed Southern
> springtime Emily was overtaken – doomed once and forever by her
> own heart. It was instantaneous overwhelming, impossible. There
> is no doubt that two predestined souls were kept apart only by her
> high sense of duty, and the necessity for preserving love
> untarnished by the inevitable destruction of another woman's life.
>
> Without stopping to look back, she fled to her own home for
> refuge – as a wild thing running . . .

Mattie's inaccuracies extended to shifting 'Title divine — is mine! / The Wife — without the Sign!' back in time to the Philadelphia spring when Emily, allegedly, was in 'the first ecstasy of renunciation', although this poem was composed some ten years later and sent to Bowles.

Millicent penned 'Bosh!' and 'ugh' down the margins of her copy. 'Oh, yeah?' she said to Mattie's gush over Emily's supposed childhood 'intimacy' with Helen Fiske (Helen Hunt Jackson), who 'would be driven into town with a pair of smashing grey horses which were dramatically walked up and down before the house [the Homestead], while the two charmers visited together behind the closed blinds'. Millicent retorts 'just the opposite' to Mattie's fancy that 'Niles could never induce [Dickinson] to publish'. And when it comes to Judge Lord, Mattie presents the poet as no more than 'his little friend'. This modest little friend would 'flit' about watering her 'frail' plants 'in the twilights'.

So wedded is Mattie to her phantom that she romances the poet's attempt to name the newborn son of Mr and Mrs Bowles. 'Only once is there any evidence of her breaking a silence like that of dead lips.' Not knowing the name in question, Mattie assumes it must be that of Aunt Emily's secret love. According to Mattie, a lovelorn Emily urges Samuel Bowles to name the boy 'by the name never like any other to her ears'. In fact, as we know, the poet asked Bowles to call his son Robert, after Browning, at the time of Elizabeth Barrett Browning's death in 1861, a time when Emily menaced the babe of poor Mrs Bowles if she refused to condone the way that Emily's letters – one in particular, not meant for wifely eyes – came whirling into her domestic fastness, determined to lasso her husband.

Mattie's Emily is a model of restraint. Too scrupulous to wound a wife, Emily remains true to Wadsworth's memory, flitting about in the 'tender shadows' of the old house. Her little form never walks, always 'flits' as she performs 'the sunny small industries of her day'. Philadelphia is a 'fatal sally' into the great world 'beyond the purple rim of the home horizon'.

The legend ballooned and floated.* Reviews were 'astonishingly good', Mattie exulted to her old friend Amy Montague. She was particularly gratified when a review of her own new collection of poems pointed to her kinship with her famous aunt. It had become a matter of pride that poetry in the Dickinson family had to do with 'fine breeding', as if breeding were a pre-condition for art. Her 'Emily book' was due out in England. Admiral Samuel Eliot Morrison,[†] Mattie heard from her editor, had stayed awake nearly all one night, reading Dickinson's letters, the only writing the editor had heard him praise unreservedly. In June, Mattie would be addressing

---

* The legend's spread was out of proportion to modest sales of only 2500 copies.
[†] Samuel Eliot Morrison was a relative and, later, an admirer of T. S. Eliot.

members of Ned's class of 1884 at their fortieth Commencement reunion. She had been invited to give other talks about Aunt Emily, in effect taking over Mabel Todd's role.

But nothing in 1924 could touch Mattie's triumph as the one and only authoritative recorder. As one reviewer said: 'It remains for the last living member of her own family to submit Emily's . . . life . . . as a beautiful inspiration.'

Mamma had never spoken of the Dickinsons to her daughter. She broke this silence on 6 June 1924 when Mabel told Millicent that there were actually two men in Emily Dickinson's life, and no distinct tragedy, 'and it scarcely influenced her life in any detail'.

'She enjoyed writing her love poems more than she enjoyed the man, I sh[oul]d be willing to say.'

Mabel spoke with the assurance of her intimacy with the poet's brother and sister. The time had come to inform Millicent on the subject of Emily Dickinson and to fire her daughter with the history of the feud. As Mabel opened her lips to talk about the past she found Millicent was already roused to fury over Mattie's raid on Mamma's five volumes.

David Todd too prodded his daughter when she visited him in the asylum. 'Are you going to sit by and do nothing, while the work on which your mother spent years is pirated and her name erased from the title-page?'

It was 'pi-racy', Millicent agreed in her somewhat Southern tones, retained from her first years in Washington. The journal *American Literature* invited Millicent to review the *Life and Letters*. 'It ought to be done, to point out the villainy of the thing,' Millicent commented to Amy Lowell. She did not, however, wish to appear 'in controversy with Mrs Bianchi; the butt of anything she chose to say. And as Walter puts it, "a wise person does not thrust his arms into a barrel of pitch if he knows it." So, as on previous occasions I must just be a good child, and sit passive, and boil with rage inside.'

Mabel herself fired a long volley of denunciation for Millicent's benefit. 'In so far as one conveys the impression that one did the work on a book when in reality it was somebody else, it is piracy. When there is misrepresentation of facts, it is falsehood, deception, perjury, fraud, deceit, sham, pretence, perfidy, distortion invention, dishonesty, treachery, counterfeit, fiction, myth, humbug, hyperbole, swindle. Fortunately through it all Emily remains inviolate. No matter how loudly chanticleer proclaims lies from the roof to the entire barnyard, it does not affect the sun.'

Millicent's sympathy for her mother in defeat endeared her to Mabel, who turned to her daughter as never before. It's a bond Millicent had craved with pent-up passion. If she, Millicent, could only protect her mother, if she could be all-important to her and not an onlooker, they might act as one.

It's a long journey in the Buick from Florida to New England. In November 1924 Mabel makes for the 'barn' in Amherst where she'd left her Chinese chest. Millicent is at her side, supporting her lame arm. There in the barn, unseen by the world, an extraordinary scene takes place as mother and daughter kneel beside the chest a quarter of a century after Mabel locked it. As the lock turns a little bell rings (a precaution in case of a thief). Then the lid is thrown back and Millicent gazes at Mamma's secret 'mine': a mass of brown envelopes filled with Dickinson poems and letters.

'We extracted the Emily things from the barn,' she confides to Amy Lowell, 'and today we have been looking them over. They are simply superb! A mine which it would be thrilling to explore. And letters from Mr Higginson and other . . . literary jackasses, who "advised strongly" against publishing anything of Emily's whatever. And in spite of all, Mamma persisted and worked away at it and brought her to light . . . Now I feel better! What an orgy we shall have when . . . M[artha] D[ickinson] B[ianchi] steps out [dies] some day!'

In 1926 Millicent Todd Bingham will publish her translation of *Principles of Human Geography* by Vidal de la Blache, who had taught her generation to look to the physical environment – steppes, savannah, forest – to explain the character of its inhabitants. This will be Millicent's last publication in the field of geography, followed by her last stint of teaching: a course on urban geography at Columbia University. In mid-career Millicent resolves to abandon her field for her mother's sake. Her idea is not so much to take care of her mother but to take up her cause.

16

THE BATTLE OF THE DAUGHTERS

By the late twenties the daughters of the feud were ready to surrender their independence as geographer and novelist. The battle for Emily Dickinson absorbed both from now on. They were evenly matched.

Mattie had the advantage of the Dickinson name and never stopped wielding it. 'My aunt, Emily Dickinson' was the refrain of her letters to her publisher, Houghton Mifflin. She was determined to preserve her legitimacy as sole Dickinson authority.

Millicent's advantage was her eloquent mother who opened the floodgates of memory to her daughter. But Mabel Todd still said nothing of adultery, so what Millicent took in of Dickinson hate and ingratitude appeared monstrous and Mamma, by contrast, sanitised. Millicent did know that her mother and Austin were bonded forever in their elevated terms, but perhaps surprisingly Millicent did *not* know, even now, that there was more to it than emotion.

Though she was too intelligent not to be aware that her mother's vehemence did not relay all the nuances of truth, the obfuscations left Millicent somewhat divided: not as to the Todd cause, but in her ambivalence towards what was spellbinding in her mother. Unlike Mattie's single-mindedness, Millicent remained uncertain as to how she might deploy her considerable powers. What displaced geography was a search for truth through typed private reminiscences in parallel with psychotherapy, starting in the spring and summer of 1927. What poor Millicent was trying to understand was the truth of her childhood, in which something illicit was covered up in secrecy and illusion – illusion conjured up by Mamma's social performance. This included the elaborate manners and dressiness of the 1890s. By 1927, when Mabel was in her seventies, she still wore headgear with aplomb and clothed herself in exquisitely delicate materials. Her white shoes were immaculate. She looked straight into the camera with a performer's pleasure in being photographed. Millicent, plainly dressed in tweeds (in deliberate contrast to Mamma) or in overalls at home, would later count fifteen white dresses, twenty-eight white 'waists' and nineteen white skirts in her mother's closet, and innumerable velvet bands to hide her throat.

Looking back, Millicent pictured herself as unlovely beside her mother, easy to ignore or leave behind, as Alden and Joe Thomas had done. Here, once again, Mamma's looming admirer looks down at her child whose round, black eyes look back rather wonderingly at Mamma's closeness to her 'King' with a creased face. As an adult, Millicent longed to expose their imposition on a child's innocence. Ideally, she would have liked to publish a work of literature she variously calls 'a study of the growth of my own soul' or 'another Comédie humaine [Balzac's realist novel] in ten volumes'.

By 1927 this private ambition mattered more than to publish another geographical book, but to tell the truth would take more courage than she had; it would also, of course, betray Mamma whom, increasingly, she saw as pathetically dependent on her inferior companion Hilder. In Mabel's blue-sky youth she'd never have considered such a man; now she inflated him. Millicent loved her mother most when she felt a call to defend her.

As for her father, she marvelled at his accepting Austin's claim on her mother. She saw this as an emotional droit de seigneur, for no one in those days crossed Austin's right to do as he pleased. Millicent cast Austin as the villain of the parental drama now consuming her attention.

One mystery she would have liked to solve was Sue Dickinson's origins. Was Mrs Dickinson, as Mabel alleged, a stable-keeper's daughter? Mattie had described her mother as her father's equal and the rock to whom the Dickinsons had turned in their hours of need.

'Actually – I hesitate to ask Mamma anything whatever,' Millicent reflected. 'The cloud of mystery which surrounded my childhood is its natural habitat – the air it breathed.' If she were to question Mamma it would open 'the blast-furnace door'.

Her many typescript reminiscences stress her divergence from her mother: a daughter who was honest, puritanical, loathing her mother's flair for performance. As a child this had made her approach Mamma's piano lessons wanting to scream and smother her own musicality. Even now her body felt 'tense and rigid', resistant to passion, she told her therapist Dr MacPherson. 'Though I respect, admire and profoundly love my wonderful husband, he does not arouse passion, nor ever has.'

Mattie, divorced finally in 1920, met in that year a young tenor called Alfred Leete Hampson at the National Arts Club in New York. She was then fifty-four; Hampson was thirty-one. He was impressed with Madame Bianchi, and became a devoted companion at The Evergreens. Mattie began to speak of 'we', of 'Alfred and I', no longer quite alone in the stripped aftermath of her marriage.

Amherst tolerated Mattie's bad-boy dependants. The town had not been averse to the foreign polish of Bianchi, and now it put up with Hampson's drinking. He was eager to help Mattie with her work. Her condition for collaboration was not accuracy; it was unquestioning loyalty. Hampson was more than happy to oblige.

Mattie's career as poet and novelist had faltered of late. Houghton Mifflin turned down her poems; taste had changed, they told her. *Les jeunes* demanded Modernism. Following the two Dickinson books in 1924, Mattie had a desert romance ready in 1925 and when that was rejected for lack of reality she whipped out a Russian novel by 1926. The press had to tell her that the second half fell off. Fortunately there was a rising public appetite for Emily Dickinson. Houghton Mifflin enquired if Mrs Bianchi had more to offer about her aunt. Encouraged to hunt amongst the leavings of the Homestead, Mattie came upon the trove of Dickinson poems that Aunt Lavinia had hidden before she died in 1899. So it was that in 1929 Martha Dickinson Bianchi and Alfred Leete Hampson

Meanwhile another centenary biographer, Josephine Pollitt, came up with a new candidate for Emily's love: none other than Major Hunt, the first husband of Helen Hunt Jackson. Pollitt plumps for Hunt on the basis of Emily's remark to Higginson that Lieutenant Hunt (as he was when he and his wife visited the Homestead in 1860) had interested her more than any other man she ever saw. What had appealed to her at the time had been a joke: there had been food on the table, with Carlo, Emily's dog, in wait for a morsel to fall. 'Your dog understands gravitation,' Hunt had said with mock sagacity.

Pollitt's husband Frederick A. Pohl, who had helped with 'tedious' research, contrived to turn a silly book into an even sillier play called *Brittle Heaven*. On stage in New York and Boston the 'tempery' wife Helen Hunt vies with the poet as to who will own the man. Helen doesn't deserve him because she's a shallow creature of the flesh; her husband prefers a chaste poet. The two women glare at each other through a dialogue of banal spats. Costumed in puffed sleeves and covered in ribbons and bows, 'Emily' was photographed as she gives Hunt a wan look while Helen fumes in the background.

In the absence of facts about the poet, banal fancies multiplied. Desperate to get Hunt away from 'Emily', Helen persuades Hunt's boss to transfer him to service in the Civil War while Helen's plea of childhood friendship prevents 'Emily' from keeping a tryst with Hunt before he leaves for the South. Two years elapse (the years, incidentally, of Dickinson's greatest fertility as a poet). Renunciation has driven the poet into a nervous decline. Then Helen reappears in Amherst to own that Emily's renunciation has won Hunt's love forever. Exalted, 'Emily' decides to go to him. She and Sister Sue are planning a secret jaunt to the battlefields when Sam Bowles arrives with the news of Hunt's death. 'Emily' sinks. Curtain.

On 10 May of the centenary year Mattie opened The Evergreens to fifty invited guests, including Mrs Dwight Morrow (whose husband, an Amherst graduate, was US ambassador to Mexico—appointed by President Coolidge, another Amherst graduate), representing Smith College. Mattie had more invitations to speak than she could manage. At Columbia's summer school she lectured on 'The Real Emily Dickinson' and the chair responded: 'We can safely leave our Emily Dickinson in your hands.' In October, a hundred and fifty women made a 'pilgrimage' to The Evergreens. Then Yale University held a 'birthday party' in December. It was accompanied by a Dickinson exhibition with Mattie's *Life and Letters* in pride of place.

Excluded from all this, Mabel Todd was not to be outdone. She threw a vast party on Dickinson's birthday, 10 December, attended by the notables of Coconut Grove. These days she covered her arms in the sheerest net and piled her white hair in an elegant chignon. Yet nothing Mabel did in the way of celebration could match Mattie's pre-eminence at this moment.

Six months later Martha Dickinson Bianchi received the first degree that Amherst conferred on a woman. At the 110th Commencement she was honoured as niece of 'that rare and original spirit, Emily Dickinson, whose poems you have brought into renewed and deserved admiration'. The occasion was reported in the press, together with a photo of Mattie in a close-fitting hat like a helmet over her eyes and a fox-fur draped over one shoulder, brushing her cheek. Her mouth has the moody look of Austin when young.

Millicent urged Mamma to challenge Mattie's prominence with an article on the literary debut of Dickinson. Millicent, in fact, wrote this, and as she put her mother's case together she felt a 'driving force'.

'Perhaps I exist only to do this,' she mused. 'I am involved without question, and I am glad to be.' Her intelligence was intrigued by the complexity of the feud, a situation 'worthy of a Henry James'.

Mother and daughter selected fifty of Dickinson's unseen letters. These they prepared to add to a revised edition of the *Letters*, to be published by Harper in 1931. It was necessary, Millicent said, 'to be supplied with ammunition', and this was Mabel Todd's claim that she owned the copyright to the Dickinson letters. She based this claim on the draft contract of 1894, still in her possession.

'Much against her will Lavinia allowed me to share the copyright,' she declared to Mr Green of Jones Library in Amherst. She repeated this to her daughter: Lavinia 'did consent, reluctantly . . . that the copyright of the *Letters* should be registered in both our names. So it was done.'

This claim should have been negated by the final, signed contract of 1894 (in which Lavinia cancelled Mabel Todd's half-copyright in the letters in the draft contract). But this final version, adverse to Mabel's interests, happened to disappear after she bought the publisher's copy* from the New York dealer Maurice Firuski. It can't be proved that she did away with it, but the publisher's copy never re-surfaced, and its non-existence freed Mabel to flourish the draft contract in her favour. It would be like her to convince herself that this draft document was the true one; that what came after, in the rising confrontation of September 1894, had been nothing but a fit of meanness on Lavinia's part that Austin, accustomed to control his sister, intended to overrule. Mabel's memory often turned Austin's intentions into actions on her behalf.

But what about the duplicate of the final contract, the one Roberts Brothers had sent to Lavinia in a big envelope that caused Austin to say its size would inflate Lavinia's self-importance?

Thirty-seven years later, when Mabel Todd's publisher, Harper, announced her expanded edition of the letters, Mattie did not come forward with Lavinia's copy of the contract. Convenient for Mabel, but did it worry her? Mattie continued to assert her claims as Aunt Lavinia's heir, citing the fraudulence of the Todds as proven in court, but Mattie did not produce Lavinia's contract – the simplest way to disqualify Todd from further publication of Dickinson letters. Was this document lost? Mabel Todd's thinking in such a situation would be to accept this as providential. God was always on her side, or should be.

After the centenary had honoured Mattie together with her aunt, Mabel Todd took the offensive with her expanded edition of the Dickinson letters. Her preface presented it as the first book ever issued about Emily

---

* In 1931 Mabel bought a carton of Roberts Brothers archives, which had been thrown out as waste paper for the mills but salvaged by a book hunter. The carton contained the whole of the Dickinson publishing papers, including the draft and final contracts in 1894.

Dickinson, prepared at the requests of the poet's brother and sister: Austin Dickinson, Lavinia Dickinson 'and I' collected letters 'which they entrusted to me' to edit and publish. At a stroke, this authorised editor displaced an unauthorised niece.

After almost four decades, Mabel Todd argued, the legend had assumed a shape unrecognisable to anyone who actually knew Emily Dickinson. It was advisable, she said, to return to sources, and here they were in this expanded re-issue: 'It is the source of material since reworked in various forms by various authors.'

She emphasised Wadsworth by printing letters about him after his death. At the same time, she declared that speculation had no place in this book that had 'in fact one purpose: to allow Emily Dickinson to speak for herself'. In this way, Todd disclaimed possession in a publication whose prime motive was, in actuality, an act of possession. Without referring to Mattie, it shot Mattie's version of her aunt's life to pieces with well-aimed rhetorical questions: who can know what Dickinson felt for others? Who can know what was momentous? Adept at graceful gestures of compliance, Todd said that she was driven to issuing this edition of the letters for the sake of others, students of Emily's life who, sensing something wrong, had begged her to tell what she knows of the 'real' Emily. Biographies 'have not lessened the confusion'. Todd found it gratifying 'to find how many people care for *my* Emily Dickinson'.

Only when her rival was flattened did Todd put forward her own strongest claim, to having done so much of the editorial toil. In the early 1890s it had been hard to get hold of letters and date them, and would have been impossible without her closeness to Austin and Lavinia. Here, at last, Todd made a comeback, pressing the case she had made at the trial. And of course there's truth to what she terms her 'fascinating, exhausting labor'.

Not satisfied with a comeback, Todd intended to wipe Susan from the record. Todd reports this omission as though it were not her initiative. It was Austin's wish. 'Such reference [to Sue] was frequent in the early letters particularly in those before his marriage. To make doubly sure, in Emily's letters to himself he erased most of such passages before the letters were given to me to edit.' In this way Todd covers herself against any future imputation that she had tampered with the letters or colluded in doing so. Austin, she insists, did this alone, even though, if we go back to the mid-1880s, we see that Mabel Todd was the active party in her campaign to have Susan out of the way. In 1931 Todd is all passivity, a model of obedience. 'In so far as the present volume is concerned, I shall continue to abide by his wishes in this particular.'

One thing Todd doesn't say is that she had ignored his wishes (and those of Lavinia and Mattie) in the matter of the daguerreotype, the sole authenticated photograph of Dickinson, taken as a schoolgirl in 1847. Todd prepared to bare the undoctored face and plain, scoop-necked dress for the first time, an act consistent with her readiness to accept the poet's arresting oddity: the pale kangaroo face with the slanted, staring eyes; the flat red hair drawn back without a curl; and the long, long neck through which words pulsed like bursts of fire. *And yet — Existence — some way back — / Stopped — struck — my ticking — through —* At a stroke Todd cut the girl free from the 'furbelows' imposed by the family. And, as always, she ignored Austin's lack of interest in his sister's genius. Her aim was to reclaim the authorised ground, and that ground was won.

Privately, Mabel Todd launched a parallel offensive. The tactical calm of her public apologia contrasts with private vituperations, mostly to Millicent who took notes and typed them for the record. One set of statements is signed in Mabel's shaky, post-stroke hand. Vinnie 'had an enormous mouth & false teeth, a crazy coot with dirty hands and never took a bath'. She had 'greatly enjoyed all her financial success from Emily during all those years before her death'. 'Vinnie ought to have given me a thousand dollars for what I had done for her. If I'd had 100 I'd have had the maple tree [on the plot of land at issue in the trial]. It was little enough to ask her.' Maggie Maher 'lied in every particular'.

It's startling to hear what she had to say about Gib Dickinson. They had appeared in the same studio photograph recreating a summer picnic in 1882. The young Mabel, buttoned to the neck in demure white tucks, her white hat shading her face, had been invited to join the Dickinsons.

Gib, aged seven, stands in the circle of his mother's arm. This fine-faced boy, who was to die a year later in a disrupted home, Mabel calls 'hideous', though she concedes he was sweet and adored by his father.

In the last month of Mabel's life, September 1932, she dictated her final statement about the feud: Susan was a drunkard like her father who had 'died in the gutter'. What Sue resented was not infidelity, 'for that she practised herself' [with Bowles]. It was that Austin fell in love. Morose, wrathful, settled in her power to make Austin unhappy, Sue was therefore furious to find love open for him. Mabel presents herself as a victim of Sue's irrational fury. That fury was handed on to Sue's daughter and it became the driving force of her life as well.

'It is hard for anyone who has not come in contact with it to imagine the force, the inexhaustible energy, the almost superhuman vitality of hate,' Mabel declared. 'It seems at times almost creative, so that the person in its grip is capable of accomplishment beyond his powers. But the trouble is that such accomplishment is neither beautiful nor true. It is a storm of destructiveness.'

Mabel died suddenly of apoplexy on 14 October 1932. Her grave in Wildwood Cemetery is within fifty yards of Austin and Susan Dickinson. A stanza from Emily Dickinson is cut into the tombstone, appropriate to her shadowing of the poet for the best part of Mabel Todd's life:

> That such have died enables us
> > The tranquiller to die:
> That such have lived, certificate
> > For immortality.

Hog Island, off the coast of Maine, was a little wilderness where Mabel and Millicent had spent their summers. There, the summer before she died, Mabel had asked her daughter for a promise. Millicent must undertake to rectify the wrong done to her mother by publishing the substantial residue of Dickinson papers in the chest. For Millicent this was the 'point of no return'.

Her husband Walter Bingham warned about taking on the feud.

'You must realize that if you do it, it may get us both before it is finished.'

There were other warnings. 'Budgie, don't you touch it!' urged Elizabeth Sawyer, her oldest friend going back to Amherst schooldays.

It was as if they had not spoken. As Millicent would say later, there was 'nothing else but to do what I could to right a grievous wrong – to my mother and to Emily Dickinson. I did not then know that I was doing a greater wrong, by getting involved in it, to Walter, and to myself.' Even Mamma had warned her not to publish anything more in Mattie's lifetime. Millicent, fired by indignation, believed that Mamma wished to protect her from Mattie, and for some time to come did not suspect the flaws in the Todd case. What she did take in was that she was in it for the long haul.

Her first venture was to complete a book Mamma had conceived before she died: a history of her efforts to bring Dickinson before the public. *Ancestors' Brocades: The Début of Emily Dickinson* was a partisan project, furthering the Todd offensive. For a start, in January 1933, Millicent delivered an address in Miami, hailing her mother as the co-discoverer as well as first editor of Dickinson's poems and letters.

Mattie contemplated a lawsuit over Mabel Todd's 'objectionable book' (the expanded edition of Dickinson's letters) which had appeared without her knowledge or consent. To her lawyers, Henry Field (who had been Aunt Lavinia's junior counsel in the lawsuit of 1898, and was now a judge) and Theodore Frothingham in New York, Mattie argued that Aunt Lavinia gave no permission to the Todds to quote one line after the publication of the original selection of letters in 1894.

There was no evidence of this, Field warned. Lavinia and Austin had turned over material to Mabel; nor was there evidence as to what happened to this material afterwards. Frothingham agreed with Field that Mattie had scant basis for a case.

Mattie also pressed her publisher Houghton Mifflin to sue Todd's publisher, Harper. Houghton Mifflin too backed off. 'I am afraid the sympathy of the literary world would be against you,' her editor Ferris Greenslet advised, 'so that the final result might be damaging to the sale of your books.' Mrs Todd was in a strong position because Lavinia's original permission to use her cache of manuscripts had not been legally revoked.

Keen to retaliate, Mattie scrambled together a rival book of letters with reminiscences. It was to be 'a personal book about Emily' and Mattie hoped to regain her authority by quashing Mabel's claim to have been the poet's 'friend'. The new book was titled *Face to Face*: as Mattie pointed out to Houghton Mifflin, however persistently Mabel had made her way into the poet's home she had never managed to see Emily Dickinson to her face.

'My Aunt Lavinia Dickinson declared Mrs Todd has never seen Emily. So that disposes of that,' said Mattie, as though victory were near.

Far from it. Ever since the adversarial biographies of 1930, Ferris Greenslet had warned Madame Bianchi not to rush out another temporary book thin on fact. 'Now that the story of Emily Dickinson's life has become a battleground, which is very regrettable but can't be helped, the critics both friendly and unfriendly will be sure to . . . judge by much higher standards of taste than would have been applied a decade ago.'

Mattie was impervious, locked in the past amid the family memorabilia and unsifted papers piled up in The Evergreens. When she offered a first-hand memory – her aunt wielding an imaginary key to a room of her own – Mattie was indeed the invaluable conduit she believed herself to be, but too often she had only hearsay to offer, like a cousin's opinion that Emily's wearing white was 'a sort of memorial to the man she loved'.

Louis Untermeyer, who had upheld Mattie's reticence, now attacked it in a front-page article in the *Saturday Review of Literature*. 'Readers waited for Emily Dickinson's niece . . . to say six definite sentences that would clarify the situation . . . Sinae rumbled, but not even a mouse of fact issued from the mountain of rumor.'

At Houghton Mifflin, Ferris Greenslet and fellow editor Mr Linscott began to doubt Mattie's story. Mr Linscott sent Greenslet an in-house memorandum:

> Myself, I am convinced that the love affair is merely a family
> legend; that Emily had tremendous admiration and respect for
> Wadsworth – but nothing more.

In vain did they urge Mattie to verify her fancies. They pointed out that her hint about Aunt Emily's wish to give the name of her secret love to baby Bowles had been discredited.* Politely, the editors reined in their irritation.

Dickinson habits of reserve had meant that nothing was discussed. And around this silence there swirled a babble of romantic hearsay. What Mattie required were readers who were too civil or too enchanted to ask awkward questions. Many reviewers did indeed continue to back the legend for its feminine appeal: the 'quaint' ways of a poet who was 'the center of a peculiarly beautiful home life'. So said the *Boston Transcript*, as did the *New York Herald Tribune*: 'It was a warm, intimate New England family, bound by ties of even more than ordinary New England affection.'

Others in the thirties were less delicate. Mattie was disconcerted by a review in *American Literature* pointing to all manner of editorial sloppiness: the incorrect use of Dickinson's middle name as 'Norcross'; the neglect to signal the approximate element in the dating; and the failure to check transcriptions against Todd's recent edition and to acknowledge it. To Mattie it was pedantic fuss, but it did not go unnoticed. The reviewer too complains of arbitrary and sometimes damaging cuts in letters, as in Mattie's fiddling with Emily's youthful boast, 'I am growing handsome very fast indeed. I expect I shall be the belle of Amherst.' Mattie had cut 'very fast indeed', blunting the over-the-top humour because she hoped to prove that Emily was saying this straight, as a 'natural, silly, happy girl'. It's a point about normality in line with the feminised daguerreotype, the curls to soften the face and the overdone ruff to hide the neck. Mattie was exercised over a black and white photograph for *Face to Face*: the portrait of the Dickinson children. She thought this image of Emily too sturdy. Contrary to the image on canvas, Emily should appear 'quaint' and 'wistful', with a pointed chin. 'This *elfin* quality has been entirely lost in the photograph because of the heavy, thick, *middle-aged* mouth.'

---

* Baby Bowles was named Charles, which coincidentally was Wadsworth's name. In fact, as we know, ED had wished the baby to be called Robert.

The inaccurate editing went on. Mattie's so-called *Complete Poems* of 1924, followed by *Further Poems* in 1929, was then followed by *Unpublished Poems* in 1935, again co-edited by the none too sober Hampson. After each new volume Houghton Mifflin brought out a new collected edition. Yet another appeared in 1937. It exasperated scholars, and in 1937 the influential critic R. P. Blackmur deplored the 'disarray of Emily Dickinson's poems'.

Mattie kept at it, encouraged by signs of public and private support. In 1933 a Dickinson exhibit at the World's Fair in Chicago had included Mattie's *Life and Letters* amongst a century's hundred best books by American women. Mattie was grateful to have Gilbert Montague's moral support against 'alien biographers of our Emily'. She was sad to live without kith or kin 'save such as we of the heart', she wrote to her old friend Amy Montague, who was Cousin Gilbert's wife. Mattie raided the poet's words to Susan Dickinson, hoping to recreate the intensity of that tie: 'Be Amy while I am Martha –' but, unlike Susan and Emily, Amy Montague showed no enthusiasm for Mattie's writings.

Millicent's husband urged her to face what she'd contrived not to know. She was nearly fifty-five years old towards the end of 1934, when reluctantly she opened Mamma's journals.

'Whatever she did would have sacrificed somebody,' Millicent thought as she read.

How much she read and how much she learnt of the sexual side of Mamma's affair she could never bring herself to say, except that Mamma's unblemished love for Austin Dickinson did mitigate Millicent's sense of sin in so far as it left her less able to judge the passion. The eloquence of the journals bound her to Mamma more than ever. Suffused by her mother's voice coming at her through all the years, Millicent was finally conjoined with Mamma as her posthumous instrument. She notes on a stray sheet: 'In the early days E.D. seemed less important and Mamma's connection with her – than my own work. Always I was subconsciously trying to get away from it all. But always brought straight back under irresistible compulsion.'

By 1935 Millicent had finished a first draft of her mother's story, the triumphant narrative of Emily Dickinson's debut, the betrayal by Lavinia Dickinson and the trial. This book would gestate another ten years while the groundswell of Millicent's distress heaved. There came a day when her mother's hate flooded through her with unprecedented power.

She dated her record of what happened 4 February 1938. That day it was snowing so fast that to Millicent's half-closed eyes it looked like a thick fog over a white world, and through that fog Mamma came towards her with her air of expectant youth. She came until she stood clear, for good and ill, to her daughter's gaze. This woman 'had an unfailing eye for the dramatic – particularly where her own person was concerned'. She had a 'superficial ebullience'; she could 'startle and delight the senses'; and all the time worked so industriously – that remarkable industry that had been 'the best foundation for a glittering superstructure'.

If Millicent's severity has an element of envy it's because Mamma had taken more pleasure in her talents than her daughter did. Mamma had lost her teeth, her right side was paralysed and she was somewhat deaf, yet she had found new forms of expression. Painting and piano cut off, she had set up a salon for conversation. 'The glow never disappeared. It scarcely dimmed at all. Her arch glances continued to the end.'

In contrast to her mother, Millicent pictures herself as a failing creature, an octopus with limp tentacles. The acute senses of its tentacles had been capable of reaching out to anything it might desire, 'but because of injury to its central mechanism, the arms hung limp, their function reduced to swinging in a restricted arc . . . It goes on living . . . but grows old without ever being the vital creature, using all its faculties to the utmost, alive to the end of the farthest tentacle, which its natural endowments enabled it to be.'

This creature can only revitalise herself, it seems, if she yields to Mamma's hate – lets it fill her being to the furthest tentacle. Alive to hate, her tentacles rear and coil in curious kinship with the enemy who is to be eliminated.

Hatred implies similarity, that is, lasting hatred does. The kind of hatred that implies incentive enough to enable it to last a life-time – strength enough to propel it beyond the grave and loop it in the hearts of a succeeding generation. The kind of congenital hatred means a feud – and a feud does not flourish among aliens . . . The most virulent kind seems to get its start in stealing of affections, and affections usually do not exist between aliens . . . Real hate is focussed . . . and focussing on a negative purpose may be carried out with as much or more determination. It's not iniquity which the hater hates; he's hating during an interval while waiting till the opportunity comes for vengeance. This waiting through a life-time does not destroy the carrier; on the contrary it seems to add the vitality to prolong life. The emotion, the hatred, keeps the hater alive and vigorous. The affection which starts a feud may be between aliens, but the hates it engenders does not continue unless between kindred souls and the closer the likeness perhaps, the more virulent the hatred.

I sympathize with Sue in so far as losing her husband is concerned. It must have been bitter.

But then, on top of that, to have that very vixen who stole your husband complete a task which you have imagined yourself the one to perform, to reap from so doing . . . a measure of permanence in the literary future – that was bitterer still. And to even have one's name left out altogether! There was real injustice.

Millicent still sees Sue through Mamma's eyes as a wife who didn't love her husband yet persecuted the woman who did love him and who released his capacity for love. 'What I wonder is – where did [Sue's] *drive* originate?' Was it hurt pride, or envy of the successful outcome of Mabel Todd's effort to launch Dickinson's poems, or both together? To tell this story of the poems from the time they were discovered until the present of 1938 was to become aware that 'the facts are not explained by any *reasonable* cause'. The cause for each separate step in the feud was hate and desire for revenge: to discredit the other side. 'Sublime, detached Emily – whose preoccupation was with eternal sentries – how purified she will sometime emerge from such a mirey slough as now holds her down!'

In a war, the calibre of recruitment is all-important. Mabel Todd had understood this. When she could not persuade Amy Lowell to take on a rival biography of Emily Dickinson, Mabel had to fall back on Taggard to get at Mattie. After Mabel's death this partisan task fell to George Frisbie Whicher, professor of English at Amherst. Together with Mabel he had helped to arm Taggard. In *This Was a Poet* (1938) he went in for the kill, bashing Mattie for factual slips, the wrong date for Mr Dickinson, Sr's death and for what Whicher calls the 'grotesque' legend. It emerges that the Wadsworth legend was grotesque only in Mattie's telling, since Whicher appropriates the legend for his own purpose, encasing it in a scaffolding of academic credibility. The strategy of the takeover required him to discredit his rival, the last of the Dickinsons whose very name authenticated her possession of the poet. Never taking his eye off Mattie as he knifed her, he seized her story. Many since Whicher have repeated the Wadsworth story for a fact, but to go back to Whicher is to see the flimsiness of its construction.

Whicher was Mabel Todd's man: he treats her deferentially, with careful acknowledgement of what she'd achieved. The feud is never mentioned but his cover declares his allegiance, stamped with the same painting of Indian Pipes as Todd had used on her covers for the Dickinson volumes of the 1890s.

That same year, 1938, Mattie made a will that shows the pain Whicher had inflicted, both in his own capacity and as a representative of Amherst College. Her will stipulates that Whicher is never to edit Emily Dickinson. Amherst College is never to own or use The Evergreens. If the property should be sold the house is to be razed to its foundations. She leaves all its contents and manuscripts to Alfred Leete Hampson, together with 'all my copyrights', the income due from them and the sole right to publication of letters written by the Dickinsons 'to which I am the sole legal heir'.

*

By 1940 more 'pilgrims' were finding their way to The Evergreens, many from the West and South. There was no sign to attract the curious, but she welcomed those who liked the poems. They were shown the memorabilia in the Emily Room. The lawn was immaculate and the old creeper still overhung the porch. Mattie brought out the grey and white cameo brooch, saying it was Aunt Emily's only adornment, fastened in the dainty ruching at the neck of her white dress. She pointed to the image of a ruched and curled poet titivated for Mattie's *Life and Letters*. Even though Todd had published the authentic image Mattie clung to this travesty.

One visitor, Pearl Strachan from England, was charmed to meet the poet's niece and repeated her words in an article: 'Madame Bianchi had the privilege of close friendship with her Aunt Emily.' Mattie related the story of the Dickinsons' descent from the Norman noble, de Caen, who came to England with William the Conqueror. Obviously Mattie's faith in this myth had remained undimmed by Whicher's ridicule. She was making a pathetic effort to recover ground with an autobiography and worked with Alfred Hampson for several hours a day. In the course of this last-ditch effort Mattie died at the age of seventy-seven, in 1943.

The death of her mother's enemy freed Millicent Todd Bingham to proceed with a double publication. In *Ancestor's Brocades* (published by Harper in 1945) Millicent repeats her mother's slanders against Sue Dickinson. She brings out the proposed division of copyright in the *Letters* of 1894, yet says nothing about the excision of this paragraph in the signed contract. Quite possibly, Mabel had destroyed that contract without telling her daughter.

With the second of the two books Millicent did something she could not risk in Mattie's lifetime: she ignored the rights to Dickinson's poetry that Alfred Leete Hampson had inherited, and in the face of Hampson's protest (backed by Mattie's old friend and lawyer Theodore Frothingham) Millicent prepared to publish her mother's cache of Dickinson's poems.

Over time Mabel had settled into certain beliefs that she had passed on to her daughter and to a new generation of readers. One of these was that a more just Lavinia had meant to reward her in the end: 'both [Austin and

Lavinia] told me she left the copyright of Emily's poems to me as financial recompense for my many years labor without pay'.

Lavinia's will, supposedly drawn up by Austin in Mabel's favour, had mysteriously disappeared. This was what Mabel alleged: the will 'was never found'. The implication was that Susan Dickinson had destroyed it. But we know that Lavinia would not have willed her copyright away from her family. Lavinia consistently rejected every move of this kind.

Millicent's publisher asked her to scour her mother's private papers and correspondence with Austin Dickinson to find authorisation in writing for Mamma's right to edit the poems of Emily Dickinson. One journal was in an envelope marked 'Private, keep out!' Millicent opened it and was nauseated: 'I found no authorization', Millicent notes. 'Instead, I met, head on, a mighty passion, so overwhelming that my knees shook and I felt as if I could not breathe. Walter read one or two letters and fell silent.'

'We'll lick it yet,' her husband comforted her.

'I think I should have collapsed if it had not been for Walter,' she said. 'The thing was so mighty, and it was so wrong! And it had spawned such primitive feelings – hatred and revenge and a curse which had reached even down to me!'

Shaken though she was, Millicent did not give up. On the contrary, she and Harper gained the support of Alexander Lindey, an authority on copyright law for the Library of Congress. He argued that to publish these poems was in the public interest. He also considered it questionable for Mattie to pass on rights to a non-member of family. Hampson continued to threaten but had not the means or will to fight a legal battle.

Bolts of Melody, with more than six hundred unknown poems by Emily Dickinson, took the public by surprise in 1945. Millicent Todd Bingham explained the delay over these poems in terms that ignored the claims of the Dickinson camp: she had been painstaking in her scholarship, re-copying from manuscript instead of relying on her mother's transcriptions, but in the many instances of poems jotted illegibly on cast-off scraps (on the inside of used envelopes – a favourite source of paper – on tiny bits of stationery pinned together, on discarded bills, on invitations and programmes, on leaves torn from old notebooks, on brown paper bags, on soiled, mildewed subscription blanks, on drugstore bargain flyers, on a wrapper of Chocolat Menier, on the reverse of recipes, on shopping lists and on the cut-off margins of newspapers), the editor had been daunted for a long time and it was only in the last three years that she had brought herself to decipher these. But what a reward, as great poems sprang into view for the first time. Mabel Todd's daughter presented herself as the prime Dickinson expert, and certainly by this time no one knew more than Millicent Todd Bingham. Her edition, though, did make two errors, acceptable at that time: as her mother had done before her, she imposed titles on untitled poems and she standardised punctuation, not grasping how vital Dickinson's punctuation may be to the way we read her.

Millicent believed that her double publication would terminate the feud. 'These feuds are now dissolved in death,' she said, the Dickinson line is 'extinct' and the task of editing what remains 'has finally reached me – the last of both their houses'. But this apparent readiness to lay down arms was a condition of victory. The distancing title of *Ancestors' Brocades* disguised an attack in the present. Millicent prints a photograph of a $505 cheque that Lavinia received as royalty. Dickinson ingratitude to Mamma still rankled. An appendix prints Lavinia's signature to the deed of Dickinson land to the Todds on 7 February 1896. Early in the book Millicent positions herself as passive under attack from an active enemy: 'I accepted', she says, the 'blight' cast on her from Mrs Dickinson and her children. But Millicent is shooting back again and again, not omitting a tedious final chapter on Mattie's errors in *The Single Hound*.

Citing her mother as co-author and acting in concert with her wishes, Millicent Todd Bingham turns out to be as adept at innuendo as Mamma, with that mastery of a sharp or flat off the true note which alters the tune. The reason given for Dickinson's solitude is the personality of members of her family. Stop. Re-play that flat. The authors, it seems, are actually suggesting that Susan drove Emily to escape her by shutting herself away for life.

A masterstroke is the authors' subtle contradiction of Mattie's allegation that the poet did not permit Mabel to see her, as her family did, 'face to face'. Millicent re-claims the intimacy with a caption to a photograph of her sweetly smiling young mother: here is Mabel 'as Emily Dickinson knew her in 1882'. Millicent doesn't actually say 'saw her', but face-to-face would be assumed by most readers.

A more blatant spin is Millicent's version of Austin's supposed request that Mabel Todd should wipe Susan from the record. After Mamma's visitation swept away resistance, Millicent seems more willing to lie on her mother's behalf: 'Family feuds were, in my mother's opinion, irrelevant.' It's made to appear as though the feud was between husband and wife, with Mabel as bystander, blameless, obedient to instructions. Millicent appears even more the bystander, with 'only the haziest idea' why her mother's work on the manuscripts had been interrupted for many years.

Puzzlingly, though, Millicent extends her unknowing – or her mother's discretion – with an incorrect recollection that the treasure chest 'was not opened until 1929', though Millicent's report to Amy Lowell reveals that it was first opened in 1924. It's simply not in character for Millicent's retentive memory to play such a trick. It has to be a fudge, but why? A possible answer lurks in a typescript reminiscence later, in 1955, where Millicent repeats the fudge: 'For twelve years [since the Todds had left Amherst in 1917] a camphorwood chest containing my mother's most precious papers had been reposing in a Springfield Storage Warehouse. I had placed it there . . . in 1917 when I packed the contents of Observatory House, Amherst, and built a little house to store them in (not finished inside).' The latter was the unfinished 'barn', and Millicent is covering up for Mamma's negligence in abandoning Dickinson's manuscripts in such an unsuitable place, unchecked, for seven years. Mabel's questionable safety net had been the transcripts she took with her to Florida, where they narrowly survived fire and flood. It would have been Millicent who realised that the originals must go into a safe form of storage.

For all Millicent's commitment to fact, loyalty to her mother took precedence. Her whole book is biased in Mamma's favour by a major omission: the fact of adultery.

The eruptive force of what must not come out left Millicent pale and strained, clutching the arm of her kindly husband. Her reminiscences, delivered in her rational voice and typed in her orderly way every few years, always dissociate her character from that of her mother: a sensitive daughter deploring all that was devious in her parents. So Millicent's untrue public statements, with no Dickinson left to oppose them, are as startling in their way as the sudden appearance of so many unknown poems. How did Millicent explain this to herself? If a daughter as intelligent as Millicent had come to believe in what she published in *Ancestors' Brocades*, the afterlife of her mother's 'spell' can't be overrated.

Millicent had been corresponding with Wallace Keep, a Dickinson relative in his seventies. While a student at Amherst College, class of 1894, he had visited Vinnie weekly. Forty years later he offered a quotable memory of her mobile face with a mimic's repertoire of expressions – the facial acrobatics of a person who is so much the performer she can't be known. This might have made her formidable if she weren't so amusing. On Keep's arrival in Amherst (in the fall of 1890, when the first volume of Dickinson poems was due) she had sidelined the youth while she fed his mother. Maggie had laid the table for two and the young Wallace had watched their lunch from a hungry distance. He recalled the next four years of supper-less Saturday evenings at the Homestead when Lavinia would grimace 'with horror and despair' to hear of poor food at his lodgings and then, holding up a candle, and followed by a train of cats, she would descend to the cellar to fetch up some apples. Coated in humour, it's a caricature that Millicent used as her opening for *Ancestors' Brocades*, an attack on her mother's enemy, touched up with Millicent's childhood recollections of a witchlike Miss Vinnie in black with knife pleats, knobbly fingers holding out an apple and huge coils of grey-streaked hair, as though all the juices of her shrivelled body had gone into that sprouting head.

Millicent sent Wallace Keep a copy of the book with a note: 'I wish to say before you read it, that I have been filled with compassion for them all, it was a devilish situation for everybody concerned. But chiefly I pity Miss Vinnie. I have tried to show that pity. But her own behavior was so incriminating that I am afraid the impression left in the reader's mind is of a treacherous old woman, nothing more. My one and only effort is to convey things as they were.'

Another reader, Mrs Franklin Harris, wrote to Millicent. The address in Coconut Grove suggests someone who had known Mamma, and so it proved, but the reason for the letter was not Mabel Loomis Todd, but to thank Millicent for her portrait of Ned Dickinson. Who now thought of Ned Dickinson, forty-seven years after his heart attack? Mrs Harris turned out to be Alice Hill, who'd been engaged to Ned at the time of the trial.

Yet another voice sounds from the past, this one rather muffled. The Norcross sisters, we recall, had refused to hand over the poet's private letters, to the annoyance of Mabel Todd who had called them 'stupid'. Her daughter calls them 'crotchety' and waves them off as unimportant. Not so: Emily Dickinson confided in her Little Cousins. Loo, who outlived her sister, did not die until 1919. When, later, Millicent called at her nursing home, she heard that Loo Norcross had kept her cousin's letters with her to the end; then had them burnt. Where Millicent deplores the folly of a 'cantankerous' old woman, it's possible to discern, through that obscuring noise, the fading voice of a tie the poet had trusted.

17

POSTHUMOUS CAMPAIGNS

Lexington Avenue, New York. Late September, 1948. In the shadows before dawn a man turns over Dickinson's papers. He has changed jobs, and his reason for doing this is 'to take care of Emily'. How do you take care of someone who has been dead for sixty years? And how does this stranger come by her papers, whatever letters he chooses to have in his apartment two floors above the narrow, store-filled avenue?

Sometimes he is up all night.

When it's time to leave for work, William (Bill) McCarthy locks his fire-proof filing cabinet and waits all day for night, when he will light his lamp and unlock his trove.

At the same time as Mattie's death gave the advantage to the Todd camp, it roused a new force. During the forties, collectors, dealers and American libraries cast their eyes on The Evergreens, for there, in disarray under flaking ceilings, lay a national treasure. Certain players in the literary marketplace quietly rolled up their sleeves. And now new players enter the stage: McCarthy and Mattie's rich cousin Gilbert Holland Montague. The rights to the papers of Emily Dickinson had changed hands and the heir, Alfred Leete Hampson, is not by temperament a fighter: he's an alcoholic in poor health and long accustomed to acquiescence. As editor he had been subordinate to Mattie – 'Madame Bianchi' as he'd called her.

Before Mattie died Cousin Gilbert had let her know that he was reading her books on Emily. As his thin lips stretched to a self-satisfied smile, the long slits of his eyes narrowed.

The effect was not altogether pleasant; his smile held an element of menace. His wife had recently died and he was inclined to public gestures in her memory, proclaiming their happiness. He wished it known that he was, after all, a man of feeling. For he was clever, vain, ambitious – a scoring ambition, intent on gain. At Harvard he'd graduated summa cum laude in political science (class of 1901, along with Robert Frost and Wallace Stevens). For a while he'd taught economics at Harvard; Franklin Delano Roosevelt had been one of his pupils. During these years he'd attended Harvard Law School and, in time, amassed $5 million as a top New York lawyer promoting private enterprise over government controls. Standard Oil was one of his clients.

It's a measure of the growing fame of Emily Dickinson that Montague, in his sixties, took her up in a serious way from 1942. Their connection led him to hint that boyhood ties with the Dickinson family had given him access to disputed and undiscovered facts. He was a collector, a shameless egotist and show-off. Born to a bankrupt father, he liked to go on about 'my butler', 'my staff' who open 'my house' – Beaulieu at Seal Harbor* in Maine – where, in July, 'my gardeners' ready delphiniums and

* Mount Desert Island.

roses for an annual tea and cocktails, four till six, attended by notables:
the Cadogans from England, American senators and four-star gener-
als – military heavyweights came each year at his bidding. With the air of
a grandee consenting to make himself 'available', he invited Alfred
Hampson to this event, and when Hampson did not rush to reply
Montague followed this up. 'My cousin, Emily Dickinson' swelled his
array of possessions.

When Millicent's books publicised the collection she held, approaches
came her way. First in line, in November 1945, Montague invited her to
dine in his Manhattan house at 15 East 37th Street. There he praised her
history of Dickinson's debut and displayed books and manuscripts so rare
that they left her, she told him, 'a-quiver' as though she had been all at
once in the great libraries of the world. The following year he came to hear
her speak at the Grolier Club in New York. She, in turn, introduced him to
what her mother had done for Amherst, in the hope of recruiting him for
the Todd camp. 'Your understanding of my efforts is, I should like you to
know, one of the sturdiest supports I have,' she wrote at first.

Meanwhile the poet Archibald MacLeish and the critic Robert Penn
Warren contacted her on behalf of the Library of Congress; so too did
William A. Jackson of the Houghton Library, Harvard, a repository of
choice manuscripts, amongst them the Keats papers and those of Melville,
the James family and the Eliots. As a Harvard alumna, Millicent was not
impervious to Jackson's interest in her Dickinson papers but explained her
promise to publish the residue in the Chinese chest. This must come first.
Yet for the sake of future scholarship she did want the papers in her possession to join eventually with those at The Evergreens as one
comprehensive collection. Privately, Millicent favoured Amherst College
as its appropriate home.

The Houghton Library was extending feelers also to the other camp. Bill
McCarthy, in charge of cataloguing, had been the enthusiast who had put
on the Yale exhibition in 1930. At that time he had offered his allegiance to
'the real Emily Dickinson', Mattie's code for the anti-Todd loyalty she
demanded of her recruits. He had gone so far as to declare himself Madame
Bianchi's 'slave for life'.

McCarthy therefore approached Mattie's heir with the right credentials. He told Hampson he'd never been so fulfilled as when he'd put together the centenary exhibition, and that his New Year resolution for 1931 had been to see more of *him*.

He said, 'even though our face-to-face meetings had been so few, I always felt that a renewed hand-clasp would erase the intervening time'.

Soon after, in February 1944, McCarthy and Hampson dined together to discuss plans for a 'shrine'. McCarthy's worship of Emily Dickinson did him no harm with Alfred Hampson, whose feelings were quite the same. Within two months of Mattie's death they were 'dear A' and 'Bill'.

Mattie's reputation reached an all-time low after Millicent's tribute to Mabel's editing. In 1946 McCarthy let Hampson know how fervently he was defending Mattie's reputation (not just for ramshackle editing but resistance, as well, to any other publication of Dickinson's works). At a literary dinner McCarthy spoke up for Mattie's 'charm, humanity, and wonder'. A partisan stance – crucial to relations with Hampson – came easily to McCarthy, who made no contact with the enemy: Millicent. Her name and her mother's remained unmentionable, as they had been in Mattie's lifetime.

Hampson, like Millicent, was not yet ready to part with manuscripts. He first wished to publish a completed version of Mattie's autobiography. Nothing came of this, but Hampson proved a sticker when it came to another posthumous task: to recover the ground his patron had lost in the feud. 'The Evergreens never forgets,' he told McCarthy. He would always insist that Mattie's *Life and Letters* and *Face to Face* were 'the only authentic pictures of Emily Dickinson'. He tried to stop Harper bringing out Millicent's edition of six hundred poems, calling Mabel Todd 'a thief' who had been 'convicted of misrepresentation and fraud in two courts'. Bibliophiles had wind of this, as did the press, Hampson was pleased to note.

Hampson then protested against acknowledgement of Millicent's help with a forthcoming edition of the poet's letters to the Hollands.* Weak and furious, Hampson signed his protest 'yours for <u>Emily</u> and <u>Martha</u>'. He was still spluttering three months later when he discovered seven remaining

---

* Edited by their granddaughter Theodora Ward.

references to Mabel Todd's pioneering work – 'a person convicted of a criminal offence . . . who was saved from prison only by clemency' – in the editor's revised preface. He exploded as though this editor had been co-opted by the enemy: her credits should not 'pander to parasites'. Yet, again, Hampson's claim to Dickinson rights proved ineffective in banning publications. These setbacks made him more susceptible to McCarthy's advice and help.

The portrait of the three Dickinson children, first published by Mabel Todd in 1894 and re-published in *Face to Face*, had become dingy with the passage of time. Parts of it were obscured. McCarthy offered to fetch it from The Evergreens and take it to the Fogg Art Museum at Harvard for restoration. Afterwards he was jubilant: cleaning revealed a book and flower in Emily's hand and a picture of a cat in Lavinia's. McCarthy raved over the 'fabulous' auburn of Emily's hair after its 'shampoo'. 'I know that however uneasy you may have been, you will be glad you trusted me with it.' Would Hampson like him to bring the portrait back to Amherst or, better still, permit the Houghton to exhibit it on the same basis as Melville's portrait, which they had on loan from his granddaughter?

McCarthy homed in on the fear of fire at The Evergreens. It was Hampson's habit to go abroad in the winter, and fear for 'Emily' (his code for her papers) had led him to pack 'Emily' in his suitcase and cart her about Europe.

Hampson was beset by other worries too: the peeling interiors of The Evergreens, the piles of unsorted papers, his proneness to hepatitis (probably alcoholic cirrhosis of the liver) and the burden of what Mattie expected of him, which he feared he was not fit to carry out. These considerations, and perhaps others, encouraged him to marry Mary Landis in 1947 when both were in their fifties.

From Hampson's point of view it was all gain. Mary was well educated, a graduate of Smith College. She would share the burden of the papers, would manage the house and would be there in sickness and in health – and in truth, there was little left of health. Best of all, she shared his regard for Mattie ('Martha', as they both now called her), whom she'd known separately.

Mary had been attracted to Hampson back in 1931 when he was not disposed to marry. His life, then, had been taken up by Mattie and their joint projects. Mary called this a turning point, for she'd turned to someone else and made a brief marriage, and by the time Hampson claimed her, all that was left for her was to prolong his existence. In short, she was to be more nurse than wife.

Nine months after the marriage Hampson was ill enough to be in hospital. He came home, pottered about, travelled again the following winter, but the precariousness of his condition brought the couple up against another problem, medical expenses. In April 1948 they resolved to do what Mattie had done occasionally in times of 'necessity': sell off a few of Emily Dickinson's letters. Where Mattie had acted through a Philadelphia dealer, the Hampsons turned to their understanding friend, McCarthy, who was so willing to help with what Mary called 'such staggering wealth'.

McCarthy warned Hampson: to sell off bits of his collection here and there would 'interfere' with selling the collection as a whole, and no one, McCarthy said, could do this better than he. A librarian was preferable to a dealer; he could do more direct marketing to collectors or libraries; he might get them $40,000. As it happened, in September 1948 McCarthy left the Houghton Library to become a dealer himself. He joined the Rosenbach Company in New York, 'to care for Emily', he told the Hampsons.

The Hampsons trusted him. They wanted 'Emily' safe for all time in a first-class institution, and required an Emily Room for the memorabilia to be transferred from the Emily Room at The Evergreens.

One weekend in mid-September 1949 McCarthy offered to stay at The Evergreens to care for Hampson when his wife was called away to nurse her father in Sea Isle City, New Jersey. McCarthy took this chance to explore the house and discovered nine letters from Helen Hunt Jackson to Emily Dickinson on a shelf in the cupboard in Mattie's room. He was thrilled by the unprecedented fact the letters revealed: the poet's agreement to publication in the case of 'Success'. There were boxes of papers in the room, which he pushed towards the bed, out of the way of the flaking ceiling. In another room he spotted Mattie's diaries. To a librarian the state of the house was a nightmare. It was also exciting, for what unknown treasure might be lurking on other shelves, or in the trunk in the Tower Room?

His fears of a leak or fire had persuaded the Hampsons to let him take 'Emily' under his protection: the manuscripts of her poems had been housed in the Rosenbach vault, while McCarthy himself stood guard over Dickinson's letters in his New York apartment, number 2A at 310 Lexington Avenue.

All through the past year McCarthy had been brooding over the letters like Tulkinghorn* in his turret, the master of secrets he alone knows. While the city slept he unlocked 'Emily' and let her out. He understood more after visits to The Evergreens in September and October 1949, as his letters to the Hampsons relate, encouraging Mary to comb the house herself: the more he and Mary could find, the more valuable the collection will be. After the first search McCarthy came armed with a borrowed flashlight. It dived into trunks and darted into dingy corners, lighting up the untouched leavings of the dead. Peering into Mattie's closet on 31 October 1949 he came upon the missing letters of Edward Dickinson and Emily Norcross from the 1820s. During another foray he discovered four letters from Emily's beloved aunt Lavinia Norcross to her sister, Emily's mother, in May 1833 after Lavinia Dickinson was born.

Back in New York City, McCarthy stayed up late, sifting and staring. 'I have had wonderful but long night hours,' he confided to the Hampsons. 'I shall have the alarm clock tomorrow ring at a quarter before 5!'

Come morning, he set about ordering and boxing 'Emily' in preparation for a sale. He told the Hampsons that he was doing this for free. 'This is something I wish to do for Emily and Martha. It is a debt I owe them for their contribution of great happiness to my life.' Rosenbach thinks him 'crazy'. In this mood of selfless generosity, McCarthy had obtained the company's right to act as exclusive dealer for the Dickinson collection. This was in January 1949. The firm was to get 10 per cent of the sale

* The lawyer in *Bleak House*.

price, and in the meantime they gave the Hampsons – in urgent need of funds – an advance of $5000. McCarthy recommended that the sellers offer control of future publication to whoever bought the papers.

'We shall, of course, get as much for the collection as possible,' McCarthy reassured the Hampsons (to whom he'd dispatched a gift of crystal tears* for the house). 'I believe there is no way you could get more.'

McCarthy's next move was very odd. He offered the lifetime collection of what he knew to be a great American poet to a Washington library of Byzantine studies. Naturally, since Dickinson doesn't fit a Byzantine collection, Dumbarton Oaks declined to have her. But why deal with an inappropriate repository when any number of distinguished American libraries might have answered McCarthy's search for a likely buyer? One possibility is that McCarthy was seeking donors of immense fortune in Robert and Mildred Bliss, who had given Dumbarton Oaks to Harvard in 1940. There's no trace of this negotiation in the files of the museum, nor in the letters of McCarthy to Mildred Bliss, and no perceptible basis for personal interest: the Bliss private library contained no books by Emily Dickinson. Whatever McCarthy had in mind, the refusal was predictable. The Hampsons were bound to be disappointed and this would have softened them up for a buyer who waited in the wings.

On 24 February 1950 McCarthy called the Hampsons to report that Mr Jackson of the Houghton Library would like to buy their collection. It's possible that this library was always in McCarthy's sights as an appropriate repository for Dickinson. Obviously he retained some tie. This is an emotional man, and his allegiance could be loyalty combined with devotion to the great poet. Conceivably, McCarthy was so obsessed with Emily Dickinson that he wrapped himself in the grandeur of acting for her. Are we looking at a Jamesian scenario of a rare inner life? Yet it turns out that, at this persuasive moment for the Hampsons, McCarthy was cycling in silent tandem with an unseen figure behind Mr Jackson.

McCarthy did not tell the Hampsons that Mr Jackson was negotiating

---

* An ornament of crystal drops in the shape of tears.

with a Harvard donor – none other than Gilbert Montague. Ten days earlier, on 13 February, Jackson had sent a letter to Montague reminding him of their common interest in Emily Dickinson and their discussions about her. Each year it had been Montague's custom to donate acquisitions worth about $1000. How was Jackson to persuade him to take on a 'considerable' donation of $50,000?* Jackson did so by holding out a tempting prospect: he assured Montague that Mrs Bingham had promised to yield up her own collection if the Library acquired Hampson's. If all went to plan, Jackson explained, the combined collection would amount to about 95 per cent of Dickinson's papers. Montague did want this, but as legal consultant to the super-rich he was accustomed to bring off a favourable deal. It appealed to him that the Todd collection would swell his benefaction at no further cost to himself, and this was linked in his mind with the triumph of a larger bargain.

Montague's motives are revealed gradually in his letters to Jackson and in the memoranda Jackson made following their conversations and phone calls. In the summer of 1950 Montague gave his opinion that the Todd hoard was worth 'in excess of $100,000', though it was only about a third as large as Hampson's collection, for which Montague was due to pay half that amount. Montague repeated this same estimate at a Boston dinner in 1953. It was not, then, an idle estimate but a considered view, one that turned on gain undeterred by morality. For if Montague believed in this figure – and it appears that he did – he intended to make a killing. By Montague's reckoning, Hampson's treasure was worth $200,000, which means that Montague thought to get it at a quarter of its market value.

Unknown to Montague, Jackson made a memorandum of what was said at this Boston dinner in 1953. Jackson had put to Montague the following corollary: in the donor's view, the two collections together were worth as much as $300,000. In other words, Montague's incentive had been to acquire *both* collections for what he believed to be a sixth of their

---

* The equivalent of about $550,000 or £360,000 in today's terms, though the buying power would differ.

combined value. To what extent he inflated his triumph is a matter for sale-room experts, but whatever the actual value of the collections in 1950, it was really Montague's perhaps inflated estimates and his expectation of bettering his initial acquisition by a third as much – a buyer's fancy, shall we say – that led to subsequent attacks on Millicent Todd Bingham. For Montague intended to hold Harvard accountable for her promise to surrender her collection. Since Jackson had indicated an expectation that her treasure would swell his donation, Montague was not inclined to let this go. To a lawyer of his temper, business and legal relations turned on the polarities of submission or resistance. If Mrs Bingham would not immediately yield up what she held he would force Harvard to sue.

To this end he devised a far-reaching claim on rights in the forthcoming agreement: Harvard was to have not only present and future rights to the Dickinson papers, the university was to own, in addition, *past* rights. This would prepare the way for attacks on the Todd camp, who would then find themselves in unlawful possession of the Dickinson papers they had held undisturbed for more than fifty years.

In the initial negotiations Montague showed the civilised face of the collector, as Jackson had known him in their dealings thus far. In fact, a piranha was swimming into the quiet Houghton pond. Montague, lashing his tail, was not abashed to own that he cared nothing for a prospective scholarly edition that mattered to Harvard and also to the poet's future. Nor in the end did money prove to have been the prime issue, as Jackson discerned; it was vanity, the beginning and end of Montague's character. In Dickinson terms, he epitomised the absurd 'Somebody', the anti-type to a 'Nobody' like the poet herself. Ironic that a creature so incapable of effacement should contrive to link his name to hers. Above all, Montague was bent on the glory of the grand public gesture. He wanted the kudos he was bound to have as sole donor of a collection remarkable for the fact that a poet of her stature had been unpublished in her lifetime. Her manuscripts had never been seen; her reclusive life tantalised the public; and many mysteries waited to be uncovered.

On 3 March 1950 Montague agreed to pay $25,000 down, and then annual $5000 instalments from the spring of 1951 to the spring of 1955. If we deduct the Hampsons' advance of $5000 and another $5000 due to Rosenbach, it appears that in the spring of 1950 the seller was due to receive only $15,000. It's not known what Hampson thought of this sum, but it's clear enough that he postponed the deal due for announcement in mid-March and then in mid-April. Hampson began acting on his own behalf in holding back on certain items. (He may have judged that he could get a better price for items sold individually.)

Montague masterminded 'a war of nerves on Hampson'. Threats were the lawyer's tactic to bring adversaries to heel, so Hampson was advised that resistance on his part would expose him to national 'disgust' in a court of law, while Rosenbach threatened to dispatch the Dickinson papers direct to the Library. Since Hampson had yielded them up to Rosenbach (through his trust in McCarthy) it was presented to Hampson as a situation beyond his control. All of this was bluff. Montague admitted in private that the legal weaponry brandished in the 'war of nerves' was 'corny'. Hampson had not yet signed an agreement; it should have been within his rights to withdraw from the terms of a sale that didn't suit him. Yet Hampson was in poor shape and apprehensive of predators (one still invisible) closing in on him from two sides.

At this point he had a haemorrhage.* An ambulance rushed him to hospital, where he struggled to go on in intensive care. Seven transfusions were needed over the next few days, from late April to early May. Bleeding, his life in danger, he gave in and signed the agreement on 6 May.

By 9 May the war was won: 'V-Emily Day', Jackson headed a letter informing Montague that the agreement was 'safely' in Rosenbach's hands. At that date Hampson was still in the dark as to the donor. The secrecy of the sale meant there was no bidding to drive up the price.

When the press release eventually went out, on 31 May 1950, there was national acclaim for Montague who received a hundred messages (he

---

* A common complication of cirrhosis of the liver is damage to the throat, resulting in haemorrhage.

counted) of congratulation, including one from General Eisenhower and a reader's letter from Mrs Morrow, who had represented Smith College at The Evergreens in 1930. She wrote:

> Next Day Hill
> Englewood, New Jersey
> May 31st '50

My dear Mr. Montague –

As one brought up on Emily Dickinson's poems I rejoice with all my heart that they have gone to a safe place – Harvard – and will be held as sacred papers for future generations to study and revere.

I congratulate you upon your magnificent gift.

> Sincerely yours,
> Elizabeth C. Morrow.

Montague answered all congratulations with a statement dictated to his secretary. He noted with annoyance one or two Harvard dignitaries who had neglected to grovel in gratitude. Temperate William Jackson was usually at hand to calm the lashing tail, but in the summer of 1950 he went to Europe, and in his absence Montague turned ugly, determined to wrest the goods from Mrs Bingham before (he feared) she sold her collection elsewhere. If another library paid upwards of $100,000 it could cut short the attention and praise feeding Montague's self-esteem. He blamed Jackson to Harvard's administrators: Jackson's policy of compromise with Mrs Bingham had been, he declared, an error. Confrontation, immediate legal confrontation before Labor Day, was the way forward. It must be brought home to Mrs Bingham that if she did not hand over the papers Harvard would sue, and her mother's shame would be publicised in court. And if Harvard declined to sue, Montague would sue Harvard itself.

To Millicent too the name of the donor came as a surprise, but she wrote to Montague expressing 'relief, for I have long feared that the Amherst collection [at The Evergreens] might be lost – or scattered!' Now 'what is, perhaps, the greatest treasure in American literature' would be safe. Montague circulated copies of this gracious letter even as he planned to do her down. Unaware of an imminent attack, she and her husband accepted an invitation to dine again at Montague's house. Part of his plan was to stop her new book. Over the last five years she had produced a picture of Dickinson in her local setting, based on family manuscripts in her mother's chest.

She had delivered *Emily Dickinson's Home: Letters of Edward Dickinson and his Family* to Harper on 1 March 1950. But by the terms of Hampson's sale to Montague, framed just over a week later on 9 March, the buyer could claim (as Mattie had done in the past, and Lavinia Dickinson before her) ownership of *all* Dickinson papers, and this meant control of all future publications of manuscript material. The sale specified that 'neither Millicent Todd Bingham nor George F. Whicher is ever to have any part in the editing of any of the manuscripts acquired by this agreement'.

This clause perpetuated the feud. The Dickinson camp, represented by the Hampsons, demanded no mention of enemy names in any Dickinson publication. No acknowledgement ever of the work done by the Todd side. Millicent Todd Bingham was to be blocked for good. More than that, she and her mother were to be erased, vindicating Susan Dickinson's failed attempt in 1901 to erase Mabel Todd's name from the title pages of the pioneering publications she had edited, co-edited, and promoted in the 1890s. Where Hampson, on his own, could exert no force, his cause was now empowered by joining his interests to those of Harvard.

Victory at last for the Dickinson camp?

In Millicent's new book she follows her mother's model of painstaking research, which was skewed whenever it came to Susan Dickinson. Susan's character is assassinated and the part she played minimised or obliterated. What looks like scrupulous research persuades us to accept the slander so that it works its will: a campaign to doctor the record for all time. If it succeeds, the ultimate victory will go to the Todd camp because the followers of the Todds (often unaware they are followers) will repeat the vilification or obliteration of the woman who had been, from youth to the end of Dickinson's days, her foremost reader. In this way the hatred of two generations will continue to influence those who are not in a position to see the want of evidence for Todd allegations.

Scholars are even more vulnerable than casual readers because those who spend years on research may be impressed with the Todds' care for scholarship and sympathise with Millicent's wrongs, which are repeated in all the statements she leaves for posterity and in tapes she made in old age. Like her mother, her voice is measured, careful to be precise, and then too like her mother she believes what she says. Where Mabel believed in her lines with the conviction of an actress, Millicent believed in them as a loyal daughter who had suffered as a child from the snubs of Susan and Mattie Dickinson.

Where Mattie's legend built up a pitiful Emily bereft, for life, of the one and only man she loved, Millicent's legend is of a pitiful Emily 'hurt', for life, by her 'cruel' sister-in-law from whom she withdrew into disillusioned seclusion. As a girl, so the Todd story goes, Susan Gilbert had a 'lush personality', charming the innocent Emily, but soon after Susan's marriage picked Susan out of the 'gutter' she began to be above herself. 'Pretence and pose came to be her most noticeable characteristics,' Millicent goes on. It was therefore impossible for the intimacy with Emily to survive. 'Emily grieved.' To support this, Millicent quotes 'I lost her' from a Dickinson poem, without proof that those words referred to Sue. After that, Sue 'pretended' to understand Emily 'better than anyone else'.

Along with Sue, the story dismisses the poet's sister Vinnie, whom it casts as a grotesque old witch, ungrateful and tight-fisted towards Mabel Todd whom, unaccountably, Vinnie trounced in court. This leaves Mabel Todd as the only worthy intimate of the poet. The price Mabel pays is to 'be caught' in 'the welter of Dickinson animosities'. Millicent deploys the passive verb, in keeping with her mother's erasure of initiatives on her own part. Mabel Todd had spoken of 'the family quarrel of endless involutions in which she wished not to become entangled'. Nothing to do with Mabel herself. The A-word has no place in the Todd legend. Instead, an innocent newcomer was 'involved', and 'became the focus of the traditional black passions for revenge which grew by what it fed on. In Mrs. Bianchi[,] the last member of the family[,] it reached a peak of fury . . . which was bent on suppressing any evidence contrary to her purpose – namely to eliminate all trace of one who had presented the poems and letters to the world.'

When it comes to eliminations of Sue's part in Emily's letters – tamperings too blatant for cover-up – Millicent takes a bold line. The heart of the matter is not the damage to Sue, as we might suppose. No, the heart of the matter is damage *by* Sue. It's Sue's fault, Millicent claims, because Sue alone was responsible for damage to the Dickinson marriage, forcing Austin to retaliate. The mutilations of the letters intrude on the reader 'so insistently that he is unable to forget the bitterness of Austin's life'. As for Emily, this brother's suffering 'was her own'. *'Emily grieved.' 'The welter of Dickinson animosities.'* Millicent's sad voice invites us to share her pity for the poet who had to live with a troublemaker in her family.

'Emily withered', the voice insists. Sue's inability to care for 'reality', only for show, 'left a permanent scar'. Emily's 'disillusionment' with Sue was 'a positive . . . element in her withdrawal'.

There is no evidence for these allegations beyond Mabel's say-so, nor is there evidence of Austin as the instigator in the matter of doctored letters. Mabel's claims to passivity never ring true: for one, that she excluded Susan from her editions of Dickinson's letters in proper obedience to Austin's wish.

The legend proliferates in commentaries, biography and, most recently, novels. Most insidious is the assertion that Emily 'endowed [Sue] with characteristics Sue did not possess'. That being so, Emily's words of love and praise count for nothing. The force-field of this camp is formidable.

'Congratulations and hallelujahs', Millicent had written to Mr Jackson about his acquisition of the other camp's papers. This hurrah to the Houghton had been well meant. Like the Hampsons, she revered Emily Dickinson. Like the Hampsons again, she recognised that the poet's papers must go to a repository with the means to preserve them. Both camps hoped that separated treasures would come together in one place. After a succession of books drawing on the Todd treasure. Millicent was willing for her collection to join with the Harvard acquisition and it was to be a gift, not a sale. Her sole condition was that she be permitted to publish two more books.

Jackson did not appear to disagree and continued to beckon Millicent to join forces, appealing to her as a scholar with the poet's interests at heart. Walter Bingham's notes after a meeting with Jackson indicate a verbal agreement: 'Harvard did not intend to stand in Mrs Bingham's way.'

Harvard, though, was in a position to set off a bomb if she would not yield – the bomb designed for her by the Hampsons. Montague was the mover behind the scenes, never permitting Harvard (and Jackson, representing Harvard) to forget what was owing to him: Mrs Bingham's hoard. Unknown to the Binghams, Jackson was pressured to change his diplomatic approach for a more confrontational one, at the same time as Montague required Harvard to serve an injunction against *Emily Dickinson's Home*, scheduled for publication in the autumn of 1950. Harper's executives were Harvard men disinclined to take legal action against their college. They therefore suspended publication of *Home* until the way was clear.

Walter Bingham then asked Harvard for an assurance that they would not object to the book.

Backed by an attorney on 11 October, Jackson stipulated that the Todd collection must come to Harvard, and that while he awaited the handover of the original manuscripts, he wished to make photostats for the newly appointed editor of a complete edition of Dickinson poems. Nothing was said about *Home*, but the Binghams still understood that there was to be a 'trade-off'.

Early in 1951 Jackson arranged to finalise the photostats in Washington, where the Binghams now lived (near where Millicent had lived as a child with her Loomis grandparents*). In preparation for his arrival Millicent sat up until one in the morning to put her negative photostats of Dickinson's poems in order. Next day Jackson collected a suitcase full of these negatives from the Binghams' apartment, 1661 Crescent Place, and took them to the Folger Library to print the negatives. Jackson was there all day, and

---

* The Loomises had lived in College Hill Terrace (now part of Belmont Street) in the Adams Morgan area of North-West Washington.

when he emerged finally at midnight he left behind the prints, parcelled and ready for mailing. He then returned the suitcase of negatives to the Binghams.

At that hour Millicent was asleep; her husband opened the door.

As the two stood face to face, Jackson chose this moment, man to man, to break the news: he can't keep his side of the trade-off.

Silence as the two men confront each other, a verbal high noon at midnight.

Silence. And then, watching Walter Bingham 'hit the ceiling', Jackson aims a second shot: a prepared statement for Bingham's wife to sign. Millicent is to give up her claim. She is to hand over all Dickinson manuscripts. He holds this in front of Bingham's eyes.

Bingham, too kind to be a fighter, struggles to comprehend what is happening. 'You mean to say that you come and get these photostats without which your editor cannot do his work, and then tell me that you can't keep your promise?'

'Oh, I did not think you would take it that way.' Jackson ducks. He can't explain his switch from temperate negotiator to the aggressor of Montague's drama.

'My wife will never sign.' Pained but defiant, Bingham shuts the door on Jackson.

Next morning he staggered to the Folger, retrieved the parcel of positive photostats before it was mailed and put it, unopened, in Millicent's closet. Shock is too tame a word for what he conveyed to his wife. She recounted this stand-off, including dialogue, in a typescript reminiscence of 1955.

Millicent was not to be bullied. Her adversaries had misread her character, mistaking civility for weakness. She thought, had they been straight they could have had the manuscripts. Montague's course, forced on Jackson, proved a disaster. It alienated Millicent and, with that, changed the fate of her collection.

On reflection, it seemed to her correct to send the photostats, so as not to obstruct scholarship, but from now on she refused to hand over her collection to Harvard.

Her parcel was returned unopened. Once confrontation was bared, only the manuscripts themselves were acceptable.

The confrontation hit Walter hard because it was not his way to say an angry word. He believed in goodness, prayed to keep himself 'unspotted from the world' and marked in his Bible 'be ye steadfast, unmovable'. To lose out to a person whose word he had trusted came as a blow with the force to undermine his existence. To the Binghams it was betrayal: they saw their intentions as decent and responsible. The pain was intensified by the fact that the betrayer, 'Harvard', happened to be their university.

Walter felt obliged to go on defending his wife. Over a lunch at the Century Club in New York, he had it out with Jackson. No luck.

One night Millicent woke at three to hear her husband pacing up and down, as she recalled four years later in her account of her husband's battles on her behalf. 'What *is* it, Walter?'

'I was trying to think what I could say to Jackson.'

The more Walter entered into the feud, the harder he breathed. In the summer of 1951, when he had to address an international psychological congress in Gothenburg, he found himself unable to stand, and returned to America in a state of collapse. With a pain in his side and needing an oxygen tent, his problem was diagnosed as a heart condition. Rheumatic fever in childhood had left his heart with a leaky valve, but what Millicent perceived was 'an agony of spirit' that he could not protect her.

Montague's threats to sue Harvard did not deter the university from granting him an honorary degree at Commencement in 1951, the fifty-year reunion of his class of 1901. When he died ten years later the most prominent accolade in the *New York Times* obituary was for donating his Dickinson collection to his alma mater, as though Montague, 'an authority' on the writings of Dickinson, had amassed the manuscripts himself.

If Montague's vanity was salved by the panoply of the degree, it was not for long. He returned to the attack by November of that year. His voice switched easily from the cultivated tone of a bibliophile turning over a rare book to the harshness of a bully: 'bring to terms'; 'compel', 'suit', 'condemnation'. He used threats to break the will of those he perceived as opponents. They might not have been opponents had Montague not positioned them as such – one of the limited categories he assigned to public relations. Faced with a battering of legal threats, Harvard had to take legal advice that defended their right not to sue Mrs Bingham as the way to win her papers. Early in 1952, when the next instalment of $5000 would soon be due, Montague resolved on a 'stand still' policy: to force Harvard to take action against Mrs Bingham, he would suspend payment of the remaining $20,000, and he would continue to suspend the sum until such a time as Mrs Bingham was beaten.

After Alfred died in May 1952 Mary Hampson inherited the Dickinson rights together with The Evergreens, but she lived as though she remained poor – too poor to repair the house or heat it in winter. Each winter she boarded in Reid Hall, an American club for women graduates in Paris where for $105 a month she was provided with a room, heating and food. Why did the sale do little or nothing – or so it appears – to improve her situation in life? While Montague paraded his largesse Mary Hampson made do and did without. In particular, she went in fear of losing her home and quailed at the prospect of a depressing end in a nursing home down the street. In vain did she appeal to Montague for advice on how to protect The Evergreens from the threat of demolition, as though he were a recruit to the Dickinson–Hampson camp, but Montague had no time for her beyond the occasional invitation to admire his garden in Maine or to dine when she passed through New York en route to her winter quarters. For a while she ventured to call him Gilbert, then reverted to Mr Montague after he announced a decision to promote her from Mrs Hampson to Mary Hampson.

The Evergreens collection of 958 manuscript poems, 200 letters, 900 selected books, and items of clothing and furniture came to the Houghton in instalments, all but McCarthy's hoard in his New York apartment. Having bonded with Dickinson, he delayed to hand her over to Harvard until Mary – taking responsibility for what McCarthy should have yielded to the buyer – had to prise manuscripts from his hold. Courteous though Mary was, she no longer trusted McCarthy.

Some time later he explained to Mary how costly it was for Harvard to publish Dickinson's poems. Harvard University Press could give her no more than a royalty of 8¾ per cent. By this stage McCarthy had less time for his dear friend at The Evergreens: these days he's 'weary'. There's an undertone of impatience to his hope that she was satisfied with the outcome. She should be. 'You <u>know</u> I am deeply devoted to you and your interests.' A further 8¾ per cent royalty for the three volumes of Dickinson letters was, McCarthy said, 'most liberal'. 'These funds will allow you to do what you can to keep The Evergreens as you and Martha would like. I am therefore happy and hope that you are.' He hoped further: in years to come, Mary might get a 20 per cent royalty on a paperback edition – an unlikely figure, as it proved. Harvard University Press offered a $1500 advance against 10 per cent royalties (with deductions for a co-publisher and the Houghton). 'A fine proposal', McCarthy urged.

In time Mary came to see how McCarthy had driven the sale. In her quietly stoic manner she reflected that he had not been quite as transparent and disinterested as he'd appeared in the forties.

Jackson came to fear that a continued policy of aggression might lead Mrs Bingham to close off their editor's access to her papers. He feared too that stress compounded by her husband's illness could bring on a breakdown, which would not be in Harvard's interests: if that happened, she and her papers could be incommunicado for as much as a year. Jackson was not in favour of Montague's ferocity and foresaw the damage he could do. Yet he could not find a way to extract himself from the course Montague continued to impose. That promise of the Todd papers in Jackson's initial overture to Montague had granted him a hold over Harvard that he never let go.

Jackson, armed with a lawyer, made a second visit to Washington. The Binghams did not yield. Jackson left saying, 'The wheels of the law grind slowly, but they grind exceedingly small.'

This threat lodged like a bullet in the Binghams and became infected as their position weakened. For in 1952 Lavinia's signed copy of the final contract of 1894 came to light at The Evergreens (filed by mistake with

Mattie's contracts).* Here was incontrovertible evidence that Vinnie had not allowed Mabel Todd a share in the copyright of Emily Dickinson's letters. Mabel had been due to have only a third-to-half share in royalties. This fact went unmentioned in her daughter's statements. She offered in its place a different fact, a claim based on the many years she and her mother had given to the transcription and dating of Dickinson manuscripts. It's the same case her mother had made at the trial half a century earlier.

Washington, June 1952. The Binghams' doctor urged Millicent to go away because her 'aura of frustration' was not conducive to Walter's recovery. She did go, to Hog Island. Sadly after three weeks, on 7 July, Walter died in her absence. His words, when Millicent took on the feud, now appeared prophetic: 'it may get us before it is finished'.

In her record of her husband's battles, Millicent had to ask herself if she sacrificed her husband on the altar of Mamma.

Inevitably, in a typescript reminiscence, Millicent fixed instead on the usual scapegoat: Susan Dickinson was the true cause of Walter's death. 'His anguish over the sacrifice of me to the vengeance of a woman scorned three-quarters of a century ago was to him a death-blow.'

The next scene opens at a professional women's club, the Cosmopolitan Club in New York. It's September 1952, and along comes Thomas H. Johnson, the new editor of the Dickinson papers. Could Mrs Bingham give him her photostats, even though she will not hand over the manuscripts to Harvard? Without her hundreds of photostats he cannot complete the task ahead. It's a personal plea, and she agrees.

Another scene amongst Millicent's reminiscences: Washington. Johnson and Millicent are in a car travelling from the Folger Library on Capitol Hill to her apartment in the North-West sector of the city. Johnson is sweating. Millicent sees the spots of perspiration on his forehead as he beseeches her to hand over her manuscripts to Harvard.

---

* Mary Hampson's Boston lawyer, Mr Dow, commented in 1960 that the other copy of the final 1894 contract, the publisher's copy, which Mabel Todd bought from the New York dealer in 1931, had 'probably been destroyed' – that is, by the Todd camp.

No, she can't. She has lost her husband and her book is banned from publication.

In 1953 Montague steps in to try his hand with obdurate Mrs Bingham. Mrs Bingham is invited to view his latest acquisition, an 1840 Webster dictionary belonging to Edward Dickinson. He would like to consult her about it.

Millicent does not take to Montague's use of a pretext for seeing her. She has no plan to visit New York, she replies.

Montague is not to be deterred, for he wants at least to know what papers still lie in the Chinese chest. Mary Hampson has been unable to tell him what is missing from the collection he bought. If he knew more precisely what Mrs Bingham retains, he might have a surer basis for legal proceedings. So he calls Mrs Bingham long-distance to announce a visit to Washington: again, there's the pretext of the dictionary. And again, politely but firmly, Mrs Bingham shuts the door: she can tell him nothing about his acquisition.

The next try is by Jackson's wife. At Christmas 1953 she will be staying with a friend in Mrs Bingham's apartment block. Would Mrs Bingham come for tea? Regretfully, Mrs Bingham cannot make it.

At length, in 1954, lawyers were brought in on both sides to knock through the impasse. Harvard was prepared to lift the ban on *Home* if Mrs Bingham would print an assent to Harvard's ownership of the rights to all Dickinson papers. Since there was no other way to publish her work, she had to agree. In November of that year Harper brought out the smaller and more exciting of the two books Millicent Bingham had by now prepared. During this period of defeat and loss she had taken out the last bundle from the chest. It contained Dickinson's drafts of letters to Judge Lord. Mabel Todd had endorsed the Wadsworth myth and kept the letters to Lord under wraps. These letters must not interfere with the cult figure who renounced the warm nearness of a lover. 'She was a creature too ethereal for marriage,' Mabel had said, 'too holy for commonplace life.'

The Emily who liked the Judge's touch does not bear out this image. She was not, after all, invariably withdrawn; not a flitting, bodiless phantom of delight; she was a physical being, confessing a physical love with extraordinary freedom to a particular man. Millicent opened a letter Emily wrote to Judge Lord after one of his visits.

'My lovely Salem smiles at me,' Millicent read. 'I seek his face so often – but I have done with guises. I confess that I love him – I rejoice that I love him – I thank the Maker of Heaven and Earth that gave him me to love – the Exaltation floods me – I cannot find my channel. The Creek turns Sea – at thought of thee . . . Incarcerate me in yourself.'

This nineteenth-century woman had felt a touch so keenly that it lingered into the night when she lay alone in bed. She could not bring herself to wash. Water would have calmed her, but she did not want calm. This is the woman of 'wild nights'. Whether it was the wildness of flesh or spirit, it's consistent with the intensity of her response to all experience, as Dorothy Wordsworth observed in her brother, the poet: 'a violence of Affection' that never sleeps. The biographer Frances Wilson, writing of wildness and desire in Dorothy herself, sees that the problem was not Dorothy's; the problem is a public who expects Dorothy to be strange and sexless. The same applies to Emily Dickinson. Having read these letters long ago, Mabel Todd had passed on her deduction to Millicent. It was that Susan, not liking sex and still less the sight of Emily in the Judge's arms, had covered it up with the chaste Wadsworth story.

Millicent understood the tenacity of legend. Ahead of others, she saw that 'by the dint of much repetition the [Wadsworth] legend has become firmly rooted'. She tried to alert readers to something genuinely startling with her title, *A Revelation*, for her book would prove that Dickinson's withdrawal from the world cannot be explained by dedication to one love for ever. Yet this book went more or less unnoticed, and curiously this persisted twenty years later when an influential Dickinson biographer said that she gave her heart 'vainly' to Judge Lord.

In May 1955 *Home* finally came out, five years after delivery. Here Millicent repeats what Austin had told her mother: at different times Emily had been devoted to different men. She'd been in love several times 'in her own way'. His sister, Austin said, had reached out toward anyone who kindled her. Again, Millicent Bingham ridicules 'the legend that Emily Dickinson became a recluse because of a broken heart'. According to Austin, the poet's seclusion had been gradual, not a reaction to parting.

Home, too, had little attention. Millicent believed it eclipsed by Johnson's three-volume edition of the poems, even though the latter came out six months later. In accord with the Hampsons' stipulations in 1950, Johnson printed no acknowledgement to Millicent Todd Bingham for abundant help, nor for *Bolts of Melody*, though her toil over six hundred poems was absorbed into this edition. Montague, ever vigilant against the Todd camp, had seen fit to enforce this two years earlier, in October 1953: Johnson's edition (still current in England as the standard edition) was 'to contain no mention whatever of Mrs. Bingham, and no expression of appreciation or thanks to her for anything she has done for [Johnson]'.

Millicent believed that the publication of *Home* was permitted because Johnson required its information for an *Interpretative Biography* of Dickinson. She took a poor view of this biography on the grounds that Johnson was a 'compiler' rather than a writer, rehashing what others thought, including the Wadsworth myth.

After fulfilling her promise to Mamma with her two last books, Millicent could do no more with her collection. Alert as ever, Montague tried one more approach in December 1955. Shameless over his role in her injuries, he wrote to her in the 'unctuous' manner she remembered. He wished Mrs Bingham to know that he could not approach Christmas without recalling the loss of her husband. He himself had borne similar loss and loneliness for many years. 'Time does not lessen either the loneliness or the grief,' she replied gravely, refusing to be drawn. Soon after, in 1956, she presented her collection of Dickinson manuscripts to Amherst College. The following year the college awarded her an honorary degree.

'As recognition of Emily Dickinson has grown apace,' said President Cole, 'it has brought with it an increasing realization of the debt owed to your mother and to you . . . by all whose minds are touched or whose hearts are quickened by that eternal and penetrating beauty of the lines written by America's greatest poet here on Main Street in Amherst Town.'

Nothing was said of the papers, to Millicent's regret (as she records in her reminiscences). She did understand that Amherst had to exercise tact in view of Harvard, and not imply that the papers had been in her gift. Amherst did not intend to fight a legal battle on behalf of the Todd camp, as Millicent continued to urge. In October 1957 she stayed at the Dickinson Homestead as a guest of Priscilla Parke, whose family had bought the house in 1916. Mary Hampson was aware of Millicent's presence next door, but there was no move towards reconciliation from either side.

How long can a feud persist? Endlessly, it seems, given the rarity of the prize. Millicent was the sole contender to experience doubt.

'Did Vinnie ask to have the manuscripts returned?' She had asked herself this question long before, in notes for a talk with her father dated 29 September–2 October 1933. 'Did Vinnie make a will leaving copyrights to Mamma?' To the second question the answer had to be a reluctant 'No', added in pencil at the time she typed up these notes in old age.

She never got over Walter's premature death. In a typescript of 1959 she remembers his arms around her at night and how he would draw her head towards his chest saying, 'that's where she belongs'. Doubts and sadness, though, did not make her less determined when she pursued descendants of the Dickinson family to probe their grievances against Cousin Mattie. In her late eighties Millicent did not neglect to preserve her record for the benefit of future biographers.

Emily Dickinson had once sent a poem to her father's sister, Catherine Sweetser, and in 1931 Mrs Sweetser's granddaughter Kate Dickinson Sweetser printed this poem in a chapter on Emily Dickinson as 'A Girl of Genius' in Sweetser's book, *Great American Girls*. Millicent came up with a sorry tale: Kate, who was lame, received a rebuke from Cousin Mattie, ordering Cousin Kate never to write about Emily again and demanding $25 due to Mattie as owner of the rights. Millicent adds a coda to the effect that when she contacted Kate a few years later, Kate was 'in much pain' and barely able to pay doctor's bills. Charitable, indignant Millicent then steps in to help Kate raise money on her jewels. Millicent is therefore in a position to report how Cousin Kate died 'with a curse on her lips' for Mattie.

Part of the cumulative force of the Todd-Bingham archive that Millicent would leave to Yale included the huge array of her mother's papers, the memoir-essays of the enfeebled octopus she had felt herself to be and a set of taped interviews in the late fifties and early sixties, the last of them, on 17 June 1963 and 31 May 1964, with Yale professor Richard Sewall.

Well before she died, Millicent set up a posthumous campaign in a way that could not fail. Her plan was to co-opt an authoritative writer of impeccable credentials for a book she had in mind. It was a venture Mamma had nearly brought off with Amy Lowell in the early twenties. In 1960 Millicent was far from accepting defeat when she appointed Sewall her literary executor. On the eve of her eightieth birthday she was devising a comeback for her camp when she granted Sewall exclusive rights to her mother's papers, Austin Dickinson's diaries and the letters of Austin and Mabel.

Her partisan agenda was clear: this executor was to 'set the whole network of Dickinson tensions in proper perspective. Eventually Mrs. Austin Dickinson's desire for revenge will appear as the drive back of (1) her husband's death, (2) Lavinia's death, (3) the malignant enmity of her daughter.' Millicent intended her executor or his appointee to unbury the truth she could never expose: 'My life . . . should have my reading of those letters [by Austin and Mabel] as its climax.'

So it came about that Sewall revived the Todd position in a full-scale biography of Emily Dickinson, published in 1974, six years after Millicent's death. In one of the two volumes Sewall fills in the family and Amherst contexts pioneered by Millicent Bingham in *Emily Dickinson's Home*, and summarises the Austin–Mabel affair from the lovers' point of view. What appears as corroborating evidence is the archive that mother and daughter had constructed and preserved over the course of ninety years.

The Todds' most effective weapon in the long term turned out to be their daughter. Mabel's persuasive grace in presenting her point of view was reinforced by the educated rigour of Millicent's voice on tape. In a tense voice, searching her memory, she took Professor Sewall through the legal history of the feud, bristling with facts and dates. These she laid out in the orderly manner of a scholar. To the unwary her testimony would appear

precise, objective, informed, and yet in every instance the Todds turn out
to be victims of the Dickinsons. To hear the tapes is to understand her
impact on a biographer. Sewall felt 'haunted' by Austin's statement that he
went to his wedding as to his execution. Only no one can know what
Austin said: the image of execution was transmitted by Mabel.

A biographer tempted by exclusive access to an archive of such eloquence and intelligence is bound to be influenced. Future readers will be
able to judge where Sewall succumbed to the vast trove of Todd untruths:
that Emily Dickinson favoured Mabel; that the poet's withdrawal into
seclusion and the violence in her poems was the result of a family split preceding Mabel's appearance; and that Austin himself 'deeded' to the Todds
the strip of land that became the basis of the court case. The biographer
even outdoes the Todds when he suggests that Dickinson's 'failure' to publish was a result of the family quarrel. This is consistent with the Todd
campaign: an 'alien', ambitious intruder into the family – Susan
Dickinson – had to be at the bottom of whatever appeared weird or wrong.
As the standard biography it was a long-term victory for the Todd camp,
shaping opinion for decades to come.

In 1972 Sewall opened the archive to Polly Longsworth when she began
to work on the lovers. *Austin and Mabel*, published in 1984, is meticulously
researched, with well-judged commentaries, but it does introduce Susan
Dickinson 'as a woman whose magnetism concealed vindictiveness' and
'whose intellect was self-serving and sometimes cruel'.

Inevitably, as the Todds' bias infiltrated commentaries it spread to other
genres: cultural history and fiction. Peter Gay's *Education of the Senses* (1984),
drawing on Mabel Todd's sexual candour, repeats the Todd untruths that
Austin Dickinson married Susan in obedience to his family and that Emily
Dickinson condoned Austin's affair. The Todd bias remains active, echoed
by Sewall's readers and the students they teach, many unaware of the
virus of hate and their role as carriers. Amongst these are recent practi-
tioners of bio-fiction. In *The Sister* by Paula Kaufmann (2006), a cruel and
spiteful Sue ends up 'hating' Emily. In *Afternoons with Emily* by Rose
MacMurray (2007), Sue has mutated from Black Moghul to death-dealing
Lucrezia Borgia. The Evergreens is Sue's 'Borgia Palace', an estranged

'Emily' warns the young narrator of the tale. 'That is where Sue will hatch her plots and do her poisonings.' She awaits her victims in the hall, a vamp in décolleté black velvet waving her fan. Can evil go further? It can. Sue 'could make mincemeat pie of the Dickinson sisters and eat it for Christmas dinner'.

In support of Susan, a 'Sister' camp came into force towards the end of the century. In 1998, when Ellen Louise Hart and Martha Nell Smith examined an ardent poem Dickinson wrote in about 1859, 'Her breast is fit for pearls', they saw the word 'Sue' erased from the verso of the pencilled draft that the poet sent to Sue, who then passed it on to Samuel and Mary Bowles. This erasure (one of many, as we know) allowed Mabel Todd to place this poem with letters to Bowles in the 1894 edition of the *Letters*, with an absurd suggestion that it was written in honour of miserable Mrs Bowles:

> Her breast is fit for pearls,
> But I was not a 'Diver' —
> Her brow is fit for thrones
> But I have not a crest,
> Her heart is fit for <u>home</u> —
> I — a Sparrow — build there ⁻
> Sweet of twigs and twine
> My perennial nest.
>
> Emily —

The important correctives of the Sister camp extend to a stand against print culture, arguing that print is liable to distort the lineation and punctuation in the vast oeuvre of manuscripts unpublished in the poet's lifetime. These scholars, led by Martha Nell Smith, make the case for posting scans of Dickinson manuscripts on the internet as the only form of publication free from editorial intervention.

This is a courageous group, and necessarily partisan. A 1998 dedication of *Open Me Carefully*, a compilation of Dickinson's writings to Sue, makes this clear: the book is for Mattie Dickinson and Mary Hampson, and to defend the love of Susan and Emily. Dickinson's outspoken ardour did embrace members of her own sex, and no one more than 'Sister'. At the same time, she was not impervious to the opposite sex. It is as vital to redress slanders on Sue's behalf as to consider the variables of Dickinson's sexual nature and changes of fashion in language. The language of love flowed freely in the correspondence of nineteenth-century women. Even so, the poet is less casual to judge from the calculated gender shift in 'Amputate my freckled bosom! / Make me bearded like a man!' Although there's no evidence that she put same-sex love into practice, the sustained improvisation of imaginative love can be more passionate and enduring than finite physical acts, and Dickinson celebrates the constancy of the unmarried 'Wife' who feels like a man. Yet nothing Dickinson feels quite fits our labels because her spark of spiritual connection carries her off even as she stirs our unseen selves.

V: OUTLIVING THE LEGEND

Mary Hampson lived to her nineties. Faithful to the last, she preserved everything left at The Evergreens. When she died in 1988 the door shut on a time capsule. The melancholy house remained much as it was in the 1880s. By June 2003 it had been uninhabited for fifteen years. When the key turned and the door opened on the shuttered hall its reds crept out of the shadow: faded red wallpaper in tatters and a worn carpet of the same colour leading the way upstairs. A relic of the Homestead was the first to emerge from the murk: a sofa that Sue had covered in dark red velvet, once the black horsehair sofa where Austin and Mabel had held together throughout 1884, defying the rows next door.

All the while, the fame of Emily Dickinson spread throughout the world. This was both sure and gradual, like an invisible path through a thicket that opens into a series of clearings. We glimpse her here and there until the poet emerges, as she foresaw a century and a half ago, one of the 'favorites' amongst the all-time few:

> Eternity's disclosure
> To favorites — a few —
> Of the Colossal substance
> Of Immortality

Unanswered and unanswerable questions resonate in the wake of lives, and no one more elusive than Emily Dickinson. She warned Higginson not to take the 'I' of her poems to be herself. Was this a cover? 'I' speaks of inward event with singular assurance: the divine Guest who keeps her company. 'The Soul that hath a Guest / Doth seldom go abroad —', she wrote at about the age of thirty-two, and then again at forty-nine: 'Immortality as a guest is sacred'. How much was genuine confession, how much dramatic monologue? The theatricality of her confessions was, at origin, a mode of rebellion against the sober, heartfelt declarations of faith expected of her milieu – the sole public drama open to a woman of her time and place. Behind her door behind the hedge a flagrant voice burst into alternative confessions: visions, 'Master', forbidden passion, wild nights.

There is no doubt of the prime drama of Dickinson's life: the incursions of 'The Spirit'. She confided to Judge Lord: 'The Spirit never twice alike, but every time another – the other more divine.' As readers of the 'price-less' future – the poet's intimates – we are allowed a glimpse (the little we can take) of the Guest from beyond our world. What happened, she tells us, is a 'Flash — / And Click — and Suddenness', as though lightning opened up a sacred place. To this place she feels a 'distinct connection'.

The 'waylaying Light' removed her from official versions of the super-natural. In this the visionary Emily Brontë was her familiar. Neither she nor Dickinson fits the pious mould because they are fearless – anything but meek. 'Life is so strong a vision' for Dickinson that nothing she sees 'can fail'. Were it not for 'partings' with those she loved, living was 'too divine'. 'Partings', she says. Not loss. The dead are near as the divine is near in the way Emily Brontë felt and affirmed: even if creation itself came to an end, 'Every existence would exist in Thee'. Others who wait on the spirit are daunted by failure when they find themselves sealed off. George Herbert protests against protracted waiting: 'I struck the board and cried / No more, I will abroad'; Hopkins cries, 'No worst, there is none'; and Eliot is depressed by the evanescence of the infinite 'thing'. He regrets the 'waste sad time / Stretching before and after'. Unlike them, Dickinson does not feel abandoned. She is an ecstatic. 'Take all away from me, but leave me Ecstasy', she said during her last illness.

Obscuring the drama of Emily Dickinson's legacy have been the dust-heaps of slander and sentimental conjecture that fortified the battlers in the war between the houses. When Mabel Todd visited the Homestead for the first time in September 1882, she imagined Emily Dickinson a Miss Havisham, a disappointed bride turned eccentric recluse. I suspect that behind Todd's conjectures and slanders lurks the real Miss Havisham of this story: a proud beauty betrayed by her chosen bridegroom, not at the altar but soon after, when David Todd resumed his philandering. Millicent stood by her mother as, in Dickens, Estella stands by Miss Havisham, becoming her creature. All the same no one formed Mabel more than Susan Dickinson during their idyll of 1881–2, when Susan invited Mabel into the family and introduced her to the poems of Emily Dickinson. There *was* a future in wait for Mabel Todd. If she appears to shadow the poet, angling for the poet's attention, and sets up her editorial workshop as Susan's rival, there was more to it: Mabel had qualities in common with the poet, a basis for identification. Both were founts of eloquence; both felt like queens; both were strong-willed, controlling; and, above all, both were workers with terrific application. Both amassed vast archives with an eye to the future.

These similarities had to be less compelling for the poet, if not irrelevant, beside her affinity for Susan who mirrored the poet as 'Nobody' in the unseen space of lives destined to be distorted. While Sue became a dependent wife, Emily held to the rare thing she was. This shadow life was as far as can be from the visibility of Mabel Todd. In appropriating Emily Dickinson for the public spotlight in which Mabel moved and had her being, Mabel did all she could to negate Sue's tie with the poet.

This has been a story of the buried life after all: Emily and Austin and Vinnie firing up at the spark Mabel touched off when she flirted with Austin's buried passions and intruded on the Homestead and coveted the shadow-world of Sue and Emily. But to touch off that spark was Austin's doing as well as Mabel's. The feud was not wholly something that was done to the Dickinsons but was in some sense a sequel to what they were.

Fifteen years after Mary Hampson's death, her dream came true. In June 2003 the house appeared sunk in gloom; the following month, it opened its door to the public as a museum. The two family houses are once again conjoined, The Evergreens an extension of the museum next door to commemorate the great poet. It is fitting to see her in relation to the intimacies and dramas of this two-house family. Visitors walk between the houses. The deep reds of The Evergreens' hall gleam in contrast to the whites and beige of the Homestead. The gloom, though, has vanished together with the dust and papers.

The poet foresaw us visitors of the future, viewing what's left: how gullible we could be as we turn over clues to the modest littleness of her person and the quaint little ambition that took its own way. A poem mocks our attempts to track her steps. That she struck out alone we do see, little tracks 'close prest'. Then her tracks disappear. Is she lost to sight? But no: her 'little Book', hat and worn shoe are found.

Relics do indeed remain: the poet's white dress on display in her room at the Homestead; her square piano, her chest of drawers and the books in the Dickinson Room at the Houghton Library; and there too the oval brooch she pinned at her throat, the brown velvet snood that held back her red hair and the crocheted wrap she wore when Mr Higginson came to call in 1870.

The only secret people keep is 'Immortality', Dickinson once said. Immortality is the mystery at the core of her story.

> Impregnable we are —
> The whole of Immortality
> Secreted in a Star

The 'Queen of Amherst' (as Mabel dubbed herself) and Dickinson's queen of immortality: where Mabel Todd's eminence resides in her editorial feat, the queen's head embossed on the poet's stationery* rules by divine right. The crown is so tall it doubles the length of the face and is surmounted by a ring of gems like stars, an emblem of power so radiant that this queen must shield our eyes with the façades she assumed: an 'old-fashioned' spinster, a shy recluse, a vulnerable mistress to a 'Master' whose bullet hits a Bird. Her secret self was other, a Noon blaze rising from the dark, and so rare that no word, no colour can convey who she is:

> Can Blaze be shown in Cochineal† —
> Or Noon — in Mazarin‡?

---

* The embossed queen appears above the 'M' of 'Master' in the final Master letter and also in the booklets.
† Scarlet dye.
‡ Royal blue.

Dickinson found love, a quickened spirit and freedom, her 'Mortal Abolition', all on her own terms. She was in many ways a moral being, a product of upright New England. In her thirties she grasped the potential disruption – to her sanity for a start – of a hidden life like a 'Bomb' in her bosom. The poetry it fuelled must be seen in terms of New England individualism, the Emersonian ethos of self-reliance which in its fullest bloom eludes classification. It's more radical and quirky than anything in Europe, more awkward and less lovable than English eccentricity; in fact, dangerous. Control was a constant necessity, reasserted through the strictures of the hymnbook verse. Though, on occasion, the gun turned on others, most of the time it went off in the poet's own head, a repeat annihilation built into her body by a Maker she called 'Master' – her real Master.

'God made me', she said in self-defence to a masked earthy Master, 'I did'nt be – myself.'

She could not be responsible for her intensity nor for the 'sickness' that determined a homebound life. Yet, of course, it was a life that made for the full-scale production of the 'Opera'. Her voice soars and the scenes of life pass and recede en route to the grave: schoolchildren at recess in a ring; the path through the grass to Sister next door; the Master drama; the loss of her father and her turn to Judge Lord; and then the setting sun and swift onset of poetic immortality. The claims of warring camps – their tampering, excisions, myth-making – can't blur the integrity of words kept as long as possible in her own hands. No other poet can speak so intimately of life after death when she calls back to us that her journey is unfinished, even now. A dash at the end of her last line leads us on. She is centuries ahead as we read, and still her voice is coming:

> Since then —— 'tis Centuries —— and yet
> Feels shorter than the Day
> I first surmised the Horses' Heads
> Were toward Eternity ——

SOURCES

The main repository of Dickinson family papers, as well as Dickinson's poems, letters, books, memorabilia and furniture, is the Houghton Library, Harvard University. There is another major Dickinson collection in the Archives and Special Collections at Amherst College. The main repository for Mabel Loomis Todd papers is the archives of Sterling Library at Yale University. This includes papers of William Austin Dickinson and of Mabel Todd's daughter, Millicent Todd Bingham, as well as the typescript record of the court case that Lavinia Dickinson brought against Mabel Loomis Todd in 1898. An off-the-record but influential deposition in the run-up to the trial, by Maggie Maher, servant to the Dickinson sisters, is in the legal archives in Worcester, Massachusetts. Jones Library in Amherst specialises in the history of the town. Susan Dickinson's papers, and those of her surviving children, Ned Dickinson and Martha Dickinson Bianchi, are at the John Hay Library of Brown University in Providence, Rhode Island. Bianchi's revealing correspondence with her publisher, Houghton Mifflin, is in the Houghton Library, as is the fascinating correspondence to do with the Library's acquisition of the Dickinson Collection, a story in which the old tensions between adversarial camps continued to function.

The sources go beyond manuscripts and print, since the poet has an impact on music, dance and theatre, including theatre director Katie Mitchell's innovative production of . . . *some trace of her*, a play inspired by *The*

Idiot by Dostoyevsky and using poems by Dickinson in the National Theatre (Cottesloe), London (2008); Martha Graham's choreography and performance of *Letter to the World* (1940, in the archives of the Martha Graham Center of Dance Records at the New York Public Library for the Performing Arts at the Lincoln Center, New York); John Adams's eerie choral setting for 'Because I could not stop for Death' in *Harmonium*; and the rare transparency of Juliet Stevenson's reading on stage at the British Library, recorded on a CD accompanying a selection of Dickinson's poems in Josephine Hart's *Catching Life by the Throat* (London: Virago, 2006; NY: Norton, 2007).

Songwriters are influenced by Dickinson. British star Pete Doherty picks up lines from 'I took one Draught of Life — / I'll tell you what I paid —' which he discusses in 'Emily Dickinson? She's hardcore', an extraordinary interview in the *Guardian* (3 Oct 2006). Carla Bruni sings (in English) 'I felt my life with both my hands / To see if it was there —' in her album *No Promises* (2008). Californian M. Ward expresses an affinity for Dickinson's combination of familiarity with the otherworldly. See interview in *Relix* music magazine (6 Jan 2009) <http:www.relix.com/Features/Interviews/SPOTLIGHT%3A_M._WARD_200901063594.html>

Abbot, John S. C. (John Stevens Cabot), *Mother at Home: Principles of Maternal Duty* (1833). Copies in Emily Dickinson Room, Houghton Library; in the Mudd Library, Yale: Lf30 833ab WB 7459; and in Library of Congress

Adams, Henry, druggist and apothecary, Amherst, record of prescriptions (1882–5). Amherst College Archives and Special Collections

Bennett, the Revd John, *Letters to a Young Lady* (1789; repr. NY, 1824). Copy in Emily Dickinson Room, Houghton Library

Bianchi, Martha Gilbert Dickinson, Papers. Houghton: MS Am 1118.96

——, Papers, John Hay Library, Brown University

——, Scrapbook, with Susan Dickinson's stories. John Hay Library, Brown University: St Armand Collection: 126. Available in Dickinson Electronic Archives (below)

——, 318 letters to Theodore Longfellow Frothingham. Houghton: bMS Am 1118.96

——, *The Cossack Lover* (NY: Duffield, 1911). Copy in Library of Congress. She also published *Russian Lyrics and Cossack Songs*

——, 'Letters of Emily Dickinson', *Atlantic Monthly* (Jan 1915). Copy in Jones Library

——, 258 letters to publisher, Houghton Mifflin (1924–42). Houghton: bMS Am 1925 (197)

————, Correspondence concerning publication of Emily Dickinson. Houghton: bMS Am 1118.97–1118.98 <http:/nrs.harvard.edu/urn-3:FHCL.Hough:hou02016>

————, Correspondence with William McCarthy (1930–43). Houghton: bMS Am 1118.97–1118.98 (123)

————, Correspondence with Amherst attorney Henry Field. Houghton: bMS Am 1118.97–1118.98 (79)

————, Correspondence with Amy Angell Collier Montague (1900–43). Manuscripts and Archives Division, New York Public Library: Montague-Collier Family Papers

————, Correspondence with Ned Dickinson. Hay Library, Brown University

————, (ed.), *The Single Hound* (1914; repr. London: Hesperus Press, 2005)

————, *The Life and Letters of Emily Dickinson* (Boston: Houghton Mifflin, 1924). Yale archives has Millicent Todd Bingham's copy with marginalia: 'Bosh!' and 'ugh' and 'oh, yeah?'

————, *Emily Dickinson: Face to Face: Unpublished Letters with Notes and Reminiscence*, with Foreword by Alfred Leete Hampson (Boston: Houghton Mifflin, 1932)

Bingham, Millicent Todd, Papers. Manuscripts and Archives, Yale University Library <http://mssa.library.yale.edu/findaids/stream.php?id=mss&colNum=0496&xml-file=mssa.ms.0496d.xml&srch=bingham%20todd&sch=ead>

————, *Ancestors' Brocades: The Literary Début of Emily Dickinson* (NY: Harper, 1945)

————, *Emily Dickinson: A Revelation* (NY: Harper, 1954)

————, *Emily Dickinson's Home: Letters of Edward Dickinson and Family* (NY: Harper, 1955; repr. Dover, 1967)

————, Correspondence with Amy Lowell. Houghton: bMS Lowell 19 (95) and 19.1 (99)

————, Letters to Theodora Ward, granddaughter of Dickinson correspondents, Dr and Mrs Holland (1945–54). Houghton: *7OM-33

————, with Raoul Blanchard (Professor of Geography, University of Grenoble), *A Geography of France* (Chicago: Rand McNally. 1919)

————, (trans. from the French), *Principles of Human Geography* by P. Vidal de La Blache (London: Constable, 1926)

————, Autobiographical typescripts. Yale: Bingham Papers, mainly box 46.

————, 'Notes for Autobiography'. Yale: Bingham Papers. Cited in Richard B. Sewall, *Life of Emily Dickinson*, i, 294–301. These rather scrappy 'Notes' do not indicate the abundance of these typescripts

————, Correspondence with Mrs George E. Pearl (Clara Pearl), daughter of Anna Newman (Mrs George H. Carleton), who lived at The Evergreens in her youth. Yale: box 84, f.258a, together with letter from Mrs Pearl to Mrs Bingham (15 Sept 1932) 'boiling' with animosity towards Martha Dickinson Bianchi. The date is a month before the attack of 'apoplexy' that killed Mabel Loomis Todd

————, 'Notes taken during the talk with my father' (typed Oct 1967, from notes she dates on TS as 29 Sept–3 Oct 1933, but the original notes go back to 1927, the year she began to abandon her academic career and join her parents' camp). Yale: box 47, f.14. David Todd's striking memories of the first transcriptions of Dickinson's poems in the late 1880s and early 1890s

————, Letters to Gilbert Montague (1945–55). Manuscripts and Archives Division, New York Public Library: Montague-Collier Family Papers, box 1

————, Article on Millicent Todd Bingham in *Current Biography* (June 1961), 10–12. Copy in Yale: Bingham Papers, box 46, f.1

————, Four tapes (3 May 1957; Dec 1958; 17 June 1963; and 31 May 1964). Historical Sound Recordings, Music Library, Sterling Library, Yale

Bowles, Samuel, 156 letters to Austin and Susan Dickinson. Houghton: bMS Am 1118.8

————, 'An annotated calendar of Samuel Bowles's letters to Austin and Susan Dickinson', by Alfred Habegger and Nellie Habegger, *Emily Dickinson Journal*, 11/2 (Fall 2002), 1–47. Dating and excerpts.

Cutter, Calvin, *Anatomy and Physiology* (repr. Boston: Mussey, 1854). Dickinson's textbook at South Hadley. Copy in Radcliffe Science Library, Oxford

Dickerman, Elizabeth (of Amherst and Smith College class of 1894), 'Portrait of Two Sisters: Emily and Lavinia Dickinson', *Smith Alumnae Quarterly*, 45/2 (Feb 1954), 79. Copy at Smith College, Northampton, Massachusetts

Dickinson Papers, including Family Papers. Houghton: bMS Am 1118.95. Arranged by first line.
1. Inventory by William McCarthy when poems first came to the Library in 1951.
2. Rearrangement of the booklets by editor, Thomas H. Johnson, in 1952.
3. Inventory of letters and contents of Dickinson Papers by Jay Leyda.
4. Rearrangement of the poems by R. W. Franklin: see *The Editing of Emily Dickinson* (1967), *The Manuscript Books* (1981) and the three-volume edition of 1998 that includes poems taken from letters (a questionable disruption of what some regard as cross-genre letter poems)

Dickinson library. Emily Dickinson Room, Houghton. This library brings together all Dickinson-owned books, belonging to both households, the Homestead and The Evergreens.

Dickinson, Edward (the poet's father), essay signed 'Coelebs' (from Hannah More's bestseller, *Coelebs in Search of a Wife*), for the *New England Enquirer.* Houghton: bMS Am 1118.95

————, Letters in Bingham, *Emily Dickinson's Home*, above

————, *A Poet's Parents: The Courtship Letters of Emily Norcross and Edward Dickinson*, ed. Vivian R. Pollak (Chapel Hill: University of North Carolina Press, 1988)

Dickinson, Edward (Ned, the poet's nephew), '"Your Prodigal": Letters from Ned Dickinson, 1879–1885', put together with commentary by Barton Levi St Armand, *New England Quarterly*, 61/3 (1988), 358–80

————, 125 letters to parents; also, letters to his sister when feud began. Hay Library, Brown University

————, 79 letters to Theodore Longfellow Frothingham. Houghton: MS Am 1996

————, Letter to his aunt, Lavinia Dickinson (1896). Houghton: MS Am 1118.96

Dickinson, Emily Elizabeth, *Poems*, ed. Mabel Loomis Todd and Thomas Wentworth Higginson (Boston: Roberts Bros, 1890). Copy in Pierpont Morgan Library, New York. Accession no: 42563. Location: E-3 87 E

————, *Poems: Second Series*, ed. Thomas Wentworth Higginson and Mabel Loomis Todd (Roberts Bros, 1891). Pierpont Morgan Library. Accession no: 42120. Location as above.

————, *Poems: Third Series*, ed. Mabel Loomis Todd (Roberts Bros, 1896). Pierpont Morgan Library. Accession: 42121. Location as above

————, 'Emily Dickinson's Letters' by T. W. Higginson (*Atlantic Monthly*, Oct 1891) in Robert N. Linscott, ed., *Selected Poems & Letters of Emily Dickinson* (1959)

————, *Open Me Carefully: Emily Dickinson's Intimate Letters to Susan Huntingdon Dickinson*, ed. Ellen Louise Hart and Martha Nell Smith (Ashfield, MA: Paris Press, 1998)

————, *Further Poems of Emily Dickinson: Withheld from Publication by her sister Lavinia, edited by her niece Martha Dickinson Bianchi and Alfred Leete Hampson* (Boston: Little, Brown, 1929). A limited edition of 465 copies

————, *Bolts of Melody*, ed. Mabel Loomis Todd and Millicent Todd Bingham (NY: Harper, 1945)

————, *The Poems of Emily Dickinson*, 3 vols, ed. Thomas H. Johnson (Cambridge, MA: Belknap Press of Harvard University Press, 1955). Little, Brown's one-volume reading edition repr. as *The Complete Poems of Emily Dickinson* (London: Faber, 1976, repr. 2003)

————, *Final Harvest*, Thomas H. Johnson's selection (Boston: Little, Brown, 1961)

————, *The Manuscript Books of Emily Dickinson*, 2 vols, ed. R. W. Franklin (Cambridge, MA: Belknap Press of Harvard University Press, 1981)

————, *The Poems of Emily Dickinson: Variorum Edition*, 3 vols, ed. R. W. Franklin (Cambridge, MA: Belknap Press of Harvard University Press, 1998)

————, *Emily Dickinson's Open Folios: Scenes of Reading, Surfaces of Writing: An Experimental Edition of Emily Dickinson's Drafts and Fragments*, ed. Marta L. Werner (Ann Arbor: University of Michigan Press, c. 1995). Associated with the poet's Otis Lord correspondence

————, *The Letters of Emily Dickinson*, i–iii, ed. Thomas H. Johnson and Theodora Van Wagenen Ward (Cambridge, MA: Belknap Press of Harvard University Press, 1958)

————, *Concordance to the Poems of Emily Dickinson*, ed. S. P. Rosenbaum (Ithaca: Cornell University Press, 1964)

————, *Concordance to the Letters of Emily Dickinson*, ed. Cynthia MacKenzie with Penny Gilbert (Boulder: University Press of Colorado, 2000)

————, manuscript letters 537, 539, 591, 948 to Maria Whitney, whose full texts were excised by Mabel Loomis Todd, in accord with Whitney's wish, in the 1894 edition of Dickinson letters. The excised texts were used for the supposedly complete Johnson edition of 1958 before the manuscripts came to light in the Houghton Library. Mabel Loomis Todd printed the last of these excised bits, on Bowles's light-giving glance, as a detached and unidentified fragment

————, Guide to Houghton collection of letters <http://oasis.harvard.edu/html/hou00202.html>

————, *The Master Letters of Emily Dickinson*, ed. R. W. Franklin (Amherst: Amherst College Press, 1986). A few lines from one of the three letters (mis-dated as 1885) had appeared in Mabel Loomis Todd's selection of 1894. Millicent Todd Bingham was the first to publish these letters in *Emily Dickinson's Home* (1955), 422–32

————, Calling card. Jones Library

————, *Emily Dickinson's Herbarium: A Facsimile Edition*, Foreword by Leslie A. Morris, Preface by Judith Farr, Introduction by Richard B. Sewall (Cambridge, MA:

Harvard/Belknap Press, 2006). Leslie A. Morris gives an authoritative, succinct and well-written history of the Dickinson Papers and how they came to Harvard

————, Early reviews. Press clippings. Yale: Mabel Loomis Todd Papers, 496C, series VII, box 101, f.242

————, 'The Likenesses of Emily Dickinson', listed with commentary by Louise B. Graves, *Harvard Library Bulletin*, vol. 1/ no. 2 (spring 1947), 248–51. Houghton: bMS Am 1118.99b (23)

————, Selected poems, read to perfection by Juliet Stevenson, originally at the British Library, recorded on CD accompanying Josephine Hart's *Catching Life by the Throat: How to Read Poetry and Why: Poems from Eight Great Poets* (London: Virago, 2006; NY: Norton, 2007)

————, *American Religious Poems: An Anthology*, ed. Harold Bloom with Jesse Zuba (NY: Library of America, 2006)

————, *American Poetry: The Nineteenth-Century*, ii, ed. John Hollander (NY: Library of America, 1993)

————, *Emily Dickinson: Poems Selected by Ted Hughes* (London: Faber, 2001)

————, *Emily Dickinson's Correspondences: A Born-Digital Textual Inquiry* (EDC), ed. Martha Nell Smith and Lara Vetter, with Louise Hart as consulting editor (Charlottesville: University of Virginia Press, 2008). 73 poems and letters from the poet's correspondence with Susan Dickinson <www.rotunda.upress.virginia.edu >

The Dickinson Electronic Archives (DEA) (1994 to the present) <www.emilydickinson.org>. This is a critical edition of select Dickinson texts, with EDC as part of it

Dickinson, Emily Norcross (poet's mother). Letters. Houghton: Dickinson Family Papers

————, *A Poet's Parents: The Courtship Letters of Emily Norcross and Edward Dickinson*, ed. Vivian R. Pollak (Chapel Hill: University of North Carolina Press, 1988)

Dickinson, Lavinia, Diary (1851). Houghton: bMS Am 1118.95

————, Letter (23 Jan 1885) to cousins Clara Newman Turner and Anna Newman Carleton about her sister's health. Houghton: bMS Am 1118.7

————, Letters to Thomas Niles. Emily Dickinson Collection, Amherst College Archives

————, Letters to Mabel Loomis Todd. Yale: box 101, f.235

————, Bill of Complaint against the Todds. Jones Library. Testimony, Dickinson *v.* Todd (Feb 1898). Houghton: MS Am 2521. Transcript of Dickinson *v.* Todd Trial. Yale: Todd Papers, 496C, series VII, box 101, f.239

————, Oral memories of Dickinson (n.d.), recorded by Mabel Loomis Todd. Yale: box 82, f.402.

Dickinson, Samuel Fowler (the poet's grandfather), Oration at Dartmouth College (26 Aug 1795). Houghton: bMS Am 1118.95

Dickinson, Susan Huntingdon Gilbert (friend of the poet's youth, her prime reader, and sister-in-law), Writings <www.emilydickinson.org/susan/table_of_contents.html>

————, Correspondence with Emily Dickinson. Digitalised in EDC

————, Papers. Hay Library, Brown University. Includes microfilm of selected papers. F5890 HAY

————, Obituary (1913) in the *Springfield Republican* newspaper. Copies in Houghton and Amherst College; also in the Dickinson Electronic Archives <www.emily-dickinson.org/susan/table_of_contents.html>

————, Correspondence with Kate Scott Turner Anthon. Houghton: bMS Am 1118.95
————, 'Annals of the Evergreens' (1892). TS memoir. Houghton: bMS Am 1118.95. Also DEA <www.emilydickinson.org/susan/table_of_contents.html>
————, 'Society at Amherst Fifty Years Ago'. TS memoir. Houghton: bMS Am 1118.95. Also DEA <www.emilydickinson.org/susan/table_of_contents.html>
————, Letter (1888) to husband Austin Dickinson. Yale: Mabel Loomis Todd Papers, 496C, series VII, box 97, f.166
————, Letters to T. W. Higginson. Emily Dickinson Collection, Amherst College Archives
————, Letters to William Hayes Ward. Houghton: bMS Am 1118.95. Amongst her writings in DEA: <www.emilydickinson.org/susan/table_of_contents.html>
Dickinson, William Austin. Recollections of Emily Dickinson. Yale. Printed by Sewall, i, 222–3
————, Drafts of letters to Susan Gilbert. Dickinson Family Papers. Houghton: bMS Am 1118.95
————, Diaries (1880–90, though no diaries survive for 1885 and 1887). Yale: Mabel Loomis Todd Papers, series VII, box 101, f.244, 245; box 102, f.246, 247, 251, 252, 253
————, Statements to Mabel Todd about his wife Susan Dickinson. Yale: Mabel Loomis Todd Papers, 496C, series VII, box 103, f.259
————, Letter to Mrs Loomis. Yale: Mabel Loomis Todd Papers. box 97, f.155
————, Letters to Mabel Loomis Todd. Yale: 496C, series VII, box 94
————, *Austin and Mabel: The Amherst Affair & Love Letters of Austin Dickinson and Mabel Loomis Todd*, by Polly Longsworth (NY: Farrar, Straus, Giroux, 1984)
————, Letters to T. W. Higginson and to E. D. Hardy of Roberts Brothers. Emily Dickinson Collection, Amherst College Archives
————, Letter to J. Clark (8 Aug 1893) about settling in Omaha. Yale: Todd Papers, 496C, box 97, folder 157
————, letters to David Todd. Yale: Mabel Loomis Todd Papers, box 97, f.161–5
Dickinson Family, Papers, library and furniture from Emily Dickinson's room. Houghton: bMS Am 1118.95. The need for preservation means that scholars can no longer examine the actual books, but in 1990, before the embargo, I did see a number of these, including the Dickinsons' Brontë collection and Emily Dickinson's geology textbook (see Hitchcock, below) with its diagrams of volcanoes
————, Dickinson Family contracts and correspondence between the Dickinson family and Roberts Brothers, Little, Brown and Company, and Houghton Mifflin and Company, concerning publication of the poet (1890s–1960s). Houghton: bMS Am 1118.18
————, Pre-1915 floor plans of the Homestead. Amherst College Archives
Dostoyevsky, Fyodor (trans. David McDuff), *The Idiot* (1868; London: Penguin Classics, 2004)
Field, Henry (attorney), Letters to MDB. Houghton: bMS Am 1118.97–1118.98 (79)
Hampson, Alfred Leete and Mary Landis Hampson, Correspondence, mostly with William McCarthy, to do with The Evergreens and the Dickinson Papers (1940s–1980s). Houghton: bMS Am 1922 <http://nrs.harvard.edu/urn-3:FHCL.Hough:hou00588> (Some of McCarthy's side to the correspondence is in Hay Library, Brown University: Evergreens Collection, box 4)

Higginson, Thomas Wentworth, Letters to Lavinia Dickinson, Thomas Niles and Mabel
    Loomis Todd. Dickinson Collection, Amherst College Archives
———, 'Emily Dickinson's Letters', *Atlantic Monthly* (Oct 1891)
Hill, Alice ('Alix') Barton (later Harris), Letter to Frothingham (1898). Houghton: MS
    Am 1996
Hitchcock, Edward, *Elementary Geology* (1840, repr. 1842). Emily Dickinson Room,
    Houghton
Holmes, Oliver Wendell, 'James Jackson: A Biographical Sketch' (1876). Countway
    Library of the History of Medicine, Harvard: B MS b6.1
Houghton Library. Search the Online Archival Search Information System (OASIS) for
    online Dickinson material and family photographs at <http://oasis.harvard.edu/
    html/hou00202.html>
Houghton Mifflin (publishers), Correspondence with Martha Dickinson Bianchi,
    1923–43. Houghton: bMS Am 1118.97–1118.98 (11)
Howe, Julia Ward, *Passion Flowers* (first collection of poems in 1854, discussed by Elaine
    Showalter, *A Jury of Her Peers*, below)
Jackson, Helen Hunt, née Fiske, *Mercy Philbrick's Choice* (Boston: Roberts, 1876)
———, *Ramona* (1884; repr. NY: Signet Classics, 2002)
———, *A Century of Dishonor: A Sketch of the United States Government's Dealings with Some
    of the Indian Tribes* (Harper, 1881; repr. Norman: University of Oklahoma Press,
    1995)
———, *Report on the Condition and Needs of the Mission Indians of Southern California* (1883)
    <www.archive.org/.../conditionofmissi00duborich/conditionofmissi00duborich
    _djvu.txt>
Jackson, James (Dickinson's Boston physician), *Letters to a Young Physician* (Boston:
    Phillips, Sampson, 1855)
———, *Another Letter to a Young Physician* (Boston: Ticknor & Fields, 1861)
———, Papers. 'Lectures on the Theory and Practice of Medicine': MS notes on
    Jackson's lectures, copied by Oliver Wendell Holmes as a medical student in 1831–3.
    Francis A. Countway Library of Medicine, Harvard
———, Papers. 'Memoria Medica' (MS casebook). Boston Medical Library in the
    Francis A. Countway Library of Medicine: f1.K.54
———, Papers. 'Notes on Medicine' MS. Boston Medical Library in the Francis A.
    Countway Library of Medicine: f1.K.53
———, Papers. 'Notes on Clinical Medicine' MS. Boston Medical Library in the
    Francis A. Countway Library of Medicine: f1.K.156
———, Prescription for Emily Dickinson. Attached to letter she sent to her brother
    asking for twice the amount. Photostat at Houghton: bMS Am 1118.99c (27 Dec
    1853). MS in Special Collections, Amherst College Library
Jackson, William A. (Librarian of the Houghton Library, Harvard). Letters to Gilbert H.
    Montague (1943–56). Two files of their correspondence (*c*. 270 letters). Houghton
    Library Office
James, Alice, *The Diary of Alice James* (repr. Penguin, 1987)
Keep, Wallace, 'Recollections of Lavinia Dickinson'. Yale: Bingham Papers, box 84, f.233
Lord, Otis Phillips, 'Memoir of Asahel Huntington', *Historical Collections of the Essex
    Institute*, 11 (July, Oct 1871)

————, Letters, obituary and documents relating to Judge Lord, also his will. Amherst College Archives: MS 761, box 9. An excellent memorial of Lord by the Bar of the Commonwealth and of the Supreme Court in Boston is in box 9, f.53.

Lowell, Amy, Correspondence with Mabel Loomis Todd and Millicent Todd Bingham. Houghton: bMS Lowell 19

Maher, Margaret (Maggie), servant to the Dickinson sisters, TS deposition (1897) preceding Dickinson v. Todd trial. Legal depository, Worcester, MA: Todd v. Dickinson, file no. 193, Location: EB101 002-008-002-005/ box 30782, in the series of Equity File Papers. Included in these papers are the testimonies of L. D. Hill and Jane Seelye

McCarthy, William (Bill), Jr, Letters to the Hampsons at The Evergreens. Hay Library, Brown University: Evergreens Collection, box 4, f.14 (for inventory) and mainly f.16. (Hampsons' letters to McCarthy are in Houghton: bMS Am 1923)

————, Correspondence with Martha Dickinson Bianchi (1930–43). Houghton: bMS Am 1118.97–1118.98 (123)

Minot, George R., 'James Jackson as a Professor of Medicine', New England Journal of Medicine, 208/5 (2 Feb 1933)

Montague, George (compiler, first cousin to Edward Dickinson, Sr), History and Genealogy of the Montague Family (Amherst: Press of E. J. Williams, 1886), revised by William Lewis Montague after a gathering of the Montagues in Amherst in 1883. Copy in Library of Congress: microfiche 1018/G292

Montague, Zebina (the poet's 'Cousin Zebina'), 'Personal History' (1852), written for the twentieth reunion of his Amherst class of 1832. Printed copy (1853) in AC. Reprinted in the family History above: entry no. 2650. Includes funeral remarks by W. S. Tyler of Amherst College (12 Jan 1881).

Montague-Collier Family Papers (Gilbert Holland Montague and Amy Angel Collier Montague). Manuscripts and Archives Division, New York Public Library

Montague, Gilbert H., Fourteen letters to Alfred Leete Hampson (1943–51). Houghton: bMS Am 1923 (14)

————, Fifty-two letters to Mary Hampson (1948–60). Houghton: bMS Am 1923 (15)

————, Letters to William A. Jackson (1943–56). Two files (c. 270 letters), Houghton Library Office. See Jackson, above

————, Correspondence regarding Emily Dickinson. New York Public Library: Manuscripts and Archives, Montague Papers, box 2

————, Letter to Millicent Todd Bingham (1955). New York Public Library: Manuscripts and Archives, Montague Papers, box 1

Niles, Thomas (Dickinson's first publisher) and Roberts Brothers colleagues, Letters to Mabel Loomis Todd and David Peck Todd. Emily Dickinson Collection, Amherst College Archives

Norcross, Frances (Fanny) L., Seven letters to Mabel Loomis Todd (1894). Emily Dickinson Collection, Amherst College Archives: Todd 329, box 18, f.16

Norcross, Lavinia (maternal aunt of Emily Dickinson), Poem addressed to her sister (Emily Dickinson's mother): 'Sister! Why that burning tear', after the death of their mother. Houghton: bMS Am 1118.95 (228)

Oates, Joyce Carol, 'EDickinsonRepliLuxe' in Wild Nights!: Stories about the Last Days of Poe, Dickinson, Twain, James, and Hemingway (NY: HarperCollins, 2008)

Pohl, Frederick and Vincent York, *Brittle Heaven: a drama in three acts* (1935). See York, below

Pollitt, Josephine, *Emily Dickinson: The Human Background of her Poetry* (NY: Harper, 1930). Copy in the Bodleian Library, Oxford

Putnam, James Jackson, *A Memoir of Dr. James Jackson* (Boston: Houghton Mifflin, 1906). Copy in Countway Medical Library, Harvard. Digitalised

Quain, Richard (ed.), *Dictionary of Medicine* (1883). Copy owned by Dr Bigelow, who attended the Dickinsons, is in Jones Library

Rich, Adrienne, 'Vesuvius At Home' in *On Lies, Secrets, Silence* (NY: Norton, 1979; London: Virago, 1980). Originally a Commencement address at Smith College. A poet's insight into a great predecessor

Root Abiah P. (later Mrs Strong), Three letters to Mabel Loomis Todd (1892–3). Emily Dickinson Collection, Amherst College Archives and Special Collections: Todd 334, box 18, f.21

Sieveking, Sir Edward Henry, *On Epilepsy and Epileptiform Seizures: Their Causes, Pathology, and Treatment* (London: John Churchill, 1858)

St Armand, Barton Levi, Collection of Dickinson Family Papers (c. 1851–1908). Hay Library, Brown University, including a vast number of items of Dickinson family memorabilia from The Evergreens

Strachan, Pearl, Interview with Martha Dickinson Bianchi at The Evergreens. *Christian Science Monitor*, Boston (4 Sept 1940)

Taggard, Genevieve, *The Life and Mind of Emily Dickinson* (NY: Knopf, 1930). Copy in Bodleian Library, Oxford

Todd, David Peck, Papers. Yale: MS 496B, series VII <http://drs.library.yale.edu:8083/fedoragsearch/rest?collection>

————, Diary (1886). Yale: box 108, f.51

————, 'A Line A Day' diaries (1893, 1894, 1895). Yale: box 108, f.55

————, Autobiographical Writings. Yale: box 110, f.67.

Todd, Mabel Loomis, Papers. Yale. <http://hdl.handle.net/10079/fa/mssa.ms.0496c>

————, Lock of hair. Yale

————, Signature as 'Mabel Loomis Dickinson' with photograph. Yale: 496C, series VII, box 103, f.262

————, Unfinished TS autobiography. Yale: 496C, series VII, box 116, f.454, and autobiographical writings c. 1930: box 116, f.456

————, 'Millicent's Life'. Yale: 496C, series III, boxes 46, 47, 48, f.49–65

————, Reminiscences in note form (n.d.). Yale: subject files: WAD, box 103, f.266

————, Correspondence with William Austin Dickinson in *Austin and Mabel: The Amherst Affair and Love Letters of Austin Dickinson and Mabel Loomis Todd*, by Polly Longsworth (NY: Farrar, Straus, Giroux, 1984)

————, Letters to Thomas Niles and Hardy of Roberts Brothers. Dickinson Collection, Amherst College Archives and Special Collections

————, Letter to curator Charles Green. Jones Library

————, Correspondence with Amy Lowell. Houghton: bMS Lowell 19 (1211) and 19.1 (1293)

————, 'Evolution of a Style' (c. 1891). Perceptive TS essay or talk on Dickinson. Yale: 496C, series VII, box 103, f.263

————, Memories of Emily Dickinson (c. 1924). Yale: box 103, f.266

————, Celebration of ED's centenary. Yale: f.398–9

————, 'ED's Literary Debut', *Harper's Magazine*, CLX (Mar 1930), 463–4. Actually written by her daughter.

————, Lecture circuit material. Yale: Mabel Loomis Todd Papers, 496F, box 14

————, Preface to *The Letters of Emily Dickinson* (Harper, 1931), ix–x

————, 'Mabel Loomis Todd Speaks' (10 and 12 October 1931). Yale: 496C, series VII, box 101, f.242

————, Journals. MS. Yale: microfilm

————, Diaries. MS. Yale: microfilm (seven reels)

————, Essay, 'Famous Lovers' (with excerpts from her correspondence with Austin Dickinson). Yale: box 103, f.270

————, Records of her associates. Yale: 496C, series VII:

on Helen Hunt Jackson: box 90, f.40

on Amy Lowell: box 90, f.50

on the Thoreau family: box 90, f.68

on Caroline Lovejoy Andrews: box 92, f.2

on Louisa May Alcott: box 92, f.1

on Higginson: box 92, f.27

on Oliver Wendell Holmes: box 92, f.35

on Julia Ward Howe: box 92, f.36

————, *Total Eclipses of the Sun* (Boston: Roberts Bros, 1894)

————, Defendants' Answer, a rebuttal of Lavinia Dickinson's Bill of Complaint, Jones Library, Amherst; Testimony, Dickinson v. Todd (Feb 1898). Houghton: MS Am 2521. Dickinson v. Todd Trial. Yale: 496C, series VII, box 101, f.239

————, TS 'Written by Mabel Loomis Todd in 1898' (statement for the Supreme Court hearing in September 1898). Yale: 496C, series VII, box 101, f.240

————, Photographs. Yale: 496E

Trial: Manuscript documents (1896–8) associated with the trials of Lavinia Dickinson v. the Todds and the Slander trial of the Todds v. Lavinia Dickinson, including the depositions of Margaret Maher, L. D. Hills, and Jane Seelye. Includes also a few pages to do with the Todds' appeal to the Supreme Court of Massachusetts. Hampshire Superior Court Civil Action No. 125 in legal depository, Worcester, MA. Additional verbatim TS records of the evidence of Dwight Palmer, David Todd, Frances Seelye, and Margaret Maher (only a photocopied fragment remains of the last) are amongst Lavinia Dickinson's Papers (16:18) in Hay Library, Brown University

Trial: Typescript records of statements made during the 1898 trials in the Superior Court of Northampton and the Supreme Court later that year. Copies in Houghton Library (Ms Am 2521) and the Todd papers, series VII, box 101, f.239, 240, at Yale. Copies of TS records also in Jones Library, Amherst and in Hay Library, Brown University

Turner, Clara Newman, 'My Personal Acquaintance with Emily Dickinson'. Houghton: bMS Am 1118.7. Printed in part in Sewall, i, 265–75 with introduction by her niece Clara Newman Pearl. A typescript of the piece and introduction together with an insert on Dickinson's domestic habits is amongst the Millicent Todd Bingham Papers. Yale: box 101, f.565

Untermeyer, Louis, 'Thoughts after a Centenary', *The Saturday Review of Literature* (20 June 1931). Copy amongst Todd Papers, Yale: 496C, series VII, box 101, f.238

Wadsworth, the Revd Charles, Letter to Dickinson (*c.* 1862), included in Johnson's edition of Dickinson's *Letters*: 248a

Wald, Jane (Curator of the Emily Dickinson Museum in Amherst), 2007 Exhibition at the Dickinson Homestead

Whitney, Maria, Archives. Smith College: box 1046, f.42

———, Five letters (from 21 Berkeley Street, Cambridge, Massachusetts) to Mabel Loomis Todd (1894). Archives and Special Collections, Amherst College Library: Todd 335, box 19, f.1

Williams, Dr Henry Willard, *Recent Advances in Ophthalmic Science: the Boylston Prize Essay for 1865* (Boston: Ticknor & Fields, 1866). Copy in the Dickinsons' library. Emily Dickinson Room, Houghton: 422

———, *A Practical Guide to Diseases of the Eye* (1867, revised 1869). 1869 edition in Widener Library, Harvard: 28.D.56

———, *The Diagnosis and Treatment of the Diseases of the Eye* (1881). Copy in Widener Library, Harvard: Med 2718.81

Williams, Tennessee, 'Person-To-Person', an introduction to *Cat on a Hot Tin Roof*, referring to Emily Dickinson

Yorke, Vincent and Frederick J. Pohl, *Brittle Heaven: An Amorous Tale of Long Ago*, a play based on the legend of the poet's life in Josephine Pollitt's *Emily Dickinson: The Human Background of her Poetry* (NY: Harper, 1930)

CRITICISM, BIOGRAPHY AND RELATED WORKS

Academy of American Poets <www.poets.org/page.php/prmID/58>, including articles relating Dickinson to music: 'Isaac Watts & Emily Dickinson: Inherited Meter', 'John Cage: The Roaring Silence' and on Copeland's song cycle, *12 Poems of Emily Dickinson*

Anderson, Bonnie, *Joyous Greetings: The First International Women's Movement, 1830–1860* (NY: OUP, 2000)

Andrews, Carol Damon, 'Thinking Musically, Writing Expectantly: New Biographical Information About Emily Dickinson', *New England Quarterly* (summer 2008). Backs Gould as the poet's lover, reviving Taggard's 1930 biography

Archer, Seth, '"I Had a Terror": Emily Dickinson's Demon', *Southwest Review* (2009), 255–73

Barker, Sebastian, Letter to *TLS* on Dickinson and religion (26 Jan 2007), following debate in the letters column, Nov 2006–Jan 2007

Benfey, Christopher, *Emily Dickinson and the Problem of Others* (Amherst: University of Massachusetts Press, 1984)

———, *Emily Dickinson, Lives of a Poet* (NY: George Braziller, 1986)

———, 'The Mystery of Emily Dickinson', *New York Review of Books* (8 Apr 1999), 39–44

———, see Liebling, *The Dickinsons of Amherst*, below

———, *A Summer of Hummingbirds: Love, Art, and Scandal in the Intersecting Worlds of Emily Dickinson, Mark Twain, Harriet Beecher Stowe, and Martin Johnson Heade* (NY: Penguin, 2008)

Bennett, Paula, *Emily Dickinson: Woman Poet* (London: Harvester, 1990)

————, *My Life, a Loaded Gun: Dickinson, Plath, Rich, and Female Creativity* (Urbana: University of Illinois Press, c. 1986)

Bloom, Harold, *The Western Canon* (NY: Harcourt, 1994), 299–300

Boswell, Jeanetta, *Emily Dickinson: A Bibliography of Secondary Sources, 1890–1987* (Jefferson, NC: McFarland, 1989). This casts a wide net, including radio, films, tributes, recordings, fiction and foreign-language editions

Brock-Broido, Lucie, *The Master Letters: Poems* (NY: Knopf, 2002)

Capps, Jack L., *Emily Dickinson's Reading, 1836–1886* (Cambridge, MA: Harvard University Press, 1966)

Cody, John, *After Great Pain: The Inner Life of Emily Dickinson* (Cambridge, MA: Belknap Press of Harvard University, 1971)

Cott, Nancy, *The Bonds of Womanhood: 'Women's Sphere' in New England, 1780–1835* (New Haven: Yale University Press, 1977)

D'Arienzo, Daria, and Margaret R. Dakin, 'An even better home at Amherst', *Amherst* (spring 2007), 26–33. On Dickinson's letters and poems to the Tuckermans.

Davis, Philip, 'A Shakespearean Grammar' in *Shakespeare Thinking* (London: Continuum 2007)

————, 'The Shakespeared Brain', *Literary Review* (July 2008)

Deppman, Jed, *Trying to Think with Emily Dickinson* (Amherst: University of Massachusetts Press, 2008)

Eberwein, Jane Donahue (ed.), *An Emily Dickinson Encyclopaedia* (Westport, CT: Greenwood Press, 1998)

————, and Cindy MacKenzie (eds), *Reading Emily Dickinson's Letters: Critical Essays* (Amherst: University of Massachusetts Press, 2009)

Emily Dickinson International Society Bulletin

The Emily Dickinson Journal (Johns Hopkins University Press)

Erkkila, Betsy, *The Wicked Sisters: Women Poets, Literary History, and Discord* (NY: OUP, 1992)

————, 'Emily Dickinson and Class', *American Literary History*, 4 (1992), 1–27

Farr, Judith, *The Passion of Emily Dickinson* (Cambridge, MA: Harvard University Press, 1992)

Fenton, James, 'Don't ask, don't tell', London *Guardian*: Saturday Review (4 Nov 2006)

Franklin, R. W., *The Editing of Emily Dickinson: a Reconsideration* (Madison: University of Wisconsin Press, 1967)

Gay, Peter, *The Bourgeois Experience: Victoria to Freud*. The first volume, *Education of the Senses* (Norton, 1984) has a detailed treatment of Mabel Todd's Diary as sexual record.

Gilbert, Sandra M. and Susan Gubar, *The Madwoman in the Attic: The Woman Writer and the Nineteenth Century Literary Imagination* (New Haven: Yale University Press, 1979)

Green, Elizabeth Alden, *Mary Lyon and Mount Holyoke* (Hanover, NH: University Press of New England, 1979)

Habegger, Alfred, *My Wars are Laid Away in Books: The Life of Emily Dickinson* (NY: Random House, 2001)

————, 'Some Problems in Reading Emily Dickinson', *Journal of English Language and Literature*, vol. 51 (Nihan University, Tokyo, 2003)

————, 'Evangelicalism and Its Discontents: Hannah Porter versus Emily Dickinson', *New England Quarterly*, vol. 70 (Sept 1997), 386–414

Hall, David D. (ed.), *The Antinomian Controversy, 1636–1638: A Documentary History* (Middletown CT: Wesleyan University Press, 1968)

Hart, Ellen Louise, 'The Encoding of Homoerotic Desire: Emily Dickinson's Letters and Poems to Susan Dickinson, 1850–1886', *Tulsa Studies in Women's Literature*, 9/2 (fall 1990), 251–72

Hart, Josephine, *Catching Life by the Throat: How to Read Poetry and Why* (London: Virago, 2006; NY: Norton, 2007). Including a section on Dickinson, together with seven other major poets

Hirschhorn, Norbert, 'Was it Tuberculosis? Another glimpse of Emily Dickinson's health', *New England Quarterly*, 72/1 (1999), 102–18

———, TS 'Translation of Medications from Adams Pharmacy Scrapbook', Health and Medicine folder, Jones Library Special Collections

———, and Polly Longsworth, '"Medicine Posthumous": A New Look at Emily Dickinson's Medical Conditions', *New England Quarterly*, 69 (June 1996), 299–316

Homans, Margaret, *Women Writers and Poetic Identity: Dorothy Wordsworth, Emily Brontë, and Emily Dickinson* (Princeton: Princeton University Press, 1980)

Jackson, Virginia, 'Thinking Dickinson Thinking Poetry' in *A Companion to Emily Dickinson*, eds Smith and Loeffelholz, 205–21

Jenkins, MacGregor, *Emily Dickinson: Friend and Neighbour* (Boston: Little, Brown, 1930)

Juhasz, Suzanne, *The Undiscovered Continent: Emily Dickinson and the Space of the Mind* (Bloomington: University of Indiana Press, 1993)

———, Martha Nell Smith and Cristanne Miller, *Comic Power in Emily Dickinson* (Austin: University of Texas Press, 1993)

Karlin, Daniel, 'Recurring Woman', *London Review of Books* (24 Aug 2000), 21–2. Questioning review of Franklin's variorum edition

Kaufmann, Paola (trans. William Rowlandson), *The Sister: A novel on the hidden world of Emily Dickinson* (2003; Richmond, Surrey: Alma Books, 2006)

Kelley, Mary, *Private Woman, Public Stage: Literary Domesticity in Nineteenth-Century America* (NY: OUP, 1984)

Lang, Amy, *Prophetic Women: Anne Hutchinson and the Problem of Dissent in the Literature of New England* (Berkeley: University of California Press, 1987)

Leyda, Jay, *The Years and Hours of Emily Dickinson* (New Haven: Yale University Press, 1960)

Liebling, Jerome, *The Dickinsons of Amherst* (Hanover, NH: University Press of New England, 2001). Photographs with essays by Christopher Benfey, Polly Longsworth and Barton Levi St Armand

Loeffelholz, Mary, *From School to Salon: Reading Nineteenth-Century American Women's Poetry* (Princeton: Princeton University Press, 2004)

———, and Martha Nell Smith (eds), *A Companion to Emily Dickinson* (Oxford: Wiley-Blackwell, 2008)

Loeschke, Maravene S., *The Path Between: An Historical Novel of the Dickinson Family of Amherst* (Columbia, MD: C. H. Fairfax, 1988)

Longsworth, Polly, *Austin and Mabel*. See Primary Sources

———, *The World of Emily Dickinson* (NY: Norton, 1990, paperback 1997)

———, 'The "Latitude of Home": Life in the Homestead and the Evergreens' in Liebling, above

———, see Hirschhorn, above

MacMurray, Rose, *Afternoons with Emily* (NY: Little, Brown, 2007)

McNeil, Helen, *Emily Dickinson* (London, Virago, 1986; NY: Pantheon, 1986)

Malcolm, Janet, *The Journalist and the Murderer* (1990; London: Granta, 1997)

Martin, Wendy (ed.), *The Cambridge Companion to Emily Dickinson* (2002)

Matteson, John, *Eden's Outcasts: The Story of Louisa May Alcott and her Father* (NY: Norton, 2007)

Mendelson, Edward, *The Things That Matter: What Seven Classic Novels Have to Say About the Stages of Life* (NY: Pantheon, 2006). Chapter on Emily Brontë is suggestive of Dickinson's affinities for her

Messmer, Marietta, *'A vice for voices': Reading Emily Dickinson's Correspondence* (Amherst: University of Massachusetts Press, 2001)

Miller, Cristanne, *Emily Dickinson: A Poet's Grammar* (Cambridge, MA: Harvard University Press, 1987)

———, 'The Sound of Shifting Paradigms, or Hearing Dickinson in the Twenty-First Century' in Pollak (ed.), *A Historical Guide to Emily Dickinson*, 201–34

———, 'Dickinson's Structured Rhythms' in Smith and Loeffelholz (eds), *A Companion to Emily Dickinson*, 391–414.

———, with Suzanne Juhasz and Martha Nell Smith, *Comic Power in Emily Dickinson* (University of Texas Press, 1993)

Mitchell, Domhnall, *Measurements of Possibility: Emily Dickinson's Manuscripts* (Amherst: Massachusetts University Press, 2005)

———, and Maria Stuart (eds), *International Reception of Emily Dickinson* (London: Continuum, 2009)

Mizruchi, Susan L., *Becoming Multicultural: Culture, Economy, and the Novel, 1860–1920* in *Cambridge History of American Literature*, ed. Sacvan Bercovitch, iii: Prose Writing, 1860–1920 (Cambridge: CUP, 2005)

———, *The Rise of Multicultural America: Economy and Print Culture, 1865–1915* (Chapel Hill: University of North Carolina Press, 2009). Separate publication of the above

Moers, Ellen, *Literary Women* (London: The Women's Press, 1978)

Morris, Leslie A., Foreword to *Emily Dickinson's Herbarium* (above) has a succinct history of the Dickinson Papers and how they came to Harvard

Morse, Jonathan, 'Bibliographical Essay' in Pollak (ed.) *A Historical Guide to Emily Dickinson*, 255–83

Murray, Aífe, 'Miss Margaret's Emily Dickinson', *Signs* (spring 1999), vol. 24/3, 697–732

———, *Maid as Muse: How Servants Changed Emily Dickinson's Life and Language* (Lebanon, NH: University of New Hampshire Press, 2010)

Oates, Joyce Carol, 'The Woman in White', *New York Review of Books* (25 Sept 2008). Review of Wineapple, *White Heat*

Ostriker, Alicia Suskin, *Stealing the Language: The Emergence of Women's Poetry in America* (Boston: Beacon Press, 1986; London: The Women's Press, 1986)

Paglia, Camille, 'Amherst's Madame de Sade' in *Sexual Personae: Art and Decadence from Nefertiti to Emily Dickinson* (New Haven: Yale University Press, 1990)

Patterson, Rebecca, *The Riddle of Emily Dickinson* (Boston: Houghton Mifflin, 1951)

Petrino, Elizabeth A., *Emily Dickinson and Her Contemporaries: Women's Verse in America* (Hanover, NH: University Press of New England, 1998)

Phillips, Kate, *Helen Hunt Jackson: A Literary Life* (Berkeley: University of California Press, 2003)

Pollak, Vivian R., 'American Women Poets Reading Dickinson: The Example of Helen Hunt Jackson' in Gudrun Grabher, Roland Hagenbüchle and Cristanne Miller (eds), *The Emily Dickinson Handbook* (Amherst: University of Massachusetts Press, 1998), 323–41

———, (ed.), *A Historical Guide to Emily Dickinson* (NY: OUP, 2004). Includes 'A Brief Biography' by Vivian Pollak and Marianne Noble

Porter, Roy, *The Greatest Benefit to Mankind: A Medical History of Humanity from Antiquity to the Present* (London: Harper, 1997)

Powers, Wendy Ann, 'Emily Brontë and Emily Dickinson: Parallel Lives on Opposing Shores', *Brontë Studies*, vol. 32/2 (July 2007), 145–9

Raine, Craig, 'Ordinary, Sacred Things' and subsequent debate on Dickinson and religion in the letters column of *TLS* (24 Nov 2006–Jan 2007)

Rector, Liam, 'Bidart's *The Sacrifice*' in *On Frank Bidart: Fastening the Voice to the Page*, ed. Liam Rector and Tree Swenson (Ann Arbor: University of Michigan Press, 2007), 130–1. Suggestive comments on the 'connective tissue' of reinvented punctuation.

Richardson, Robert D., *Emerson: The Mind on Fire* (Berkeley: University of California Press, 1995)

Scott, D. F., *The History of Epileptic Therapy* (Carnforth: Parthenon, 1993)

Sewall, Richard Benson, *The Life of Emily Dickinson*, 2 vols (NY: Farrar, Giroux, 1974; London: Faber, 1974; repr. Harvard University Press, 1994). Appendix II to the first volume prints a few of a vast Yale collection of documents relevant to the 'War between the Houses'. In section 4 of Appendix II, Sewall offers a 'synthesis' of three typescripts of Mabel Todd's reminiscences in the Yale archive, under the title of one of them, 'Scurrilous but True'. Scurrilous they are, but not true. Fascinating for the distortions of Todd's slander as it thickened over many decades. Section 5 of Appendix II is notes taken by Millicent Todd Bingham during an interview with her father in September–October 1933, after her mother's death, when Millicent was taking on her mother's campaign. Section 6 is an extract from only one of Millicent's massive collection of TS reminiscences at Yale.

———, *The Lyman Letters: New Light on Emily Dickinson and her Family* (Amherst: University of Massachusetts Press, 1965). Copy in Library of Congress

———, (ed.), *Emily Dickinson: A Collection of Critical Essays* (Englewood Cliffs: Prentice-Hall, 1963)

———, and Martin Wand, '"Eyes Be Blind, Heart Be Still": A New Perspective on Emily Dickinson's Eye Problem', *New England Quarterly*, 52/3 (Sept 1979), 400–6

Seymour, Miranda, 'Emily's Tryst', *New York Times* (24 Aug 2008). Review of Wineapple, *White Heat*

Showalter, Elaine, lecture on American women writers. Oxford (11 May 2006)

———, *A Jury of Her Peers: American Women Writers from Anne Bradstreet to Annie Proulx* (London: Virago, 2009)

———, *The Female Malady* (London: Virago, 1985)

Smith, Martha Nell, *Rowing in Eden: Rereading Emily Dickinson* (Austin: University of Texas Press, 1992)

———, *A User's Guide to Emily Dickinson* (Oxford: Blackwell, 2011)

———, with Cristanne Miller and Suzanne Juhasz, *Comic Power in Emily Dickinson* (Austin: University of Texas Press, 1993)

————, and Ellen Louise Hart (eds), *Open Me Carefully: Emily Dickinson's Intimate Letters to Susan Huntingdon Dickinson*. In Primary Sources

————, and Mary Loeffelholz (eds), *A Companion to Emily Dickinson* (Oxford: Blackwell, 2008), including essays by the editors

The Smith College Monthly (Nov 1941). Special Dickinson issue

Spender, Dale, *Man Made Language* (London: Routledge & Kegan Paul, 1985)

St Armand, Barton Levi, 'Keeper of the Keys: Mary Hampson, the Evergreens, and the Art Within' in Jerome Liebling et al., *The Dickinsons of Amherst* (Hanover, NH: University Press of New England, 2001), 107–67

————, *Emily Dickinson and Her Culture: The Soul's Society* (Cambridge: CUP, 1986)

————, '"Your Prodigal": Letters from Ned Dickinson, 1879–1885', *New England Quarterly*, 61/3 (September 1988)

Stuart, Maria (ed.), *International Reception of Emily Dickinson* (London: Continuum, 2009)

Temkin, Owsei, *The Falling Sickness: History of Epilepsy from the Greeks to the Beginnings of Modern Neurology* (1945; Johns Hopkins University Press, 1971, second edn)

Tufariello, Catherine, '"The Remembering Wine": Emerson's Influence on Whitman and Dickinson' in *The Cambridge Companion to Ralph Waldo Emerson*, ed. Joel Porte and Sandra Morris (Cambridge: CUP, 1999)

Vendler, Helen, *Poets Thinking: Pope, Whitman, Dickinson, Yeats* (Cambridge, MA: Harvard University Press, 2006)

Walsh, John Evangelist, *This Brief Tragedy: Unravelling the Todd–Dickinson Affair* (NY: Grove Weidenfeld, 1991)

Wand, Martin and Richard B. Sewall, 'Eyes Be Blind, Heart Be Still: A New Perspective on Emily Dickinson's Eye Problem', *New England Quarterly*, 52/3 (1979), 400–6.

Ward, Theodora (granddaughter of Dr and Mrs Holland), 'The Finest Secret', *Harvard Library Bulletin*, vol. 98, 90–106

Whicher, George Frisbie, *This Was a Poet: Emily Dickinson* (NY: Scribners, 1938, repr. University of Michigan: Ann Arbor Paperbacks, 1957, repr. 1960)

Wineapple, Brenda, *White Heat: The Friendship of Emily Dickinson and Thomas Wentworth Higginson* (NY: Knopf, 2008)

Wolff, Cynthia Griffin, *Emily Dickinson* (NY: Perseus Books, 1986)

Wolosky, Shira, *Emily Dickinson: A Voice of War* (New Haven: Yale University Press, 1984)

————, 'Emily Dickinson' in *The Cambridge History of American Literature*, ed. Sacvan Bercovitch, iv: Nineteenth-Century Poetry 1800–1910 (Cambridge: CUP, 2004)

NOTES

The notes below include all three major publications of Emily Dickinson's manuscripts, since all are in use: the first complete scholarly edition, which Johnson brought out in 1955; the variorum edition by Franklin in 1998, which re-dated some poems, added poems from the letters and altered Johnson's chronological numbering; and the digital and selective presentation of EDC (Emily Dickinson Correspondences) that eliminate editorial interventions between Dickinson manuscripts and the reader. The approximate dates below, from Franklin's edition, may be too minutely identified not to remain questionable in some cases.

ABBREVIATIONS

AB	*Ancestors' Brocades: The Literary Début of Emily Dickinson* by Millicent Todd Bingham (1945)
AC	Archives and Special Collections, Amherst College Library
ALH	Alfred Leete Hampson, heir of MDB's Dickinson Papers in 1943
A&M	*Austin and Mabel: The Amherst Affair and Love Letters of Austin Dickinson and Mabel Loomis Todd*, by Polly Longsworth (NY: Farrar, Straus, 1984; repr. Amherst: University of Massachusetts Press, 1999)
BFN	Benjamin Franklin Newman, student of law in Edward Dickinson's office
Brown	Martha Dickinson Bianchi Papers, John Hay Library, Brown University, Providence, RI
DEA	Dickinson Electronic Archives
DFP	Dickinson Family Papers, Houghton Library, Harvard University: bMS Am 1118.95
DPT	David Peck Todd, astronomer and MLT's husband
ED	Emily Dickinson
EDC	Emily Dickinson Correspondences
EDR	Emily Dickinson Room, Houghton Library, Harvard University. Includes Dickinson library.
FF	*Face to Face* by MDB (1932)

Fr	*The Poems of ED: Variorum Edition*, i–iii, ed. R. W. Franklin (Cambridge, MA: Belknap Press of Harvard University Press, 1998). The numbers are those of the poems, not the pages. The same numbers apply to a one-volume reading edition. Some editorial decisions are inevitably contested
Habegger	Alfred Habegger, *My Wars Are Laid Away in Books: The Life of ED* (NY: Random House, 2001)
HH	Helen Hunt Jackson, renowned New England writer on the wrongs of Native Americans; schoolfellow of ED in Amherst; later, friend and supporter.
HM	Houghton Mifflin, MDB's publisher. Correspondence in Houghton: bMS Am 1925
Home	*ED's Home* by Millicent Todd Bingham (1955)
Houghton	The Houghton Library, Harvard University
J	J plus a number represents the numbering of poems by ED in editions by Thomas H. Johnson. He was appointed in 1950 by Harvard University Press to be first authoritative editor of the complete corpus of ED. He produced scholarly editions in 1955 (poems) and 1958 (letters – see L), as well as the *Final Harvest* selection of 1960 and the readable one-volume paperback of the poems from Faber, the best and most complete of the editions available in the UK. Everything published subsequent to Johnson's editions is based on his work which was based (though unacknowledged) on the transcriptions and extensive groundwork of Mabel Loomis Todd and Millicent Todd Bingham.
Jones	Jones Library, Amherst
LD	Lavinia Dickinson, ED's sister
L	*The Letters of ED*, i–iii, ed. Thomas H. Johnson and Theodora Ward (Cambridge, MA: Belknap Press of Harvard Univ Press, 1958). The numbers refer to letters, not pages
LL	*Life and Letters* of ED by MDB (1924)
MB	*The Manuscript Books of Emily Dickinson*, ed. R. W. Franklin (Cambridge, MA: Harvard/Belknap, 1981)
MDB	Martha Dickinson Bianchi, ED's niece. Daughter of WAD and SHD
MH	Mary Hampson, inheritor and occupant of The Evergreens
MLT	Mabel Loomis Todd, ED's first editor. Mistress of WAD
MTB	Millicent Todd Bingham, MLT's daughter
NYPL	New York Public Library
PML	Pierpont Morgan Library, New York
Sewall	Richard B. Sewall, *A Life of ED*, 2 vols (1974; repr. Harvard University Press)
SHD	Susan Huntingdon Dickinson, née Susan Huntingdon Gilbert, friend, sister-in-law, and prime reader of ED
Trial MSS	Manuscript documents (1896–8) associated with the trials of Lavinia Dickinson *v.* the Todds and the Slander trial of MLT *v.* Lavinia Dickinson, including the depositions of Margaret Maher, L. D. Hills,

and Jane Seelye. Includes also a few pages to do with the Todds'
appeal to the Supreme Court of Massachusetts. Hampshire Superior
Court Civil Action No. 125 in legal depository, Worcester, MA

Trial TSS   Typescript records of what happened in court during the 1898 trials
in the Superior Court of Northampton and the Massachusetts
Supreme Court later that year. Copies with the Dickinson family
papers, Houghton Library, and the Todd papers, Sterling Library,
Yale.

TWH   Thomas Wentworth Higginson, mentor to ED
WAD   William Austin Dickinson, ED's brother
Yale   Manuscripts and Archives, Sterling Library, Yale University: MLT
Papers, 496C; MTB Papers, 496D; photographs 496E.

I: A POET NEXT DOOR

3 *four thousand*: Franklin, *The Editing of ED*, 4–5.
3 *wallpaper incident*: Edward (Ned) Dickinson to 'Mopsy', his sister Martha Dickinson,
who was at Miss Porter's school in Farmington, Connecticut (26 Jan [1885]),
marked 'am'). Brown: St Armand Collection: 33.
4 *'the paternal mansion'*: SB to WAD, enquiring after ED. Houghton.
4 *brown brick*: TWH to his wife (1870), L342a.
4 *'Exterior'*: 'This was a Poet —' (c. late 1862), J448/Fr446.
4 *'The Soul selects her own Society'*: (c. 1862), J303/Fr409/EDC.
5 *'The Soul that hath a Guest'*: (c. 1863). J674/Fr592.
5 *'Fortune'*: 'This was a Poet—' (c. late 1862). J448/Fr446.
5 *'Names of Sicknesses'*: To Mrs Holland, L873. At this time, late 1883, the doctor called
her sickness 'nervous prostration'. It was soon after Gib's death, but ED refers to
'The Crisis of the sorrow of so many years'.
5 *said to be different*: 'Since Gib's death Emily was differently ill & alarmingly so'. LD to
Clara Newman Turner and Anna Newman (23 Jan 1885). Houghton: bMS Am
1118.7.
6 *'My Life had stood . . .'*: (c. late 1863), J754/Fr764.
7 *'Existence'*: (c. spring 1863). J443 has the correct capital E (transcribed in the lower
case in Fr522).
7 *hints and guesses*: T. S. Eliot, *Four Quartets*. He refers to what ED called the 'Flash'.
7 *'Bomb'; 'Hold'; 'calm'*: 'I tie my Hat' (c. spring 1863). J443. *MB*, 555. Fr522 omits the
penultimate stanza since in the booklet (number 24) there is a line under it, cus-
tomarily used to indicate the end of a poem, but ED copied this stanza within the
text of 'I tie my Hat' and it's continuous with the preceding line. It's a climactic
stanza, a sequel to the first climax in the poem ('struck — my ticking —
through —'), fitting the explosive content of the alternative world within.
Johnson's transcription of this important poem should be restored.
7 *'yellow eye'*: 'My Life had stood — a Loaded Gun —', op. cit.
7 *'buckled lips'*: 'The reticent volcano' (n.d.). J1748/ Fr1776. Transcribed by MLT and
published in 1896.

7 *'Abyss has no Biographer —'*: L899. Vendler, 71, associates abyss with the 'fissure' and 'rupture' of life's 'serial plot'. This appears an internal paradigm of the family plot disrupted by a feud.

7 *'I'm Nobody!'*: (*c.* late 1861). J288/Fr260.

7 *'Wife — without the Sign!'*: 'Title divine — is mine!' (*c.* 1861). J1072/Fr194.

8 *'I tie my Hat'*: (*c.* spring 1863). The poem is transcribed here from *MB* 553–5, the manuscript source for J443. (The transcription in Fr522 eliminates the penultimate stanza, which is relevant to the counter-domestic point of the poem.)

8 *'eyes were full of . . .'*: *The Mill on the Floss* (1860), book II, ch. 5.

9 *'What have I done?'*: 'Millicent's Life', vol. iii (24 Sept 1881). Yale: box 116, f.454. Also, MLT's Journals (24 Sept 1881). Yale: microfilm.

10 *donor*: James B. Germaine of Albany. MTB, TS notes for a talk with her father, 1967. Yale: box 47, f.14. Germaine left his money elsewhere.

10 *card-dropping etiquette*: Unfinished TS autobiography. Yale.

10 *Mrs Stearns*: MS memorial tribute (n.d.). Yale: box 78, f.315.

10 *MLT's hair*: a lock in Yale collection.

11 *thinnest white dress*: MLT Journals. Yale: microfilm, reel 8.

11 *'Exultation is the going'*: pencil fair copy, addressed 'Sue' (*c.* early 1860). J76/ Fr143.

11 *'Her talk . . .'; 'quick . . .'; 'seizes . . .'*: From SHD's obituary for ED in the *Springfield Republican* (May 1886). The tense of the verbs is changed from past to present.

11 *MLT on Schubert*: Yale: box 77, f.310. (37 MS pages.)

12 *Emma offering scalloped oysters*: Austen, *Emma* (1815).

12 *WAD 'delicate'*: MLT, Journals, III, 185 (10 Nov 1882). Yale: microfilm.

12 *'on the heights'*: MLT, Journals, V (1886): a retrospect. Yale: microfilm.

12 *MLT's voice rang out; 'Miss Emily'*: MLT, Journals, III, 174 (15 Sept 1882). Yale: microfilm, reel 8.

13 *'endure'*: 'Elysium is as far as to'. J1760/Fr1590. MLT had the impression that this poem was composed during her visit, *c.* 1882.

13 *Austin's diary*: Yale.

14 *'always watching'*: Home, 413.

14 *'She writes the strangest poems'*: MLT, Journals, III, 174. Yale: microfilm.

15 *'we all love you'*: L311.

16 *'sew alone'*: L310.

16 *'at the White Heat'*: (*c.* 1862). J365/Fr401. One of three copies was sent to TWH.

16 *'torrid spirit'; 'Domingo'*: L855. Domingo was associated with the production of rum and with its power to intoxicate.

16 *books with 'more'*: The Mill on the Floss, book IV, ch. 3.

16 *'still — Volcano — Life'*: (*c.* spring 1863). J601/Fr517.

17 *control*: Juhasz, *The Undiscovered Continent*, 172–3.

17 *'Fire rocks'*: 'On my volcano grows the Grass'. J1677/Fr1743. Transcribed by SHD.

17 *'Will my great Sister . . .'*: (*c.* 1883). L854.

17 *'Your little mental gallantries . . .'*: (*c.* 1883). L856.

II: 'A STILL — VOLCANO — LIFE'

1: THE FIRST FAMILY

21 *pure and terrible*: (July 1874). L418. After her father's death.

21 *I do not expect . . . pleasure*: Sewall, i, 47.

21 *LD mimicked father*: MLT's notes of LD's anecdotes. Yale: box 82, f.402.

21 *saw things . . . just as they were*: WAD, recollections of ED. Yale. Sewall, i, 222–3.

21 *startling*: LD to ED's editor, Niles (3 Apr 1893). AC.

21 *the Soul's Superior instants*: (c. 1863). J306/Fr630.

21 *simulate*: J443/Fr522.

22 *a sweet little song*: L7.

22 *Kangaroo*: L268. See the vivid poem 'Kangaroo', by D. H. Lawrence.

22 *freckles*: ED mentioned them to Mrs Bowles (c. Aug 1861), L235. She also mentions 'my freckled bosom' in 'Rearrange a "Wife's" Affections', though in a poem it could be invention. In her youth the scoop-necked dresses of the 1840s would have exposed her chest to the sun (unlike the buttoned-up, collared style of the 1860s and her famous white dress).

22 *ED's voice*: Elicited by MLT. In her TS essay, 'ED: Poet and Woman'. Yale.

22 *WAD's similar interrogative lift*: Evident in letters to MLT.

23 *Wild nights — Wild nights!*: (c. late 1861). J249/Fr269.

23 *Aunt Elizabeth registered as male*: Habegger, 129.

23 *only male relative on the female side*: ED to Mrs Holland (Aug 1876). L473.

23 *Bennett's advice book*: EDR.

23 *letter to the World*: (c. spring 1863). J441/Fr519.

23 *for what is each instant . . .*: L656 (c. early Sept 1880).

23 *Oh! Caroline . . .*: Caroline Dutch, Habegger deduces. She later taught ED at Amherst Academy.

24 *I am sensible . . .* and *I think . . .*: Cited in Habegger, 42, 43.

25 *kiss*' and '*-s*': Cited in Habegger, 54.

25 *Requirement*'; '*unmentioned*'; '*Fathoms . . .*': (c. early 1864). J732/Fr857. Habegger, 56, speculates plausibly that the poem looks back to her parents' union.

26 *I think you will learn . . .*: *Jane Eyre*, ch. 14.

26 *If you were God . . .*: To Elbridge Bowdoin. L28.

26 *Oh what an afternoon . . .*: (c. early 1860). J148/Fr146. Habegger, 226, notes how ED 'made heaven the beneficiary'.

26 The Mother At Home: By John Stevens Cabot Abbott. Copies in EDR, Mudd Library, Yale, and Library of Congress.

26 *rigid discipline*'; '*unimpassioned*': Ibid, 63–4.

27 *perusing such papers only . . .*: L63.

28 *fire*': Reported by Lavinia Norcross to Emily's mother. She had fetched little Emily at the time of Lavinia's birth and was driving with her to Monson when a terrific storm broke. McCarthy discovered letters from Lavinia Norcross to her sister, and mentions this incident in his letter to Mary Landis Hampson (20 Sept 1949). Houghton: bMs Am 118.97–118.98 (123)

28 *cordiality*', etc: To Clara Newman Turner (c. 1884). L926. Cited by Sewall, i, 269.

28 *'Born — Bridalled — Shrouded —'*: 'Title divine — is mine!' (*c.* 1861). J1072/Fr194. See also ch. 4.

28 *Mrs Dickinson's 'burning tear'*: Verse by her sister Lavinia Norcross. Habegger, 67.

29 The Belle of Amherst: (1976) by William Luce.

30 *language of her own*: Cogently argued by Cristanne Miller, *ED: A Poet's Grammar*.

30 *'Father steps . . .'*: Cited by Ward, 'Secret', 91.

30 *WAD to boarding school*: (1846) Williston Seminary in Easthampton, Massachusetts.

30 *'looking very stately'*: L45.

31 *genealogy and dates of the Dickinson family in sixteenth and seventeenth centuries*: <http://homepages. rootsweb.ancestry.com/~marshall/esmd83.htm>

31 *date of the voyage; sons killed*: Ibid. The sons were killed in King Philip's War.

32 *'Cousin Zebina . . .'*: L4.

32 *fear of fits and croup*: (16 Feb 1838). Houghton. Quoted in Habegger, 98.

32 *'coming out'*: MDB, *FF*, 87–8.

32 *seat of the sciences and 'It is still ours . . .'*: Oration (1795) at Dartmouth. DFP. Houghton

32 *'depression of spirits'*: Catharine Dickinson Sweetser (29 Apr 1838), cited by Habegger, 106.

33 *'Swelling of the Ground'*: 'Because I could not stop for Death —' (*c.* 1862). J712/Fr479.

33 *ED recalling Sophia*: To Abiah Root (28 Mar 1846). L32.

34 *Abiah Root*: Attended the Academy *c.* 1843–4.

34 *Mrs Fiske's death*: Habegger, 170–1.

34 *'the early spiritual influences . . .'*: To Maria Whitney (*c.* May 1883). L824, cited Fr1605.

34 *'It was given to me . . .'*: (*c.* late 1862). J454/Fr455.

35 *'no verse . . .'*: L751.

35 *Amherst in ED's girlhood, prayer meetings and 'low sad tones' etc*: SHD, TS of 'Amherst Half a Century Ago'. DFP. Houghton.

36 *ED in the cellar*: MLT's notes on LD's recollections. Yale: box 82, f.402.

36 *'I miss you . . .'*: L3.

36 *'entertain . . .'*: L5.

37 *'letter to the World'*: (*c.* 1863). J441/Fr519.

37 *'I am always in love . . .'*: to Abiah Root (14 Mar 1847). L45.

38 *'press you to my arms'*: L12.

38 *mad letter; 'God is sitting here' etc*: L31.

38 *'I love to be surly . . .'*: To Jane Humphrey in the same month (23 Jan 1850). L30.

2: A SCIENTIFIC EDUCATION

39 *ED on the classics side*: She returned to the English side in 1846–7 for her final year in high school. (During that year SHD was on the classics side.)

39 *specimens*: ED, *Herbarium*.

39 Elementary Geology: Copy in EDR.

40 *'eternity of matter'*: Ibid., 274.

40 *'the future destruction . . .'*: Ibid., 281.

40 *'red hot lava . . .'*: Ibid., 228.

40 *'Etna's scarlets'*: 'More Life — went out — when He went' (*c.* autumn 1862). J422/Fr415.

40 *'Lava step'*: 'Volcanoes be in Sicily' (transcribed by SHD). J1705/Fr1691.

41 *ED's school compositions*: WAD's recollections. Yale. Sewall, i, 222–3.

41 *'the sillyest creature . . .'*: To Jane Humphrey (1842). L3.

42 *ED's piano*: EDR. Replica at the Homestead.

42 *'too busy . . .'*: To TWH (1862). L261.

42 *first women's college*: Elizabeth Reid's Bedford College for Women opened in London in 1849. It was designed in opposition to the conservative Queen's College run by men and aiming at the education of governesses (destined for exploitation and misery – see Kathryn Hughes, *The Victorian Governess*). Bedford had an all-women board of governors. A women's medical college opened in Philadelphia in 1850.

42 *number enrolled at South Hadley*: Green, *Mary Lyon*, points out that this was the fall intake in 1847, and that over the course of the academic year this number would have dwindled. The intake was a good deal higher than the one hundred and thirty-five men enrolled in Amherst College.

43 *'wholesome & abundant'*: L18.

43 *'"Faith" is a fine invention'*: (c. 1860). J185/Fr202.

43 *ED remained seated*: Clara Newman Turner, 'My Personal Acquaintance with ED'. Houghton. Sewall, i, 265–75. There has been some rather puzzling scepticism about the veracity of this anecdote. It's puzzling because other anecdotal information from MLT has been accepted uncritically, though she doesn't always tell the truth. There are fashions in who might be trusted. In this case the language of the anecdote does fit ED's style. Scholars are rightly sceptical of a similar anecdote from MDB, suggesting open defiance, for ED took care not to give offence in religious matters.

43 *'Have you said your prayers?'*: ED must have reported this to LD, who repeated the retort to a teacher at Smith College, Miss Jordan, who was interviewed by MTB (3–4 Nov 1934) in preparation for *AB*. Although Miss Jordan was sometimes given to partisan gossip, the retort does ring true. Sewall, i, 263.

43 *meeting on 17 Jan*: Green, *Mary Lyon*, 248–9.

44 *'many sweet girls'*: L20.

44 *Miss Lyon discouraged exclusive friendships*: Later in the century Miss Porter, at her fashionable school in Farmington, Connecticut, resisted the close friendship of Minny Temple, Henry James's cousin, and Helena de Kay (Gilder).

44 *'Miss Fiske told . . .'*: L16.

44 *'pulmonary episodes'*: Norbert Hirschhorn and Polly Longsworth, 'Medicine Posthumous: A New Look at ED's Medical Condition', *New England Quarterly*, 69 (June 1996), 299–316.

44 *ED not tubercular as an adult*: In the flow of a lively anecdote about her father when ED was in her forties (L401), she tossed off an announcement, accompanied by a dramatising exclamation mark, that she was 'in consumption' as a baby. In tone and context, the remark is too airy to be convincing but has gained credence by the weighty tone of critics who take it out of context, saying that she was 'diagnosed' with the disease.

45 *'struck'*: 'I tie my Hat', op. cit.

45 *'A desolate feeling . . .'*: L22.

46 *'real ogres'*: MLT's notes of LD's snippets of memory. Yale: box 82, f.402.

46 *Hannah Porter*: Three College letters were sent to Porter. Habegger, 28–30, opened up this aspect as part of his well-judged consideration of 'the massive presence of Calvinist evangelicalism in ED's life'. See too Habegger, 'Evangelicalism and its Discontents: Hannah Porter versus ED', *New England Quarterly*, 70 (Sept 1997), 386–414.

47 *read* Jane Eyre: ED borrowed the novel at the end of 1849. That winter she acquired Carlo, a Newfoundland dog.

47 *Lavinia at boarding school*: LD went to Wheaten Female Seminary in Ipswich, Massachusetts.

48 *'we do not have much poetry . . .'*: To WAD (15 Dec 1851). L65.

48 *friction with mother*: MLT's notes on LD's snippets of memory. Yale: box 82, f.402.

49 *failure of friendships*: L15.

49 *'silent' letters*: (23 Jan 1850). L30.

50 *'Experiment to me'*: Sent first to SHD (c. 1865). J1073/Fr1081.

50 *accused Jane etc*: L81, L86.

50 *ED and Shakespeare*: Emily Fowler Ford's recollections of their girlhood for MLT's edition of ED's *Letters* (1894), 129–30.

51 *'the integrity of the private mind'*: Essay: 'Self-Reliance'.

51 *Anne Hutchinson and dissent*: Ronald Bush, Oxford lecture on ED (18 Jan 2006).

52 *Hawthorne on women's public utterance*: 'Woman' in *Hawthorne* (NY: The Library of America). Amy Lang, *Anne Hutchinson and Dissent in New England* (Univ of California Press, 1988).

53 *'the infinitude of the private man'*: 'Self-Reliance'. The source is Emerson's *Journal*: 'In all my lectures, I have taught one doctrine, namely, the infinitude of the private man . . .'. (7 Apr 1840).

53 *gave her Emerson*: ED to Jane Humphrey (23 Jan 1850). L30. First edition (1847). EDR.

53 *'touched the secret Spring'*: ED to Judge Otis Lord (30 Apr 1882). L750.

53 *'stinging rhetoric'; 'bullets'*: *Journals* (24 June 1840). ED had no access to his journals but, since Emerson repeats his message over and over, she would have picked up these injunctions elsewhere.

53 *'In silence . . .'*: Ibid. (11 June 1840).

53 *'I tire of shams, I rush to be'*: Quoted in Santayana's essay on 'Emerson the Poet', *Santayana on America*, ed. Richard Colton Lyon (NY: Harcourt, 1968)

54 *'I shall'*: (23 Jan 1850). L30.

54 *letter to Joel Norcross*: L29 (11 Jan 1850). MLT did not include this in her selection of 1894. It did not fit the Dickinson image she was promoting.

54 *'a lie . . .'*: Habegger, 228, suggests a broken promise.

55 *lava and fire associated with feminists of 1848; volcanic cartoon; the Vésuviennes*: Bonnie Anderson, 'Volcano Time' in *Joyous Greetings*, ch. 7.

55 *'No law . . .'*: 'Self-Reliance'.

56 *'She felt a dangerous power . . .'*: Benfey, *A Summer of Hummingbirds*, 127.

56 *April 1850 letter to Jane Humphrey*: L35.

58 *'married'*: (22 June 1851). L44.

58 *'often wrote'*: ED to the Revd Edward Everett Hale (13 Jan 1854). L153.

58 *a retrospect on BFN's message*: L153.

58 '*My dying Tutor* . . .': To TWH (7 June 1862). L265.

58 '*If I live* . . .': To TWH (1876). L457. In this letter she speaks of BFN as 'my earliest friend', and she's thinking of his death in the context of her father's 'lonely Life and his lonelier Death'.

58 '*Title divine — is mine!*': Sent to SB (*c.* 1861) and SHD (*c.* 1865). J1072/Fr194/EDC.

58 '*Newton is dead*': (27 Mar 1853). L110.

58 *ED's letter to BFN's minister*: L153, op. cit.

59 '*My life closed* . . .': J1732/ Fr1773. Undated. Transcribed by MLT, who eliminated dashes.

59 '*boots* and *whiskers*': To Abiah Root (17 May 1850). L36.

59 '*Papa above*': (*c.* early 1860). J10/Fr151.

59 *Jacob wrestles*: Genesis: xxxiii, 24–32.

59 '*worsted God*': 'A little East of Jordan' (*c.* early 1860). J59/Fr145.

60 '*The Soul selects* . . .': J303/Fr409/EDC, op. cit.

60 *timely mentor*: Charlotte Brontë too had this luck when she became the pupil of M. Heger in 1842–3.

60 '*new — and small*' *etc*: J454/Fr455. See p. 34, above. The following paragraph picks up this poem.

3: SISTER

61 *did not disguise*: Her outcries are similar to Florence Nightingale's in *Cassandra*. They have to do with the artifice of women's assumed character and middle-class ways of life in the mid-nineteenth century. In *Florence Nightingale: The Making of an Icon* (London: Viking; NY: Farrar, 2008), 356, Mark Bostridge speaks of an intensity verging on madness.

61 '*blessed*' *night*: To Jane Humphrey (3 Apr 1850). L35.

61 '*in rebellion*': Ibid.

61 '*the author in me*': draft letter to SHD. DFP. Houghton: bMS Am 1118.95.

61 '*little ninny*': L45.

62 '*Topknot*' *etc*: L37. The name is presumably a reference to the topknot of hair worn by high-caste males in ancient Japan.

62 *Susan Gilbert's birth*: 19 Dec 1830, nine days after ED. I'm indebted to Martha Nell Smith's brief biography of SHD on the internet site for her.

62 *Thomas Gilbert's bankruptcy*: MLT in 'MLT Speaks' (1931), who was bent on slander and whose testimony can't therefore be trusted, says that SHD's brother, Dwight Gilbert, paid the town for their father's upkeep in the 'poorhouse'. There is no other evidence, so far, that he was ever in a poorhouse, and the allegation is likely to have been part of MLT's claim that SHD had despicable origins.

64 *Again* . . . '*in love*': In the same way she'd been 'in love' with her teachers at school. It could be more than a crush but less than acknowledged lesbian love. There were elements of romantic ardour in nineteenth-century attachments – Dorothy Wordsworth's for her brother, Tennyson's for Arthur Hallam, Charlotte Brontë's for Ellen Nussey – that don't fit sexual labels because the demonstrativeness and the declarations of love were largely emotional.

64 '*little world of sisters*'; '*sainted* Mary': L38.

64 *Vinnie's diary*: For 1851. DFP. Houghton: bMS Am 1118.95.

65 *'You won't cry . . .'*: L88.

65 *'stupid', 'I fancy . . .'*: L56.

65 *would not permit anything to <u>blossom</u>*: L92.

66 *favourite passage in* Shirley: unspecified, alas.

66 *'Dollie is stuffed with sawdust'*: (8 June 1851). L42.

66 *'For our sakes . . .'*: To WAD (29 June 1851). L45.

67 *men's clothes and 'P.O.M. Meetings'*: SHD, 'Amherst Half a Century Ago'.

67 *Lyman and the Dickinsons*: Habegger's well-researched account, 184–7.

68 *Vinnie's kisses*: *The Lyman Letters*; Habegger, 185.

68 *Hester Prynne's hair*: Hawthorne, *The Scarlet Letter*.

68 *WAD 'long fainting . . .'*: Draft letter to SHD, after spring 1853. DFP. Houghton: bMS Am 1118.95.

68 *WAD as schoolmaster*: Spring 1851 until summer 1852. After that read law in father's office until he entered Harvard Law School in spring 1853.

69 *WAD's comic virulence*: L43.

69 *'Lady Susan'*: (24 July 1850). WAD goes in for this fantasy in a letter of condolence to Sue on the death of her sister. Houghton.

69 *'very high style of rapture'*: To WAD (22 June 1851). L115.

69 *Martha's eyes alight*: (Sept 1851). L52.

70 *drafts of WAD's letters to Martha Gilbert*: Home, 162. After forty years he gave them to MLT, who passed them on to her daughter.

70 *'She thinks a great deal . . .'*: (11 Nov 1851). L62.

70 *'I give all your messages . . .'*: (15 Dec 1851). L65.

70 *Amity Street*: The vicinity of Amherst Academy and Amherst House, where Sue had lived with her parents from the ages of two till six, and where the Todds would board on their arrival in the early 1880s.

70 *'You and I . . .'*: L93.

71 *'hard heart of stone'; 'a big <u>future</u>'*: L85.

71 *plantain leaf in herbarium*: Herbarium, 56. In her Preface, Judith Farr notes that ED's arrangement of her botanical finds provides 'a kind of colloquy among specimens'.

72 *'I so love to be a child'*: To Abiah Root (c. late 1850). L39.

72 *crack time away; 'I need her . . .'*: L85.

72 *'Has it occurred to you . . .'*: *A&M*, 85.

73 *volume of* Poems: SHD had dated it Jan 1853.

73 *'some punkins'; 'I am really lonely . . .'*: *A&M*, 85.

74 *'On this wondrous sea'*: J4/Fr3. Preceded only by ED's two valentines, this is the earliest serious poem to survive.

74 *Sue . . . appreciated Mr Dickinson*: ED's report to WAD (16 May 1853), saying that their father felt Sue appreciated him more than almost anyone else. L123.

75 *'Forgive me now Mattie . . .'*: DFP. Houghton: bMS Am 1118.95. The word 'spoiled' is unclear.

75 *WAD's capacity for hero worship*: SHD, 'Annals of the Evergreens'.

76 *ED advised WAD*: L65.

76 *pure and terrible*: See opening paragraph of ch. 1.

76 *'affliction'; 'Micawber'*: L49.

76 *'Sue has eaten broth . . .'*: L167.

77 *'Sue — you can go . . .'*: L173.

78 *'How did Sue look?' etc*: ED to SHD. L177.

78 *women without dowries*: the Wollstonecraft sisters, the Brontë sisters, MLT, the Temple sisters are some examples of those who did not expect to marry or who faced the difficulty.

78 *Mr Cratchett's*: At the corner of 6th and D streets. Houghton Mifflin to MDB (1 May 1930). Houghton: bMs Am 118.97–1118.98 (11)

79 *Wadsworth*: See vivid portraits by Benfey, *Hummingbirds*, 121–2, and Wineapple, *White Heat*, 71.

79 *'dark secrets'*: Recalled after Wadsworth's death in 1882 to James D. Clark. L776. Cited by Habegger, 331.

79 *'Jennie — my Jenny Humphrey . . .' etc*: (16 Oct 1855). L180.

80 *'gone-to-Kansas'; 'deathless me'*: To Mrs Holland. L182. Cited by Sewall, ii, 466.

80 *Mrs Dickinson on the sofa*: Pollak and Noble, 'A Brief Biography' in *A Historical Guide*, 23, note her 'need for more emotional support' from her husband.

81 *'My Wheel is in the dark'*: Sent to SHD (*c.* early 1859). J10/Fr61. It's what Yeats termed the dark of the moon: the inchoate creative act. Eliot called it the 'first voice' of poetry (in 'Three Voices of Poetry'). The poem also speaks of traversing 'the unfrequented road', reminding one of Frost's later choice: the road least travelled by. Vendler, 65, discusses this poem in her essay on ED's 'serial plot'.

81 *lamp, book*: 'I was the slightest in the House' (*c.* 1862). J486/Fr473.

81 *'Banker'*: 'I never lost as much but twice' (*c.* 1858). J49/Fr39.

82 *'So stationed . . .'*: 'I was the slightest in the House', op. cit.

82 *Chaucer*: 'Truth'.

82 *Yeats*: 'A General Introduction to my Work' (1937).

82 *'Noteless'; 'I could not bear . . .'*: 'I was the slightest in the House', op. cit.

82 *'shrill morning call'*: (24 Dec 1851). L66.

82 *dedication to father*: 'Sleep is supposed to be'. J13/Fr35.

82 *'wild, erratic natures'*: 'The Heart's Astronomy'. Elaine Showalter, lecture on American women writers (Oxford, 11 May 2006) and *A Jury of Her Peers: American Women Writers from Ann Bradstreet to Annie Proulx* (Virago, 2009), 77–80.

83 *Samuel Howe and Florence Nightingale*: Mark Bostridge, *Florence Nightingale*, 86.

83 *'troubled . . .'*: WAD's draft of a letter to SHD. DFP. Houghton: bMS Am 1118.95. Even if he didn't send a fair copy, this is likely to have been a basis for discussion.

83 *The Evergreens*: Designed by William Fenno Pratt of Northampton, Massachusetts.

84 *Aurora Leigh*: Ellen Moers makes connections with ED in *Literary Women* (London: The Women's Press, 1978), 55–62, 165–70, 244–5, 285–6.

84 *'I think I was enchanted . . .'; 'Foreign Lady'; 'Mighty Metres . . .'*: (*c.* 1863). J593/Fr627.

84 *ED's hairstyle*: Recalled by LD in the 1890s when she rejected the daguerreotype as the appropriate image of ED. LD wrote to her cousin John Graves, 'Emily and I always wore our hair this way because it was the way Elizabeth Barrett Browning did.'

85 *Memoirs of Rachel*: By Mme A. de Barrera. Inscribed 'Emily Dickinson' by SHD. EDR.

85 *ED's poem on Currer Bell*: 'All overgrown by cunning moss' (*c.* early 1860, possibly 31 March, the fifth anniversary of CB's death). J148/Fr146.

85 *not 'at all like . . .'; trumpet; 'condensed . . .'*: Charlotte Brontë, Biographical Notice to the posthumous edition of her sisters' works (London: Smith Elder, 1850). Gaskell, *Life of Charlotte Brontë*, ch. 14.

86 *'more electric . . .'*: To Mrs Holland (early May 1883). L822. Mary F. Robinson's life of Emily Brontë was published in Roberts Brothers Famous Women Series (15 Apr 1883).

86 *'the Maid in black'*: (*c.* late 1859). L209.

86 *Kate Scott Turner*: Born in 1831. Married Campbell Ladd Turner in 1855, who died two years later. She and ED corresponded between 1859 and 1866, the year when Kate married John Anthon.

86 *ED improvising at the piano*: Letter (1914) from Kate Scott Turner (Anthon) to MDB after SHD's death, recalling that visit. DFP. Houghton: bMS Am 1118.95.

87 *'Condor Kate'*: (*c.* summer 1860). L222.

87 *'my girls' etc*: (*c.* Mar 1859). L203. Written after Kate's departure on 18 Feb.

87 *'unnatural evenings' etc*: To Kate Scott Turner (*c.* late 1859). L209.

87 *'When Katie kneels . . .'*: L208.

88 *Emerson at The Evergreens*: Sewall, ii, 468. There is no evidence whether ED attended the lecture.

88 The Angel in the House: Popular Victorian poem by Coventry Patmore (Boston, 1856).

88 *SHD's note to ED*: DFP. Houghton: bMS Am 1118.95.

89 *'By such and such . . .'*: (*c.* late 1858). J38/Fr47.

90 *'Fortunate for us . . .'*: To WAD. L87.

90 *'not* like us'*: L78.

90 *SHD's copy of Goethe*: EDR.

90 *booklets*: Known to scholars as 'fascicles', but this word is not ED's. It was introduced by MLT in 1890 when she co-edited the first selection of ED's poems, four years after the poet's death. The booklets are also known as 'packets' but this gives the wrong impression. What ED intends is a home-made book of about six pages of notepaper that the author folded and threaded together.

90 *'One Sister'*: (*c.* 1858–9). J14/Fr5/L197/EDC. The copy sent to SHD (possibly, Johnson suggests, for her twenty-eighth birthday on 19 Dec 1858) was signed 'Emilie' and is pasted into MDB's copy of *The Single Hound*, the first selection of poems published by MDB in 1914, immediately after her mother's death.

91 *'Domingo'*: L833, op. cit.

91 *'the little tippler'*: 'I taste a liquor never brewed' (*c.* 1861). J214/Fr207.

91 *poem to 'Dollie'*: 'I often passed the Village' (*c.* 1858). J51/Fr41. ED acquired the 1857 edition of *Wuthering Heights*, which is presumably when she read it.

92 *erotic*: See Martha Nell Smith, *Rowing in Eden*, and Louise Hart and Martha Nell Smith (eds), *Open Me Carefully*, who make a strong case for same-sex love. See also EDC.

92 *'No Words . . .' etc*: (*c.* 1884). L913.

4: 'WIFE WITHOUT THE SIGN'

93 *'Bomb'*: 'I tie my Hat' (*c.* 1863). J443. Fr omits the semi-final stanza including the 'Bomb' in the breast, which should not be detached from the speaker's domestic aspect. That would seem to be the point of the poem. Johnson transcribes it correctly.

94 *'Existence'*: Franklin transcribes what looks like a capital E as lower case. ED tends to use capitals for important abstract nouns.

94 *'Fire . . . gun'*: 'I have never seen "Volcanoes" —' (*c.* 1860). J175/Fr165.

94 *'a quiet — Earthquake style —'*: 'A still — Volcano — Life' (*c.* spring 1863). J601/Fr517.

94 *'buckled'*: 'The reticent volcano' (n.d. – MS believed lost). J1748/Fr1776.

94 *'Tell the truth but tell it slant'*: (*c.* 1872). J1129/Fr1263.

94 *'I am alive I guess'*: (*c.* summer 1863). J470/Fr605.

94 *'I felt my life with both my hands'*: (*c.* summer 1862). J351/Fr357.

94 *'twinkled back'*: Ibid.

94 *He touched me; I groped . . .*: 'He touched me' (*c.* summer 1862). J506/Fr349.

94 *'Rowing in Eden'*: 'Wild nights — Wild nights!', op. cit.

95 *mistake to read . . . literally*: Benfey, *Hummingbirds*, 245, concludes: 'Her "master letters" seem, in retrospect, experiments in enacting a grand passion on the page.'

95 *'They were disobedient . . .'*: (*c.* spring 1858). L187. First 'Master' letter.

96 *'Oh did I offend . . .'*: L248. Dated by Johnson 'early 1862' but now thought to be early 1861. Second 'Master' letter.

96 *'Tomahawk . . .'*: Ibid.

96 *'Fuschzia . . .' and 'Cactus . . .'*: 'I tend my flowers for thee' (*c.* autumn 1862). J339/Fr367.

96 *ED's weight*: MLT, Journals, V (1 Sept 1886). Yale: microfilm.

97 *third 'Master' letter*: L233.

97 *'nail in my breast'*: (*c.* late May 1863). L281.

97 *closer to exercises in composition*: Susan Howe, *My Emily Dickinson* (Berkeley: North Atlantic, 1985), 24–7: 'These three letters were probably self-conscious exercises in prose by one writer playing with, listening to, and learning from others.'

97 *'words obey my call'*: 'Words', *The Green Helmet and Other Poems* (1910).

98 *'I cannot dance upon my toes' etc*: (*c.* 1862). J326/Fr381.

99 *'Face out of Paradise'*: L489.

99 *Bret Harte*: SB introduced him to the Dickinsons.

99 *'shaggy manner'*: 'Annals of Evergreens'.

99 *SHD's submission of 'Nobody knows'*: Habegger, 389. J35/Fr11.

99 *'Has girl . . .'*: SHD to ED (n.d.). DFP. Houghton: bMS Am 1118.95.

99 *one of Bowles's earliest letters*: Habegger dug up the date of this birth: 15 May 1859.

100 *'I have made [women] shed many tears'*: Cited by Farr, 205, from SB's biographer, George Merriam (1884): a woman who visited SB's newspaper in 1865 reported his words.

101 *'trial . . .' and 'torture . . .'*: To SHD (26 Feb [1864]).

101 *'the late flirtatious widow'*: To WAD (n.d., probably 1863).

101 *'Mrs Bowles . . .'*: SB to WAD (16 Jan [1859]).

102 *'I would not, if I could . . .'*: SB to WAD ([Feb 1859]).

102 *limp along; 'Utica schoolgirls'*: To WAD (Oct 1861).

102 *'wanton & fickle'*: To SHD (26 Feb [1864]).

102 *SB did not want to be drawn too far*: This is a guess on the basis that had SB a just estimate of ED's poems, he'd have expressed it in letters to her brother and Sue, and that ED herself would have reflected this in her letters to him. Then, too, she might not have taken up with Higginson had she had better hopes of SB.

102 *'the Queen Recluse . . .'*: To WAD (9 Jan 1863).

102 *'spiritual manifestations'*: SB to the Dickinsons (2 Jan [1859]).

102 *'for the sister . . .'*: To WAD (4 Feb 1859). Houghton.

102 *'a savage, turbulent state . . .'*: to WAD (2 May 1863).

102 *'If it had no pencil'*: (*c*. early 1861). J921/Fr184. Letter amongst those sent to the Bowles family. Habegger, who favours Wadsworth as 'Master', suggests it was sent to Mary. Unlikely because of the erotic charge. ED was not attracted to Mary.

103 *'Two swimmers'*: (*c*. spring 1861). J201/Fr227.

103 *intruder on a marriage*: 'Wife — without the Sign!' op. cit.

103 *'I'm "wife" . . .'*: 'I'm "wife" — I've finished that' (*c*. spring 1861). J199/Fr225.

104 *'A wife — at Daybreak . . .'*: (*c*. 1861). J461/Fr185.

104 *general conception etc*: Draws on Virginia Woolf's essay *'Jane Eyre* and *Wuthering Heights'*.

104 *'the endless . . . hereafter'*: Nelly Dean seeing Catherine dead in *Wuthering Heights*, ch. 16.

105 *'Vesuvius at Home'*: 'Volcanoes be in Sicily', op. cit.

106 *'I cant thank you any more . . .'*: (*c*. early 1862). L252.

107 *'Could you leave "Charlie". . .'*: (*c*. early Mar 1862). L253.

107 *'Title divine'*: J1072/Fr194. L250, where the date is *c*. early 1862.

107 *'Here's what . . .'*: L250.

107 *SB's confidence to WAD*: When Bowles had visited The Evergreens with his wife in 1861.

108 *'have as much as ever . . .'*: SB to WAD. Habegger's transcript of these letters on the internet.

108 *'I've nothing Else . . .'*: (*c*. spring 1861). J224/Fr253.

108 *SB and 'Lady-writers'*: Farr, 205, takes this from Merriam.

108 *SB's 'bullet' and the third Master letter*: Neat link by Farr.

108 *'Arabian'*: L662.

108 *'manikins'*: Farr, 185.

108 *'little gems'*: (13 July 1862). SB refers again to her poems as 'gems' in a letter (3 Dec 1864): 'gems for the "Springfield Musket"'.

109 *'puzzled'*: J224/Fr253.

109 *'little tippler'*: op. cit.

109 *'Safe in their alabaster chambers'*: (*c*. 1859, 1861). J216/Fr124/EDC. (Fr and EDC include SHD's critique.)

109 *Fidelia Cooke*: Habegger, 383–4.

109 The Household Book of Poetry: ed. Charles Anderson Dana (1819–97), sixth edition (NY, 1860). EDR.

109 *'to New England'*: (*c*. summer 1861). L233. The third 'Master' letter.

109 *Shakespeare's sonnets in the mid-space*: Stephen Greenblatt, *Will in the World* (Pimlico, 2005), 249.

109 *Ann Wroe*: Being Shelley (London: Cape, 2007), 83.

110 *'letter to the World'*: 'This is my letter to the world' (*c.* spring 1863). J441/Fr519.

111 *the need to speak*: Poet Liam Rector describes dashes as 'the connective tissue which begins to function like words themselves'. We hear 'the need to speak'. 'Bidart's *The Sacrifice'*, *On Frank Bidart: Fastening the Voice to the Page*, ed. Liam Rector and Tree Swenson (Ann Arbor: University of Michigan Press, 2007), 130–1.

111 *'a terror . . .'*: (25 Apr 1862). L261. Farr, who makes a strong case for SB as Master, suggests that ED's upheaval was occasioned by his decision to go to Europe.

111 *'palsy'*: To TWH (7 June 1861). L265.

112 *'half angel, half demon'*: MDB heard this from Ned. Cited by Farr, 215.

112 *'Hearts in Amherst – ache . . .'*: L259.

113 *'I cannot see you'*: L276.

113 *'Keep the Yorkshire Girls . . .' and 'Please to need me . . .'*: L299 and L300.

113 *'Ethiop within'*: 'More Life — went out —' (*c.* 1862). J422/Fr415.

113 *'Ourself behind ourself, concealed —'*: 'One need not be' (*c.* 1862; *c.* early 1864 copy sent to Sue). J670/Fr407.

5: 'SNARL IN THE BRAIN'

114 *'Snarl in the Brain'*: ED to Loo (*c.* late May 1863). L281.

114 *'Existence'*: J443, op cit.

114 *DNA as tragedy*: I owe this to Laura Sims, University of Oxford, when we discussed biography across the table at the Helen Gardner Feast, St Hilda's College (9 Feb 2007).

114 *'My loss . . .'*: Final stanza of 'My first well Day — since many ill —' (*c.* spring 1863, copied in booklet 28). J574/Fr288. Earlier (Nov 1862) ED sent a version of the quoted single stanza to SB (at the time of his return from his convalescent journey to Europe). L275. The Bowles version disguises the personal source ('My') in 'you', as though speaking for a sick Bowles. Seth Archer quotes the same stanza in his 2009 article on panic attacks, noting that 'anxiety, panic, and mental anguish somehow brought her closer to this beloved sense of immortality'.

114 *'As One does Sickness over'*: J957/Fr917.

115 *'A Clock stopped'*: (*c.* late 1861). J287/Fr259.

115 *'Agony'; 'Convulsion'*: 'I like a look of Agony'. J241/Fr339.

115 *'Transport' taught 'by throe'*: 'Water is taught by thirst' (*c.* 1859). J135/Fr93.

115 *'Spasmodic'; 'uncontrolled'*: L265.

115 *Mark Bostridge on posthumous diagnoses*: *Florence Nightingale*, 324.

115 *'Dying!'*: (*c.* spring 1861). J158/Fr222.

115 *'some strange Race'*: 'I felt a Funeral, in my Brain' (*c.* summer 1862). J280/Fr340.

116 *'I felt a Funeral, in my Brain'; 'dropped down'*: Ibid. See Vendler, 73, on extinction of consciousness.

116 *'Cleaving'*: (*c.* early 1864). J937 and 992/Fr867. Sent to SHD, who was in the know. Vendler, 71. Habegger, 477, cites this poem as an example of ED's poetic registration of 'the fear that one may be coming apart'. He adds: 'No other American writer of her time explored with equal sensitivity and mastery the experience of fragmentation.'

116 *'off my head'*: 'If ever the lid gets off my head' (*c.* summer 1863). J1727/Fr585.

116 *'scalps'*: 'He fumbles at your soul' (*c.* late 1862). J315/Fr477/EDC and 'Nature —— sometimes sears a Sapling ——' (*c.* late 1862). J314/Fr457.

116 *'Nature —— sometimes sears a Sapling ——'*: Ibid.

116 *'Dread'*: 'I lived on Dread ——' (*c.* late 1862). J770/Fr498.

116 *'to simulate is stinging work'*: J443, op. cit.

116 *'Presentiment'*: 'Presentiment —— is that long shadow —— on the Lawn ——' (*c.* late 1862). J764/Fr841.

117 *'Winds'; 'Thunderbolt'; 'Universe'*: 'He fumbles at your Soul', op. cit. Cristanne Miller, *Emily Dickinson: A Poet's Grammar*, 115, comments perceptively: 'As a narrative event, the poem may reveal the speaker's attempt to outlive an overwhelming experience by articulating it in a universalized verbal and pronominal form: this happens to "you," not (just?) her. The present tense may imply that she continuously relives the sequence even while trying to distance herself from it by representing it as universal, or prophetic of someone else's life.'

117 *'electric gale'*: 'With Pinions of Disdain' (*c.* 1877). J1431/Fr1448.

117 *'by birth a Bachelor'*: L204. Aged 28. Recent research on epilepsy by Dr Jane Mellanby in the Department of Experimental Psychology, University of Oxford, has found that epileptic monkeys are demoted in the social hierarchy and unlikely to mate.

117 *'The Brain within its Groove'*: (*c.* 1862). J556/Fr563. Deppman, 94–8.

117 *'Murder by degrees'; 'mashes . . .'*: 'The Whole of it came not at once ——' (*c.* late 1862). J762/Fr485. Similar to 'stuns you by degrees' in 'He fumbles at your Soul', op. cit.

117 *'straighten'; 'bubble Cool'*: 'He fumbles at your Soul', op. cit.

117 *'Assassin'; 'borrows a Revolver'*: 'One need not be a Chamber —— to be Haunted ——' (*c.* 1862). J670/Fr407. (This scene is from a version of *c.* early 1864, sent to Sue.) A line quoted above, at the close of ch. 4, 'Ourself behind ourself, concealed', is from this poem. The haunted house, the divided self, and the confrontation are uncannily like Henry James's psychological ghost tale, 'The Jolly Corner', a story T. S. Eliot later related to his hero's haunted self in *The Family Reunion*.

117 *poems that recount the . . . stages*: See Vendler, 67, on the *and thens* of a torturer's chamber.

118 *'The Maddest . . .'*: 'It struck me —— every Day ——' (*c.* 1863). J362/Fr636.

118 *'Fog'*: 'There is a Languor of the Life' (*c.* summer 1863). J396/Fr552.

118 *'Languor'*: Ibid.

118 *'the Hour of Lead'*: 'After great pain' (*c.* autumn 1862). J341/Fr372. Also 'Boots of Lead' creak over the Soul in the brain's funeral. Fr340.

118 *understanding of epilepsy*: Temkin, *The Falling Sickness* (1945, rev. 1971), ix: 'There is no unanimity about the range of the concept of epilepsy, and the nature of the disease is still obscure.' Sieveking, *On Epilepsy* (1858), notes that the nineteenth-century advances in physiology were not matched by understanding of the nervous system.

118 *Dr Holmes on epilepsy*: *Medical Essays* (Boston: Houghton Mifflin, 1891), 192.

118 *Julius Caesar*: I:ii.

118 *'epilepsy' in Othello*: IV:i.

118 *'the throe of Othello'*: (20 June 1877). L506.

119 *'reticent'*: 'The reticent volcano' (transcribed by MLT). J1748/ Fr1776.

119 *'when upon a pain Titanic . . .'*: 'I have never seen "Volcanoes" ——' (*c.* 1860). J175/Fr165.

119 *'gunshot'; 'spasmodic throes' etc*: Sieveking at the time in *On Epilepsy*, 4, 74, 108–9.

119 *Jackson not to be consulted for anything trivial*: To her brother ED mentioned a trouble she and her sister shared. I agree with Dr Norbert Hirschhorn ('Was It Tuberculosis?', *New England Quarterly*, 1999) that this was a blind. Lavinia was physically robust. Habegger, 262, suggests it was LD alone who (according to her diary) 'called at Dr Jackson's' but it's more likely that she accompanied her frailer sister.

119 Letters to a Young Physician: See 60–7, 85, 211, 229.

120 *advice not to remove*: Jackson, *Another Letter*, 116.

120 *'idiot medications'*: Oliver Wendell Holmes, student notes from Jackson's medical lectures (1833).

120 *'liability to the epileptic paroxysm'*: Jackson, *Another Letter*, 48–9.

120 *'dreadful'*: Ibid., 49.

120 *tastes should be indulged*: Ibid., 83.

120 *Patients ready to be brave*: James Jackson Putnam, *Memoirs of James Jackson* (1905).

121 *Dr Jackson and ED's way of life*: This suggestion came from Siamon Gordon. Henry James imagines something similar, the lift the truth (that she's incurable) gives to Milly Theale, whose wise doctor opens up to her certain possibilities for living in *The Wings of the Dove*.

121 *delivered the prescription to her father*: (7 Oct 1851). L55. 'Father has the recipe.'

121 *'I have tried . . .'*: Ibid.

121 *prescription survives*: pinned to L148, to WAD (27 Dec 1853). Reproduced in *Home*, 332. Editors Johnson and Ward add note about 'a simple skin lotion, prescribed even today for rough or chapped hands'.

121 *glycerine as treatment for epilepsy*: 'Medicinal Uses of Glycerine in the 19th Century', TS in Health and Medicine folder, Jones Library, derived from *Health at Home or Hall's Family Doctor* by William Whitty Hall (Hartford, CT: James Betts and Company, 1874).

122 *Hirschhorn on prescription for glycerine*: 'Was It Tuberculosis?', *New England Quarterly*, 72/1 (1999), 110–11.

122 *'unsanitary'*: Sieveking, 245.

123 *'consolation . . .'*: Jackson, *Another Letter*, 92.

123 *'Somebody . . .'*: (c. spring 1861). J158 / Fr222.

123 *epilepsy often misdiagnosed*: *The Spiral Staircase*, Karen Armstrong's autobiography, reveals that the nuns in her convent blame her for exhibitionism since doctors find nothing the matter.

124 *'Struck, was I . . .'*: (c. early 1864). J925/Fr841.

124 *'I like a look of Agony'*: (c. summer 1862). J241/Fr339.

124 *'Torrid Noons'*: 'The farthest Thunder' (c. 1884). J1581/Fr1665. The 'Missiles' of 'torrid Noons' were sent to SHD in L914.

125 *'It dont sound so terrible . . .'*: (c. autumn 1862). J426/Fr384. Miller, *ED: A Poet's Grammar*, 78–82, offers a sensitive analysis of poems that absent any reference for 'it'. Miller picks out 'It was not Death, for I stood up' as a poem which attempts to 'mark the boundaries' of 'an unnamed, powerful event' and 'circles its central theme, the identity of "it"'.

125 *'I fit for them — I seek the Dark . . .'*: (c. 1866). J1109/Fr1129. Apart from her, doctors alone use this verbal construction. ED must have sent this to SHD because it was published with SHD's cache, *The Single Hound*, 1914.

125 *grammar undergoing transformation*: an illuminating analysis in Miller, *ED: A Poet's Grammar*.

125 *to 'do'*: 'A still — Volcano — Life'. J601/Fr517.

125 *'a purer food'; 'transport . . .'*: 'I fit for them', op. cit.

126 *'While we were fearing . . .'*: (*c.* 1874). J1277/Fr1317.

126 *consultation with Dr Williams*: Information in ED's letters, Leyda, Hirschhorn and A&M.

126 *eye-wash*: Adams Drugstore, Amherst, Prescription records 1882–5. AC. The prescription is for 'Dickinson'; a likelihood but no guarantee this is ED.

126 *'Bereaved of all . . .'; 'Cups . . .'; 'I waked . . .'*: (*c.* early 1864). J784/Fr886.

127 *address of Dr Williams's consulting room*: Habegger, 484. The house no longer exists. The site is between Commonwealth Avenue and Newbury Street, across the road from the public gardens. Later the site of Ritz-Carlton Hotel, now part of TAJ hotel chain.

127 *scotoma*: noted by Jackson, *Letters to a Young Physician*.

127 *'like so many sphinxes'*: Charcot, *Leçons sur les maladies du système nerveux faites à la Salpêtrière*. Cited by Porter, 546–7.

127 *ophthalmoscope newly in use for searching out diseases of the brain*: Porter, 506.

127 *'hyperaesthesia of the retina'*: In his textbooks Dr Williams steers clear of epilepsy. Too mysterious for his factual manner.

127 *photo-sensitivity*: Dr Williams' textbook, *The Diagnosis and Treatment of the Diseases of the Eye*, notes that hyperaesthesia of the eye occurs in delicate subjects, marked by photophobia, neuralgia and seeing luminous spots of different colours. Vision is unimpaired. Avoidance of the glare of light from snow, together with little use of the eyes, can be effectual. In women, he says, there are cases of intense photophobia. One treatment is to be away from home. In 'hysterical hyperaesthesia' women are said to complain of persistent images on the retina and discomfort from light. The tone is misogynist, as though this were women's nonsense. He does not consider if there could be a physical cause.

128 *'forget the color of the Day'*: 'Severer Service of myself' (*c.* early 1864). J786/Fr887.

128 *'glittering Retinue . . .'; 'put a Head away'; 'No Drug for Consciousness'; 'Affliction'; 'Being's Malady'*: Ibid. Habegger, 485, picks up the aural nuance of 'glittering Retinue'.

128 *'Before I got my eye put out'*: (*c.* summer 1862). J327/Fr336. I quote the first version sent to TWH because the capitals are more revealing.

129 *doctor wipes her cheeks*: To SHD. L292.

129 *'Perception . . .'*: (*c.* 1865). J1071/Fr 1103.

129 *Coleridge*: *Biographia Literaria* (1815–16), ch. 13: 'On the Imagination'.

130 *'Emily wants to be well'*: L293.

130 *'Down thoughts'*: To Loo. L290.

130 *'Siberia'*: L290. In Fr994 (*c.* 1865) it feels to the speaker as if 'the mind were going blind —'.

130 *Alice James on doctors*: *The Diary of Alice James* (27 Sept 1890). Penguin classics, 142. Showalter, *The Female Malady*, 144.

131 *'hystero-epilepsy'*: This supposed condition was thought to be connected with menstruation (D. F. Scott, *The History of Epileptic Theory*). There is a suggestive article on the subject in a standard medical dictionary owned by Dr Bigelow of Amherst

who treated the Dickinsons in the 1880s, now in Jones Library. See also Temkin, 370, and Showalter, *The Female Malady*, 150.

131 *'It struck me'*: (*c.* 1863). J362/Fr636.

132 *intermarriage*: Letter from Gilbert Montague to ALH about MDB seeking information about their families. He refers also to intermarriage with the Gilberts. Houghton: bMS Am 1923 (14).

132 *Zebina's paralysis*: According to Sieveking, 29, the left side can be paralysed during a fit, and in rare cases this can be permanent.

133 *'Poor Harriet and Zebina'*: L279.

133 *caller's report of Ned's fit*: Elizabeth T. Seeyle to her husband Julius Seeyle (11 Feb 1877), who was College President. Seelye Papers, AC: box 5, folder 13.

133 *rheumatic fever*: *Home*, 466. Called here inflammatory rheumatism.

134 *'crumb'*: (*c.* late May 1877). L501.

134 *'scintillation'*: To Mrs Holland (*c.* early 1877). L491.

134 *Mattie and WAD ashamed of each other*: L492.

135 *MLT on epilepsy and WAD's nervous make-up*: Journals, V (18 Oct 1891), 98–9. Yale.

135 *broken crockery*: Reported to MLT when she was preparing the first edition of ED's letters (1894).

136 *'Loaded Gun'*: op. cit.

136 *'power to kill'*: Benfey, *Hummingbirds*, notes the source in Byron, 'The Prisoner of Chillon', a poem to which ED alludes in her 'Master' letters.

6: TELLING

137 *'rearrange'; 'Amputate . . .'; 'bandaged'*: 'Rearrange a "Wife's" Affection!' (*c.* late 1861). J1737/Fr267.

138 *'as Firmament to Fin'*: L265.

138 *"Tis so appalling . . .'*: (*c.* summer 1862). J281/Fr341.

138 *Men dying 'externally' etc*: 'We dream — it is good we are dreaming' (*c.* summer 1863). J531/Fr584. This poem is discussed by Miller, *A Poet's Grammar*, 80. I'm indebted to Linn Cary Mehta for an observation that ED wrote more death poems during the Civil War.

139 *'perfectness'; 'situates'*: 'Perception of an Object costs', op. cit: ch. 5.

139 *'surge' in the brain*: Philip Davis, 'The Shakespeared Brain', *Literary Review* (July 2008).

139 *John Adams and ED*: Thanks to music critic Philip Clark for playing *Harmonium*.

139 *Adams's objective treatment of ED*: I owe this again to Philip Clark.

139 *pop stars*: M. Ward, for one (in *Post-War*); the Italian Carla Bruni, for another. The latter's album released in 2007 included adaptations of ED, Yeats and Auden, sung 'in a smoky, quivering English accent'. M.Ward is one of the singer-songwriters discussed by Laura Barton in 'This be the verse', *Guardian* (13 Oct 2006). Portrait of Bruni's pop career (before marrying the French premier Sarkozy) in the London *Times* (19 Dec 2007).

139 *Doherty nicking ED and Dostoyevsky*: 'Emily Dickinson? She's hardcore', interview with Laura Barton, *Guardian* (5 Oct 2006).

140 *'I took one Draught of Life . . .'*: J1725/Fr396.

140 *ED resented editorial interference*: 'The Snake', she said, was robbed of her.

140 *poems provisional, with continued alterations in booklets*: Wineapple, *White Heat*, 74.

141 *a persuasive case*: EDC as part of the Dickinson Electronic Archives. Led by Martha Nell Smith, the Dickinson Editing Collective has an ongoing project to publish thirty of ED's MSS (together with transcription and commentary) on the internet. The idea is to eliminate editorial interventions between ED and her readers.

141 *'Caxton killed Anon'*: 'Anon', ed. Brenda Silver, in the Virginia Woolf issue of *Twentieth Century Literature* (fall/winter 1979).

141 *'. . . some trace of her'*: The Cottesloe at the National Theatre, London (Oct 2008).

141 *alternative to publication*: Martha Nell Smith, *Rowing in Eden*. See too Petrino, 20.

142 *'Publication . . . is the Auction . . .'*: (c. late 1863). J709/Fr788.

143 *'donkeys'*: LL, 81. 'Donkeys, Davy,' she said, alluding to *David Copperfield* where David's eccentric aunt Betsy Trotwood gives this alarm when donkeys stray into her garden.

143 *'The Soul selects . . .'*: op. cit.

143 *'Rare . . .'; 'sovreign People'*: (c. 1865). L336/Fr893.

143 *'altitude of me —'*: ''Twas just this time . . .' (c. summer 1862). J445/Fr344.

143 *'Mine . . . White Election!'*: J528/Fr411.

144 *'I grope'*: To SB (early summer 1862). L266.

144 *SHD and Peruvian mines*: (c. 1862). L258.

144 *Bowles and North African mines*: (c. 1875). L438: 'your Numidian Haunts'. At the time of the Roman Republic, the province of Numidia stretched across present-day Algeria and Tunisia. Cited by Farr, 188, as amongst ED's erotic metaphors.

144 *'I have lost a Sister . . .'*: L395.

144 *'a hedge away'*: See poem celebrating SHD's birthday, end ch. 3.

144 *'own a Susan of my own'*: L531 is a letter-poem sent to SHD and signed 'Emily'. Fr1436. Farr, 128, surmises that ED's phrase was only a gesture of acknowledgement of their amorous past.

145 *Sue as stranger*: (c. 1877). L530.

145 *so the story goes*: Remembered by Gertrude Graves, 'A Cousin's Memories of ED', Boston *Sunday Globe* (12 Jan 1930). Cited by Johnson as note to L515.

145 *'Your "Rascal"'*: (c. 1877). L515.

145 *'Are you — Nobody — too?'*: (c. late 1861). J288/Fr260.

145 *'We will preserve . . .'*: L230.

146 *'My heart . . .' etc*: (c. summer 1860). L220.

146 *'Because I could not say it . . .'*: 'Through the strait pass of suffering'. L251/Fr187.

146 *'mad'*: To Mrs Holland (c. 20 Jan 1856). L182.

146 *'few pleasures so deep . . .'*: L265.

146 *'wayward'; 'I had no Monarch . . .'*: L271.

147 *'I went to school . . .'*: L261.

147 *'punish'*: Houghton: *65M –121.

147 *'Sweetest of Renowns . . .'*: (c. spring 1876). L458.

148 *'plaintive'*: TWH's word. Editor's note to L274.

148 *'Did I displease . . .'*: L274.

148 *'Will you instruct . . .'*: (c. 1873). L396.

148 *'Dare you. . .'*: Ch. 3, op. cit.

148 *Higginson to ED*: DFP. Houghton: bMS Am 1118.95. Signature cut out in the ms has been restored. L330a (minus date).

149 *'partially cracked . . .'*: Editor's note to L481.

149 *ED to Chickering*: (early 1883). L798.

149 *'unsuitable'; 'too ethereal'*: ED's schoolmate Emily Fowler Ford's account of a conversation with Dr Holland in ED, *Letters* (1931), 131. (Emily Ford was herself the author of two volumes of verse. She disparaged ED, calling her poems 'air-plants' with 'no roots in the earth'. She judged that 'these lyrical ejaculations, these breathed out projectiles, sharp as lances' would, if published, fall on idle ears.)

150 *Dr Holland's belittling attitudes to women*: I owe these details to Habegger, 383, who discovered Holland's revealing unsigned essay, 'Women in Literature' (1858).

150 *'out of gear'*: (c. 20 Jan 1856). L182.

150 *'I was sick, little sister . . .'*: L385.

150 *SHD and 'sick Days'*: L383, 384.

150 *no golden fleece, and Jason a sham*: 'Finding is the first Act' (c. early 1865). J870/Fr910.

150 *'because they talk . . .'*: L271.

150 *'drained'*: TWH to his wife. L342b.

151 *'abnormal'*: TWH recalled the interview twenty years later, *Atlantic Monthly*, lxviii (Oct 1891), 453.

151 *'Infinity'*: From 'Show me Eternity' (c. 1884). L830/Fr1658.

151 *'Only Woman . . .'*: (c. 1875). L447.

151 *twice the number*: she sent SHD 276 poems.

152 *'Safe . . .'*: For history of the drafts, see Elizabeth A. Petrino, ch. entitled 'Alabaster Chambers'. ED wrote two more endings for the poem.

152 *SHD's note on 'Safe' to ED*: DFP. Houghton: bMS Am 1118.95. In note to L238.

152 *'I shall not murmur'*: J1410/Fr1429

153 *SHD's rarity*: Recalling 'Rare to the Rare' in ch. 3, op. cit. L336, a poem-letter.

153 *'To see you . . .'*: L346.

153 *'Egypt . . .'*: L430. *Antony and Cleopatra*, III: xi, 56–61.

153 *Helen Fiske in Amherst*: see ch. 1.

153 *Helen Hunt*: Kate Phillips, 141–7, 308–9.

155 *'The Birds begun at Four o'clock'*: (c. 1863). J783/Fr504.

7: ROMANCING JUDGE LORD

156 *'Dear Family'*: DFP. Houghton: bMS Am 1118.95.

156 *Edward Dickinson's funeral*: *Springfield Daily Republican* and funeral sermon. Copies in DFP. Houghton: bMS Am 1118.95.

157 *text from Samuel*: 1 Sam 20:1.

157 *'melted to tears'*: funeral sermon, quoting letter to the Revd Mr Colton who had brought on the conversion of the group of seventy in 1850, including SHD.

157 *'I would like it to not end'*: L418.

157 *'I say unto you'*: L432.

157 *'a House of Snow'*: Ibid.

157 *Mr Dickinson and the birds*: L644.

157 *'Palace'*: 'From his slim Palace in the Dust'. J1300/Fr1339.

157 *'Marl House'*: (*c*. Jan 1875). L432.

157 *'He giveth . . .'*: Psalms 147, v.9. Allusion in L668.

158 *'spectacular . . .'*: L696.

158 *'George Who — ?'*: 'That sums all Politics to me' (late autumn 1884). L950.

158 *LD more hurried*: L667.

158 *Tenderness*: 'the only God I know'. L689.

158 *hands-on care*: ED's list of what she did does not include the hands-on nursing. L668.

158 *the sisters' bond*: (*c*. 1873). L391.

158 *royal purple*: MTB's 'Biographical Notes' in *Home*, 486–7.

158 *court martial*: ED, *Letters*, ed. MLT (1931), 175.

158 *'Eagles'*: MTB's 'Biographical Notes' in *Home*, 486–7.

158 *'Aunt Glegg'*: L650.

159 *'the dear Lords'*: L392.

159 *enquire*: Letters to LD (*c*. 1875–7), DFP. Houghton: bMS Am 1118.95.

159 *granddaughter*: Theodora Ward, *Harvard Library Bulletin*, 98. Ward edited the letters ED sent to her grandparents, and assisted Johnson's edition of the collected letters.

160 *Benfey*: *A Summer of Hummingbirds*, 206.

160 *'Profile of a Tree . . .'*: L645. Fragment with no name attached that was amongst the Lord material. Photograph in Werner, *Open Folios*.

160 *ED's letters to Lord*: Drafts amongst her papers, some fragments, some in pencil, some fair copies. It can't be assumed with certainty that she sent them in exactly this form as part of their weekly correspondence. One of ED's drafts was in an envelope addressed in Lord's hand to Vinnie and sent via Austin's law office. Presumably Lord's sister-in-law and niece, who deplored the tie with ED, destroyed ED's letters after Lord's death. Lord's letters to ED were also presumably destroyed along with those of other correspondents. Werner, 47, 'unedits' fragments and drafts, and questions the status Johnson gave them as letters. It's uncertain how MLT came to have this collection, which includes a few fragments that don't obviously apply to Lord. Werner, stressing textual instability, looks at words as an aesthetic construct on the page. This tends to deflect their specified erotic charge. There is, however, too much circumstantial evidence to fade out ED's attachment to Judge Lord. Critics who foreground what was undoubtedly an intense tie to Susan are tempted to minimise her attractions to men. In my view she was susceptible to both sexes but with a verbal excitement and abandon that elude current categories.

160 *Abbie Farley*: Twenty years later she married William C. West from a leading Salem family.

160 *will of Otis P. Lord*: AC: MSS 761aa-bb, box 9.

160 *'Little hussy'*: Recalled by Mrs Miriam Stockton, the chief heir of Abbie Farley West (died 1932), talking to MTB in 1936. *ED: A Revelation*, 23.

160 *SHG's warning against ED to MLT*: Note to L757. Source in MLT, 'Scurrilous but True' (1932), quoted in Sewall, i, 195. Quoted by MTB, *Revelation*, 59,

161 *'Fumigation . . .'*: L1041.

161 *'merciless'; 'dynamite . . .'*: 'In Memory of Otis P. Lord' (1884) by the Bar of the Commonwealth and of the Supreme Court at Boston. AC, box 9, f.53.

161 *'the secret springs of action'; 'he that becomes master . . .'*: The Hon Asahel Huntington Memorial Address to the Essex Institute, Salem (5 Sept 1871). Cited in *ED: A Revelation*, 44–6.

161 *'a perfect figure-head . . .'*: 'Annals of Evergreens' (1892).

162 *ED's courtroom language*: (c. 1878). L559.

162 *'hunger'; 'Dont you know . . .' etc*: (c. 1878). L562

162 *'does Judge Lord belong to the Church?'; 'I had never tried . . .'*: (c. 1878). L560.

163 *'I fear I must ask . . .'; 'Should you ask . . .'*: (Oct 1879). L619.

163 *'little devices . . .'; 'glee'; 'How fleet . . .'*: (c. 1881). L695/J1513/Fr1557.

163 *'sweet Salem'*: L751.

164 *'How could I . . .'*: L645.

164 *intensified in late summer 1880*: Benfey, *A Summer of Hummingbirds*, 206.

164 *'your distant hope'; 'heavenly hour'; 'unvail'*: L645.

164 *'I have done with guises'*: L559.

165 *'fair home'*: L645.

165 *racy talk*: Obituary recollections by colleagues on the bench. AC. MSS 761aa-bb, box 9.

165 *'I will not wash . . .' etc*: (1880). L645.

165 *prison-house*: Wordsworth, 'Ode on Intimations of Immortality'.

165 *'Ethiop within'*: 'More Life — went out — when He went' (c. autumn 1862). J422/Fr415.

165 *'Cobweb attitudes'; 'such was not . . .'*: 'To hang our head — ostensibly —' (c. 1859). Fr160 /J105.

165 The Belle of Amherst: By William Booth Luce, with Julie Harris in the role of ED.

165 *spoof of ED legend in Being John Malkovich*: Noted by Daniel Karlin, reviewing Fr (1999).

165 Joyce Carol Oates, *'EDickinsonRepliLuxe'*: *Wild Nights!* Thanks to novelist Sheila Kohler for the gift.

166 *extraordinarily frank in its strange allusiveness and innuendo*: Comment by Isobel Dixon.

166 *'. . . To write to you . . .'*: L750.

166 *'impregnable chances . . .'*: L750. See also L749, where it has a differently ambiguous connotation in a letter to the Boston editor, Niles, where the question of publication has come up.

167 *'Papa . . .'*: L750.

167 *'Emily Jumbo'*: (c. Nov 1882). L780.

167 *Jumbo in the circus*: Benfey, *A Summer of Hummingbirds*, 217.

167 *'I will try . . .'; 'dear Home'; 'So delicate . . .'; 'tender Priest . . .'; 'a treasure . . .'; 'While others . . .'*: (3 Dec 1882). L790.

168 *'the cause'*: L691.

168 *'would be right'*: It's the moral language of Strether, the New England hero of Henry James, as he backs away from commitment to a congenial partner, Maria Gostrey. The situation is not entirely clear: why is it not 'right'? The closing scene of *The Ambassadors*.

168 *'Fire rocks'*: J1677/Fr1743, op. cit.

168 *bridegroom*: See ch. 4, above.

8: SPLIT IN THE FAMILY

169 Middlemarch's *'glory'*: (*c*. Apr 1873). L389.

169 *'the Lane to the Indes . . .'*: To SHD (*c*. Mar 1876). L456.

169 *'like a vulture'*: L962. Cross's *Life* was published in 1885.

169 *stories of the Wilder and Loomis ancestry*: MLT, unfinished TS autobiography. Yale: box 116, f.452.

171 *Thoreau invited Loomis to the Maine Woods*: Letters from Thoreau to Loomis were discovered belatedly. Yale: box 46, f.9.

171 *'Richard Coeur de Lion'*: MLT, unfinished TS autobiography. Yale: box 116, f. 452. I'm guessing here that MLT had this from her mother.

172 *story based on her younger self*: 'Friendly Enemies': (1889). Yale: box 77, f.310. She wrote this story when she returned to the Boston Conservatory for further training in 1889–90.

173 *DPT's bent for gadgetry*: Benfey, *A Summer of Hummingbirds*, 181.

174 *'a strong intuition' etc*: Journals, cited *A&M*, 51.

175 *'climax . . .'*: Journals. Yale: microfilm, reel 8.

176 *'give up everything . . .'*: Henry James, *The Golden Bowl* (1904), ch. 27.

176 *Todds' private life at Amherst House*: MLT, Journals, III (1881). Yale: microfilm.

176 *'At first I used to suffer . . .'*: Journal (Feb 1890). Yale: microfilm. Cited *A&M*, 50.

176 *'absolutely blind . . .'*: Cited *A&M*, 51.

177 *WAD 'could be forever trusted'*: MLT, Journals (15 Sept 1882). Yale: microfilm, reel 8.

177 *'I have simply felt . . .'; 'innocent'; 'caged eagle'*: *A&M*, 58.

178 *Millicent's first encounters with Amherst and 'Gildud'*: MLT's fragmentary biography of MTB which is really more an autobiography. TS. Yale.

178 *'I have not the quality of motherhood . . .'*: 'Millicent's Life'.

179 *MLT's exchange with Ned*: MLT, Journals, III (2 Mar 1882), 161. Yale: microfilm.

181 *'Cynic . . .'*: L689.

181 *'thrown open . . .'*: *A&M*, 135.

181 *'Why should I . . .'*: WAD to MLT (*c*. Nov 1882). *A&M*, 134

181 *'the most delicate courtesy'*: MLT, Journals, V (16 Dec 1885). Yale: microfilm, reel 8.

182 *LD's imitations*: 'Annals of The Evergreens'.

183 *Gib born*: (1 August 1875).

183 *'Our' child*: L1018.

183 *'panting with secrets'*: L868.

183 *'Weren't you chasing Pussy?'*: L664.

183 *'Tudor . . .'*: To SHD. L938.

184 *'Oh I love you . . .'; 'It was no fault . . .' etc*: *A&M*, 138.

184 *'The evening . . .' etc*: *A&M*, 149 (8 Jan 1883).

184 *'cruel' etc*: *A&M*, 149 (8 Jan 1883).

185 *'feeling of wrath'*: *A&M*, 152 (28 Jan 1883).

185 *'I trust you . . .'*: *A&M*, 156.

185 *'famished . . .'*: *A&M*, 154.

186 *winter use of the dining room at the Homestead*: I'm grateful to Jane Wald, curator of the Emily Dickinson Museum, for this information.

187 *tryst*: On that occasion, DPT was there.

187 *'she had come to stay'*: *A&M*, 143 (15 Dec 1882).

187 *'I have come to stay'*: A&M, 151.

187 *'As I told you . . . come to stay'*: Third repetition not included in A&M. MLT letters to WAD. Yale.

187 *'I came to stay'*: A&M, 160 (25 Apr 1883).

187 *gift of arbutus; 'I am sorry . . .'; 'This week . . .'*: A&M, 160–1.

188 *WAD on meeting MLT in Boston*: WAD to MLT (12 July 1883). A&M, 165. Sewall, i, 179.

189 *'I suffer . . .'*: A&M, 166.

189 *LD's letter*: A&M, 160–1.

189 *'shine & affection'; 'I shall sing . . .'*: LD to MLT (n.d. and '12 July'). Yale.

190 *'I thank God . . .'; 'Yes, darling'; 'before the veil . . .'; 'white heat . . .'*: A&M, 171–3.

191 *WAD's letters to David Todd*: Yale: 496C, series VII, box 97.

191 *'than all the Trustees . . .'*: Interviewed by MTB. Yale. Cited by Sewall, i, appendix II, 294.

192 *'sweetly unmoral'*: Journals (1911). MLT acknowledged her disappointment in the marriage only decades later, as something she was too proud to discuss even in her journal where her usual mode was 'blue sky'.

192 *'Black Moghul'*: A&M.

192 *'Perhaps the dear, grieved Heart . . .'*: L869.

192 *'has not leave to last'; boats*: L871.

193 *'My life as a sort of consecration . . .'*: Quoted in A&M, 173.

III: MABEL'S REIGN

9: EMILY'S STAND

197 *'Never eaqualled'*: WAD's diary (17 Nov 1884). Yale: box 101, f.245.

197 *'most perfect . . .'*: WAD's diary (Sun, 14 Oct 1888). Yale: box 102, f.251.

197 *records of lovemaking*: Diaries at Yale. Discussed in A&M, 180, and Peter Gay, *Education of the Senses*, 461–2, where Gay finds that MLT used 'o' for orgasm after a progressive number during the year, e.g. on 28 Apr 1881 she notes: 'Happiest of nights with David – my own. 15 (o)'. On 22 Sept 1882, soon after the Rubicon moment with WAD, she was in Washington with DPT and notes numbers 40 and 41.

197 *'at the other house . . .'*: WAD's diary (1886), Yale: box 102, f.247.

197 *'A most . . . two hours'*: MLT's diary (1886). Yale: microfilm, reel 1.

198 *'we met . . .'*: Letter (6 Aug 1885). A&M, 235–6. WAD's diary for Thursday 7 August 1884 corroborates this: 'at the other house pm till 4 _ = = = = and then at office'. An uninterpretable M-like mark above the parallel lines.

199 *'all will be well'*: (29 Dec 1883). A&M, 178.

199 *'Conventionalism . . .'*: (early 1884). A&M, 186.

199 *'dream . . .'*: a poem entitled 'P.S. First' (c. 1883).

200 *Maggie's witness*: Deposition before a trial of 1898. See below, ch. 12.

200 *'Such superhuman . . .'*: Letter to his sister at school (Mar 1885). A&M, 202.

200 *'talk you over . . .'*: (12 July 1885). Yale.

201 *second writing table*: Longsworth, *The World of ED*, 84.

202 *door closed*: Maher's deposition before the 1898 trial.

203 *'snare . . .'*: L736.

203 *pressed*: Herbarium, 32.

204 *'Trophy is a snare'*: (late Sept 1882, the same month as MLT's singing). L769.

204 *'entangled Antony'*: (21 Mar 1885). L978.

205 *'Will Brother and Sister's dear friend . . .'*: (c. 1883). L831.

205 *'America'*: (summer 1885). L1004.

206 *'adder's tongue . . .'*: MLT's diary (8 May 1885). Yale: microfilm.

206 *'Their dappled importunity'*: (c. 1885). Fr1677. Franklin's note about the MS links it with the diary entry above.

207 *'You are a great poet'*: L444a.

207 *'like a great ox . . .'*: L476c.

207 *'You say . . .'*: L476c.

207 A Masque of Poets: Copy in PML: 42123, location: E-387E.

207 *'I will copy . . .'*: (29 Apr 1878, from her home in Colorado Springs). L573a.

207 *'Success is counted sweetest'*: (c. 1859). J67/Fr112/EDC.

207 *'Now . . .'*: (25 Oct 1878). L573b.

208 *'she wished . . .'*: L749b.

209 *'efface'*: L814.

209 *'I thank you . . .'*: L813b.

209 *sample poems*: Including 'The Wind begun to rock the Grass' and 'Ample make this Bed'.

209 *Niles's rejection of ED*: L814a.

210 *dull*: John Matteson, *Eden's Outcasts: The Story of Louisa May Alcott and her Father* (NY: Norton, 2007), 335. According to biographer Susan Cheever (in conversation), Alcott herself thought it dull, resistant as she was to writing for children.

210 *HH and the Native Americans*: Susan L. Mizruchi, *Cambridge History of American Literature*, vol. iii, 549–52; Showalter, *A Jury of Peers*, 200–3; and Loeffelholz, *From School to Salon*, 131–61.

211 *'What portfolios . . .'*: L937a.

211 *'I hope . . .'; 'tender permission'*: (c. early 1878). MLT omitted these lines in her 1894 edition of ED's letters and Johnson printed this less interesting truncated version in L537 and L591. Houghton: MS Am 111.10 (4). The MSS were lost then rediscovered amongst the Houghton collection.

211 *'light a world'*: ED to Whitney (c. autumn 1884). Cut as above from L948. MS rediscovered.

212 *'phosphorescence'*: SHD quoted this. Amongst her section of DFP, Houghton bMS Am 1118.95, recording an oral remark of ED's to Ned (7 Mar 1883).

212 *LD heard; 'Emily . . .'*: L752. ED reports this exchange verbatim to Lord (14 May 1882).

213 *'rapture'; 'return' etc*: L752.

214 *'Still own thee'*: (c. early 1884). J1633/Fr1654. Not published until 1945.

214 *'A caller comes'*: L967.

214 *'dart'; 'anguish . . .'*: L891.

214 *'place of shafts'*: L892.

214 *'Abyss has no Biographer* — ': L899, op. cit., Part I.

214 *'My heart . . .'*: Shakespeare, *Julius Caesar*. ED didn't specify this line when she referred to this oration, but it's the most apt.

214 *'I never knew . . .'*: L901.

214 *'waylaying Light'*: L937.

214 *'When Jesus . . .'*: L932.

215 *interiors of the Lessey house*: photographs in the Todd collection, Yale.

215 *'a great darkness coming'*: (early Aug 1884, looking back to 14 June). L907.

217 *'The little boy . . .'*: L907.

217 *'The going from a world we know'*: (early Aug 1884). J1603/Fr1662/L907. From destroyed letter to Loo and Fanny about her illness. Copied by Fanny for MLT's selection of *Letters* (1894). The punctuation would have been regularised, and Fanny would have edited out anything too revealing.

217 *'Show me Eternity'*: (c. 1884). Follows letter signed 'Sister'. L912/Fr1658.

217 *'No Words ripple . . .'*: L913.

217 *cardinal flower*: L909.

218 *'Go to Mine . . .'; 'No vacillating God'; 'Remember . . .'*: L908.

218 *'Dart' of enemy spear*: A code word for death elsewhere in ED's poetry.

218 *'adjourning Heart'*: When Hawthorne asks which is the most contaminating of sins, it turns out to be an adjourning heart: removing or withholding the self from family or community. Chillingworth, Dimmesdale, Young Goodman Brown, Ethan Brand and the Puritan minister who assumes a black veil through which he looks on the woman who was to be his wife – all are guilty of breaking their ties with 'the human heart'.

219 *Nellie Sweetser*: L916. Cornelia Peck had married Howard Sweetser in 1860. The Sweetser family lived on a large plot behind that of the Homestead, and socially they were on a par.

219 *'trust'; 'Right'*: L953.

219 *'a sneak . . .'*: WAD to MLT (c. 25 Oct 1884). *A&M*, 199.

219 *'vulgar minded people'*: WAD to MLT (c. 10 Oct 1884). *A&M*, 197.

220 *WAD to Mrs Loomis*: (n.d.). Yale: MLT Papers, box 97, f.155.

220 *'There is nothing . . .'*: (c. 25 Oct 1884). *A&M*, 199.

220 *'Parting . . . reluctantly'*: L946.

221 *'The Dyings . . .'*: (autumn 1884). L939.

221 *rows*: DPT's recollection, MTB, 'Notes taken during the talk with my father' (1927). Yale: box 47, f.14. Cited by Sewall, i, appendix II.

221 *wallpaper incident*: Ned to 'Mopsy', his sister Mattie who was at Miss Porter's school in Farmington, Connecticut (26 Jan [1885]), marked 'am'). Hay Library, Brown University, Providence: St Armand Collection: 33.

221 *'wild'; 'cruelty . . .' etc*: Ibid. St A: 34. The time is noted: '11.15' p.m.

222 *'most forlorn . . .'*: To MDB (29 Jan 1885). Ibid. St A: 35.

222 *'gasps out'; 'the Cripples'*: Ned to Frothingham (3 Mar 1885). St Armand, *New England Quarterly* (1988), 373.

222 *'Little dud David'*: DPT's recollection, MTB, 'Notes taken during the talk with my father' (1927). Yale: box 47, f.14. Cited by Sewall, i, appendix II, section 5. Sewall cites a later date, Sept–Oct 1933, which is the date MTB gives when she types the interview finally in the years before her death. It looks as though MTB started interviewing her father during that critical year for her when she began receiving psychotherapy.

222 *'strange relation'; 'more remarkable . . .' etc*: Journals. Yale: microfilm, reel 8.

223 *four-way*: *A&M*, 203.

223 *'cynical, carping . . .'*: MLT, Journals, IV (July 1885), 102. Yale: microfilm.

223 *'I kiss you . . .'*: (3 July 1885). *A&M*, 220.

223 *'when it comes right'*: WAD to MLT (7 June, the day after she sailed, 1885). *A&M*, 208.

223 *'kiss you & caress . . .' and '— and then . . .'*: To DPT (9 Aug 1885) and to WAD (18 Aug 1885). *A&M*, 239.

224 *'Dear heart . . .'*: MLT to WAD from Lucerne (3 Aug 1885). *A&M*, 232.

224 *'Dear Boy'*: L1000.

225 *ED's refusal to sign the deed*: Evident when DPT was cross-questioned in a trial over MLT's claim on Dickinson land twelve years later. Under pressure he admitted that the Todds had not bought their plot (as Mabel gave out), but had it deeded to them as a gift 'after Miss Emily died'. See ch. 13, below.

225 *'You will look after Mother?'*: L999.

225 *'Why should we censure Othello . . .'*: L1016. Dated by MLT, and included in her first selection of ED letters, 1894.

226 *'client' note*: Yale: 496C, box 94.

226 *'I will come . . .'*: Yale. Not in *A&M*.

226 *'Thistles'*: L1033. Matthew 7.16.

227 *'The tie between us . . .'*: (c. late 1885). L1024.

227 *'Emerging . . .'*: Ibid.

227 *'solace'*: (c. early 1886). L1029 and L1030.

227 *'Because I would not stop for Death'*: (c. late 1862). J712/Fr479.

227 *'the great intrusion of Death'*: (autumn 1884). L940.

227 *'I do not think . . .'*: L668.

227 *drugstore record of prescriptions*: Several other Dickinsons lived in the vicinity, and I've inferred that the patient who appears most frequently and is called simply 'Dickinson' or 'Miss Dickinson' is ED, since all other Dickinsons are indicated by full name, 'Mrs', or initials.

227 *Dr Bigelow's copy of* Dictionary of Medicine: Jones Library, Amherst.

228 *MLT in black in the church choir*: Diary (16 May 1886). Yale: microfilm, reel 1.

228 *'utterly'; 'cried frantically'*: MLT, diary (18 May 1886). Yale: microfilm, reel 1.

228 *MLT perceptive and prescient*: Comment by Lennie Goodings at Virago.

228 *Poe's tale*: 'The Fall of the House of Usher'.

228 *MLT in black and haggard*: A neighbour, Mrs Jameson, noticed this.

228 *'Don't say a word'*: (n.d.). *A&M*.

228 *meadow*: Described by MTB in her notes for an autobiography. Sewall, i, appendix II, 296.

228 *Painted red*: It was red with green trimmings. *AB*, 4. The house still stands, though it's been moved in toto from the southern to the northern side of the street, the side nearer to the Homestead. The house is no longer visible from Main Street, surrounded now by mature trees, and the Dickinson meadow is filled with houses.

229 *'a little house . . .'*: Yale — one of the three TS mss in the Yale archive, synthesised by Sewall, i, 'Scurrilous but True', appendix II, 285.

229 ménage à trois: *A&M*, 242. Thanks to Keith Carradine for the alert.

229 *'with the witness'*: WAD's diary (1886). Yale: box 102, f.247. Siamon Gordon noted his use of the legal word.

229 *Mabel's diary for 1886*: Yale: microfilm, reel 1.

229 *'more than any other man'*: Interview with MTB (1927). Sewall, i, appendix II.

229 *'a sort of unspoken sympathy'*: MLT Papers (6 July 1885). Yale: 496C. Not in *A&M*.

229 *'clear the track'*: WAD to MLT (12 July 1886). *A&M*, 250.

229 *DPT humming an aria*: Peter Gay, 94.

229 *outside stair*: *A&M*, 242.

230 *'awful omni-presence'; 'the somewhat terrible center . . .'*: A few fragments of autobiography (from massive collection). Yale. Transcribed by Sewall, i, appendix II, 297–8.

230 *'the quaint little girl . . .'*: (c. late Sept 1882). L769. MTB was then aged two. The date suggests that the child accompanied Mabel's first visit to the Homestead, and that though ED did not appear to Mabel, she was face to face with the child.

230 *tassels*: '25 August 1927', autobiographical TSS. Yale: box 56, f.6. After typing, MTB adds in pencil that someone must have told her this detail, i.e. she questions her memory, but the dangling, the bending to a small child who's often about the house, rings true. Who could have told her? Mamma never saw ED.

10: LADY MACBETH OF AMHERST

231 *'Mabel Loomis Dickinson'*: Yale: 496E, series I, box 4, f.57. The envelope is undated.

231 *'presentiment'*: (2 Nov 1885). *A&M*, 244.

232 *farewell letter*: (5 June). Yale. Not in *A&M*.

232 *An angel*: (c. spring 1885). *A&M*, 204.

232 *'pure white'*: (14 June 1886). *A&M*, 247.

234 *MLT's report of what WAD told her of his marriage*: Journals, V (16 Dec 1885). Yale. Also a summary on a strip of paper, preserved with her papers at Yale: 496C, series VII, box 103, f.259. The spider's web cliché is repeated in both sources.

234 *inscribed book*: EDR.

234 *ED's exchange with Dr Holland*: Quoted by ED to SHD. L714.

234 *Sue's visit to ED*: ED to Dr Holland. L715.

235 *'And you alone . . .'*: (6 July 1885). Yale. Not in *A&M*.

235 *'It seems unfair . . .'*: (Feb 1883). *A&M*, 154.

235 *MLT asked WAD for reasons*: *A&M*, 185.

235 *MLT in Washington*: (early 1884). Ibid.

235 *'to use as a shield'*: WAD to MLT, repeating her plea. Ibid.

236 *'a lady to the core'*: (19 Aug 1887). *A&M*, 288.

236 *Ned's nerves*: To MDB (1 Feb 1885). Hay Library. St Armand, *New England Quarterly* (1988), 373.

236 *'storm-centre'; 'stiffened up'*: To MDB (11 Jan and 3 Mar 1885). Ibid.

236 *'Is it not better . . .'*: (early 1884). *A&M*, 186.

236 *'my sweet wife'*: *A&M*, 235.

237 *'wicked' etc*: *A&M*, 240–1.

237 *'encumbrances', 'annoyances'*: (15 Dec 1885). *A&M*, 244–5.

237 *'deprivations . . .'*: (2 Nov 1885). *A&M*, 244.

237 *'one turn of God's hand'*: (15 Dec 1885), op. cit.

237 *'The World hath not known . . .'*: (c. late 1885). L1024.

238 *'You will not . . .'*: *A&M*, 244–5.

238 *'star of presentiment . . .'*: (2 Nov 1885). *A&M*, 244.

238 *potentially dangerous*: Browning's Porphyria (in the dramatic monologue 'Porphyria's Lover') and Othello's Desdemona are loved by men who kill them.

239 *'divine possibilities . . .'*: MLT to WAD (7 June 1887). Yale. Not in *A&M*.

239 *'of-course feeling . . .'*: (c. 10 June 1887). Yale. Not in *A&M*.

240 *'unconscious'*: Polly Longsworth, *A&M*, 286.

241 *'morbid'; 'hatred . . .'*: *A&M*, 286–7.

241 *'If any divine visitation . . .'*: *A&M*, 290.

241 *'my angel wife'*: (18 June 1887), when she was en route for Japan. *A&M*, 270.

242 *'There is nothing else . . .'*: (16 July 1887). *A&M*, 280–1.

242 *'the power' of her love*: *A&M*, 280.

242 *Seelye not impressed with DPT*: WAD to MLT (3 July 1887). *A&M*, 273–4.

242 *'I am pitifully helpless . . .'*: (31 July 1887). *A&M*, 286.

242 *'turn it over'*: *A&M*, 298.

243 *'I want to rush away . . .'*: (2 Nov 1885). *A&M*, 244.

243 *'clearly'*: (6 July 1885). Yale. Not in *A&M*.

243 *'hoggery . . .'*: (13 Nov 1887). DFP. Houghton: bMS Am 1118.95.

244 *'volume of Emerson . . .'*: (16 Nov 1887), from Memphis, Tennessee. *A&M*, 300.

244 *'frightened'*: WAD to MLT (28 Mar 1888). *A&M*, 304.

245 *SHD to WAD from Maine*: (4 Aug 1888). DFP. Houghton: bMS Am 1118.95.

245 *MLT's appearance in 1888*: MLT's photo album. Yale: 496E.

245 *'thunderbolt'; 'I was crushed'*: *A&M*, 310.

245 *'that heavy incubus' etc*: Journals (22 Oct 1888), 33. Yale: microfilm.

246 *'It almost seems to me . . .'*: *A&M*, 310–12.

247 *'heart-breaking discourtesies'*: MLT to WAD (14 Apr 1889). *A&M*, 319.

247 *MLT and the Handel and Haydn Society*: Journals (winter 1990). Yale: microfilm.

247 *MLT on her 'dear men'*: Journals, V, 44, 49. Yale: microfilm.

248 *'face to face with . . . horror'*: (30 Nov 1889). *A&M*, 328.

248 *Mrs Coonley*: A cousin of Eben Loomis.

249 *'mentally and spiritually . . .'*: (1890). *A&M*, 296.

249 *'wonderful effect'*: Journals, V (30 Nov 1890), 73. Yale: microfilm.

249 *creative offspring*: I'm indebted to poet and agent Isobel Dixon for this.

11: MABEL IN EXCELSIS

250 *'my work . . .'*: MDB, Introduction to *Further Poems*.

250 *'A Damascus blade . . .'; 'swift . . .'*: Obituary, *Springfield Republican* (18 May 1886). Copy in AC.

251 *SHD sent poem to Gilder*: (31 Dec 1886). Century Collection, Manuscript Division of the New York Public Library, cited *AB*, 88.

251 *'un-presentable'*: SHD to TWH (c. 1890). AC: ED collection: Todd, 110–11.

251 *'Alcohol' and 'pearl'*: Cited by Benfey in 'The Mystery of ED', *NYRB* (1999).

251 *'wayward'*: TWH, Preface to *Poems* (1890).

251 *'wayward' stuck*: See Charles R. Anderson, *Emily Dickinson's Poetry: Stairway of Surprise* (1960; repr. NY: Anchor, 1966).

252 *'sometimes weary . . .'*: LD to Amherst friend, Mrs Dickerman, quoted in her daughter, Elizabeth Dickerman (of Amherst, Smith class of 1894, whose mother had been close friend of LD). 'Portrait of Two Sisters: Emily and Lavinia Dickinson', *Smith Alumnae Quarterly* (Feb 1954), 79. Copy in Smith College archives.

252 *MLT's daily visits to LD*: Diary, November 1888. Yale: microfilm.

253 *'No publisher . . .'*: MLT recalled these words in 'ED's Literary Debut', *Harper's Magazine*, CLX (Mar 1930), 463–4.

253 *commercial rather than private publication*: *A&M*, 294.

253 *MLT's typewriter*: Exhibited at the Homestead in Oct 2007. ED collection, Jones Library.

254 *Assignation 'up stairs'*: MLT, Diary (16 Oct 1888). Yale.

255 *Far off in the future . . .*: Sewall and *A&M*, for instance, relay the Todd story.

255 *'gave it up definitely. Then . . .'*: MLT to TWH (16 Dec 1890). AC.

256 *Look like the innocent flower: Macbeth*. Letter from Lady Macbeth to her husband.

256 *'uplifted'*: (1890). *A&M*, 296.

257 *baskets of poems; transcribing at Vinnie's; hustled out of sight*: Recalled by DPT. MTB, 'Notes taken during the talk with my father' (typed Oct 1967). Yale.

257 *Miss Graves's mistakes*: Franklin, *Editing ED*, 13–14.

257 *DPT helped to sort*: DPT's reminiscence of MLT's editing, as told to MTB (Sept 1934). He was by then mentally ill, but what he says rings true. Yale.

257 *'comets of thought'*: MLT to Mr E. D. Hardy (Dec 1894), who replaced Niles (following his death in May 1894) at Roberts Bros, when she proposed they publish a Dickinson yearbook with her 'comets of thought' for each day. AC.

257 *DPT and Olive Schreiner*: Niles to MLT (13 Oct 1891). AC. MLT had read *The Story of an African Farm* in 1888. Her diary notes that she didn't like it.

258 *TWH came to discuss transcripts*: Diary. Yale: microfilm. Wineapple, *White Heat*, 276. There's conflicting evidence (from MLT) that she called on him at his home at 25 Buckingham Street, Cambridge, or perhaps these were different occasions. Wineapple suggests plausibly that 'Mabel enhanced her role as Dickinson's perspicacious sponsor'.

258 *MLT's version of meeting with TWH; TWH astonished*: MLT, Journals, IV, 75. Yale.

258 *'I don't know . . .'*: WAD to MLT (25 Apr 1890). *A&M*, 358.

258 *'unwise to perpetuate . . .'*: Niles to TWH (10 June 1890) from Arlington in Boston. AC. Confirmed in MLT, Journals, V, 78. Yale.

259 *reader's report*: enclosed in reply from Mr Niles. AC.

259 *'I died for Beauty'*: (c. 1862). J449/Fr448.

259 *LD as 'Maltese pussycat'*: MLT, Journals, V, 77. Yale: microfilm.

260 *MLT justified her editing*: Journals, V (30 Nov 1890).

260 *'a shaft of light . . .'*: Quoted by MLT in her essay 'The Evolution of a Style'. Yale.

260 *'I never lost as much but twice'*: (c. autumn 1858). J49/Fr39.

261 *'As she stood . . .'*: *The Commonwealth*, Boston (20 Feb 1892), cited *AB*, 196.

261 *'kill'*: MLT, Journals, V, 80. Yale.

261 *never met face to face; 'flitting'*: Admitted under legal cross-questioning. See ch. 12.

261 *Howells on ED*: review for *Harper's* (Jan 1891).

262 *Elihu Vedder on ED*: DFP. Houghton: bMS Am 1118.95, box 8.

262 *'love at first sight'*: (12 Jan 1892). DFP. Houghton: bMS Am 1118.95.

262 *Christina Rossetti on ED*: Niles to MLT (17 Feb 1891). AC.

262 *Alice James on ED*: (6 Jan 1892). *Diary of Alice James*, 227.

262 *'I'm Nobody'*: (c. late 1861). J288/Fr260.

263 London Daily News *on ED*: (Dec 1891).

263 *reviews*: MLT employed a cutting service, and kept a scrapbook. AC: box 20, f.1.

263 *'You are the only person . . .'*: TWH to MLT (15 Dec 1890). Todd Papers, AC.

263 *stopped speaking*: MLT, Journals, V (16 June 1891), 86.

263 *'for her' and 'I think . . .'*: SHD to TWH (c. 1890). AC: Todd, 110–11.

263 *'laziness'*: Journals, V (30 Nov 1890). Yale. Well-chosen lines quoted in *A&M*.

263 *'Just lost'*: In pencil addressed 'Sue'. First published, entitled 'Called Back', in the *Independent*, 43 (12 Mar 1891), 1, repr. J160/Fr132. MS in the Univ of Virginia. Early in 1861 ED made another fair copy for booklet 10. Contesting correspondence in *AB*, 114–20.

263 *the wind from 'beyond the world'*: '2nd Debate between the Body and Soul' (1911) in *Inventions of the March Hare*, ed. Christopher Ricks (Faber and Harcourt, 1996).

264 *'waste'*: Burnt Norton: V.

264 *plan to use the prose*: To Higginson, op. cit.; also to William Hayes Ward (8 Feb 1891). Lowell Collection, Houghton. Letters to Ward in DEA: <www.emilydickinson. org/susan/table_of_contents.html>.

265 *eighty poems*: Houghton. 'Notes Towards a Volume of Emily Dickinson's Writings'. <www.emilydickinson.org/susan/table_of_contents.html>.

265 *fifty-nine*: Before the ED collection was bought by Harvard, Mary Hampson found this small packet of poems copied by SHD, about half of them unpublished and half in *The Single Hound*. Fr1686–1744.

265 *spirit of strife*: Phrase from Tolstoy, *Anna Karenina*.

265 *LD's legal protest to Ward*: (21 Mar 1891). DFP. Houghton: bMS Am 1118.95.

266 *Ward declined*: Ward to WAD (21 Mar 1891). DFP. Houghton: bMS Am 1118.95.

266 *'Indian Pipes and Witch Hazel'*: TWH to Niles (27 July 1891). AC.

266 *'fascicules'*: LD talked of 'the little volumes'. Thomas Johnson called them 'packets'. But 'fascicles' has so far won out in Dickinson scholarship.

266 *letters 'a private trust . . .'*: Franklin, *Editing ED*, 84.

266 *Mrs Ford*: She died soon after.

267 *mutilation of 'One sister . . .'*: See figures 8, 9 and 10 in Franklin, *The Editing of ED*.

267 *allegation it was WAD who did the mutilations*: In *Open Me Carefully*, Smith and Hart ascribe the mutilation to Todd who was trying 'to hide Susan's central role in Dickinson's writing process' and to 'suppress any trace of Susan as Emily's primary audience'.

267 *revival of Lady Macbeth imperatives*: MLT to WAD. *A&M*, 371.

267 *MLT omitted correspondence with SHD*: MLT did have occasion to refer to the reproachful letter Emily sent when Sue, as a single young woman, went silent out west. 'Perhaps this is the point at which our paths diverge', Emily writes to Sue in 1854. Hardly representative of the lifelong tie that followed Sue's return and capitulation to marriage. This sentence would of course appear to support MLT's argument that the two women were mostly estranged.

268 *cut references to sickness*: Home, 54.

268 *Norcross cousins shielded ED from biographical intrusion*: Conceivably, they wished to conceal confidential comments about Lavinia, the feud, or Mabel Todd herself, but

in such a case it would have been simple to eliminate the relevant letters rather than the entire batch.

268 *Fanny Norcross to MLT*: Todd 329. AC. Box 18, f.16. *AB*, 282–3.

269 *MLT's unpublished essay on the letters*: 'The Evolution of a Style'. Yale.

270 *'Think of . . .'*: MLT to E. D. Hardy (3 Dec 1894). AC.

270 *'a peculiarly delicate. . .'*: MLT to Niles (26 Feb 1894). AC.

270 *'in the cold impartiality of print'*: Ibid.

270 *Hardy succeeded Niles*: Niles died in Perugia in May 1894.

271 *'This may all seem . . queer . . .'*: WAD to Hardy (25 Sept 1894). AC.

272 *'in a heap'*: WAD to Hardy (22 August 1894). AC. The aggressive tone covers the fact that WAD is in fact climbing down. This letter accepts joint royalties.

272 *another run of copies*: ALH, Foreword to *FF*, xiv, alleges that of the second printing of 1500 copies, 1200 were returned. This is hearsay only, part of the anti-Todd campaign to suggest that MLT's 1894 edition of the *Letters* shouldn't count.

272 *crusader*: LD to Niles (27 July 1891). AC.

272 *'Thermopylae'*: ED to MLT (19 July 1884). See ch. 9, above.

273 *'whimsical' etc*: Preface to *Poems* (1890).

273 *'definitely posed . . .'*: MLT, Journals, V (18 Oct 1891), 98. Yale. Cited Sewall, i, 227.

273 *Habegger's persuasive analysis of 'This is my Letter . . .'*: Talk: 'Some Problems'.

273 *MLT's review column*: (Nov 1890). In Scrapbook, AC. She reviewed her own edition, together with three other Roberts Bros books.

274 *ED unlike the daguerreotype*: MLT to Niles (13 July 1893). AC. The portrait of the three Dickinson children is in EDR and a copy now hangs in the parlour of the Homestead.

274 *'soften the eye . . .' and 'altogether softened'*: MLT to Niles (17 Jan 1894). AC.

275 *'neuralgic darts . . .'; 'the hardly human dumbness'*: *The Critic* (1891). MLT's Scrapbook, op. cit.

275 *'picturesque' life; 'gentle . . .'*: MLT's review column in *Home Magazine* (Nov 1890).

275 *'startling . . . poetic bombs'*: 'Evolution of a Style' (*c.* 1894). Yale.

276 *'no comprehension . . .'*: WAD to TWH, quoted in Dickerman, 'Portrait of Two Sisters', op. cit.

276 *'inciting voice', etc*: To Charles Clark (mid June 1883). L827.

276 *'Joan of Arc'*: LD to Niles (27 July 1891). AC. Cited by Jane Ward in her 2007 exhibition at the Homestead.

IV: THE WAR BETWEEN THE HOUSES

12: LAVINIA'S STAND

279 *not a cent*: Miss Vryling Wilder Buffam to MTB (16 Nov 1938). *AB*, 368.

280 *DPT bathed LD*: MLT, Diary (21 Dec 1894). Yale: microfilm, reel 3.

280 *'had the best' of both men's lives*: *A&M*, 372.

281 *relief*: Ned to Frothingham (Mar 1898) says that 'recent changes in the family' had rendered his life 'endurable' before the case arose. DFP. Houghton: bMS Am 1118.95.

281 *'My best friend . . .'*: 'A Line A Day Diary' (16 and 17 Aug 1895). Yale: 496B, series VII, box 108, f.55.

281 *'degrading . . .'*: Maggie Maher recalled this exchange. Trial mss.

281 *'My Austin . . .'; 'I feel . . .'; 'I want . . .'*: Diary. Yale: microfilm.

282 *'on a volcano . . .'; 'real . . . self'*: Journals (May 1896), 136. Yale: microfilm, reel 9.

282 *'of pain'; 'Youth is my role'*: Journals, VII (Sept 1896).

282 *'signet royal . . .'*: Journals, VIII (1897).

282 *Omaha plan*: WAD to J. Clark (8 Aug 1893). Yale: 496C, box 97, f.157. Sewall, i, 184, notes that the letter is a draft and may not have been sent.

283 *'A deaf God'*: *A&M*, 375.

283 *'And if my life . . .'; 'My advancements . . .'*: *A&M*, 361.

284 *money meant a lot*: When advancement of the needy is debated in E. M. Forster's *Howard's End* (1910), it's suggested that the most effective gift to an able but poor aspirant is not, in the first instance, education; it's a certain number of pounds.

284 *'no treason' and 'Ever be . . .'*: (Aug 1885). See ch. 9, above.

284 *WAD's bequest to MLT*: Yale: box 97, f.153.

285 *nearly $34,000*: LD Papers, Hay Library. Inventory of the estate (Apr 1896) added up to $33,890.

285 *'slippery . . .' etc*: Diary (6 Oct 1895). Yale. Cited by Walsh, 185.

286 *measurements of meadow*: Original deed in MLT's hand. Trial mss. The 290-foot measurement is the length of the adjoining Dell. This means that she was extending the width of her plot to 54 feet, and not the mere 13 feet she alleged in her later recollections.

287 *Bumpus longed to make love*: *A&M*, 412.

287 *MLT's exchange with Spaulding*: 'Mabel Todd Speaks' TS (10 Oct 1931). Yale: box 101, f.242.

288 *scene in the dining room*: Reconstructed from statements before and during the ensuing court case.

288 *Maggie told LD*: Mr Palmer, WAD's executor, saw the deed in a business magazine and confronted Maggie about it in the Amherst post office.

290 *'paper'*: Mr Spaulding corroborated this in court on 3 Mar 1898.

291 *'mere trifles . . .'*: *A&M*, 408.

291 *'witchesmare'*: Ned to friend Theodore Frothingham in the aftermath of the court case (7 Mar 1898): '16 years witchesmare', which therefore goes back to 1882. As in 'nightmare'. Like his aunt, Ned invents a word. An alternative reading of the ms word could be 'witchesmere'. Houghton: bMS Am 1996 (2). In demonising MLT at the time of the court case, Ned pays her back for slurs on his mother.

291 *Ned to LD*: DFP. Houghton: bMS Am 1118.95.

292* *a thousand dollars her due*: 'Mabel Todd Speaks', op. cit.

292* *royalty statements on first edition of ED's letters*: LD Papers, Hay Library.

293 *'wallop'*: MLT, Diary (27 May 1897). Yale: microfilm, reel 3. Quoted in *A&M*, 414.

293 *Mr Hills's claim*: Deposition taken by LD's counsel, Mr Field (1897). Trial mss.

293 *'leeches'*: *Springfield Republican* (4 Mar 1898), reporting the case.

293 *Miss Seelye's report of Maggie's words*: Deposition taken by Mr Field (1897). Mss.

294 *'All right'*: MLT reports in her Diary (20 Dec 1897). Yale: microfilm, reel 3.

294 *'too good a case . . .'*: 'MLT Speaks', op. cit.

294 *WAD repudiates his children*: recalled by MLT, Ibid.

295 *evidence of Maggie Maher*: Trial mss.

13: THE TRIAL

See *A&M*, 'The Law Suit and the Trial', 409–13. This informed summary has the advantage of being available. Other sources are the trial mss and 'MLT Speaks'.

299 *'fool'; 'Paddy'; 'pack of lies'; 'disgust'*: 'MLT Speaks' (10 Oct 1931). Yale: box 101, f.242. Some material synthesised by Sewall, i, appendix II, section 4.

299 *MDB locked the piano*: Ibid.

300 *to sue as a form of therapy*: Janet Malcolm makes a brilliant comparison with Freud's talking cure in *The Journalist and the Murderer* (New Yorker, 1990).

300 *date of Amherst Slander Case*: Summonses (dated 26 Feb 1898). Trial MSS.

300 *Hills pleading sick*: He did not record slander evidence but did record a deposition for the land trial. It's unclear whether Miss Seelye testified at the land or the slander trial.

301 *land trial records*: Trial MSS: Hampshire Superior Court Civil Action No. 125, including depositions by Maggie Maher, Jane Seelye and Mr Hills; Houghton Ms Am 2521; newspaper cuttings in the Houghton's box of family papers, bMS Am 1118.95 and newspaper cuttings (the *Springfield Republican* and the *Hartford Courant*) at Yale: 496C, series VII, box 101, f.241; copies of the Bill of Complaint and the Defendants' Answer in Jones Library, Amherst. Official Transcript, Yale: box 101, f.239, including another copy of the Bill of Complaint, a summary of the land trial in the Superior Court: 'Report of the Evidence', and the Supreme Court summary.

301 *LD's courtroom outfit*: 'MLT Speaks', op. cit.

301 *LD's hairstyle*: LD to her cousin, John Graves of Boston. DFP. Houghton: bMS Am 1118.95.

302 *'ridiculous'*: *AB*, 359; Sewall, i, appendix II, 262.

302 *MLT's courtroom hat*: 'MLT Speaks', op. cit.

303 *wrinkles; teeth*: MLT's reminiscences in *AB*.

303 *Field remembered LD*: Letter to MDB (26 Nov 1932). Correspondence concerning the publication of ED. Houghton: MS Am 1118.97–1118.98.

303 *deceive the elect; 'make anybody believe . . .'*: MLT, Journals, VIII. Yale: microfilm, reel 9.

304 *LD's 'forlorn look'*: 'MLT Speaks', op. cit.

306 *'lesson . . .'*: Ned to Frothingham (Mar 1898). DFP. Houghton: bMS Am 1118.95.

306 *asked her to edit her poems*: *Hartford Courant* (2 Mar 1898), reporting the case.

309 *Taft's summing-up*: *Springfield Republican* (4 Mar 1898). *A&M*, 422.

309 *'pounded'*: MLT's word. Diary (3 Mar 1898). Yale: microfilm, reel 3.

309 *3 April*: MLT records the judgment in her diary on 15 Apr. Yale: microfilm, reel 3.

310 *'Something was done . . .'*: Ibid.

310 *'kills me daily'*: Diary (21 Apr 1898). Ibid.

310 *Harvard Law School*: 'MLT Speaks', op. cit. MLT often lied, but this rings true.

310 *'own legs'*: 'MLT Speaks' (10 Oct 1931). Yale: box 101, f.242.

311 *Mrs Washington Cable*: A friend of MLT.

311 *Supreme Court case*: It was case no. 172, argued in Sept 1898 and set out in the *Massachusetts Supreme Court Reports*, 183.

312 *'I am . . . crushed'*: Diary (29 Nov 1898).

312 *sensitive as a leaf; a chain; 'I shall die . . .'*: Journals, VIII. Yale: microfilm, reel 9.

14: DEFEATS OF THE FIRST GENERATION

313 *fourth volume*: MLT repeats this intention in her recollections thirty-three years later. MLT's note in 1931: 'I was in the midst of preparing a fourth volume . . .'.

313 *'disgrace . . .'*: Ned to Theodore Frothingham (Mar 1898). Houghton: bMS Am 1996 (2).

313 *escaped to Europe*: summer 1897, with the trial due, then, for the autumn.

313 *'witchesmare'*: Ned to Frothingham (7 Mar 1898), op. cit.

314 *'taking his usual drive . . .'*: Letters to MDB (11 Jan 1885). Hay Library, St A. 36.

314 *Potomac*: Letters to MDB. Hay Library, St A. 36.

314 *'smooth front'*: Ned to MDB (26 Jan 1885). St Armand, *New England Quarterly* (1988), 373.

314 *'without . . . a row'*: Ned to Frothingham (17 Jan 1898).

314 *'rains . . .'*: Ned to Frothingham (15 Dec 1897).

314 *Alix*: St Armand calls her 'Alix'. *The Dickinsons of Amherst*, 135.

314 *so dear a girl*: Ned to Frothingham (17 Jan 1898).

315 *'too happy to be wise . . .'*: SHD to Frothingham (4 Jan 1898).

315 *'pinch . . .'*: Ned to Frothingham (17 Jan 1898).

315 *Ned's agony*: His cousin, daughter of Martha Gilbert Smith, speaks of his 'agony' in a condolence letter to SHD. Hay Library.

315 *fiction of earlier date*: MDB to Frothingham (2 May 1913): 'Sixteen years ago tomorrow Ned died.'

315 *the case killed Ned*: Plausible suggestion in *A&M*, 423. Frothingham sent roses to Alice Hill, who replied to thank him on 11 May 1898 (Houghton: bMS Am 1996 (4)).

315 *'After Ned's death . . .'*: Letter to MTB (20 Feb 1935), cited Sewall, i, 261. See also Mary Lee Hall to Genevieve Taggard, biographer of ED (4 Nov 1929 and 14 Sept 1930), Yale: Todd-Bingham archive. Cited in Sewall, i, appendix II, 254.

317 *LD tore out . . .*: DFP. Houghton: bMS Am 1118.95.

317 *'Did Miss Vinnie . . .'*: letter to Mary Lee Hall (20 Mar 1934). Cited Sewall, i, appendix II, 260.

317 *'Millicent, you never . . .'*: (20 Feb 1935). Cited Sewall, i, appendix II, 261.

318 *'decided not to breathe . . .' etc*: An attentive recorder, MLT made a collection of LD's sayings. Yale: series V, box 82, f.402.

318 *'to spare expense . . .'*: To Norcross cousins (7 Oct 1863). L285.

318 *LD's poems*: folder, typed and dated 1898. DFP. Houghton: bMS Am 1118.95.

319 *MLT noted LD's death*: Journals, VIII. Yale: microfilm, reel 9.

319 *MLT and the medium*: Journals, IX. Yale: microfilm, reel 9.

319 *Bleak House*: MLT, Diary (26 July 1897). Yale: microfilm, reel 3.

321 *Amy Angell Collier*: Correspondence in Montague Papers, MS division, New York Public Library.

322 *'heartbreaking associations'*: MDB to Frothingham (1903). DFP.

322 *'victims . . .'*: MDB to Frothingham (25 May 1907). DFP.

322 *'slanders' etc*: to Frothingham (22 Mar 1907). DFP.

322 *'seriously ill'*: MDB to Frothingham (25 May 1907). DFP.

323 *'some'; 'fraudulent business . . .'*: Montague, recalling this talk, to Mary Hampson (7 Aug 1952). Contracts and Correspondence, Houghton: bMS Am 1118.18.

323 *'spell'; 'hypnotic'; 'clasping . . .'*: Essay, 'New Year's Eve, 1900'. Yale.

324 *MLT on DPT's affairs; 'justification'*: Journals, cited by *A&M*, 50–1.

325 *'Austin was mine . . .'*: Essay, 'New Year's Eve, 1900', op. cit.

325 *'Sue hated . . . love'*: MLT's reminiscences in note form. Yale: subject files: WAD, 496C, series VII, box 103, f.266 (n.d.).

325 *'God . . .'; 'killing'; 'irrevocably'; 'wickedest . . .'*: Essay, 'New Year's Eve, 1900', op. cit.

325 *Sue's death*: SHD died of a heart condition at the age of eighty-two.

15: TWO DAUGHTERS

326 *MTB's memories*: Yale: Bingham Papers, 496D. Autobiographical TSS, mainly in box 46.

326 *'my early childhood . . .'*: MTB, aged eighty-four, to her mother's friend Mr Green, curator of Jones Library, Amherst (28 Jan 1965). Jones Library, Special Collections.

327 *sees ED 'every day'*: MTB, taped recollections. Sterling Library, Yale: Historical Recordings. For LD in the kitchen, see *AB*, 14–15.

327 *MTB's memories of the dining room, Maggie and LD*: 'Reminiscences: 23–30 August 1927'. Yale: box 46, f.6.

327 *'That they could be human . . .'*: Ibid.

327 *'dear quaking voice'*: (21 July 1933). Yale: box 46, f.1.

328 *MLT's rouge*: (21 July 1933, nine months after MLT's death). Yale: box 46, f.7.

328 *'X woman'*: (15 July 1905). Yale: box 46, f.6.

328 *'primly placed'*: Ibid.

329 *'all that Mamma has left now'*: MTB recalled making this remark to 'the snake' of Amherst, Mrs Grosvenor. 'Reminiscences', op. cit.

329 *'obnoxious . . .'; 'Deliver . . .'*: Memoir of 1905. Autobiographical pieces, op. cit.

330 *'imperial Girl'*: (June 1885). L987.

330 *jaunty hat*: ED to MDB (late 1882). L787. The photograph (Houghton) which prompted this note has inscribed on the back: 'Mattie Dickinson, 19 November 1882'.

330 *'freedom . . .'*: *FF*, 66.

330 *'live in vain'*: L403.

331 *'martial . . .'*: To MDB (Oct 1884). L942.

331 *'worse'*: Journals, V (Oct 1891), 87. Yale: microfilm.

331 *'I knew . . .'*: To SHD. L886.

331 The Single Hound: Reissued, with MDB's Preface, by Hesperus (London, 2005).

332 *MDB to Frothingham after SHD's death*: (13 Feb 1914). DFP. Houghton: bMS Am 1118.95.

332 *'Your praise is good . . .'*: (c. summer 1861). L238. Quoted by MDB in Preface, *The Single Hound*.

333 *'Adventure most unto itself . . .'*: Became last stanza of 'This consciousness that is aware' (c. 1864–5). J822/Fr817. The MS addressed to 'Sue' and signed 'Emily' was pasted into MDB's copy of this volume. *The Single Hound*, 7.

333 *'I fit for them'*: *The Single Hound*, 94.

333 *'The Devil . . .'*: (c. 1879). J1479/Fr1510. *The Single Hound*, 107, preferring the alternative 'finest' to 'best' friend in line 2. This alternative is more pleasing to the ear and subtler as to sense.

333 *Kate Scott Turner Anthon's recollections*: Letter (8 Oct 1914) from Whitebridge, Grasmere,

England, to MDB on receiving copy of *The Single Hound*. DFP. Houghton: bMS Am 1118.95.

334 *'Vesuvius at Home'*: 'Volcanoes be in Sicily' (transcribed by SHD). J1705/Fr1691. Adrienne Rich used the phrase as title for her brilliant essay on ED.

334 *volcanic narrative; Pompeii*: 'I have never seen "Volcanoes" —' (c. spring 1860). J175/Fr165.

334 *'beloved old spot'*: To Frothingham (6 Dec 1914). DFP. Houghton: bMS Am 1118.95.

334 *'some of the days . . .'*: Ibid.

334 *'Just the changing lights . . .'*: To Frothingham (13 Feb 1914).

334 *'to us'*: To Frothingham (6 Dec 1914), op. cit.

334 *'a passionate attachment' in Germany*: MTB, TS reminiscence, '12 May 1959'. Yale: box 46, f.8. MTB does not name this woman on paper, but details she relays on tape correlate with a companion in Germany called Marta Milinowsky, who had an American mother and was head of the piano department at Vassar until 1958.

335 *'humbled'*: '12 May 1959'. Yale: box 46, f.8.

335 *Joseph Thomas*: Ibid.

335 *MTB's geography of France*: (Chicago: Rand McNally, 1919).

336 *privilege*: letter to Mr Green of Jones Library after Bingham's death in 1952.

337 *'It revolts . . . me'*: Autobiographical TSS, 'Reminiscences: 28 August 1927'. Yale: box 46, f.6.

338* *'re-editing'*: MDB's claim in letter to McCarthy (23 Nov 1930). Houghton: Correspondence with McCarthy: bMS Am 1118.97–1118.98 (123).

339 *'scarcely seen'*: To SHD (Feb 1884), on being shown a photo of MDB at 18. L886. MDB is not mentioned by name in this letter but the editor surmises the reference must be to her.

340 *'of course'*: Amy Lowell to MLT (23 Jan 1923). Houghton: bMS Lowell 19.

340 *'will perform a life . . .'*: MLT to Amy Lowell (8 Sept 1923). Houghton: bMS Lowell 19 (1211).

340 *'my dear mis-read Emily'*: To Amy Lowell (17 Sept 1923). Ibid.

340 *'dear Miss Lowell'*: (26 Nov 1923). Ibid.

340 *asked MTB to put a stop to DPT*: Letter (30 Jan 1924). Ibid.

340 *Wadsworth's image in the twentieth century*: One example is Albert J. Gelpi in *Emily Dickinson: The Mind of the Poet* (Cambridge, MA: Harvard, 1965): 'Wadsworth would seem the unquestionable choice for Master.' The first ED biographer of the twenty-first century, Alfred Habegger, in a talk, 'Some Problems', is rightly sceptical of 'the patently spurious elements in Bianchi's highly colored version of the romance where she suggests that ED fell instantly in love and then loftily renounced her married lover'.

340 *MDB's Wadsworth legend*: LL, 46–50. MDB misdates 1855 visit to Philadelphia as 1853.

341 *ED on Wadsworth*: L727, 764 and 737.

341 *'best earthly friend'*: To James D. Clark (March 1883). L807.

341 *'It's easy to invent a Life'*: (c. 1863). J724/Fr747.

341 *MTB's copy of LL*: Yale. Ridicule of HHJ embellishment, 74.

342 *'astonishingly good' reviews*: To Amy Montague (9 June 1924). Montague Papers.

342 *MDB's new collection of poems*: *The Wandering Eros*, published by HM, following her ED books.

342 *Samuel Eliot Morrison*: HM to MDB (14 Oct 1924). Houghton: bMS Am 1925.

343 *Ned's class*: To Amy Montague (9 June 1924). Montague Papers.

343 *review of MDB's poems*: clipping in HM correspondence. Houghton: bMS Am 1925 (197).

343 *1924 as the first time Mamma spoke of the Dickinsons*: MTB, historical recording (1964). Sterling Library, Yale.

343 *ED 'enjoyed . . .'*: Yale: subject files: WAD, 496C, series VII, box 103, f.266 (n.d.).

343 *'Are you going . . .'*: MTB's TS recollections, 'Veterans Day, 1955', op. cit.

343 *MTB on 'pi-racy'*: Tape relating the legal battles in the feud, 1964. Historical recordings, Yale.

343 *'It ought to be done . . .'*: (27 July 1924). Houghton MS Lowell 19 (95).

343 *'In so far . . .'*: In conversation with MTB (1931). Yale: 496D, box 103, f.602.

344 *the lock's bell*: MTB, introduction to *Bolts of Melody* (1945).

344 *'extracted the Emily things . . .'*: MTB to Amy Lowell (13 Nov 1924). Lowell Papers, op. cit.

16: THE BATTLE OF THE DAUGHTERS

346 *'growth . . .'; 'Comédie humaine'*: 'Reminicences' (28 Aug 1927). Yale: box 46, f.6.

347 *'I hesitate to ask . . .'*: 'Reminiscences' (29 Aug 1927). Yale: box 46, f.6.

347 *'Though I respect . . .'*: MTB's notes on visits to Dr MacPherson. Yale: box 48, f.32. Yale also has her notes on further visits, in 1940–52, to Dr Ehrenclou (box 48, f.37). The latter sounds banal, not up to MTB's intelligence.

347 *ALH lived at The Evergreens*: MTB, 'Veterans Day, 1955', op. cit. ALH 'had been living with [MDB] for several years'.

347 *MDB's rejected novels*: 'The Great Deliverer' and 'Andrew Djubzyke'.

348 *'an almost unbroken narrative . . .'*: MDB, introduction to ED, *Further Poems*, viii.

348 *'trembles . . . dimity apron'*: Ibid.

348 *Louis Untermeyer*: 16 March 1929. Quoted approvingly in *FF*, 52.

348 *'the veils . . .'*: MDB quotes this proudly to HM (27 Apr 1930). Houghton: bMS Am 1925.

349 *MLT opening her treasure chest in 1929*: A cagy letter (dated 7 July 1930) from MLT to Mr Green of Jones Library, Amherst, reveals that she had distributed Dickinson papers in four different places: the Springfield warehouse; a safe in Florida; a safe in New York (possibly Millicent's when she was teaching at Columbia); and 'another safe'. Jones Library.

349 *MLT supported Taggard*: MLT told MTB at this point that the two men in ED's life were Gould and Wadsworth. It's unlikely that Austin had ever named them.

349 *Mary Lee Hall as Taggard's source*: Sewall, ii, 419–22.

349 *'Hallelujah . . .'*: L34

349 *Miss Hall's gossip about Gould*: Taggard, 115, 336–7, 357.

349 *'would never have . . .'*: Taggard, 120.

350 *Josephine Pollitt*: *ED: The Human Background of her Poetry* (Harper, 1930).

350 *Brittle Heaven*: (NY: Samuel French, 1935). Pohl collaborated with Vincent Yorke. Copy in Bodleian Library. Original title was *Stardust and Thistledown*.

350 *On stage*: The play was produced at the Vanderbilt Theater, New York, and also at the Tremont Theater, Boston, during the 1933–4 season.

350 *MDB and the centenary*: Letters to HM in Houghton: bMS Am 1925 (197); letters to McCarthy, especially 23 Nov 1930, in Houghton: bMS Am 1118.97–1118.98 (123).

351 *'driving force'; 'Perhaps I exist . . .'; 'worthy of a Henry James'; 'ammunition'*: MTB, '1929'. Yale: box 47, f.14.

351 *'Much against . . .'*: MLT to Mr Green of Jones Library (5 Feb 1930). Jones Library.

352 *LD 'did consent . . .'*: Yale: box 82, f.390.

352 *MLT's preface to* Letters, 1931: Preface and drafts at Yale: 496D, box 87, f.307.

353 *MLT printed letters about Wadsworth*: His friends, the Clarks, corresponded with ED in the mid-1880s.

354 *'Existence'*: J443, op. cit.

354 *LD 'had an enormous mouth . . .' etc*: 'MLT Speaks' (10 Oct 1931). Yale: box 101, f.242.

354 *'Vinnie ought . . .'; Maggie 'lied . . .'*: Ibid.

355 *'hideous'*: Ibid.

355 *'for that she practised . . .' and 'It is hard . . .'*: To MTB who typed it (7 Sept 1932). Yale: 496D, box 103, f.602.

355 *'That such have died . . .'*: J1030/Fr1082. MLT had published this in *Poems: Third Series* (1896). The tombstone quotation is not quite accurate.

355 *'point of no return'*: 'MTB', interview in *Current Biography* (June 1961), 11.

356 *'You must realize . . .'*: MTB, 'Veterans Day, 1955', op. cit. Repeats it '1 May 1959'. Yale: box 46, f.8.

356 *'Budgie . . .'; It was as if; 'nothing else . . .'*: MTB, '1 May 1959'. Yale: box 46, f.8.

356 *warning not to publish in MDB's lifetime*: MTB, 'Veterans Day, 1955', op. cit.

356 *mother as co-discoverer*: Yale: 496D, box 46, f.1.

356 *'objectionable book'*: To HM (16 Oct 1931). HM. Houghton: bMS Am 1925 (197).

356 *Field warned*: Letter to MDB (18 Nov 1931). Houghton: bMS Am 1118.97–1118.98 (79).

357 *Todd's strong position*: Greenslet to MDB (28 Dec 1931). Ibid.

357 *'personal book . . .'*: MDB to HM (14 July 1932). Ibid.

357 *'disposes . . .'*: To HM (25 July 1932). Ibid.

357 *Greenslet's warnings to MDB*: (15 July and 19 Aug 1931). Ibid.

357 *wearing white . . . 'a memorial . . .'*: FF, 51.

357 *'Readers waited . . .'*: Untermeyer, 'Thoughts after a Centenary' (20 June 1931).

357 *memorandum*: (23 Sept 1931), just before *Letters* (1931) came out. HM correspondence. Houghton: bMS Am 1925.

358 *American Literature*: Morris U. Schappes, 'Errors in Mrs. Bianchi's Edition of ED's Letters' (1933).

358 *pedantic fuss*: MDB to Mr Linscott at HM (11 Apr 1933). HM correspondence, op. cit.

358 *MDB on photo of ED as child*: To Lovell Thompson at HM (14 Oct 1932). Ibid.

359 *The inaccurate editing went on*: Easy though it has been to ridicule the inaccuracies of these volumes, in *Further Poems* of 1929 MDB and ALH did attempt (ahead of later, professional editors Johnson and Franklin) to register the poet's lineation. In this they anticipate post-structuralist textual studies of the 1990s (continuing into the present century).

359 *'disarray . . .'*: Cited by Franklin, *The Editing of ED's Poems*.

359 *Dickinson exhibit at World's Fair*: MDB to HM (20 July 1933). HM correspondence, op. cit.

359 *MDB grateful for support*: To Amy Collier Montague (28 July 1933). Montague-Collier Papers, NYPL.

359 *'save such as we of the heart'*: (7 Apr 1934). Ibid.

359 *'Be Amy . . .'*: (7 Apr 1935). Ibid.

359 *'Whatever she did . . .'*: '10 November 1934'. Yale: box 46, f.7.

359 *'In the early days . . .'*: TS reminiscence (1935). Yale: box 45, f.8.

360 *4 Feb 1938; fog; the octopus; 'Hatred . . .'*: '4 February 1938'. Yale.

362 *Indian Pipes on the cover*: Paperback edition by University of Michigan in 1957, repr. 1960.

362 *MDB's will*: (15 November 1938). AC: MDB's Misc. MSS, folder 2.

363 *'pilgrims'*: ALH to Amy Montague (Sept 1940). Montague Papers.

363 *Pearl Strachan*: interview in the *Christian Science Monitor*, Boston (4 Sept 1940), illustrated with photo of The Evergreens and the doctored image of ED. Enclosed with the above letter to Amy Montague.

363 *worked with ALH*: ALH to Amy Montague (6 Oct 1940). Montague Papers.

363 *'both told me . . .'*: Preface to new edition of *Letters* (1931), with drafts at Yale: 496D, box 87, f.307.

364 *will 'was never found'*: 1931 is pencil date of TS fragment amongst MTB's conversations with Mamma. Yale: 496D, box 103, f.603.

364 *'no authorization'; 'lick it yet'; 'I should have collapsed . . .'*: '25 May 1959'. Yale: box 46, f.8.

364 *Alexander Lindey*: MTB, tape recording (1964) on the history of legal battles in the feud, op. cit.

365 *'feuds . . . dissolved in death'*: AB, 399.

365 *photo of cheque*: AB, 194.

365 *'blight'*: AB, 15.

365 *SHD the reason for ED's solitude*: Ibid.

366 *MTB's 1955 statement*: 'Veterans Day, 1955', op. cit.

367 *Wallace Keep*: 'Recollections of Lavinia Dickinson' (15 April 1933). Yale: 496D, box 84, f.233. AB, 29–9.

367 *MTB to Keep*: (9 May 1945). From home, 1661 Crescent Place, Washington DC.

368 *so it proved*: MLT's diaries show that Alice Hill was often with her at The Dell.

368 *'crotchety'; unimportant; 'cantankerous'*: AB, 247–8.

17: POSTHUMOUS CAMPAIGNS

This chapter is indebted to an article by Leslie A. Morris, Curator of Modern Books and Manuscripts at the Houghton Library: her Foreword to Emily Dickinson's *Herbarium*, where she notes how, after the lawsuit, 'the feud between the Dickinsons and the Todds colored all subsequent work on Emily Dickinson'.

369 *'to take care of Emily'*: MH repeats this to Gilbert Montague in a letter (1 Aug 1952) that reflects on how William (Bill) McCarthy had controlled everything. Hampson correspondence, Houghton: bMS Am 1923.

370 *Montague's appearance*: Photographs in the Houghton Library and in the NYPL.

370 *$5 million*: *New York Times* obituary (Feb 1961).

370 *boyhood ties*: Edwin De T. Bechtel echoes Montague's boast in letter to him (31 May 1950). NYPL: Montague Papers, box 2.

371 *Cadogans*: Sir Alexander and Lady Cadogan were house guests in 1946.

371 *Montague invited MTB to dine; 'a-quiver'; 'Your understanding . . .'*: NYPL: Montague Papers, box 1: Bingham correspondence.

371 *Archibald MacLeish and Robert Penn Warren*: MTB also mentions other emissaries from the Library of Congress, Verner Clapp and David Mearns.

371 *McCarthy as MDB's 'slave'*: McCarthy's correspondence with MDB. Houghton: bMS Am 1118.97–1118.98 (123).

372 *'charm . . .' of MDB*: McCarthy to ALH (2 Apr 1946). Houghton: bMS Am 1923.

372 *'The Evergreens never . . .'*: (20 Aug 1947). Ibid.

372 *'thief' etc*: To McCarthy (12 Sept 1947). Ibid.

373 *'a person convicted . . .'*: To McCarthy (6 Dec 1947). Ibid.

373 *a picture . . .*: McCarthy to ALH (5 Dec 1947 and 27 Apr 1948). Hay Library: Correspondence, box 4, f.14. MH to Montague (22 June 1950). Houghton: bMS Am 1923.

373 *'fabulous'; 'I know . . .'*: (5 Dec 1947 and 27 Apr 1948). Hay Library: box 4, f.14.

373 *'Emily' in ALH's suitcase*: ALH to McCarthy (6 Sept 1948). Houghton: bMS Am 1923 (2).

374 *Mary attracted to ALH in 1931*: To Montague (11 Dec 1958). Houghton: bMS Am 1923.

374 *'staggering wealth'*: Hampsons' letters to McCarthy in Apr 1848, particularly ALH's letter of 22 Apr and Mary's preceding letter. Houghton: bMS Am 1923.

374 *$40,000*: McCarthy to the Hampsons (Sept 1948). Hay Library.

374 *'to care for Emily'*: Ibid.

374 *McCarthy's explorations*: To Hampsons (14 Sept 1949). Houghton: bMS Am 1923.

374 *pushes papers towards the bed*: McCarthy to MH (20 Sept 1949). Houghton: bMS Am 1923. ALH alerted her to the ceiling.

375 *McCarthy's find of missing letters of Dickinson parents*: McCarthy to ALH (31 Oct 1949). Houghton. Noted by Leslie A. Morris in Foreword to ED's *Herbarium*.

375 *letters from Lavinia Norcross*: McCarthy to MH (20 Sept 1949). Houghton. He had found the letters the previous night.

375 *'long night hours'*: (26 Aug 1949). Houghton: bMS Am 1923.

375 *'This is something . . .'; 'crazy'*: McCarthy to the Hampsons (Sept 1948). Hay Library.

376 *crystal tears*: Sent in Nov 1947, possibly as a wedding present. Houghton: bMS Am 1923.

376 *'no way you could get more'*: (4 Jan 1949). Houghton: bMS Am 1923.

376 *Dumbarton Oaks*: In Georgetown. At the time of the sale a different representative of the Rosenbach Company was in correspondence with Mrs Bliss; McCarthy made his offers to her later, between 1951 and 1953: almost all his offers were rare books, mostly on gardens and garden design. What negotiation existed during the winter of 1949–50 must have been oral and casual. In her Foreword to ED's *Herbarium*, Leslie A. Morris mentions a call in early Feb 1950 from the Director of Dumbarton Oaks, John Thacher, to William Jackson, rejecting the Dickinson collection and suggesting that Jackson take over.

376 *McCarthy seeking donors of immense fortune*: Suggested by David Redden in conversation at Sotheby's, New York (18 Sept 2009).

376 *no books by ED*: Checked by James Carder, the present curator. Afterwards, Mildred Bliss did contribute toward the ED Room at the Houghton Library.

376 *24 Feb 1950*: McCarthy correspondence. Houghton: bMS Am 1923.

376 *McCarthy did not tell*: A letter from ALH to Montague (1 June 1950) shows that

he had been in the dark until the day before when the sale was announced to the public. NYPL: Montague Papers, box 2: Correspondence regarding Dickinson.

377 *$50,000*: Leslie A. Morris of the Houghton Library, in conversation (4 Sept 2009). In trying to estimate the value of this sum paid in 1950, it may be worth noting, for comparison, that in 1946 Sotheby's in London sold thirty-four manuscripts for £50,000 and 673 illuminated manuscripts for £100,000. A collector in the early fifties, Mildred Bliss of Dumbarton Oaks, paid (the Rosenbach Company) as much as $750 and $2200 for two rare books. In Jan 1952 she paid $975 for a 378-page MS by an obscure eleventh-century scribe; $1008 for seven rare books; and in 1952 her account for nine rare books was nearly $3000.

377 *'in excess of $100,000'*: (18 July 1950). Houghton office: Montague files.

377 *Montague's 1953 estimate of the market value of ED's papers*: Boston dinner of the Massachusetts Historical Society under the auspices of the Club of Odd Volumes (to which both men belonged) on 13 Oct 1953, recorded in Jackson's memorandum on 14 Oct. Houghton office: Montague files. (The memorandum is unsigned but one of the three copies is initialled 'W.A.J.'.) Jackson does not record his own opinion.

378 *experts*: David Redden, head of manuscript sales at Sotheby's, New York, considers $50,000 a good sum at the time, comparable to 'millions' in today's terms.

379 *'war of nerves . . .'; 'disgust'*: Montague to Jackson (17 Apr 1950). Houghton office: Montague files.

379 *'corny'*: Montague to Jackson (17 Apr 1950), op. cit.

379 *ALH's haemorrhage*: Jackson to Montague (3 May 1950). Houghton office: Montague files.

379 *'safely'*: Letter to Montague. Houghton office: Montague files.

379 *ALH did not know name of donor*: Congratulatory letter to Montague (1 June 1950) indicates that the announcement on 31 May had revealed this to him. NYPL: Montague Papers, box 2.

379 *31 May*: MTB taped interview (1964). Yale: Historical Sound Recordings.

380 *General Eisenhower to Montague*: List of correspondents (1 June 1950). NYPL: Montague Papers, box 2, Correspondence regarding ED.

380 *Morrow to Montague*: Ibid.

380 *mother's shame*: Jackson's note to himself (5 Feb 1952, following a telephone discussion with Montague) that he should not allow Montague to pressure the Library 'to expose to the world the mystery of events leading to [Mrs Bingham's] acquisition of the papers'. Houghton office: Montague files.

381 *MTB's 'relief . . .'; 'greatest treasure . . .'*: (31 May 1950). Cited by Leslie A. Morris in Foreword to ED's *Herbarium*. Houghton office: Montague files.

381 *MTB accepted Montague's invitation*: (11 July 1950). NYPL: Montague Papers, box 2.

381 *'neither . . .'*: Quoted by Leslie A. Morris, Foreword to ED's *Herbarium*.

382 *MTB's legend*: Quotations from *AB*, 93, 218, 219; Home, 409.

382 *SHD's 'lush personality'*: *AB*, 219.

382 *'Emily grieved'*: Ibid.

382 *'I lost her'*: 'Now I knew I lost her' (c. 1872). J1219/Fr1274. Not addressed or signed. If this poem is autobiographical, there are other candidates for loss: Mrs Holland (whom ED reproached for not writing after her move to New York in

1870), or Kate Turner Anthon whose friendship with ED ended after she remarried.

382 *LD as old witch: AB*, ch. 1: 'Dramatis Personae', 14.

382 *passive: Revelation*, 60.

382 *'became the focus . . .'*: MTB, '1951'. Yale: box 47, f.14.

383 *'a positive . . . withdrawal': Revelation*, 3.

383 *'endowed [Sue] with characteristics . . .': Revelation*, 3.

383 *'Congratulations and hallelujahs'*: Letter (18 May 1950). Cited by Leslie A. Morris, Foreword to ED's *Herbarium*.

383 *a gift*: In March 1950 MTB did tell Jackson she might have to sell the papers, but she thought of a gift most of the time. Jackson advised Montague of this shift, and Montague still went on with the agreement. This was to be Harvard's main defence in the ensuing battle with Montague.

385 *'trade-off'*: MTB, taped interview (1964), op. cit.

385 *confrontations of Jackson and the Binghams, 1951*: MTB gives a detailed account in 'Veterans Day, 1955', op. cit.

386 *'be ye steadfast . . .'*: Philippians, 4:8.

387 *'stand still'*: (1 Feb 1952). Houghton office: Montague files.

387 *instalments; McCarthy's reluctance*: Leslie A. Morris, Foreword to *Herbarium*.

388 *McCarthy's comments on royalties*: (14 June 1955). Houghton: bMS Am 1923.

388 *McCarthy had driven the sale*: MH to Montague (1952), op. cit.

389 *'aura of frustration'*: MTB, 'Veterans Day, 1955', op. cit.

389 *SHD as scapegoat*: TS reminiscence (1959). Yale.

389 *'His anguish . . .'*: MTB, TS '25 May 1959'. Yale: box 46, f.8.

391 *'My lovely Salem'*: (c. 1878). L559.

391 *'a violence of Affection'*: Dorothy Wordsworth's *Journal*, cited by Frances Wilson, *The Ballad of Dorothy Wordsworth* (Faber, 2008), 36.

391 *MTB attacks romantic legend: Revelation*, 3, 8, 58.

391 *'vainly'*: Sewall, i, 184.

391 *'in her own way'; reached out: Home*, 374–5.

392 *'the legend . . .'*: Ibid., 373.

392 *Montague enforced MTB's erasure*: Montague files: Jackson's memorandum (14 Oct 1953); Montague to Boston lawyer, Ames (14 Oct 1953); Montague letter (22 Oct 1953) with 'to contain no mention . . .'. It was authorised by the Harvard Corporation at this time.

392 *'compiler'*: '16 May 1959'. Yale: box 47, f.16.

392 *'unctuous'*: MTB, 'Veterans Day, 1955', op. cit.

392 *final exchange of Montague and MTB*: NYPL: Montague Papers, box 1: Bingham correspondence (14 and 17 Dec 1955).

393 *'Did Vinnie . . .'*: Yale: box 47, f.14.

393 *'No'*: MTB's 'Notes for talk with my father'. DPT died in 1939. MTB died in 1968. Notes typed up with the date Oct 1967. 'No' was therefore added during the last year of MTB's life. Yale: box 47, f.14.

393 *'that's where she belongs'*: TS memoir, '25 May 1959', op. cit.

393 *to probe their grievances*: See Clara Pearl to MTB (15 Sept 1932). Yale: box 84, f.258a. Clara was Mrs George E. Pearl, and her mother, the former Anna Newton, was

Mrs George H. Carleton. Much of Mrs Pearl's information came from a memoir of ED and family by Anna's elder sister Clara Newman (Mrs Sidney Turner). See also Kate Dickinson Sweetser, below.

393 *'curse on her lips'*: MTB, 'Veterans Day, 1955', op. cit.

394 *taped interviews*: Historical Sound Recordings, music section of Sterling Library, Yale. TS transcription of the 1963 interview. Yale: 496D, box 46, f.13.

394 *appointed Sewall her literary executor*: See 'the care of Richard Sewall': MTB, '28 July 1964'. Yale: box 46, f.9.

394 *'set the whole . . .'*: MTB, '4–6 Jan 1960' and '7 Feb 1960'. Yale: box 46, f.9.

395 *Sewall's* Life of ED: The second volume follows Mabel Todd's approach in her edition of Dickinson's letters: they were organised on the basis of assorted recipients (with the earlier correspondences preceding later ones). To see the poet as an amalgam of separate relationships and correspondences was appropriate in 1892–4, at a time when batches of letters were in the process of being collected from Dickinson's living correspondents who loomed large: their willingness and information were making the edition possible. Eighty years later this approach leaves the poet more elusive than ever.

395 *'magnetism concealed vindictiveness'*: A&M, 67–8.

395 *Peter Gay on WAD's obedience*: Senses, 106.

395 *SHD cruel and spiteful; 'hating'*: Kaufmann, 109, 226.

395 *'Borgia Palace'*: Afternoons, 98, 103, 105.

396 *'black velvet; 'micemeat pie . . .'*: Ibid.

396 *false attribution of 'Her breast is fit for pearls'*: Open Me Carefully: Emily Dickinson's Intimate Letters to Susan Huntington Dickinson (Ashfield, MA: Paris Press, 1998), 9. The copy sent to Sue remained incorrectly placed in the Bowles section in MLT's 1931 edition of ED's Letters, 202–3. J84/Fr121.

V: OUTLIVING THE LEGEND

401 *The Evergreens in June 2003*: I visited the house with a collector of women's books, Lisa Baskin, and biographers Frances Spalding and Gretchen Holbrook Gerzina who spoke of 'a stain seeping through twelve layers of wallpaper'. We were unaware that this was the last month to see the house in its original state.

401 *'Eternity's disclosure . . .'*: 'The Soul's Superior instants' (c. 1863). Sent to SHD. J306/Fr630.

401 *'I' not herself*: (July 1862). L268. 'When I state myself, as the Representative of the Verse – it does not mean – me – but a supposed person.'

401 *'The Soul that hath a Guest'*: (c. 1863). J674/Fr592. Quoted in Part I, above.

401 *'Immortality as a guest is sacred'*: (c. June 1880). L644.

402 *'The Spirit never twice alike . . .'*: (30 Apr 1882). L750. ED seems to conflate the Spirit with her worship of Lord.

402 *'priceless'*: (c. June 1880). L664.

402 *'Flash'*: 'The Soul's distinct connection' (c. early 1865). J974/Fr901.

402 *'waylaying Light'*: To HH (Sept 1884). L937. 'The farthest Thunder that I heard' (c. 1884). J1581/Fr1665.

402 *ED's kinship to Emily Brontë*: ED talks of Emily Brontë to Maria Whitney (*c.* summer 1884). L948. 'Did you read Emily Brontë's marvellous verse?', followed by the stanza beginning 'Though earth and man were gone'. ED talks of her again as 'gigantic Emily Brontë' in letter to Mrs Holland (*c.* 1881). L742.

402 *anything but meek*: See, for instance, Brontë's address to the deity as 'Comrade' and 'slave' as well as 'King' in 'Oh thy bright eyes must answer now', *Poems* (1846). ED owned this volume.

402 *'Life . . . vision'*: To Whitney (*c.* summer 1883). L860.

402 *'I struck the board . . .'*: 'The Collar', *The Temple* (1633).

402 *'No worst . . .'*: 'Terrible Sonnets'.

402 *infinite 'thing'*: 'Preludes: IV' (*c.* 1912)

402 *'waste sad time'*: *Burnt Norton*: V (1934–5).

402 *an ecstatic*: Josephine Hart, deviser of poetry readings by celebrated actors at the British Library. *Catching Life By the Throat* (London: Virago; NY: Norton, 2007)

402 *'Take all away . . .'*: (2 Jan 1885). L960.

402 *Miss Havisham*: MLT imagined ED as a Miss Havisham (from Dickens, *Great Expectations*) on 15 Sept 1882. Journals, III, 174. Yale: microfilm, reel 8.

403 *MH's dream of The Evergreens as a memorial museum*: MH to Montague (17 June 1952). Houghton: bMS Am 1923. In 1991 the house passed to the Martha Dickinson Bianchi Trust. Ownership of the house passed to Amherst College on 1 July 2003.

403 *papers*: A fantastic collection of papers and memorabilia (deriving from Susan, Ned and Mattie) went to the Hay Library at Brown University in Providence, Rhode Island.

404 *'close prest'; 'little Book'*: ''Twas the old — road — through pain —' (*c.* 1862). J344/Fr376.

404 *'Impregnable we are'*: (*c.* 1884). L935.

404 *'Queen of Amherst'*: 'MLT Speaks' (10 Oct 1931). Yale: 496C, box 10, f.242.

404 *ED as queen of immortality*: She also calls herself 'Queen of Calvary' in 'I dreaded that first Robin' (*c.* 1862). J348/Fr347.

404 *queen's head embossed on stationery*: Facsimile edition of *The Master Letters of Emily Dickinson*. Farr, 189.

404 *ring of gems like stars*: See 'Row of Stars' in 'I lost a World' (*c.* 1861). J181/Fr209.

404 *'old-fashioned'*: See ch. 3, above: 'I'm so old-fashioned', said ED at twenty-three.

404 *'Can Blaze . . .'*: 'I found the words' (*c.* 1862). J581/Fr436.

405 *'God made me'*: (*c.* summer 1861). L233. The third 'Master' letter.

405 *'Opera'*: 'I cannot dance opon my toes'. See ch. 4, above.

405 *'Since then . . .'*: Final stanza of 'Because I could not stop for Death —' (*c.* late 1862). J712/Fr479.

ACKNOWLEDGEMENTS

My first debt is to my mother Rhoda Press who, far off 'at the bottom of Africa', read Dickinson with an affinity for her visitations (the 'flash'), sufferings, intense friendships and private oeuvre of poems.

This book goes back to the late eighties when I planned a book of women's lives. It was to include Emily Dickinson as well as Charlotte Brontë and Minny Temple, cousin to Henry James and model for his American girl. Research on all three began in 1990, and initial findings prompted longer biographies. New York agent Georges Borchardt welcomed a Dickinson proposal in 1999, reshaped in 2005. He offered, as always, support for evolving ideas, together with astute questions and words of wisdom. Virago publisher Lennie Goodings took this on with an infectious commitment to great poetry and to Dickinson in particular. Her inspired editing has made a difference to what emerged, and I've been fortunate too in Zoe Gullen who handled the copy-editing and much else with care and judgement. Thanks to London agent Isobel Dixon for her supportive involvement, and to Penguin (NY) publisher Kathryn Court for another decisive acceptance, backed by helpful contributions from co-editor Alexis Washam.

No biography is possible without others' work. Speculation about Dickinson, her family and milieu is dependent on the work of editors followed by biographers, social historians and critics over the last hundred and twenty years. This book is indebted to Alfred Habegger's feats of corrective research in *My Wars Are Laid Away in Books*, especially his work on the figures surrounding Dickinson's childhood. This admirable biography refuses to lose the poet to biographical contexts, even while bringing these convincingly to life. A story of the feud must be dependent on meticulous research in Polly Longsworth's *Austin and Mabel*.

I've returned many times to the treasures of the Houghton Library. This time the curator Leslie A. Morris extended the scope of the story by directing attention to Martha Dickinson Bianchi's newly catalogued correspondence with her publisher, and by making available the fascinating correspondence between her predecessor William Jackson and the donor Gilbert Montague. Chapter 17 grew out of her pioneering essay on the contest over ownership of the Dickinson papers. In the Houghton reading room Susan Halpert, ably assisted by colleagues, has been expert as ever at tracking manuscripts, a model of swift helpfulness.

My cousin Jennifer Roth, of Sotheby's, New York, asked the head of rare books and manuscripts, David Redden, to discuss the sale of the Dickinson Papers. It was generous of him to share his wealth of experience.

Thanks too to rights departments for permissions to quote, in particular to Scarlett R. Huffman of Harvard University Press for her promptness and kindness, and to archivists at the following libraries: Manuscripts and Rare Books at Yale, and Richard Warren of the Historical Sound Recordings in the Music Library at Yale; Margaret R. Dakin and Daria D'Arienzo in Amherst College Library; Tevis Kimball in Jones Library, Amherst; the Manuscript Division of the New York Public Library; Jane Wald, Director of the Emily Dickinson Museum; Timothy Engels at Brown University Library; Nicholas Graham of the Massachusetts Historical Society; James Carder of Dumbarton Oaks; and Jack Eckert of the Countway Library of Medicine, Harvard. Living in Washington, DC during the final stages of this book, I luxuriated in the grandeur and bounty of the Library of Congress.

The chapters on the trial of 1898 could not have emerged without Karen V. Kukil, editor of Sylvia Plath's *Journals* and Associate Curator of Special Collections, Smith College, who came to my rescue over an apparently lost deposition. She tracked this down with help from Nancy A. Foley, First Assistant Clerk of the Court House, Northampton Superior Court.

There were stimulating exchanges and comments from academics, writers and friends, including Mark Bostridge, Lucasta Miller, Diane Middlebrook and members of her women's salon, Eva Hoffman, Susan Jones,

Michael Gorra, Linn Cary Mehta, Carol Sanger, Faith and Stephen Williams, and Tree Swenson, Director of the Academy of American Poets. Her husband Liam Rector, founder of the writing seminars at Bennington College, created a rare place where it was possible to try out ideas. Bennington students and writers were quick to share their thoughts, particularly Alice Mattison, April Bernard, Martha Cooley, novelists Sheila Kohler and Jill McCorkle who alerted me to Tennessee Williams's comments on Dickinson; also Susan Cheever who discussed Boston publisher Thomas Niles. Dickinson scholars Cristanne Miller and Martha Nell Smith have been enlightening and generous.

Musician Philip Clark shared his taste for musical 'improvisation', suggestive for Dickinson's poetry. He also introduced me to John Adams's settings for 'Because I could not stop for death' and 'Wild Nights' in *Harmonium*.

'An ecstatic' was the way Emily Dickinson was described by Josephine Hart, deviser of poetry readings by celebrated actors at the British Library. Her apt word stayed with me.

For expertise on epilepsy, I'm grateful to Dr Jane Mellanby in the Department of Experimental Psychology, University of Oxford, and at a later stage Professor Samuel F. Berkovic, FRS, Director of the Epilepsy Research Centre at the University of Melbourne.

Writer Pamela Norris, who read a draft of the whole book, made detailed comments with her usual grace of mind. Everything she said was telling.

Finally I must thank Siamon Gordon for his hypothesis about the effect of Dickinson's physician in formulating her way of life. Thanks is due even more for his readiness to discuss each chapter from start to finish. In many ways, this is his book as much as mine.

PERMISSIONS

INDEX

POEMS: INDEX OF FIRST LINES